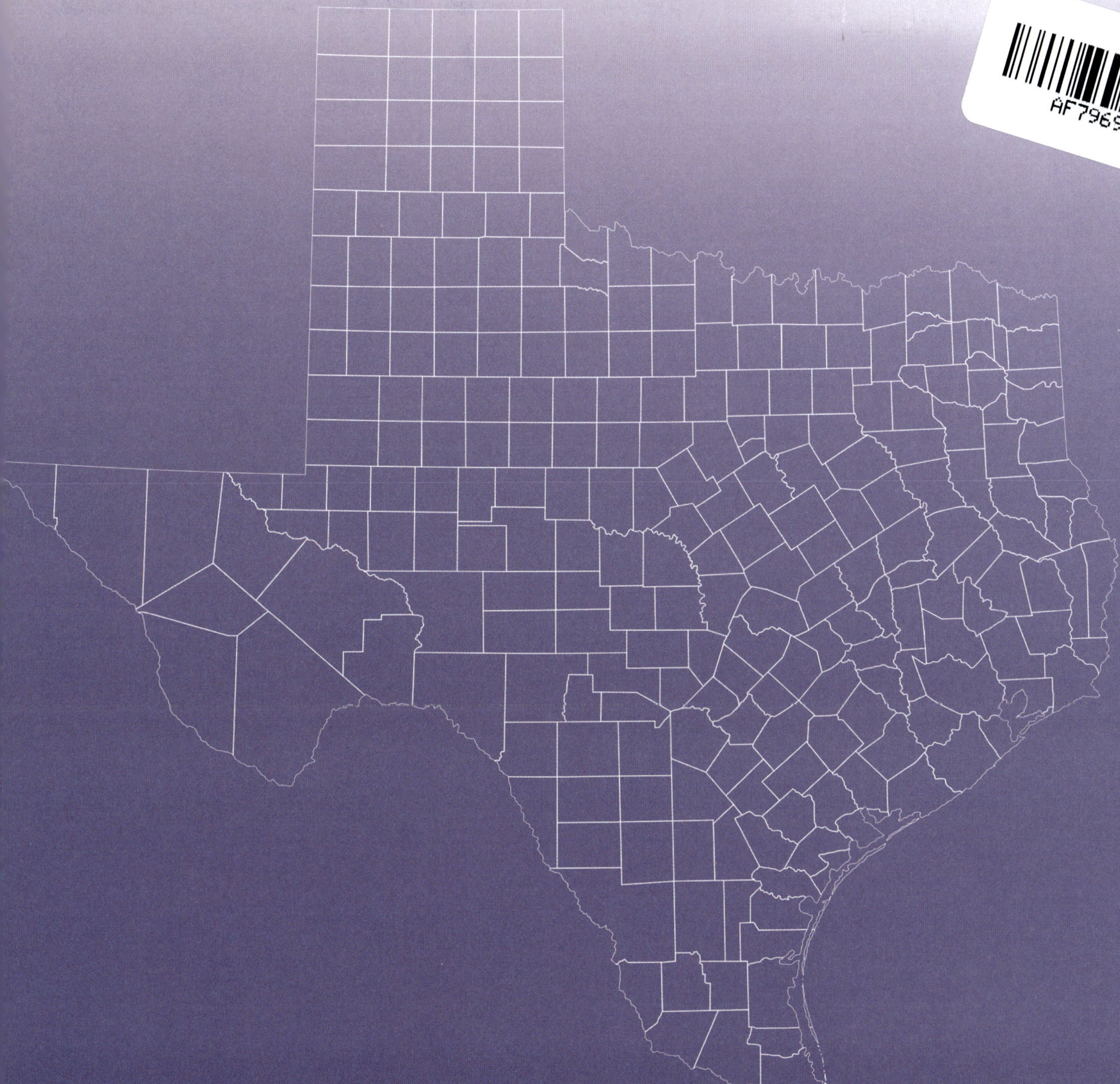

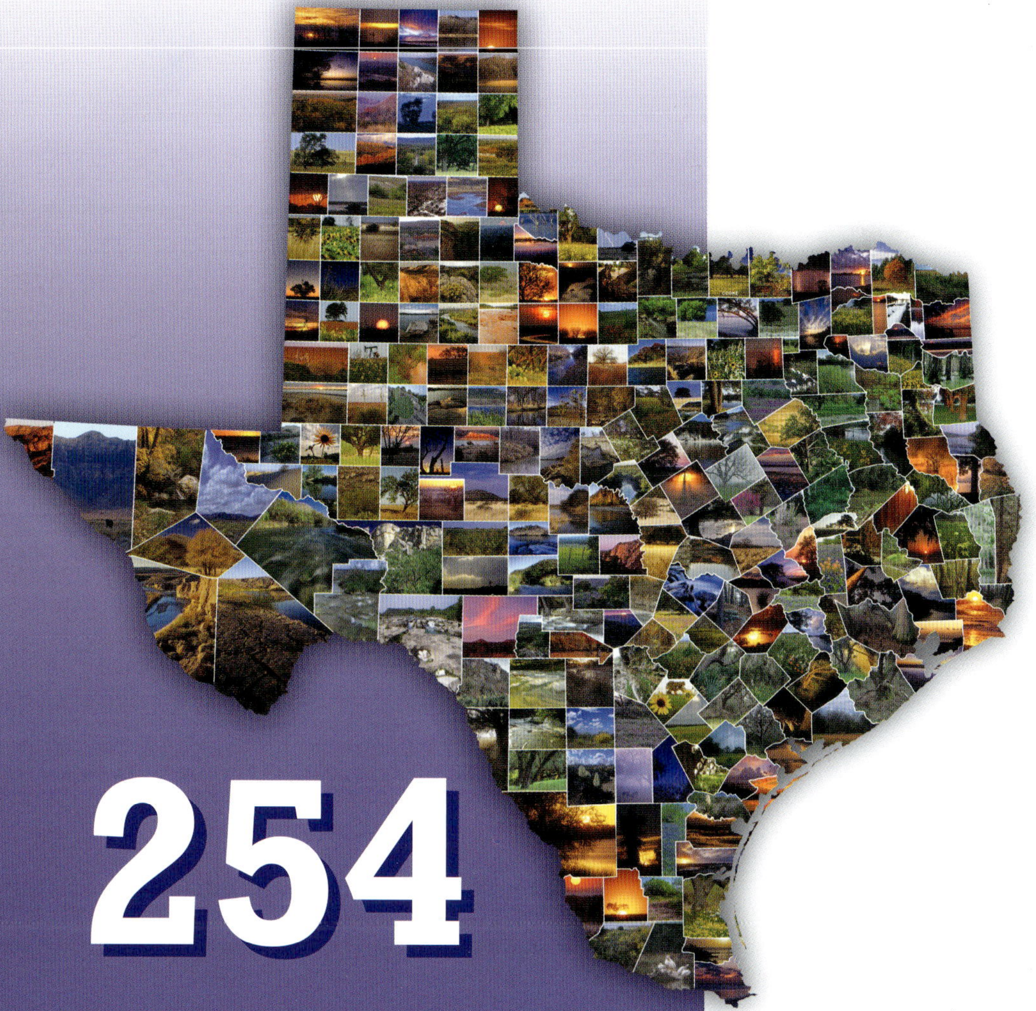

254

A Photographer's Journey through Every Texas County

Ronn Varnell & Lance Varnell

SCHIFFER PUBLISHING
4880 Lower Valley Road • Atglen, PA 19310

Library of Congress Control Number: 2020943534

Edited by Ian Robertson
Designed by Justin Watkinson
Cover design by Molly Shields
Type set in Rockwell/Brandon Grotesque/Minion Pro

ISBN: 978-0-7643-6163-0
Printed in India

Published by Schiffer Publishing, Ltd.
4880 Lower Valley Road
Atglen, PA 19310
Phone: (610) 593-1777; Fax: (610) 593-2002
E-mail: Info@schifferbooks.com
Web: www.schifferbooks.com

Special thanks to these people and organizations for their efforts in helping this work to become a reality:

Daniel Hamilton

James Pharoan

Billy Stewart

Eric Kolflat

Tom Forbes

Teri Crane

Seamus Rail

Erica Varnell

Andrea Brauer

Mike Brauer

David Benbennick

Wikipedia

Texas State Historical Association

Contents

Introduction

When some folks describe Texas, they usually say, "Everything is bigger in Texas." Not to brag, but it's close to right. For example, if you're in Texarkana, Texas (in the northeastern corner of the state), you're closer to Chicago than you are to El Paso (in the western corner). If you think that's a Texas tall tale, grab a map and check it out.

That's a big state. Not to be outdone by the state, some of the Texas counties have bragging rights as well. Brewster County, in the western part of the state, is more than three times the size of the state of Delaware, and more than 500 square miles larger than Connecticut. Not only are some of the counties huge, but there's a lot of them; the state is made up of 254 counties. That explains the title.

It's a big state and a big photo project. Just the photography alone took a little more than fifteen years to complete. This is a book comprises 254 photographs—one from each county in the state. They are not just photos of cities or landmarks, or industrial sites, which you might think would best describe a county. Each is a beautiful landscape photograph illustrating that even in the most urban or rugged county, nature's beauty is always there, and Texas has been blessed abundantly.

When putting the book together, we followed a formula. On each page there is a small map showing the location of the county, along with text outlining when the county was formed, whom it was named for, and a short fact we think you will find interesting. This isn't an atlas or history book; it is a collection of Texas landscape photography.

Lance began photographing Texas in 1992. Although he has photographed throughout the United States and in a variety of foreign countries, his favorite place for photography was Texas.

As an avid hiker, backpacker, and camper, Lance has, over the years, developed a special relationship with maps and atlases. It was this fascination that started him on the journey that has taken him to all 254 counties in Texas and lasted for more than fifteen years.

Lance says that on a day in 1996, while poring through a Texas atlas, his attention was drawn to a map with a grid of all the Texas counties. With an artist's eye for shapes and colors, it came to him that it would be an interesting project to drop a landscape photo into the shape of each of the counties. This was all the kick start the project needed. At the time he had other projects and assignments that occupied a great deal of his time ,and paid the bills, so working full time on the project was out of the question. Fifteen years later he had the photos he needed. Now the task was to put it all together into a mural. Lance enlisted the help of Daniel Hamilton, a graphics artist. Two hundred fifty-four photographs called for a large canvas, so they chose an 8-by-8-foot mural printed on vinyl.

The obvious extension of that project is this book, a collection of all 254 photographs used to create the mural.

According to Lance, "You can find the beauty of nature and something interesting to photograph anywhere you go." "Admittedly," he adds, "not all areas of Texas are pho-to-graphic hotspots, but as I have heard it said, there are no boring subjects, only boring photographers." The last photo of the project was shot on January 11, 2012. It was a long and sometimes frustrating process, but when asked what his favorite photograph in the collection is, he says, "I don't have a favorite photo, but I did love the journey."

Tragically, only a few months after this book was finished, Lance was diagnosed with a rare disorder of the optic nerve. Today Lance is blind.

Ronn Varnell September 2019

When a photographer loses his eyesight, an opportunity for reflection—on everything—surfaces. There seemed to be many more questions than anything else. Will there be any more hiking? How will I experience the places that have meant so much to me? What is my relationship to wilderness now? Things change, although the most important of them will always be there.

There have been many character-building experiences given to me over the years. These were not delivered to my doorstep. When we venture out to find these things, we take them, and their benefit is not measured in monetary terms. We find ourselves with a brand of fuel that sustains us indefinitely, perfectly—one day. A notion of giving back to the source of this life hits us. How do we do this? How do we direct our energies in such a way? This land sustains us, all of us. When considering this thought, it becomes apparent that we don't even need to stop being selfish to go down this road. It should be the most natural of things. There are many places that have helped me build a foundation. There is love for all of them. Texas happens to be the place that contains some of the most significant.

Lance Varnell December 2019

Anderson County

Gus Engling Wildlife Management Area

Anderson County was organized in 1846 and is named in honor of Kenneth L. Anderson, who was vice president of the Republic of Texas. In 1826, David G. Burnet received a grant from the Mexican legislature to settle three hundred families in what is now Anderson County. Most of the settlers in the county came from the southern states and from Missouri.

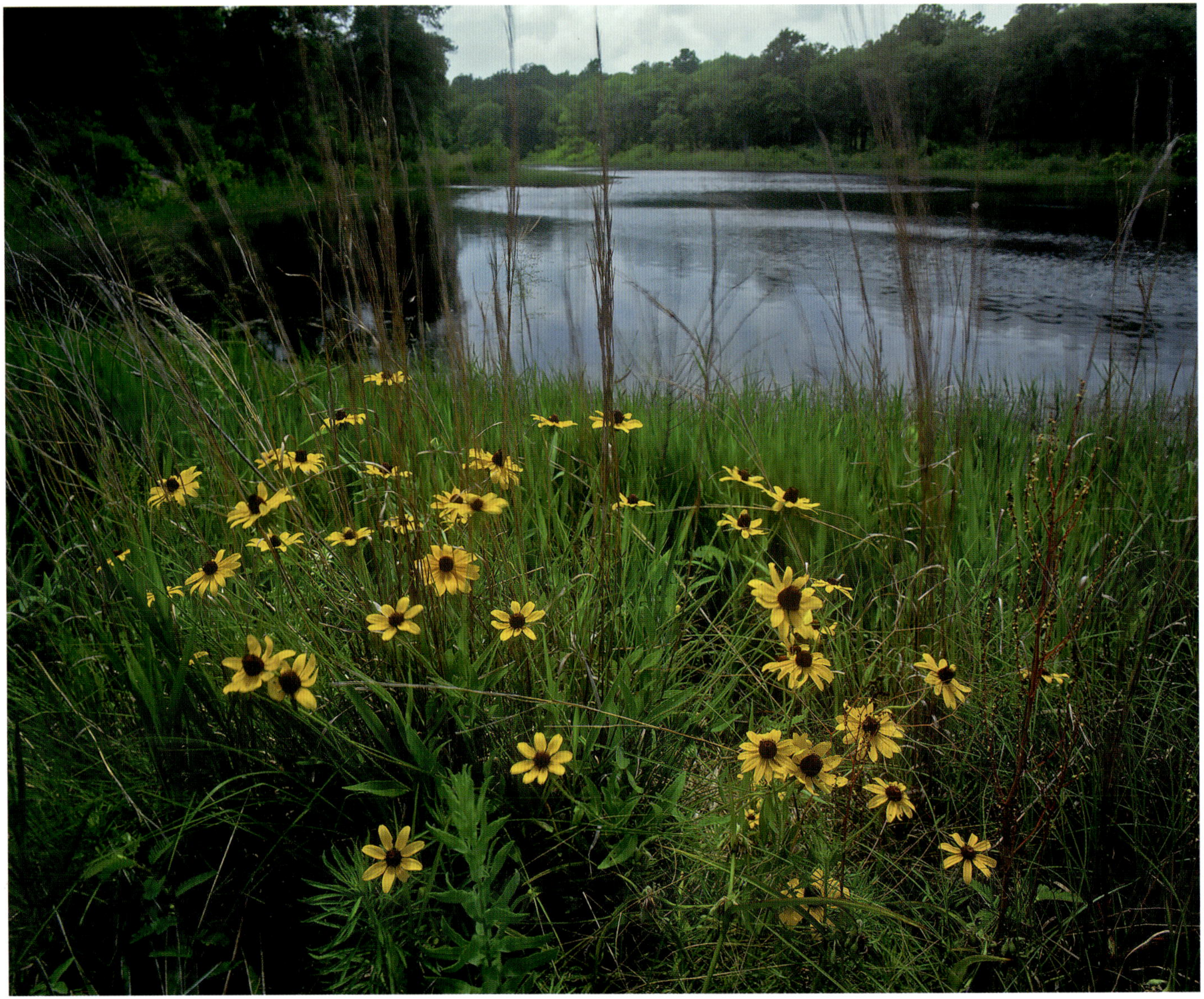

Andrews County

Sunset over Shafter Playa Lake

Andrews is named for Richard Andrews, a soldier of the Texas Revolution. The county was created on August 21, 1876, from Tom Green County and was organized in 1910. Around 1900, to entice voters, the community of Shafter Lake gave free lots to cowboys to enable them to vote for that town in its bid to become the county seat.

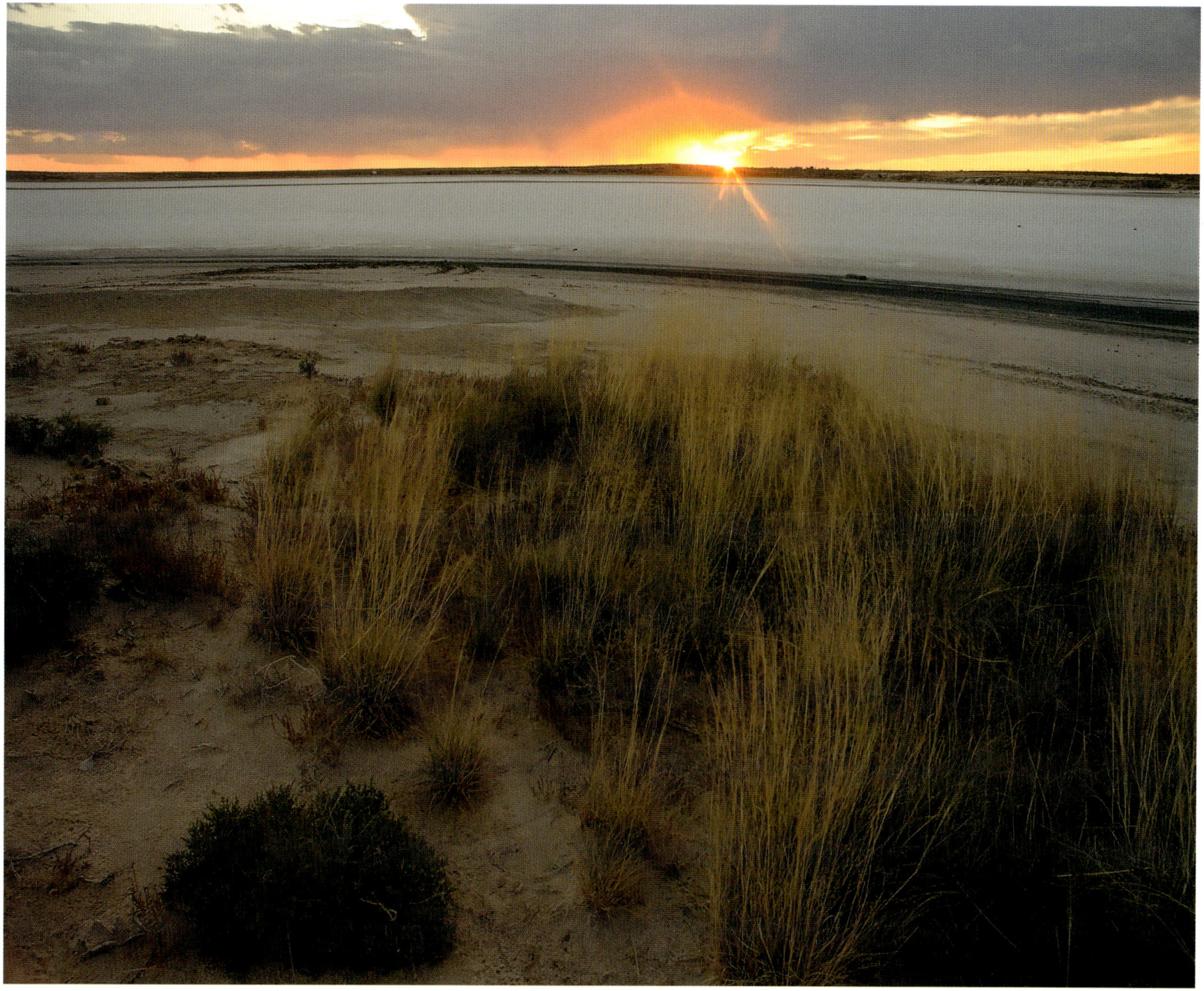

Angelina County

Autumn Wildflowers in the Angelina National Forest

The county was formed in 1846 from Nacogdoches County. It is named for a Hasinai Native American woman who assisted early Spanish missionaries and was given the name Angelina by them. In 1861, Angelina County was the only county in East Texas, and one of only a handful of other Texas counties to reject secession.

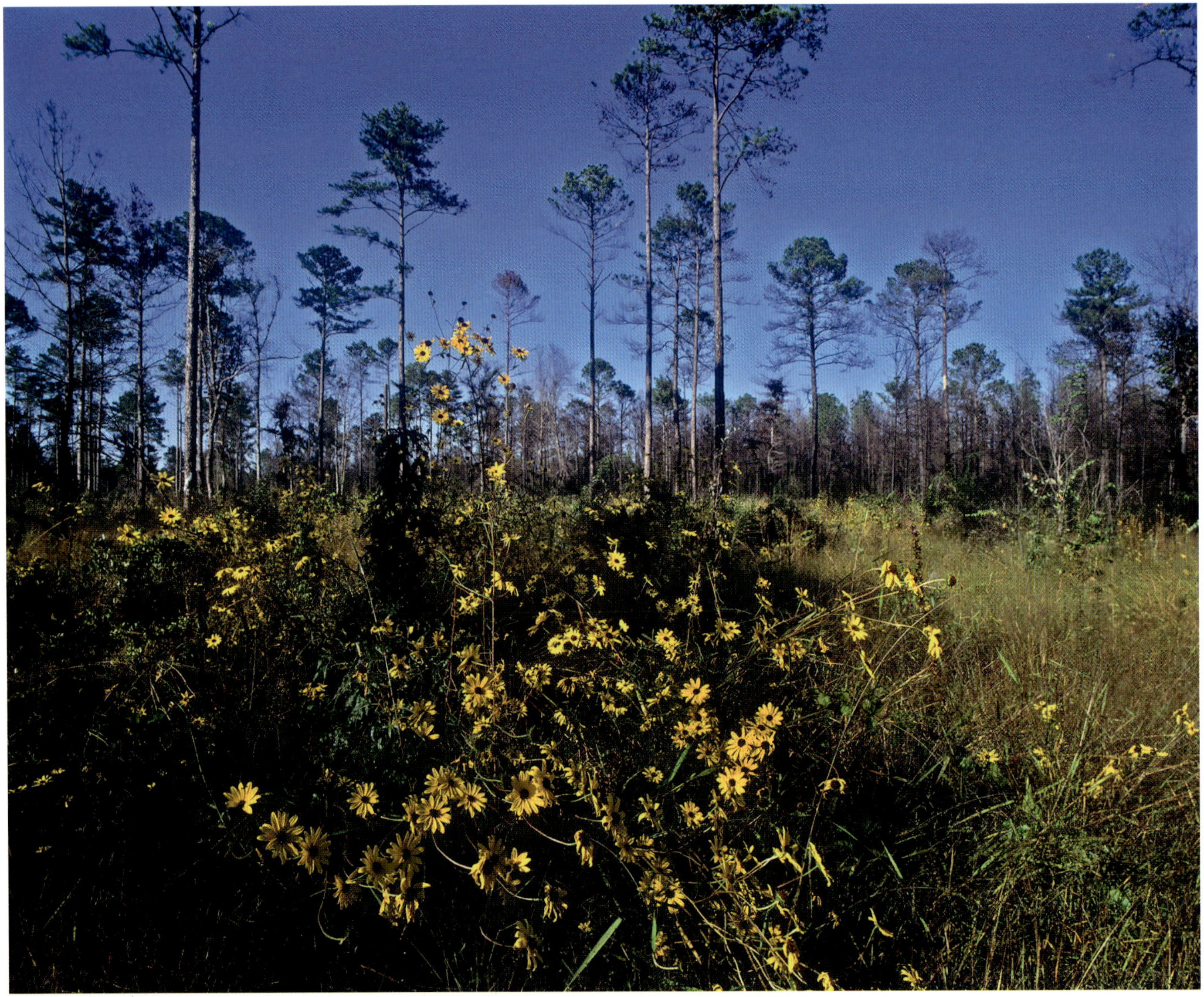

Aransas County

Sunset over Coastal Marshland

The county was formed in 1871 from Refugio County and was organized the following year. It was named for the Rio Nuestra Señora de Aranzazu, a Spanish outpost in early Texas. The first European to see this land was probably Alonso Álvarez de Pineda, who sailed along the coast of Texas in summer 1519 and also discovered Aransas Bay.

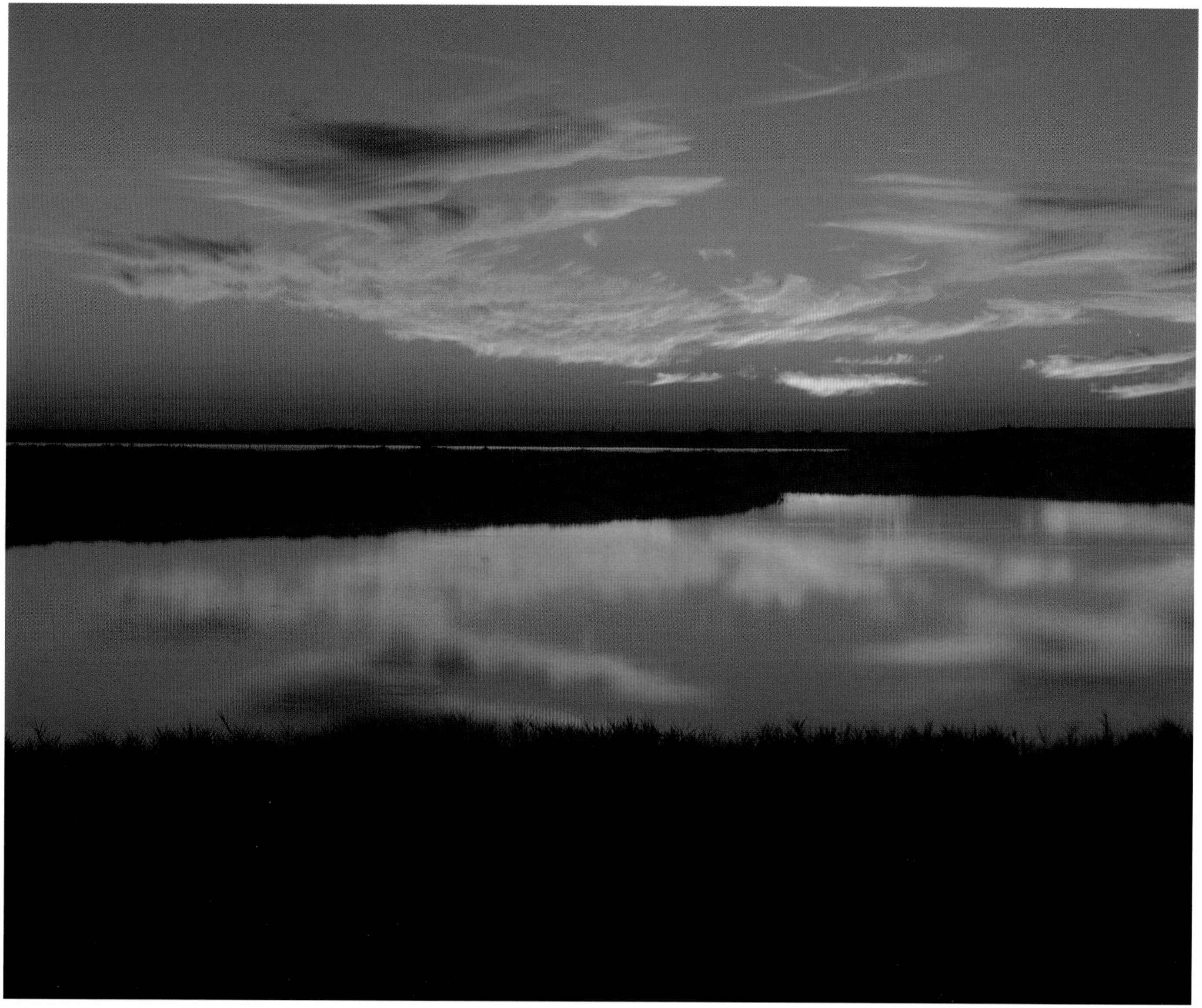

Archer County

Wichita River and Willow Tree

The county was formed in 1858 and organized in 1880. It is named for Branch Tanner Archer, a commissioner for the Republic of Texas. Before white settlement, Apaches, Wichitas, Tawakonis, Kichais, Caddoes, Comanches, and later Kiowas camped and hunted in the area now known as Archer County. Today ranching plays an essential part in the economy of the county.

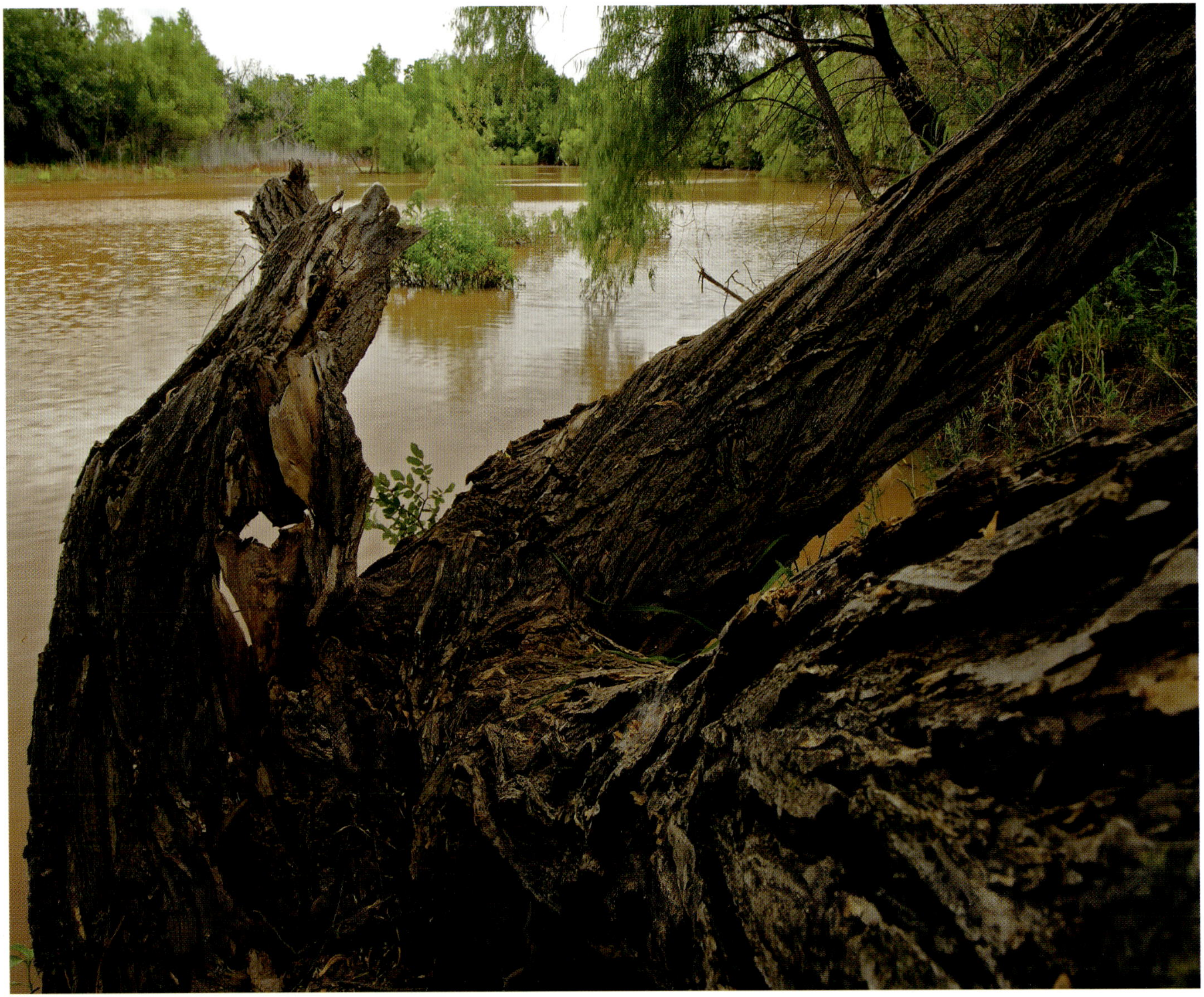

Armstrong County

Palo Duro Canyon State Park

Armstrong County was formed from a part of Bexar County in 1876 and was organized in 1890. It was named for one of several pioneering Armstrong families in Texas. Tom Blasingame, the so-called "oldest living cowboy in the history of the American West," worked in Armstrong County for seventy-three years.

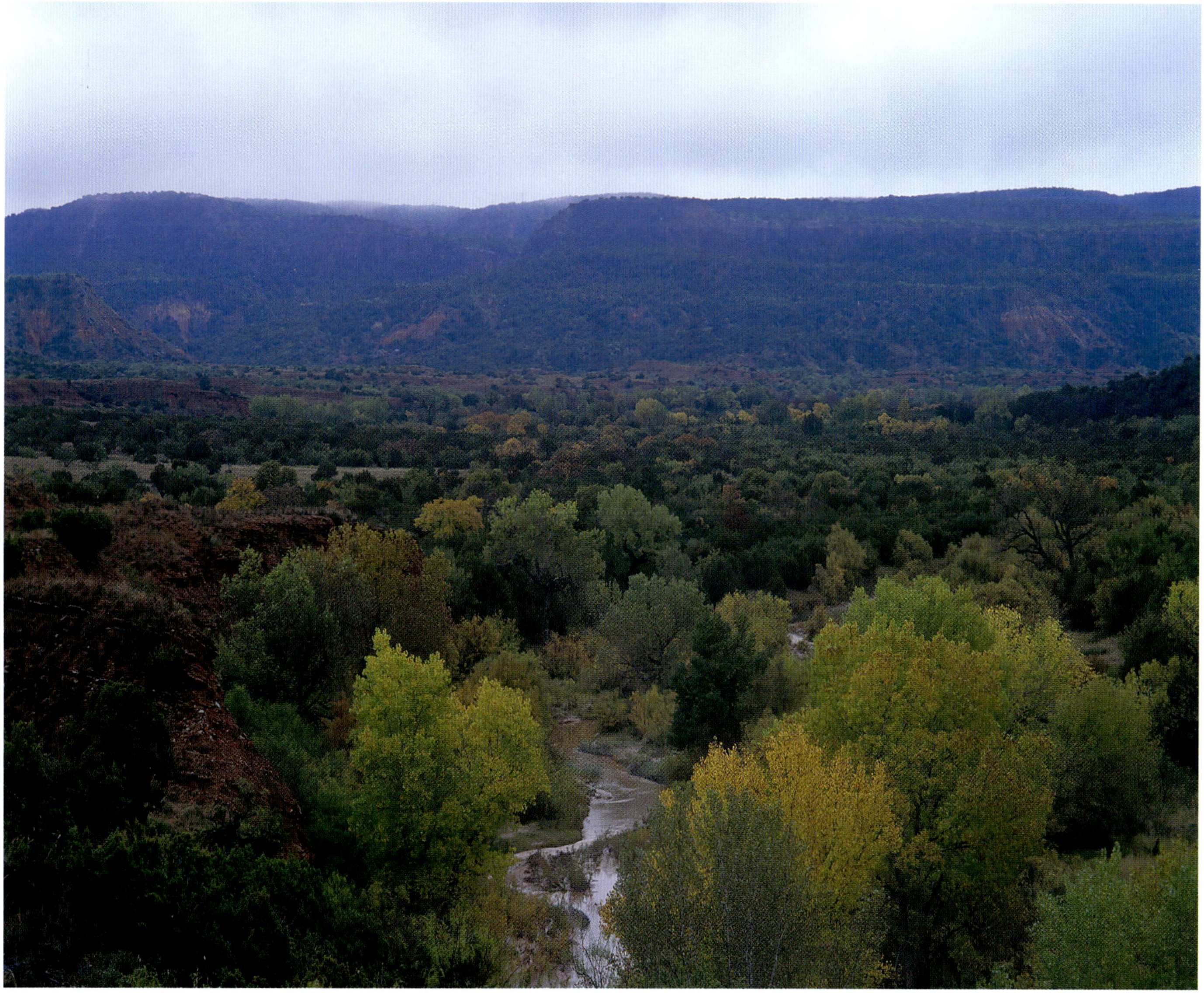

Atascosa County

Wildflowers, Prickly Pear, and Mesquite

Formed from part of Bexar County in 1856, the county is named for the Atascosa River. The Atascosa River runs 92 miles southeast through Atascosa County and into Live Oak County, where it drains into the Frio River.

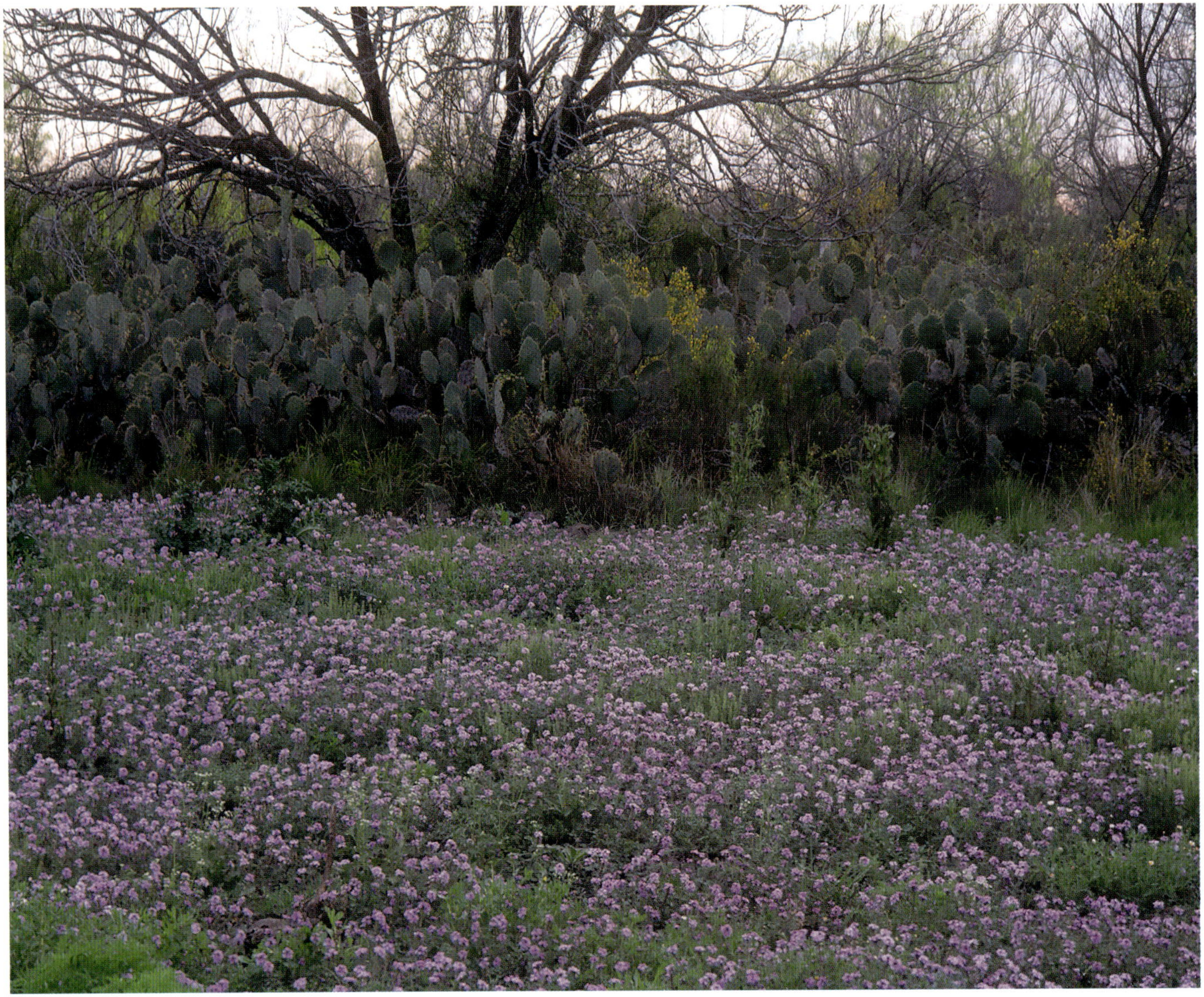

Austin County

Sunset over the Brazos River in Stephen F. Austin State Park

Austin County is named for Stephen F. Austin. It was formed in 1836. Known as the "Father of Texas," Stephen F. Austin led the second and ultimately successful colonization of the region by bringing three hundred families from the United States to the area in 1825.

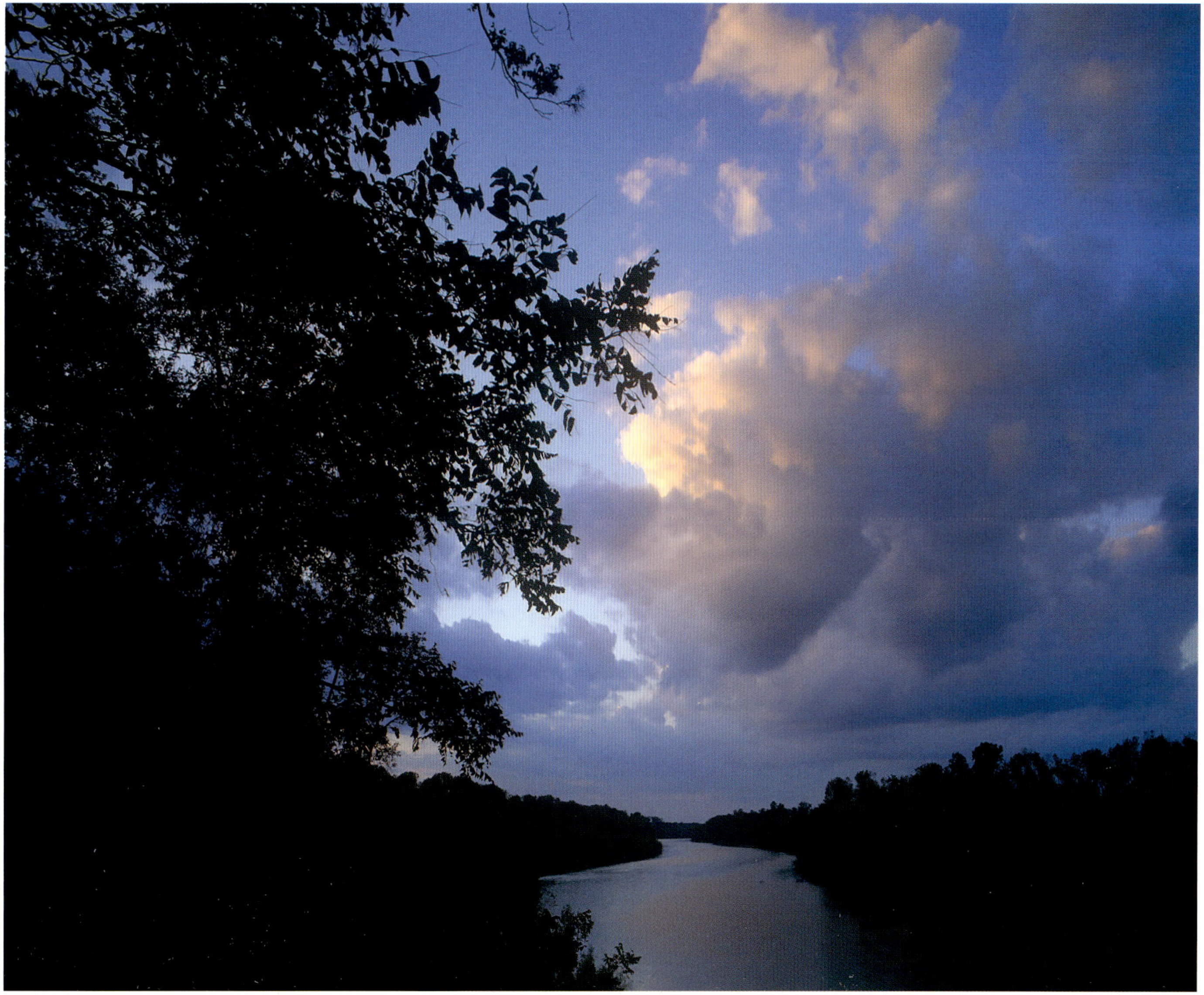

Bailey County

Late Afternoon in Muleshoe National Wildlife Refuge

Bailey County was established in 1876 and is named for Peter James Bailey III, a soldier and defender of the Alamo. Bailey County is one of the thirty dry counties in the state of Texas.

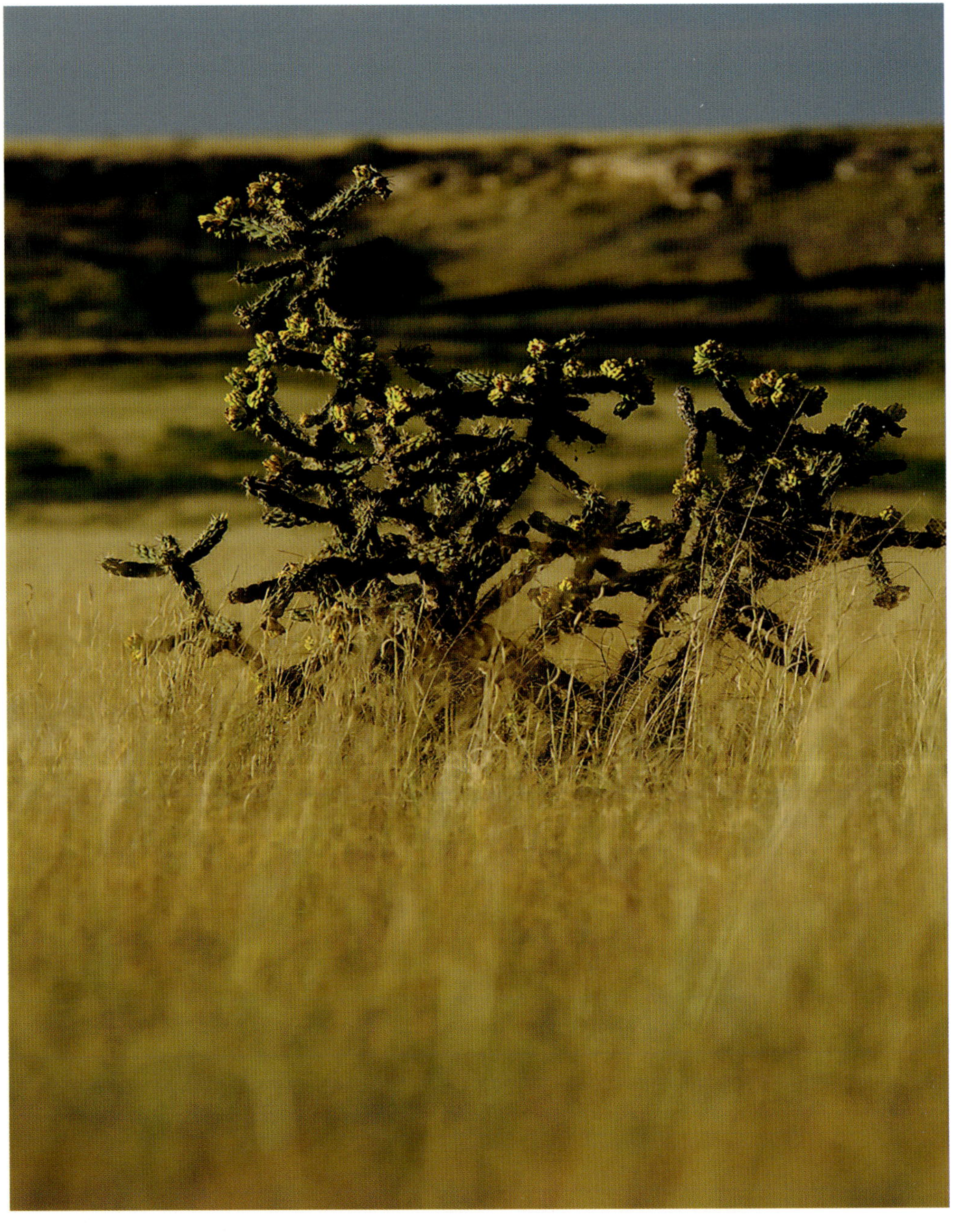

Bandera County

Lost Maples State Natural Area

The county was formed in 1856 from parts of Bexar and Uvalde Counties and is named for Bandera Pass. *Bandera* is the Spanish word for "flag." The community of Bandera is officially recognized by Texas legislature as the "Cowboy Capital of the World."

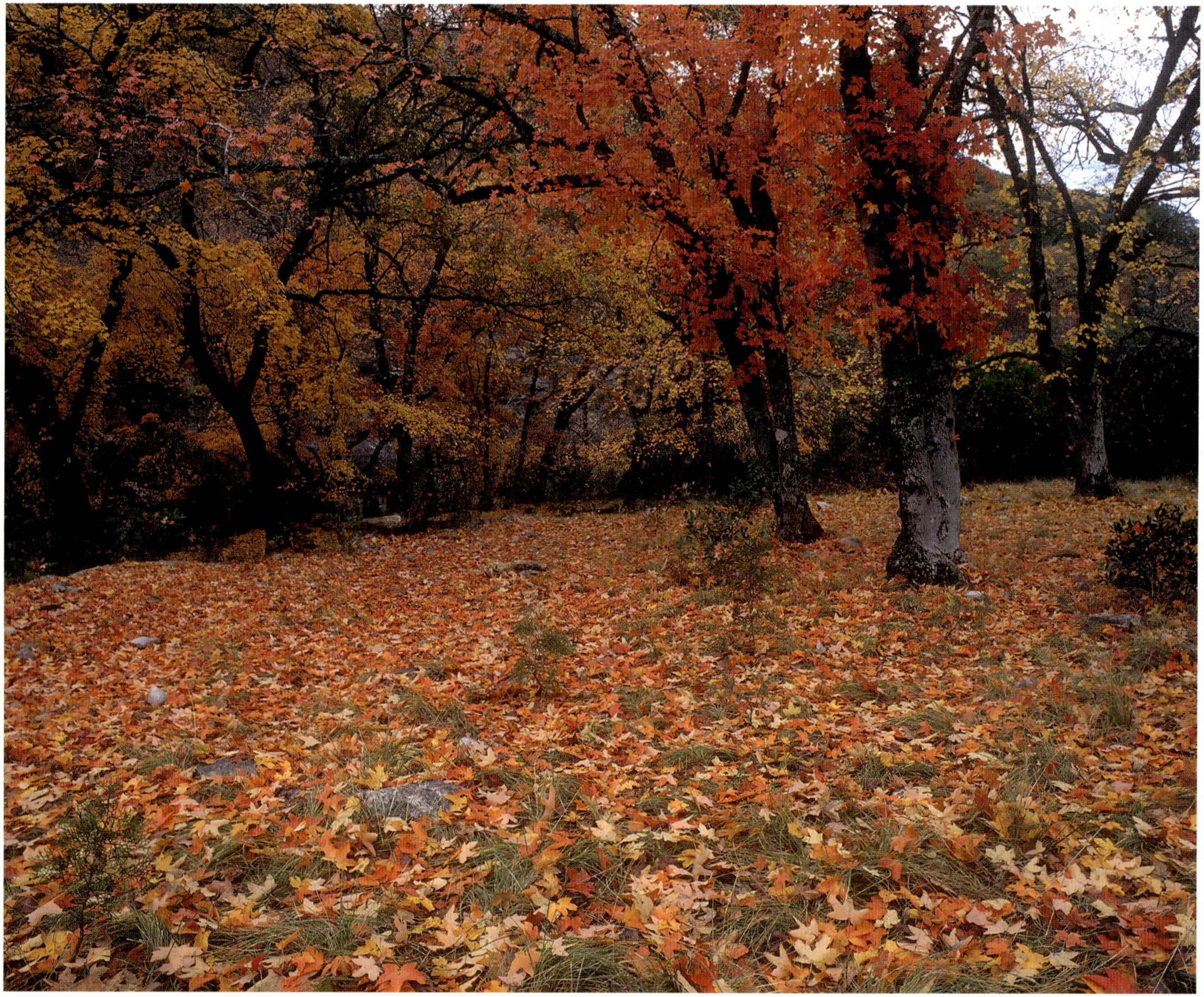

Bastrop County

Bastrop State Park in the Lost Pines Region

The area was organized as a county in 1837 and is named for Felipe Enrique Neri, Baron de Bastrop, an early Dutch settler who assisted Stephen F. Austin in obtaining land grants in Texas. In September 2011, Bastrop County suffered the most destructive wildfire in Texas history, which destroyed more than 1,600 homes.

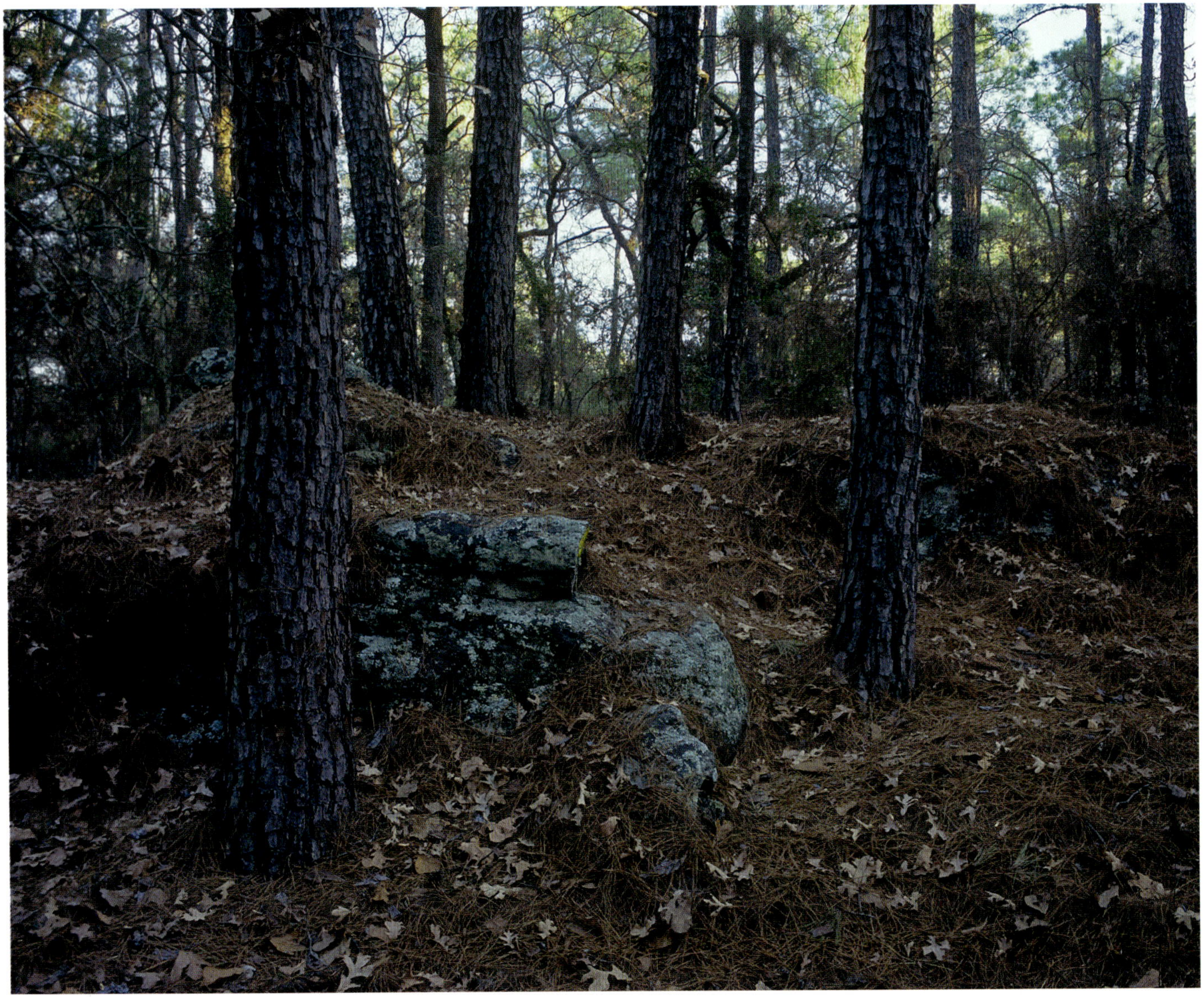

Baylor County

Wichita River Sunrise

The county was created in 1858 and organized in 1879. It is named for Henry Weidner Baylor, a surgeon in the Texas Rangers during the Mexican-American War. Before it was settled, the area that is now Baylor County lay within the range of the Wanderers, a nomadic Comanche band who relied on buffalo for food, clothing, shelter, tools, and ornaments.

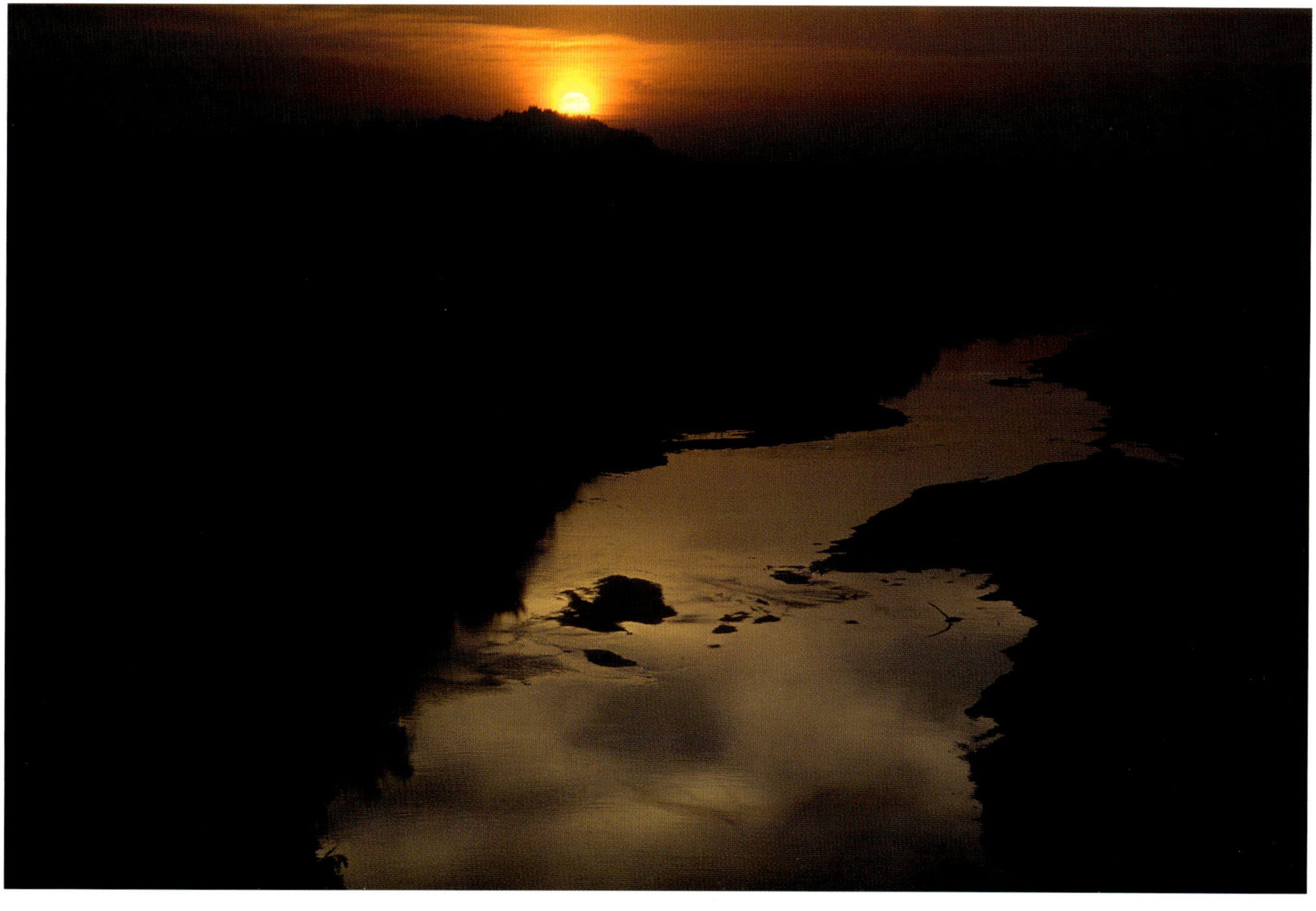

Bee County

Live Oak in Afternoon Light

The county was founded on December 8, 1857, and was organized the following year. It is named for Barnard E. Bee Sr., a secretary of state of the Republic of Texas. The early European settlers of this area were mainly Irish immigrants, but toward the end of the 1840s and early 1850s, more settlers from the southern states began to move in and build settlements.

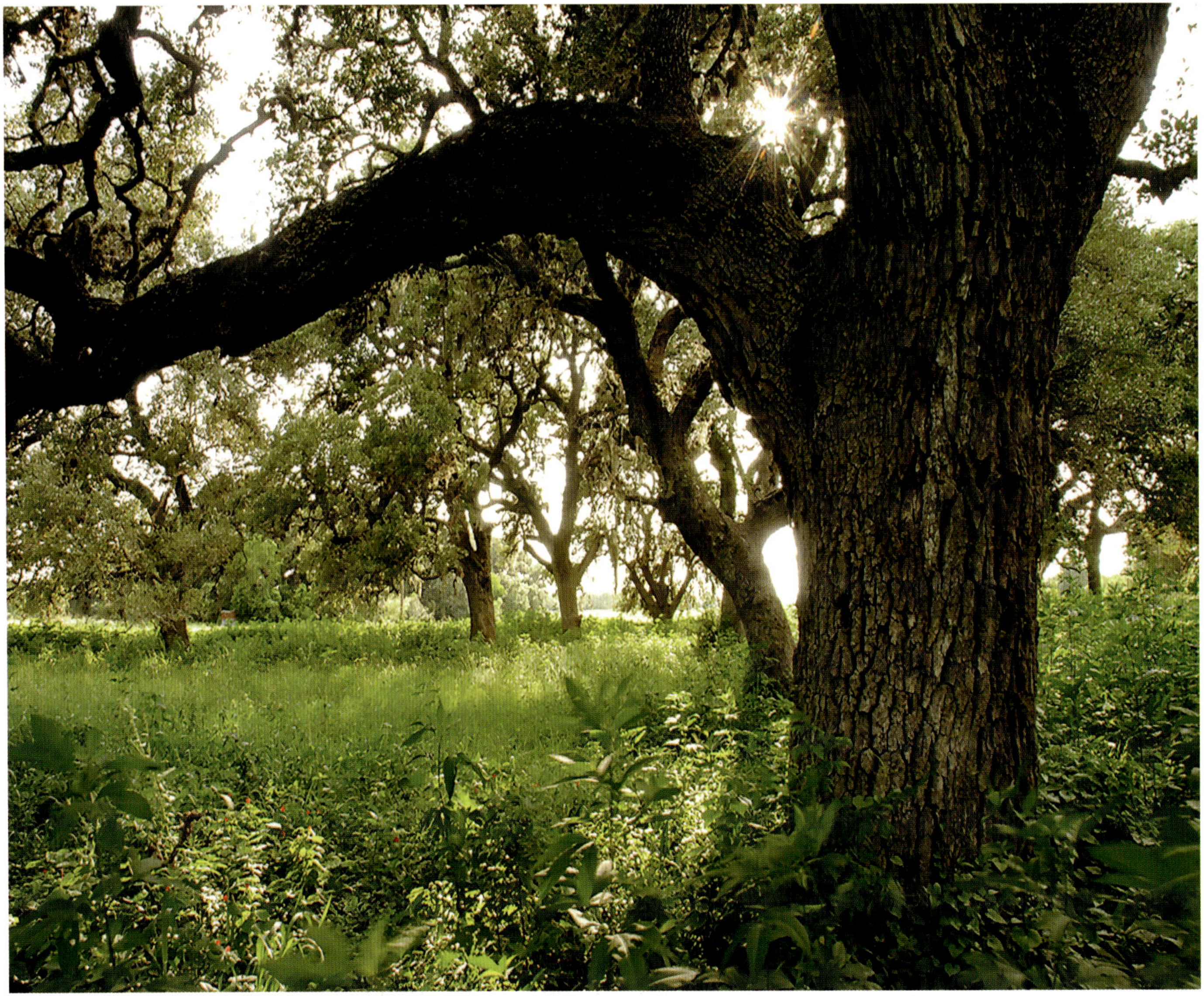

Bell County

Leon River at Sunrise

The county was founded in 1850 and is named for Peter Hansborough Bell, the third governor of Texas. Bell County is the home of Fort Hood, a military training base that opened in 1942.

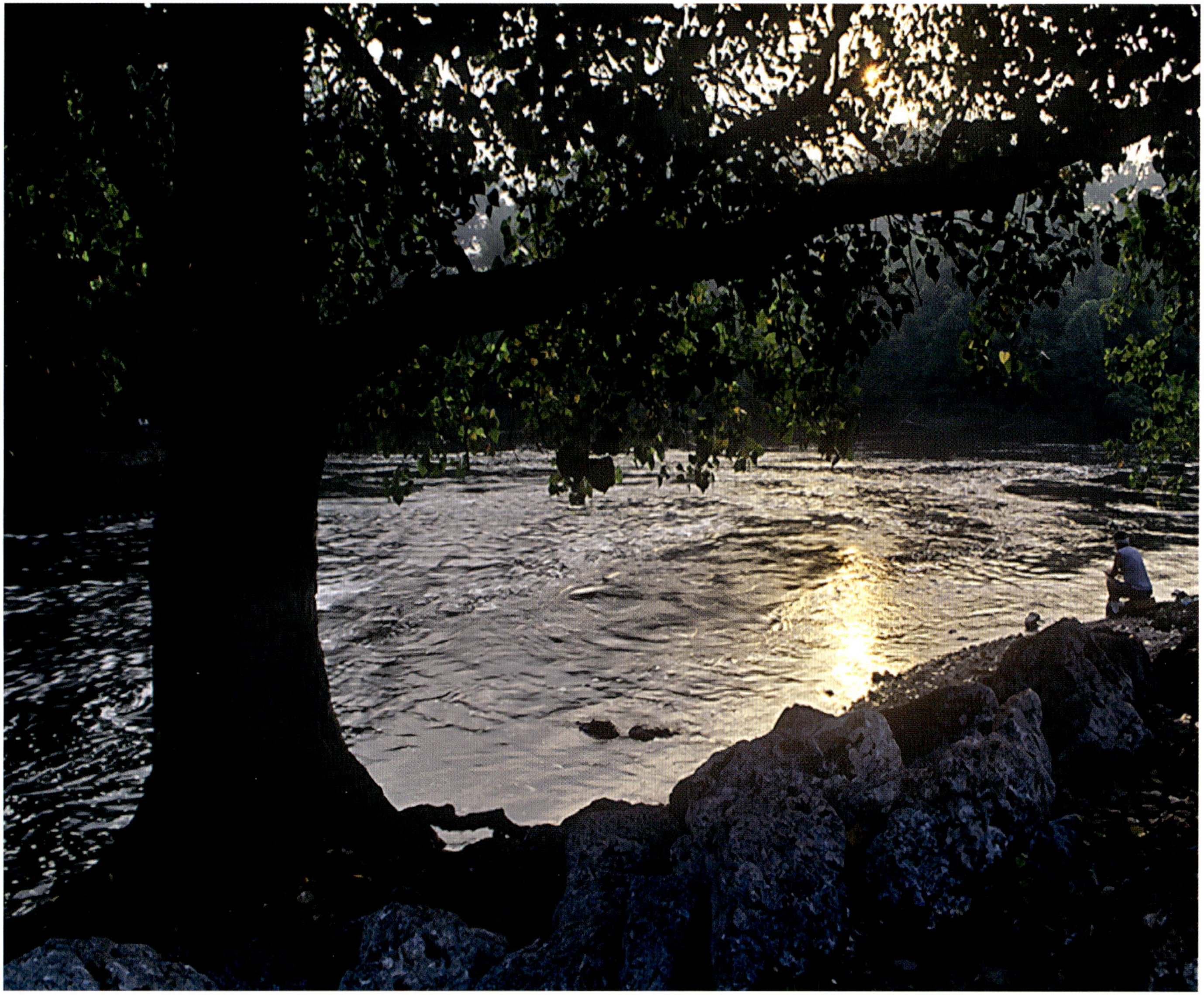

Bexar County

Government Canyon State Natural Area

Bexar County (pronounced "Bear" in Texas) was established in 1836 and is named for San Antonio de Bexar, the major presidio in Mexican Texas, named in turn for the San Antonio River and the Spanish viceroy's family, who were Dukes of Bejar in Spain. Bexar is one of the original Texas counties. The Alamo is in San Antonio, which is in Bexar County.

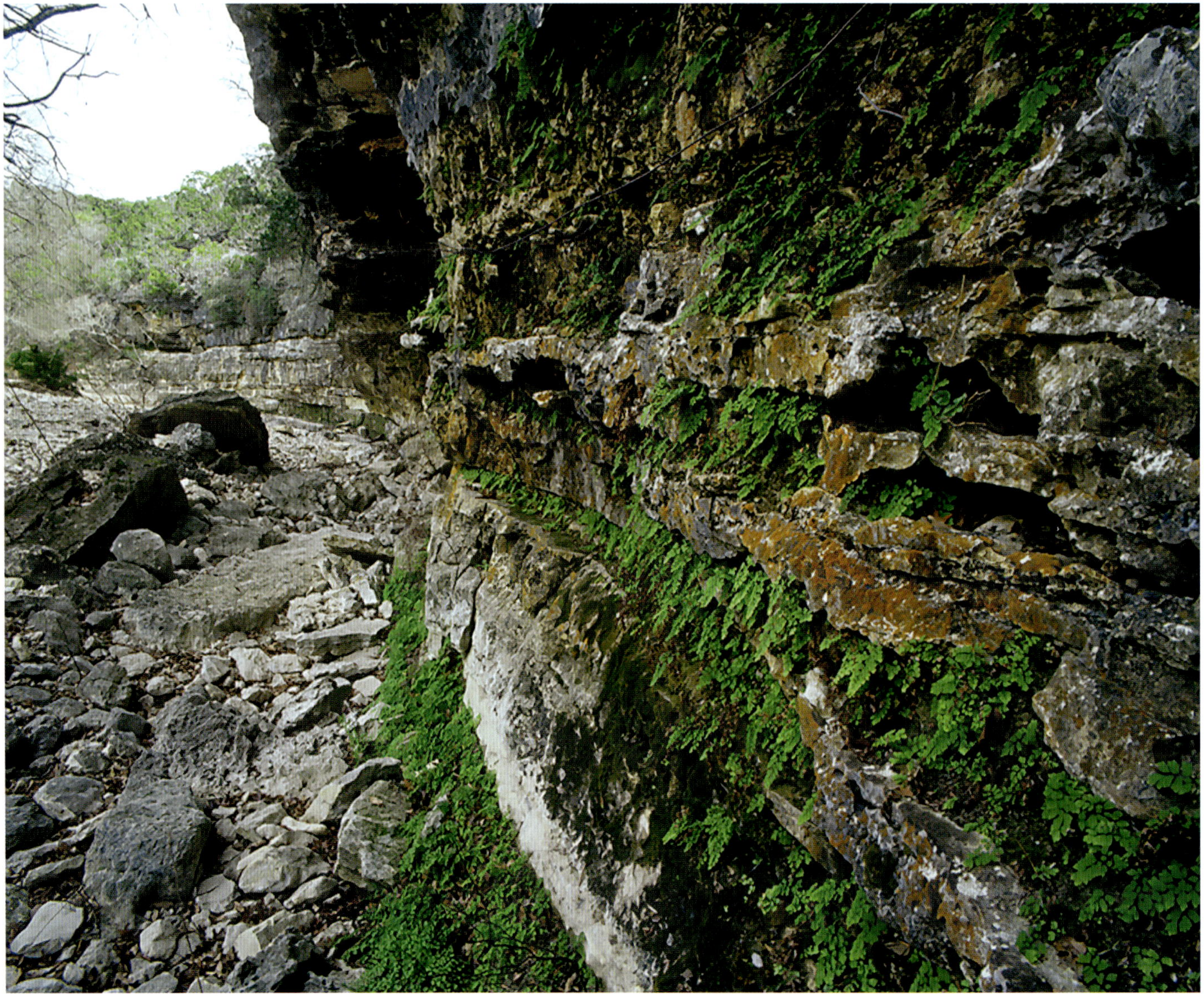

Blanco County

Pedernales Falls State Park

Named for the Blanco River (Spanish for "white"), the county was established in 1858. In the 1850s, Samuel Ealy Johnson Sr.—grandfather of President Lyndon B. Johnson—and his brother Jesse Thomas Johnson founded a cattle business in Johnson City. The town is named for their nephew, James Polk Johnson. The Johnson family emigrated from Alabama.

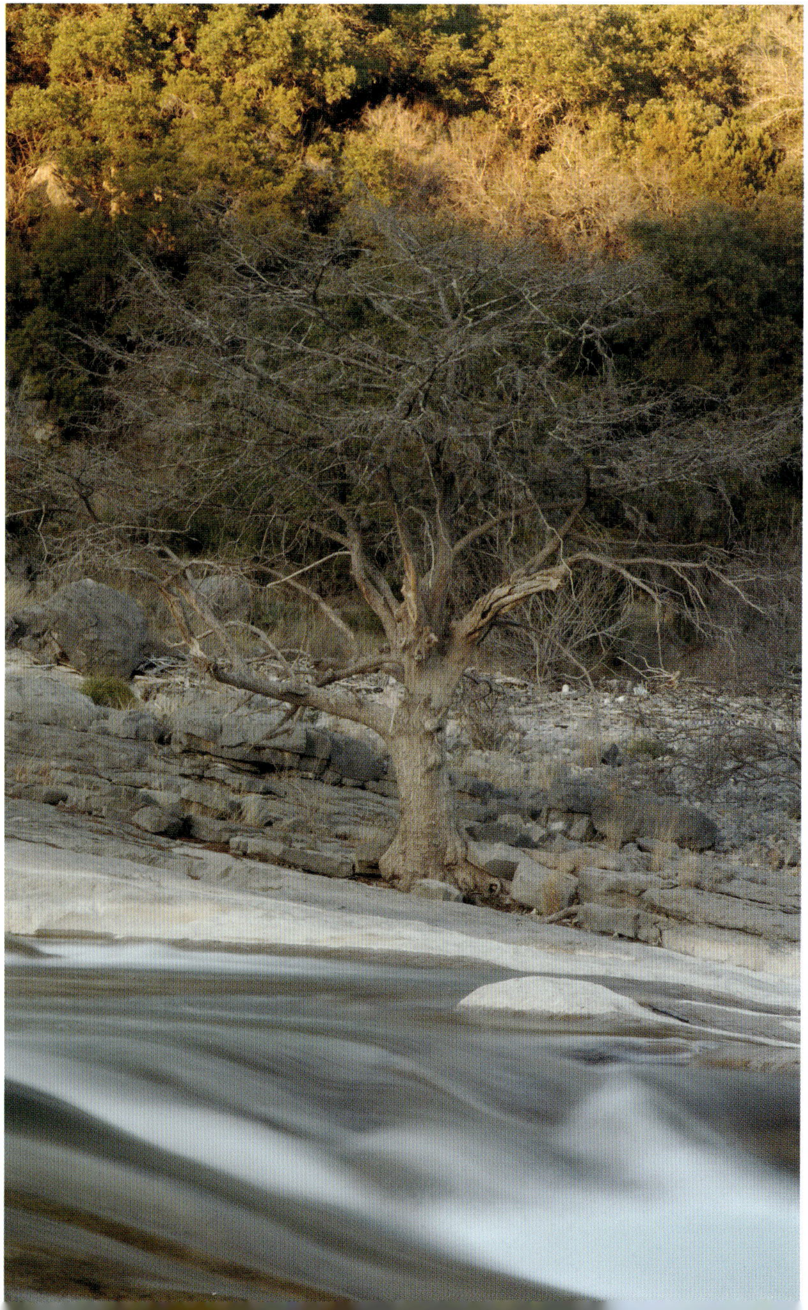

Borden County

Headwaters of the Colorado River near the Community of Union

Borden County was established in 1876. The county was named for businessman Gail Borden Jr., the inventor of condensed milk.

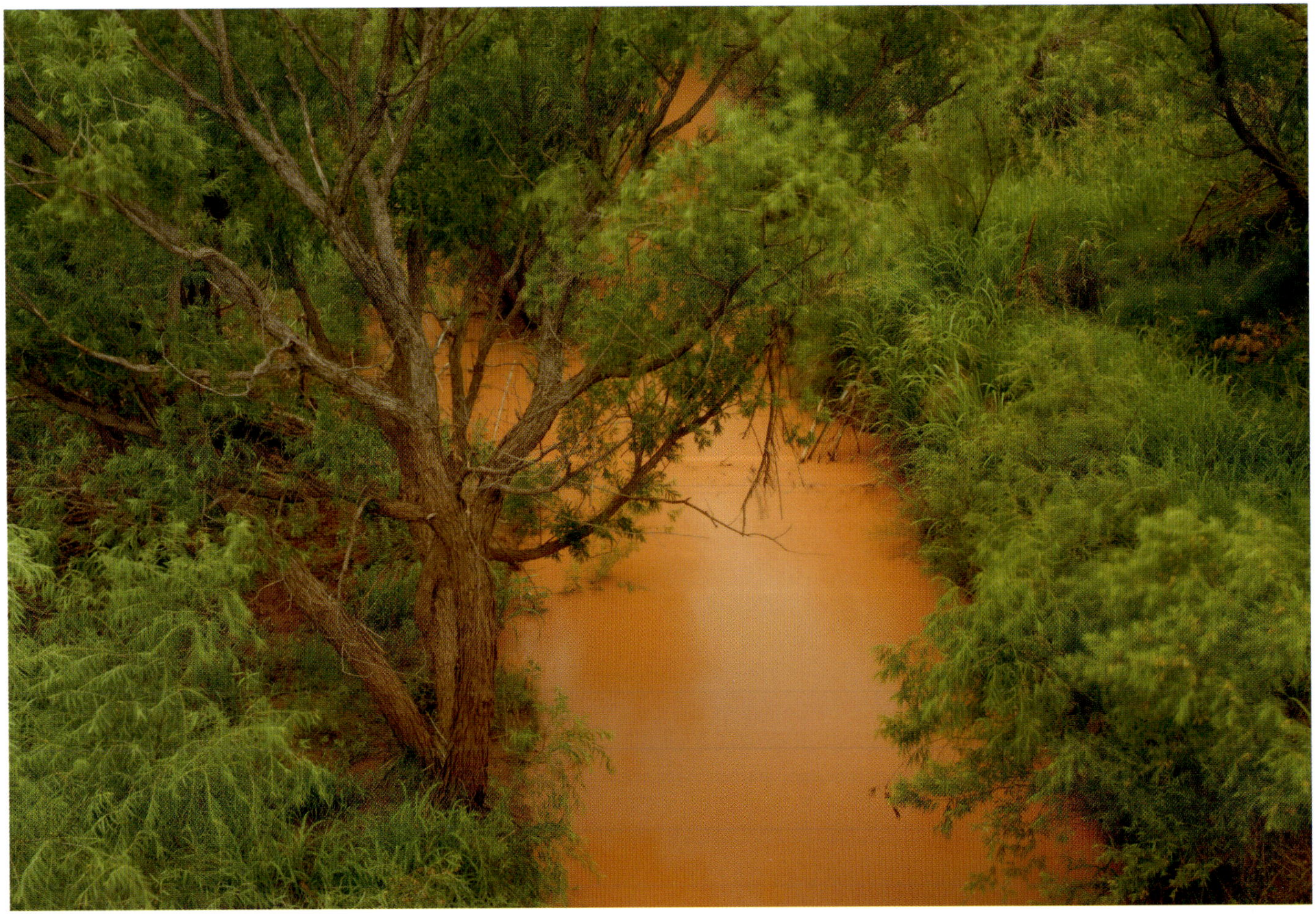

Bosque County

Meridian State Park

This county is named for the Bosque River. *Bosque* is the Spanish word for "forest." The county was founded in 1854. Notable residents have included Jacob De Cordova, an early member of the Texas House of Representatives; Calvin M. Cueton, Texas chief justice from 1921 to 1940; and James E. Ferguson, the twenty-sixth governor of the state of Texas, from 1915 to 1917.

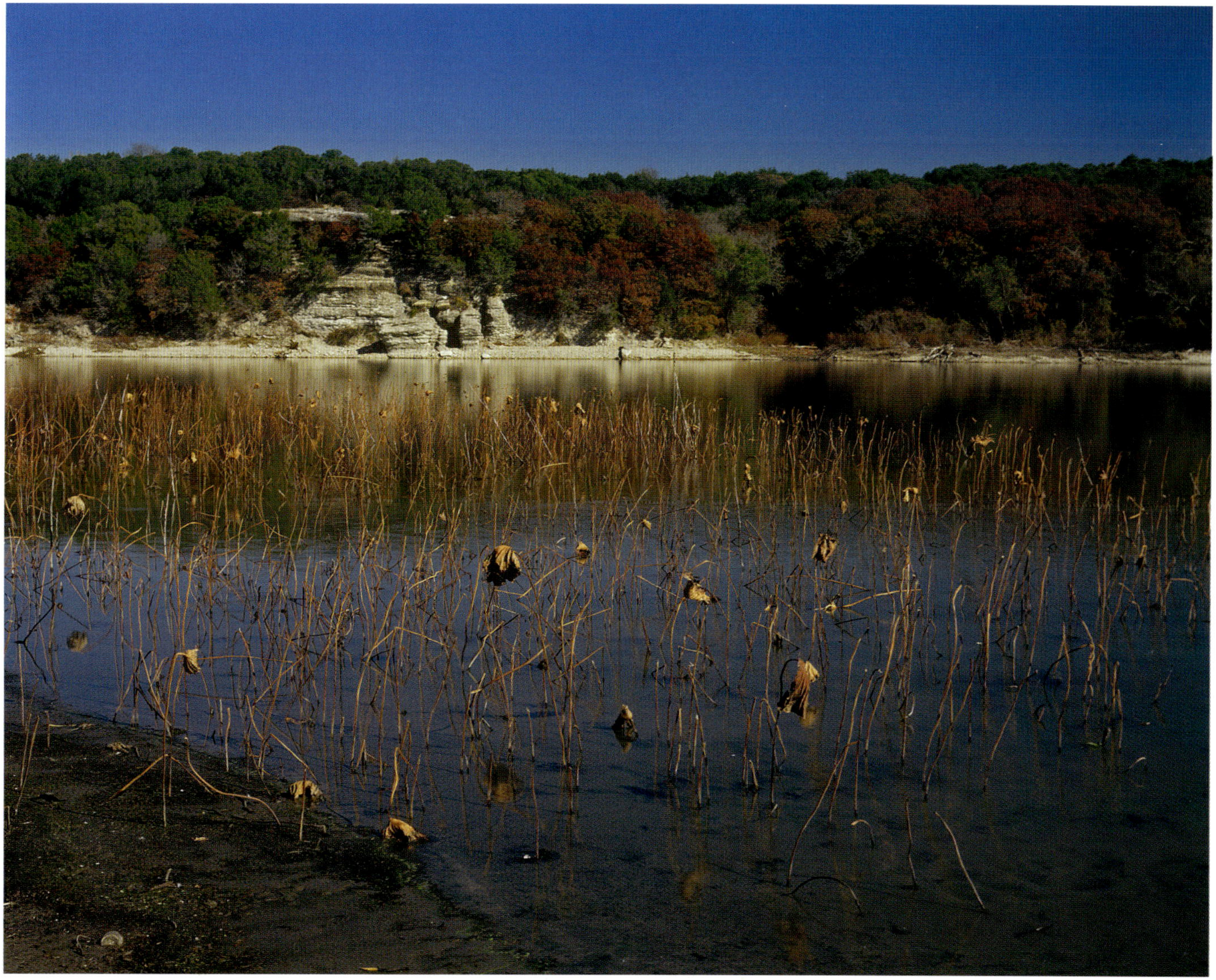

Bowie County

Springtime Scene near the Oklahoma Border

Bowie County was established in 1840 and is named for the famous knife fighter Jim Bowie, who died at the Alamo. French explorer Jean Baptiste Benard de La Harpe founded the military fort Le Poste des Cadodaquious in 1719. The fort remained in continuous use until 1770.

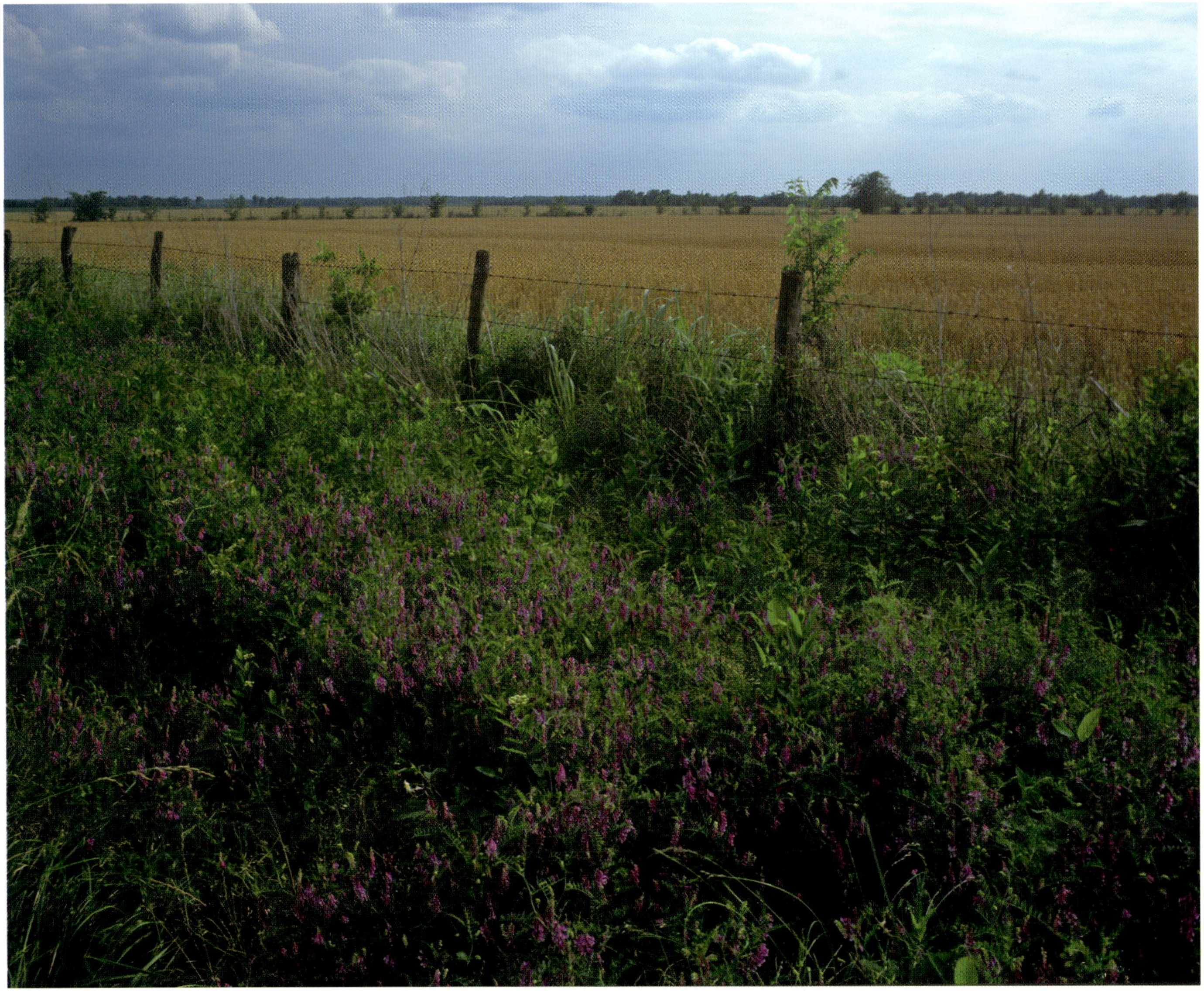

Brazoria County

Peach Point Wildlife Management Area

The county was named for Brazoria, Texas, an early port on the Brazos River. It was established in 1836 as one of the original twenty-three counties. Stephen F. Austin's original burial place is in Gulf Prairie Cemetery, in the town of Jones Creek, Texas, on what was his brother-in-law's "Peach Point Plantation." His remains were exhumed in 1910, to be reinterred at the state capital in Austin. The town of West Columbia served as the first capital of Texas, dating to prerevolutionary days.

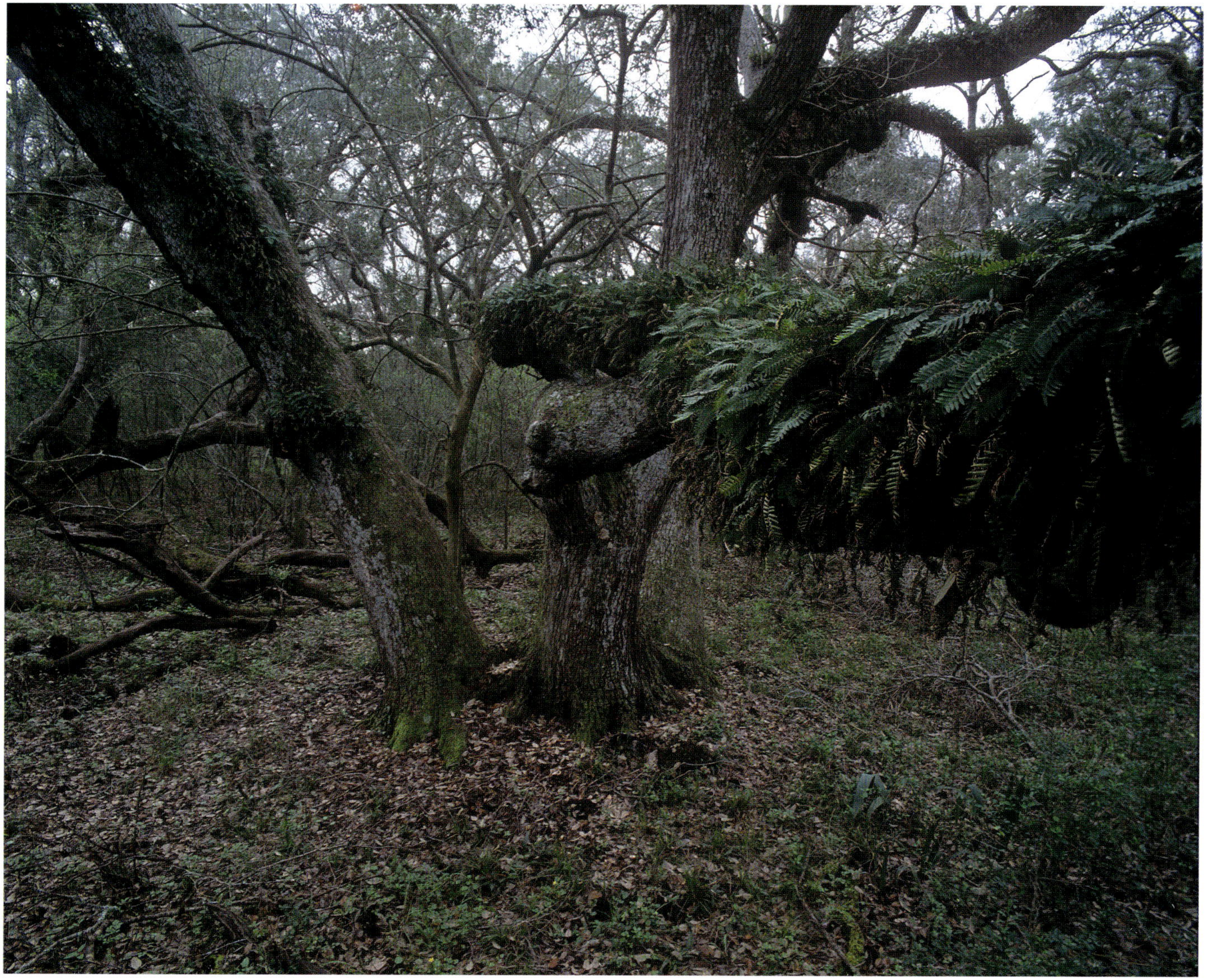

Brazos County

Ranchland Sunset in the Southern Portion of the County

Established in 1841, the county is named for the Brazos River. Formerly one of the state's poorer counties, the county donated 2,416 acres of land in the 1870s to create Texas A&M University. That donation has enabled the county to be among the state's most financially successful.

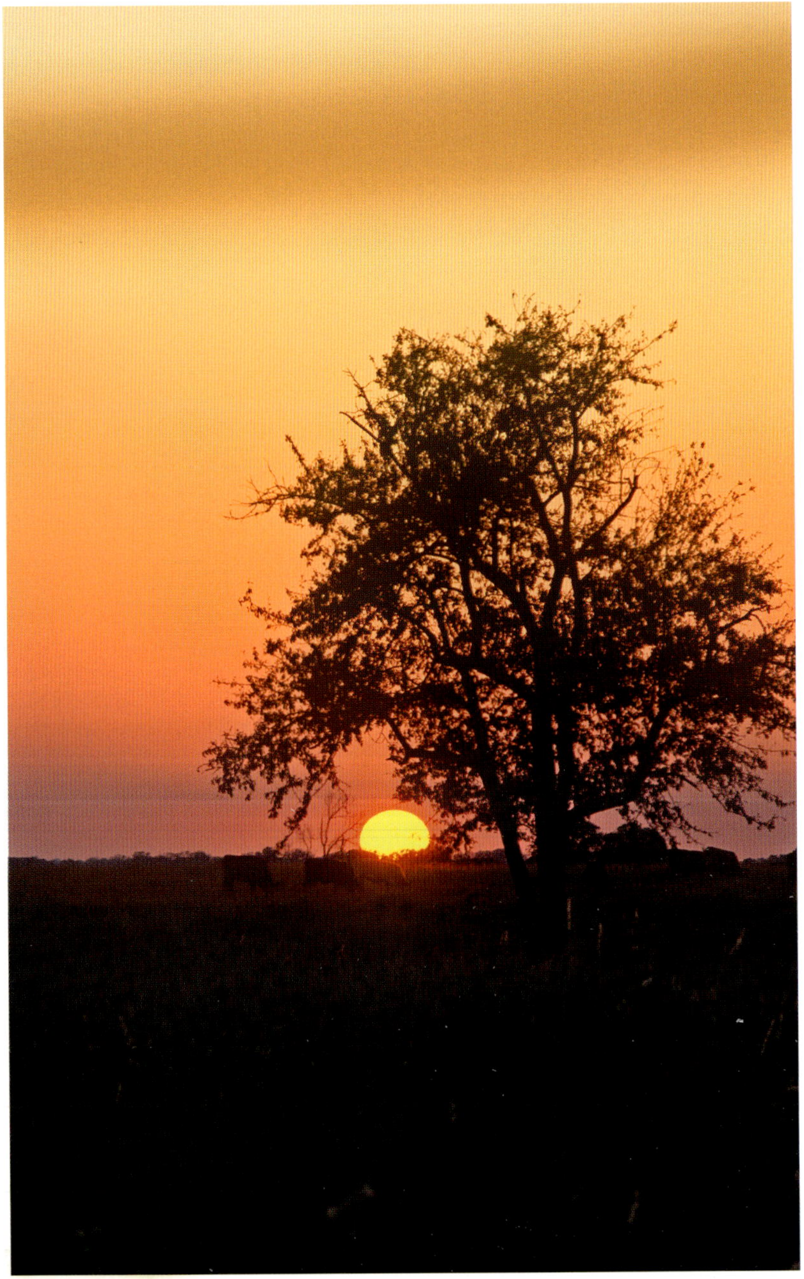

Brewster County

Rio Grande River near Mariscal Canyon in Big Bend

Brewster County was founded in 1887. The county's namesake was Henry Percy Brewster (1816–1884), a secretary of war for the Republic of Texas and a soldier in the Civil War. Big Bend National Park is in Brewster County. The park's 800,000 acres have national significance as the largest protected area of Chihuahuan Desert topography and ecology in the United States. This county is the largest in Texas.

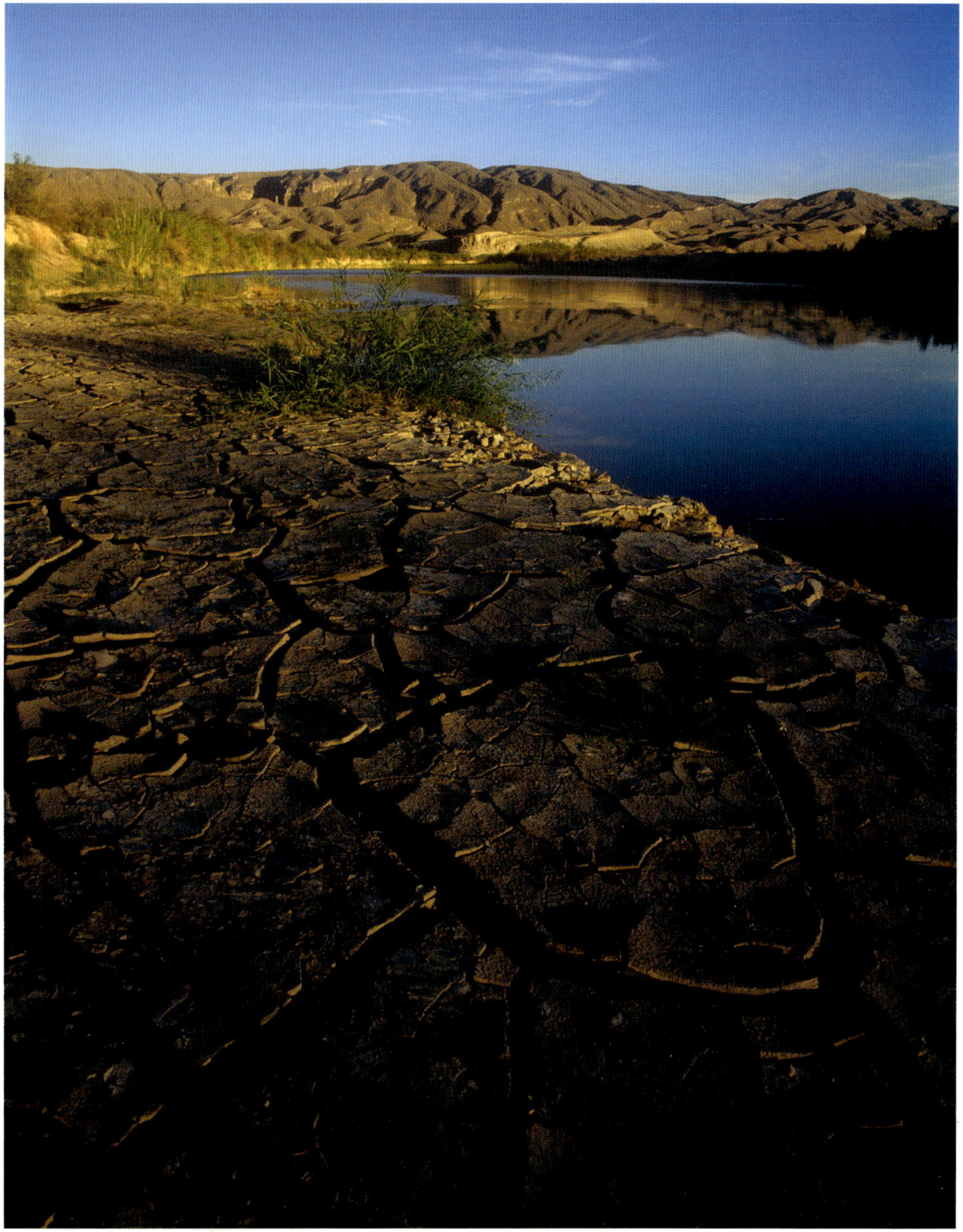

Briscoe County

Cap Rock Canyons State Park

The county is named for Andrew Briscoe (1810–1849), a signatory of the Texan Declaration of Independence and a soldier during the Texan Revolution. The county was established in 1876. At one time the vast JA Ranch, founded by Charles Goodnight and John George Adair, reached into Briscoe County.

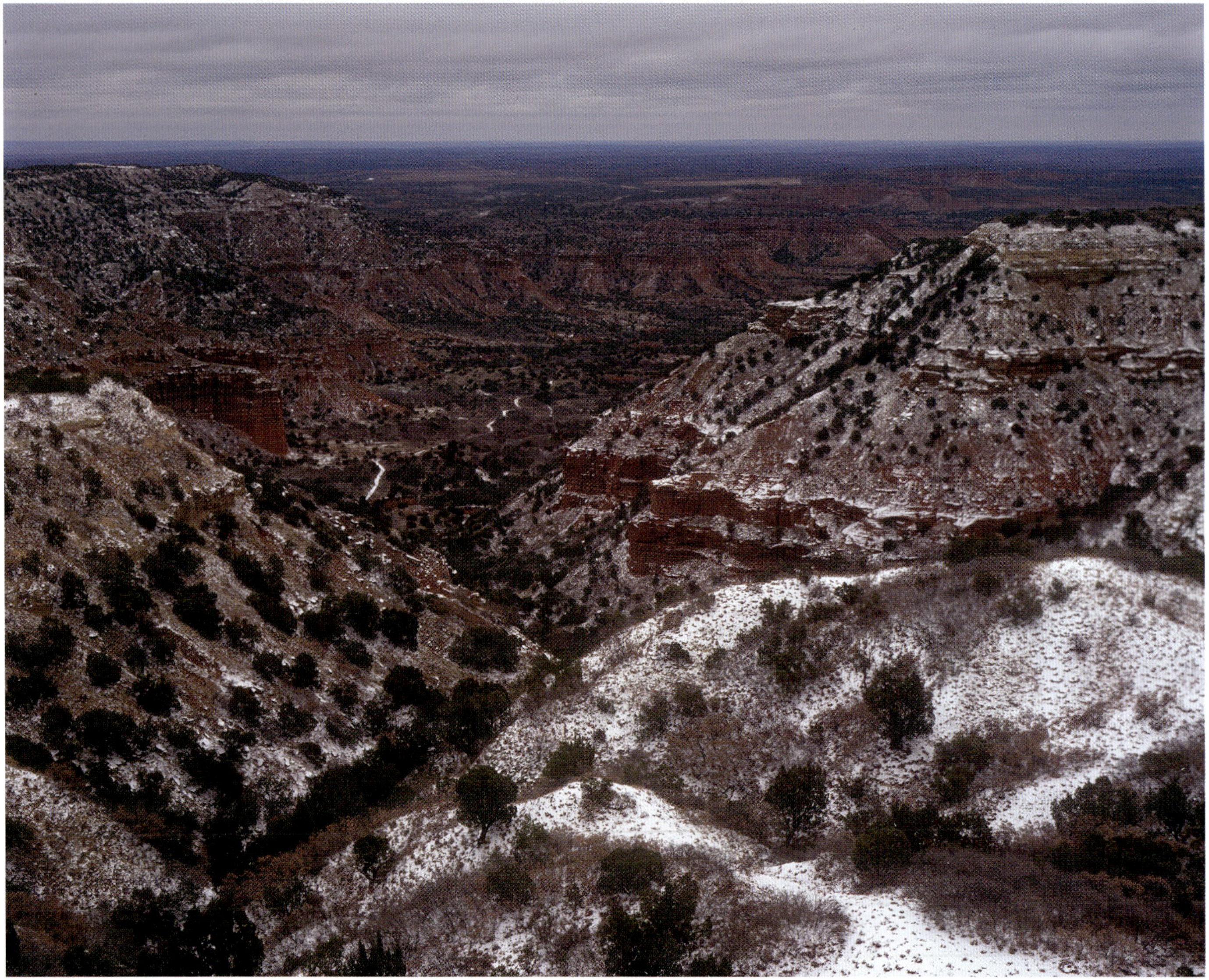

Brooks County

Wildflowers and Mesquite

Brooks County was established in 1911 and is named for James Abijah Brooks, a Texas Ranger and state legislator. Brooks rapidly gained a reputation as a Ranger who would quickly draw his gun rather than negotiate. In 1886, while pursuing outlaws in the Indian Territory, Brooks became involved in a gunfight that almost cost him his life and resulted in one man being killed.

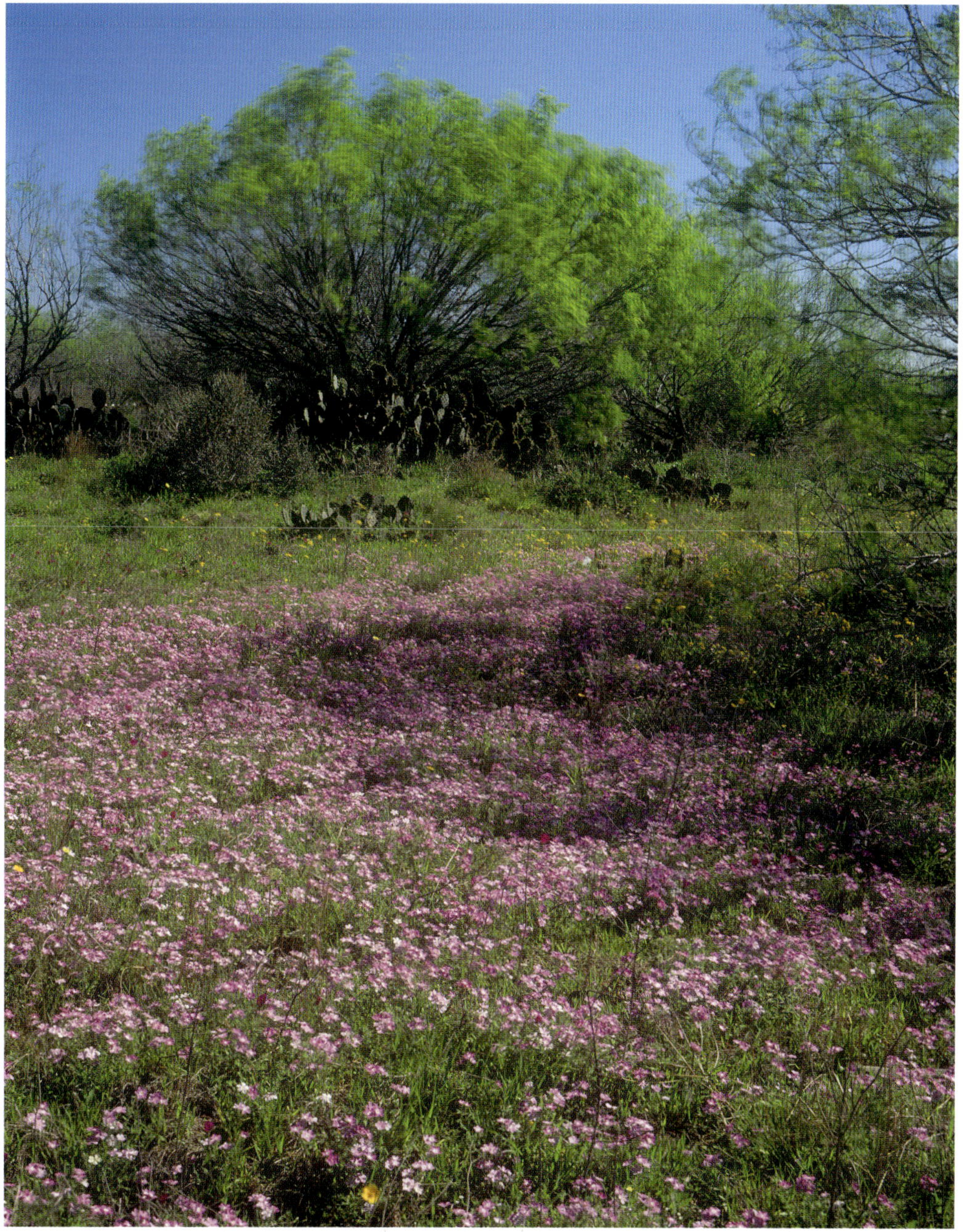

Brown County

Lake Brownwood State Park

The county is named for Henry Stevenson Brown, a commander at the Battle of Velasco. The county was formed in 1856. The famous outlaw John Wesley Hardin and gang celebrated his twenty-first birthday in Brown County. Lawman Charles Webb drew his gun, provoking a gunfight that ended Webb's life. A lynch mob was formed, but Hardin and his family were put into protective custody. The crowd broke into the jail and hanged his brother Joe and two cousins, but Hardin was able to escape.

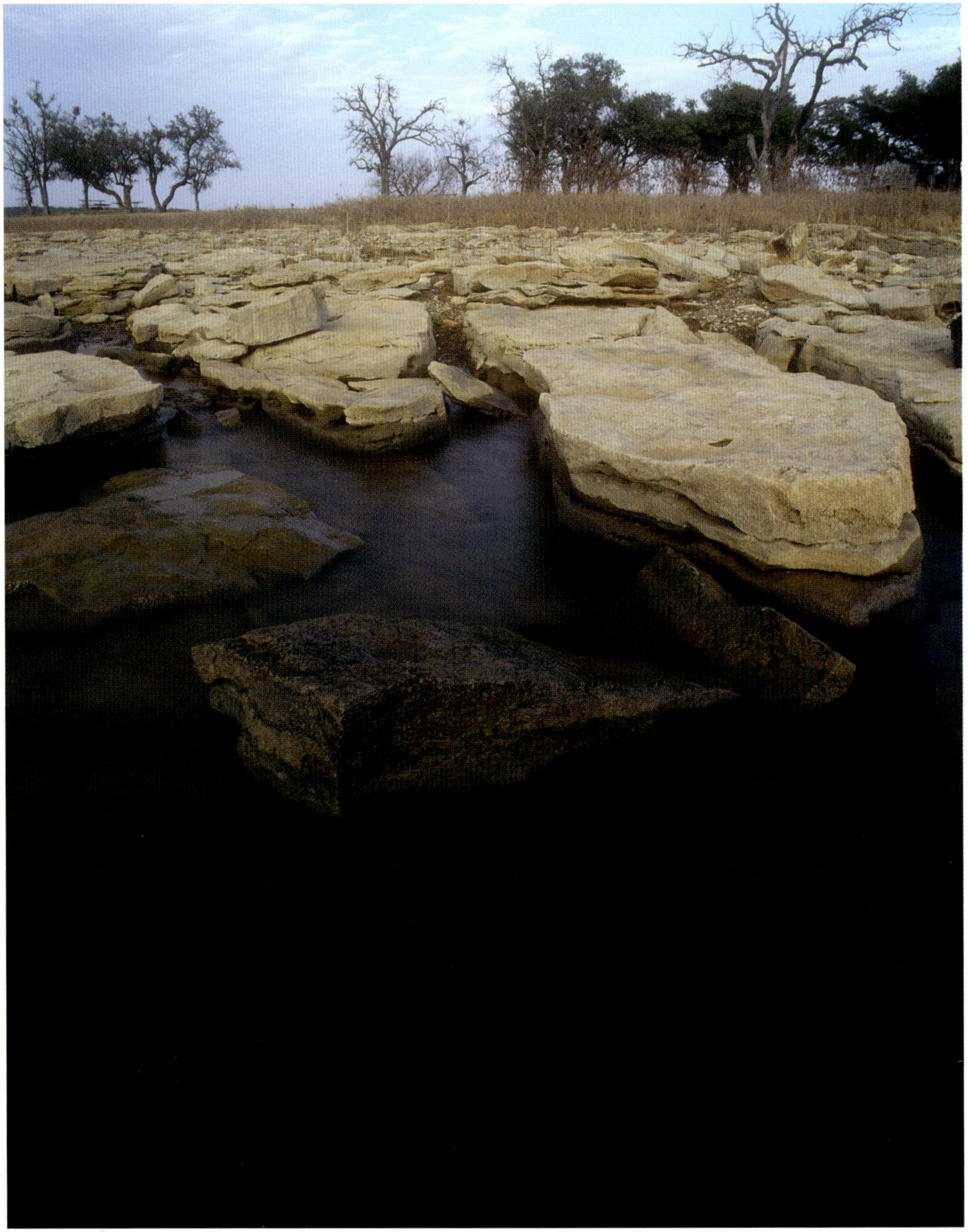

Burleson County

Lake Somerville State Park, Birch Creek Unit

The county was formed in 1846 and is named for Edward Burleson (1798–1851), a general of the Texas Revolution and vice president of the Republic of Texas. During the Civil War, Burleson County farmers experimented with the cultivation of unfamiliar food crops such as wheat to circumvent the Union navy's blockade of the Texas coast.

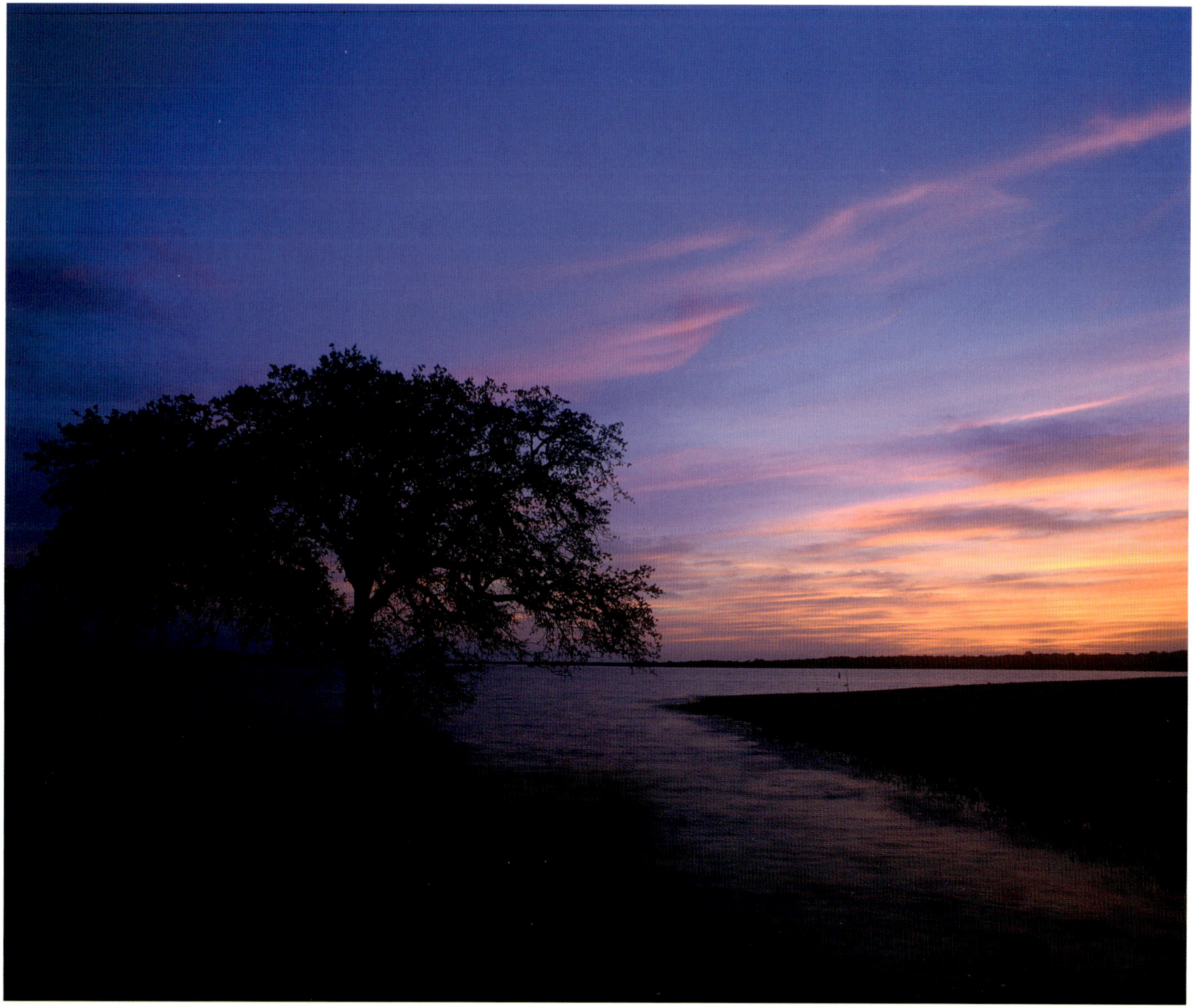

Burnet County

Balcones Canyon Lands National Wildlife Refuge

David Gouverneur Burnet, for whom the county is named, was the first president of the Republic of Texas, taking office in 1836. The county was formed in 1852. In Texas, Burnet is pronounced with the emphasis on the first syllable (BURN-it).

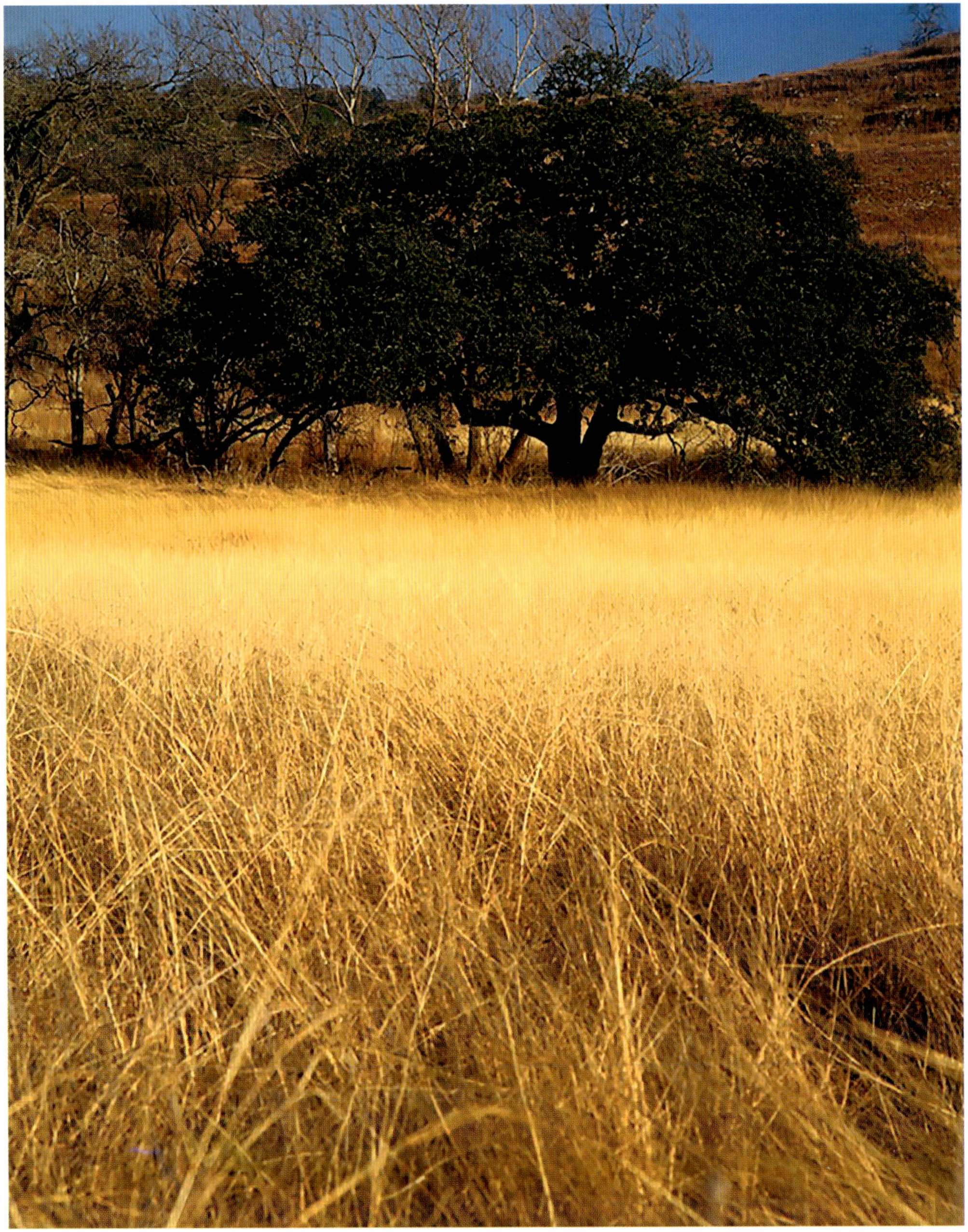

Caldwell County

Pecan Trees and Wildflowers

Established in 1848, the county is named for Mathew Caldwell, a signer of the Texas Declaration of Independence and a soldier during the Texas Revolution. In 1861, the county voted 434–188 in favor of secession from the Union. Several hundred men from Caldwell County served in the Confederate Army.

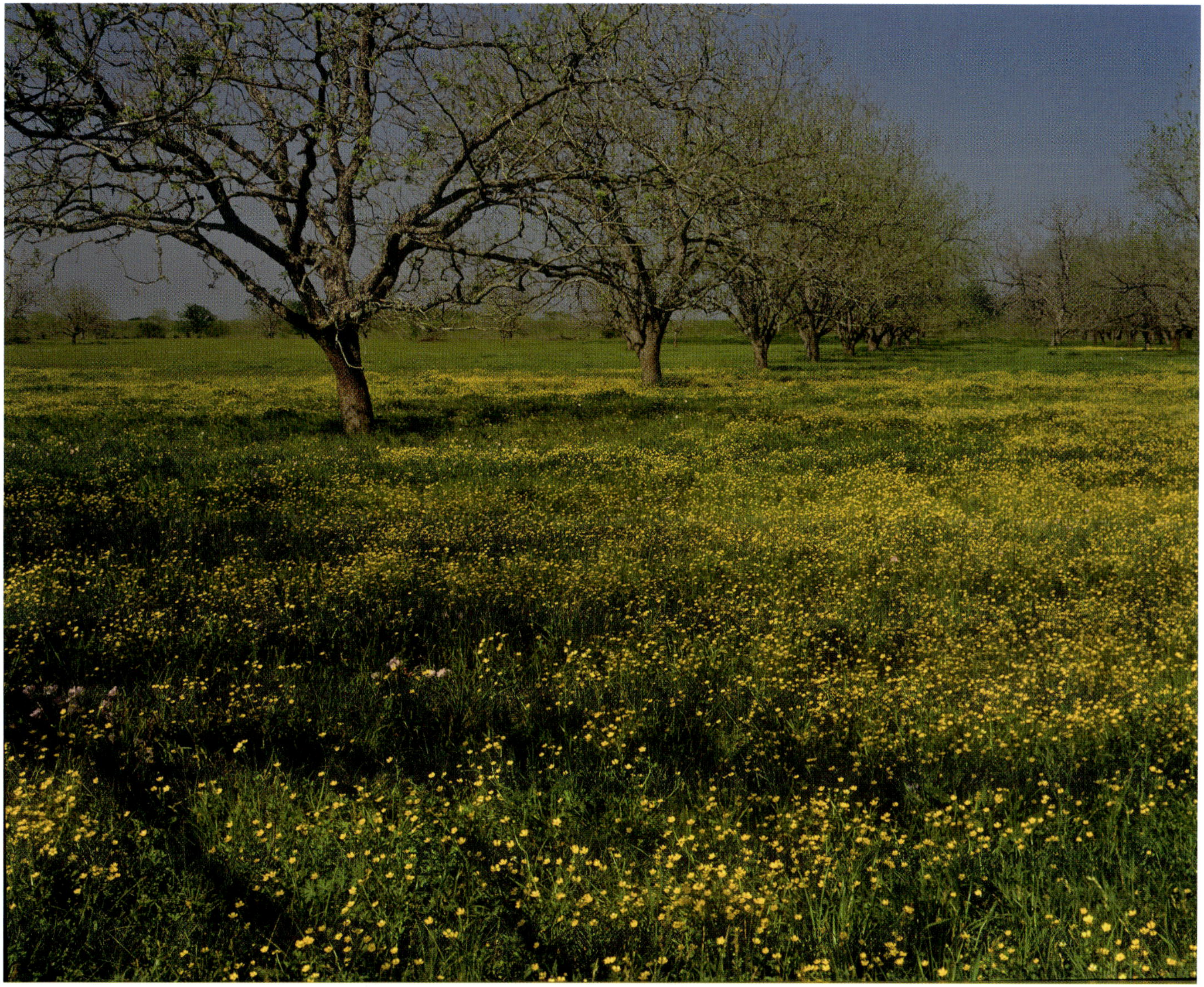

Calhoun County

Stormy Sunrise over the Gulf in Matagorda Island State Park

The county was formed in 1846 and is named for John C. Calhoun, the seventh vice president of the United States. In 1983, Matagorda Island State Park and Wildlife Management Area was established. The park is run by the Texas Parks and Wildlife Department under an agreement between the United States Department of the Interior and the State of Texas.

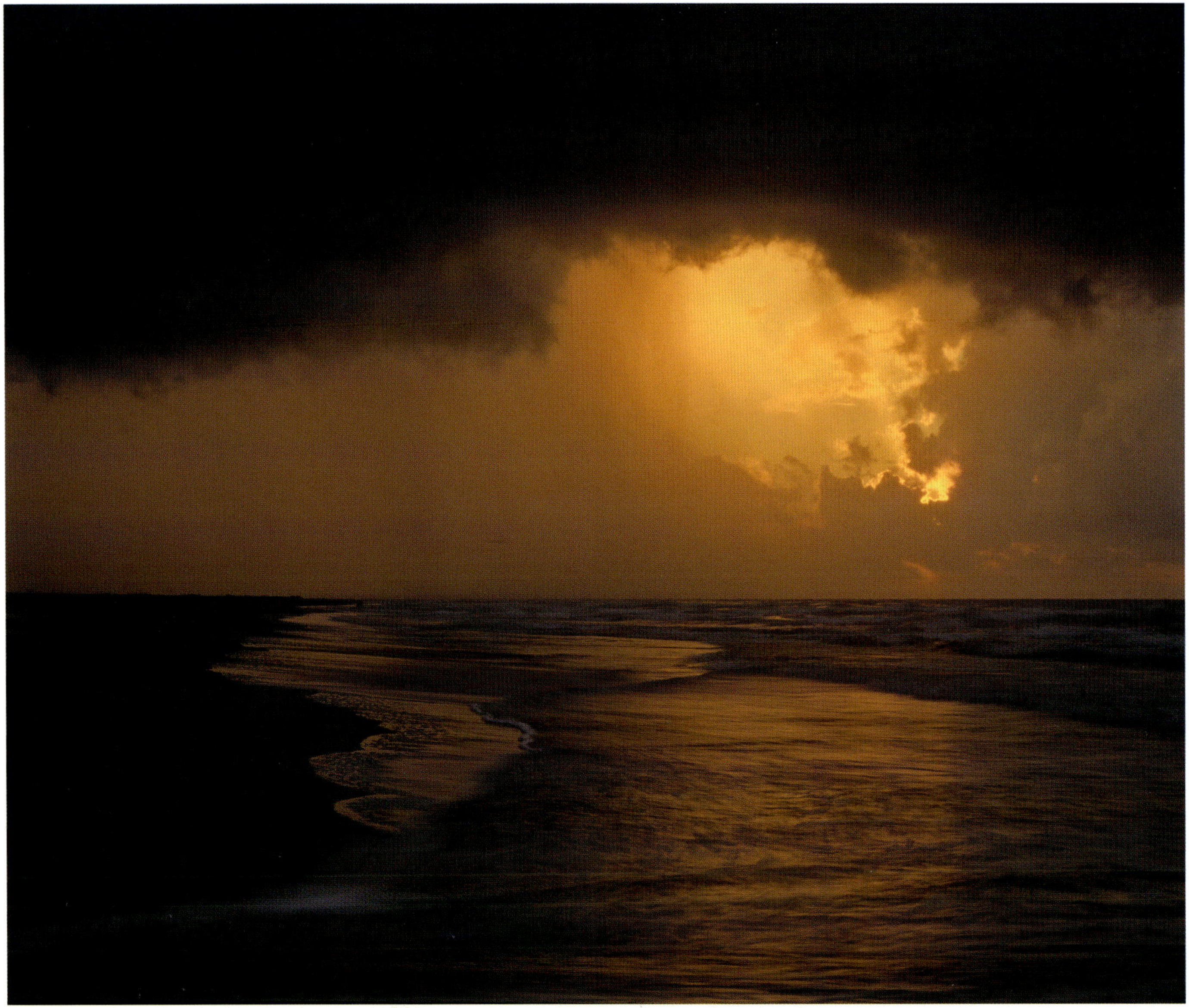

Callahan County

Sunny Winter Day in the Central Portion of the State

The county is named for James Hughes Callahan, a soldier during the Texas Revolution, and was founded in 1858. Because of the threat of a Comanche attack, little permanent settlement took place in the area until after the Civil War.

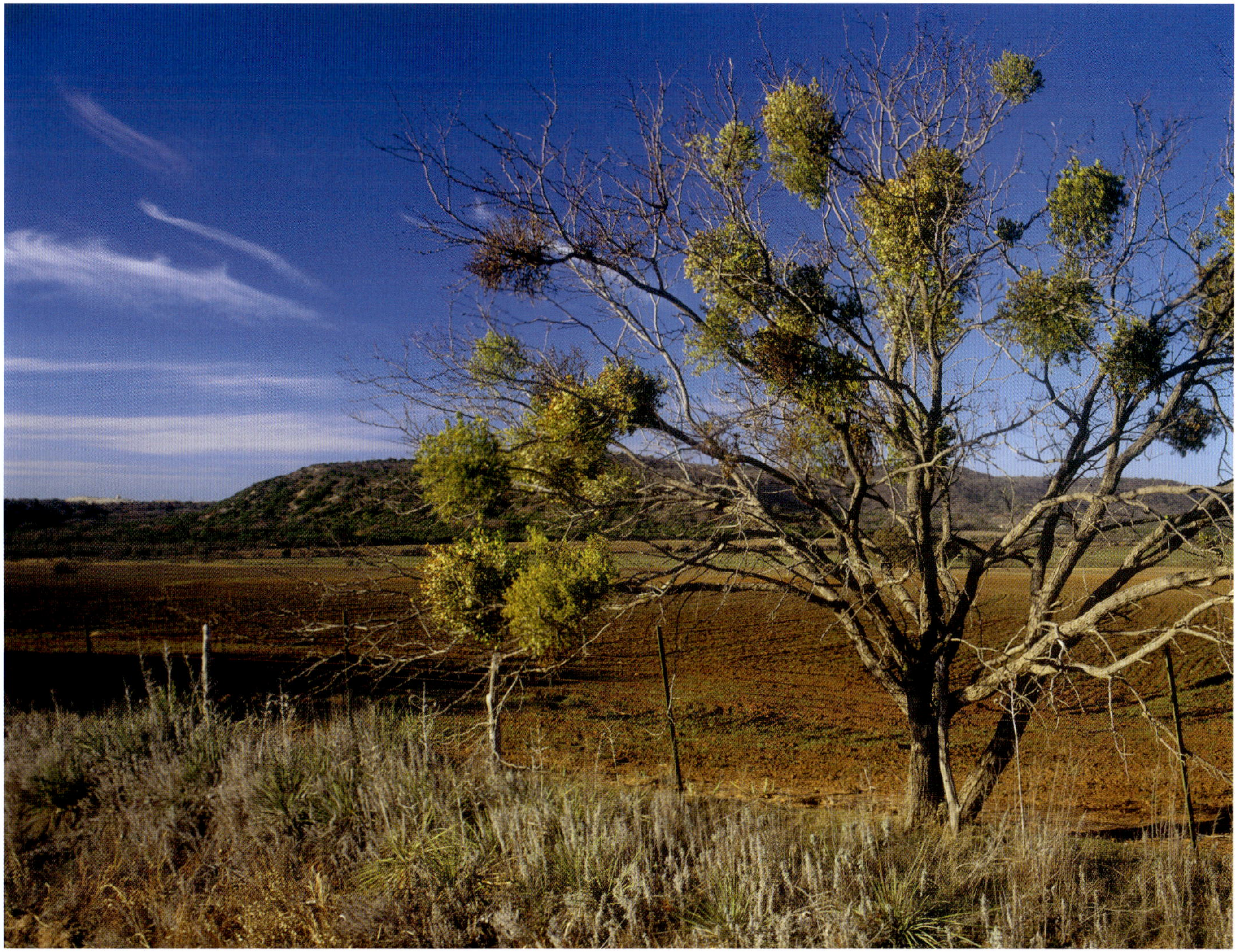

Cameron County

Sunset over Laguna Madre on South Padre Island

Cameron County was formed in 1848 and was named for Ewen Cameron, a soldier during the Texas Revolution. Several protected areas, including Palo Alto Battlefield National Historical Park, are in Cameron County. It is the southernmost county in the state.

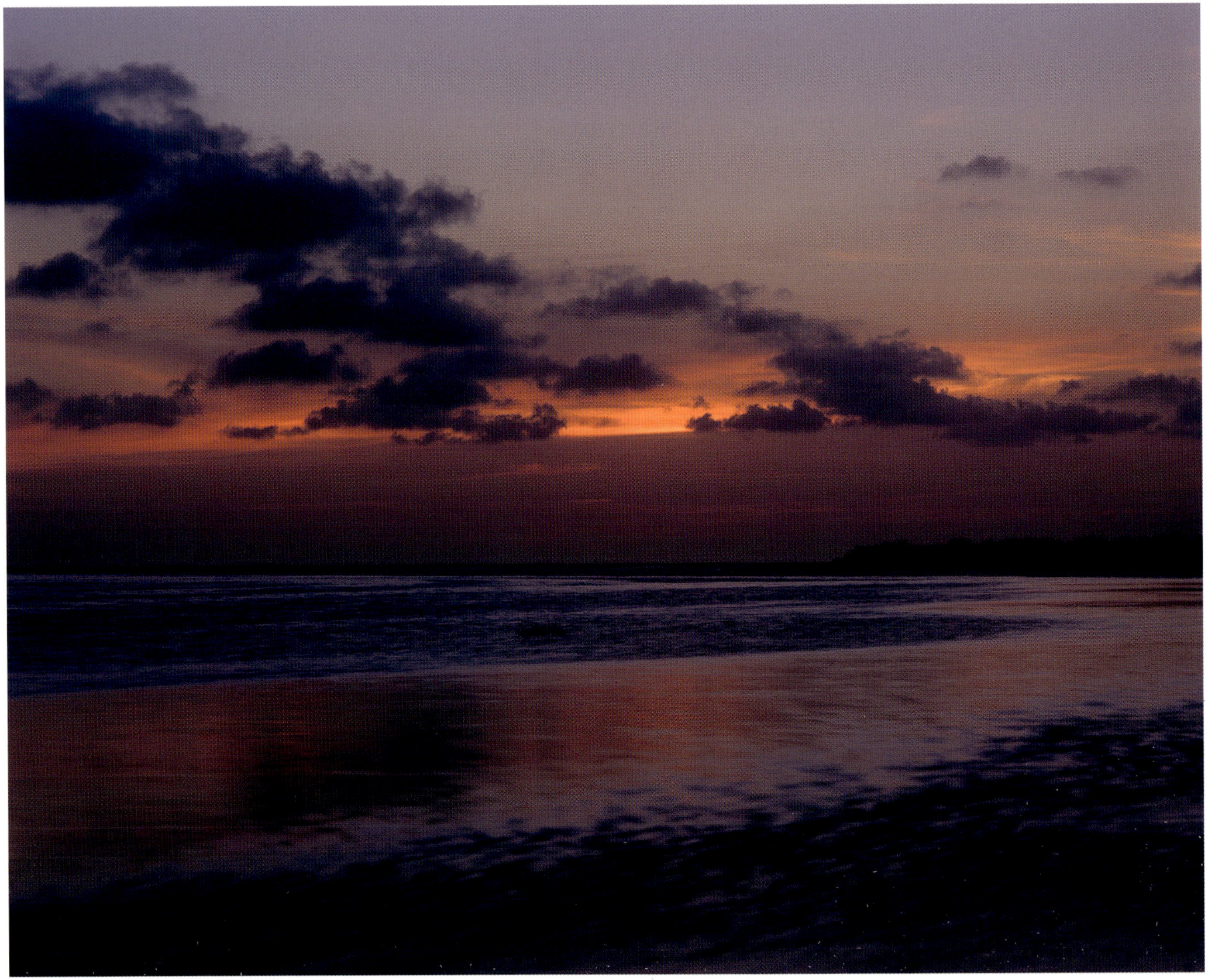

Camp County

Sunrise over Lake Bob Sandlin

The county was established in 1874 and is named for John Lafayette Camp (1828–1891), a Texas state senator. Anglo settlement began in the late 1830s, with most of the early settlers coming from Georgia, Alabama, and Tennessee.

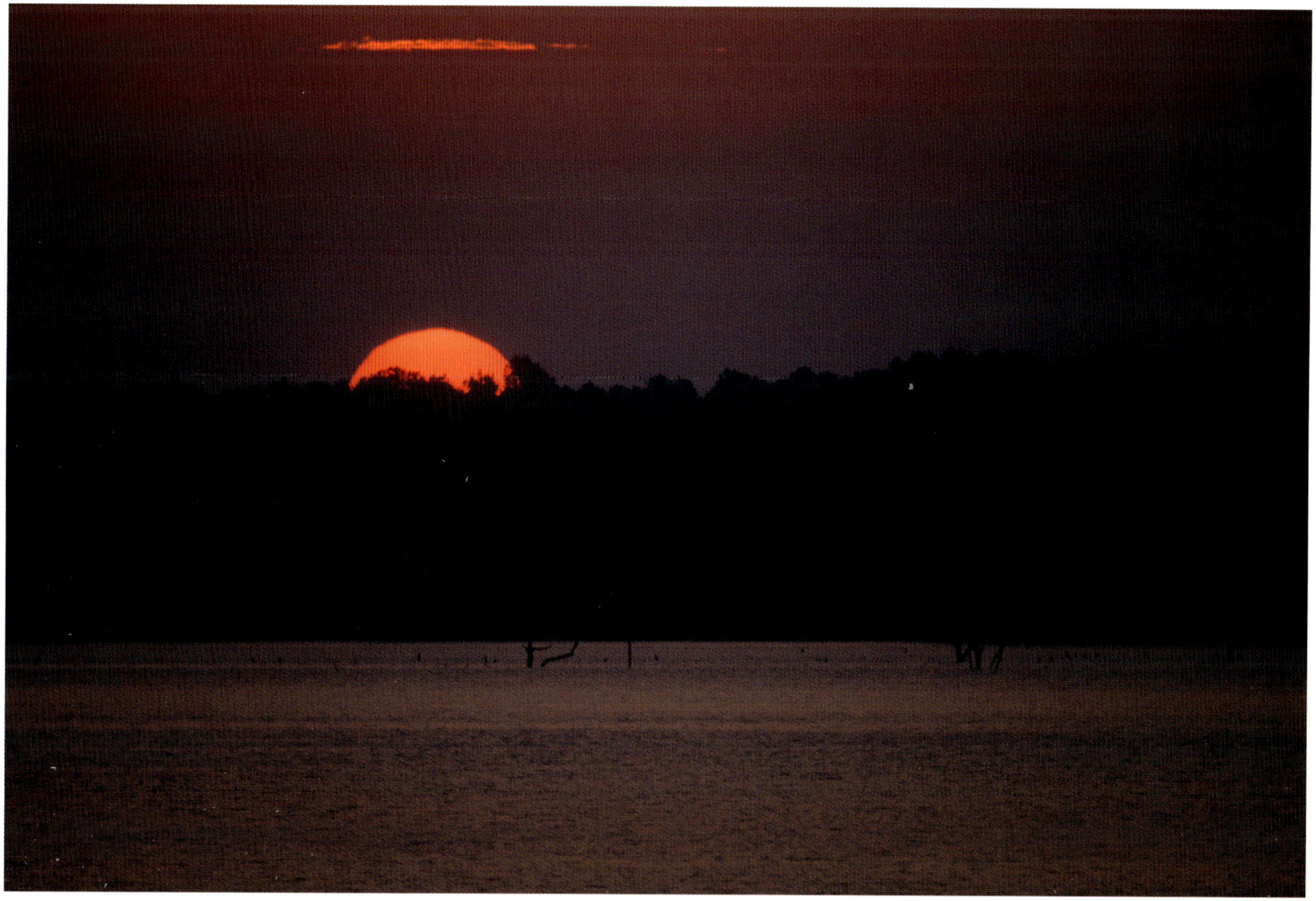

Carson County

Dawn over a Cotton Field

Carson County was formed in 1876. Since 1921, when oil was first discovered in Carson County, more than 178 million barrels of oil have been produced from county lands. Samuel Price Carson, the first secretary of state of the Republic of Texas (1836–1838), was the county's namesake.

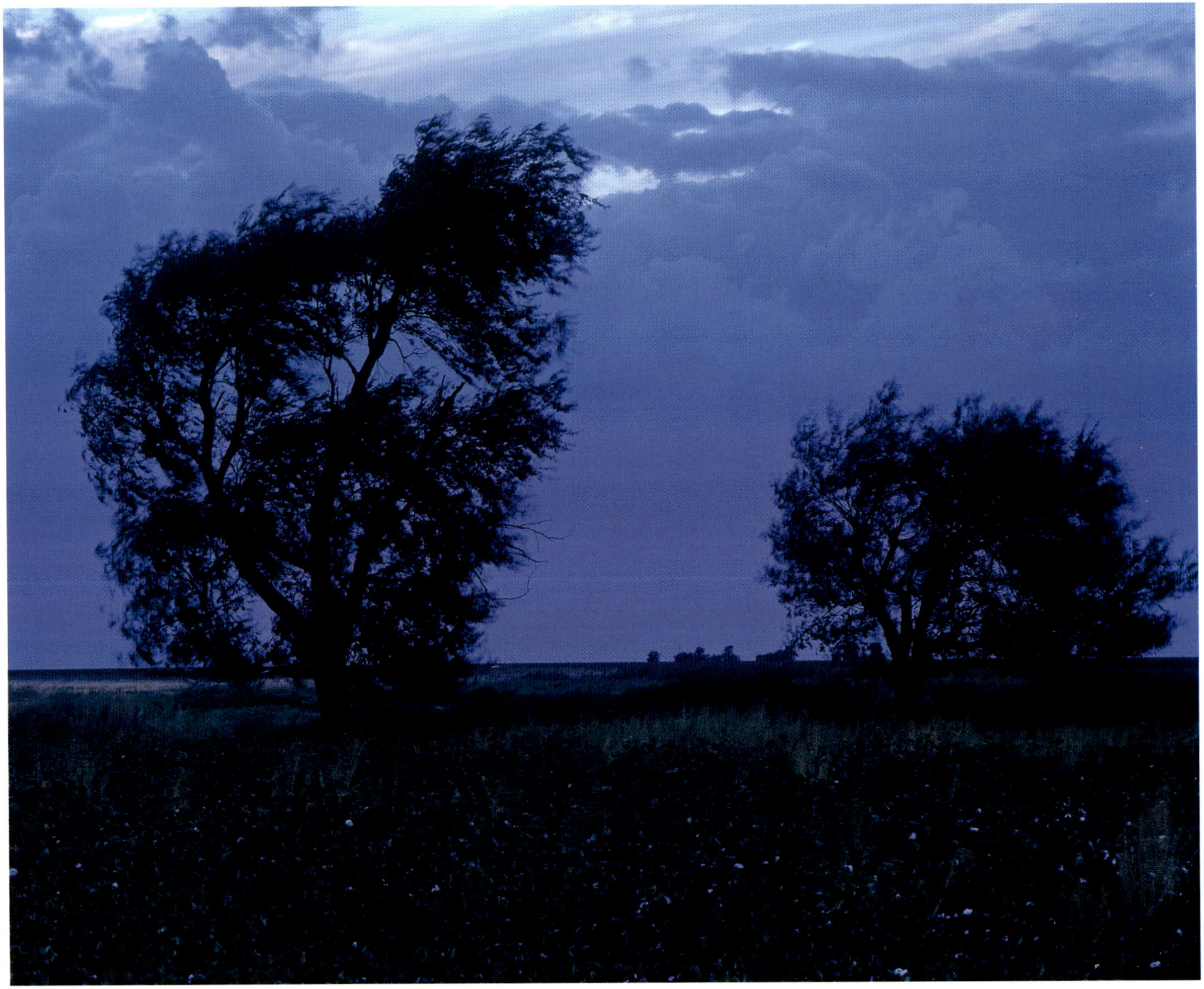

Cass County

Atlanta State Park

The county was founded in 1846. It was named for Lewis Cass (1782–1866), a senator from Michigan who favored the annexation of Texas to the United States. The first European entry into what would become Cass County occurred between 1687, when Henri Joutel traveled north in search of Henri de Tonti, and 1690, when Tonti returned to Texas in search of survivors of the LaSalle expedition.

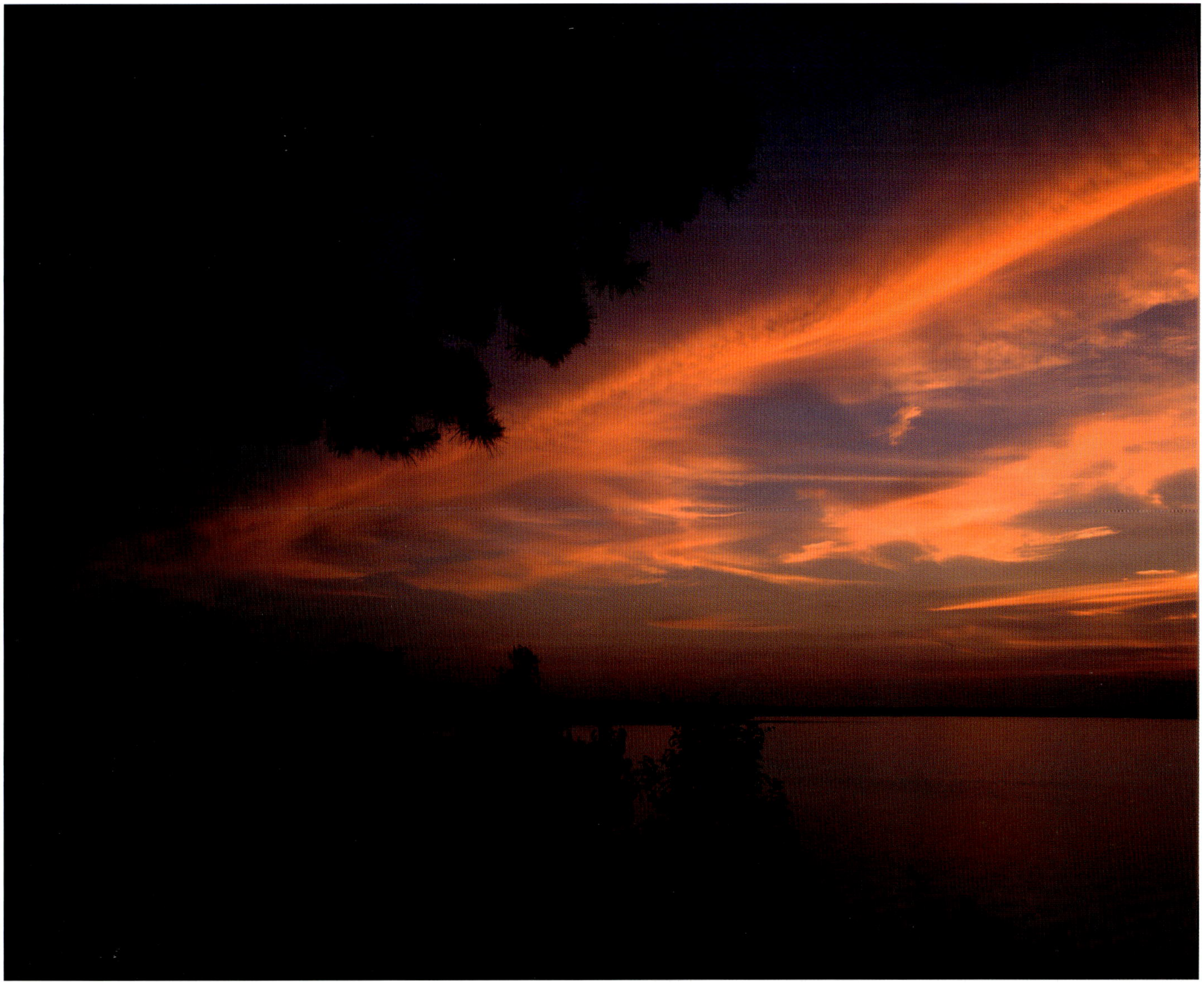

Castro County

Morning Sun over a Prarie, Pothole Lake

Castro County was named for Henri Castro (1786–1865), a French consul general for the Republic of Texas and founder of a colony in Texas. The county was established in 1876. Soon after 1900, Panhandle ranches began to sell lands to arriving settlers, and the advent of German farmers in the eastern part of the county between 1902 and 1906 helped stimulate farming on a large scale.

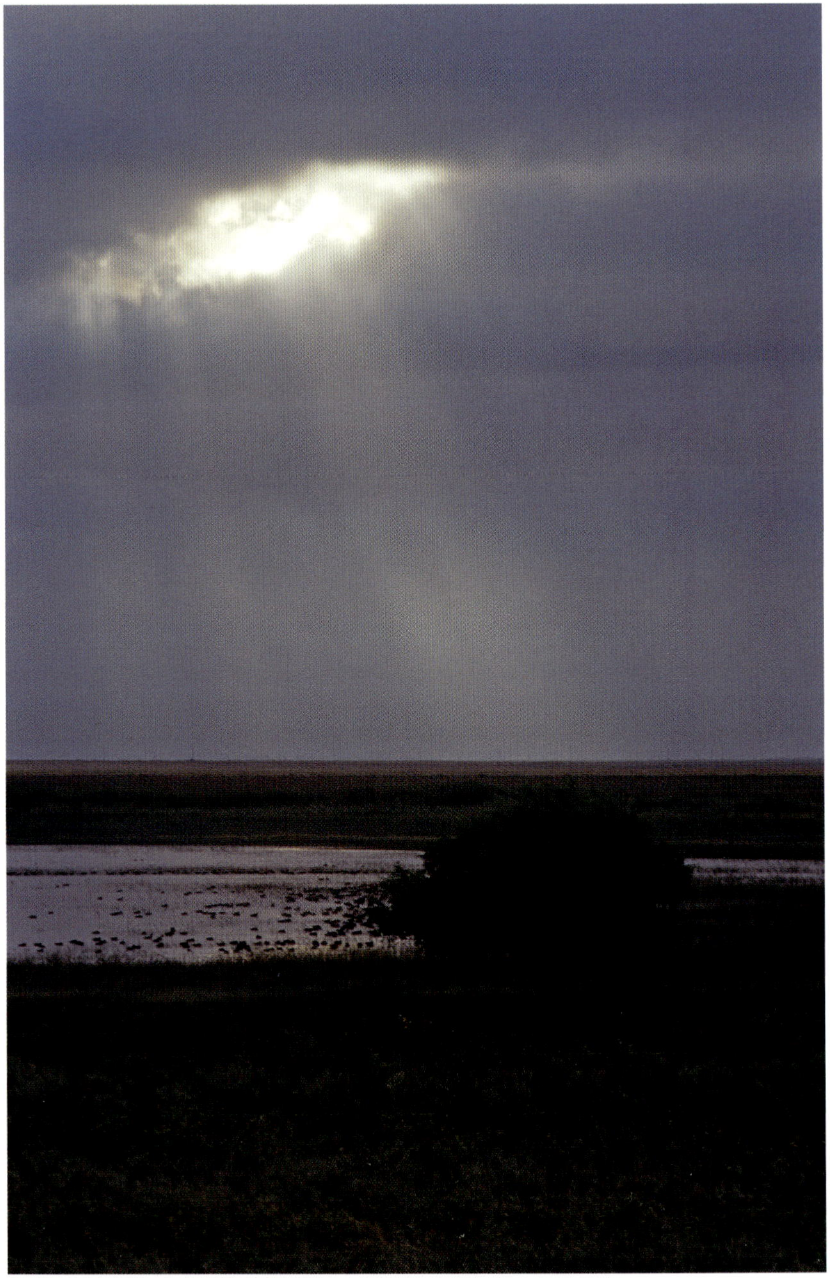

Chambers County

Sunset over East Galveston Bay in Anahuac National Wildlife Refuge

The county was established in 1858 and is named for Thomas Jefferson Chambers, a lawyer and surveyor who helped resolve land disputes for Americans in Mexican Texas. The Anahuac National Wildlife Refuge is in Chambers County.

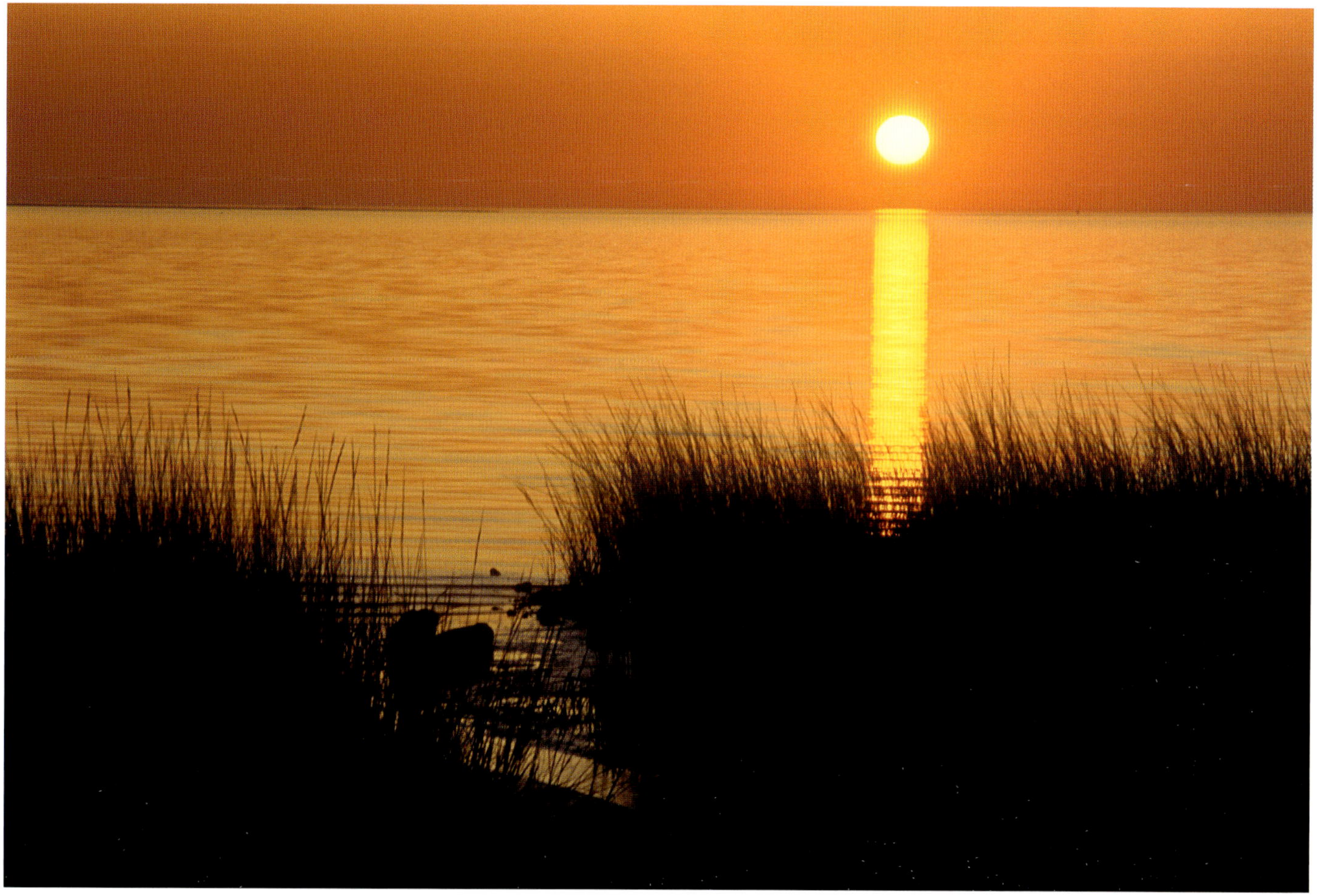

Cherokee County

Neches River

The county was established in 1846 and is named for the Cherokee Native American tribe. Sam Houston, the adopted son of Chief Oolooteka of the Cherokee, on January 14, 1836, negotiated a treaty between Chief Bowl of the Cherokee and the Republic of Texas. On December 16, 1837, the Texas Senate declared the treaty null and void, and encroachment of Cherokee lands continued.

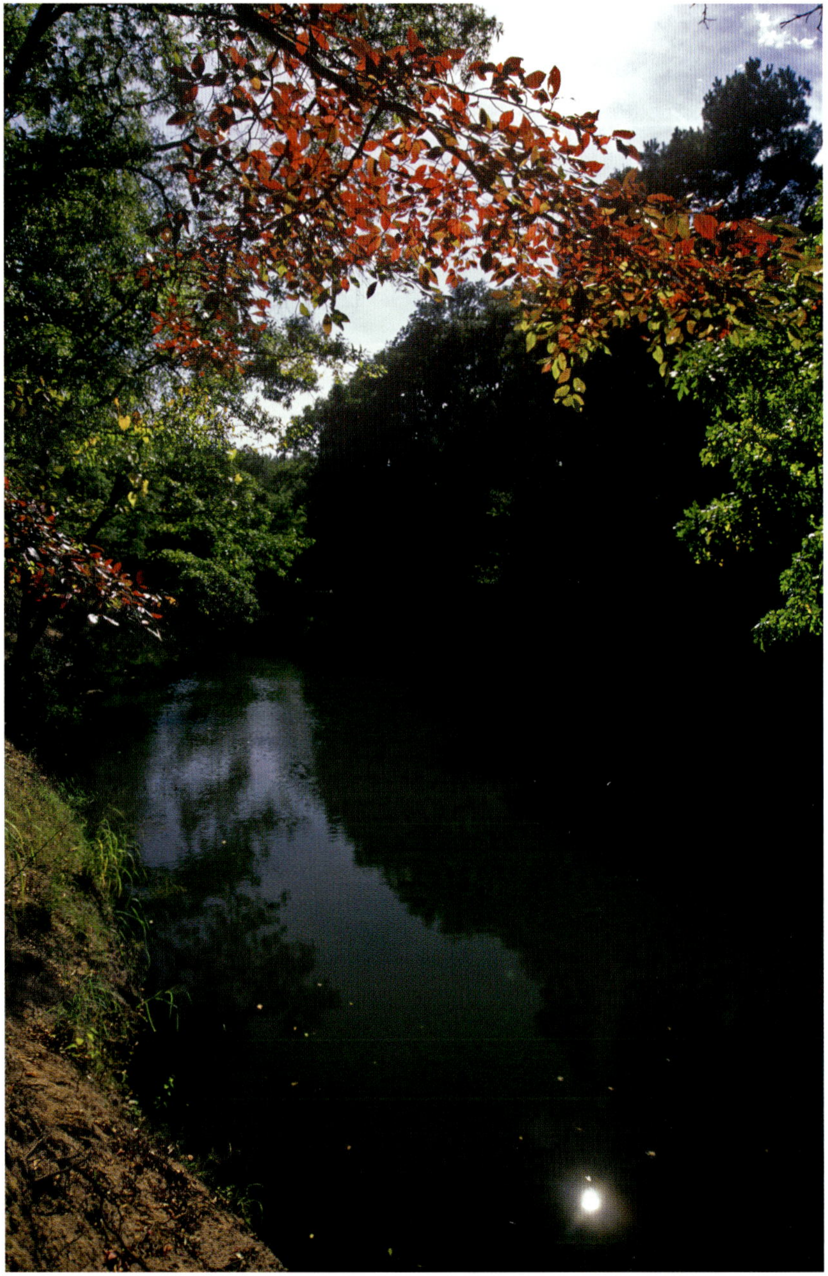

Childress County

Sunset through Mesquite Trees near the City of Childress

Named for George Campbell Childress (1804–1841)—one of the authors of the Texas Declaration of Independence—this county was formed in 1876. The Shoe Nail Ranch, owned by Chicago meat packer Gustavus Franklin Swift, was started in 1883, in the northern part of the county.

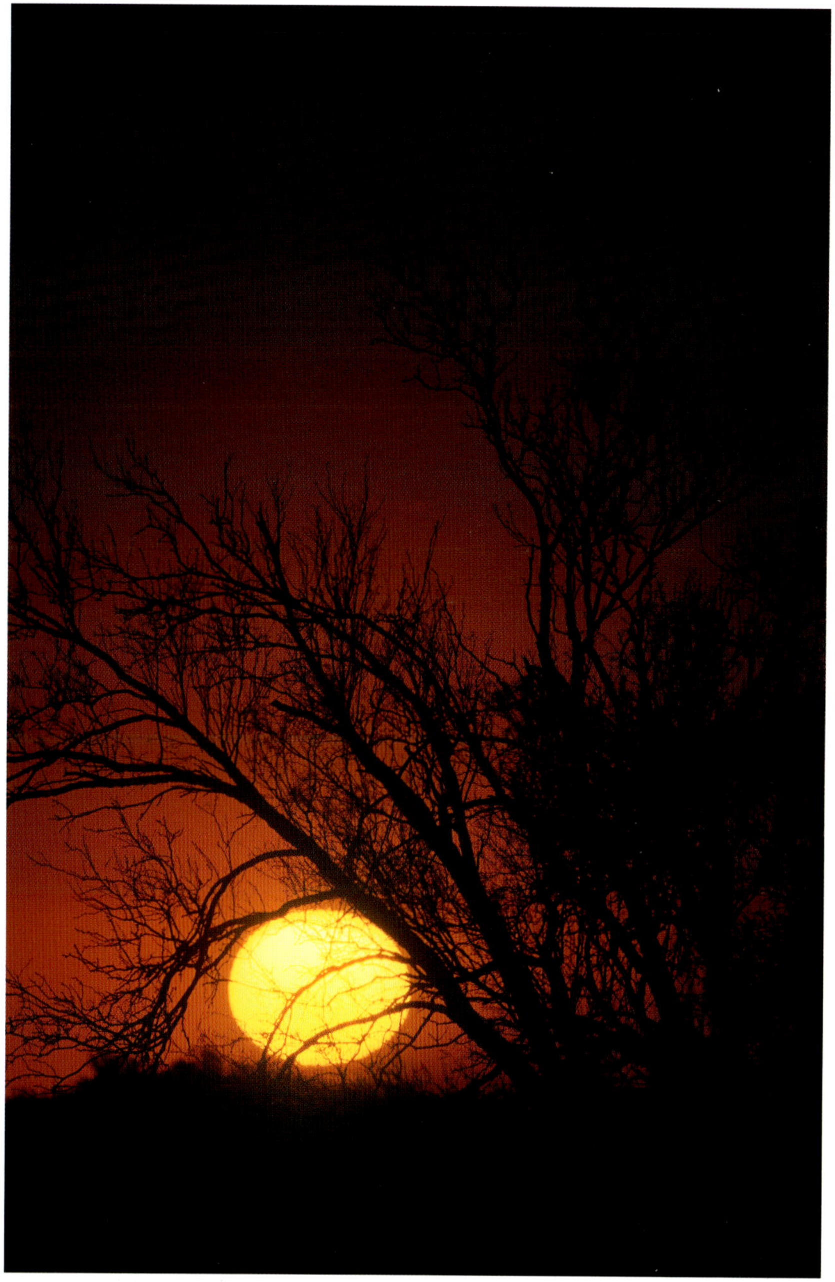

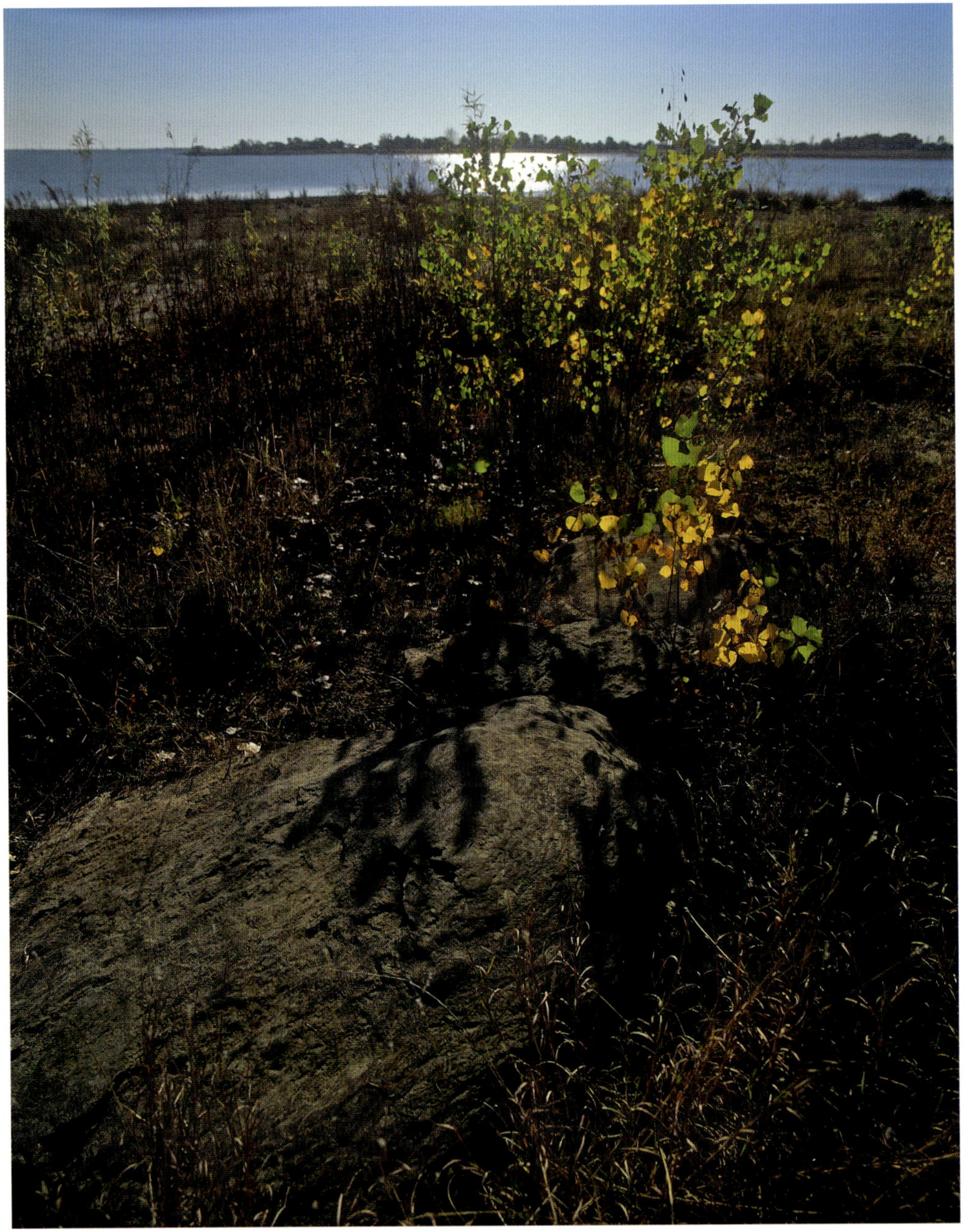

Clay County

Lake Arrowhead State Park

Formed in 1857, the county is named for Henry Clay, US senator from Kentucky and ninth secretary of state of the United States (1825–1829). On the eve of the Civil War, Henrietta, the largest community in Clay County, had ten homes and a general store. Indians remained a constant threat at this time, and the Army conducted regular patrols of the area. The county was largely abandoned in 1862 because of the removal of federal military protection.

Cochran County

Sunrise and Windmill

The county was named for Robert E. Cochran (1810–1836), a defender of the Alamo. Cochran County was founded in 1876. The 1890 census does not show any residents in the county, and in 1900, only twenty-five people lived there. In 1901 George Washington Littlefield bought 238,858 acres for his ranch.

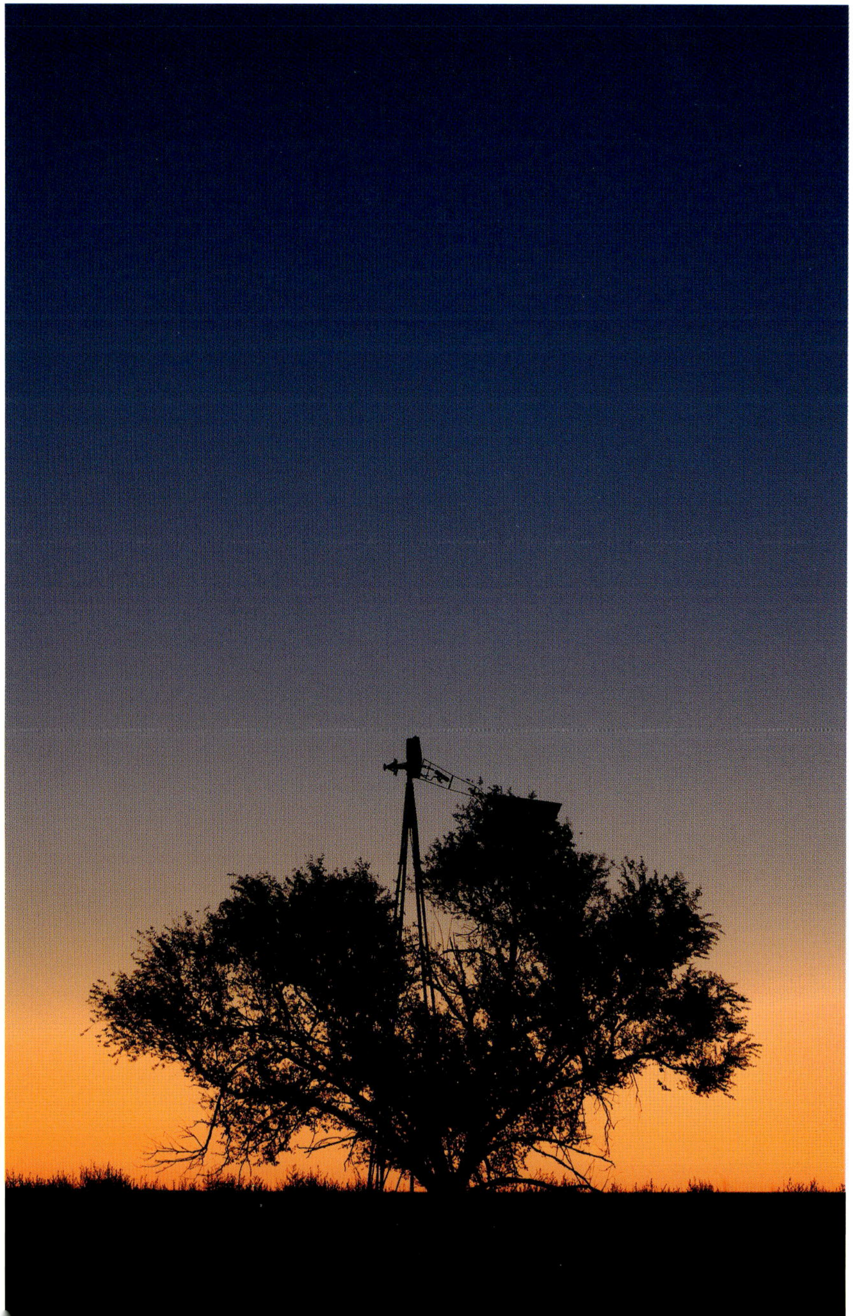

Coke County

E. V. Spence Reservoir from Wildcat Creek Park

The county is named for Richard Coke, the fifteenth governor of Texas (1874–1876). The county was formed in 1889. In 1891, after an election, the new town of Robert Lee became the county seat. Confederate General Robert E. Lee had once served at Fort Chadbourne in the county.

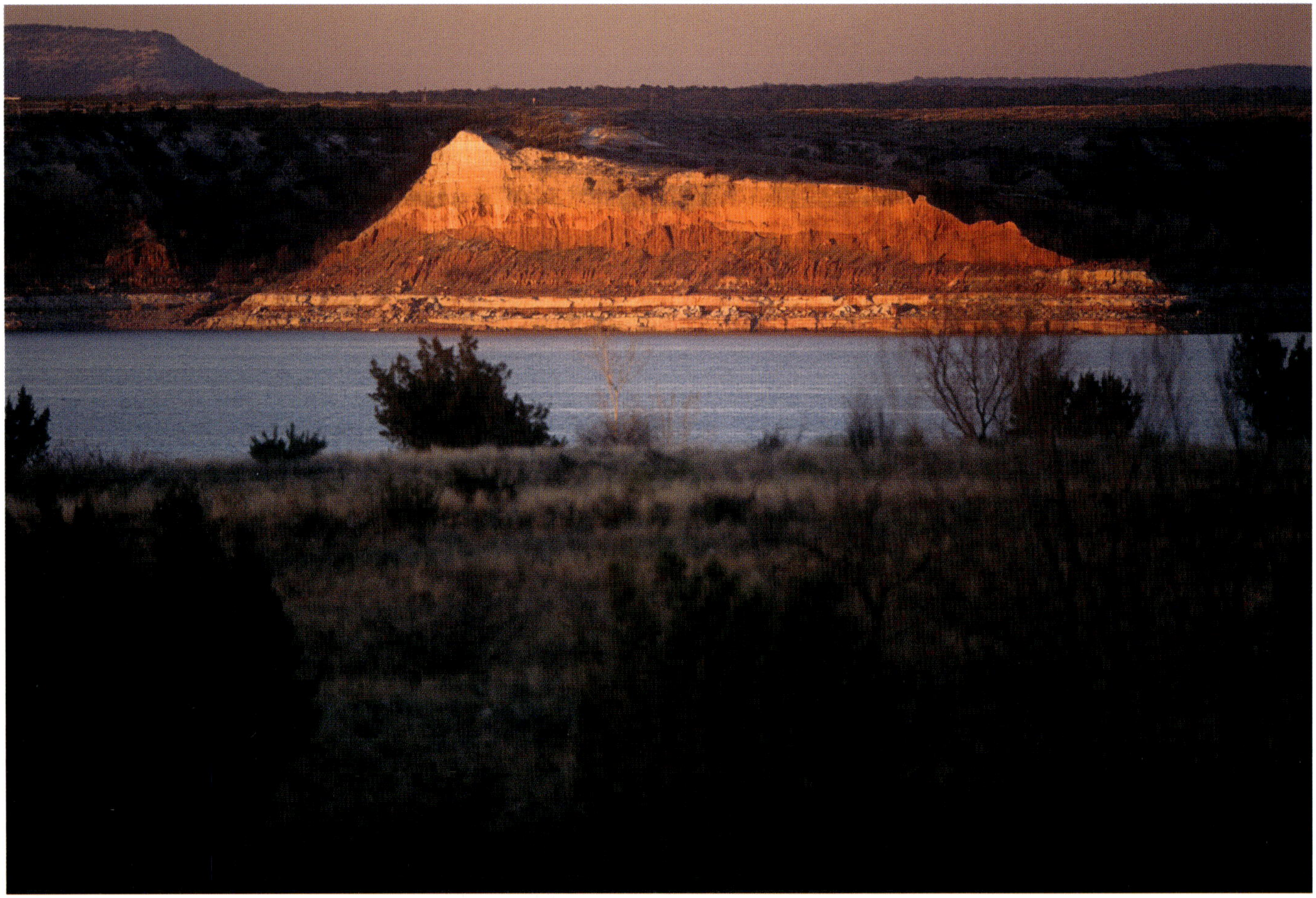

Coleman County

Hords Creek Lake

Formed in 1858, the county was named for Robert M. Coleman, a signer of the Texas Declaration of Independence and a soldier at the Battle of San Jacinto. In 1917, oil was discovered on the J. P. Morris ranch. By 1948, the oil fields were producing more than one million barrels per year.

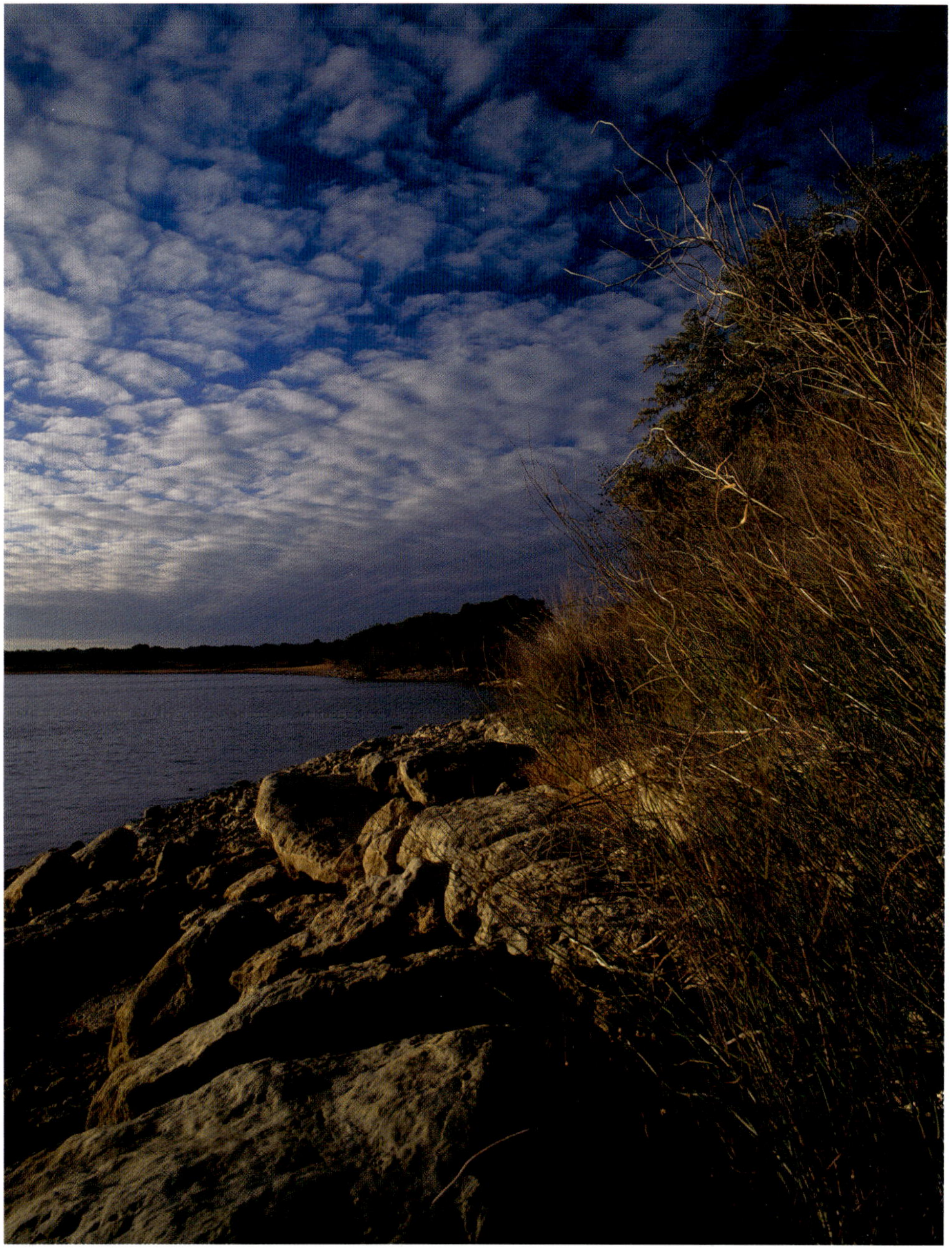

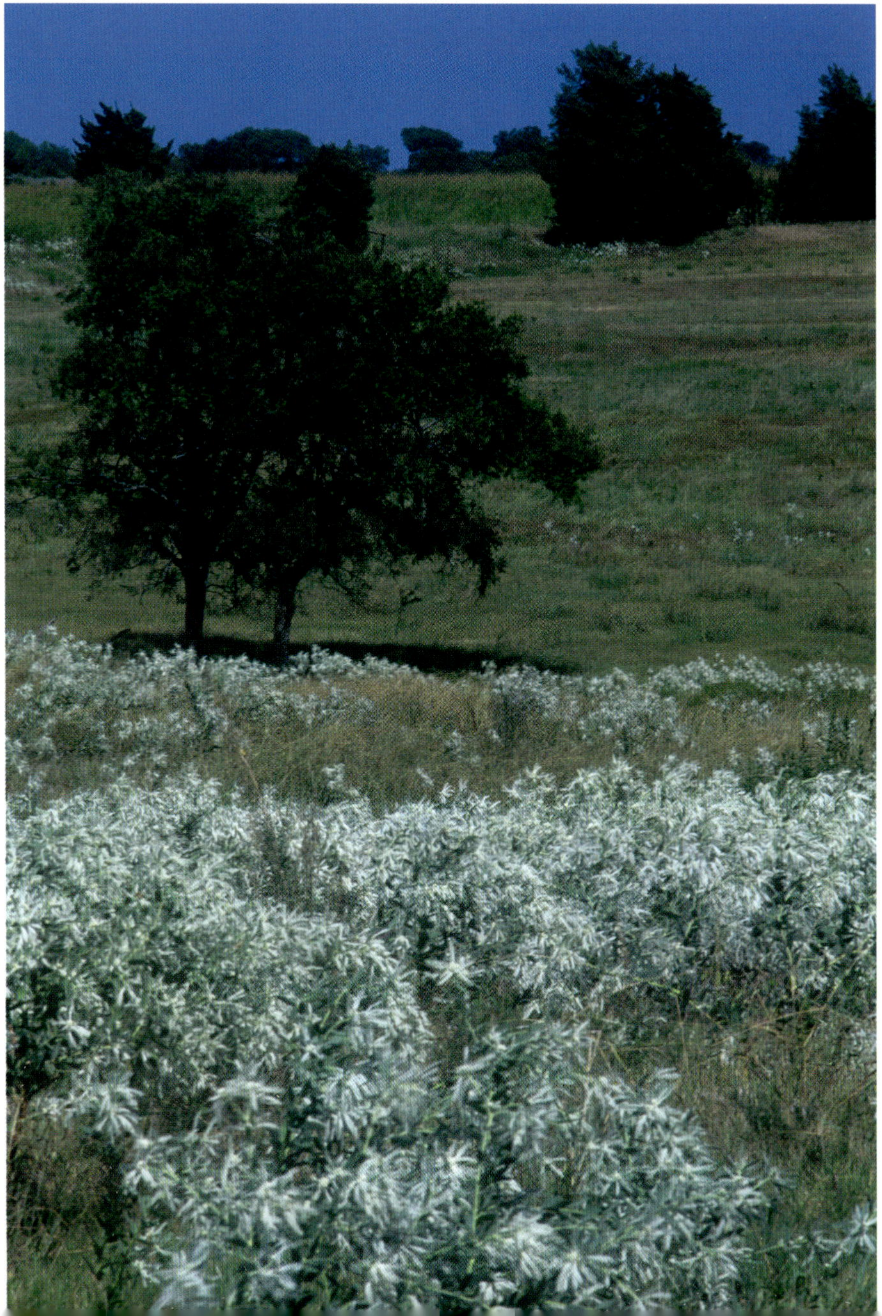

Collin County

A Sunny Afternoon on Ranchland near the Dallas-Ft. Worth Metroplex

The county is named for Collin McKinney (1766–1861), an author of the Texas Declaration of Independence and the oldest person to sign it. The county was organized in 1846. In 1861, when the Civil War broke out, James W. Throckmorton, a native of McKinney and a Texas state senator, urged against secession, and his influence resulted in Collin County's vote of 948 to 405 against secession. Once Texas joined the Confederacy, more than 1,500 residents of the county enlisted in defense of the South, led by Throckmorton, who rose to the rank of brigadier general.

COLLINGSWORTH COUNTY

Collingsworth County

Morning near the Oklahoma Border

The county was founded in 1876 and is named for James Collinsworth, a signer of the Texas Declaration of Independence and first chief justice of the Republic of Texas. The difference in the spelling of the name of the county and the spelling of the founder's name is due to an error in the bill creating the county.

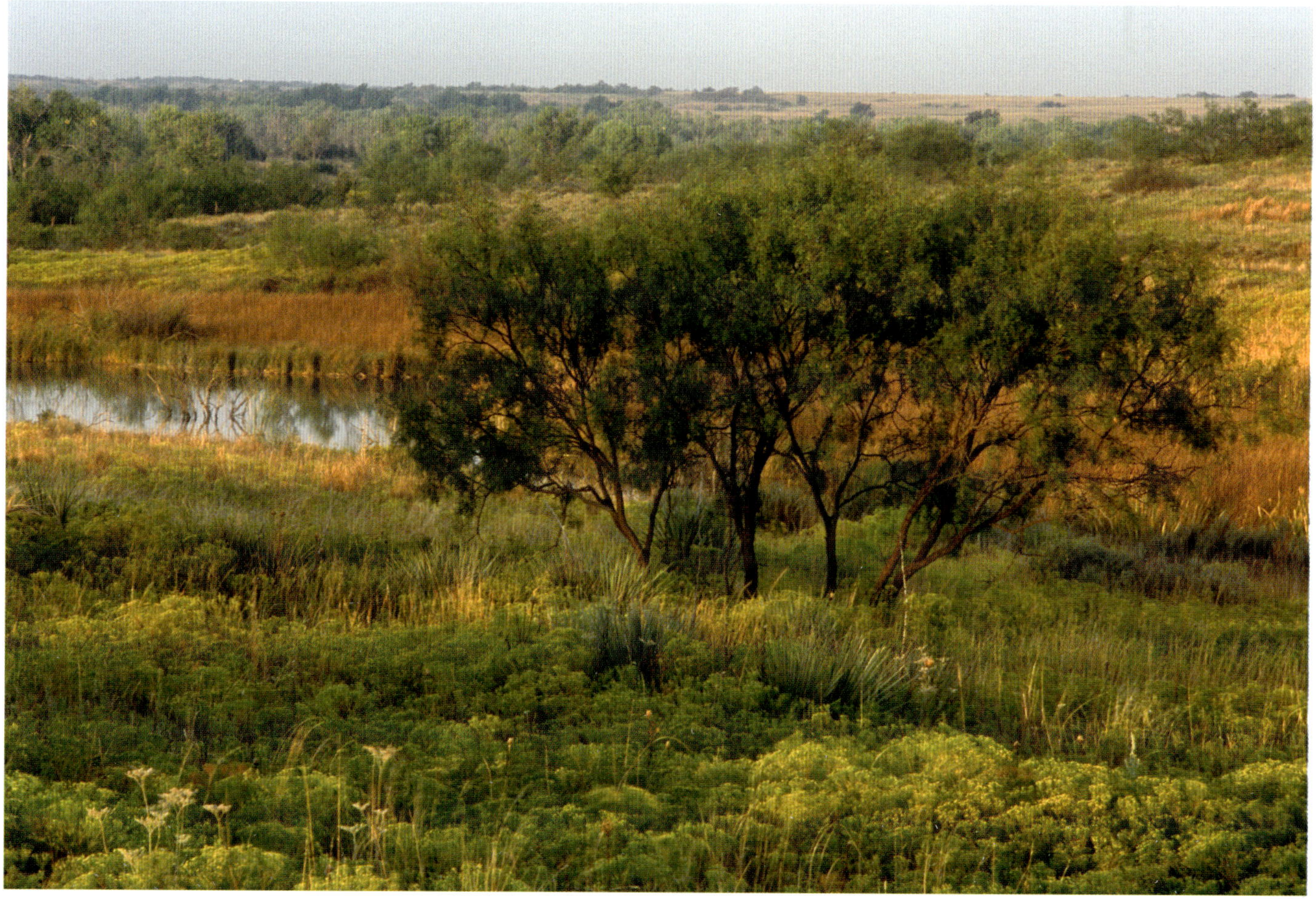

Colorado County

Atwater Prairie Chicken National Wildlife Refuge

The county is named for the Colorado River; *colorado* is Spanish for "red." The county was founded in 1836. The first settlers were members of Stephen F. Austin's "Old Three Hundred" families.

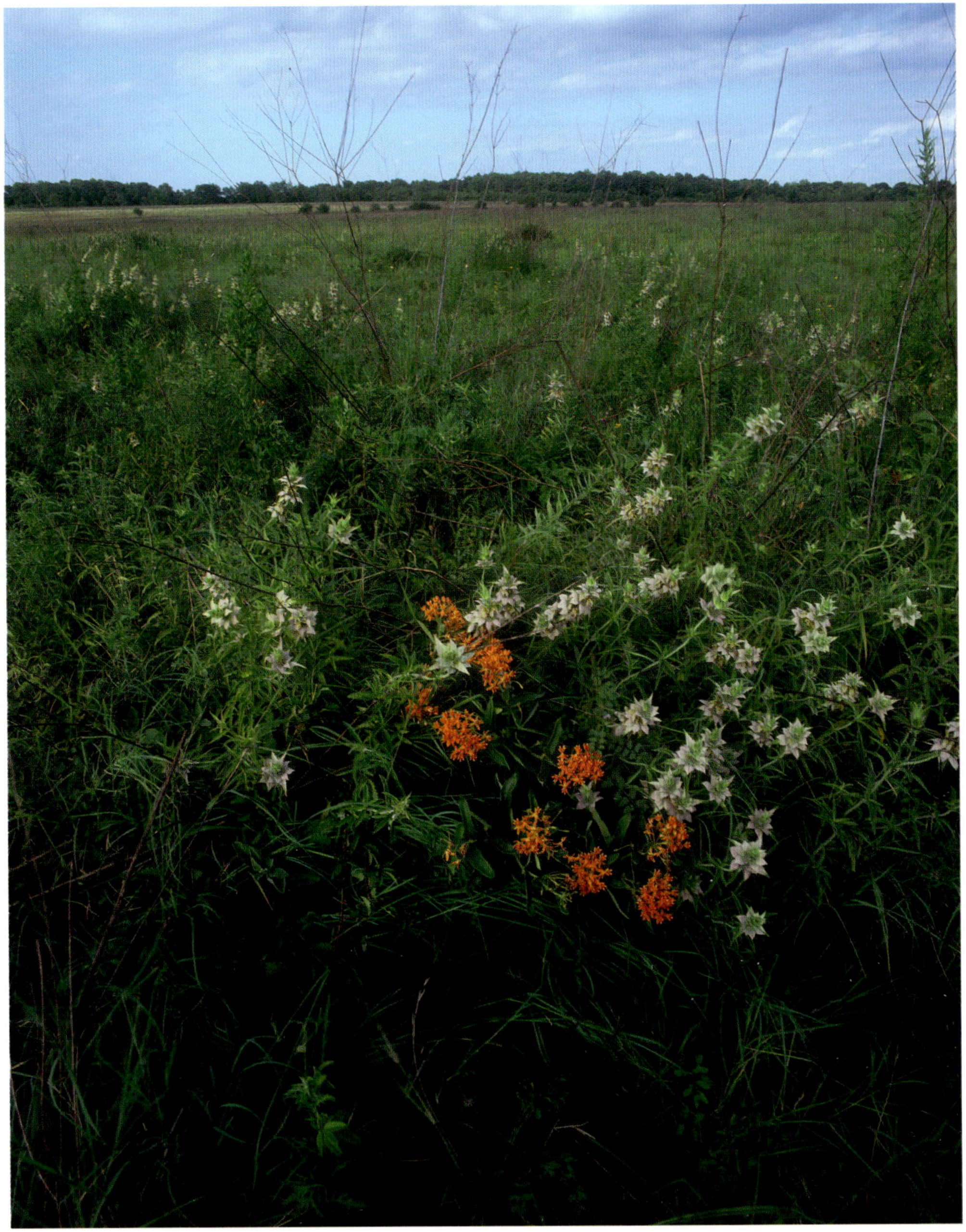

Comal County

Honey Creek State Natural Area

The county was formed in 1846 and is named for the Comal River. *Comal* is Spanish for "basin." In 1842, the Fisher-Miller Land Grant set aside 3 million acres to settle six hundred families and single men of German, Dutch, Swiss, Danish, Swedish, and Norwegian ancestry in Texas.

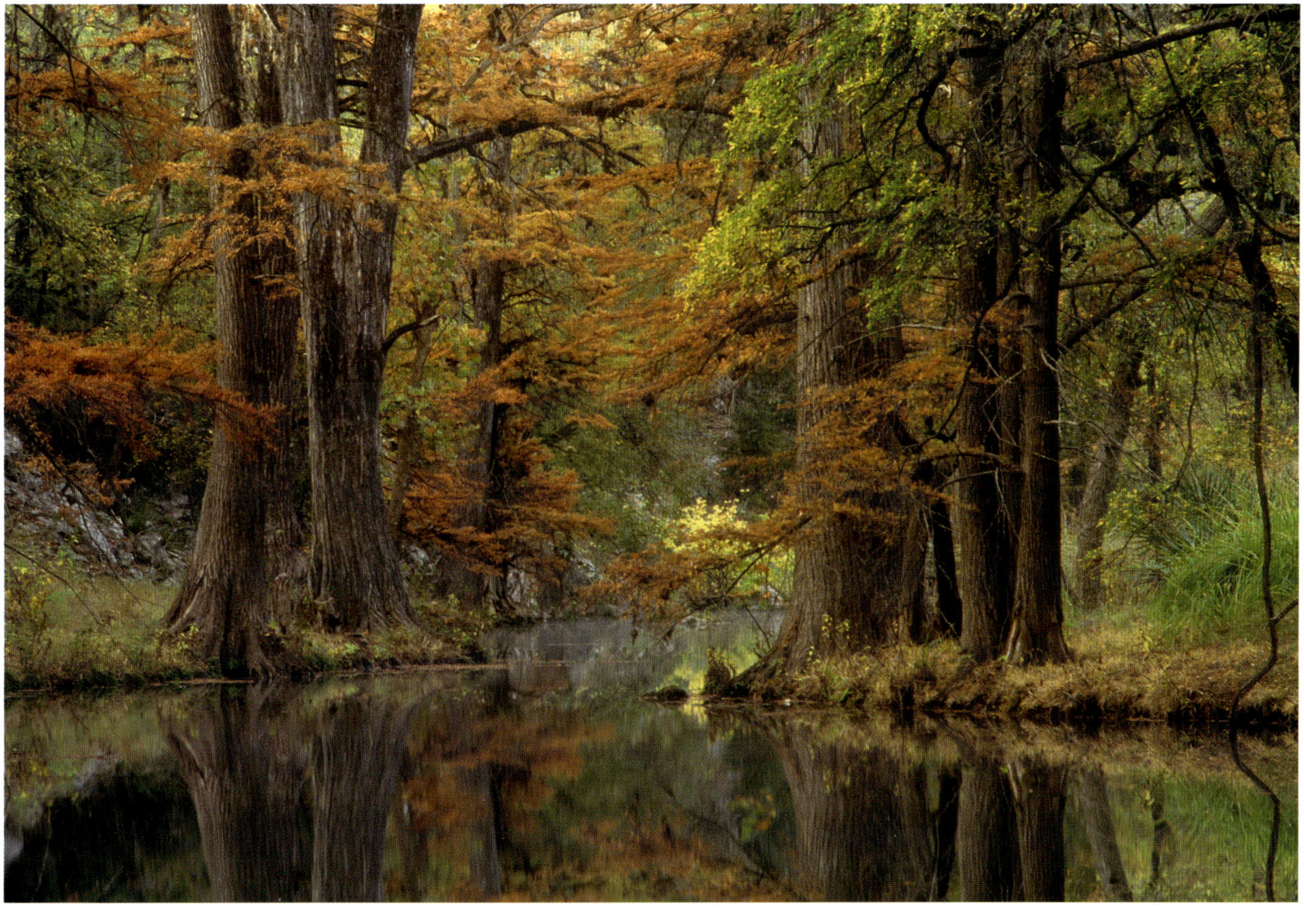

Comanche County

Typical Ranchland Scene on an Autumn Day

Comanche County was formed in 1856 and is named for the Comanche Native American tribe. As of 1982, Comanche was ranked second in Texas for peanut production, with the production of more than 45 million pounds.

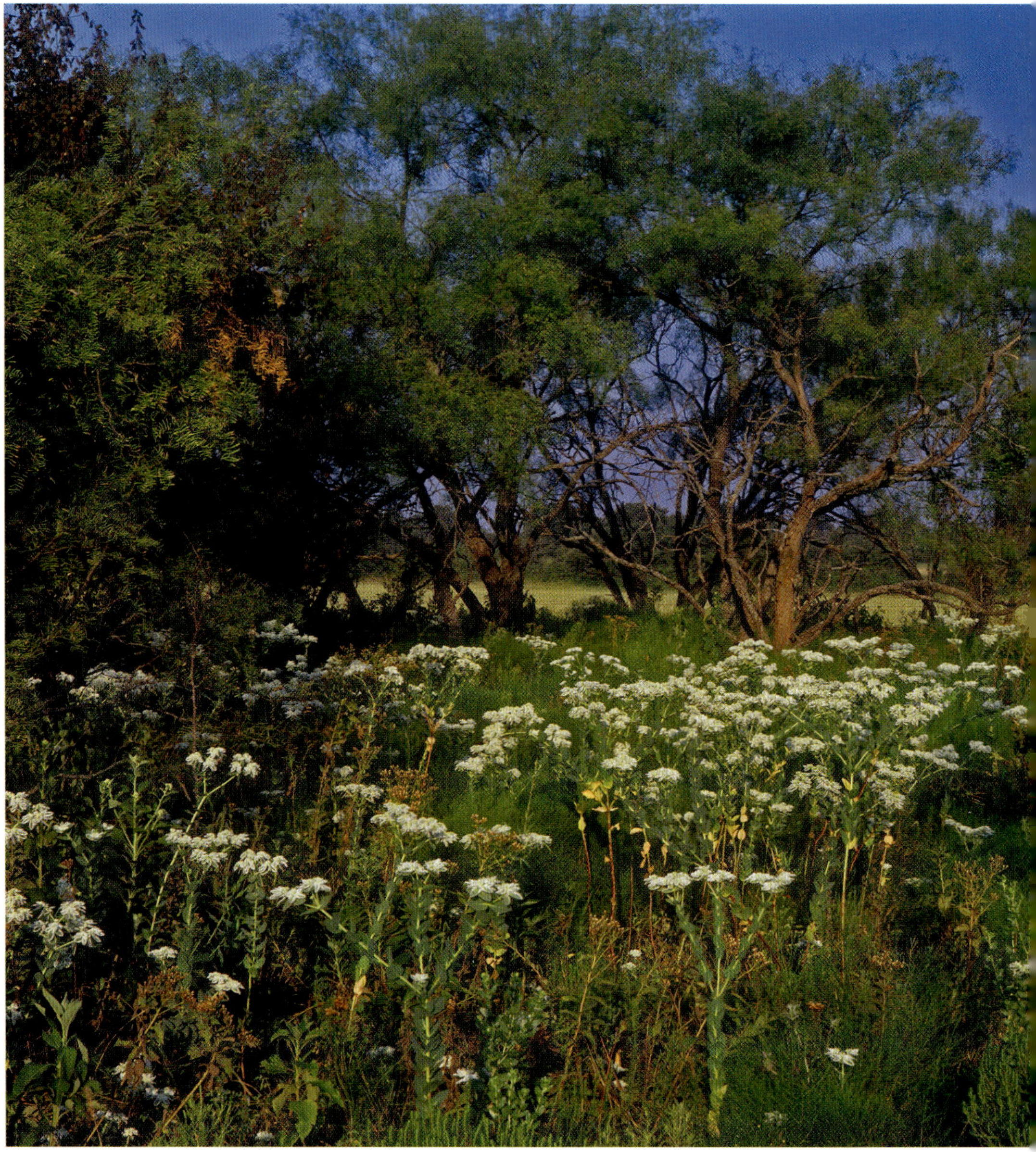

Concho County

Thorny Mix of Vegetation near Paint Rock

The Concho River—which is Spanish for "shell"—provides the name for the county. It was founded in 1858. About a mile west of Paint Rock—the county seat—some of the most famous Indian pictographs in Texas can be found.

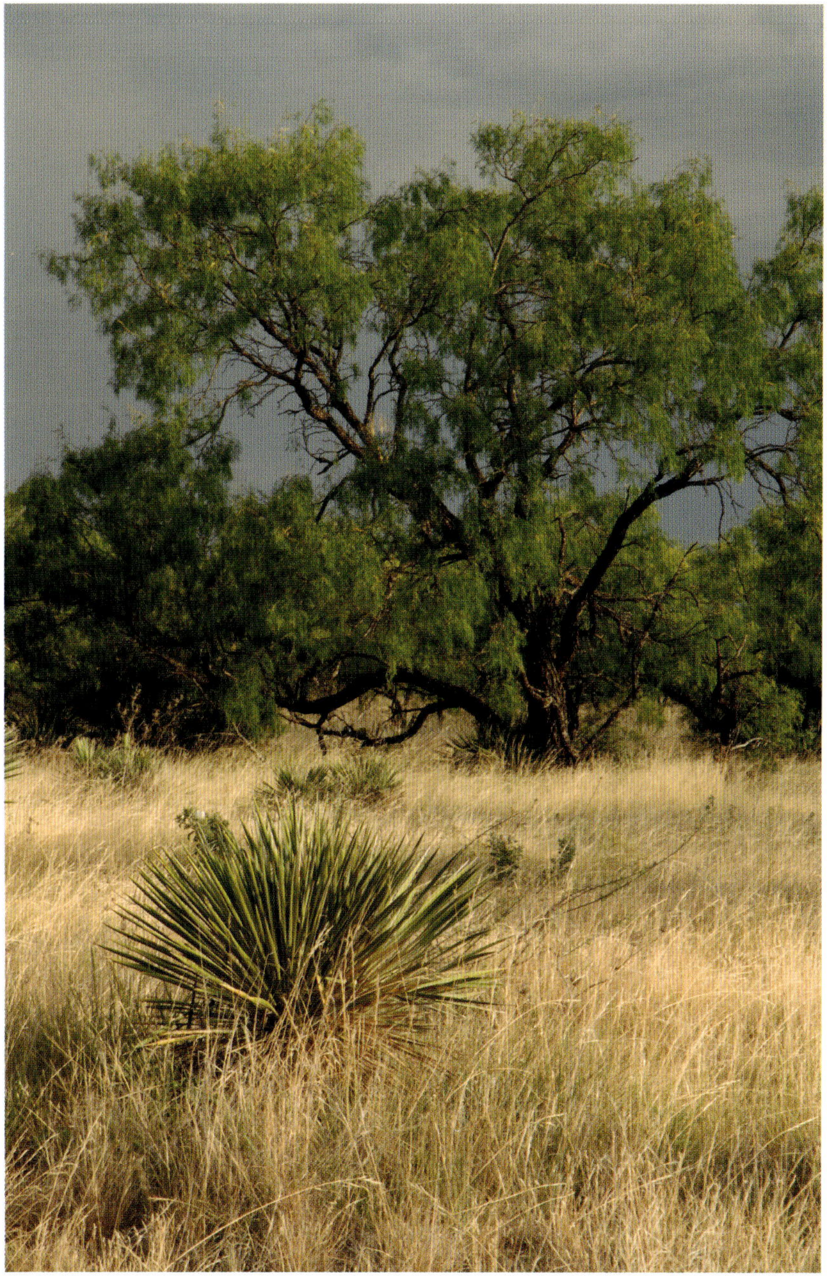

Cooke County

November Wildflowers

This county was formed in 1845 and is named for William Gordon Cooke, a soldier during the Texas Revolution. The county was crossed by several early trails, including the Mormon Trail—a branch of the Chisholm Trail—and the Butterfield Overland Mail route.

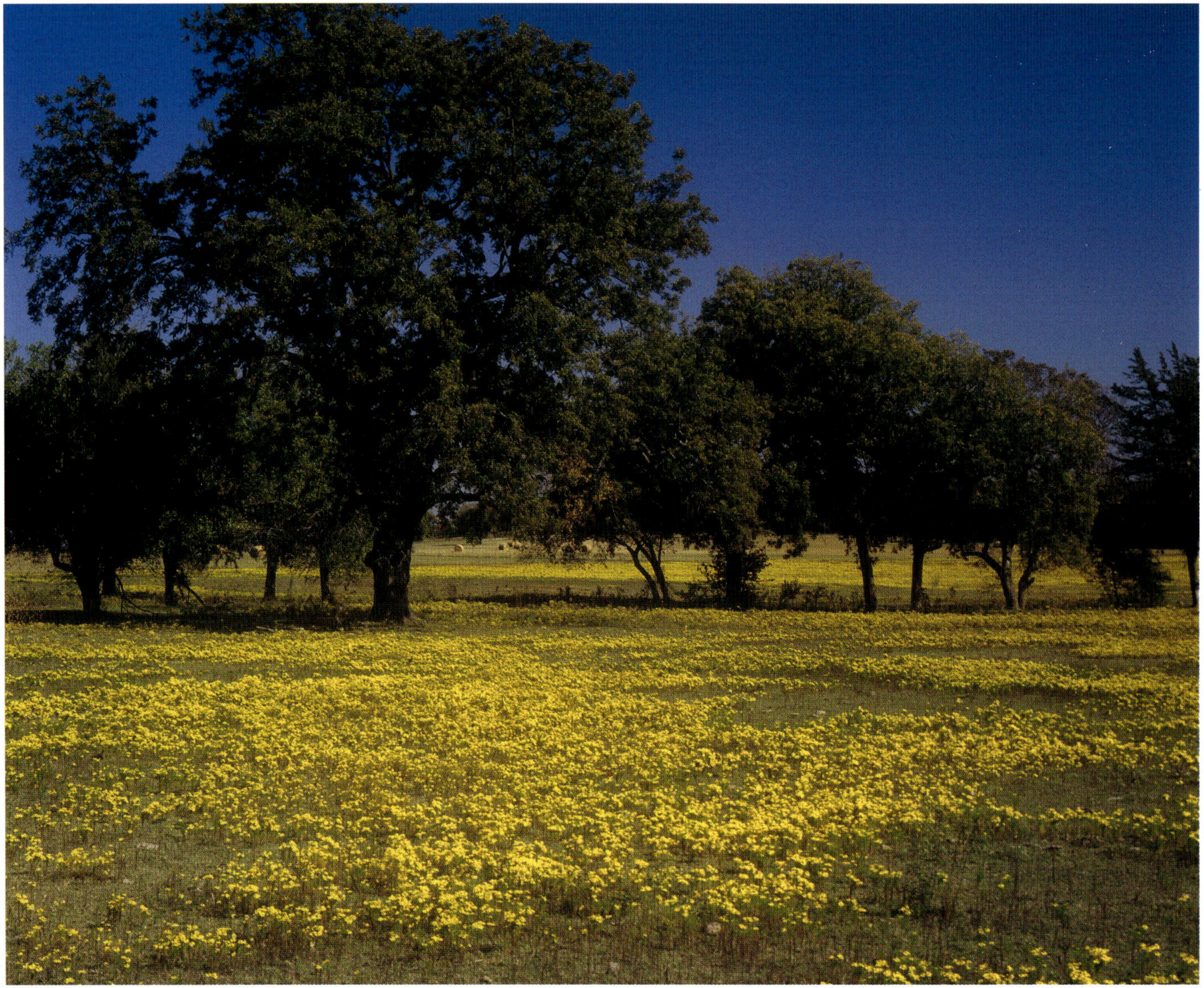

Coryell County

Late-Afternoon Sun on an Autumn Day

This county is named for James Coryell, a frontiersman and Texas Ranger who was killed by Native Americans. The county was organized in 1854. When the General Colonization Law went into effect in 1824, followed by the 1825 State Colonization Law of Coahuila y Tejas, Robert Leftwich obtained a grant to settle eight hundred families in the area.

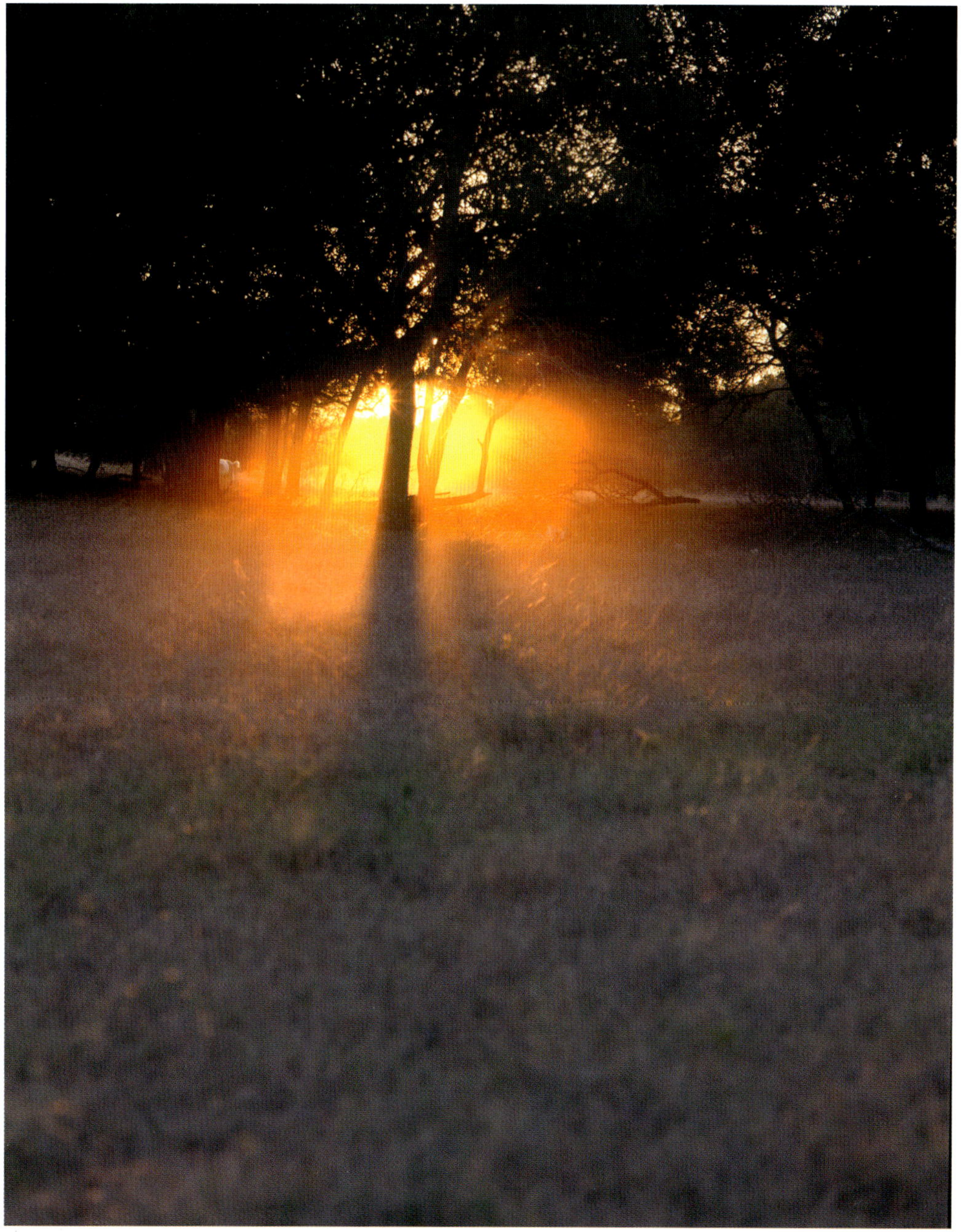

Cottle County

Sunset in the Matador Wildlife Management Area

The county was formed in 1876 and is named for George Washington Cottle, who died defending the Alamo. While the county was founded in 1876, a killing on the county line in 1889 induced residents to petition for county organization so that the suspect's trial could be held in the county. Cottle County was organized in 1892, with Paducah as the county seat.

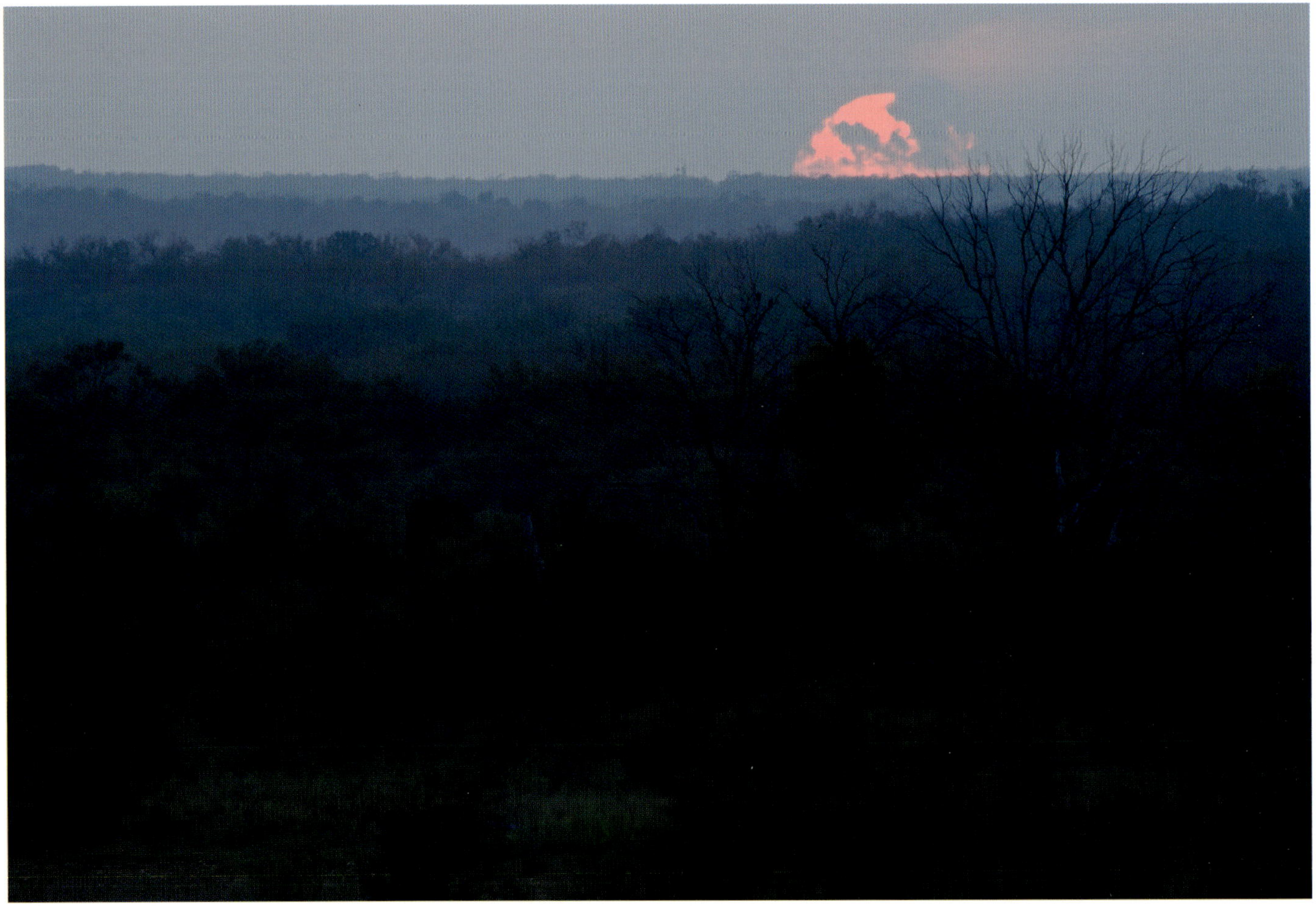

Crane County

Pecos River

The county is named for William Carey Crane, an early president of Baylor University. Although the county was founded in 1887, settlement came only years later, and the county was not organized until 1927.

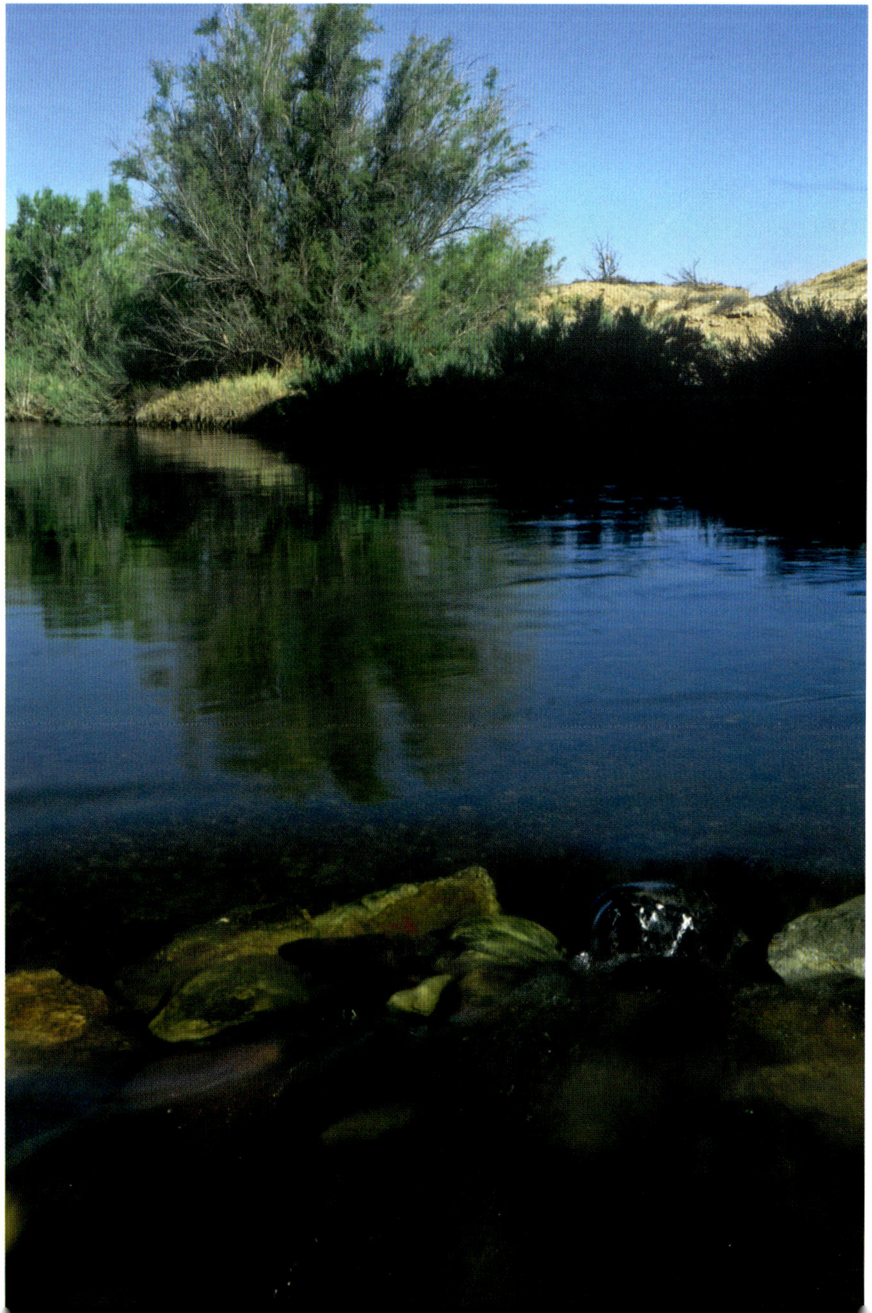

Crockett County

Limestone Bluffs near the Pecos River

Founded in 1875, the county is named for David Crockett, the legendary frontiersman who died at the Battle of the Alamo. In 1590, Spanish explorer Gaspar Castaño de Sosa led a mining expedition of 170 that passed through the western section of Crockett County to reach the Pecos River.

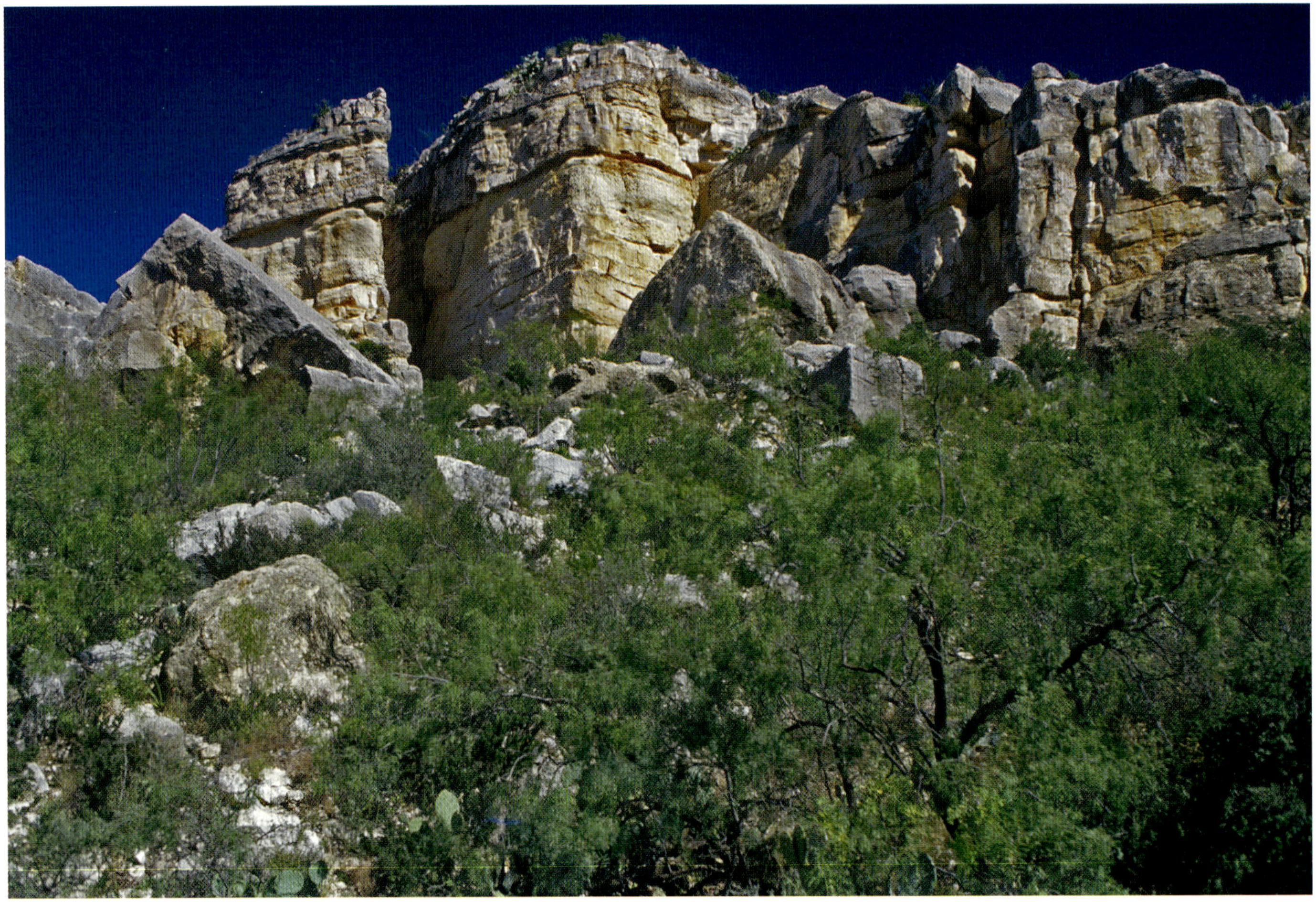

Crosby County

Late Afternoon among the Badlands of the Panhandle

The county is named for Stephen Crosby, a Texas land commissioner. The county was founded in 1876. In 1871, Ranald S. Mackenzie fought Quanah Parker and other Comanches at the Battle of Blanco Canyon. The campaign established the Mackenzie Trail, used by the first settlers in Crosby County in the late 1870s.

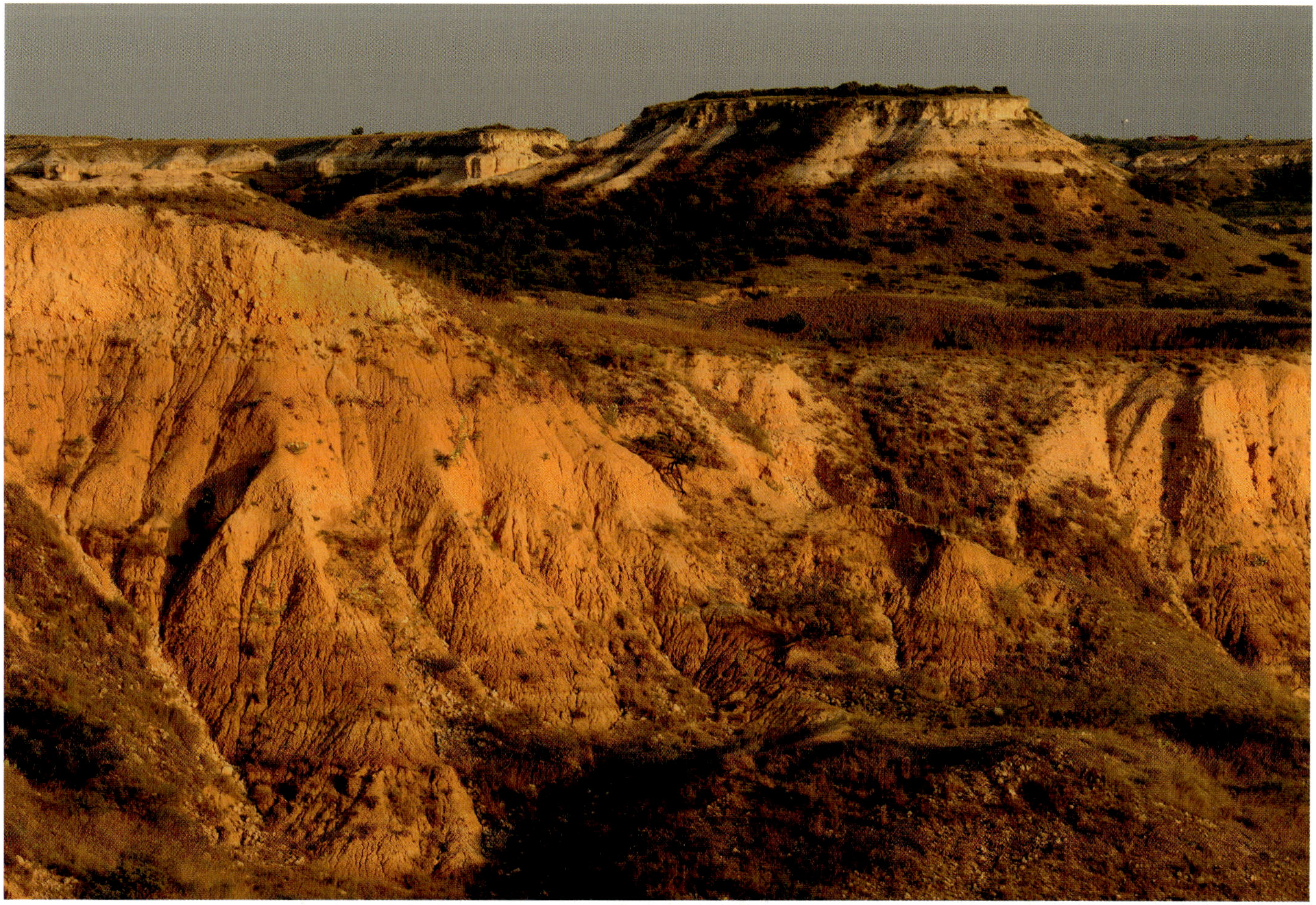

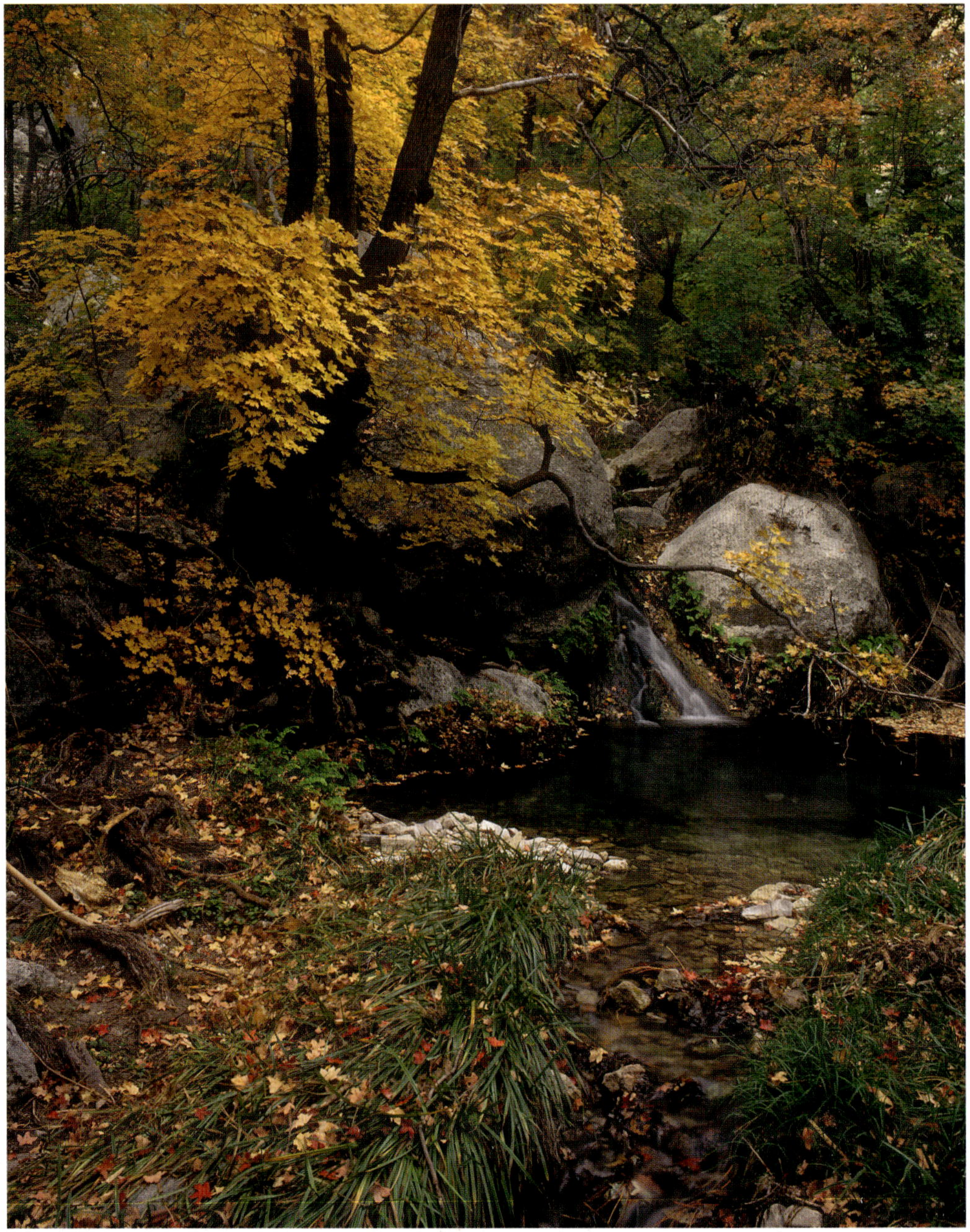

Culberson County

Smith Spring in Guadalupe Mountains National Park

The county was founded in 1911. It was named for David Browning Culberson, a lawyer, US congressman, and soldier in the Civil War. Both the San Antonio–San Diego Mail Line and Butterfield Overland Mail served the area between 1857 and 1861. These mail coaches provided a means for travelers to reach California in twenty-seven days if the passenger had the $200 for a one-way fare and was courageous enough to withstand the weather and dangers along the route.

Dallam County

Winter Sunrise

The county was founded in 1876 and was named for James Wilmer Dallam, a lawyer and newspaper publisher who had a close association with the Supreme Court of Texas. The first settlement in the area followed in 1870, which resulted in the Red River War of 1874 and 1875 with native Comanche and Kiowa tribes.

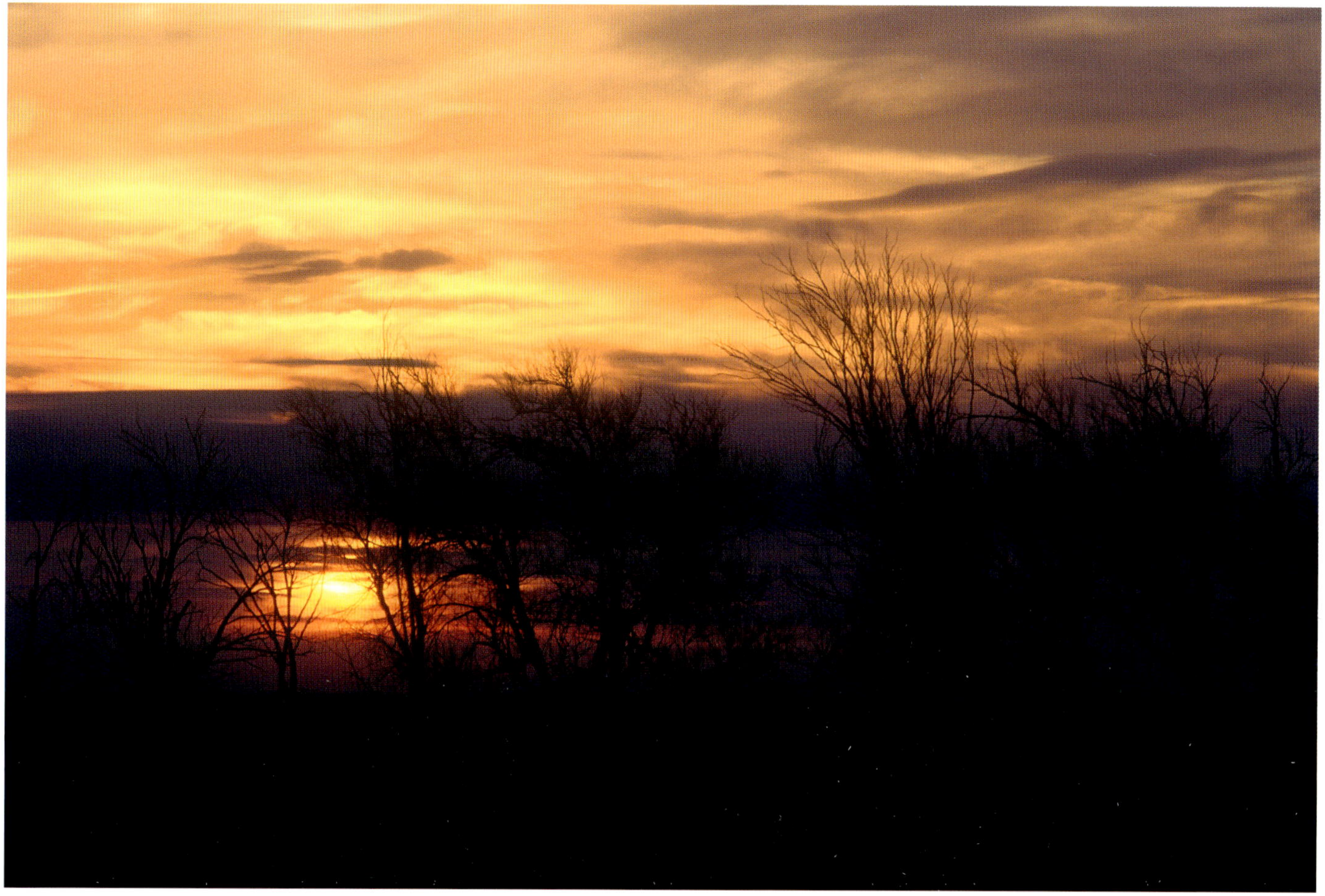

Dallas County

Cedar Hill State Park

The county was named for George Mifflin Dallas, the eleventh vice president of the United States, and was founded in 1846. The first to settle in the county was John Neely Bryan, who arrived in November 1841 with his dog and a Cherokee friend known as Ned.

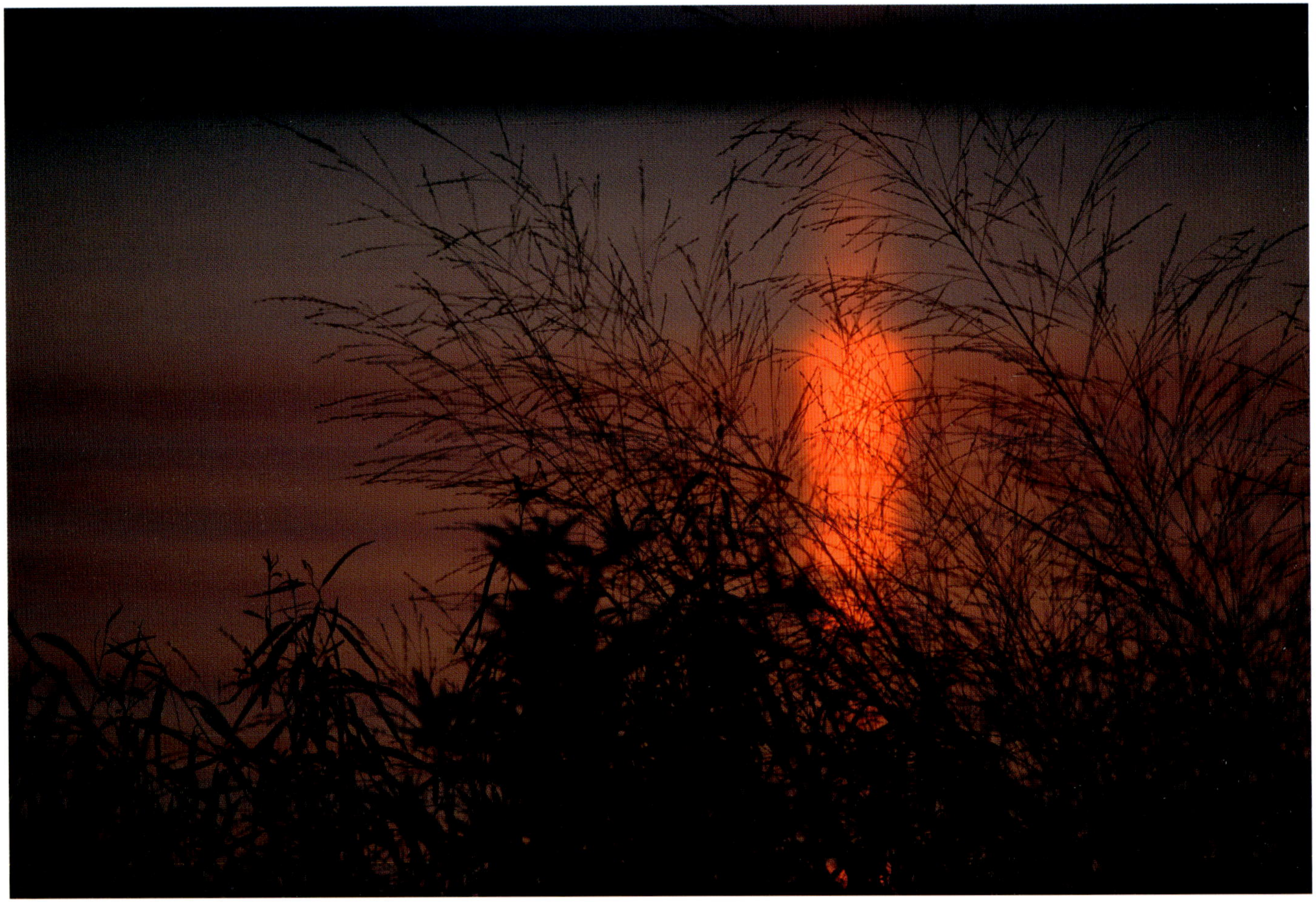

Dawson County

Pumpjack and Sunflowers

The county was founded in 1876 and is named for Nicholas Mosby Dawson, a soldier of the Texan Revolution and victim of the Dawson Massacre, in which thirty-six Texan militiamen were killed by Mexican soldiers on September 17, 1842. In 1943, the discovery well for the Spraberry Trend, the third-largest oil field in the United States, was drilled in Dawson County on land owned by farmer Abner Spraberry.

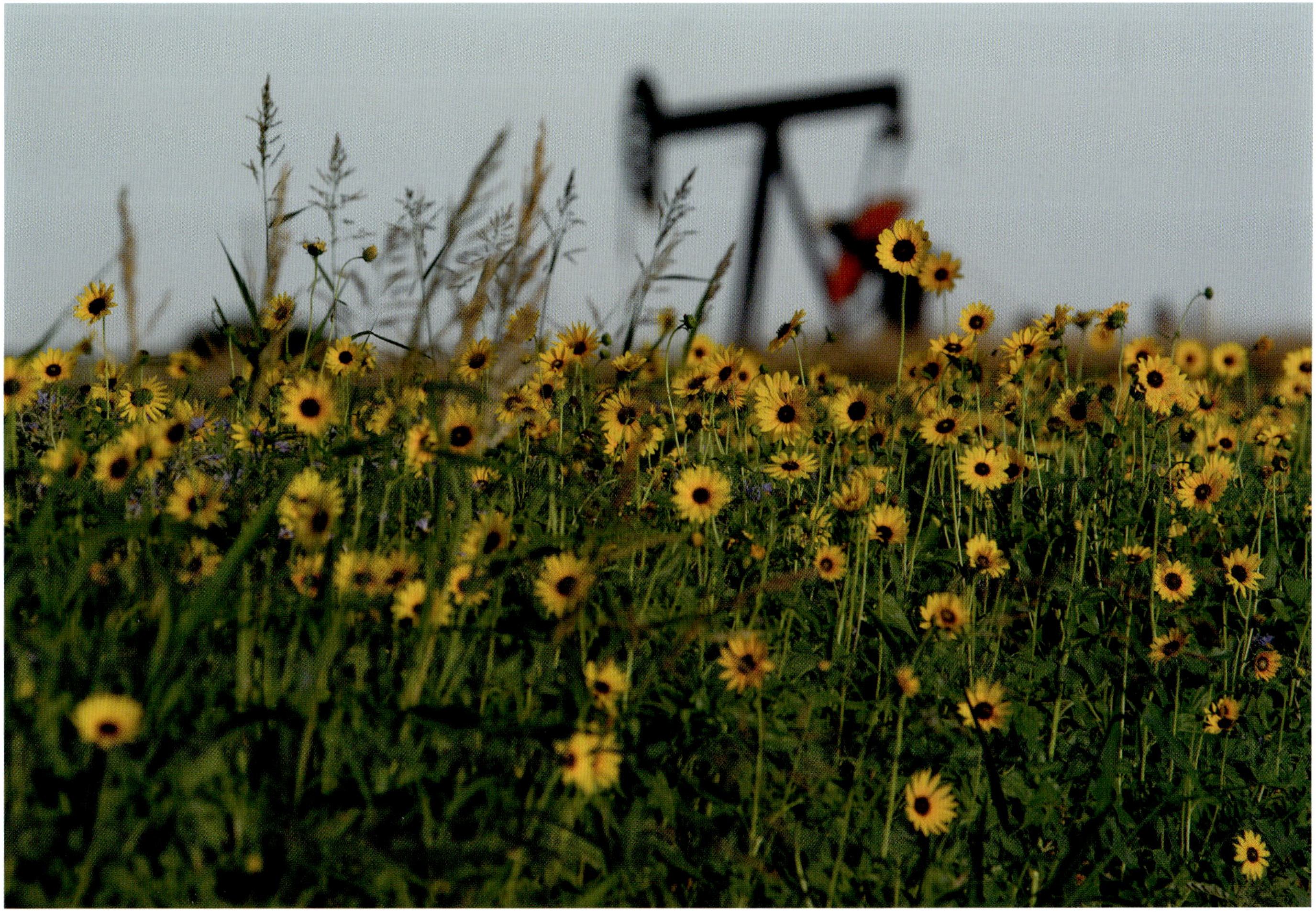

Deaf Smith County

Solitary Copse of Trees and Windmill

Erastus "Deaf" Smith (1787–1837), a scout during the Texan Revolution, provides the name for the county, which was founded in 1876. After the war, Deaf Smith led a company of Texas Rangers. His first name was generally pronounced "deef."

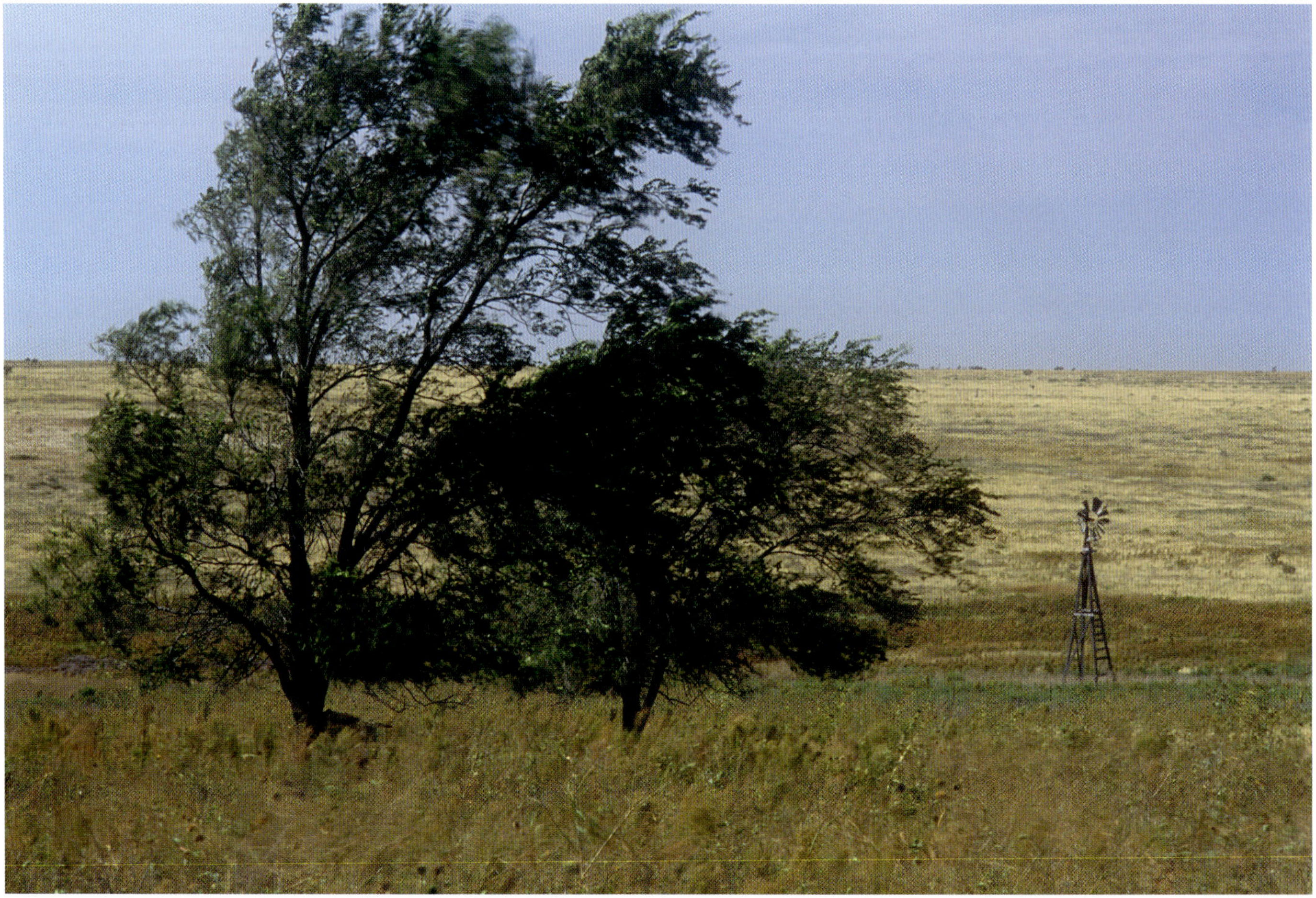

Delta County

Sunset in Cooper Lake State Park

The county was founded in 1870 and was named for its triangular shape, much like the Greek letter delta. Nat Corbet, a former resident of New York, established the first store in the county, in the community of Ben Franklin, in 1845.

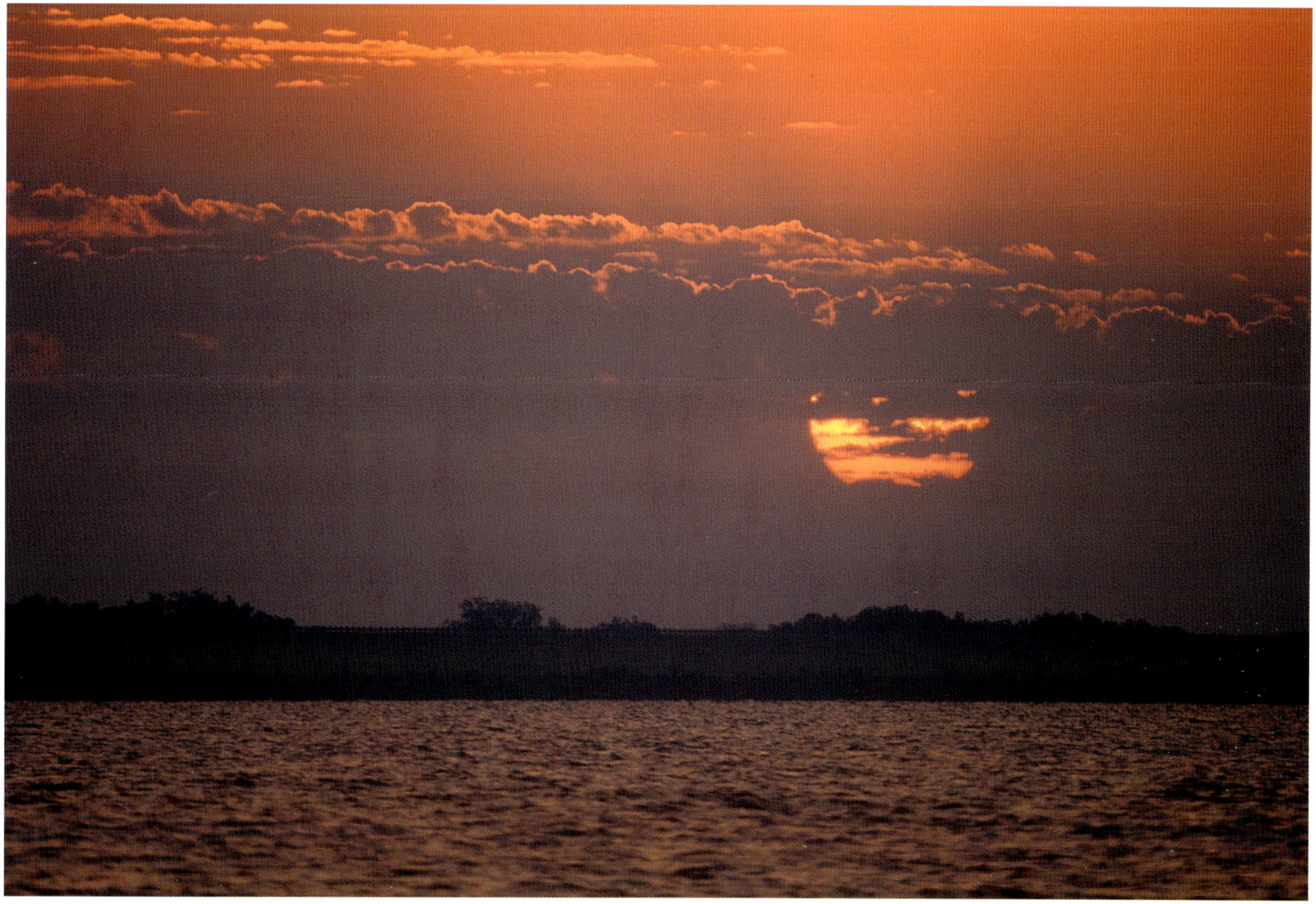

Denton County

Lake Grapevine

Denton County was named for John Bunyan Denton (1806–1841), a preacher, lawyer, and soldier killed during a raid on a Native American camp. The county was formed in 1846. The Denton County Courthouse, on the square in the city of Denton, was built in 1896. Today the building houses various government offices, as well as a museum.

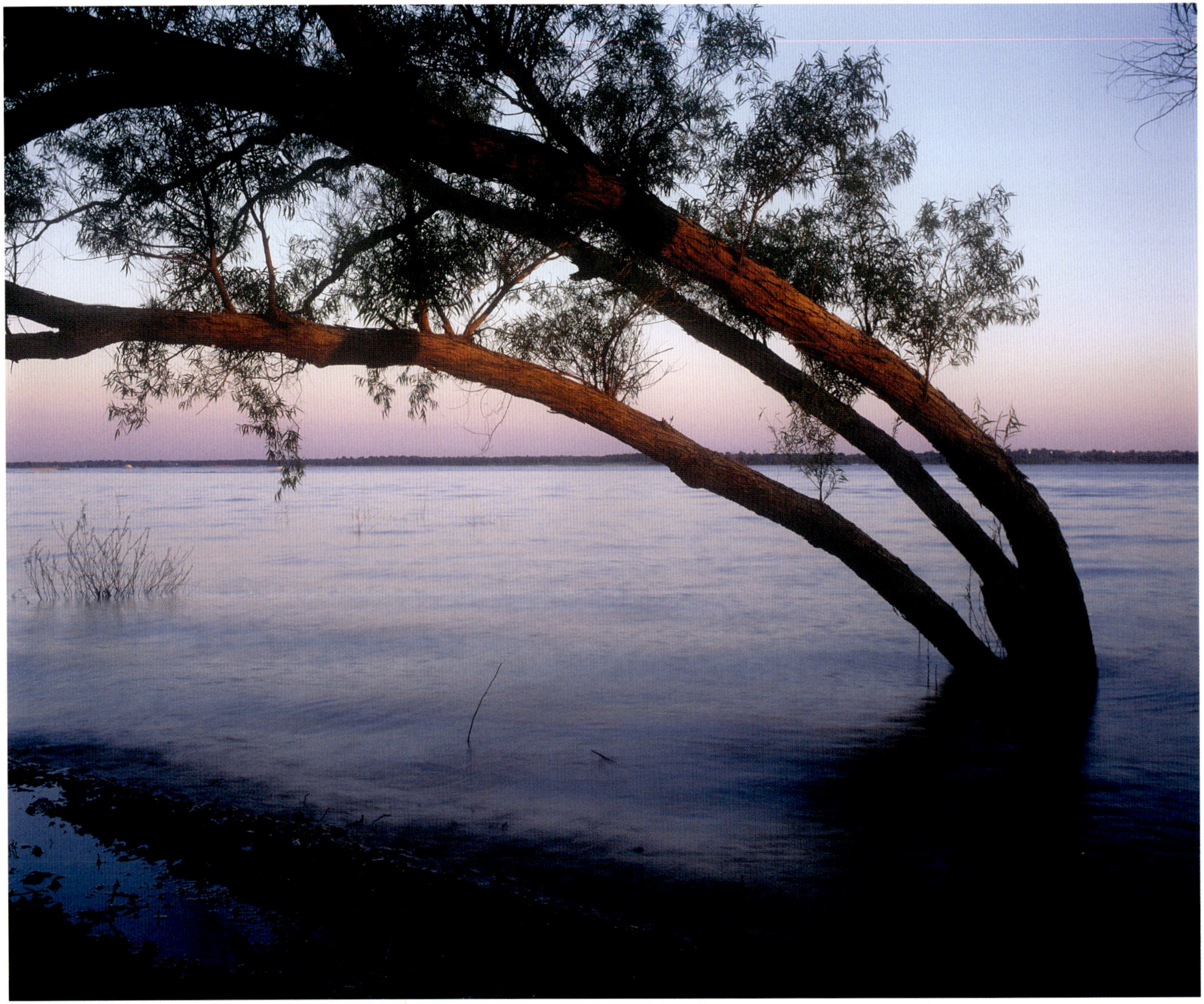

DeWitt County

Massive Live Oak and Sunflowers

The county was founded in 1846 and is named for Green DeWitt, an organizer who founded an early colony in Texas. The notorious Sutton-Taylor feud began as a Reconstruction-era county law enforcement issue between the Taylor family and lawman William E. Sutton. It eventually involved both the Taylor and Sutton families, the Texas State Police, the Texas Rangers, and John Wesley Hardin. The feud, which lasted a decade and cost thirty-five lives, has been called the longest and bloodiest in Texas history.

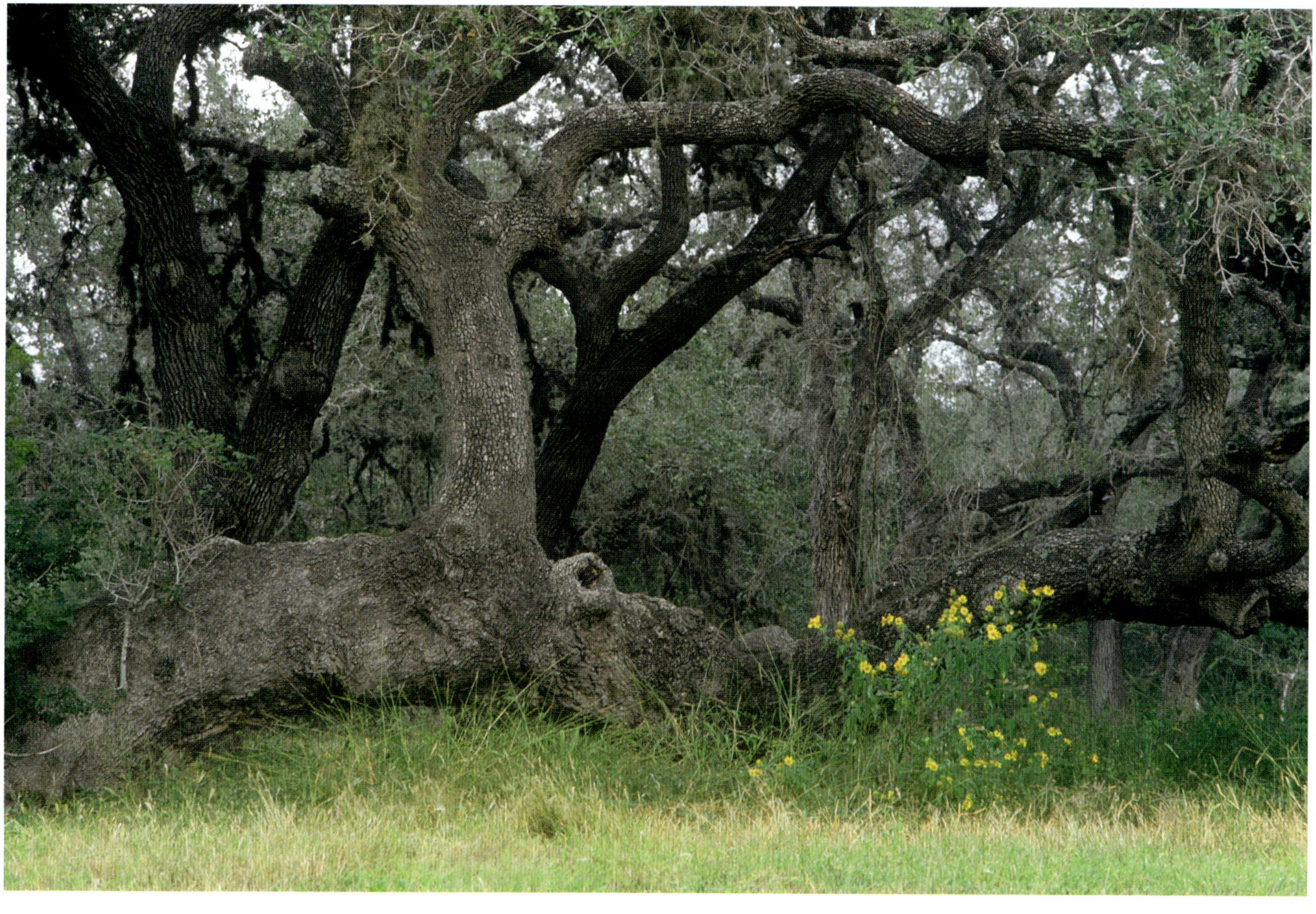

Dickens County

Rabbit Brush Growing from Boulder

The county was formed in 1876 and was named for J. A. Dickens, who died at the Battle of the Alamo. Until the first years of the twentieth century, settlers shunned the area because of its remoteness and minimal rainfall. Instead of farms, vast cattle ranches took up most of the land.

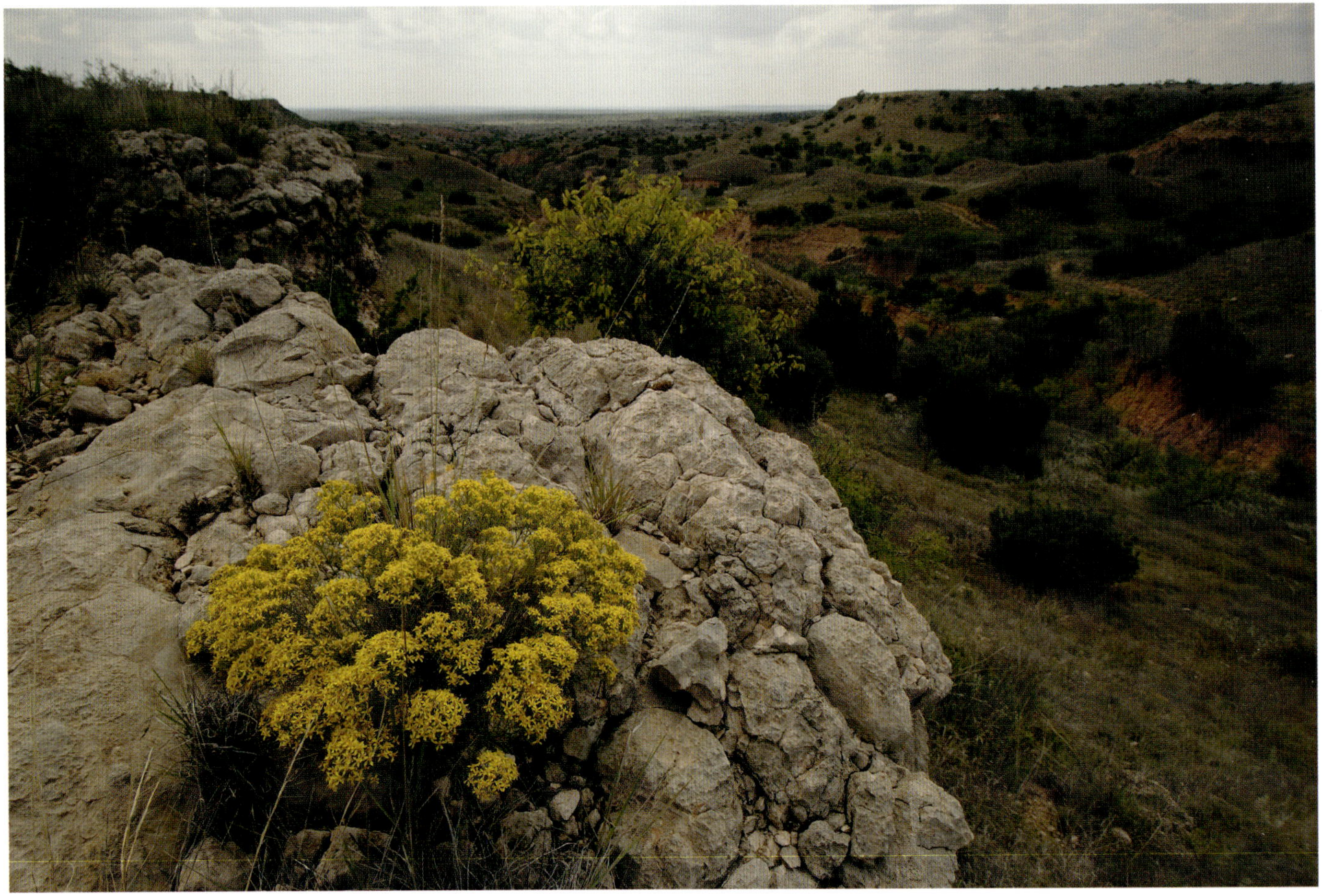

Dimmit County

Morning Light on Oak Trees

The county is named for Philip Dimmitt, a significant figure in the Texas Revolution. The county was founded in 1858. The area between the Rio Grande and the Nueces River, in what was to become Dimmit County, was a disputed territory known as the Wild Horse Desert, where neither the Republic of Texas nor the Mexican government had explicit control. Ownership was in dispute until the Mexican-American War. The area became filled with lawless characters who kept many peaceable settlers out of the area.

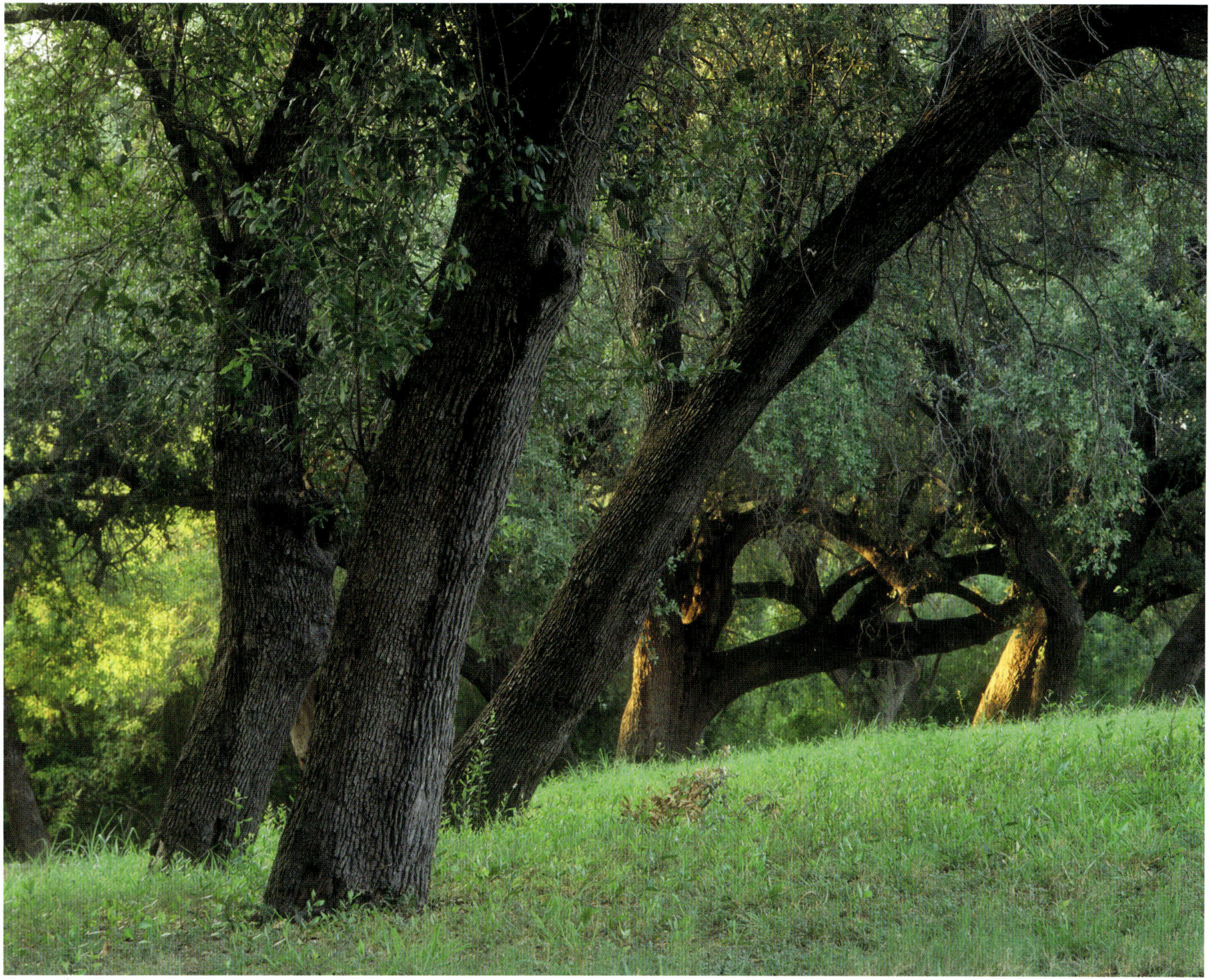

Donley County

Grove of Cottonwood Trees after a Rainstorm

The county was named for Stockton P. Donley, a frontier lawyer and Texas Supreme Court justice. The county was founded in 1876. Legendary cattle baron Charles Goodnight spent his later years in Donley County. It was also the home of historian Harley True Burton, author of *A History of the JA Ranch*, which Goodnight formerly co-owned. Burton was president of Clarendon College and the mayor of Clarendon from 1955 to 1963. The JA Ranch is in the counties of Donley, Hall, Briscoe, and Armstrong.

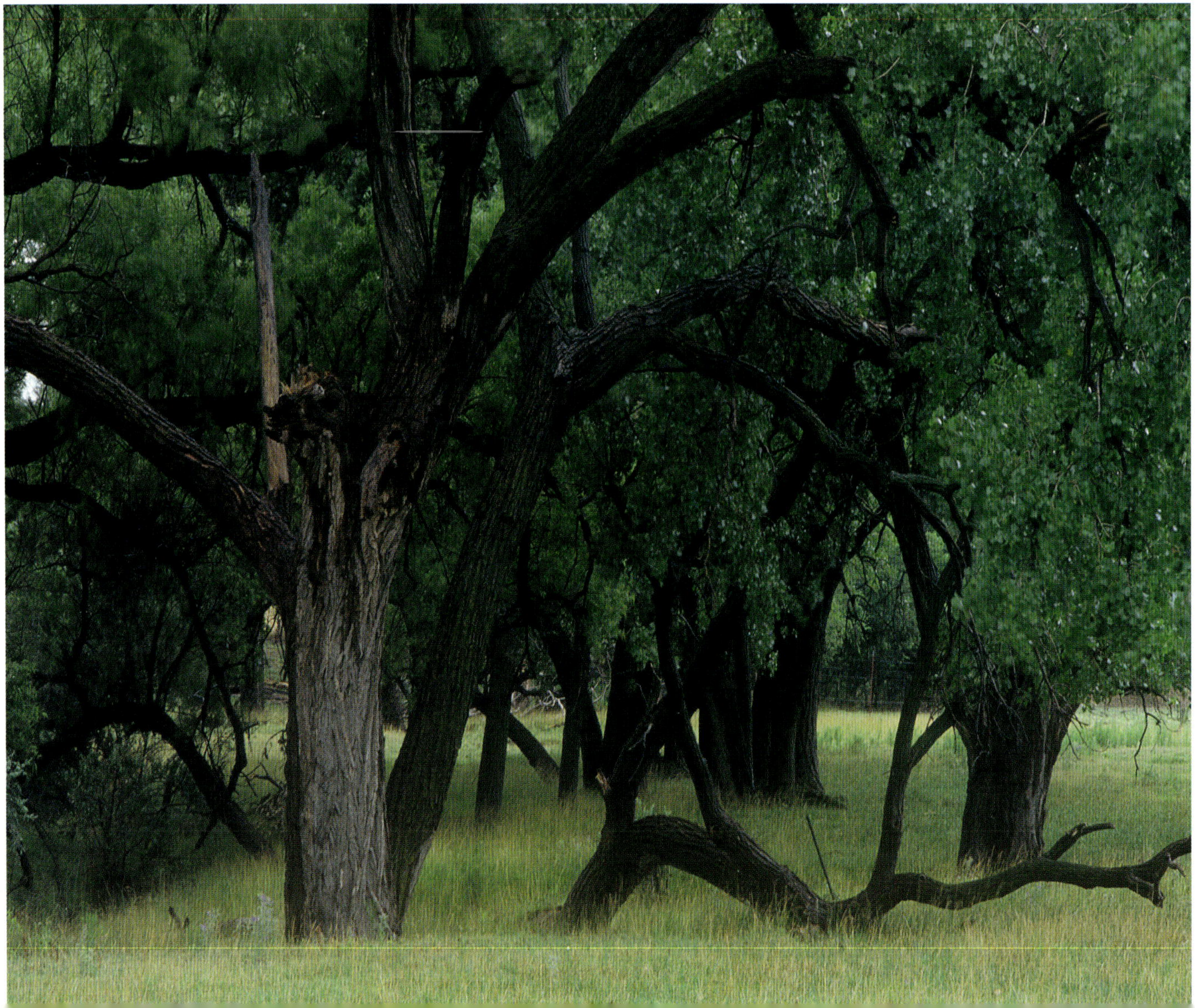

Duval County

Sunset and Yucca

The county was founded in 1858 and organized in 1876. It is named for Burr H. Duval, a soldier in the Texas Revolution who died in the Goliad Massacre. After the Texas-Mexican Railway was built in 1881, the county's San Diego station was important for hides, wool, and cotton.

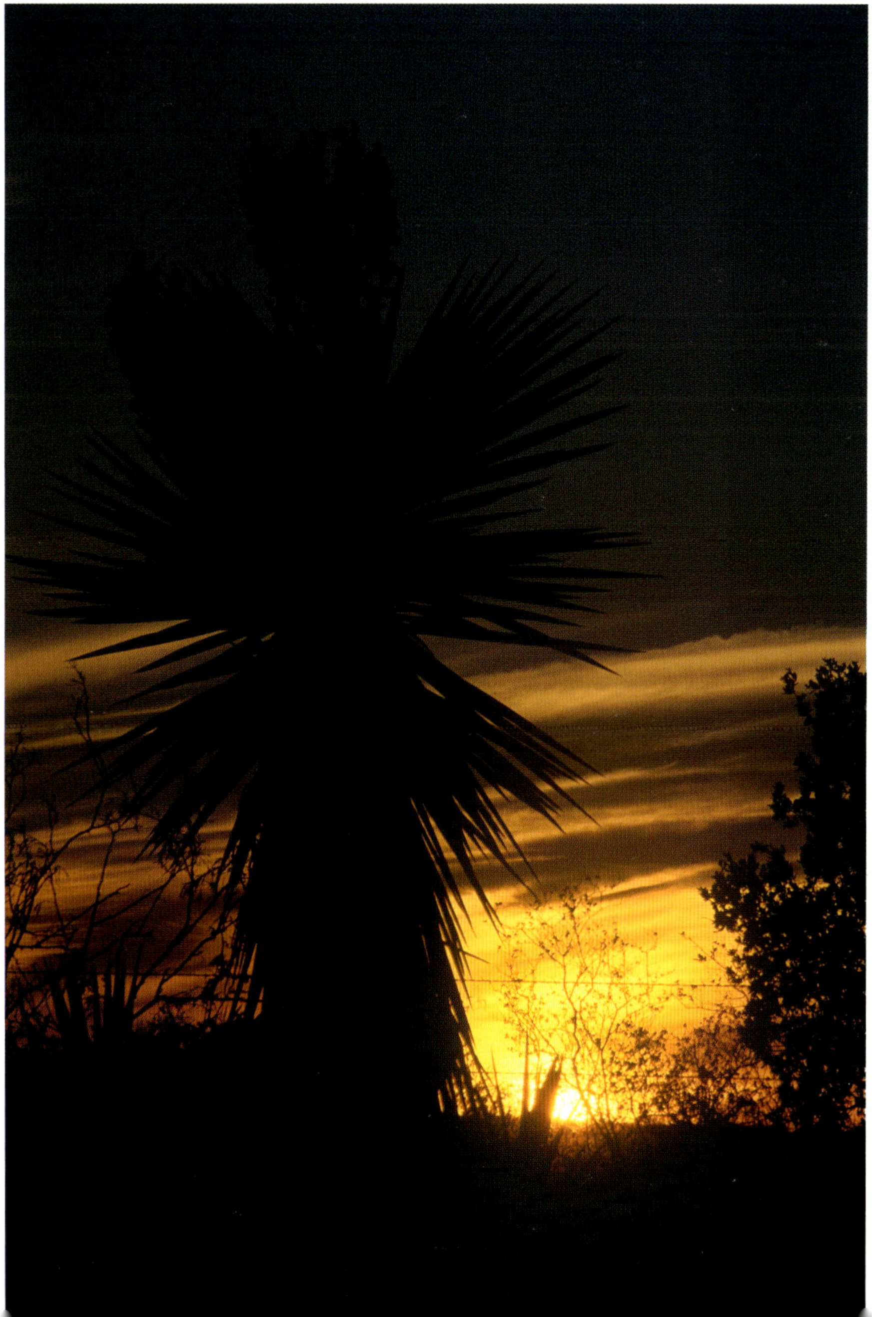

Eastland County

Lake Leon

The county was founded in 1858 and organized in 1873. It is named for William Mosby Eastland, a soldier during the Texas Revolution. Eastland County is known for the legend of "Old Rip," a horned toad that lived many years sealed in the cornerstone of the previous Eastland courthouse, built in 1897.

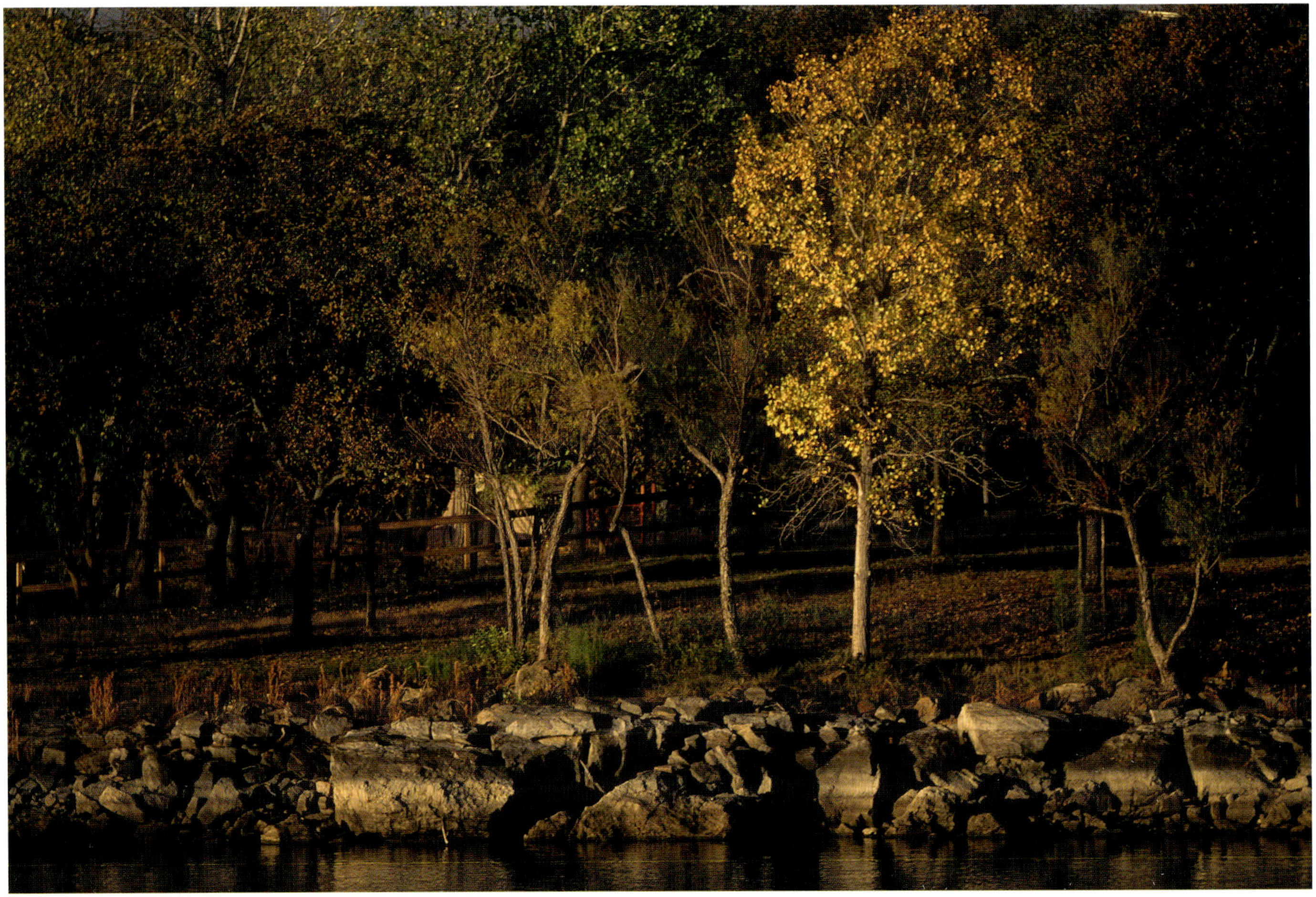

Ector County

Sunflower in Odessa's Comanche Trail Park

The county was founded in 1887 and organized in 1891. It was named for Mathew Ector, a Confederate general in the American Civil War. A Stonehenge replica is on the campus of the University of Texas of the Permian Basin in Odessa, in Ector County. The roughly twenty stone blocks—similar in size, shape, and appearance to the ancient Stonehenge in southwestern England—were unveiled in summer 2004.

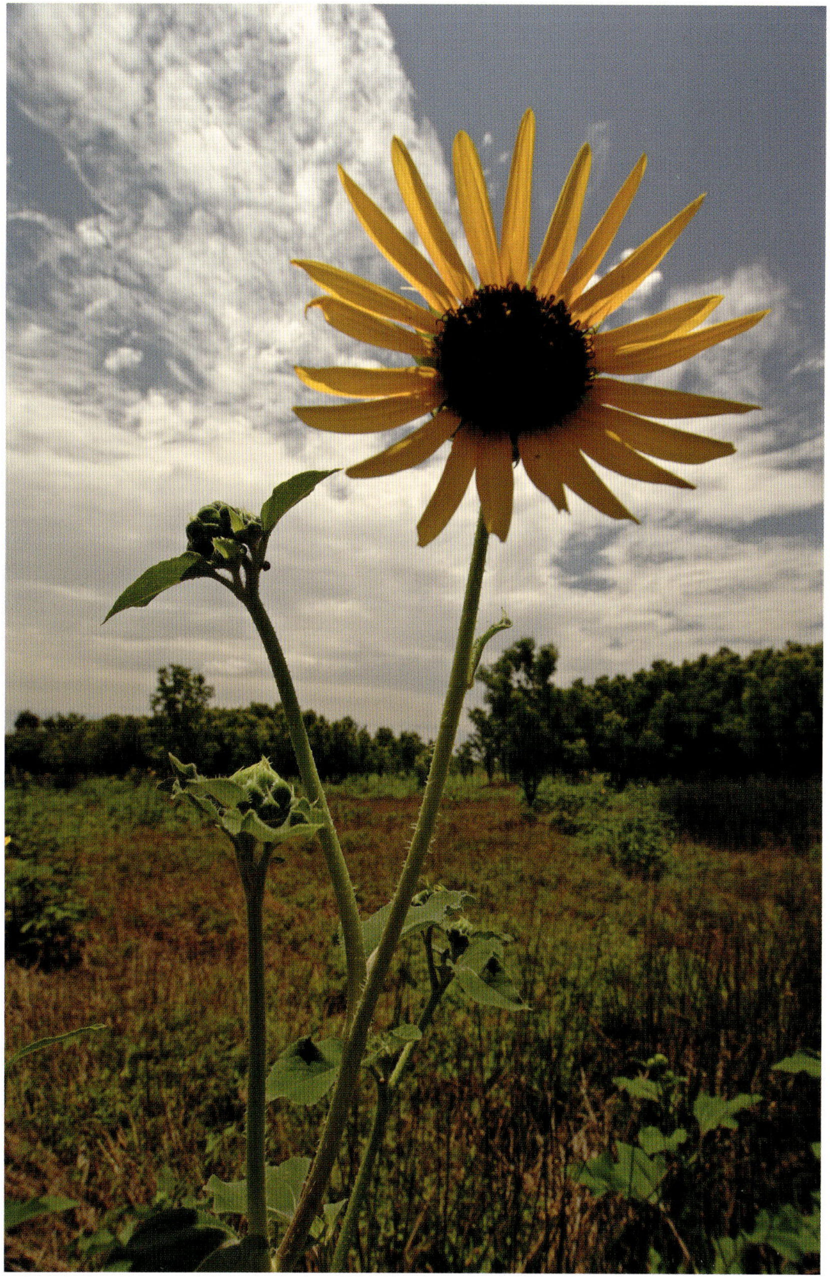

Edwards County

Sunset over the Hills of the Edwards Plateau

The county was created in 1858 and organized in 1883. It is named for Haden Edwards, an early settler. Devil's Sinkhole State Natural Area, near Rockprings, is home to the largest single-chambered cavern and the third deepest in the state.

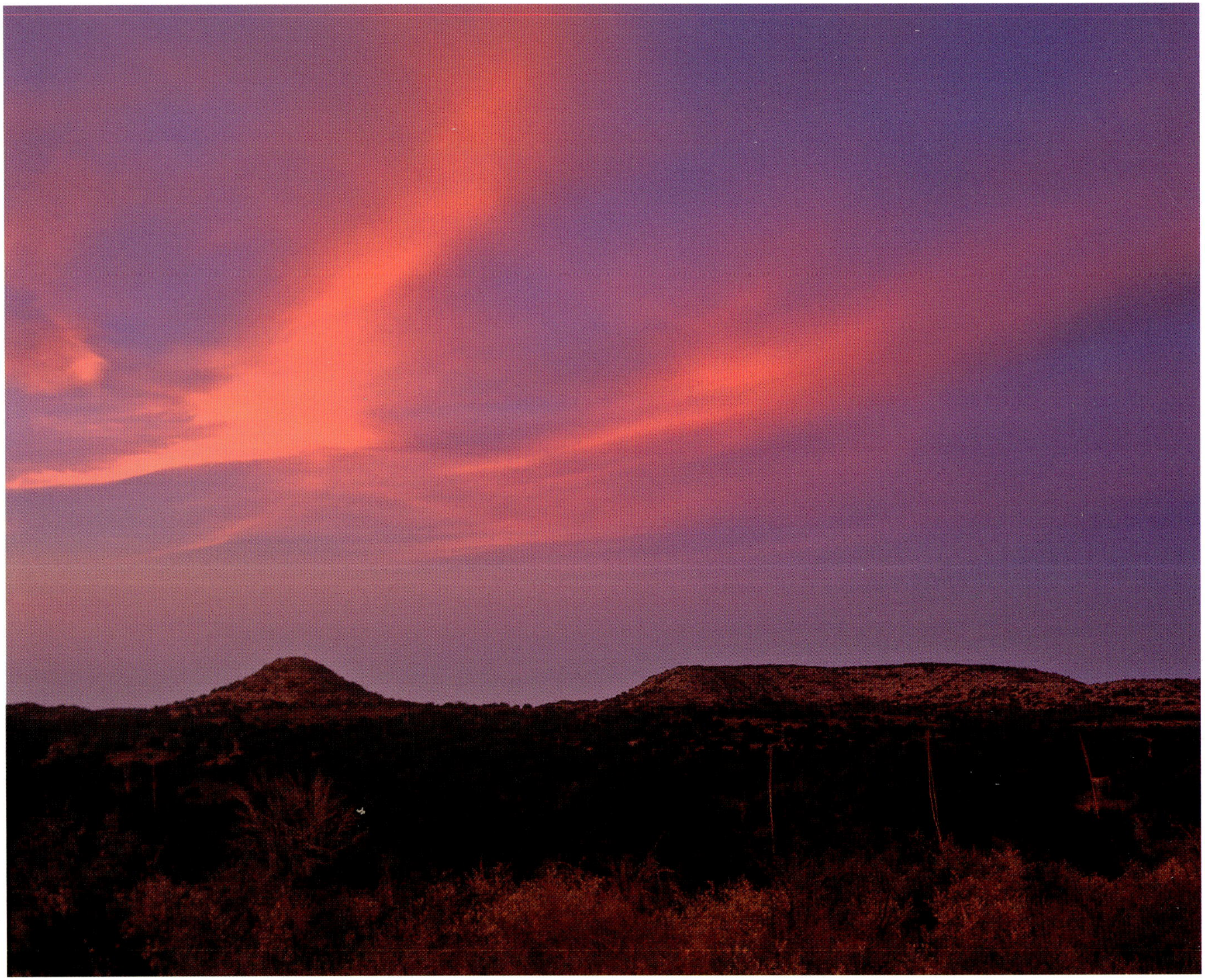

Ellis County

Wildflowers South of Dallas

The county was founded in 1849 and organized the next year. It is named for Richard Ellis, president of the convention that produced the Texas Declaration of Independence. Notable individuals from Ellis County include country singer and songwriter Ernest Tubb and the notorious Clyde Barrow of Bonnie and Clyde.

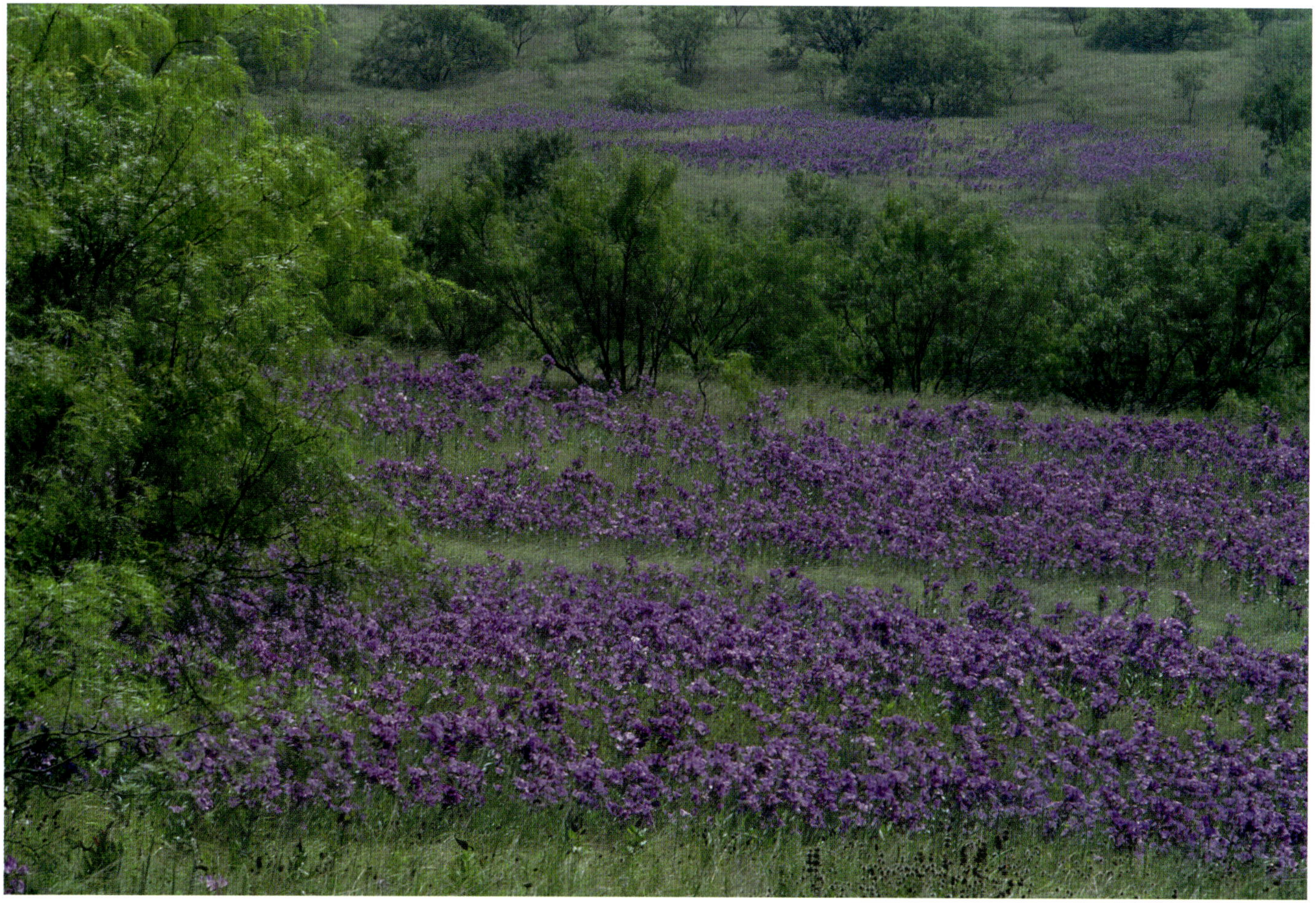

El Paso County

Hueco Tanks State Park

The county was created in 1850 and organized in 1871. It was named for the pass the Rio Grande created through the mountains on either side of the river. El Paso is a shortened version of "El Paso del Norte," which is Spanish for "the Pass of the North." Before the Civil War, slavery was an almost insignificant factor in El Paso County's agricultural economy, since there were only fifteen slaves in the area at that time.

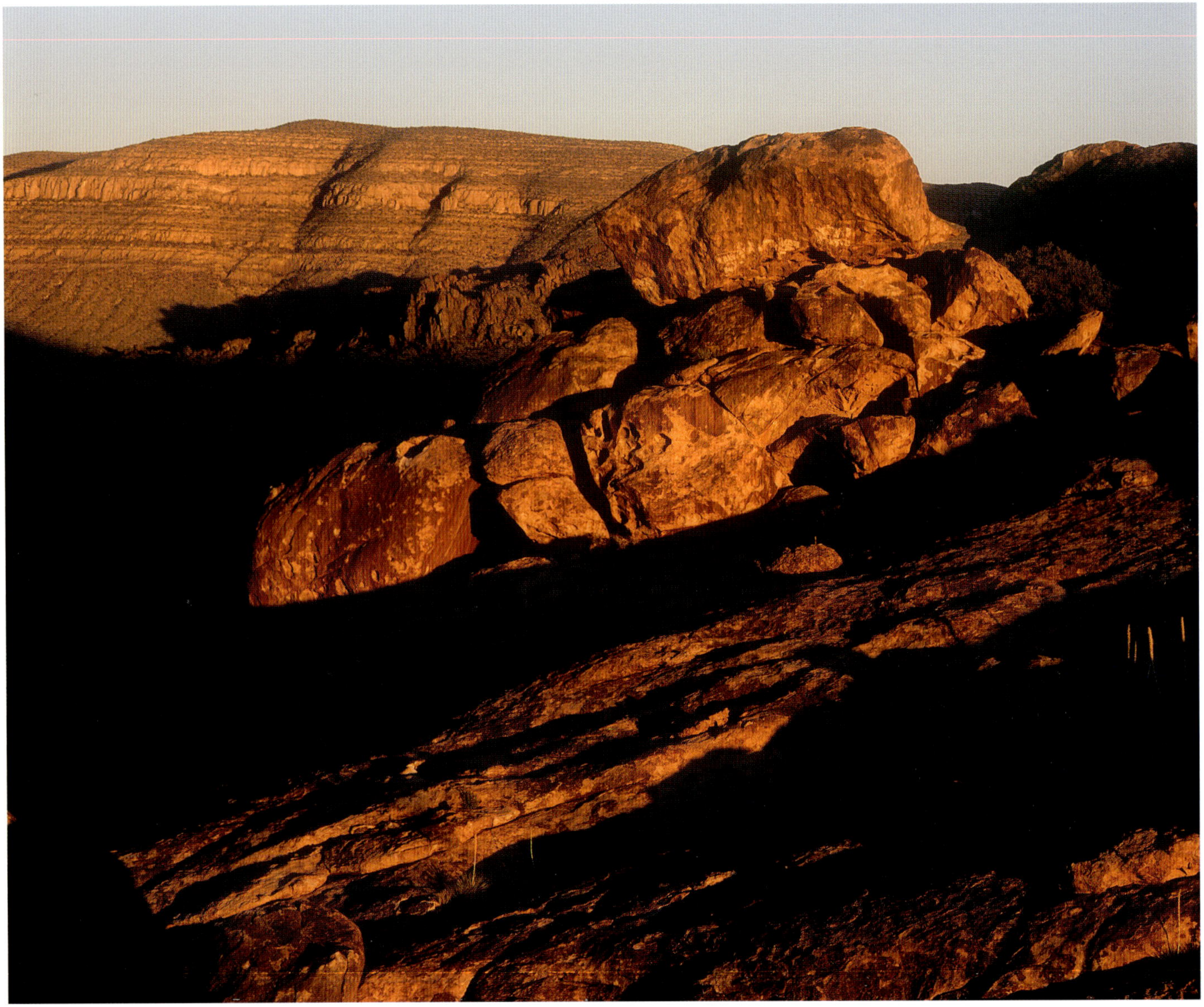

Erath County

Indian Blanket and Mesquite Trunk

The county is named for George Bernard Erath, an early surveyor and a soldier at the Battle of San Jacinto. The county was founded in 1856. Cotton became the dominant crop between 1875 and 1915, with the most abundant crop recorded in 1906. The industry was helped in 1879, when the Texas Central Railroad reached Dublin, and in 1889, when the Fort Worth and Rio Grande Railroad was completed through Stephenville.

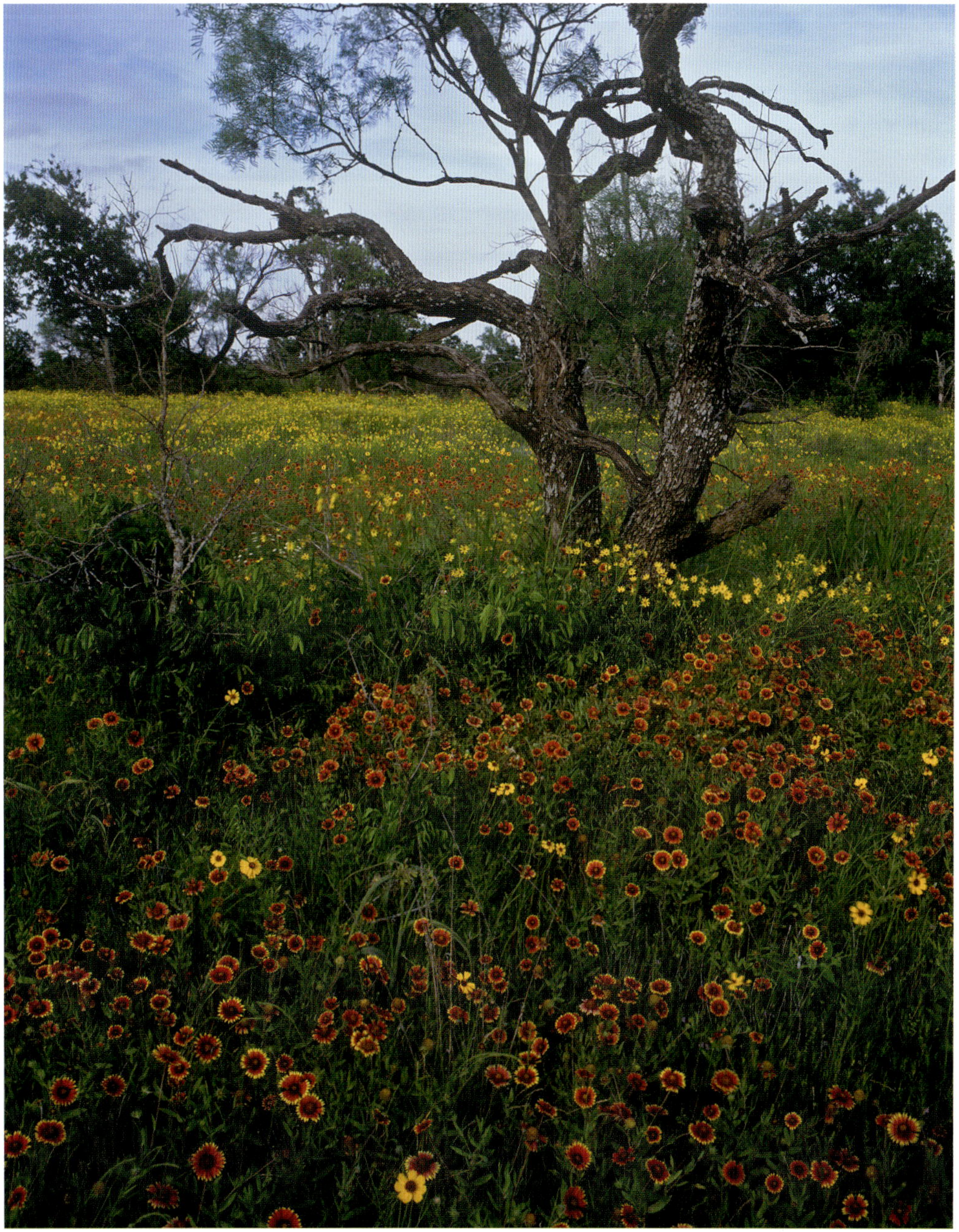

Falls County

Blooming Redbud Tree

The county was named for the original 10-foot-tall waterfall on the Brazos River that existed until the river changed course during a storm in 1866. The county was formed in 1850. Sterling C. Robertson and Robert Leftwich received a grant from the Mexican legislature to settle eight hundred families in the area.

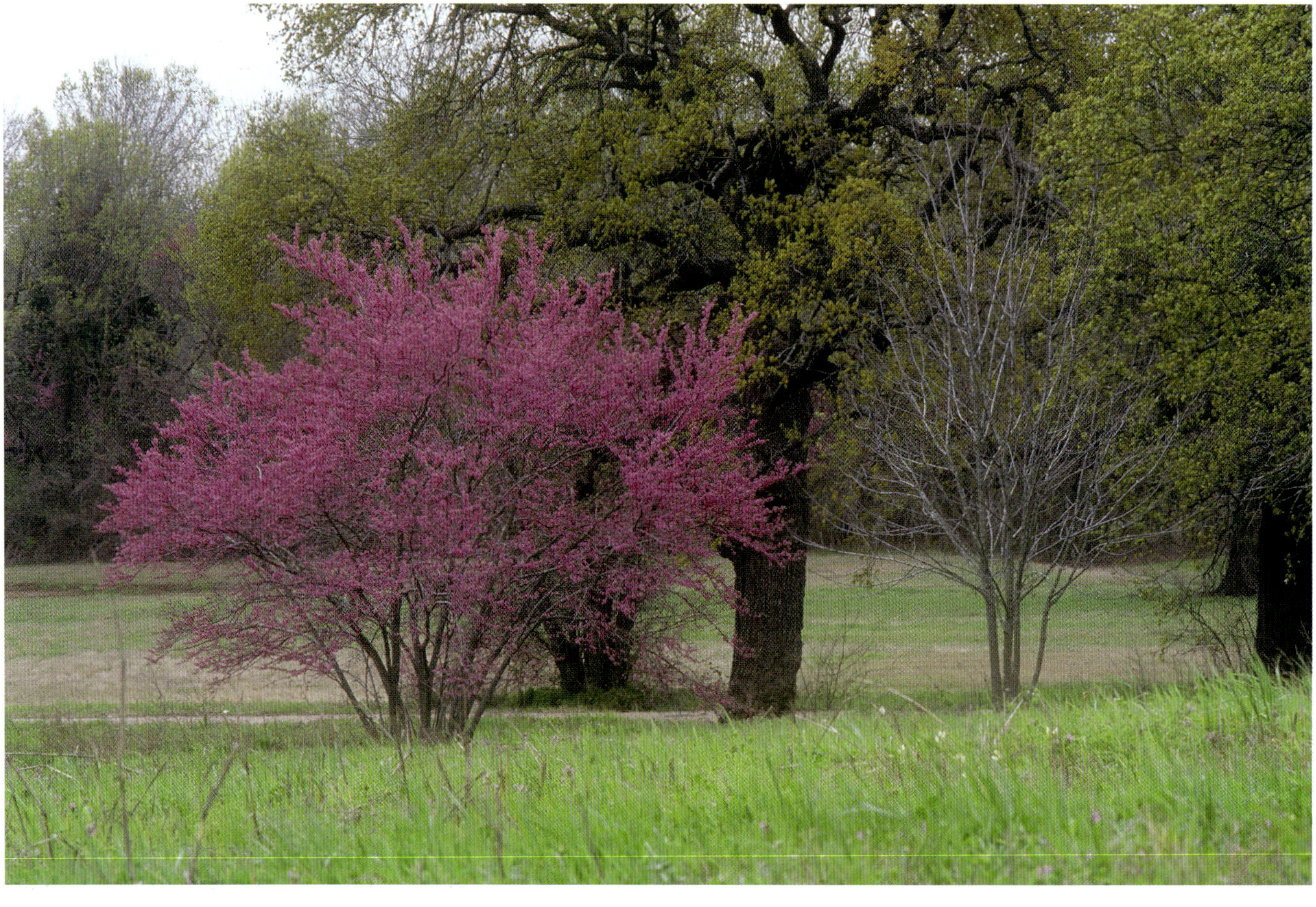

Fannin County

Early-Morning Storm

Founded in 1837, the county is named for James Walker Fannin Jr. (1805–1836), the commander of the Texans killed in the Goliad Massacre. Caddo National Grassland is a national grassland consisting of two separate sections in northeastern and southeastern Fannin County. The parcel of land was purchased in the 1930s and comprises more than 17,000 protected acres.

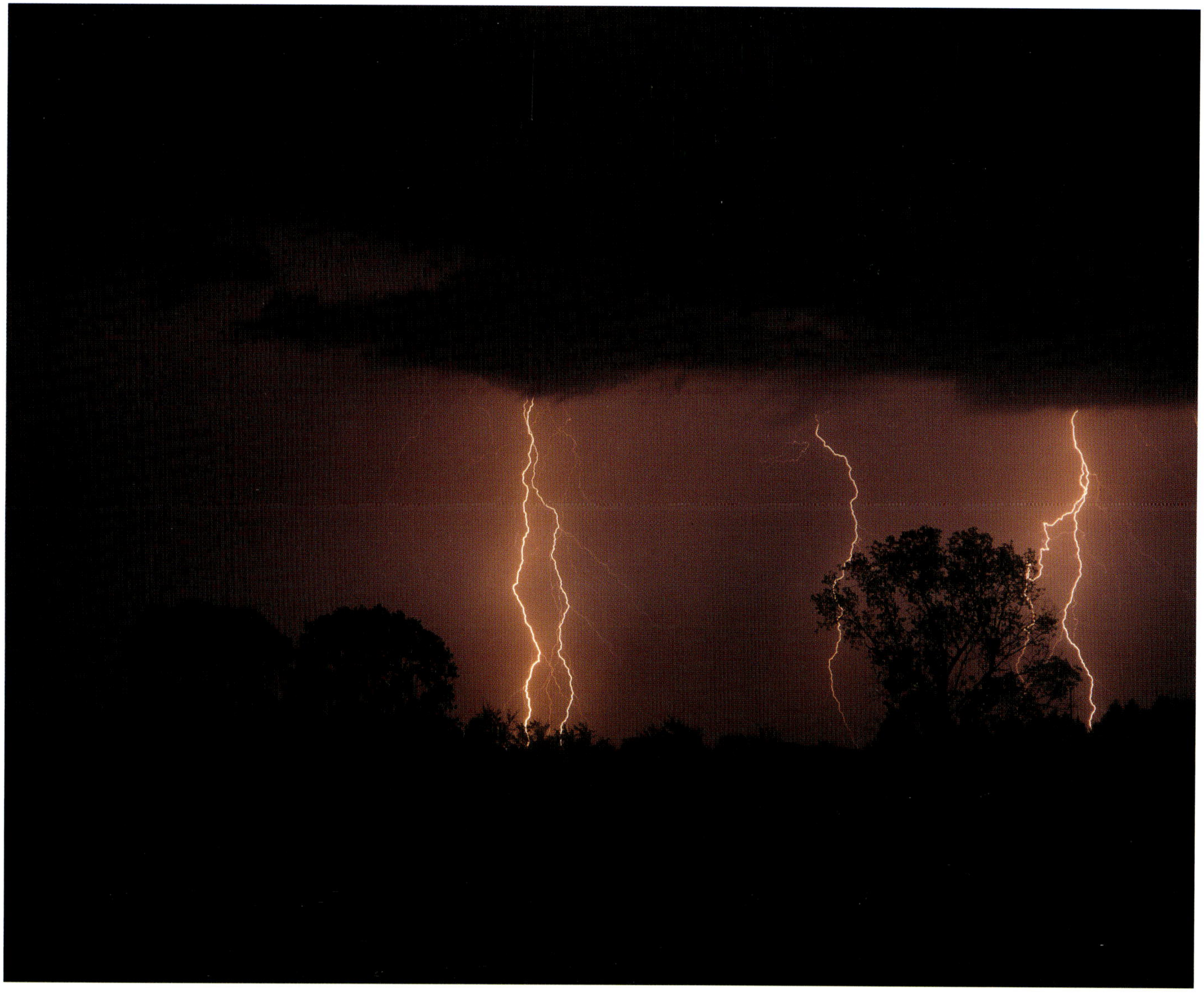

Fayette County

Sunset Sky and Windmill

The county is named for Gilbert du Motier, Marquis de Lafayette (1757–1834), the French-born general and hero of the Revolutionary War. The county was formed in 1837. Fayette County is the location of the famous "Chicken Ranch," which was the basis of the musical play and feature film *The Best Little Whorehouse in Texas.*

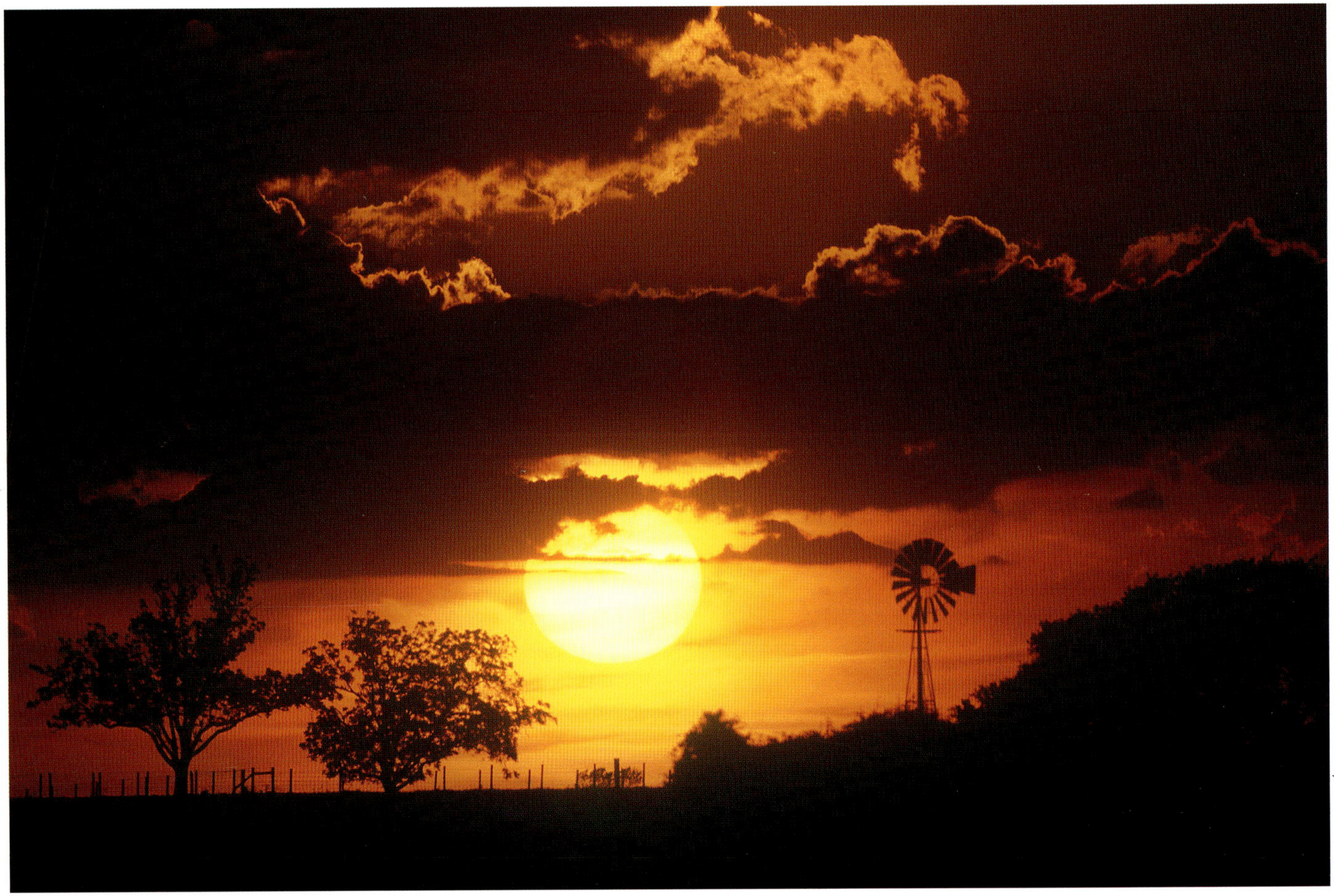

Fisher County

Windblown Winter Scene

Fisher County was created in 1876 and organized in 1886. It is named for Samuel Rhoads Fisher, a signer of the Texas Declaration of Independence and a secretary of the Navy of the Republic of Texas. The town of Roby eventually won the county seat election over Fisher, but it was later discovered that one of the voters—a Mr. Bill Purp—was actually a dog whose owner lived near Roby.

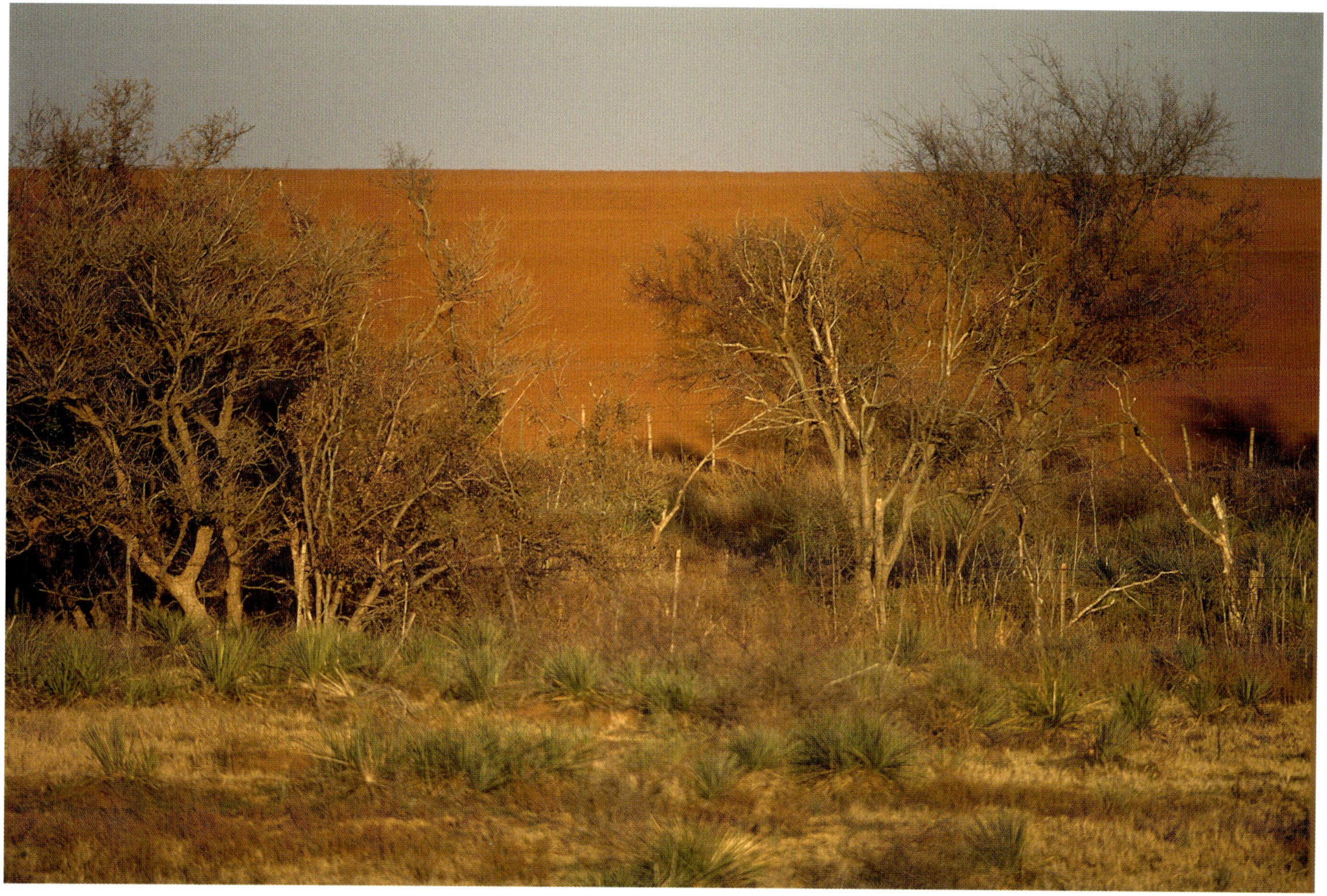

Floyd County

Along the Cap Rock Canyons Trailway

The county was created in 1876 and organized in 1890. It was named for Dolphin Ward Floyd, who died defending the Alamo. Floyd County is in what many call the wind corridor of the United States. The wind corridor stretches from the Panhandle of Texas up into Minnesota, including some of the most wind-rich states in the country.

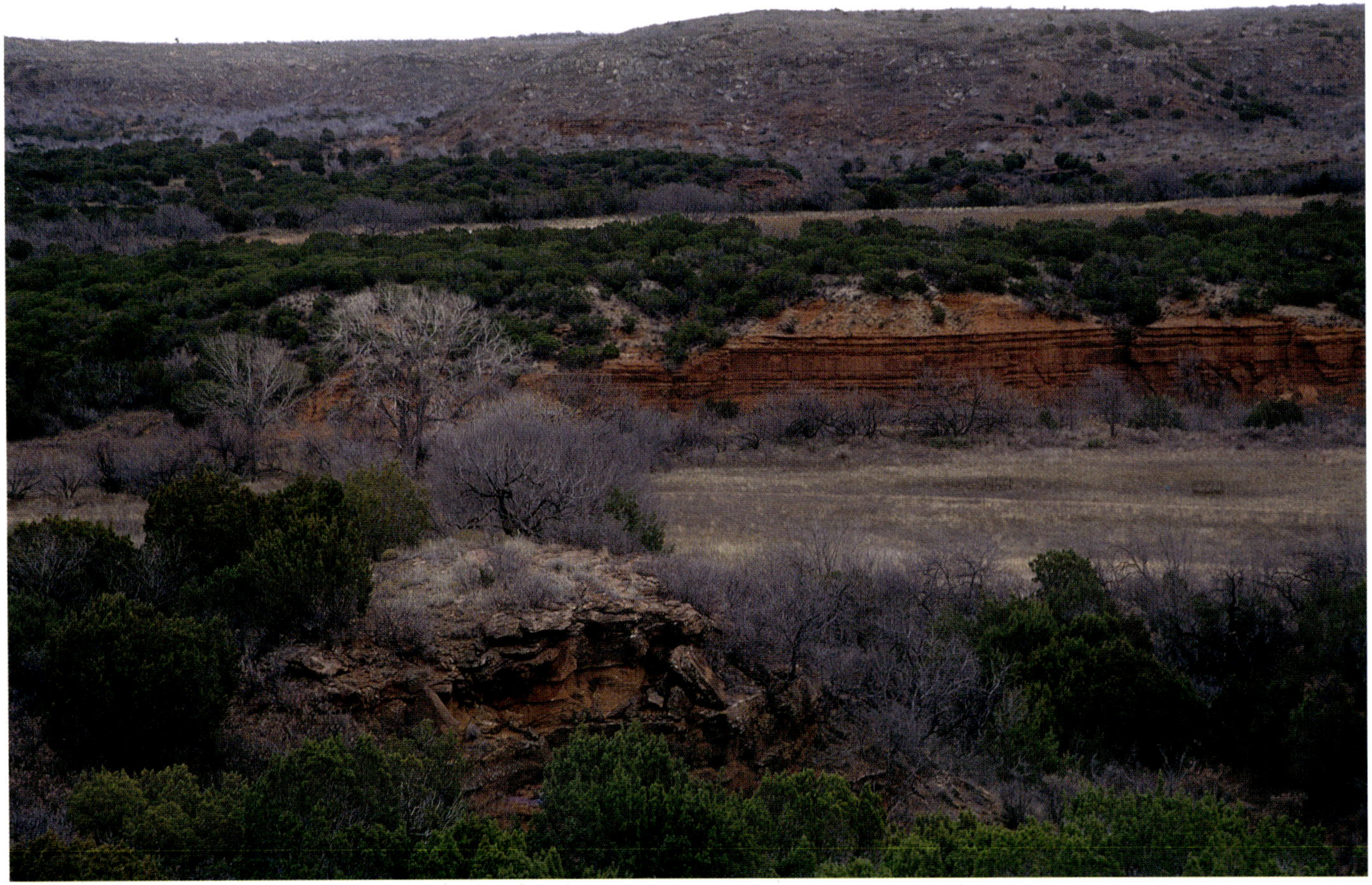

Foard County

Sunset over the Pease River

Founded in 1876, the county was named for Robert Levi Foard, an attorney and Confederate major in the Civil War. Droughts and other adversities reduced crop production and drove some farmers from their lands in the second decade of the twentieth century. By 1920, the number of farms in Foard County had dropped to 629, and the population had declined to 4,700.

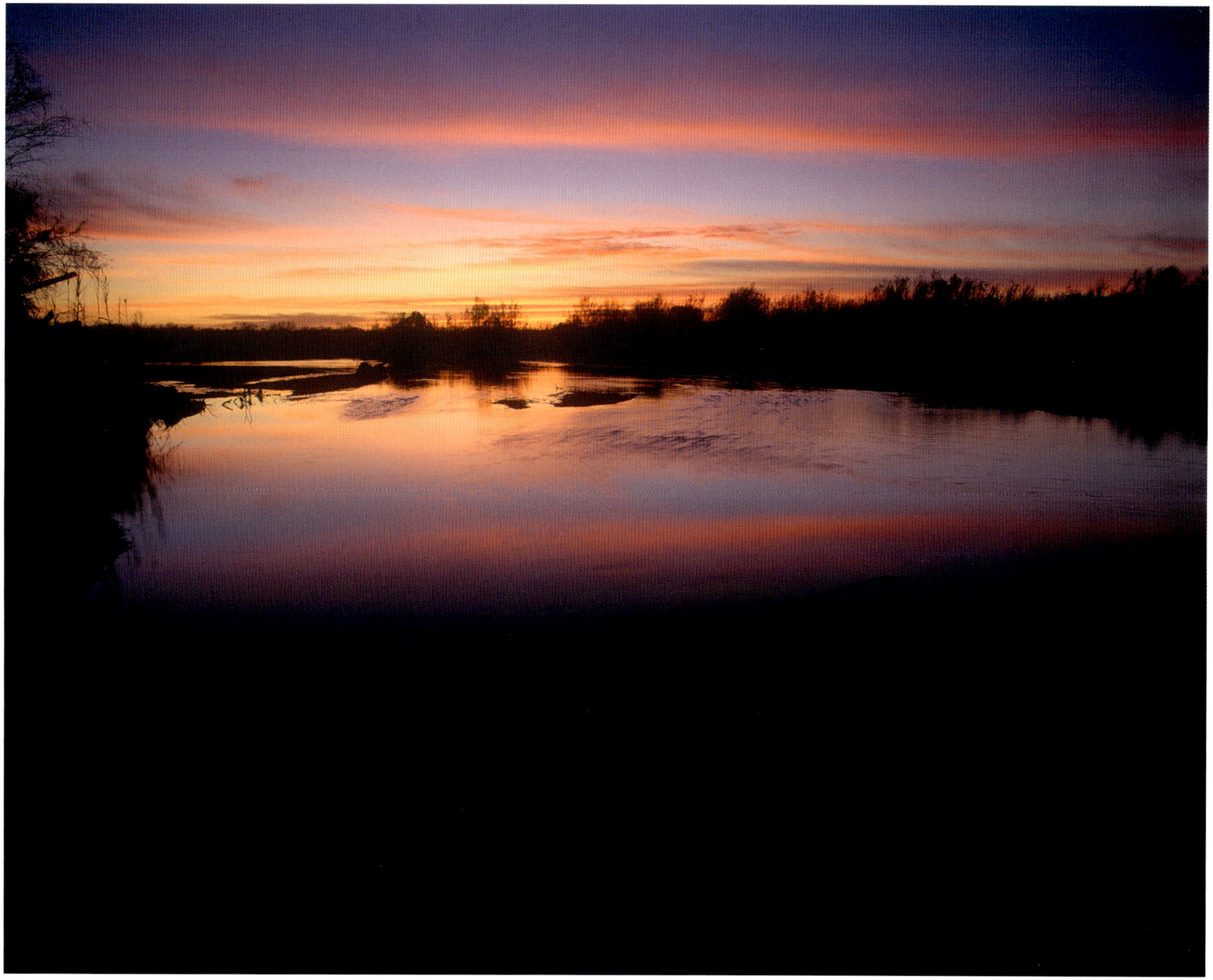

Fort Bend County

Foggy Morning at Brazos Bend State Park

The county was founded in 1837 and organized the following year. It was named for a blockhouse at a bend of the Brazos River; the fort was the start of the community in the early days. By the 1880s factional tensions were fierce, mainly along racial lines. The Jaybirds, representing the majority of the whites, were struggling to regain control from the Woodpeckers, who were made up of some whites consistently elected to office by the majority of African Americans. The political feud culminated in a gun battle at the courthouse on August 16, 1889, which routed the Woodpeckers from the seat of government.

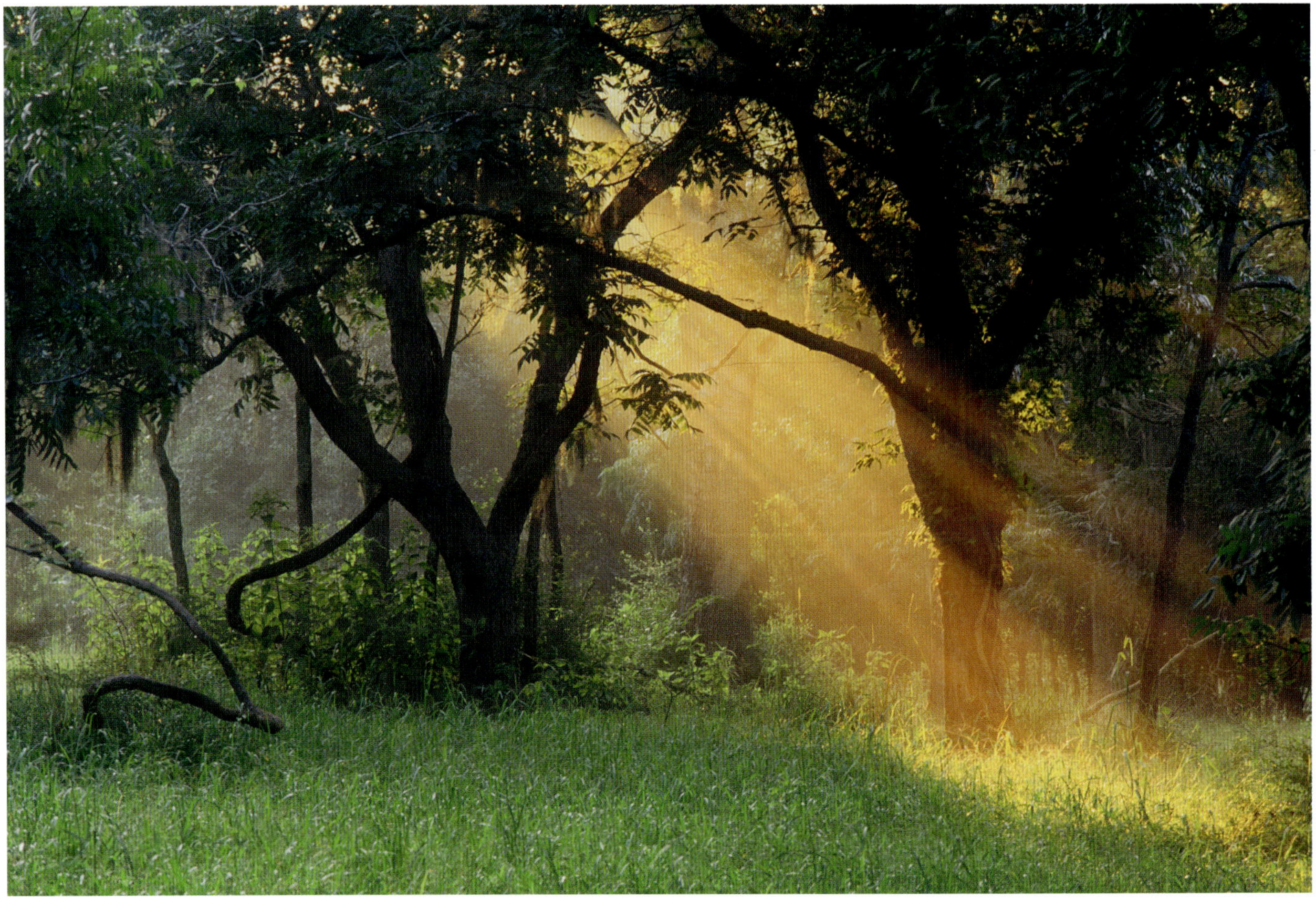

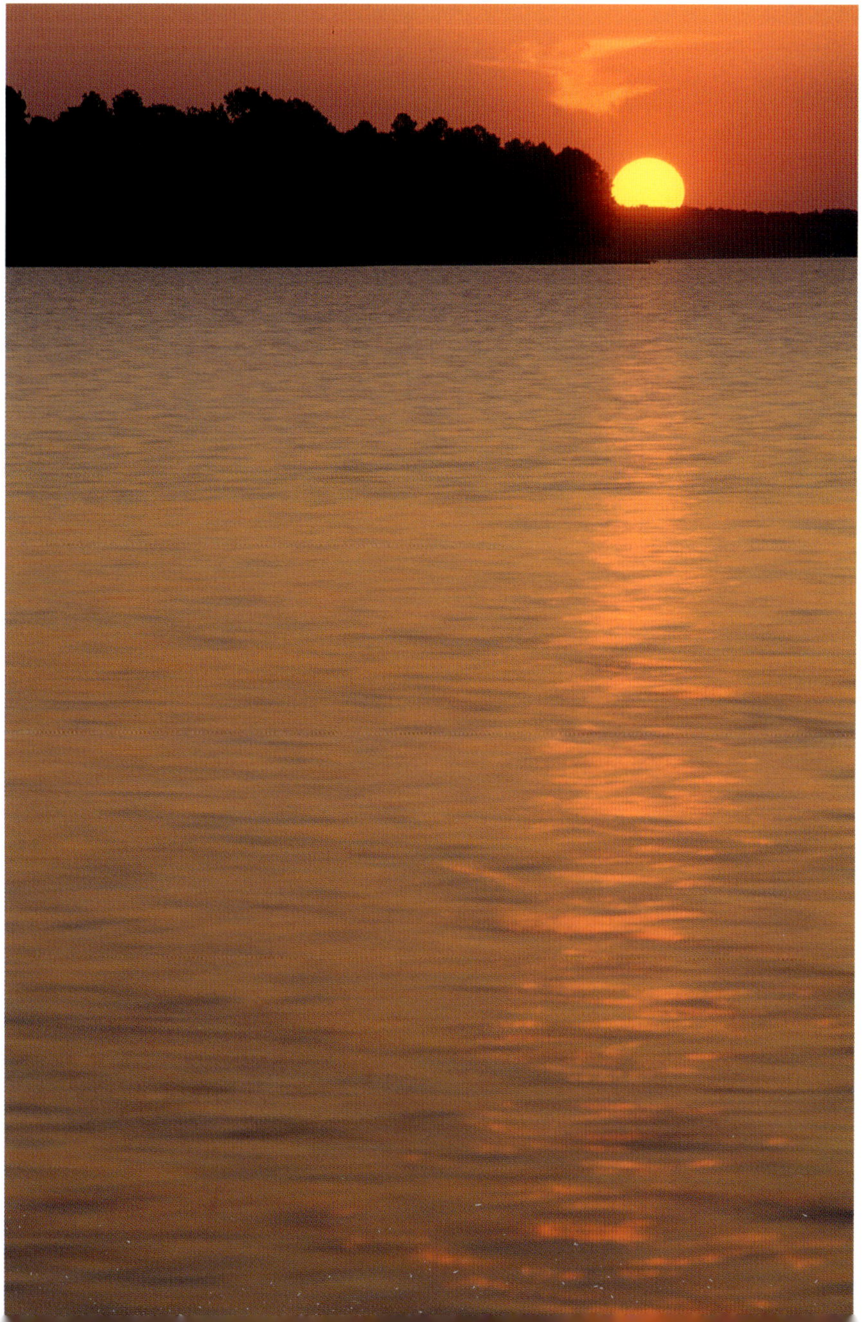

Franklin County

Sunset over Lake Cypress Springs

Franklin County was established in 1875. Although the origin of the county's name is not recorded, it is generally believed to have been named after Judge Benjamin C. Franklin, the first appointed justice in the Republic of Texas. The county's economy was based on agriculture, with corn and cotton followed by more than half a million peach trees in production in the 1920s, watermelons in the 1930s, and the state's record production of cane syrup in the 1940s.

Freestone County

Fairfield Lake State Park

The county was created in 1850 and was named for a type of peach grown in the area. The threat of Indian hostilities kept most from homesteading in Freestone County until the Treaty of Bird's Fort in 1843. Within three years of the treaty, colonization—primarily from southern states—had been so successful that the counties surrounding Freestone had already been organized.

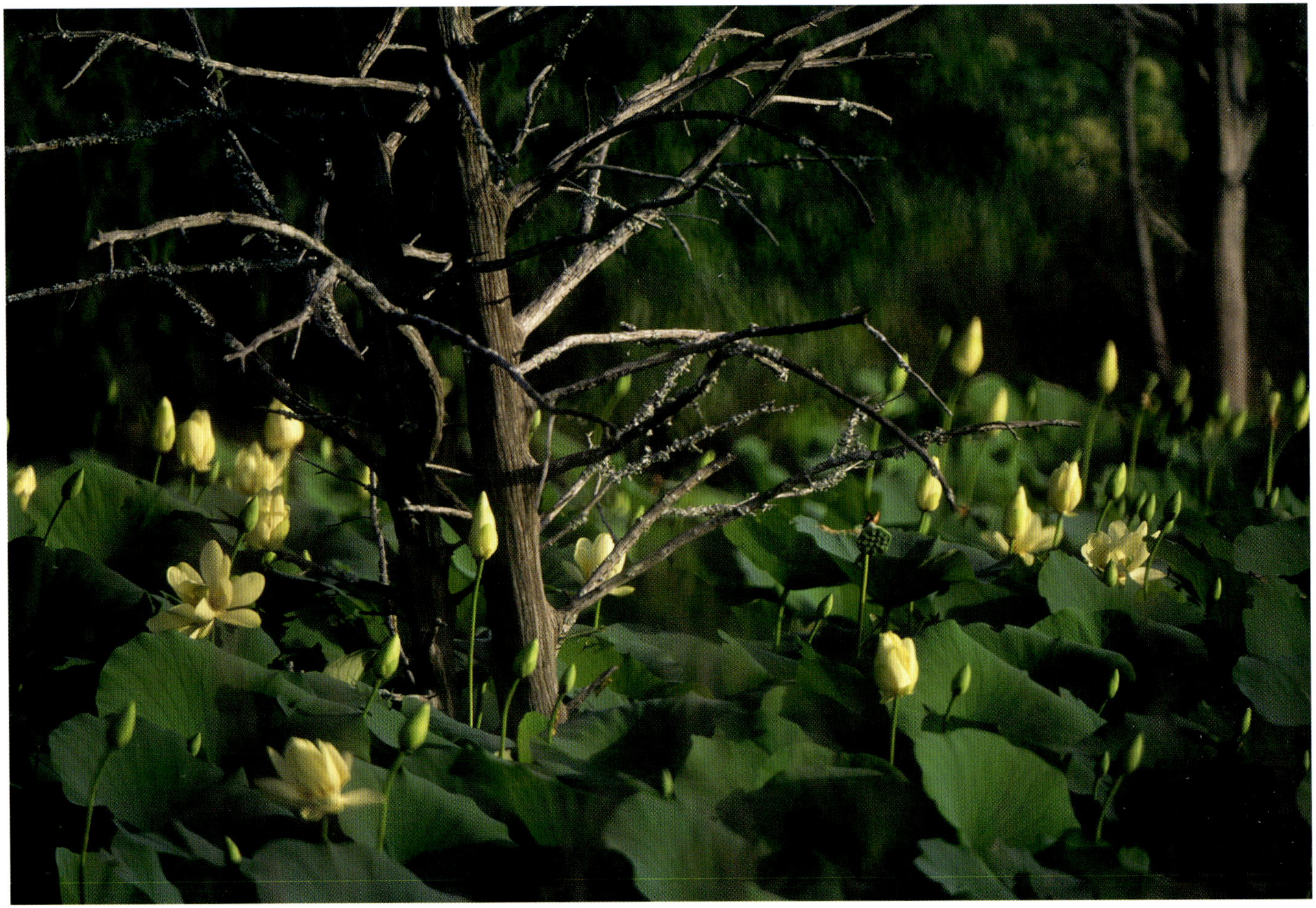

Frio County

Springtime Scene Southwest of San Antonio

The county was formed in 1858. It is named for the Frio River (*frío* is Spanish for "cold"). The decade between 1870 and 1880 was a period of rapid development. The county population rose dramatically from a reported 300 in 1870 to 2,100 in 1880. The fourteen farmers reported as operating in the Siestadera-Bigfoot area of northeastern Frio County in 1870 were actually stock raisers of cattle or sheep, along with farmers who raised small vegetable gardens and some corn production for domestic consumption. Frio City developed as a "cowboy capital" and outpost cultural center of Southwest Texas.

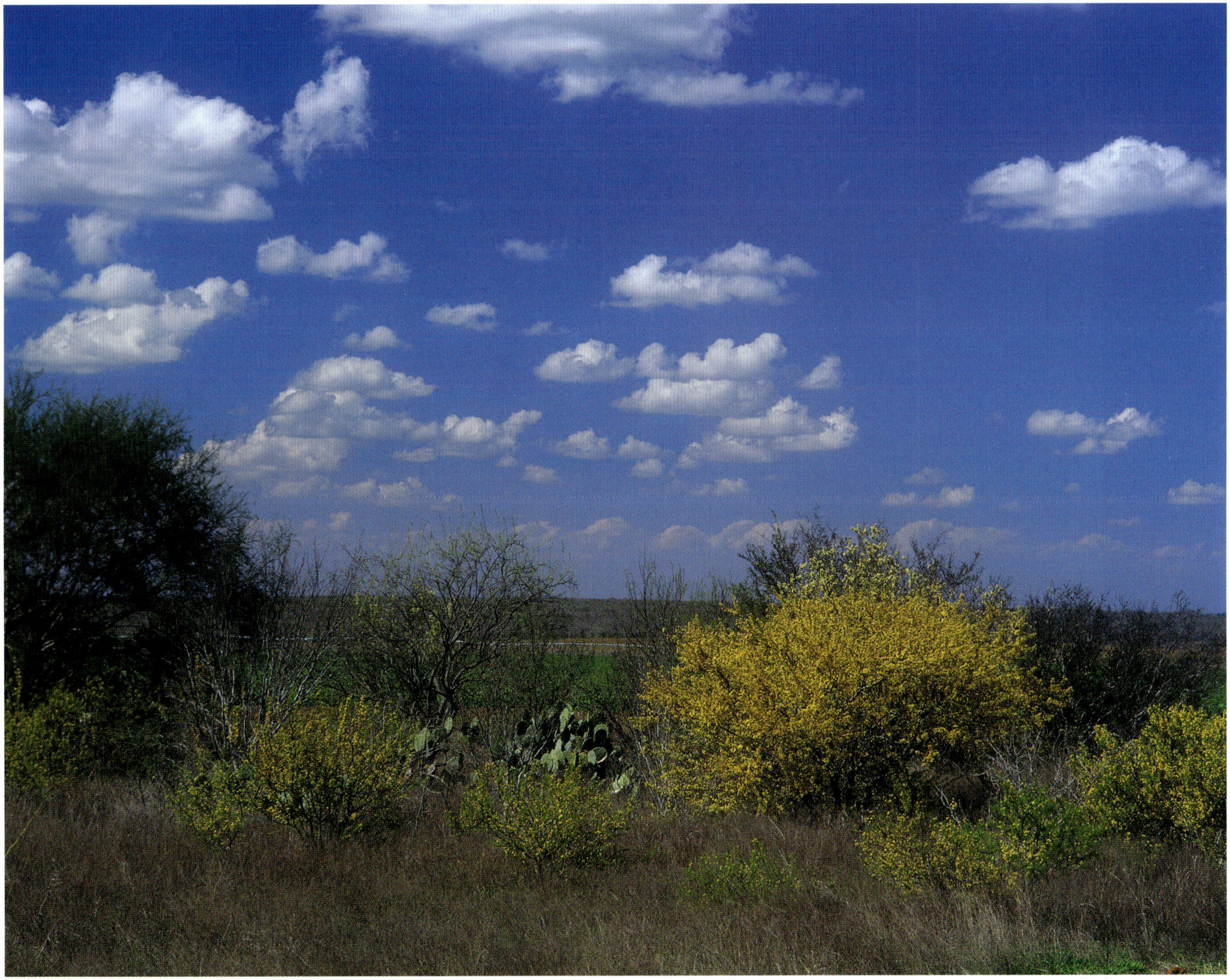

Gaines County

Cotton Field and Tumbleweed

The county was created in 1876 and named for James Gaines, a merchant who signed the Texas Declaration of Independence. Entertainers Larry Gatlin and Tanya Tucker call Gains County home.

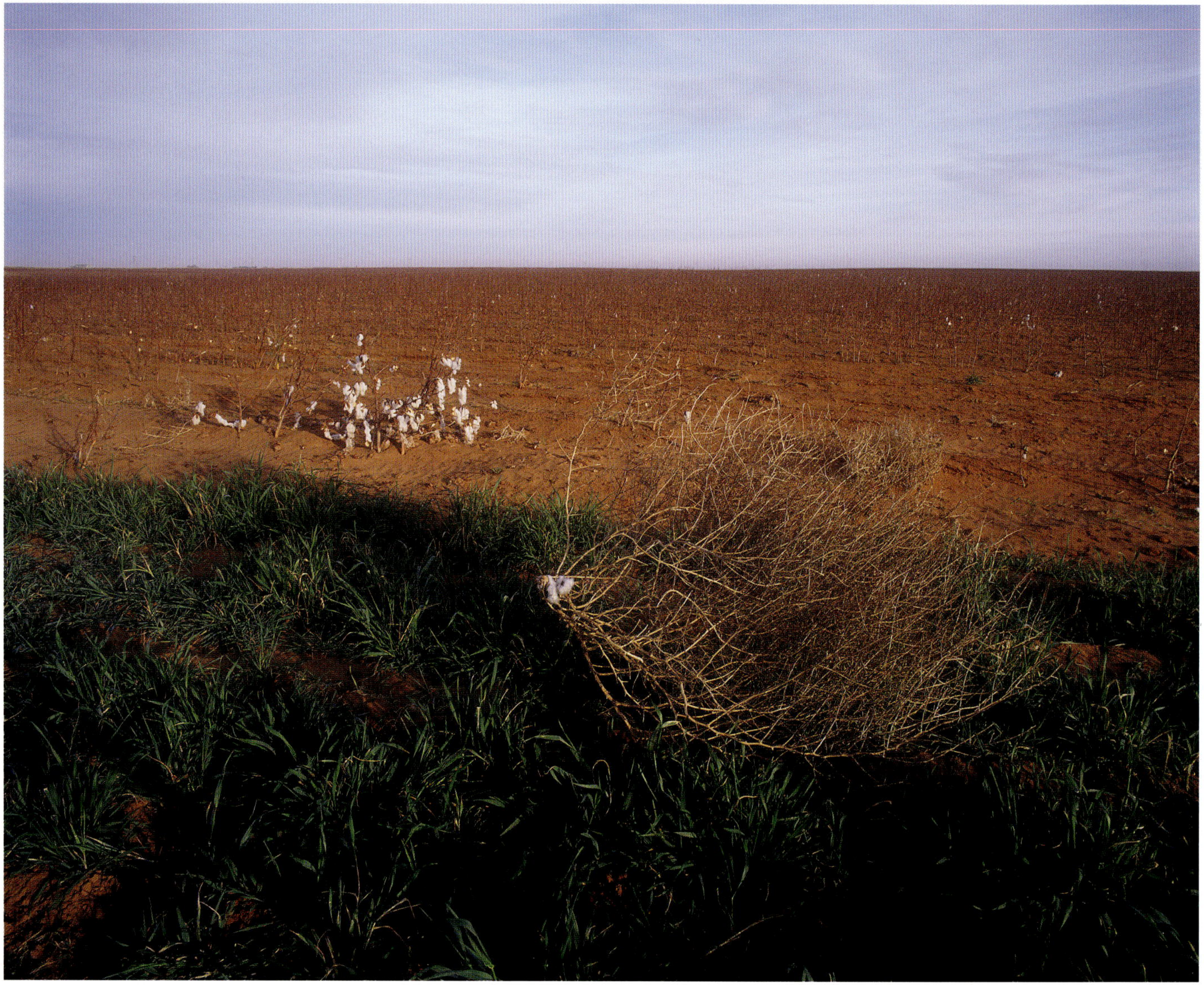

Galveston County

Sunrise over the Gulf at Galveston Island State Park

Galveston County was formed in 1838 and is named for Bernardo de Gálvez, Spanish governor of the Louisiana Territory. The 1900 Galveston Hurricane devastated the county, killing an estimated six thousand people on the island alone and others throughout the rest of the county. The Port of Galveston was closed for some time for rebuilding.

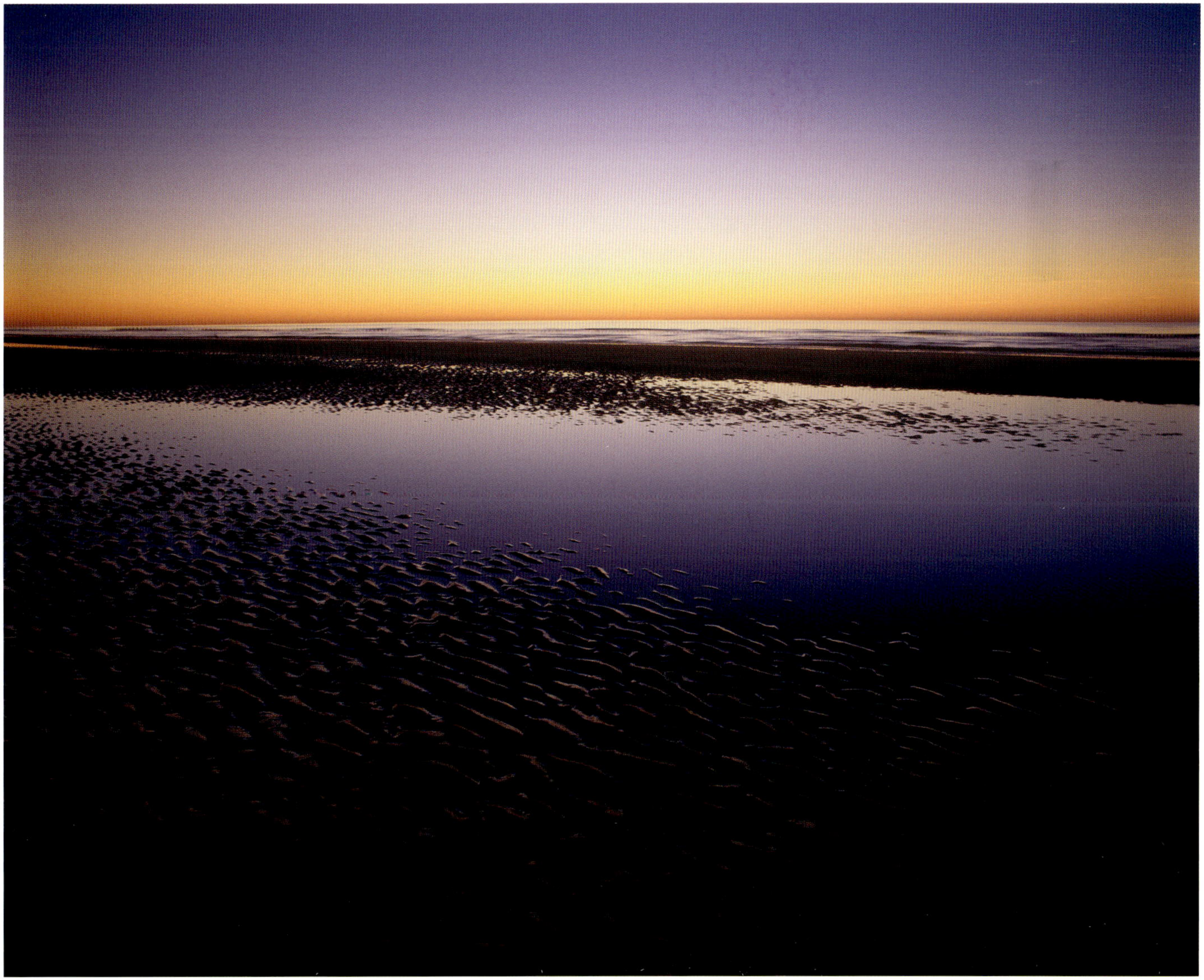

Garza County

Lake Alan Henry at the Sam Wahl Recreation Area

The county was created in 1876 and organized in 1907. Garza County is named for a pioneer Bexar County family because it was once a part of that county. Beginning in 1909, C. W. Post built a cotton gin and attempted to improve agriculture production through rainmaking involving the heavy use of explosives fired from kites and towers along the rim of the Caprock Escarpment.

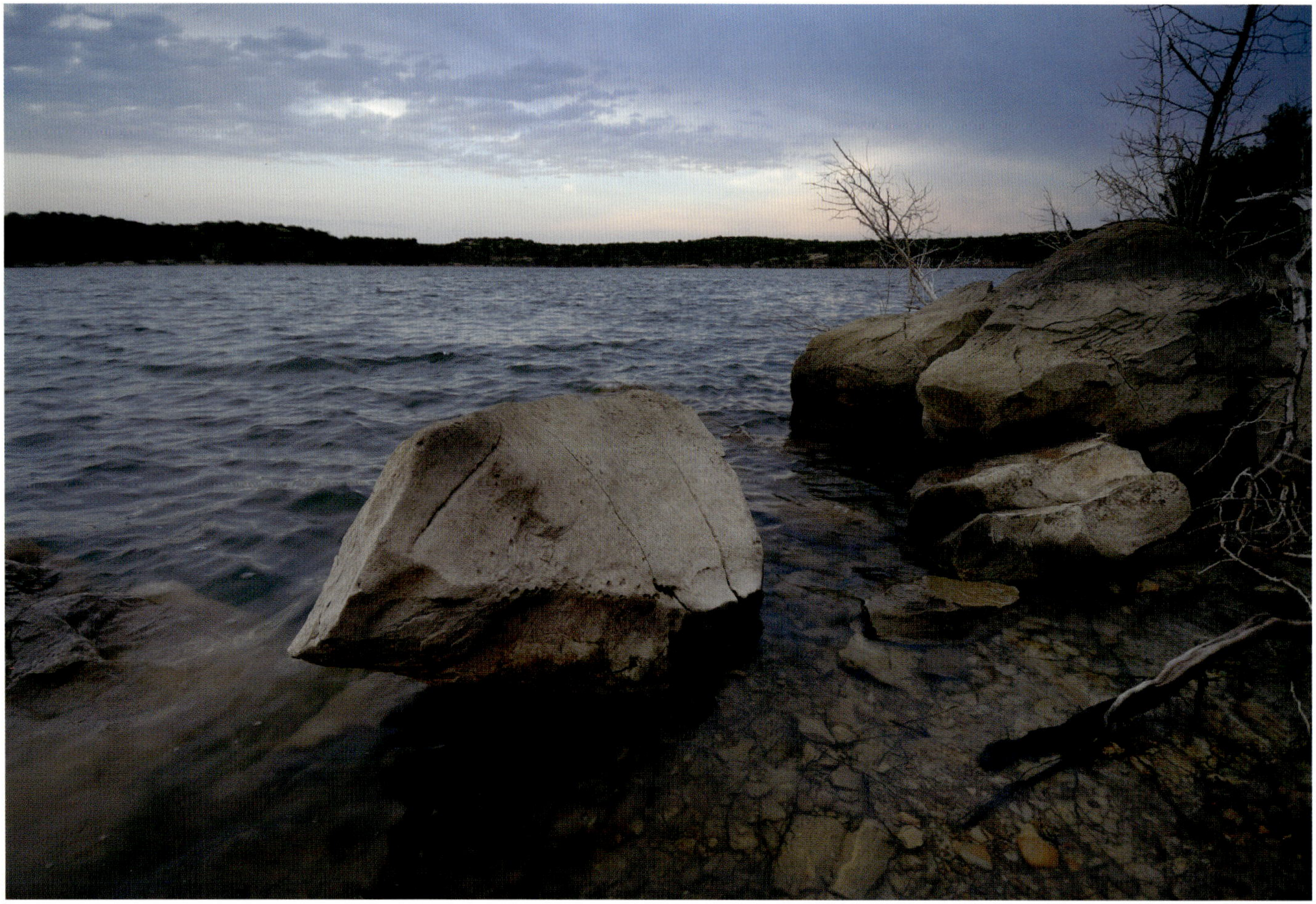

Gillespie County

Bluebonnets along the Willow City Loop

The county was named for Robert Addison Gillespie, a merchant, Mexican-American War soldier, and Texas Ranger. The county was created in 1848. In 1908, future president of the United States Lyndon B. Johnson was born in a small farmhouse on the Pedernales River. Johnson became the vice president of the United States in 1961 and subsequently president following the assassination of President John F. Kennedy two years later. Johnson's ranch at Stonewall was known as the "Texas White House."

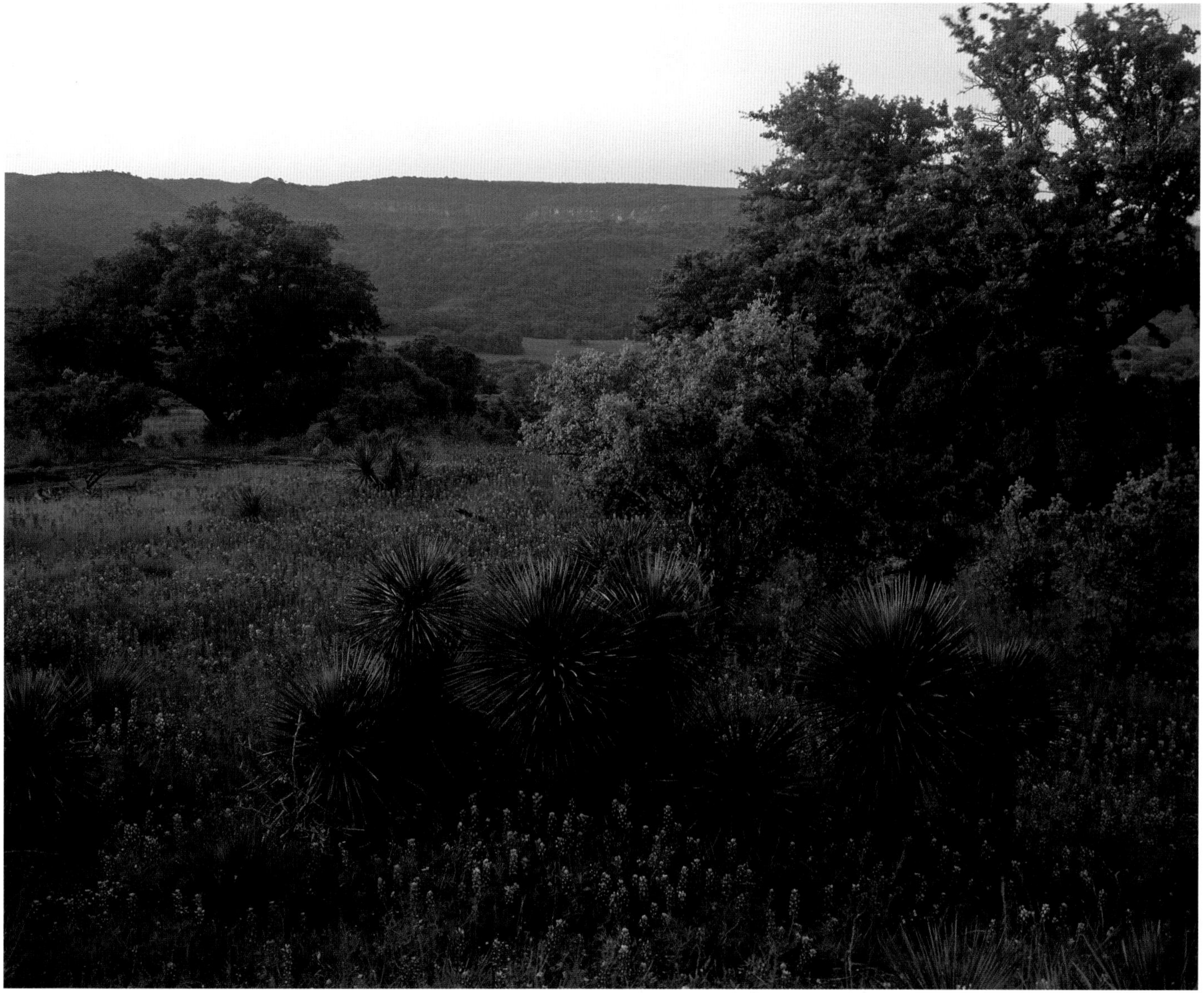

Glasscock County

Sunset and Mesquite

The county was created in 1887. It was named for George Washington Glasscock, an early settler of the Austin, Texas, area. The Spraberry Trend—the third-largest oil field in the United States by remaining reserves—underlies much of the county.

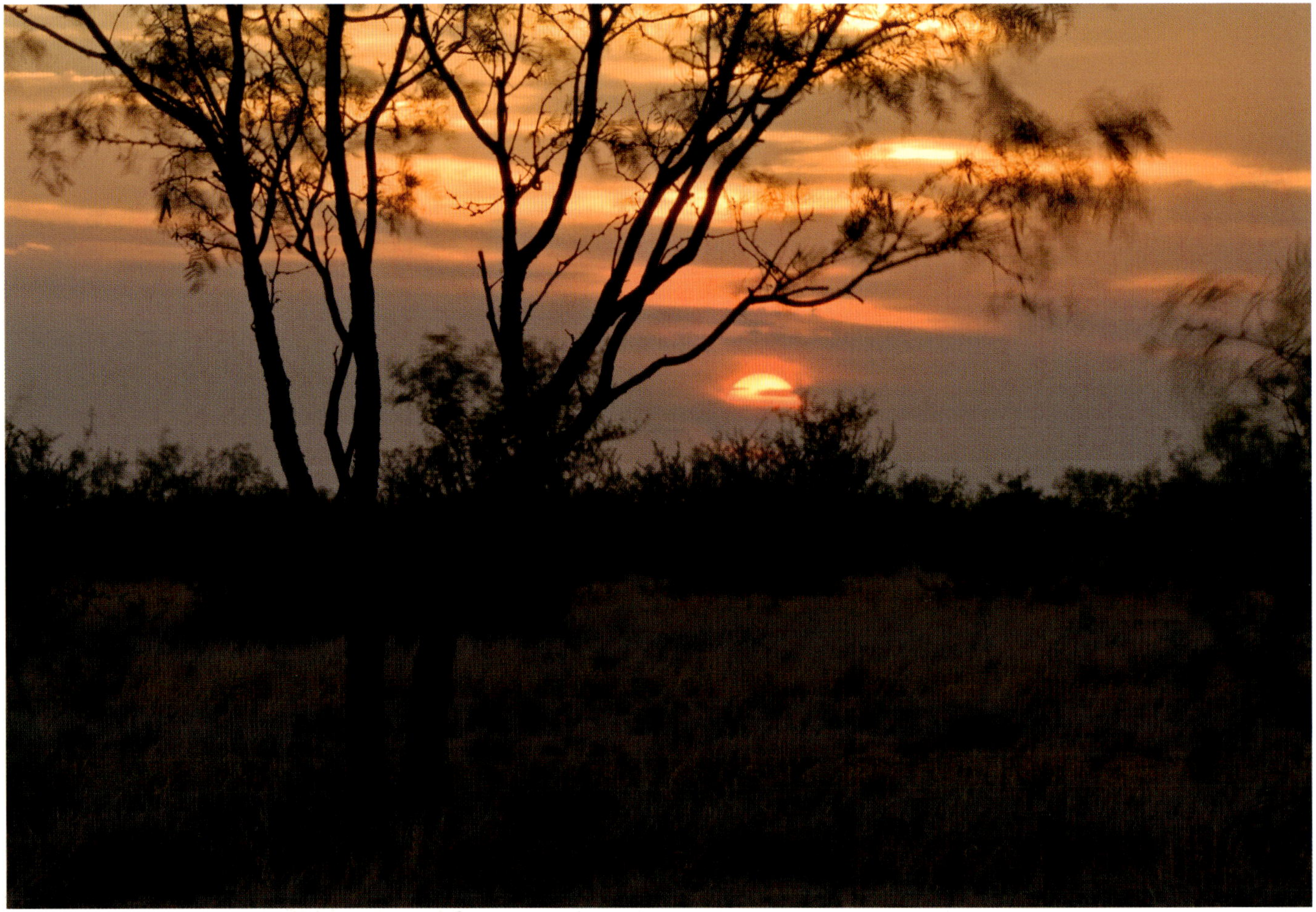

Goliad County

Spring Thunderstorm

The county is named for Father Miguel Hidalgo; "Goliad" is an anagram of Hidalgo, minus the silent *H*. The county was created in 1836; in that year, Col. James Fannin and his Texan soldiers were executed by the Mexican army under orders from General Antonio López de Santa Anna in what became known as the Goliad Massacre.

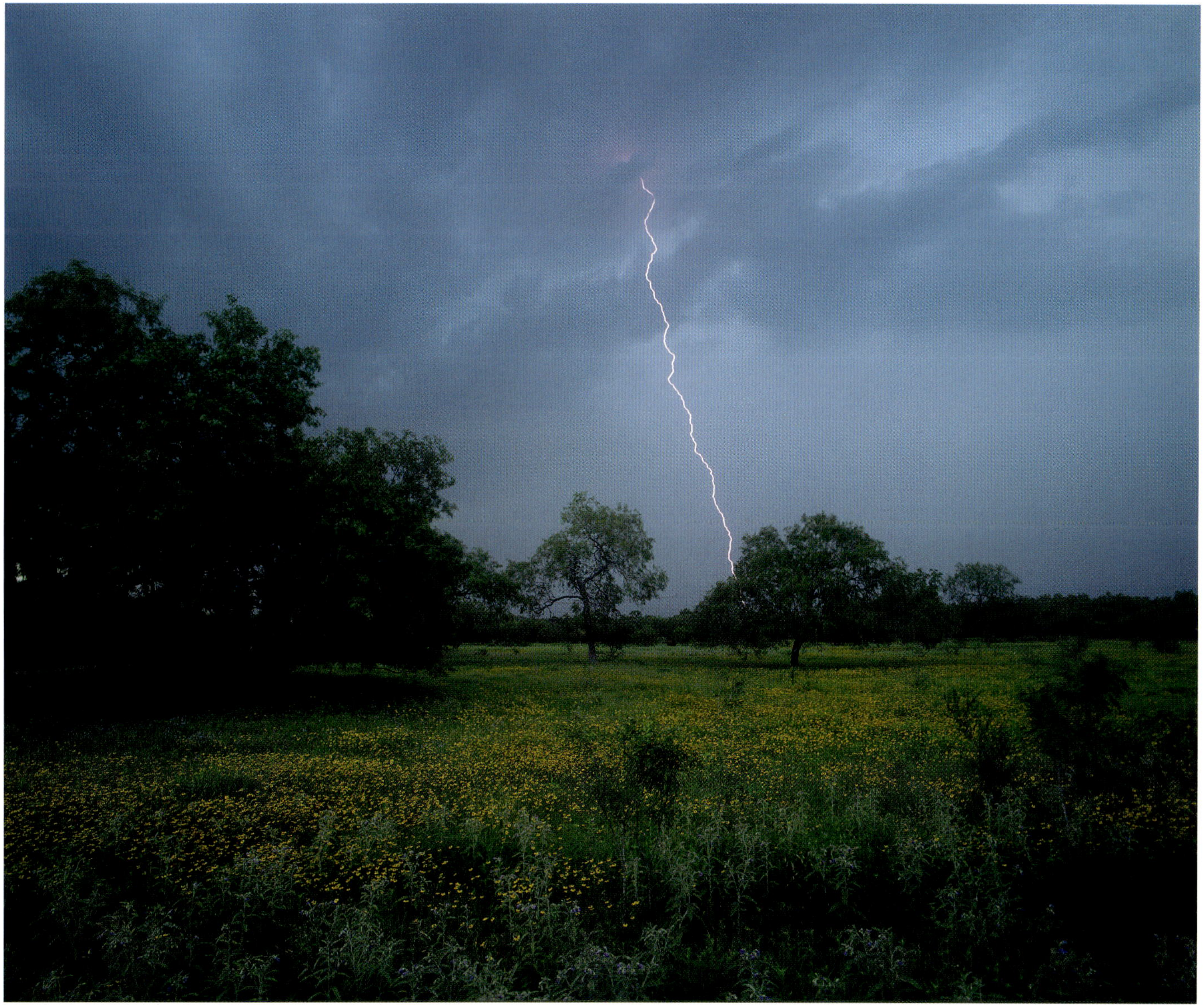

Gonzales County

Ottine Swamp in Palmetto State Park

The county is named for its county seat, the city of Gonzales. The county was created in 1836. Gonzales College was the first institution in Texas to confer bachelor of arts degrees on women.

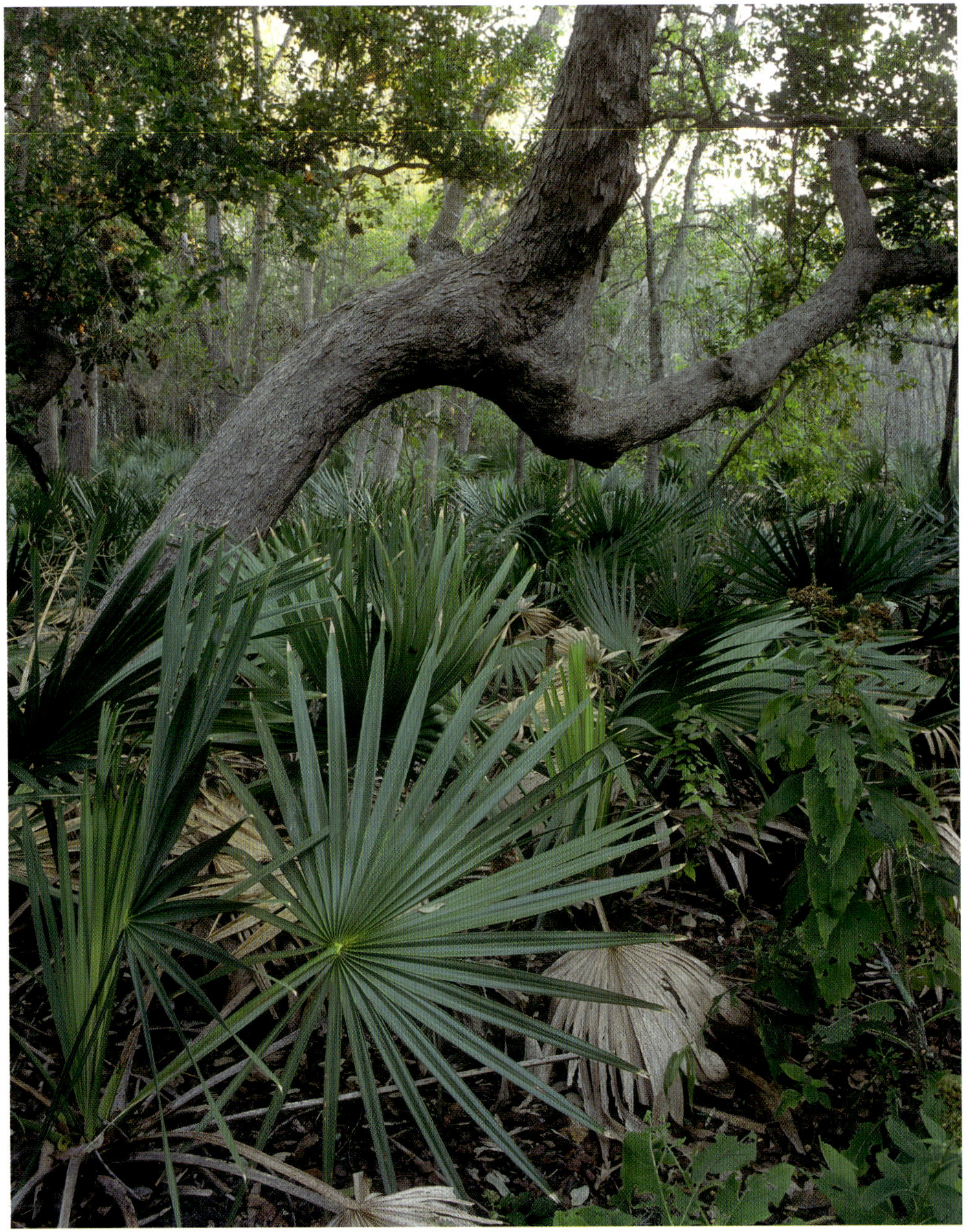

Gray County

McClellan Creek National Grassland

The county was created in 1876 and was named for Peter W. Gray, a Confederate lawyer and soldier in the American Civil War. The county's prehistoric Plains Apache inhabitants gave way to the Apaches, who in turn were displaced by the Comanches and Kiowas. These people dominated the Panhandle until they were crushed in the Red River War of 1874 and were removed to the Indian Territory.

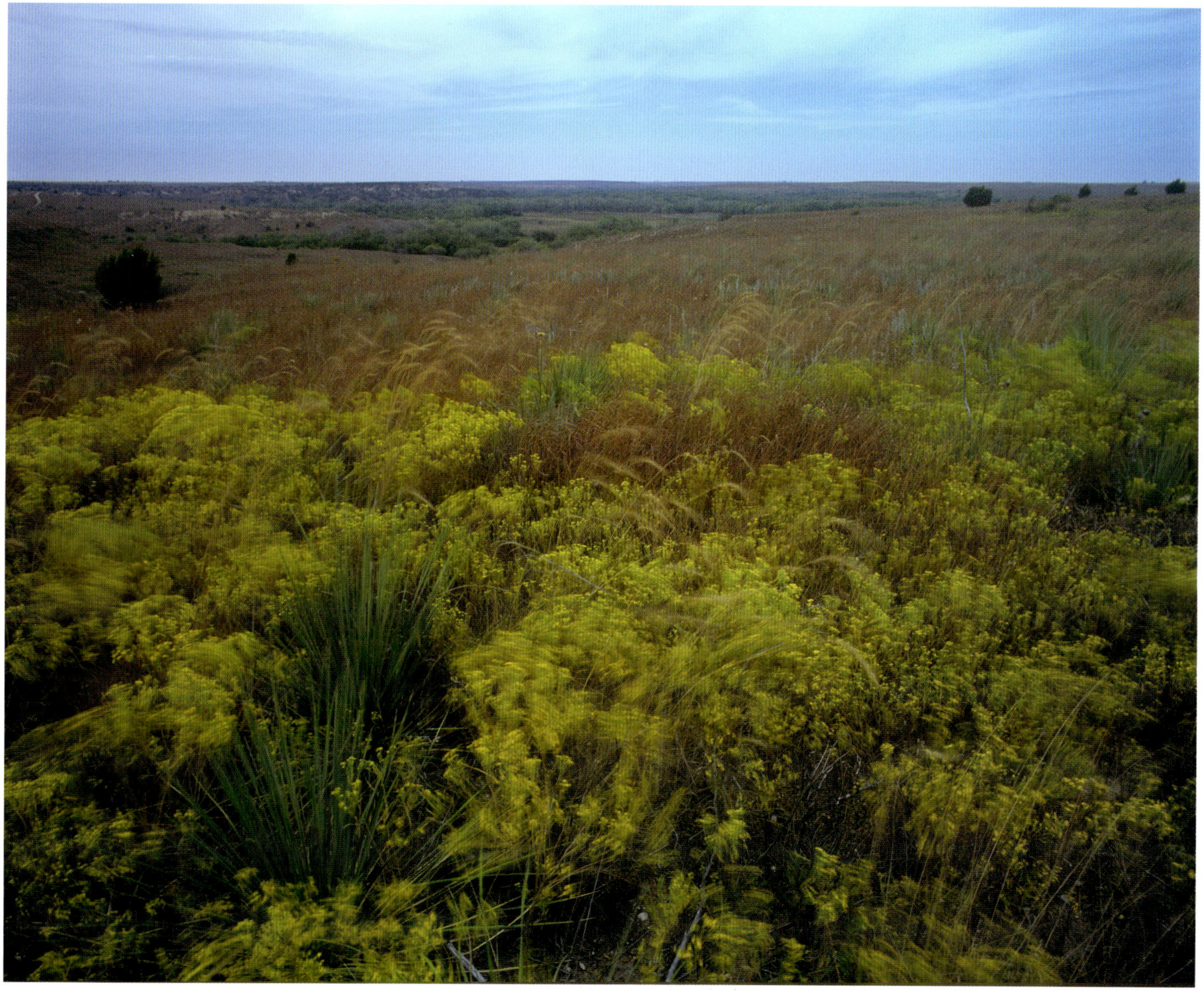

Grayson County

Fall Color on a Sunny November Day

The county was founded in 1846 and is named for Peter Wagener Grayson, an attorney general of the Republic of Texas. In 1938, construction of a dam on the Red River was authorized by the US Congress; the dam was completed in part through the use of labor provided by German prisoners of war.

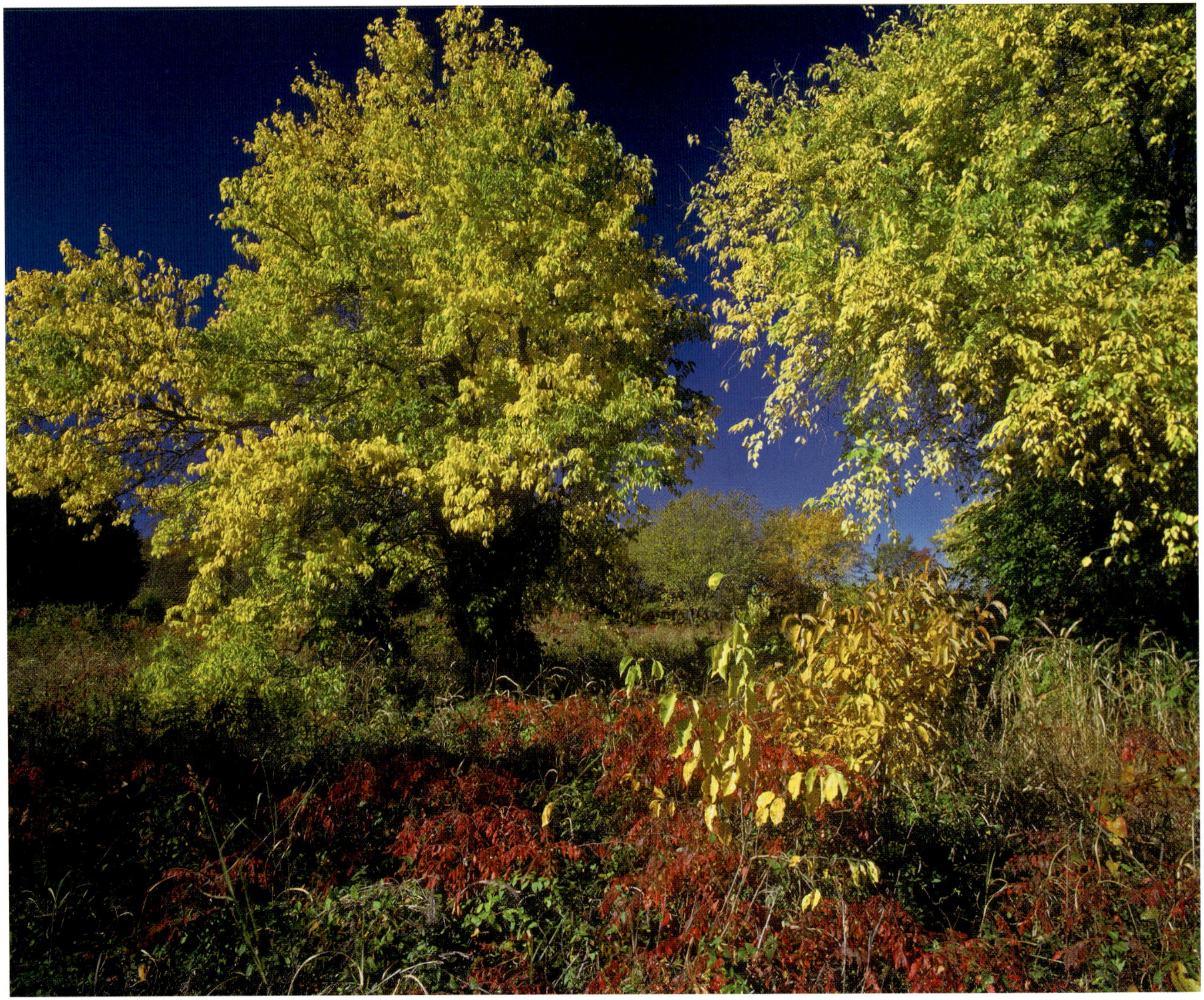

Gregg County

Wildflowers among the Pines

The county is named for John Gregg, a Confederate general killed in action during the American Civil War. The county was formed in 1873. Discovery of oil near Kilgore, Texas, in October 1920 was the beginning of an oil boom that attracted workers to the county and expanded the population by more than 500 percent by 1940.

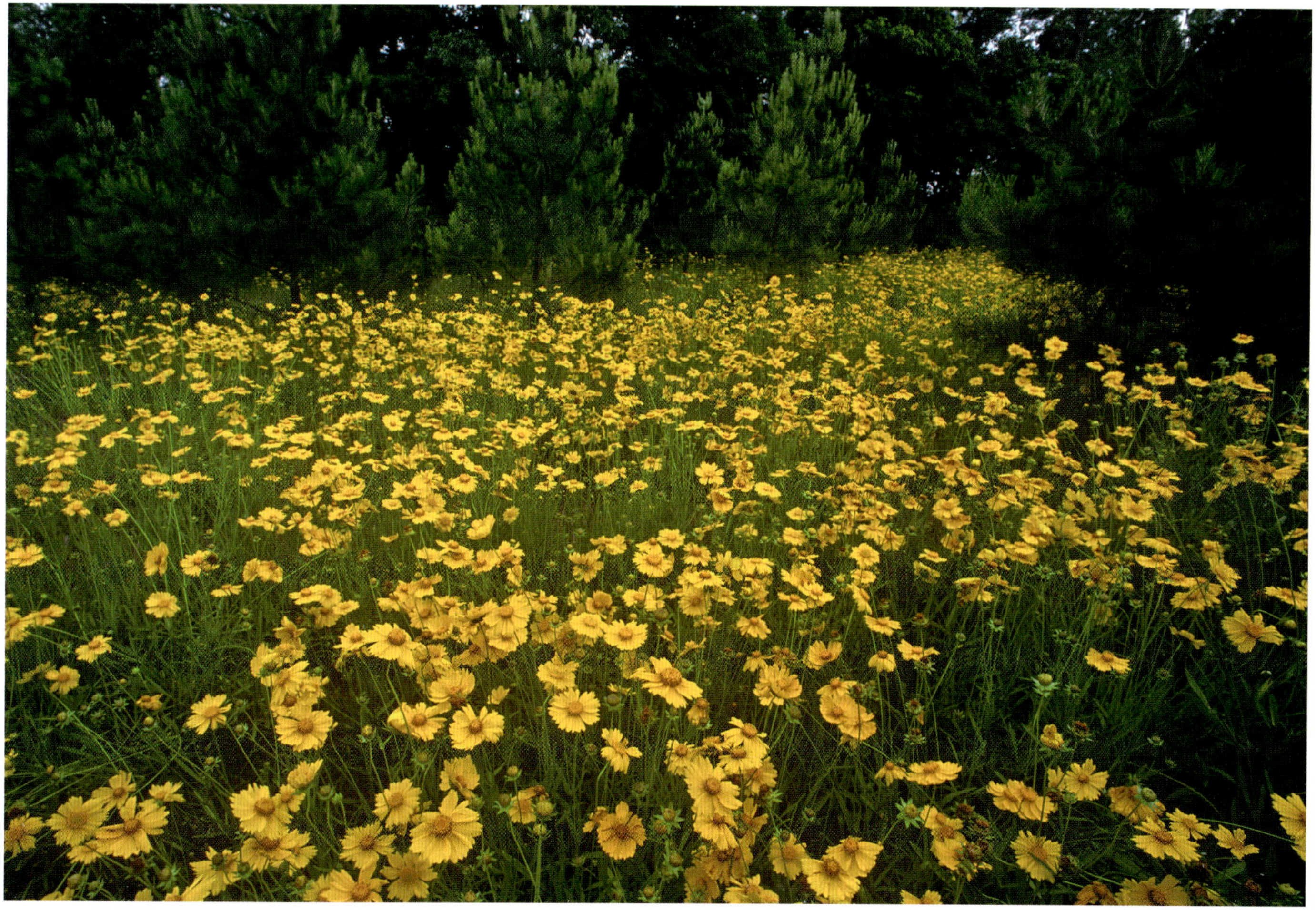

Grimes County

Indian Paintbrush
and Bluebonnets
along Highway 105

The county was formed in 1846. It was named for Jesse Grimes, a signer of the Texas Declaration of Independence and an early settler of the county. It is likely that the first European to set foot within what is now Grimes County was the ill-fated French explorer René Robert Cavelier, Sieur de La Salle, who may have crossed the area early in 1687, traveling from Matagorda Bay in a final attempt to reach the Mississippi River.

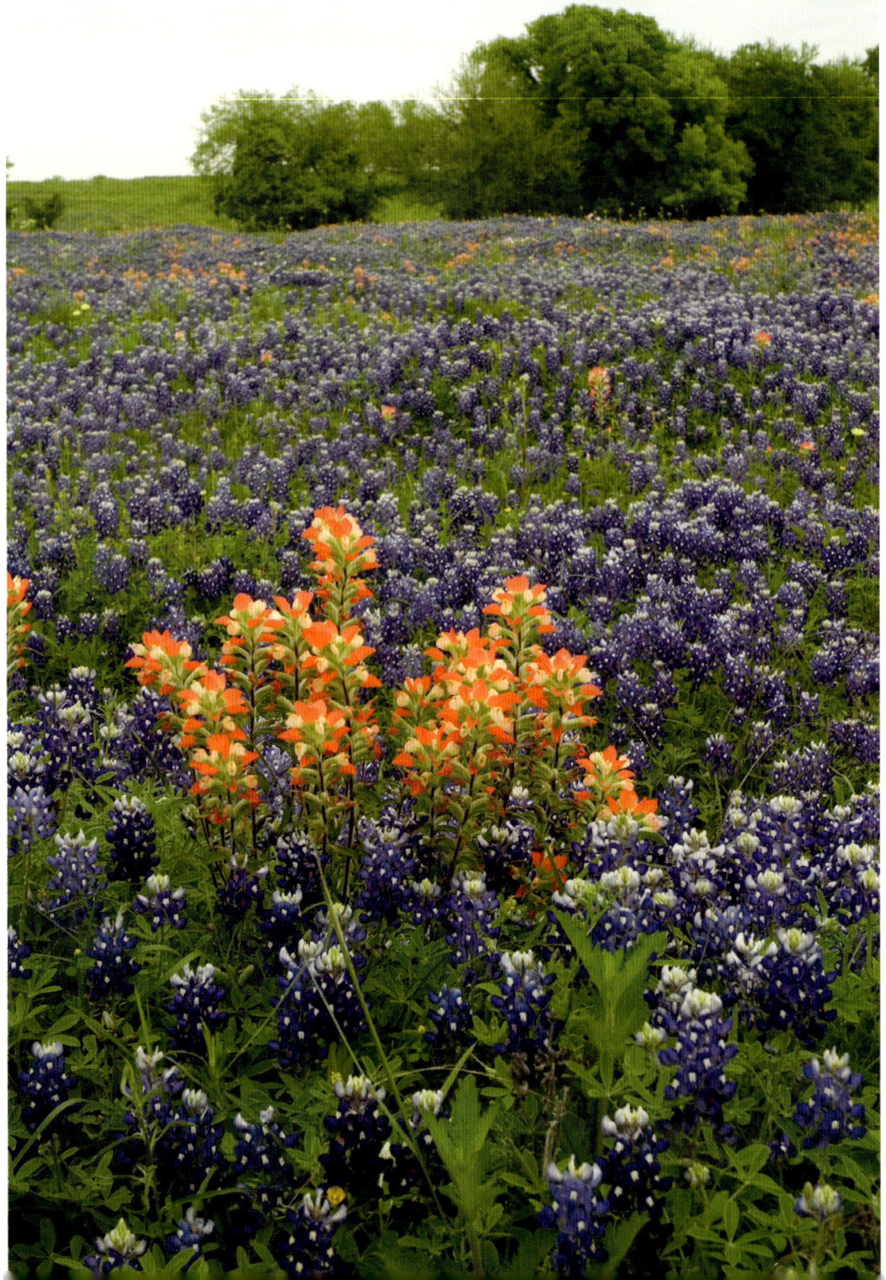

Guadalupe County

Wildflowers and Wheat Field

The county was founded in 1846 and is named for the Guadalupe River. In 1861, the people of the county voted 314–22 in favor of secession from the Union. Guadalupe County sent several troops to fight for the Army of the Confederate States.

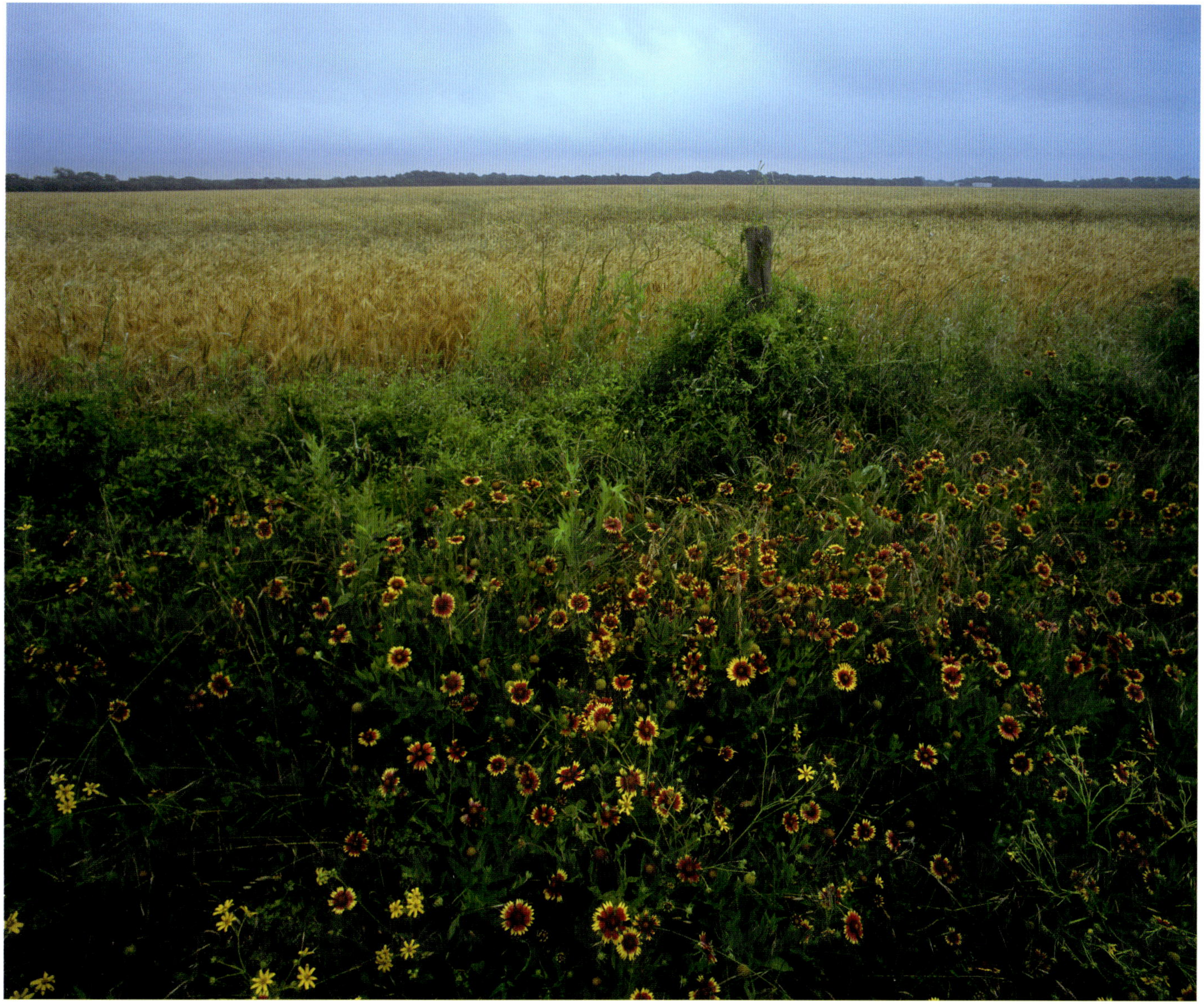

Hale County

Brilliant Lighting on Hayfield

The county was created in 1876. It is named for Lieutenant John C. Hale. In 1969, country artist Jimmy Dean, brother Don Dean, and cousin-in-law Troy Pritchard formed the Jimmy Dean Sausage Company and opened the Jimmy Dean Meat Company in Plainview.

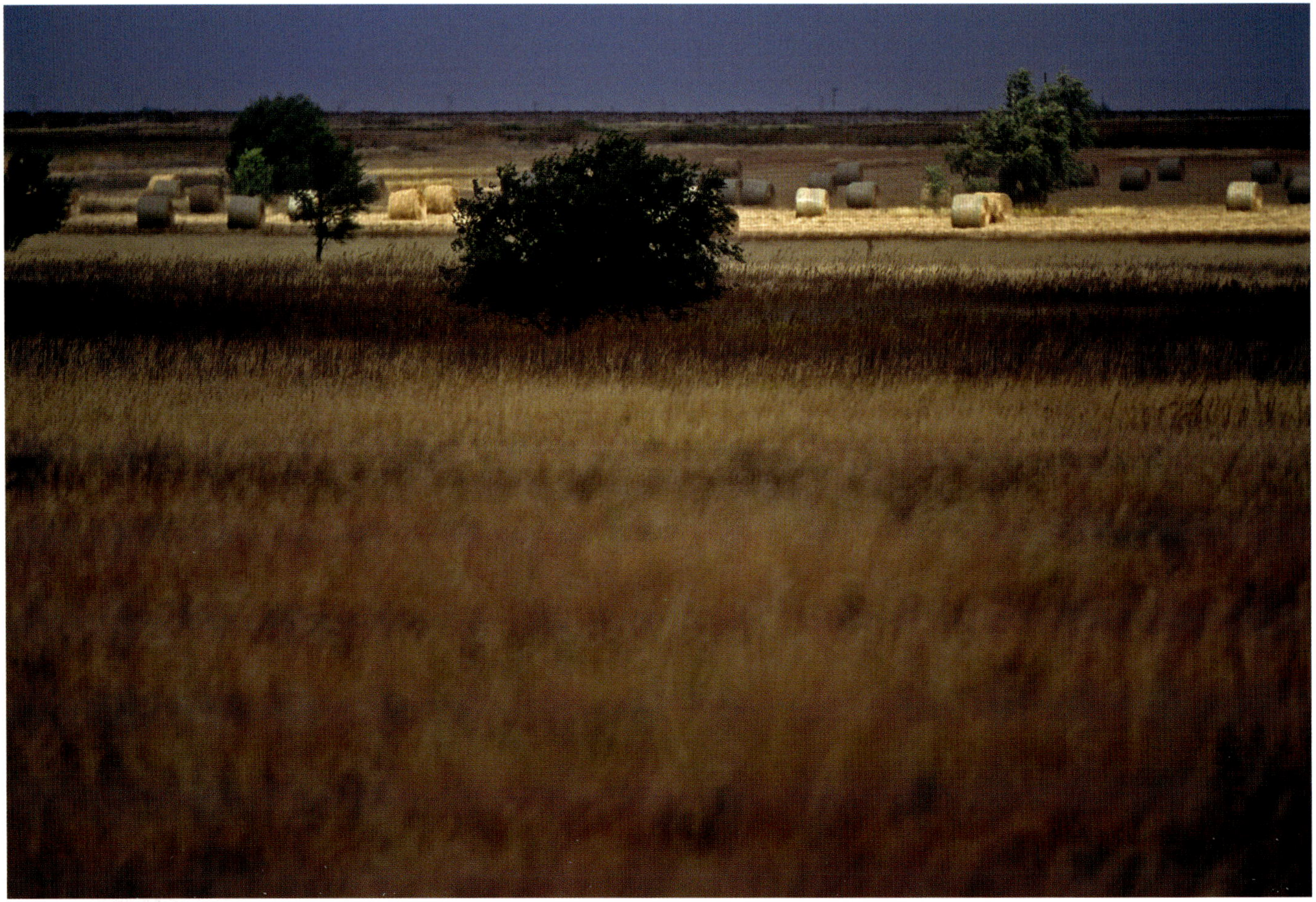

Hall County

Prairie Dog Town Fork of the Red River

The county was created in 1876 and organized in 1890. It is named for Warren D. C. Hall, a secretary of war for the Republic of Texas. The county is the home of country music legend Bob Wills, the "King of Western Swing."

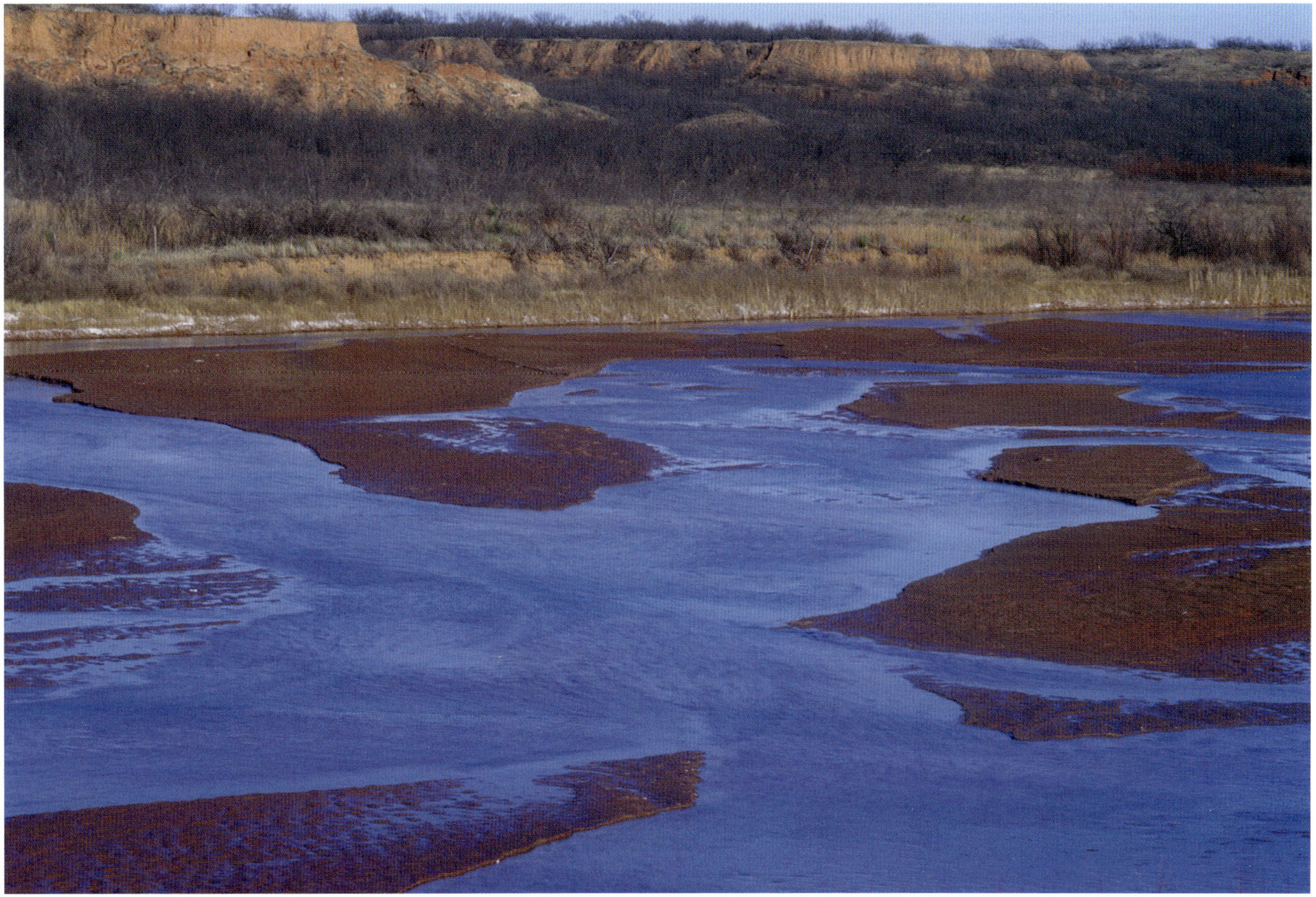

Hamilton County

Sunset Sky over Pasture

The county was created in 1858. It is named for James Hamilton Jr., a former governor of South Carolina who gave financial aid to the Republic of Texas. In 1950, Ollie P. Roberts (also known as Ollie L. Roberts, "Brushy Bill" Roberts, or William Henry Roberts)—a resident of Hico during the late 1940s—claimed to have been the outlaw Billy the Kid. The assertion is based on a legend that Patrick F. Garrett helped Billy fake his own death. The Hico Chamber of Commerce responded by opening a Billy the Kid Museum.

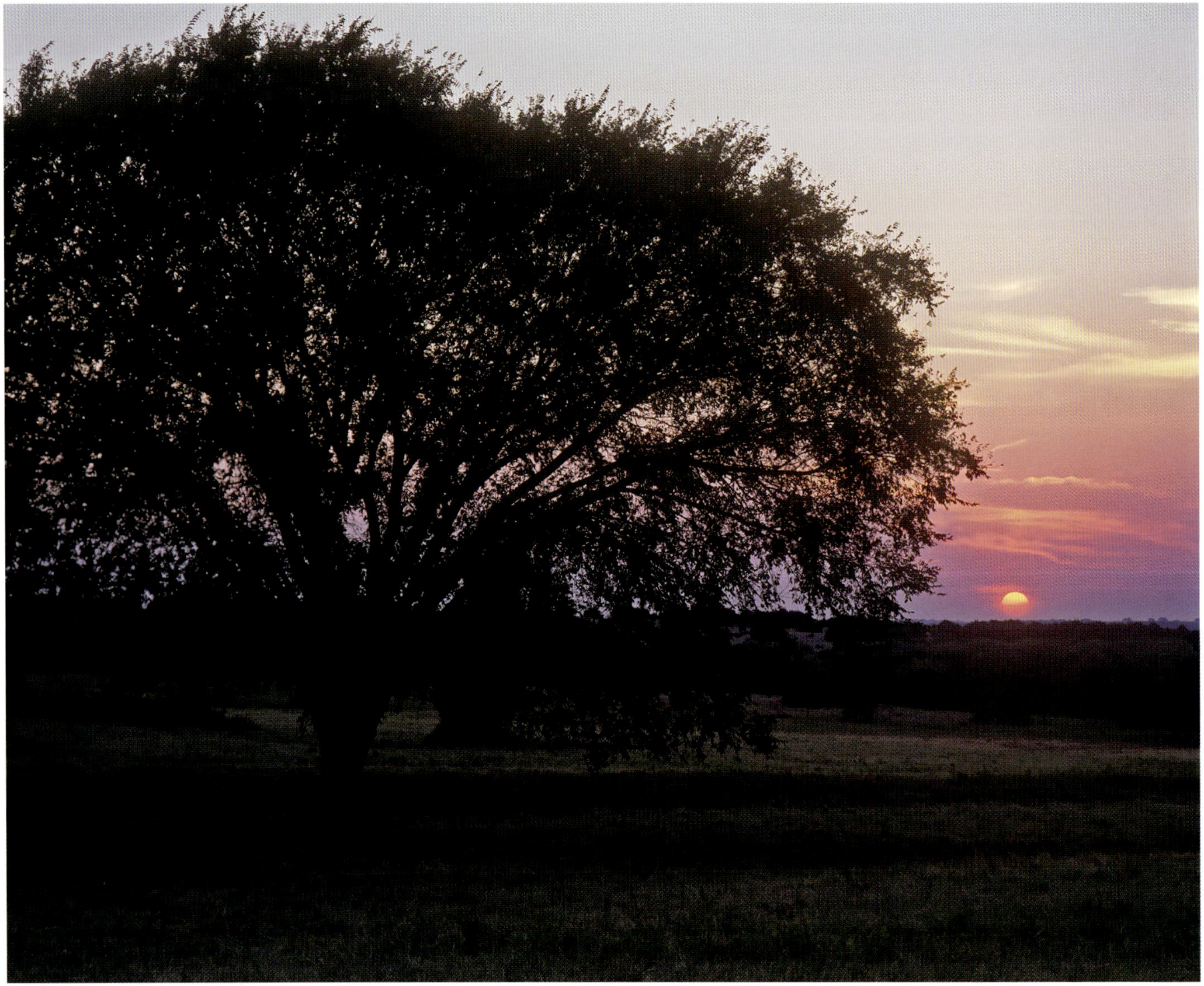

Hansford County

Sunset over Palo Duro Reservoir

The county was created in 1876 and organized in 1889. It is named for John M. Hansford, a Texas state congressman and judge. In 1873, English brothers James Hamilton Cator and Arthur J. L. (Bob) Cator were sent by their father, British naval captain John Bertie Cator, to Kansas in search of financial opportunity. The brothers soon found their true calling as buffalo hunters and established an outpost along the North Palo Duro Creek. They named this camp Zulu, and it soon became known as Zulu Stockade.

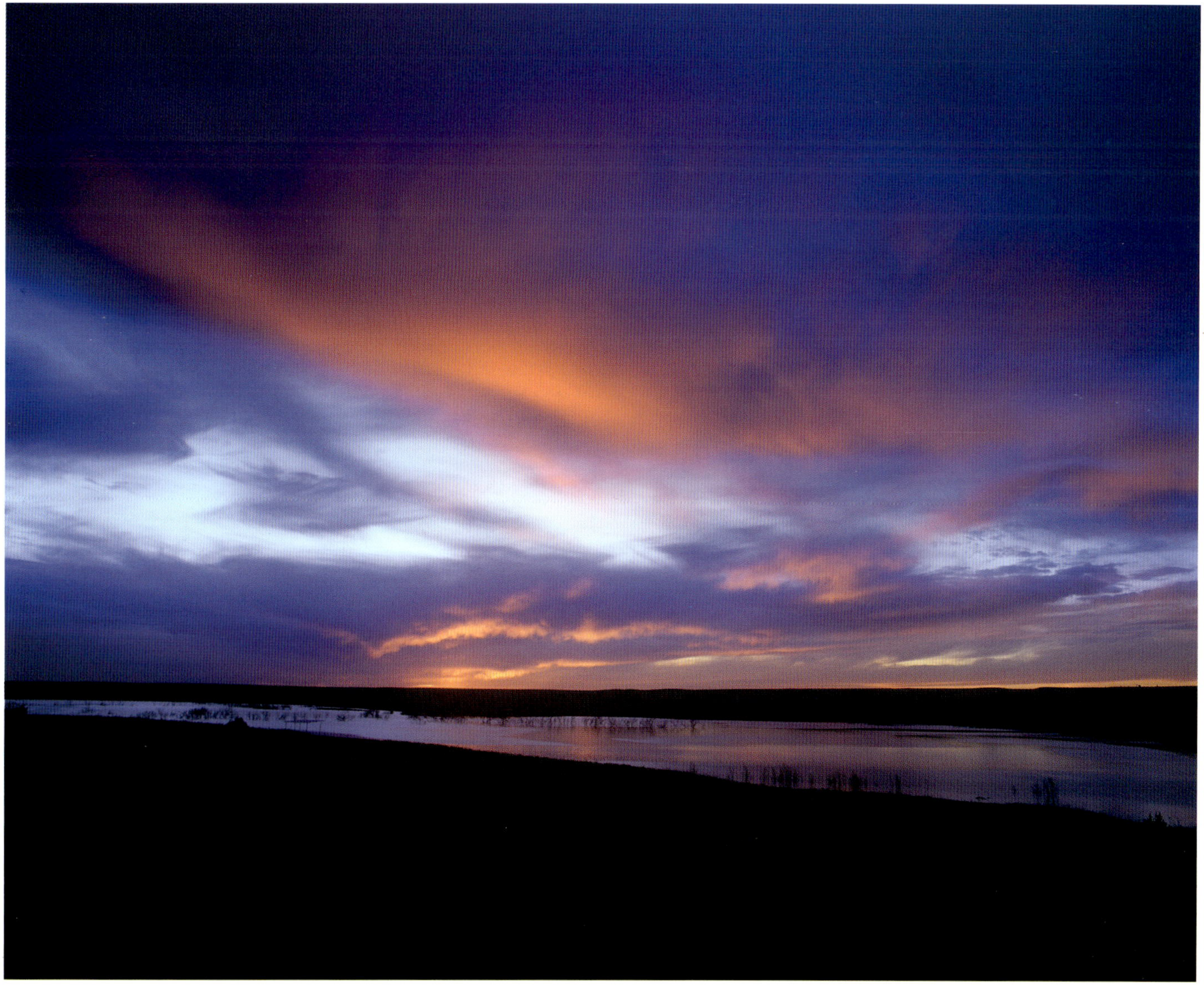

Hardeman County

Copper Breaks State Park

The county was created in 1858 and organized in 1884. It is named for two brothers, Bailey Hardeman and Thomas Jones Hardeman, early Texas politicians and legislators. The Prairie Dog Town Fork of the Red River joins with Buck Creek in the northwestern corner of the county to form the Red River, which flows east to create the northern border of the county, separating it from Oklahoma.

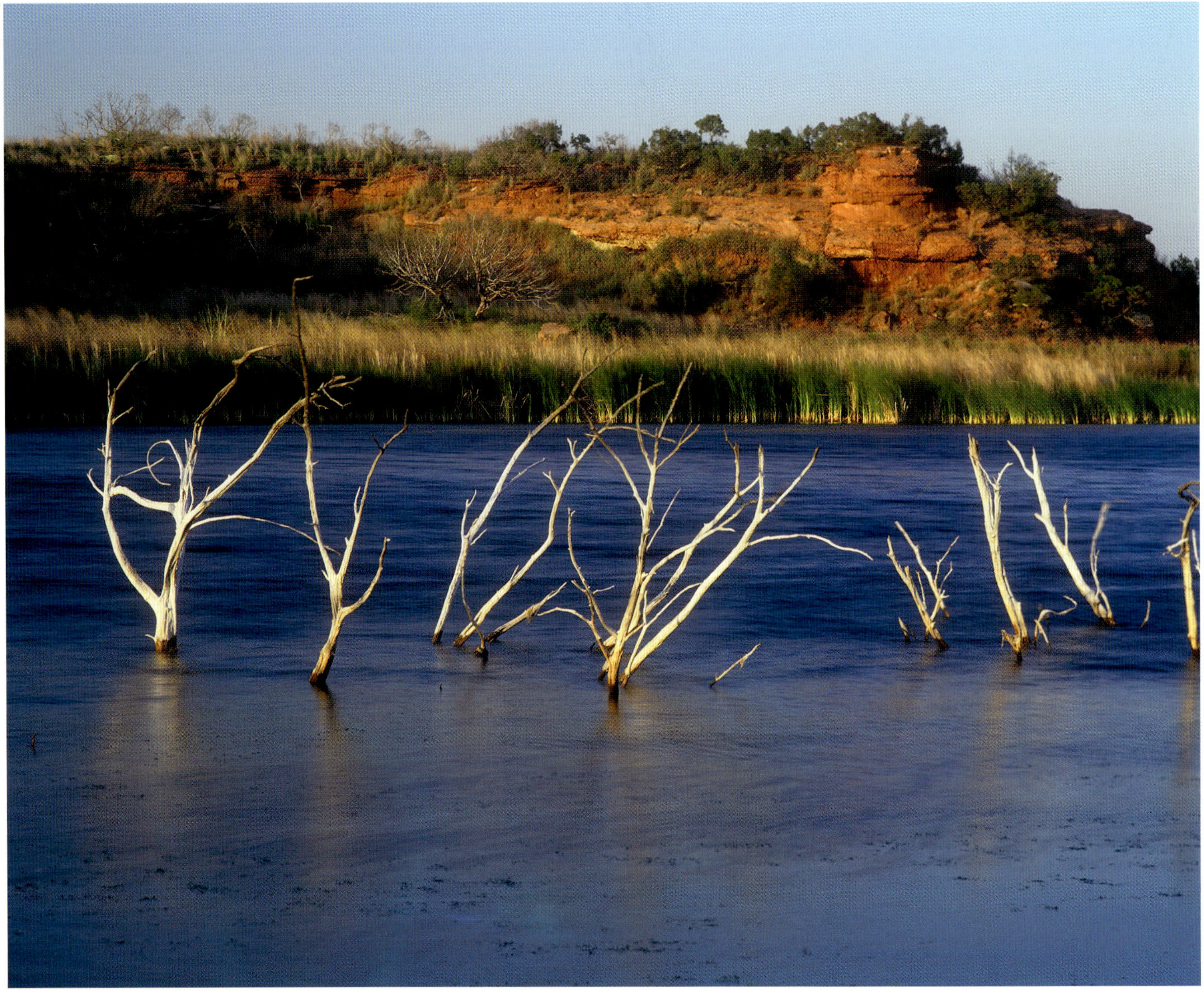

Hardin County

Village Creek State Park

The county is named for the family of William Hardin from Liberty County, Texas. The county was formed in 1858. As early as 1878, loggers floated timber cut from the county's hardwood, longleaf, and loblolly pine forests down local streams to the Neches River and Beaumont. By 1881 at least two lumber-processing mills were operating in the county.

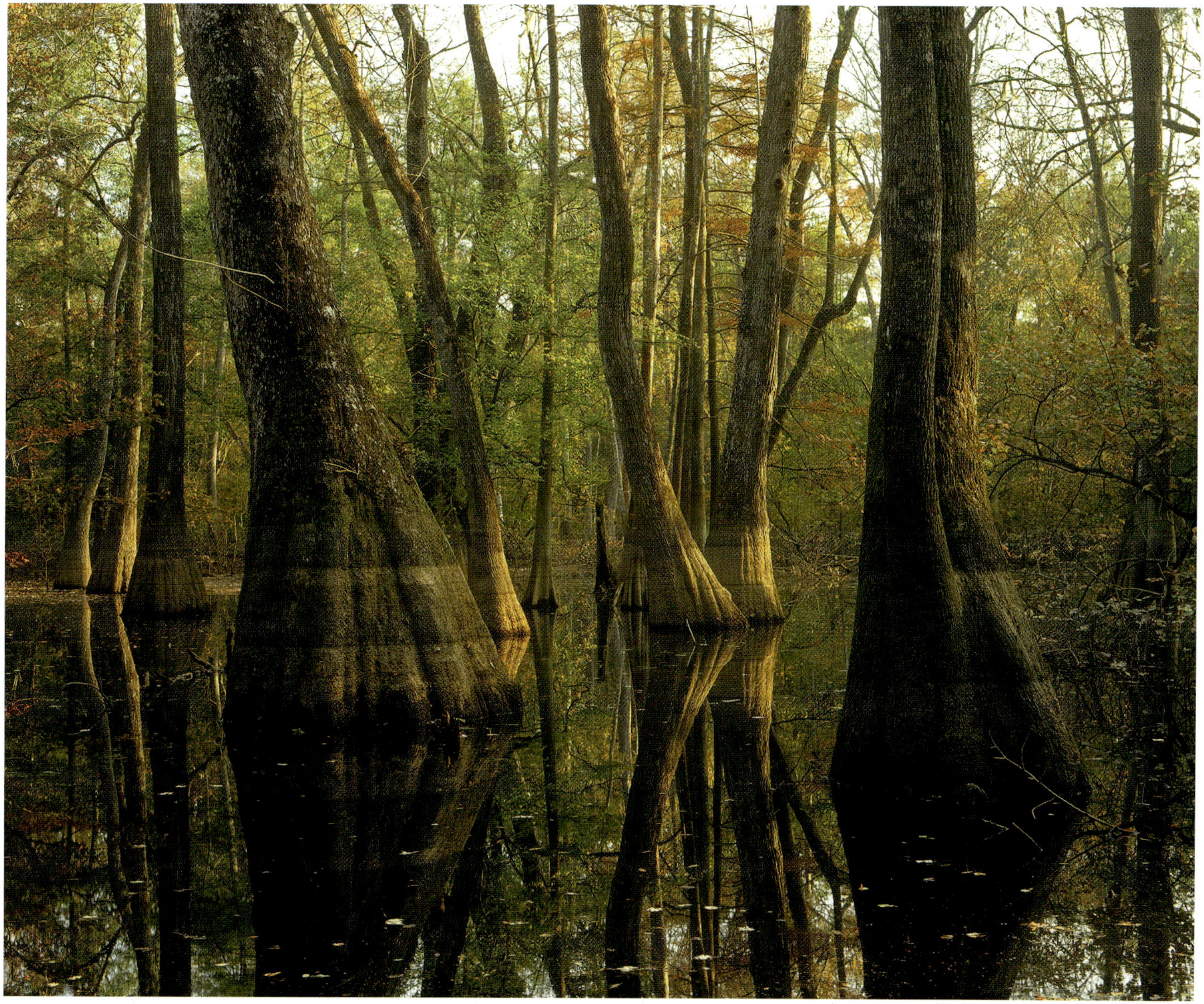

Harris County

Cypress Trees in Jesse H. Jones Park

The county was founded in 1836 and organized in 1837. It was named for John Richardson Harris, an early settler of the area. Owing to the city of Houston, Harris County is the most populous county in Texas and the third-most-populous county in the United States.

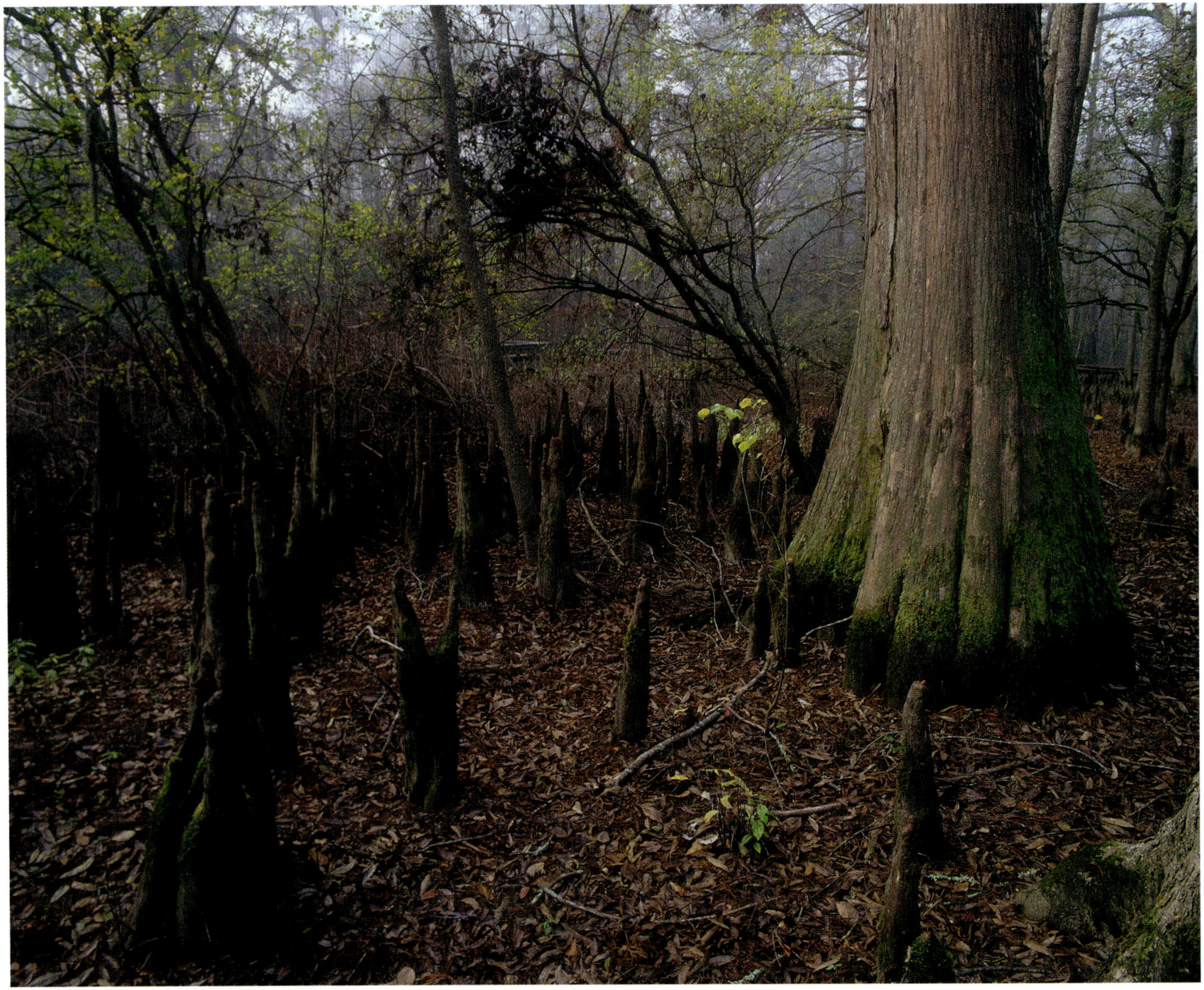

Harrison County

Caddo Lake

The county was created in 1839 and was named for Jonas Harrison, a lawyer and Texas revolutionary. Mysterious and exotic Caddo Lake is in northern Harrison and southern Marion Counties in Texas, and western Caddo Parish in Louisiana.

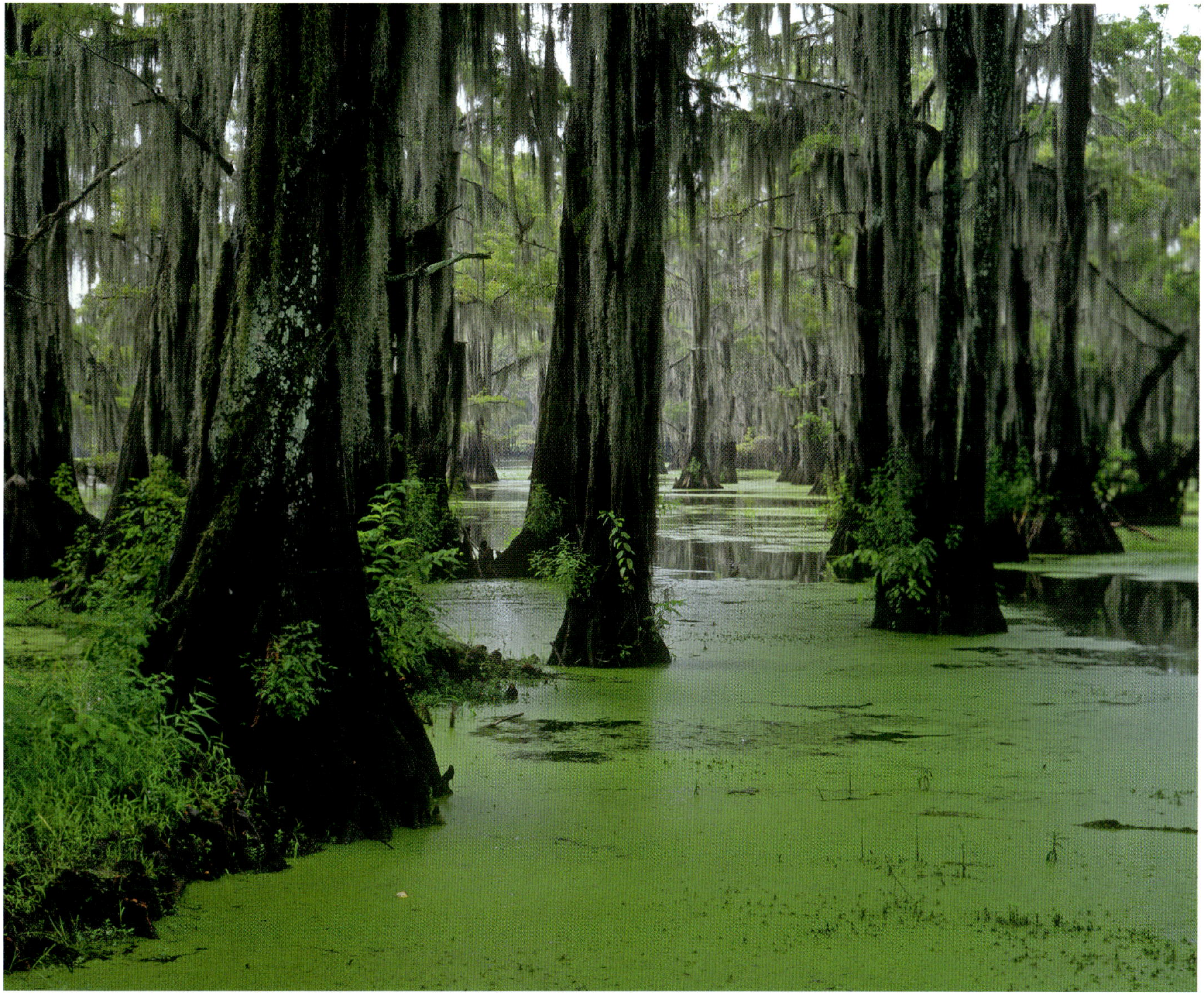

Hartley County

Sunrise over Flooded Field

The county was created in 1876. It was named for Oliver C. Hartley and his brother, Rufus K. Hartley, two early Texas legislators and lawyers. The grim days of the Dust Bowl and Great Depression set the area back during the 1930s. The establishment of Dalhart Army Air Field in northern Hartley County during World War II helped revive the economy.

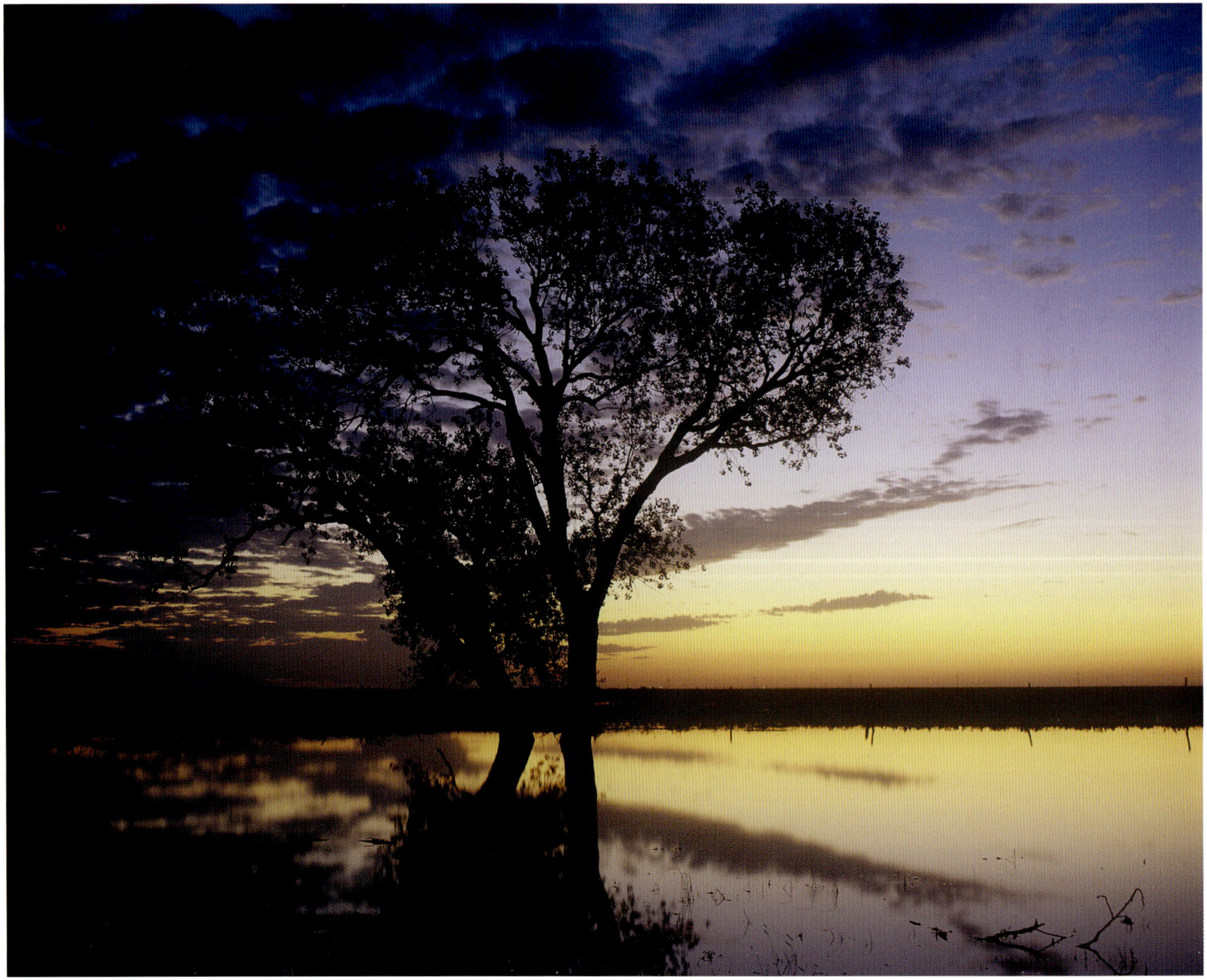

Haskell County

Sunset over an Irrigated Field

The county was created in 1858. It was named for Charles Ready Haskell, who was killed in the Goliad Massacre. Though the first oil wells in the county were drilled in 1929, extensive production did not begin until after World War II. Subsequently the petroleum industry became prominent in the local economy.

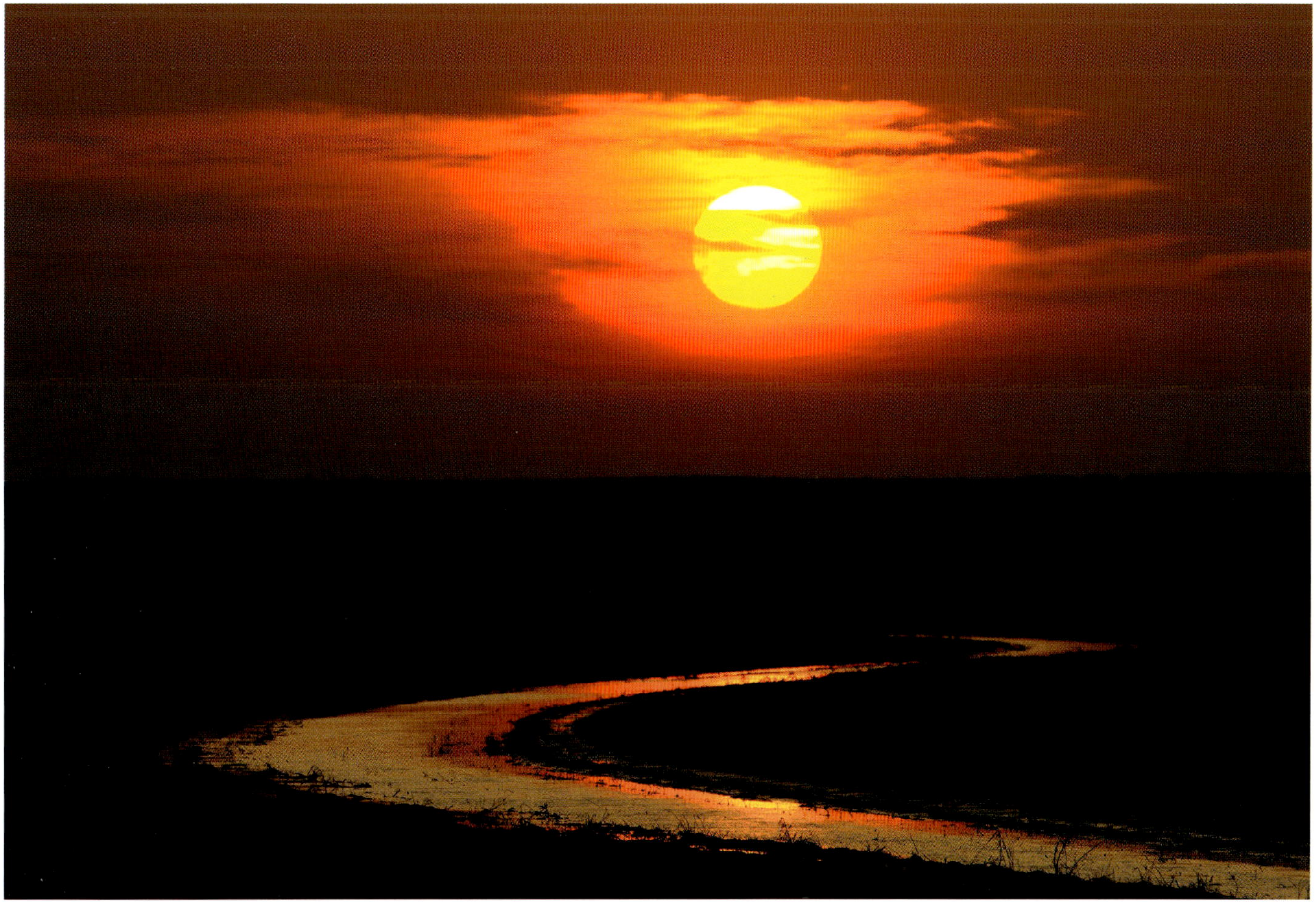

Hays County

Mixed Wildflower Field

The county is named for John Coffee Hays, a Texas Ranger and Mexican-American War officer. The county was formed in 1848. In 1942, the construction of San Marcos Army Air Field began, and it was renamed Gary Air Force Base in 1953, to honor Second Lieutenant Arthur Edward Gary, the first San Marcos resident killed in World War II.

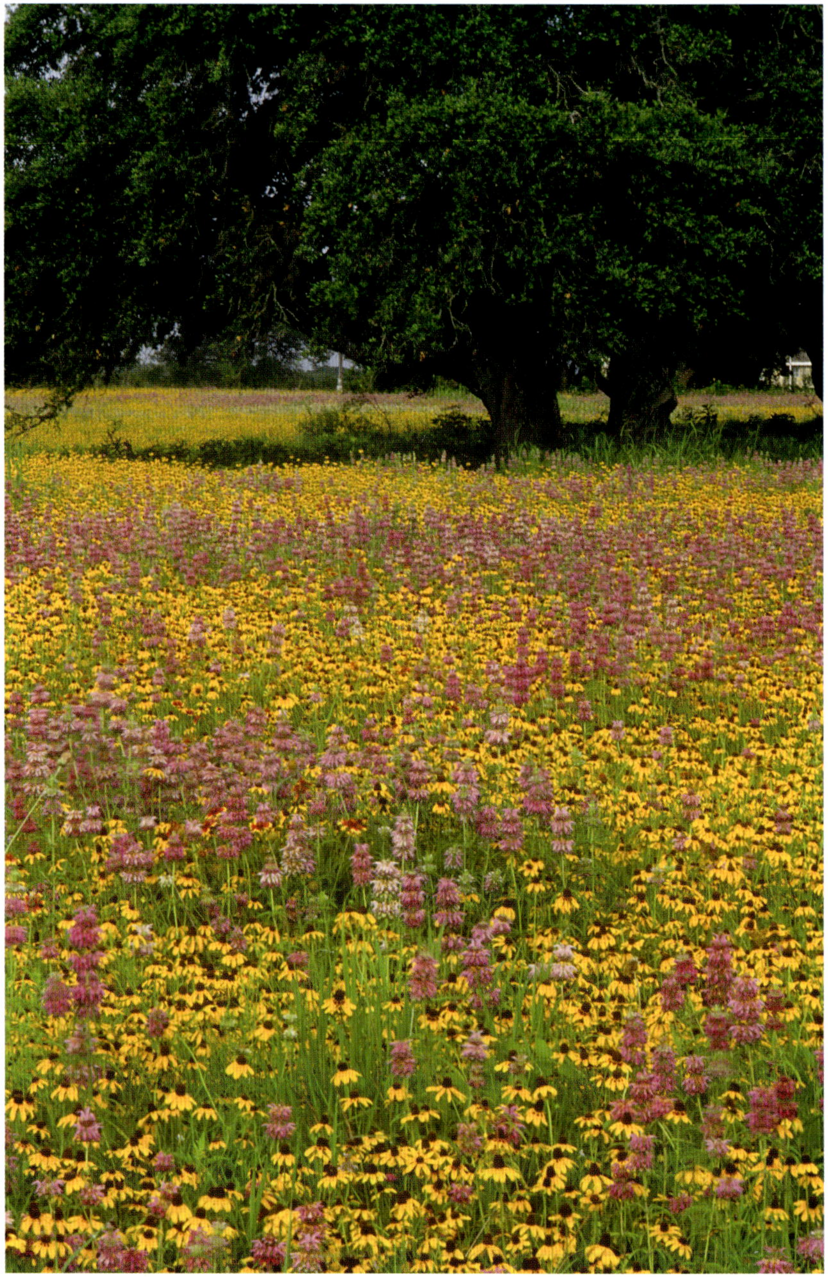

Hemphill County

Lake Marvin in Black Kettle National Grassland

The county was created in 1876 and organized in 1887. It carries the name of John Hemphill, a judge and Confederate congressman. On July 4, 1888, the first rodeo in Texas and perhaps the world was held on Main Street of the Hemphill community of Canadian. It began as a competition among some of the larger ranches in the area. The annual Fourth of July Rodeo continues to this day.

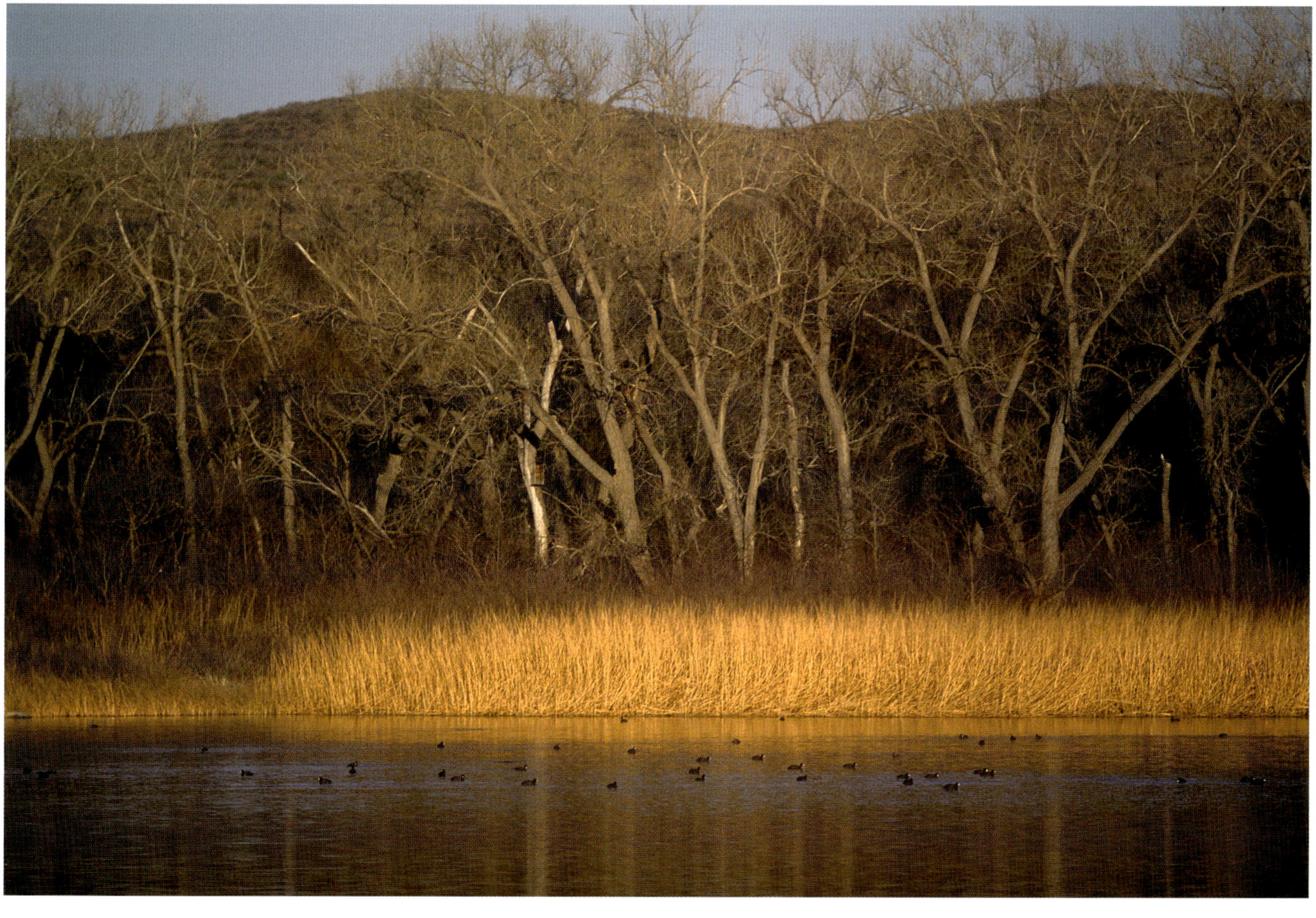

Henderson County

Lush Springtime Meadow

The county is named in honor of James Pinckney Henderson, the first attorney general of the Republic of Texas and later secretary of state for the republic. The county was created in 1846. Early Spanish and French explorers reported that the Native American people in the area called themselves the Tejas, which some claim is the origin of the name Texas.

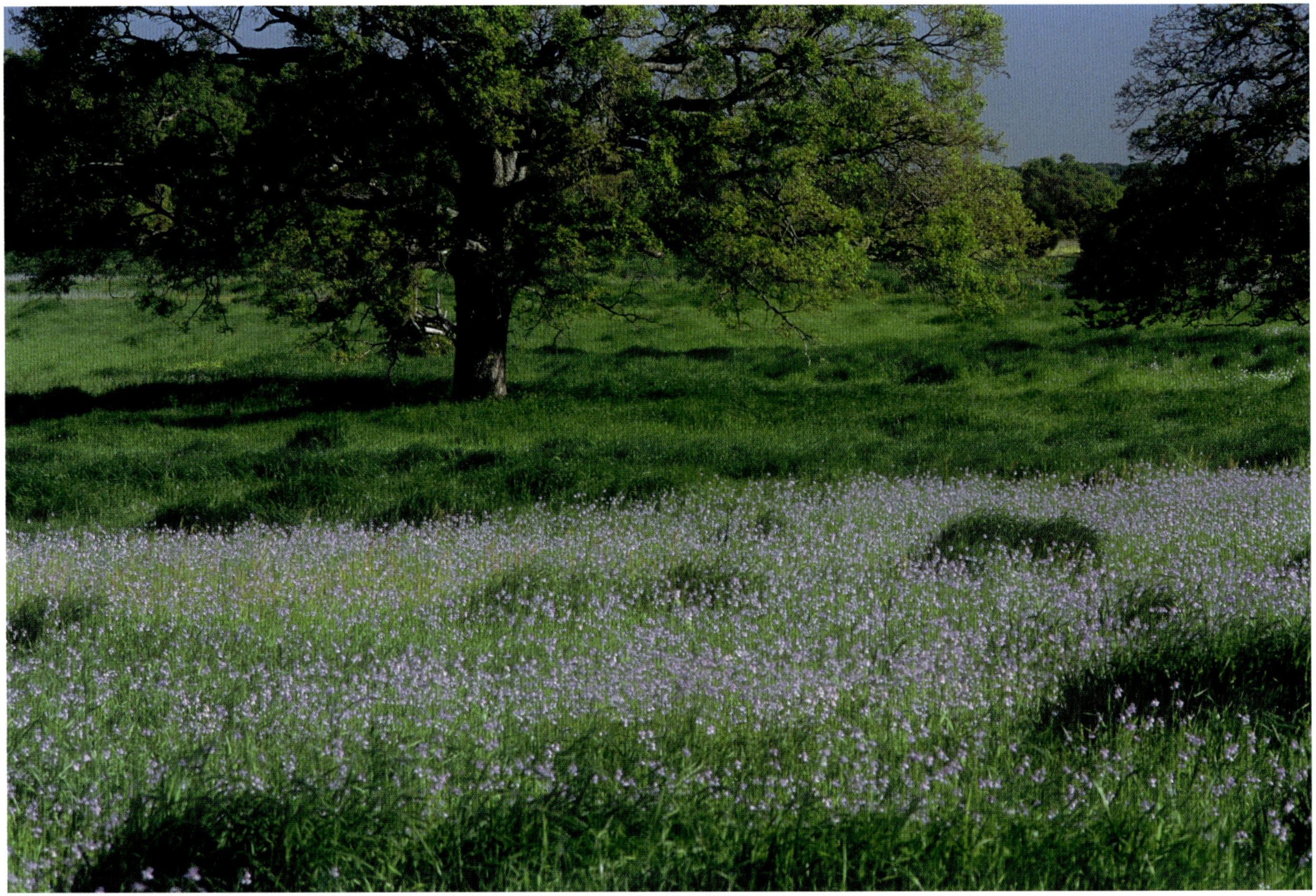

Hidalgo County

Santa Ana National Wildlife Refuge

The county is named for Miguel Hidalgo y Costilla, the priest who raised the call for Mexico's independence from Spain. The county was founded in 1852. Citrus fruits were produced on a commercial basis starting around 1907, when W. A. Fitch planted a commercial-scale grapefruit orchard near Mercedes. Texas red grapefruit is a popular export.

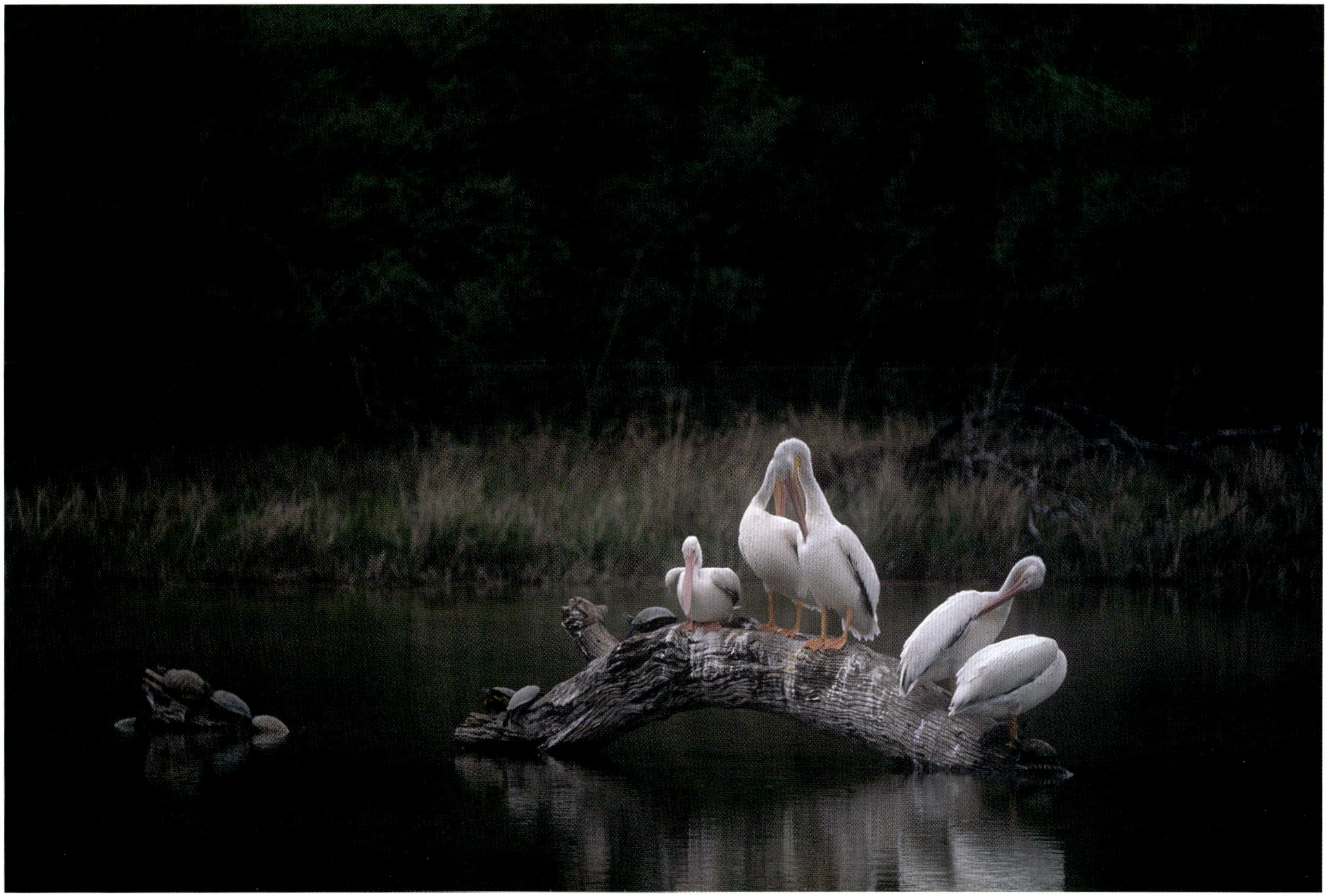

Hill County

Nolan River

The county is named for George Washington Hill, secretary of war and secretary of the navy for the Republic of Texas. The county was formed in 1853. Hill County overwhelmingly approved secession (by a vote of 376 to 63), and the county remained loyal to the South throughout the Civil War. Home guards were established in May 1861, and during the war Hill County supported three cavalry units that saw action primarily in Louisiana and Arkansas.

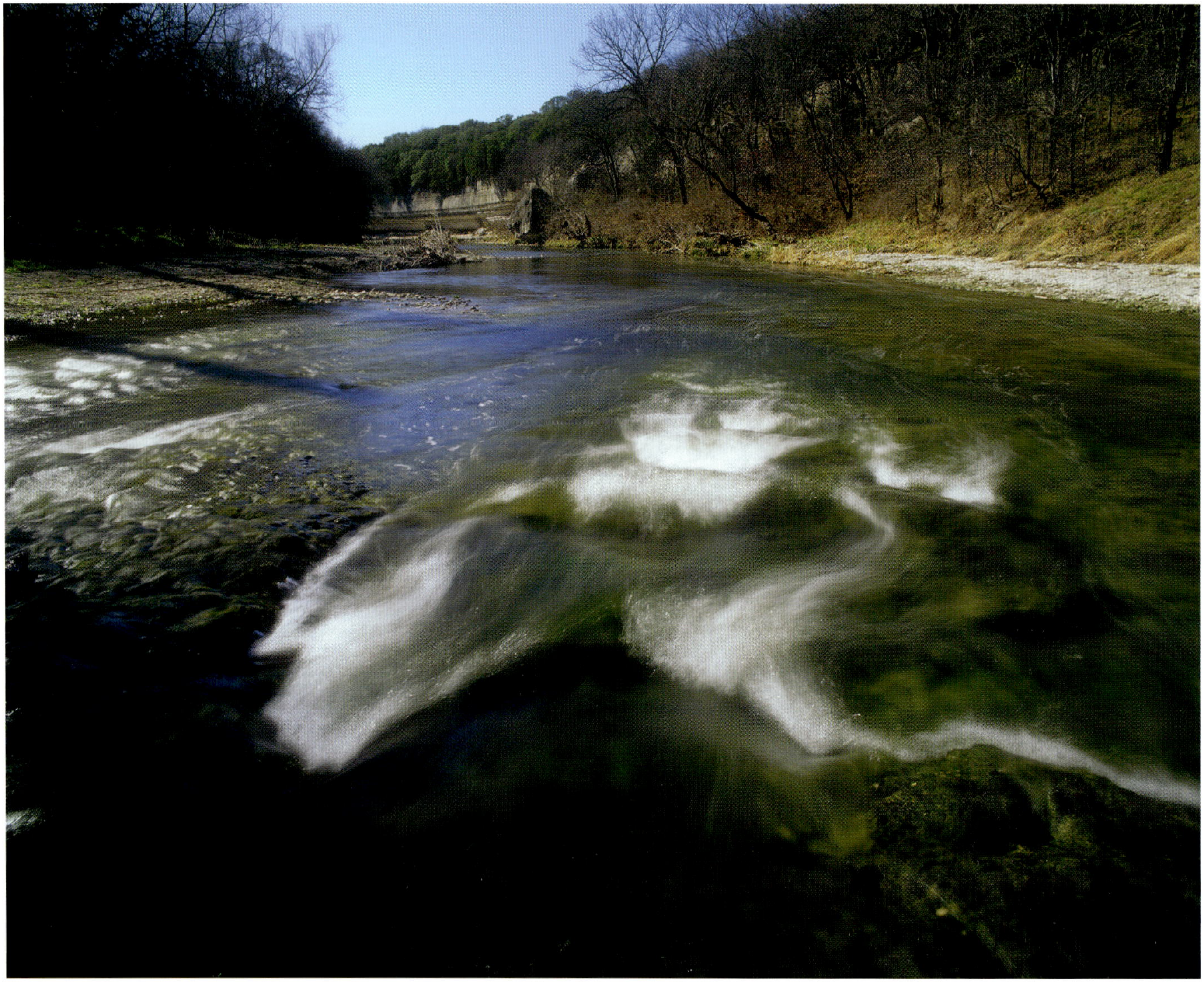

Hockley County

Yucca Painted with a Flashlight at Dawn

The county was created in 1876 but was not organized until 1921. It is named for George Washington Hockley, a secretary of war of the Republic of Texas. Only 87 acres in the county were planted in cotton in 1920, but by 1929, cotton culture occupied more than 95,000 acres of county land.

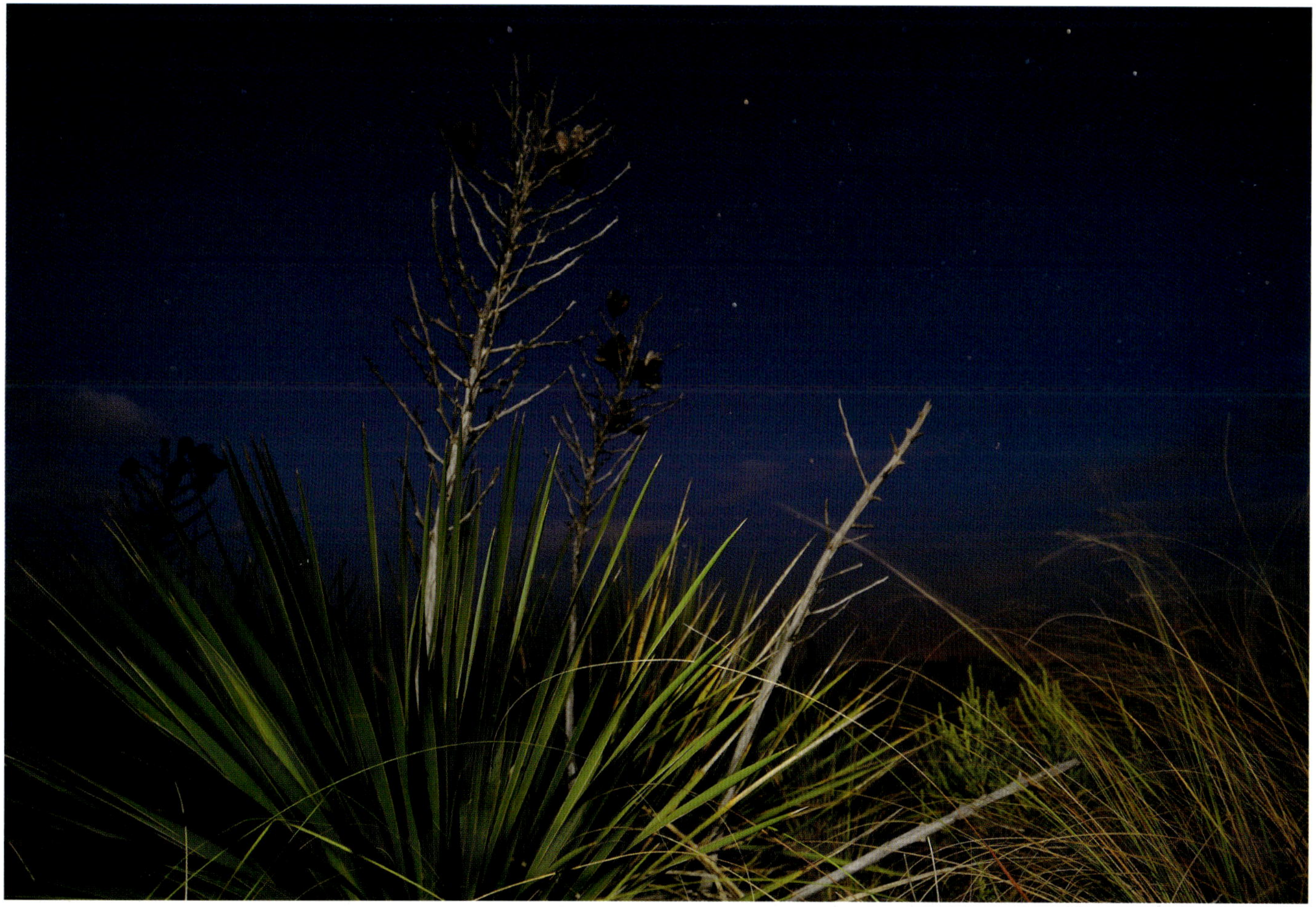

Hood County

Lone Tree on a Hill

The county was formed in 1866 and is named for John Bell Hood (1831–1879), a Confederate lieutenant general and the commander of Hood's Texas Brigade. In 1982, 84 percent of the land in Hood County was used for farming and ranching. Pecans were grown on 5,000 acres, making Hood County a leader in pecan production.

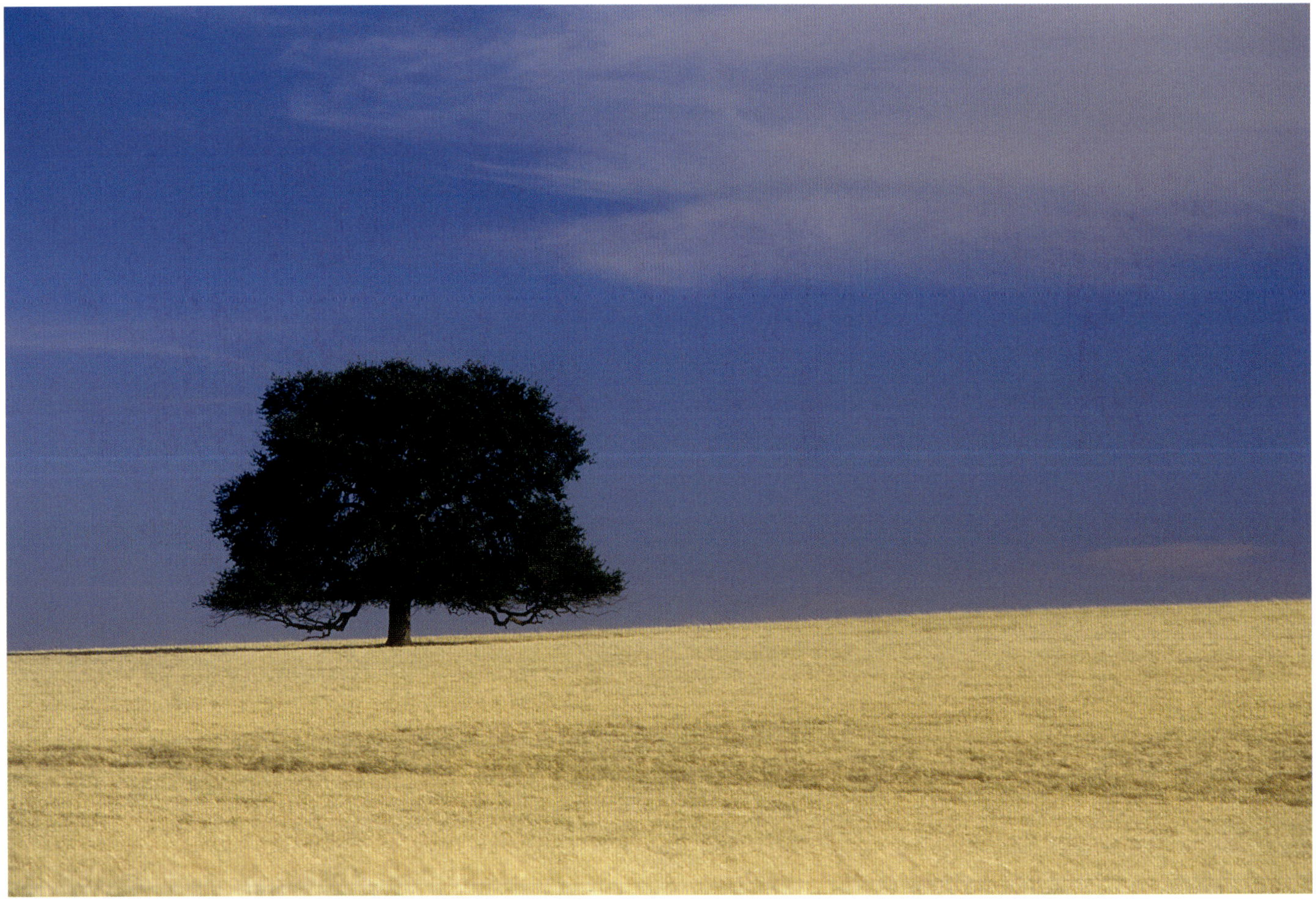

Hopkins County

Goldenrod along a Fence Line

The county is named for David Hopkins, an early settler. The county was established in 1846. The area that became Hopkins County was initially occupied by the Caddo Indians, who were later displaced by the Cherokees. Troops dispatched by the Republic of Texas under the command of General Kelsey H. Douglass defeated the Cherokees in 1839. This event encouraged settlers, now relatively safe from Indian attacks, to move into what is now Hopkins County.

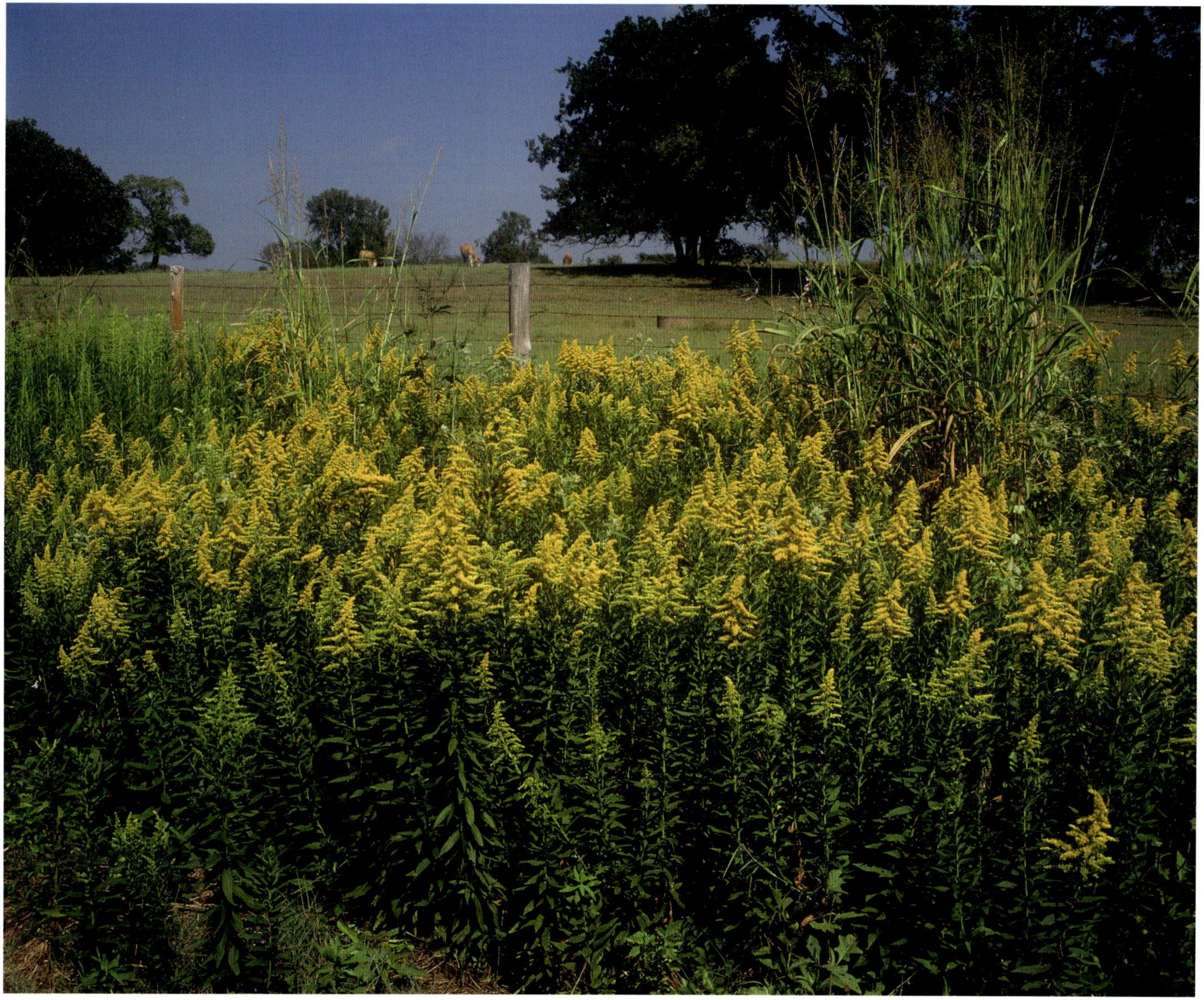

Houston County

Big Slough Wilderness of the Davy Crockett National Forrest

The county is named for Sam Houston (1793–1863), general of the Texas Revolution, commander at the Battle of San Jacinto, later president of the Republic of Texas, and a US senator and governor of the state of Texas. Houston County was founded in 1837, the first new county created under the Republic of Texas. The original boundaries of Houston County also included all of present-day Anderson and Trinity Counties and portions of present-day Henderson and Polk Counties.

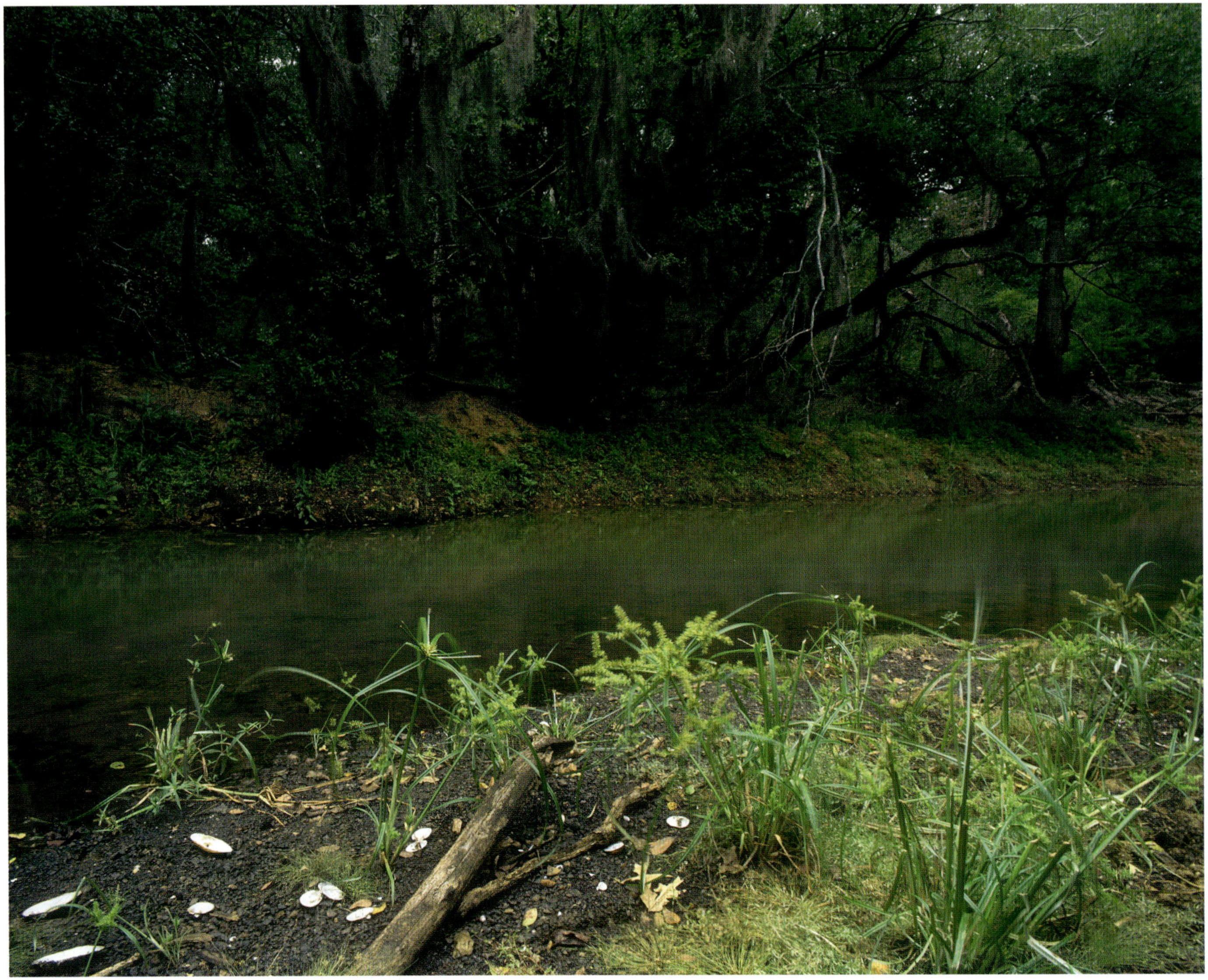

Howard County

Big Spring State Park

The county was created in 1876 and organized in 1882. It is named for Volney E. Howard, a US congressman from Texas. In 1919 and 1920, S. E. J. Cox set off a speculative boom after he encouraged investors to put up money for land. His efforts resulted in no producing wells, and in 1923 Cox, along with his famous employer, the polar explorer Dr. Frederick A. Cook, was convicted of oil land fraud.

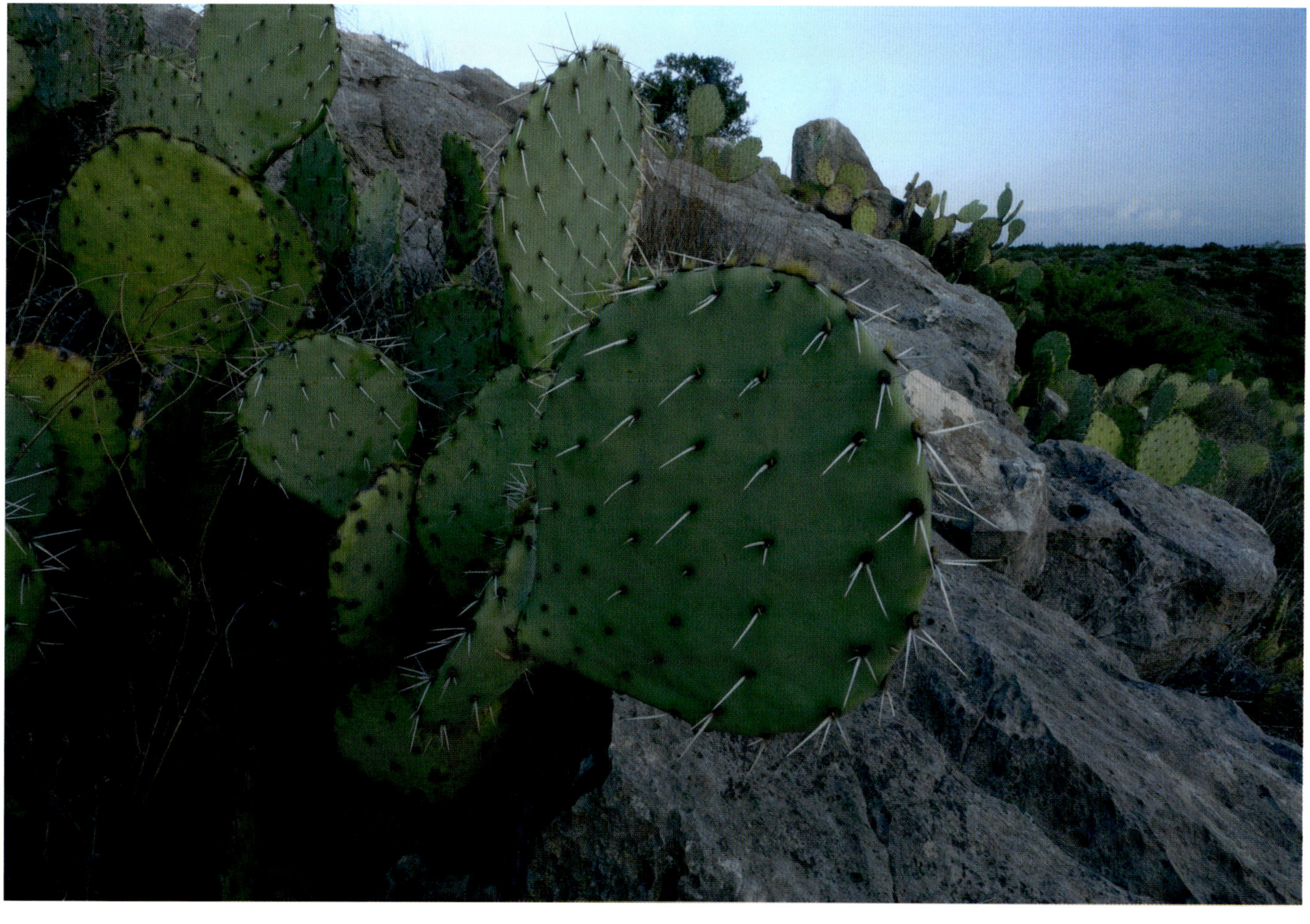

Hudspeth County

Late-Afternoon Light on the Guadalupe Mountains

The county was named for Claude Benton Hudspeth, a US congressman, rancher, and newspaper publisher. It was organized in 1917. Men from San Elizario and the other villages along the Rio Grande near El Paso had become dependent on the salt trade for their livelihoods. After the Civil War they built a road from Fort Quitman to the Salt Basin in northeastern Hudspeth County. Anglo politicians tried to capitalize on this trade by asserting ownership of the salt lakes and levying fees on the traders. The result was the seven-year San Elizario Salt War, which heightened tensions between Mexicans and Americans in the 1870s.

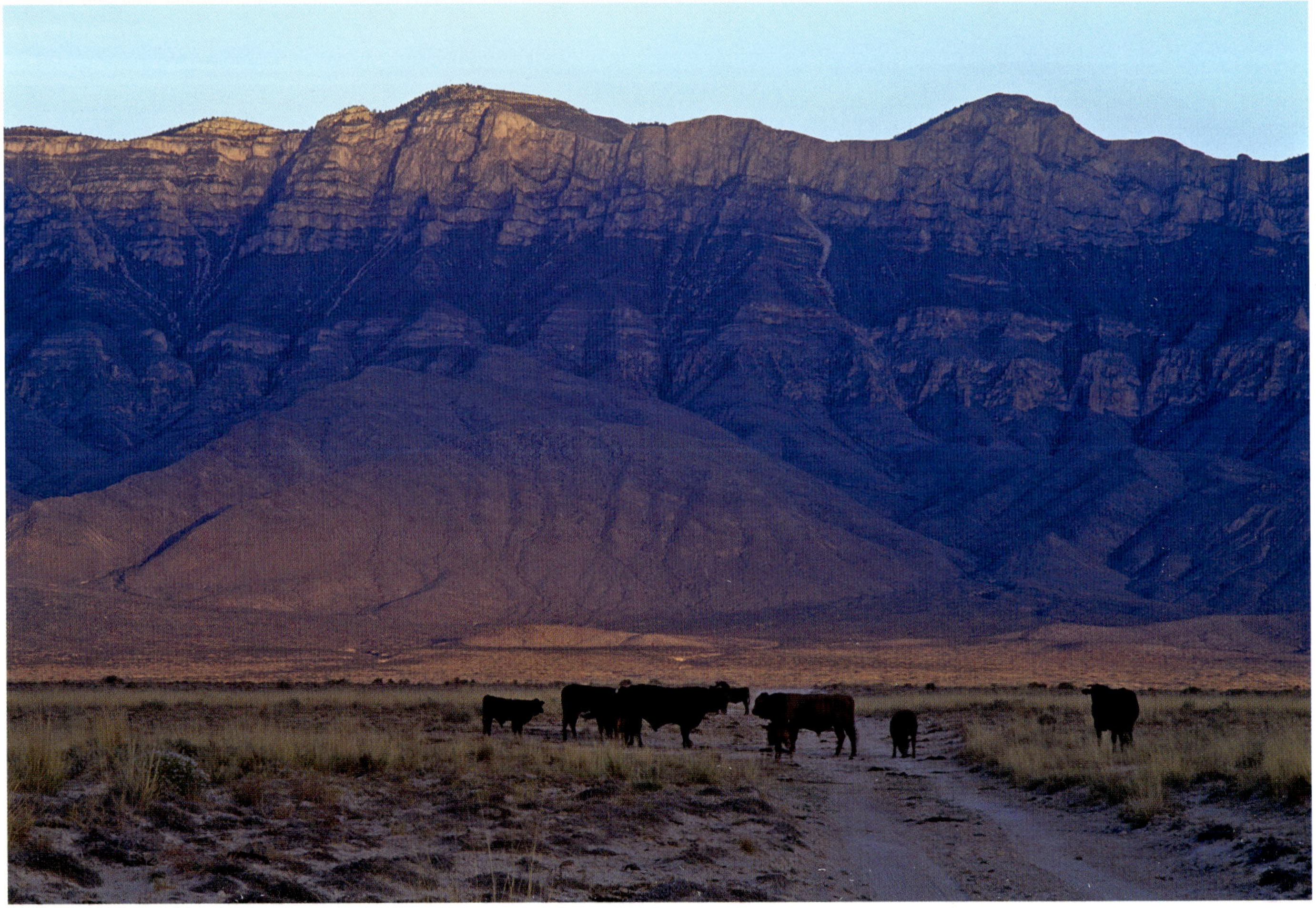

Hunt County

Sunrise over Lake Tawakoni

Founded in 1846, the county is named for Memucan Hunt Jr. (1807–1856), a secretary of the navy for the Republic of Texas. Audie Murphy—actor, Medal of Honor recipient, and the most decorated soldier in World War II—was born in Hunt County.

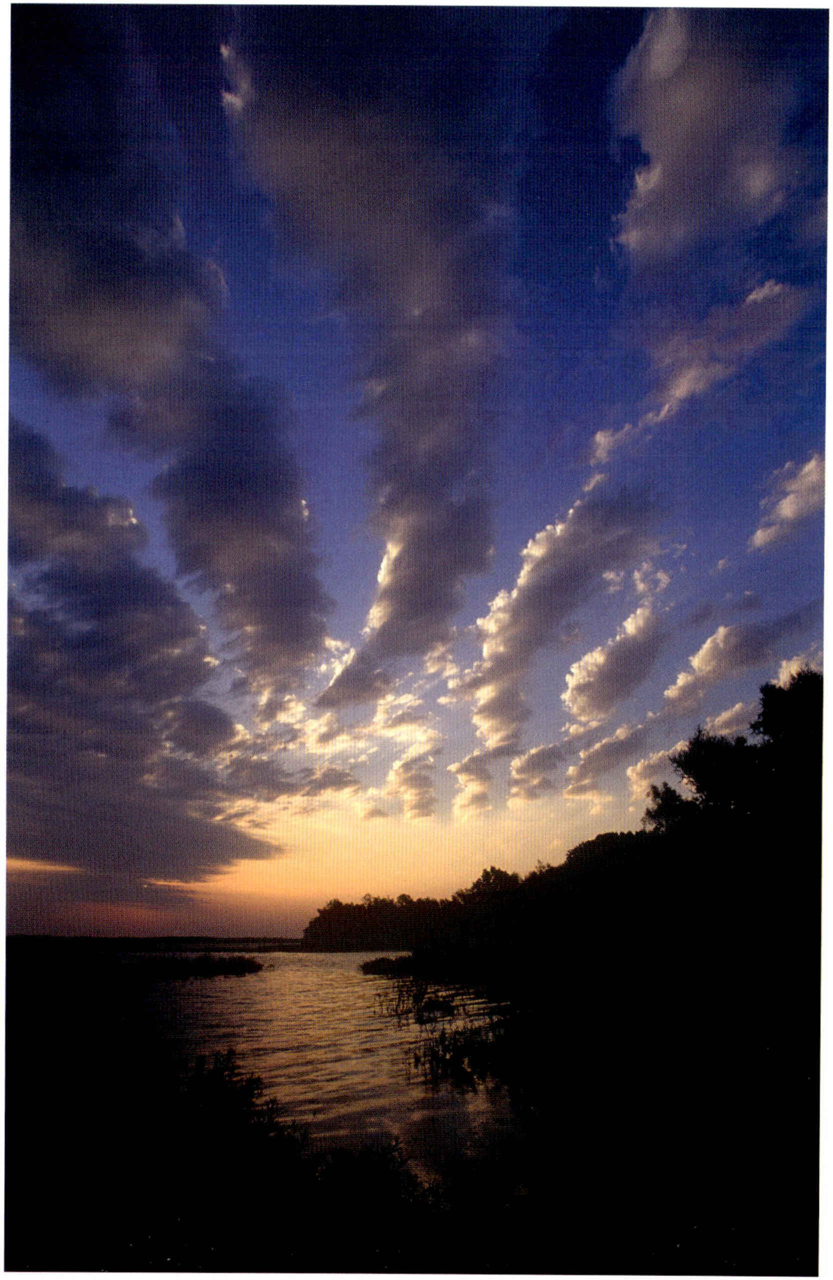

Hutchinson County

Lake Meredith National Recreation Area

Andrew Hutchinson—an early settler and attorney—is the namesake for the county, which was formed in 1876. Bent, St. Vrain, and Company established a trading post in this area to tap into Indian trading. Known as Fort Adobe, it was blown up by traders three years later due to Indian raids. The ruins became known as "Adobe Walls."

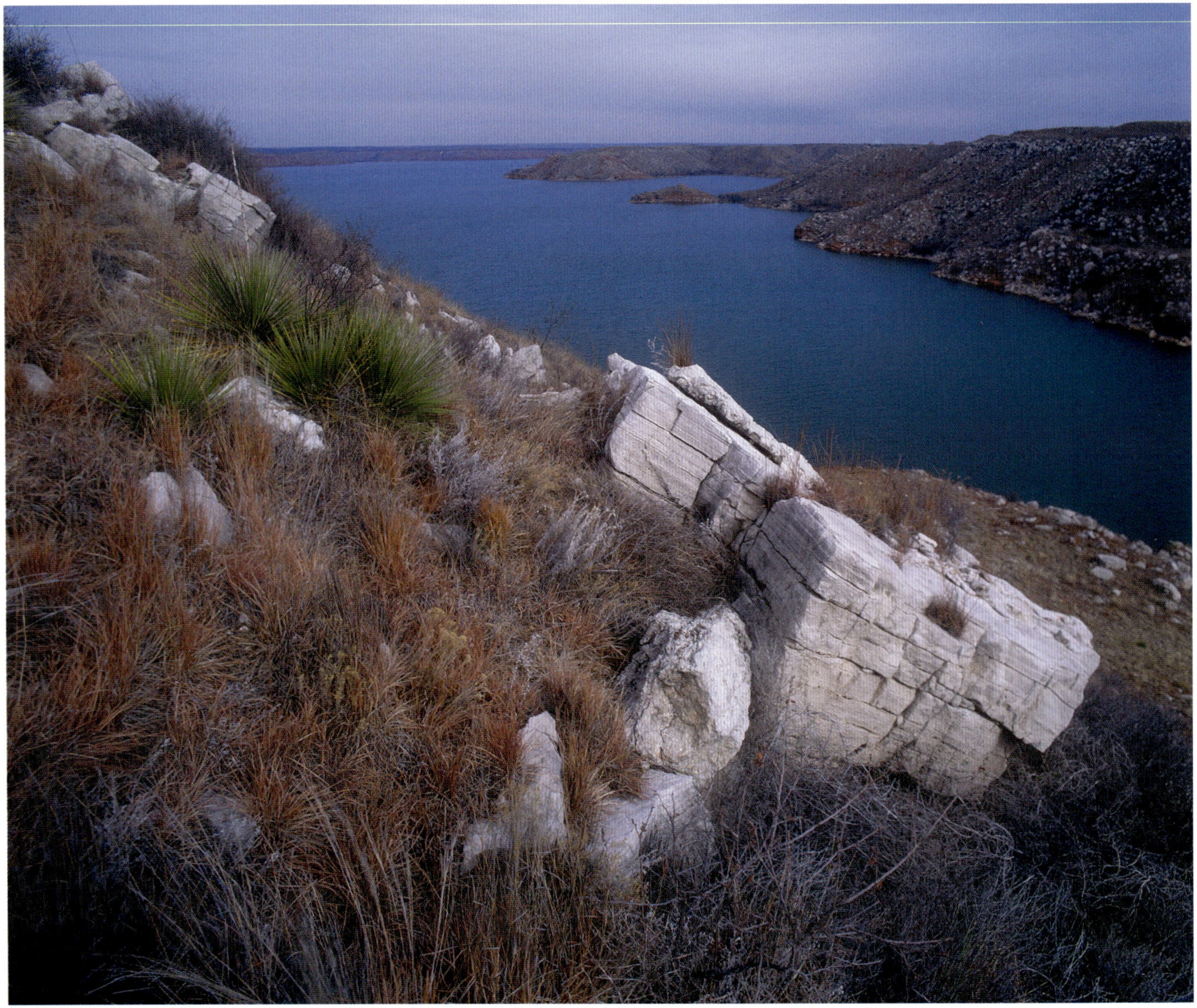

Irion County

Foggy Sunrise and Mesquite Trees

The county was named for Robert Anderson Irion, a secretary of state of the Republic of Texas, and was formed in 1889. On January 8, 1865, the battle of Dove Creek was fought at the junction of Spring and Dove Creeks between 1,400 Kickapoo Indians and 370 state border guards under Captain Henry Fossett. The Kickapoos were eastern Indians who had been uprooted by the American government and removed to reservations in the Indian Territory; they were attempting to move to Mexico when intercepted by Fossett's troops. Thirty-six whites were killed and sixty were wounded in the battle; Indian casualties totaled eleven dead and thirty-one wounded.

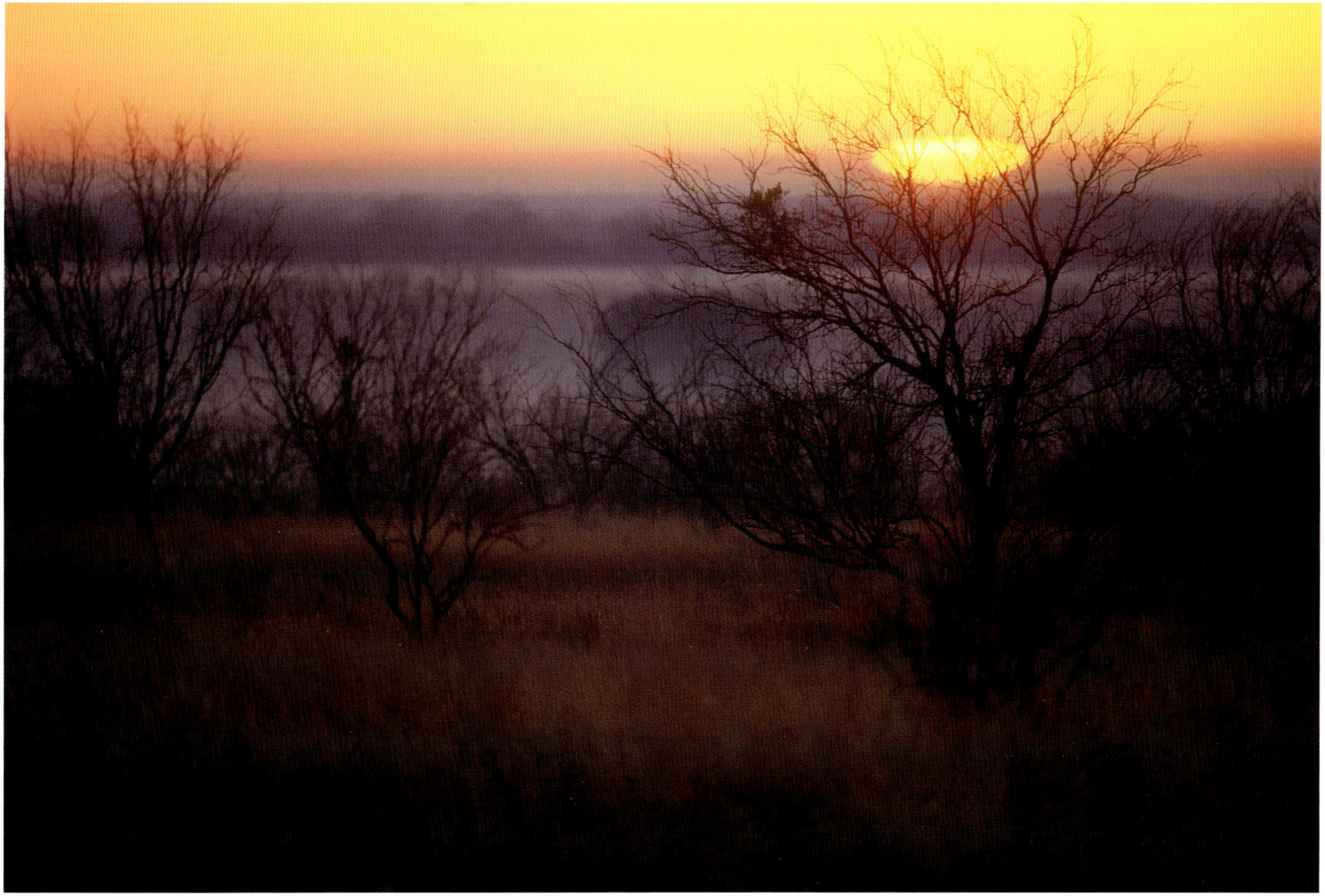

Jack County

Lost Creek in Fort Richardson State Park

Jack County was formed in 1856 and is named for Patrick and William Jack—brothers, participants in the "Anahuac Disturbance," and veterans of the Texas Revolution. The Anahuac Disturbance was an uprising of settlers in and around Anahuac in 1832 and 1835 that helped precipitate the Texas Revolution. This eventually led to the territory's secession from Mexico and the founding of the Republic of Texas.

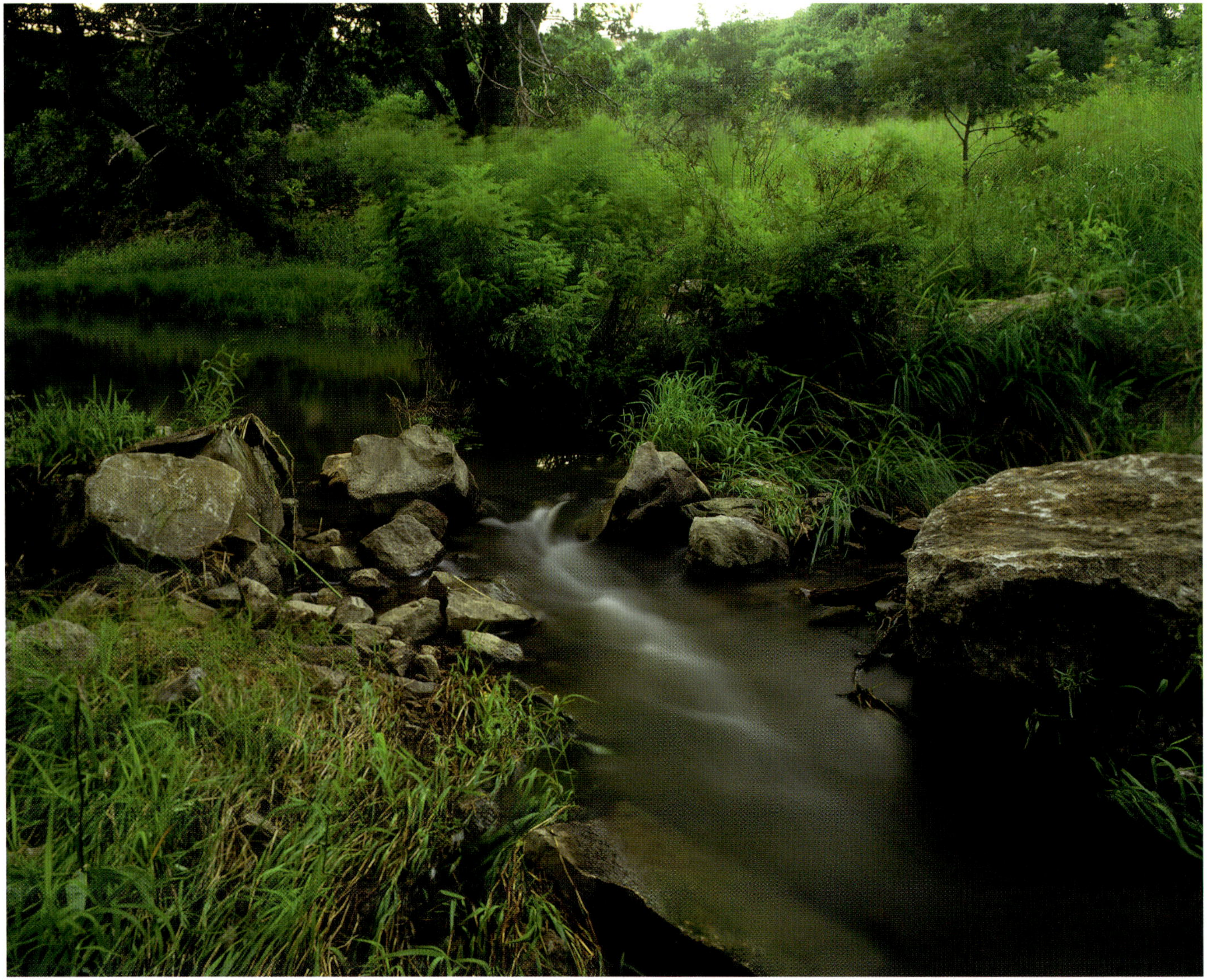

Jackson County

Lake Texana State Park

The county was named for Andrew Jackson, the hero of the Battle of New Orleans and the seventh president of the United States (1829–1837). The county was created in 1835 as a municipality in Mexico and in 1836 was organized as a county of the Republic of Texas. Six of Stephen F. Austin's Old Three Hundred families settled in the future county. So many of the early colonists came from Alabama that for a time the municipality became known as the "Alabama Settlement."

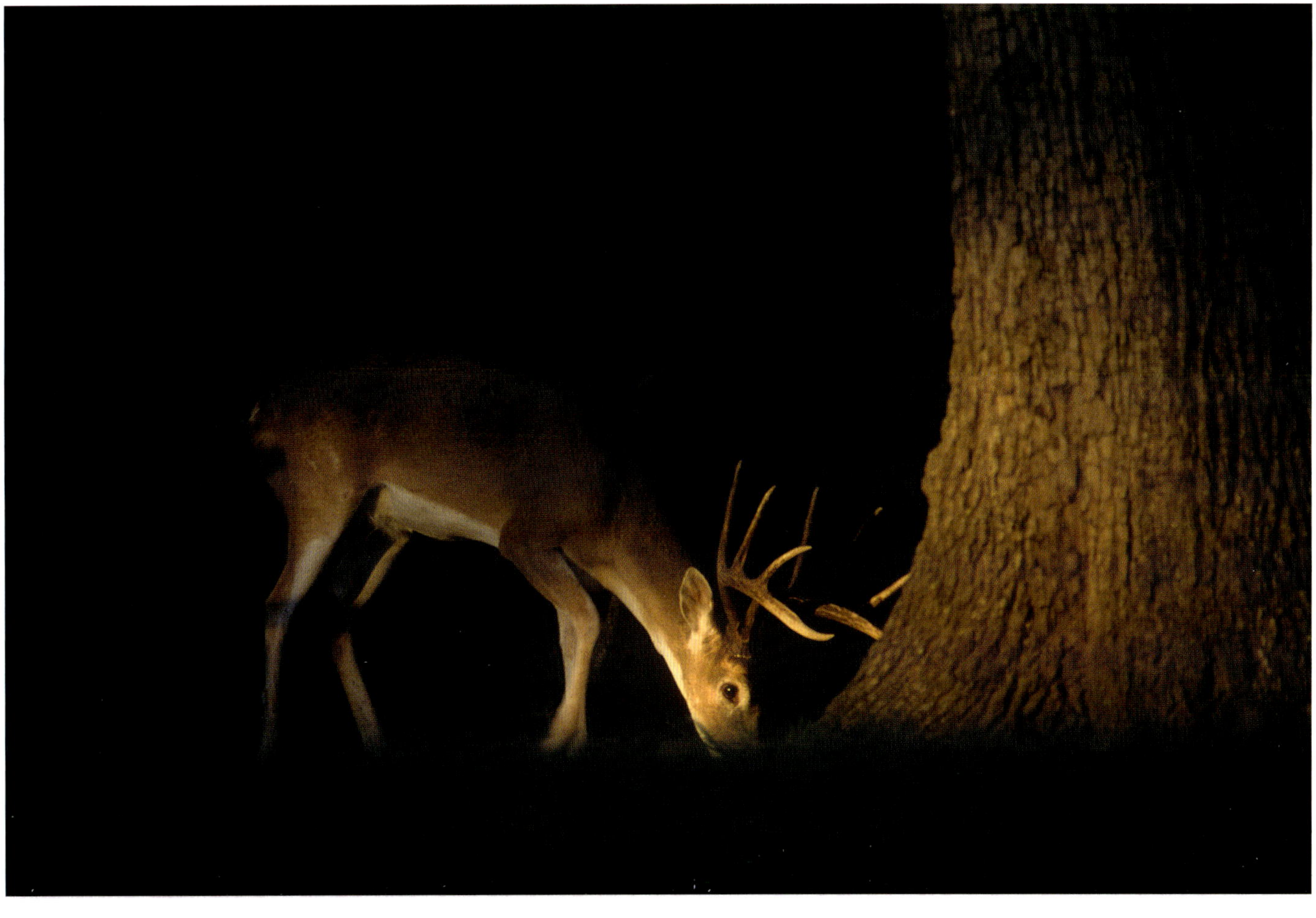

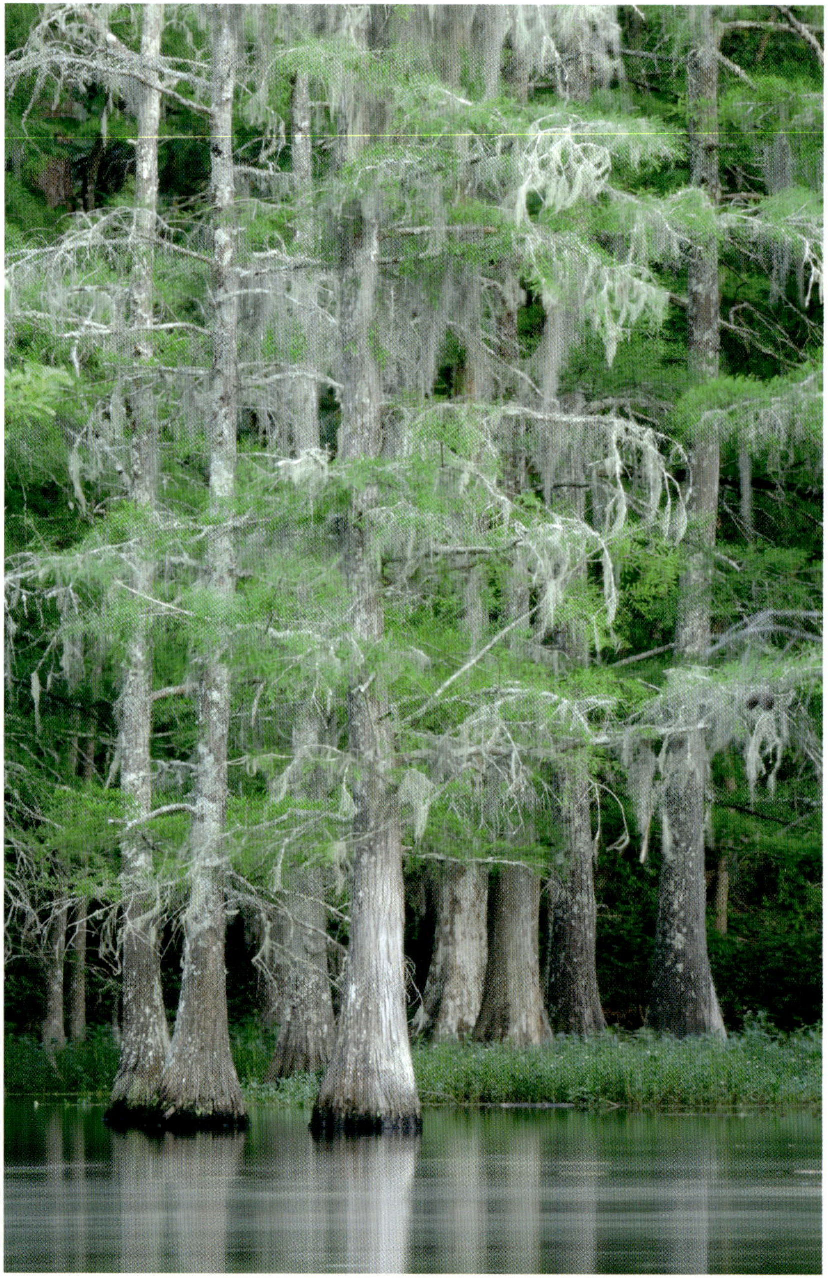

Jasper County

Martin Dies Jr. State Park

The county is named for William Jasper (1750–1779), an American Revolutionary War hero. The county was formed in 1836. Jasper County is one of the original thirty-six Texas counties.

Jeff Davis County

Cottonwoods along Limpia Creek

The county was formed in 1887. It is named for Jefferson Davis, president of the Confederate States of America (1861–1865). Fort Davis was established in 1854. The land was leased from surveyor John James at three hundred dollars per year. The fort was surrendered to the Confederacy in 1861 and abandoned in 1862, after the Confederate defeat at Glorieta Pass, New Mexico, but was reoccupied by US troops on July 1, 1867.

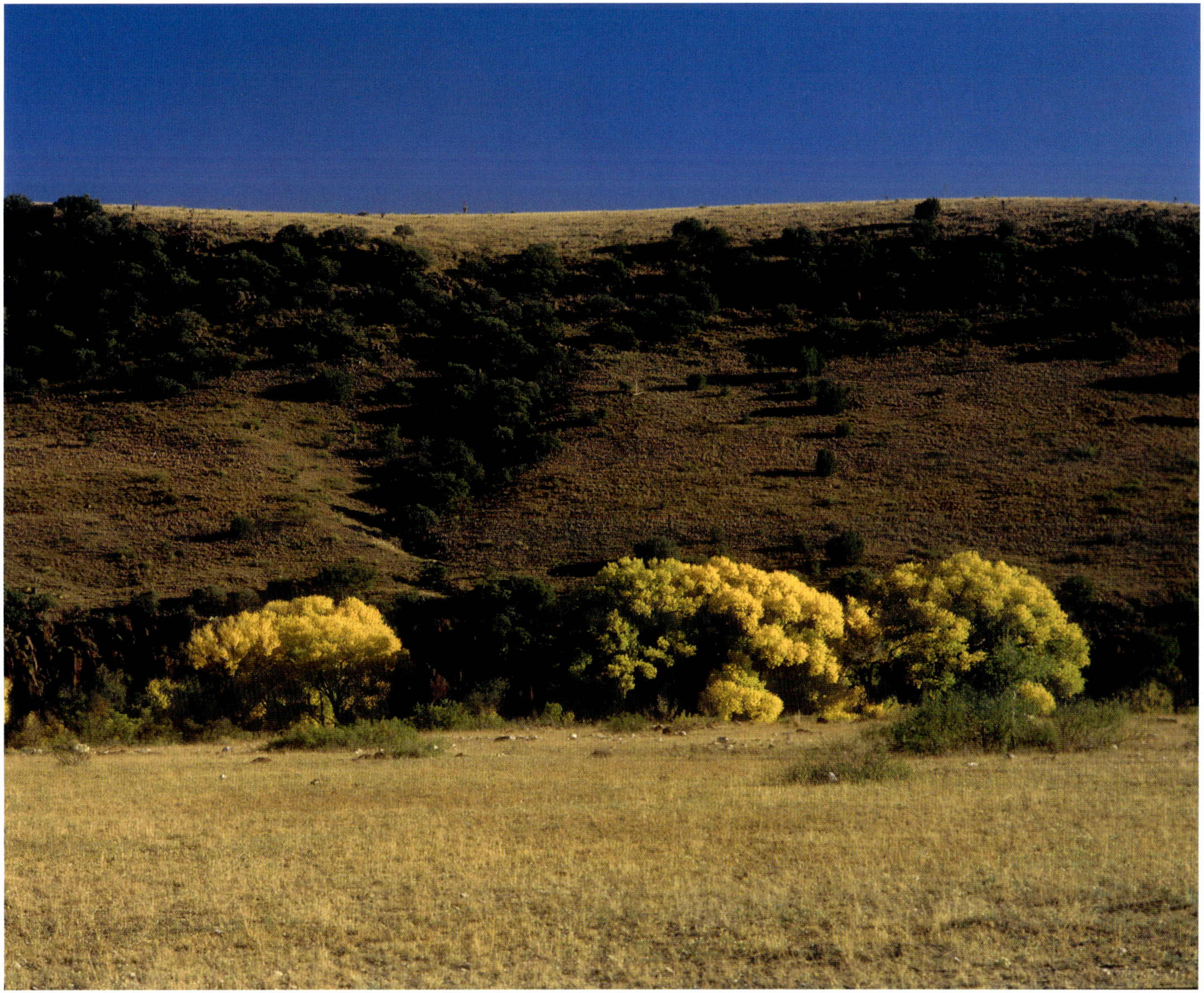

Jefferson County

Sunset near High Island

Thomas Jefferson, the third president of the United States and the principal author of the Declaration of Independence, is the namesake for this county, which was formed in 1836. In 1863, during the American Civil War, the battle of Sabine Pass ended federal efforts to penetrate the interior via the Sabine River.

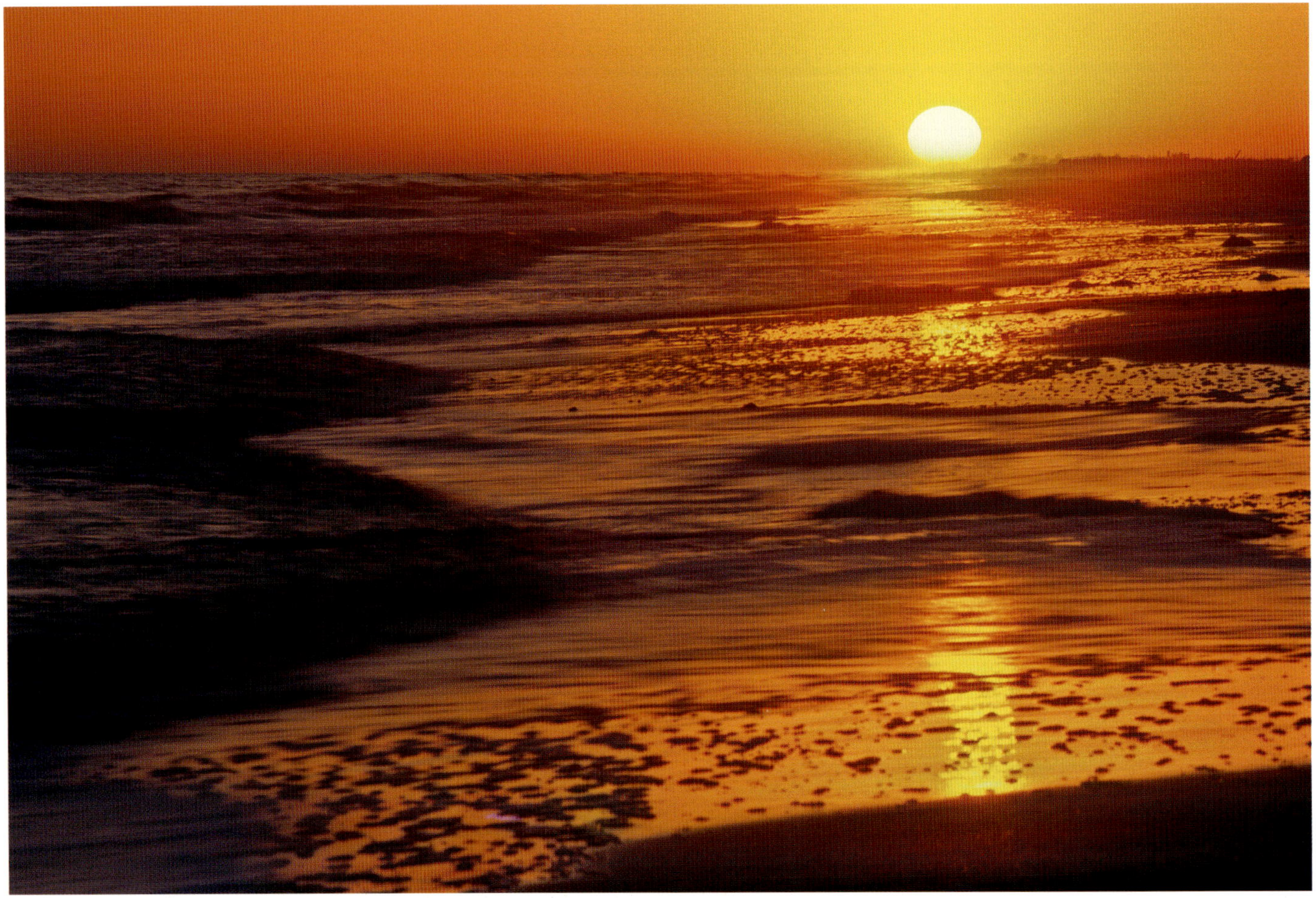

Jim Hogg County

Spring Sunrise

The county was formed in 1913 and is named for James Stephen Hogg, the twentieth (and first native-born) governor of Texas. In the decades after World War II, the county's economy continued to be primarily devoted to ranching and petroleum production. Although the number of ranches continued to decline, mainly as the result of consolidations, the number of cattle increased steadily, reaching nearly 50,000 head by the early 1980s.

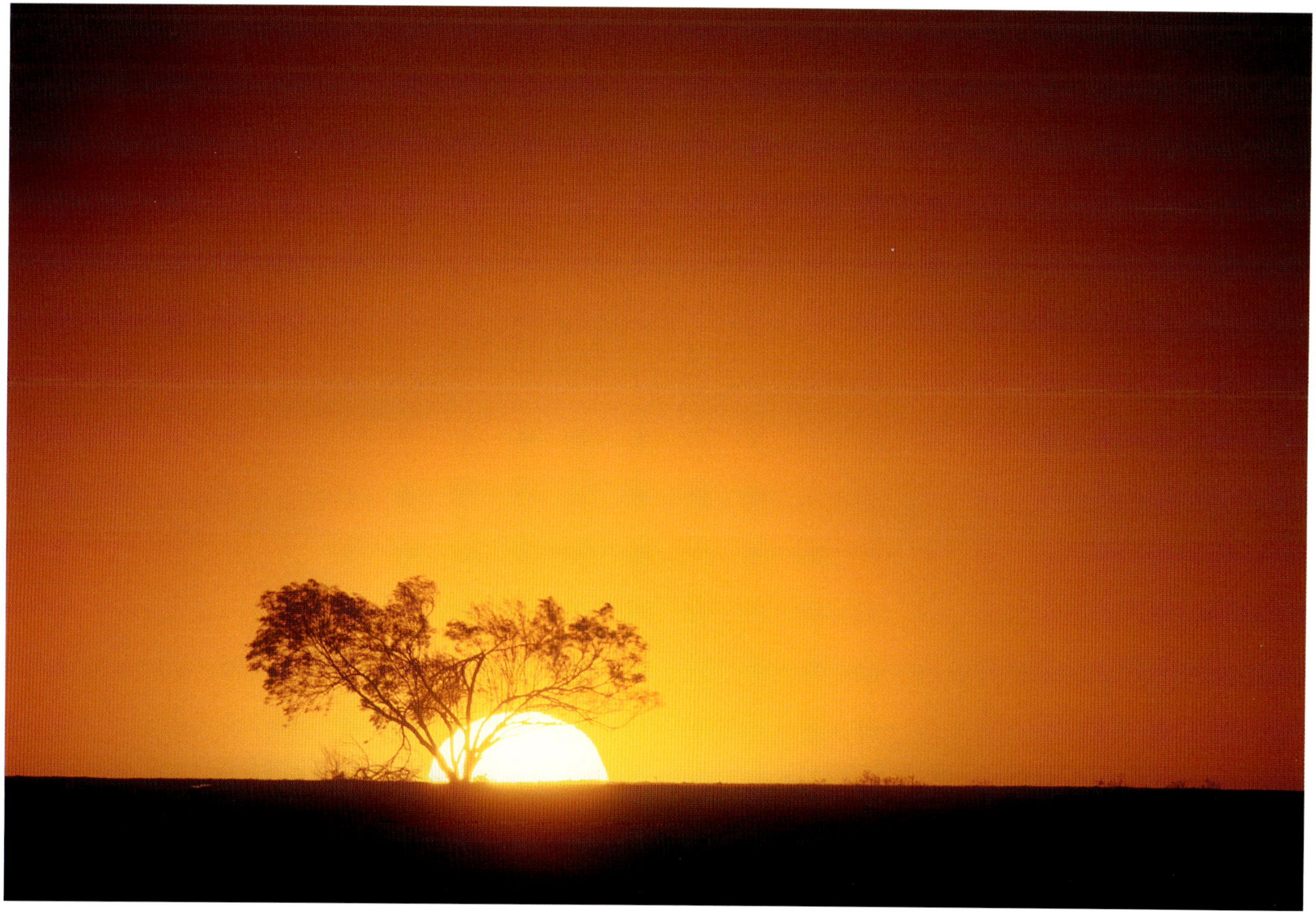

Jim Wells County

Bluebonnets and Mesquite Trees

The county is named for James Babbage Wells Jr., judge and Democratic Party boss in South Texas. The county was formed in 1911. The area that is now Jim Wells County has been the site of human habitation for perhaps 11,000 years. Among the oldest artifacts found in the region are stone implements and human remains dating from the Paleo-Indian period (9,200–6,000 BCE).

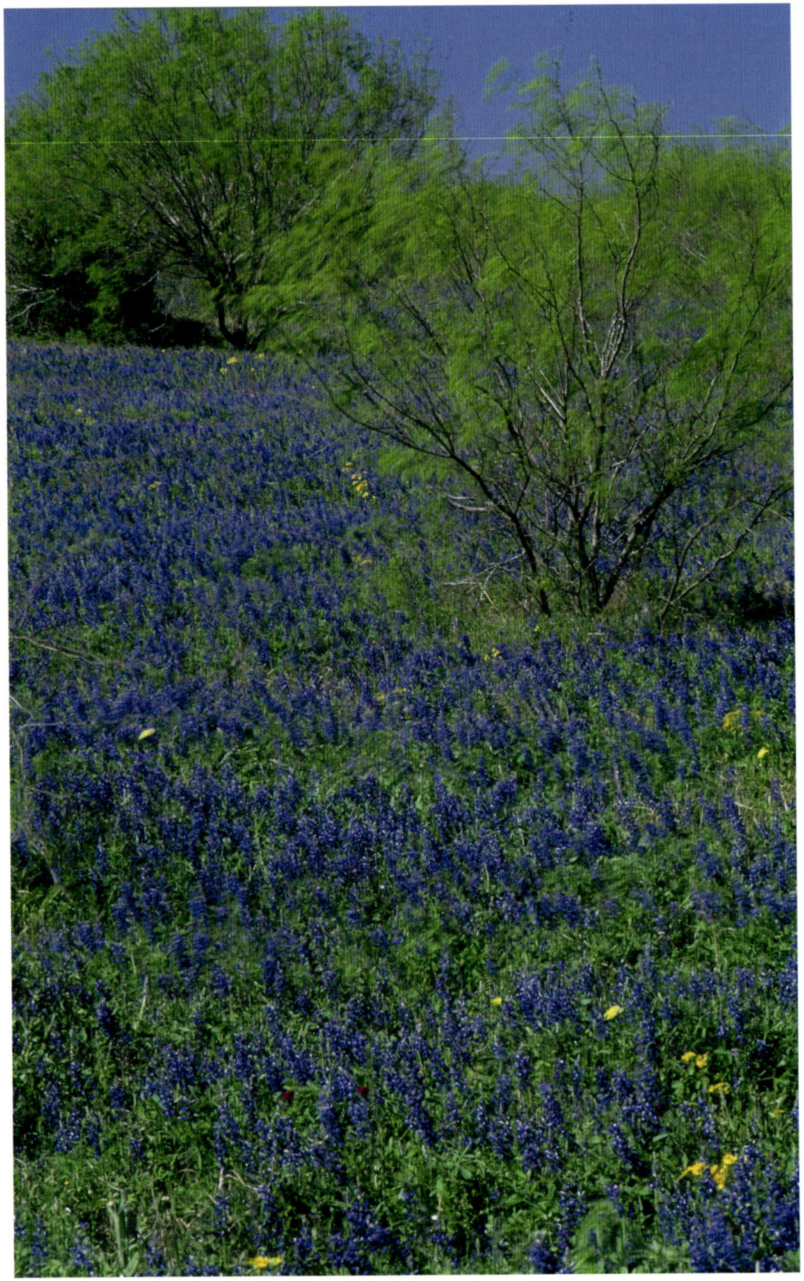

Johnson County

Cleburne State Park

Named for Middleton Tate Johnson—a Texas Ranger, a soldier in the Mexican-American War, and senator for the Republic of Texas—the county was established in 1854. The oldest settlements in Johnson County were in the eastern portion. The site of Alvarado was settled in 1851, and the town was platted in 1853. Grandview (formerly two words)—founded around 1860—was the second community established.

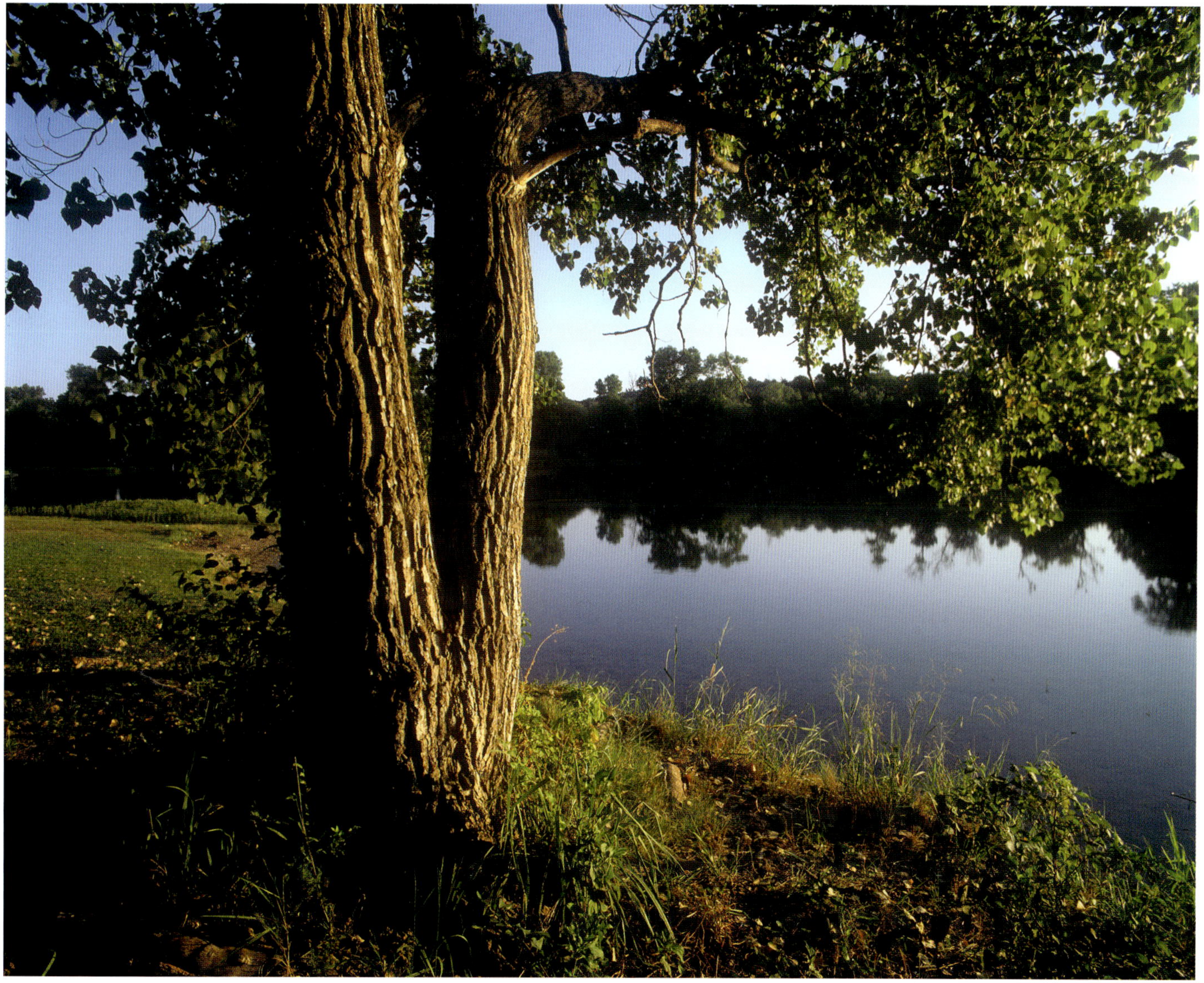

Jones County

Prickly Pear Cactus and Mesquite on the Grounds of Fort Phantom Hill

This county is named for Anson Jones, the fifth president of the Republic of Texas (1844–1846). It was formed in 1854. The earliest white settlement of Jones County was in 1851, when Fort Phantom Hill, near the site of present-day Hawley, was established as one of a line of forts from the Red River to the Rio Grande. These military outposts guarded the frontier and furnished protection to California gold-seeking forty-niners following the Randolph B. Marcy Trail across Texas.

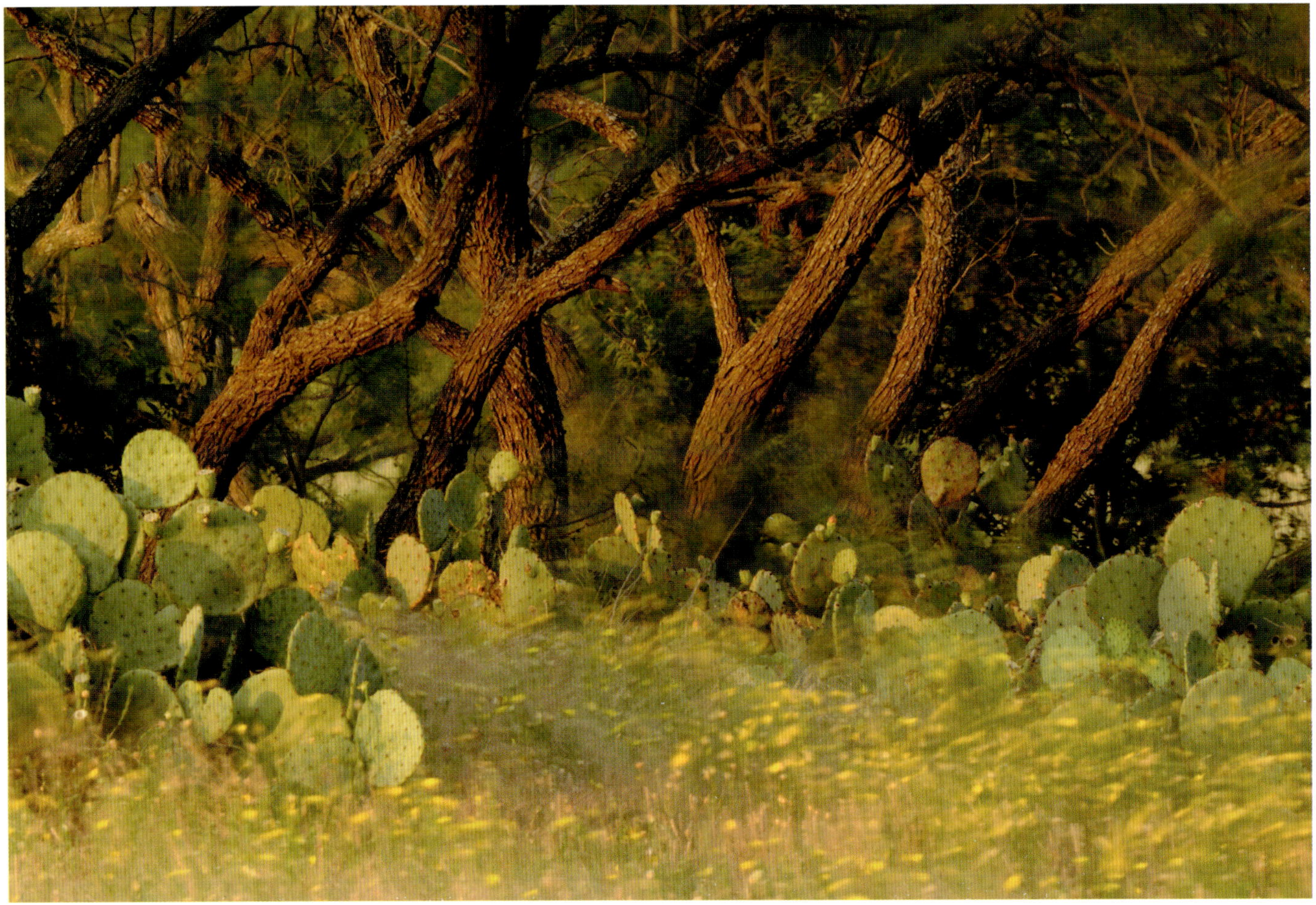

Karnes County

Prairie and Passing Rainstorm

Established in 1854, the county was named for Henry Karnes, a soldier in the Texas Revolution. By 1853, Anglo settlers, led by Thomas Ruckman and Lewis S. Owings—who had founded Helena—petitioned the state legislature to form a new county from portions of Bexar, Gonzales, DeWitt, Goliad, and San Patricio Counties.

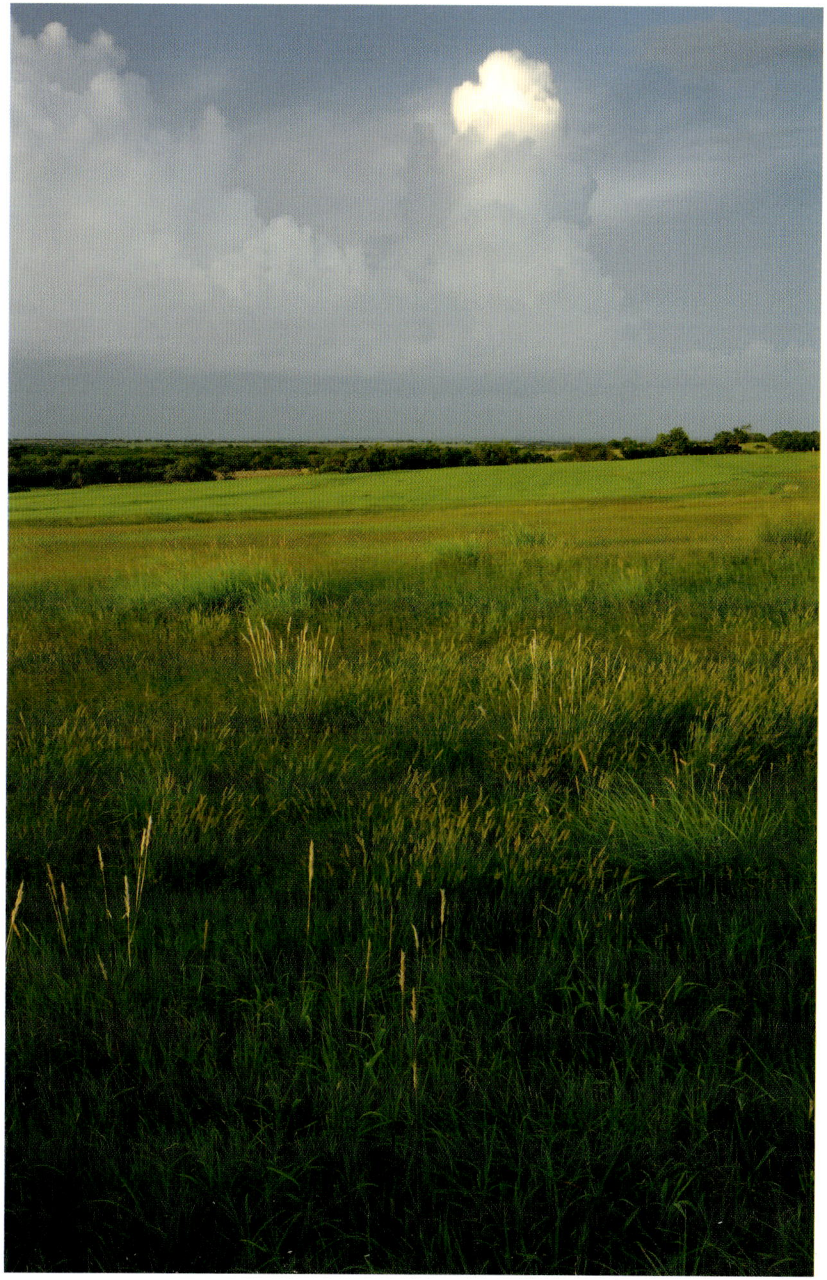

Kaufman County

Cattle Egrets and Farm Pond

The county is named for David Spangler Kaufman, a Jewish Texas state senator and the second Jewish member of the United States House of Representatives. The county was founded in 1848. In 1861, by a three-fourths majority, Kaufman County's citizens voted in favor of the state's secession from the Union. During the four years of the Civil War, the county contributed several companies of soldiers, most of whom fought in Elkanah B. Greer's regiment.

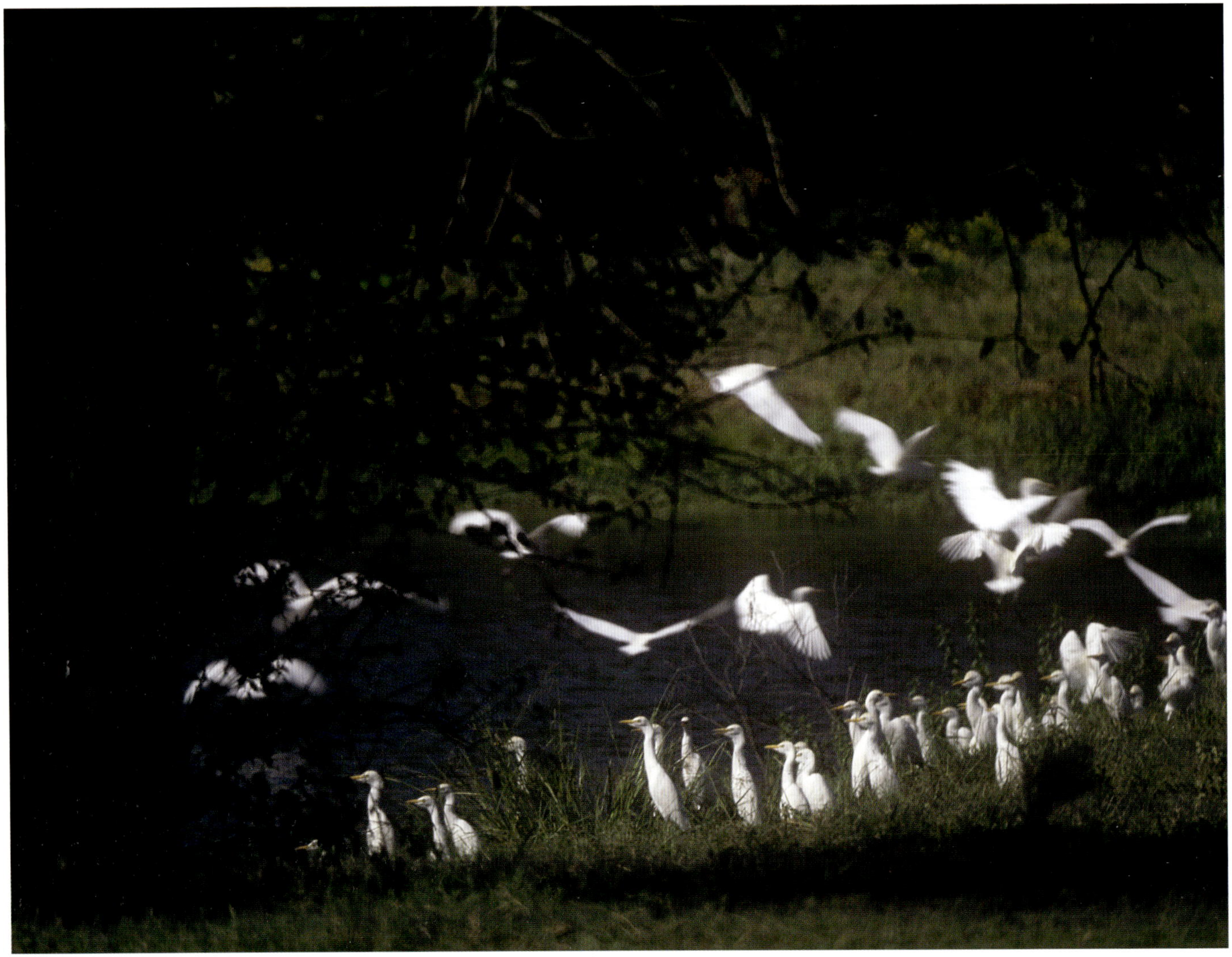

Kendall County

Hill Country Sunset

Kendall County is named for George Wilkins Kendall, an early journalist and sheep rancher who gained national fame as a war correspondent during the Mexican-American War. The county was organized in 1862. In 1861, Unionists from Kerr, Gillespie, and Kendall Counties participated in the formation of the Union League, a secret organization to support President Abraham Lincoln's policies.

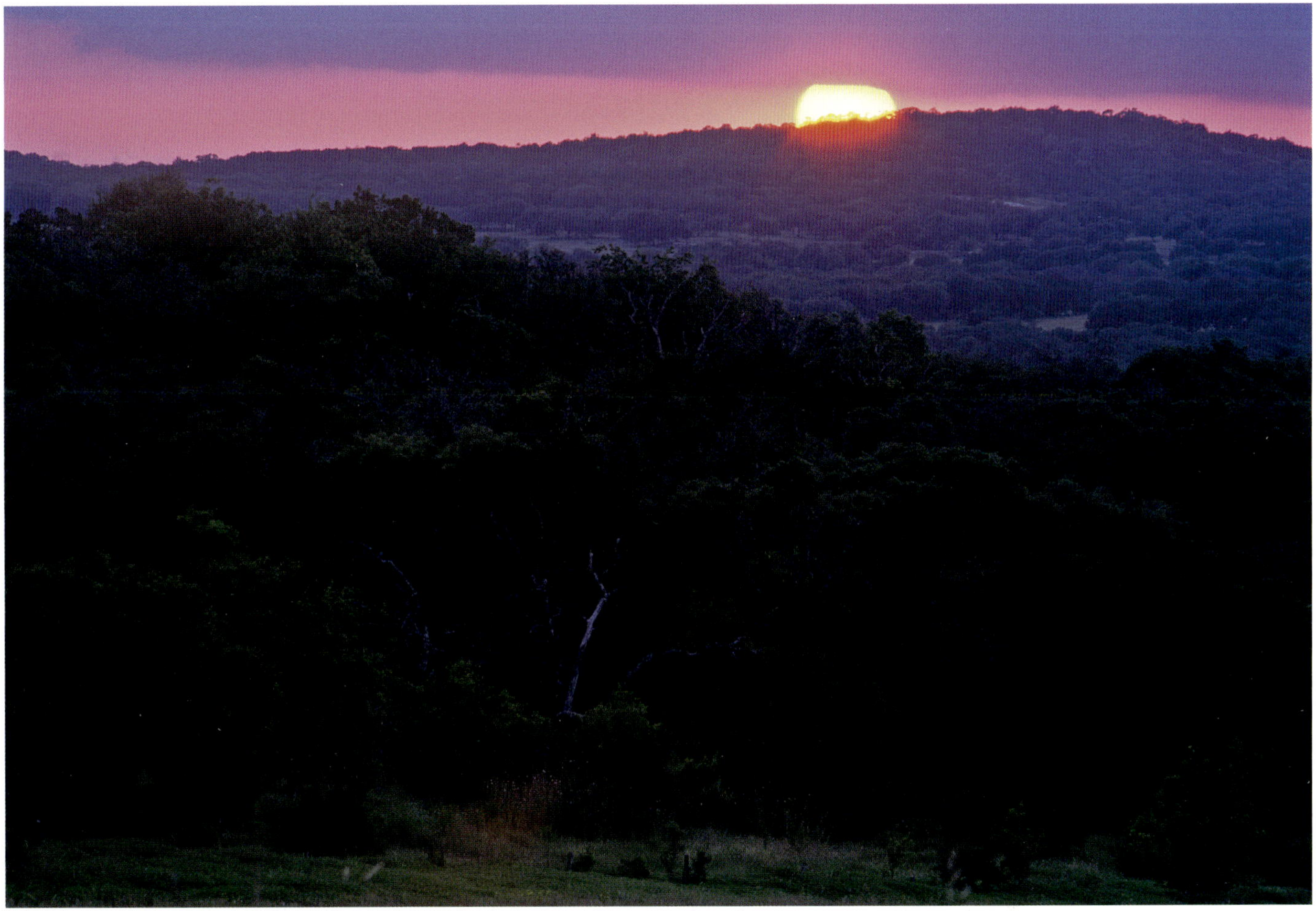

Kenedy County

Wildflowers and Mesquite Tree

The county was founded in 1921 and is named for Mifflin Kenedy, an early rancher and land speculator. The King Ranch, of which Mifflin Kenedy was a partner prior to 1868, covers a large part of the county.

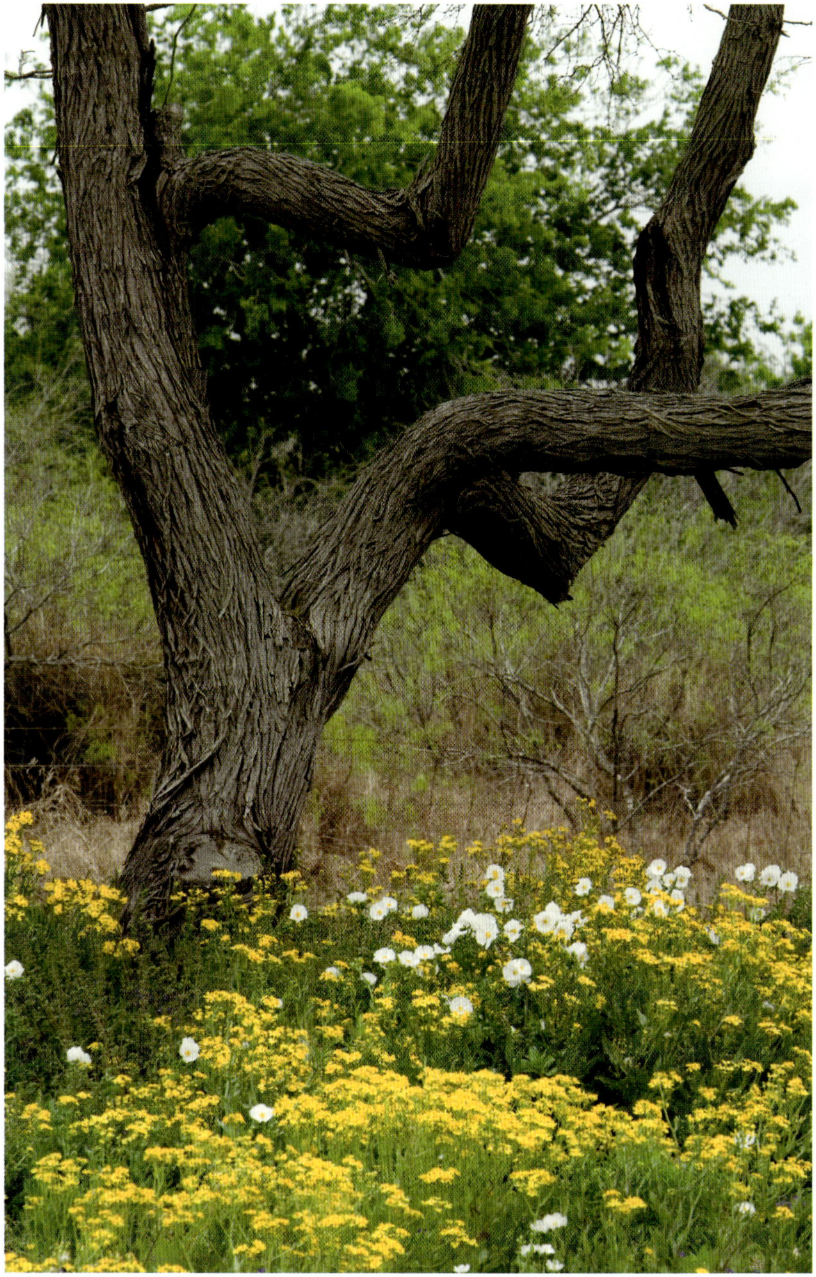

Kent County

Swallows over the Double Mountain Fork of the Brazos River

Andrew Kent, who died at the Battle of the Alamo, is the namesake for the county, which was formed in 1876. By 1930, Kent County became less dominated by the cattle industry and more focused on crop production. In 1920, the census counted fewer than 18,000 cattle. Cotton—the most important crop—was planted on more than 19,000 acres, and more than 7,000 acres were planted in corn and wheat that year.

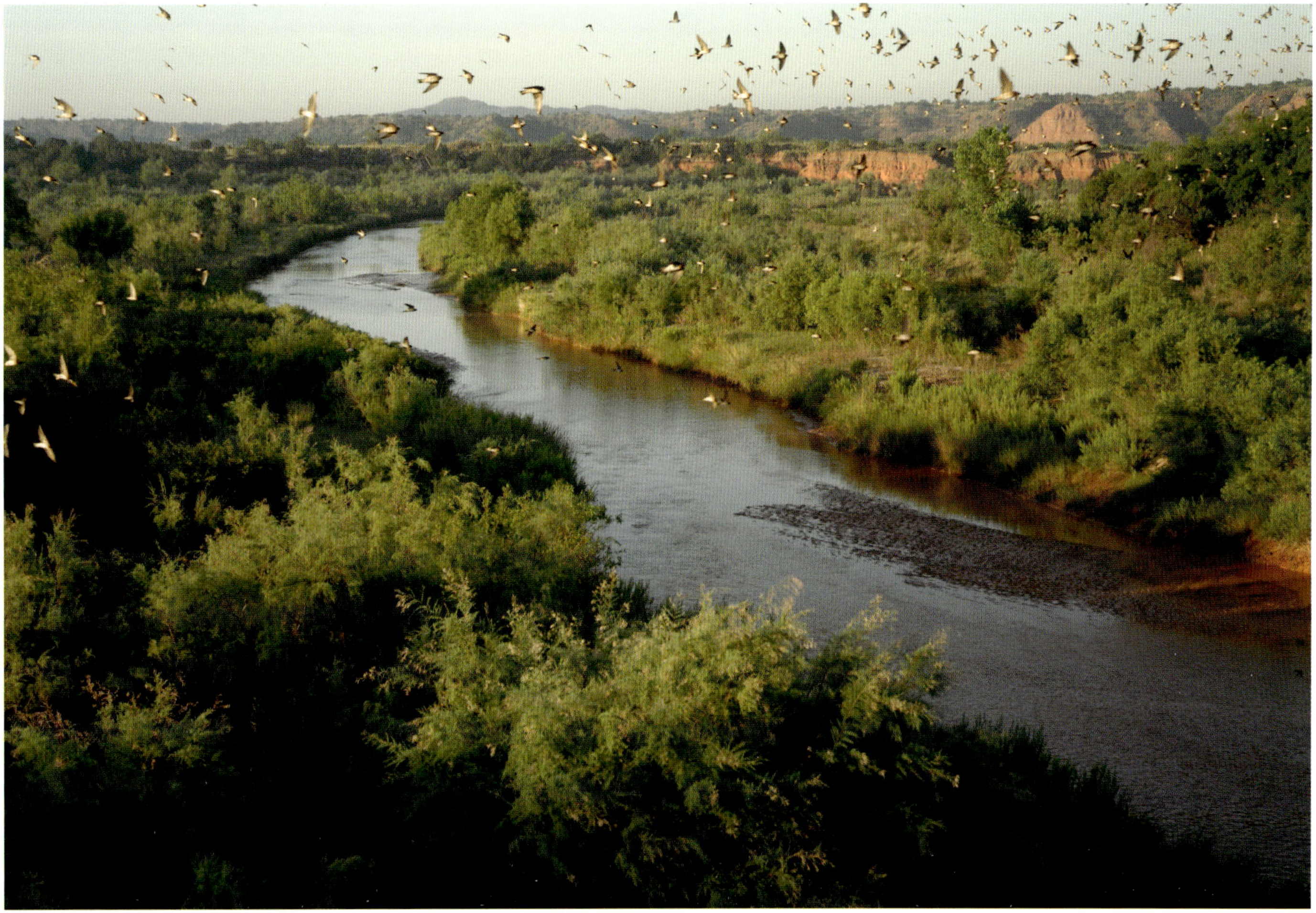

Kerr County

Late Afternoon along the Guadalupe River

Named for James Kerr, an early colonist in Texas and a soldier in the Texas Revolution, the county was formed in 1856. Shortly before the establishment of the county, the Texas State Convention of Germans met in San Antonio on May 14–15, 1854, and adopted a political, social, and religious platform that included the abolition of slavery and capital punishment.

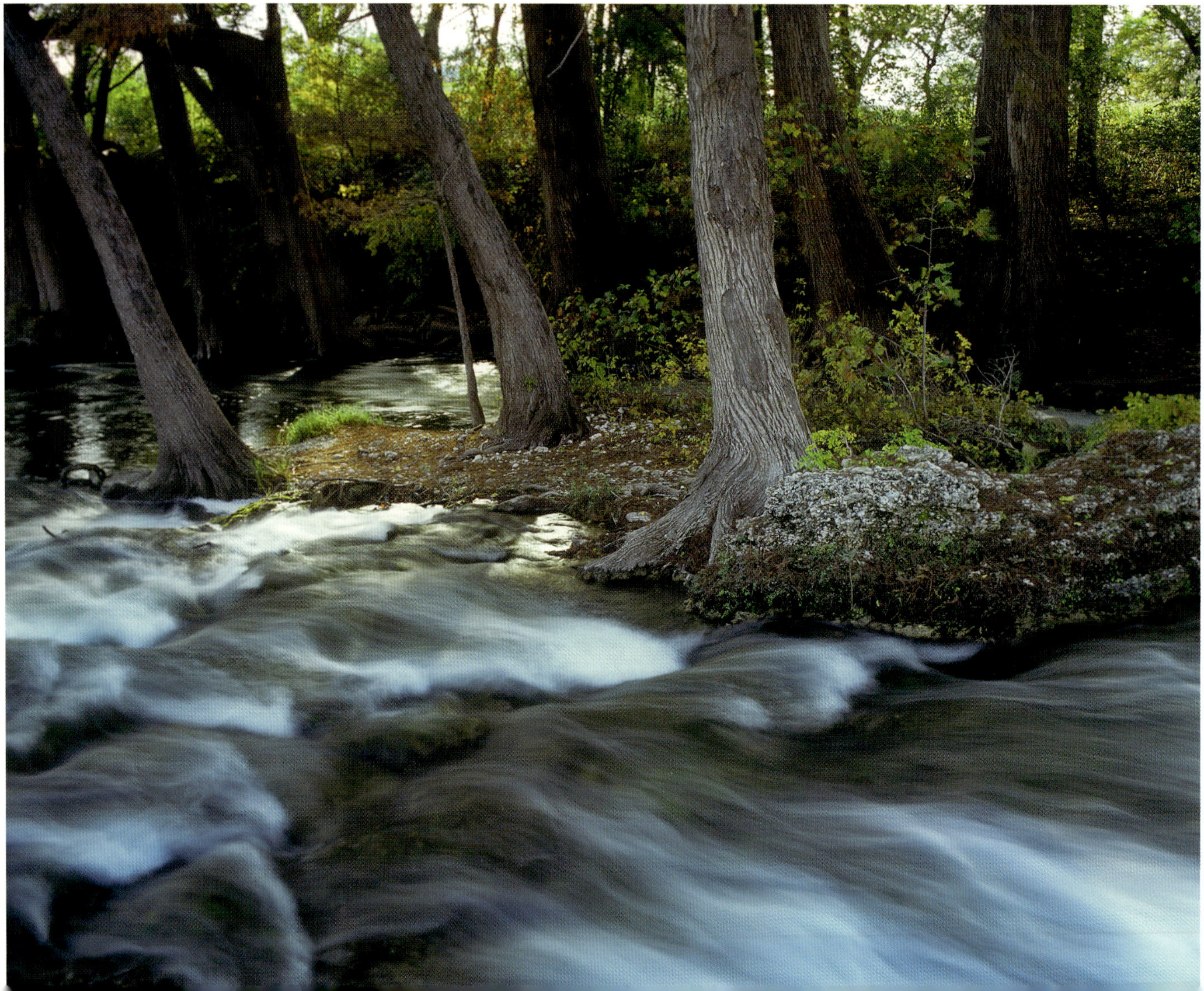

Kimble County

South Llano River State Park

The county is named for George C. Kimbell, who died at the Battle of the Alamo. The spelling differs due to an error in the bill creating the county, which was passed in 1858. Kimble County continued to grow during the early twentieth century. The population in 1900 was 2,500. The twentieth century brought many amenities to the county that were previously unavailable. Four Mile Dam was completed in 1904. The first telephone system came to Junction in 1905, and the first banks opened a year later. Electric lights came to Junction in 1917, and gas stations were introduced soon after.

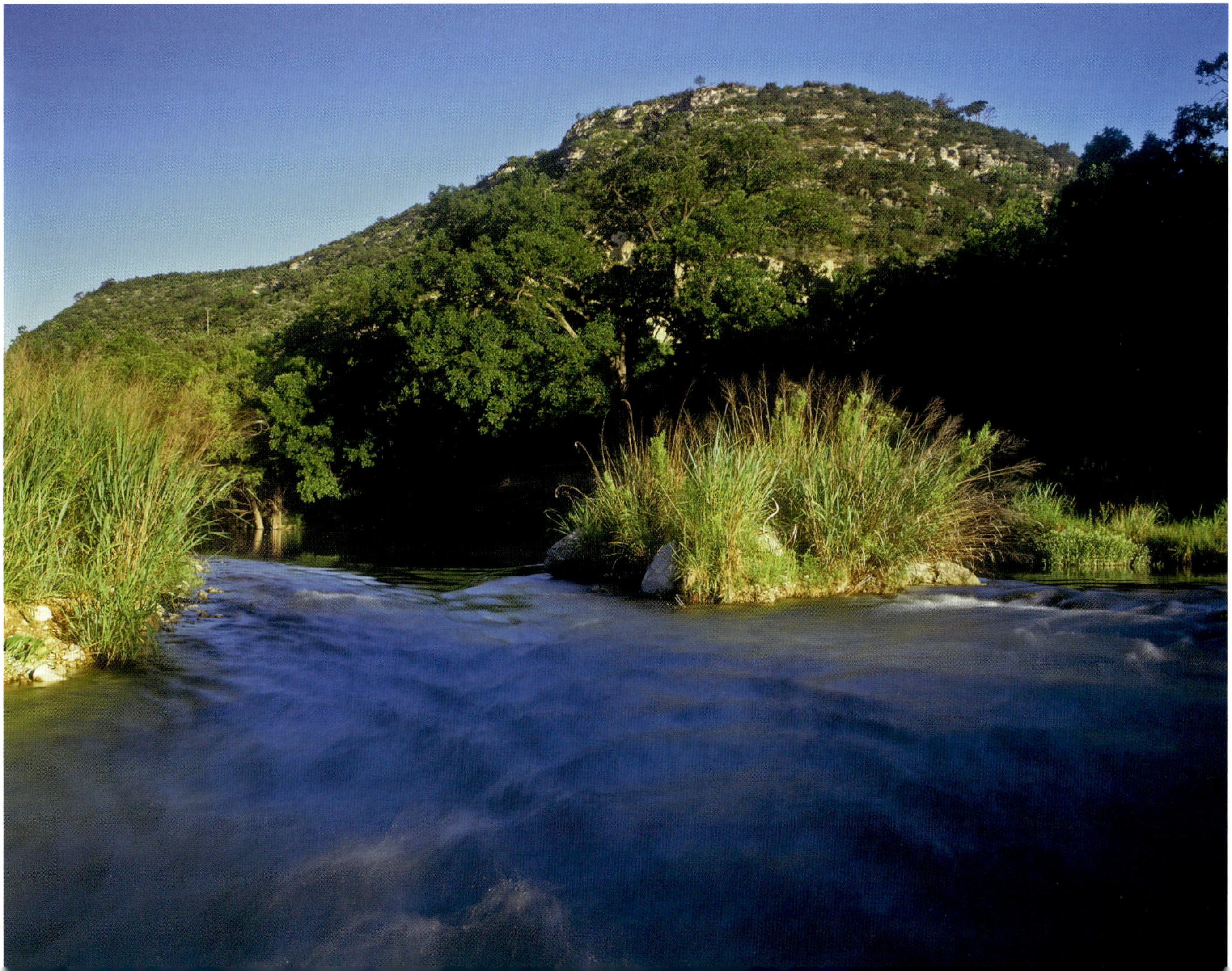

King County

Rugged Ranchland of the Panhandle

The county was founded in 1876 and is named for William Phillip King, who died at the Battle of the Alamo. Apache and Comanche were early Native American tribes in the area. The Red River War of 1874–1875 was a United States Army campaign to force the removal of Indians in Texas and their relocation to reservations to open the region to white settlers.

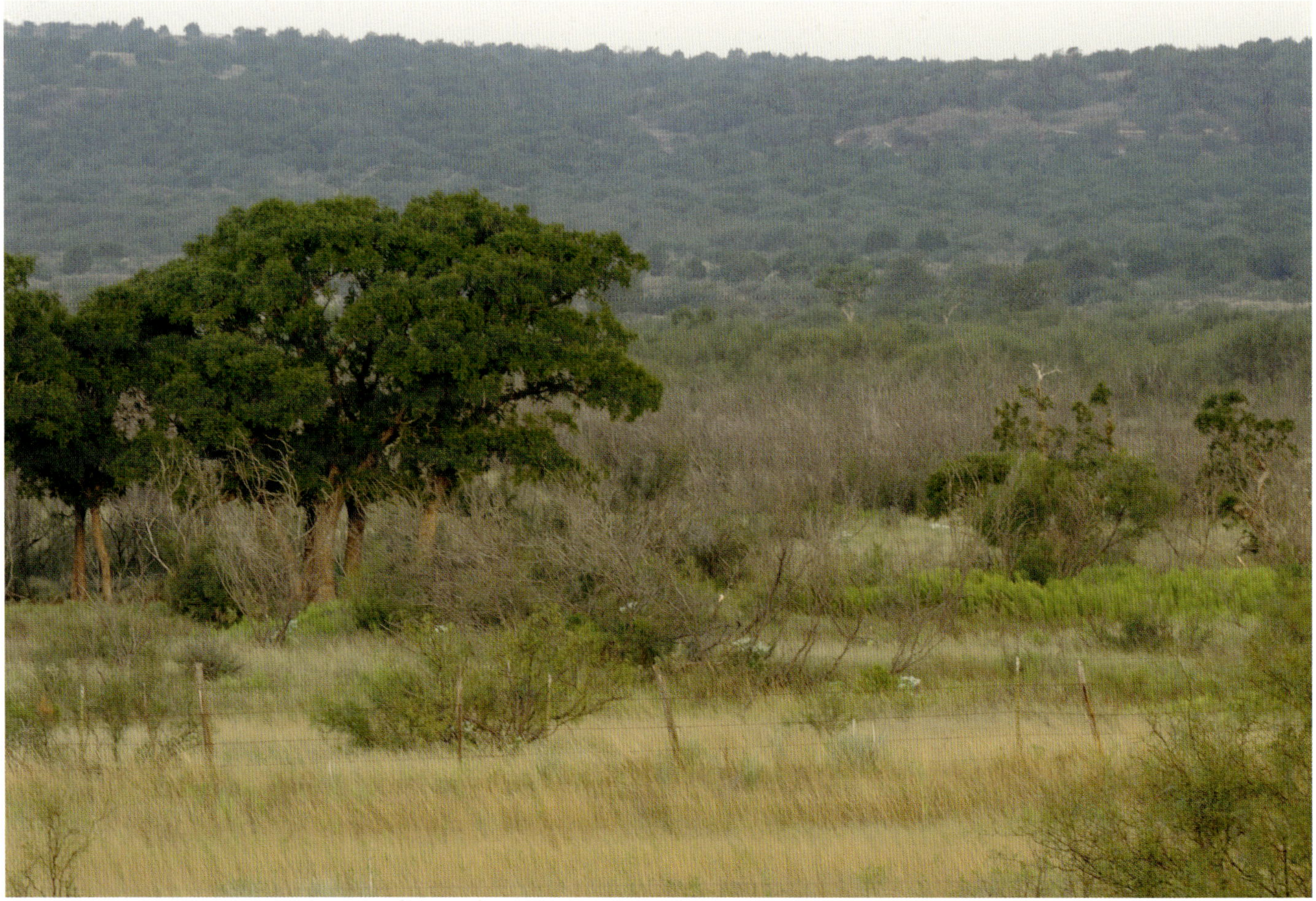

Kinney County

Limestone Outcrop and Prickly Pear Cactus

Named for Henry Lawrence Kinney, a Texas state senator and land speculator, the county was formed in 1850. James T. "Happy" Shahan constructed Alamo Village on his ranch near Brackettville during the late 1950s for the filming of the 1960 John Wayne epic *The Alamo*. Preserved as a tourist attraction, Alamo Village continued to serve as a set for hundreds of movies and documentaries.

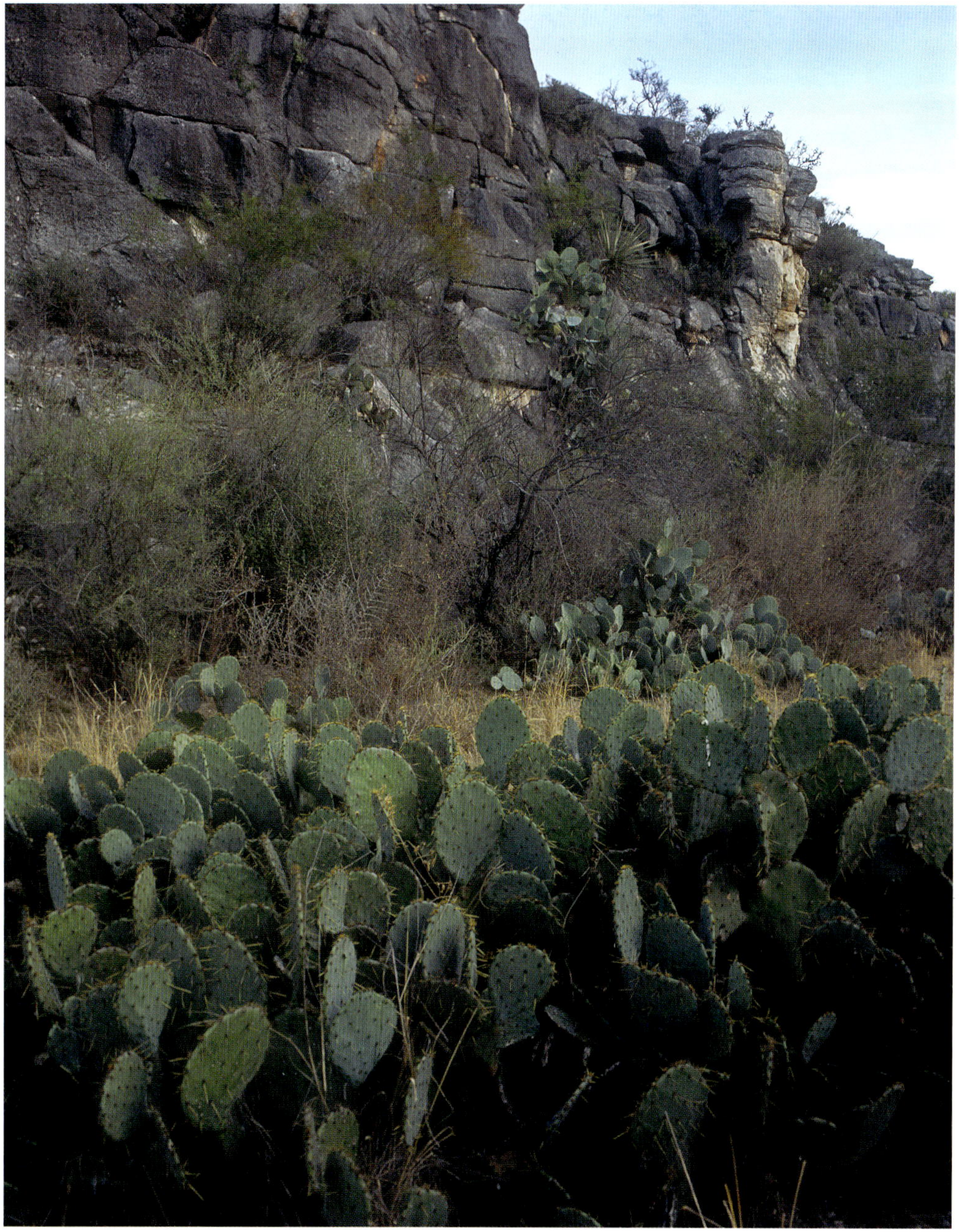

Kleberg County

Sunset over the Gulf of Mexico

The county was named for Robert Justus Kleberg, an early German settler and soldier at the Battle of San Jacinto. The county was established in 1913. The county's namesake, Robert Kleberg, supported the cause of the Confederacy. When the Civil War broke out, he raised a company of militia, but because of his advanced age he was not received into active service.

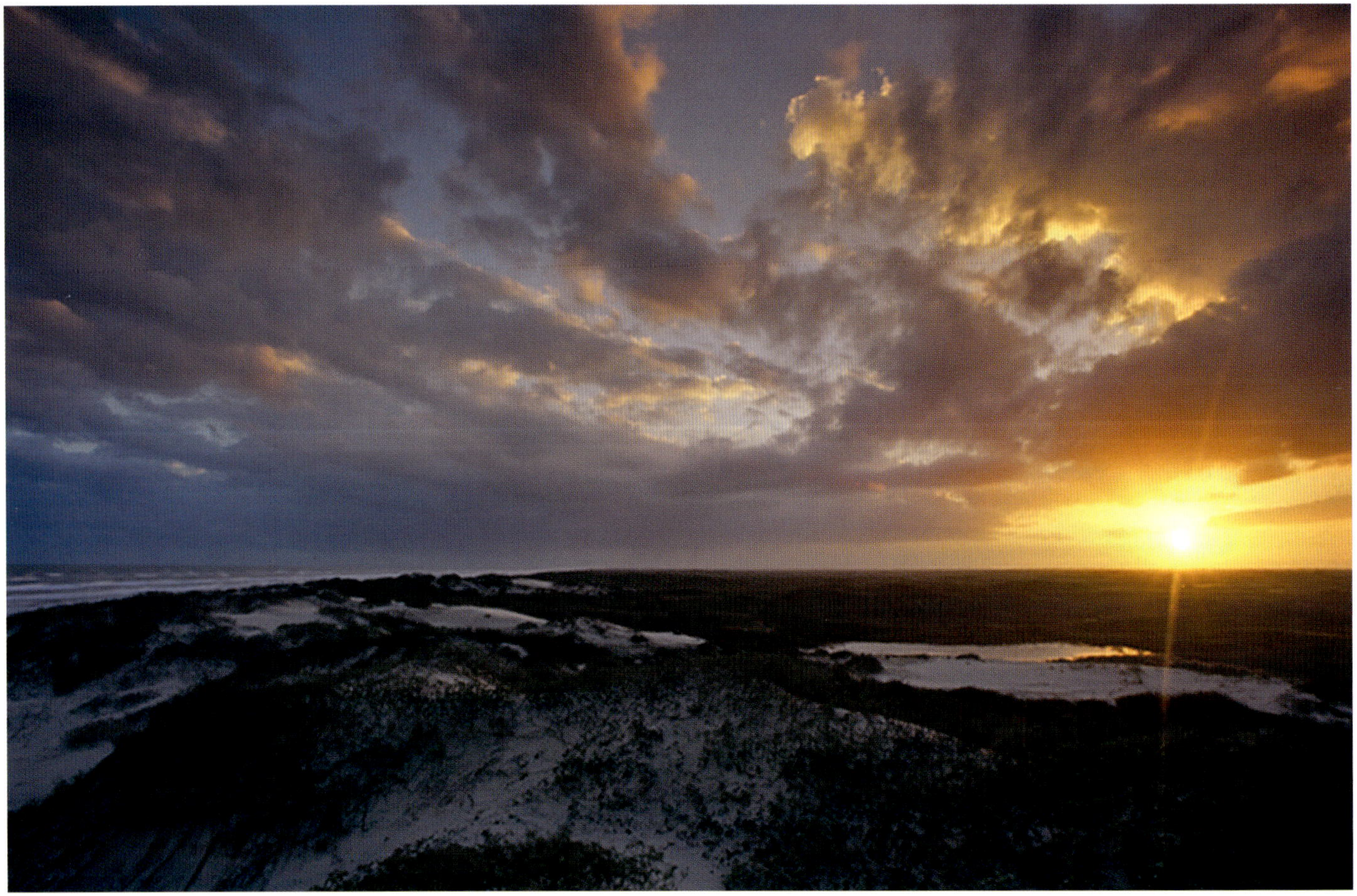

Knox County

An Autumn Sunrise

Formed in 1858, the county is named for Henry Knox, the first secretary of war of the United States. In 1855, elements of the Second United States Cavalry, commanded by Colonels Albert Sidney Johnston and Robert E. Lee, patrolled the vicinity. Both Johnston and Lee later became prominent Confederate generals.

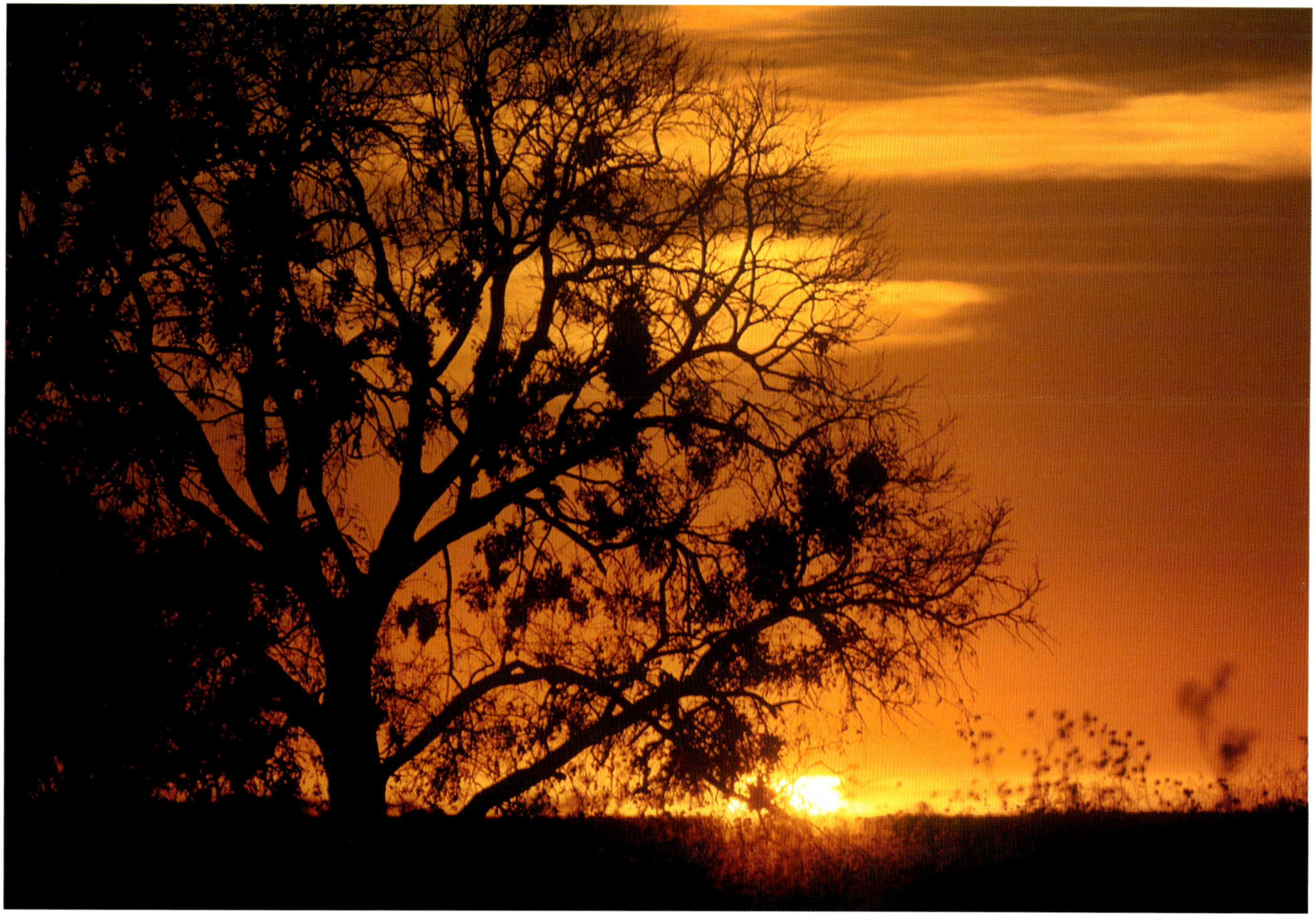

La Salle County

Blooming Yucca

The county is named for René Robert Cavelier Sieur de La Salle, the French explorer who traveled through Texas. The county was formed in 1858. In the early 1880s, the International Great Northern Railroad laid tracks to the county. Around this time, outlaws were gradually eliminated from the area, and the last Indian raid happened in 1878.

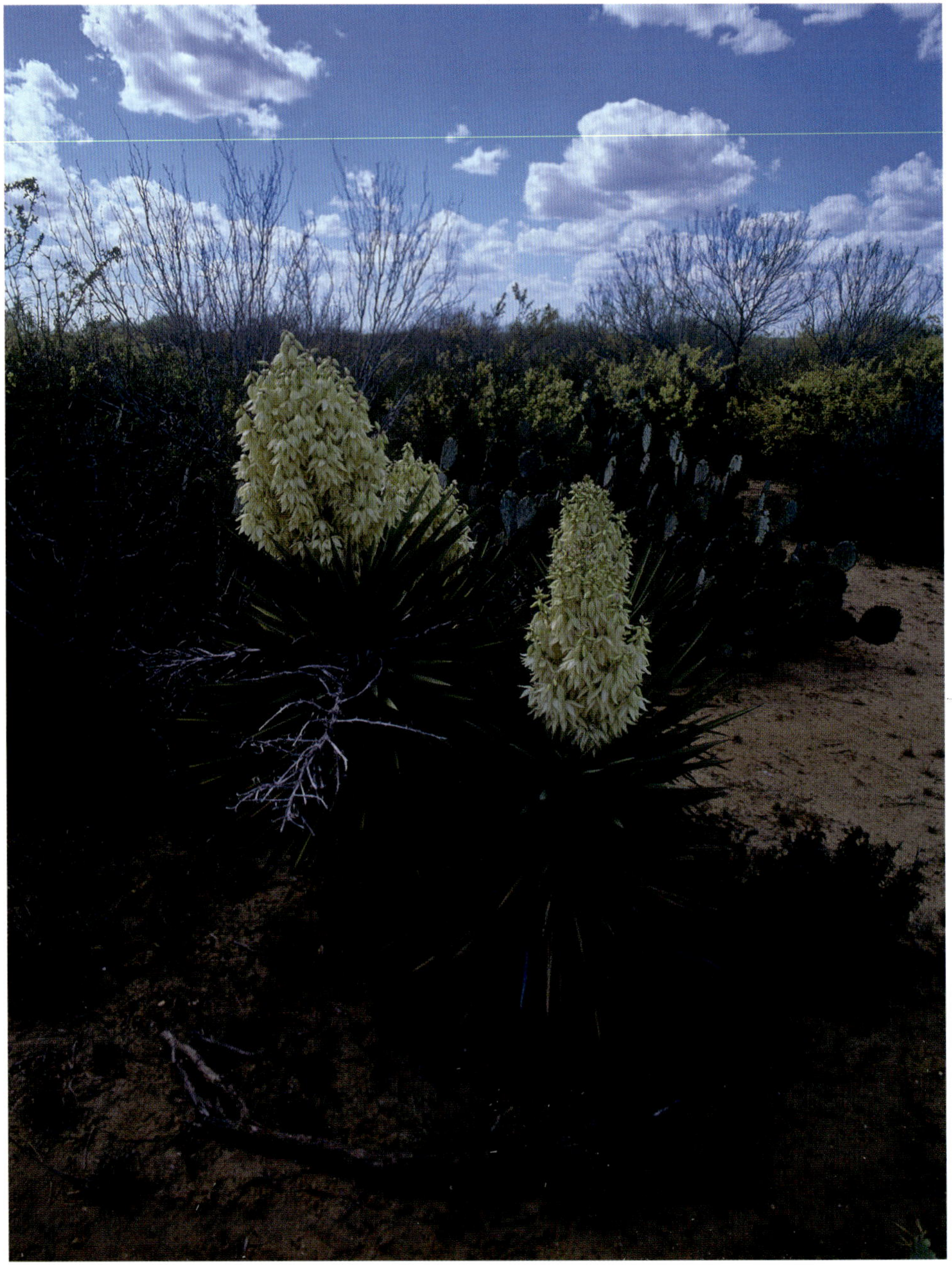

Lamar County

Sunset over Pat Mayse Lake

The county is named for Mirabeau Buonaparte Lamar, the third president of the Republic of Texas. Lamar County was formed in 1840. The county was well situated to play a significant role in the transportation of goods and merchandise in North Texas. As early as 1844, the Texas Congress passed an act to form a commission to plan and build the Central National Road of the Republic of Texas. This road proceeded from the Red River, near Wright's Landing in Red River County, across Lamar County to Paris, and then southwest to Dallas, where it connected with other major roads of the period.

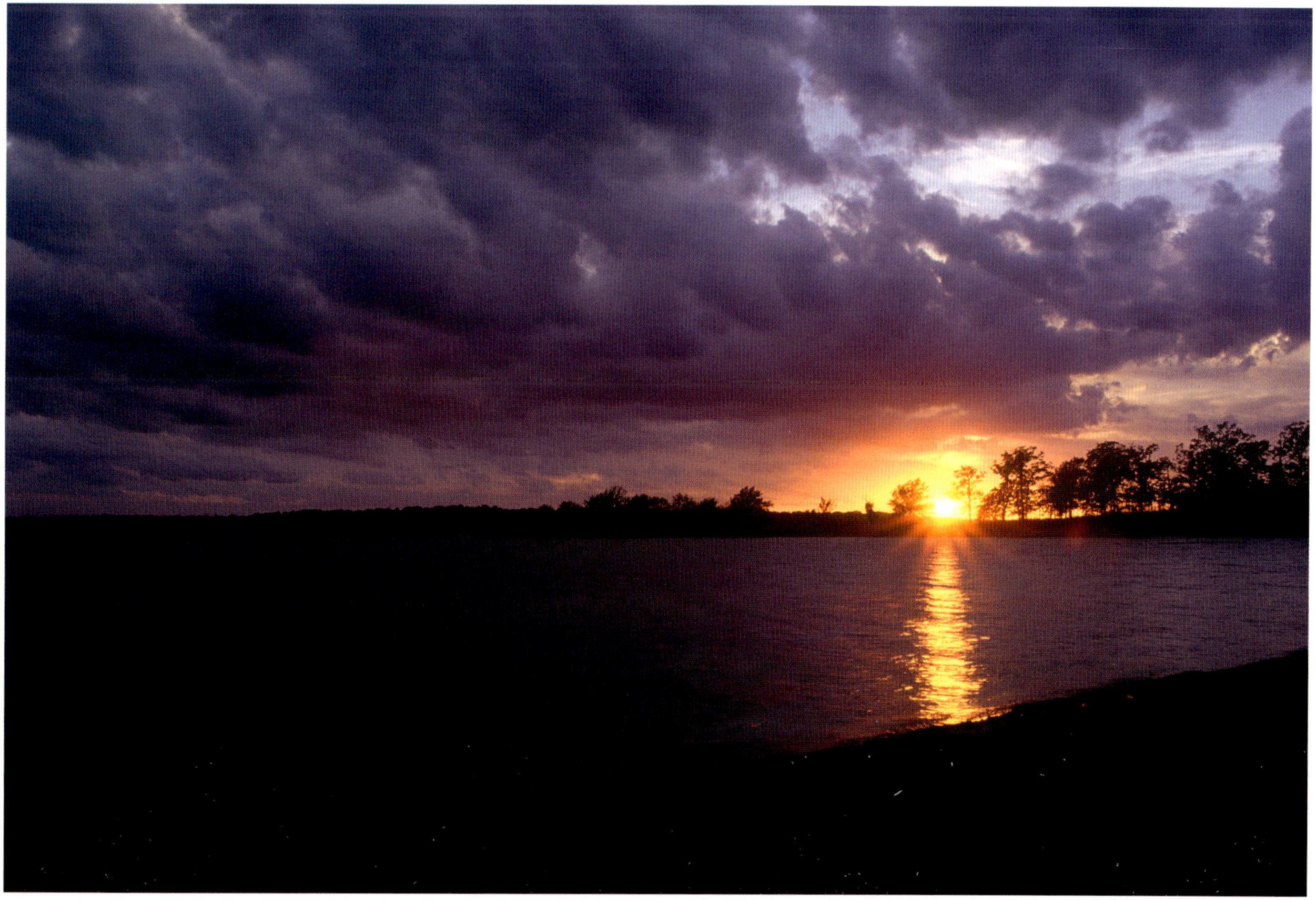

Lamb County

Crop of Sunflowers in the Panhandle

The county was organized in 1876 and is named for George A. Lamb, who died at the Battle of San Jacinto. Ranching arrived in the area when the vast XIT Ranch—occupying more than 3 million acres of land—was established in 1885.

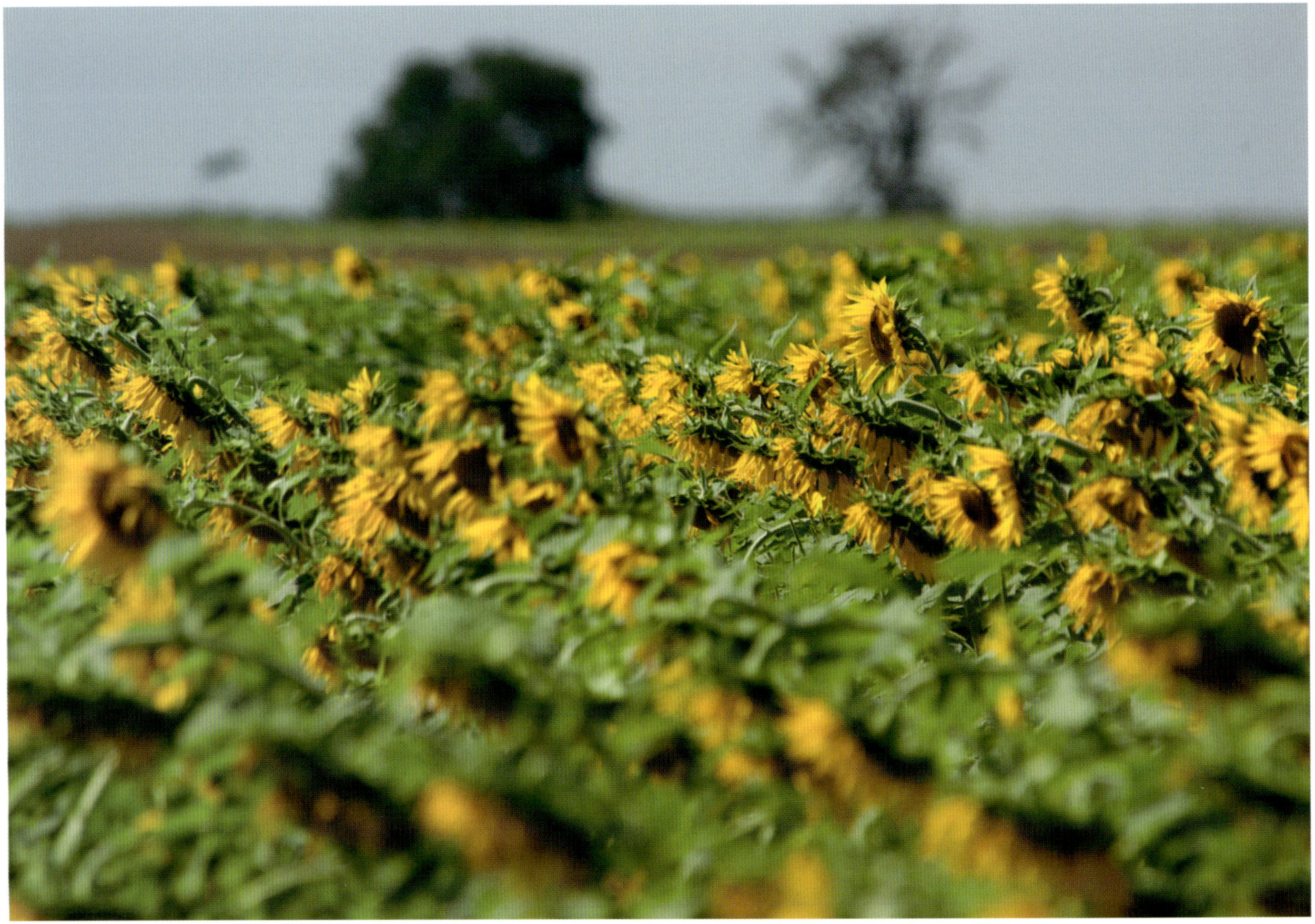

Lampasas County

Hill Country Scene along FM 581 near Lometa

Formed in 1856, the county is named for the Lampasas River (*lampasas* is Spanish for "lilies"). On February 10, 1873, Governor Davis issued a proclamation prohibiting the carrying of sidearms in Lampasas. On March 14 of that year, Captain Thomas Williams and seven state policemen entered Lampasas to enforce the proclamation. The state police immediately arrested Bill Bowen for carrying a gun in town. Bowen persuaded Captain Williams and two of his men to enter Jerry Scott's Lampasas Saloon, which led to a gunfight between the state police and the Horrell brothers and their associates. Three officers were killed in the saloon, and a fourth was fatally wounded while trying to escape.

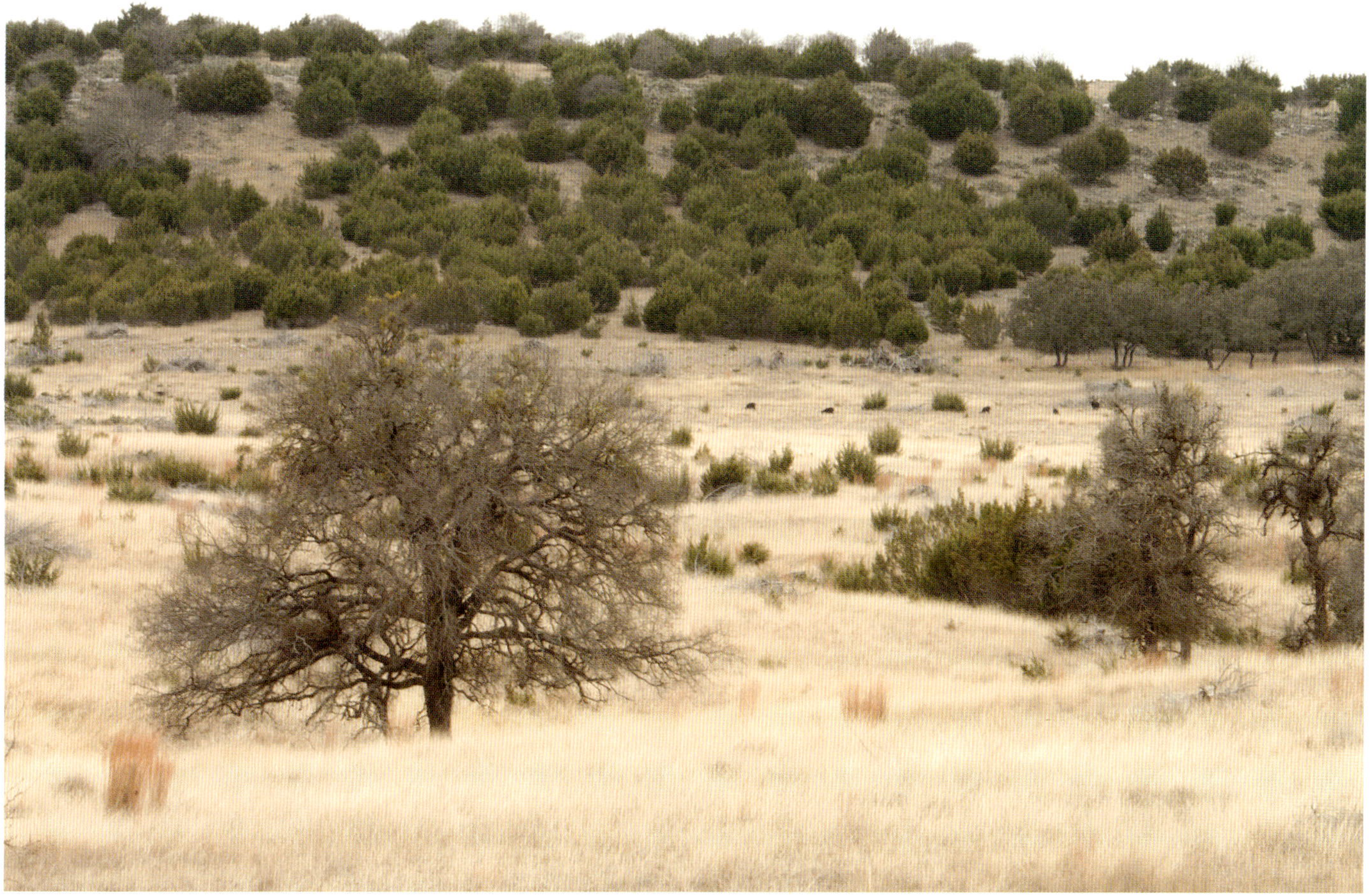

Lavaca County

Sunflowers and Oak Trees

Formed in 1842, the county is named for the Lavaca River. *La vaca* is Spanish for "the cow." On the eve of the Civil War, Lavaca County was in most ways typical of the counties of the region: decidedly southern in character and outlook, with a rapidly developing plantation economy. Not surprisingly, given its large number of slaveholders, the citizenry overwhelmingly supported the Southern cause. Nearly 95 percent of those who went to the polls voted for secession. Lavaca County men volunteered for the Confederate army in large numbers, many of them serving in Whitfield's Legion, the Eighth Texas Cavalry.

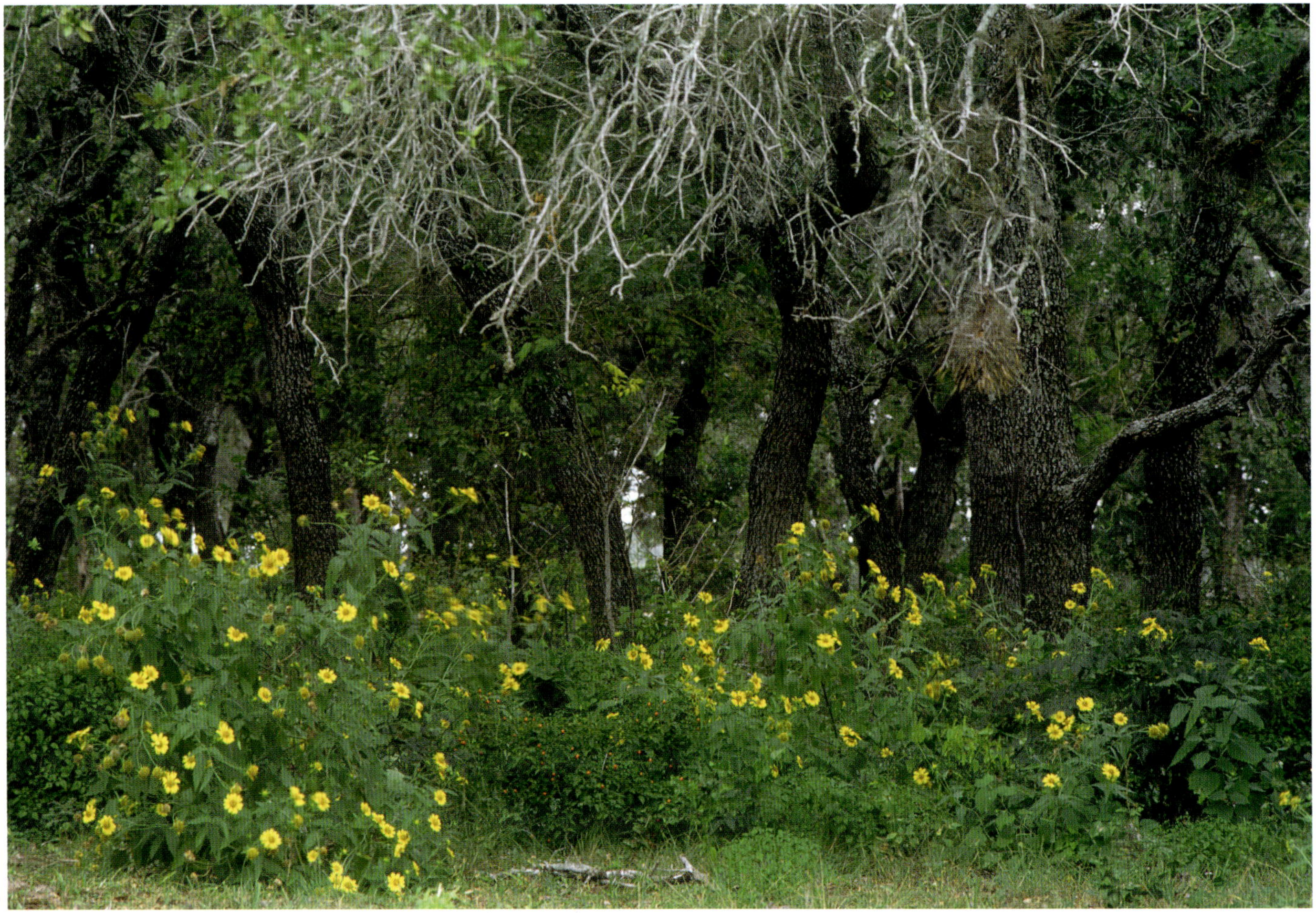

Lee County

Lake Somerville State Park, Nails Creek Unit

Lee County is named for Robert E. Lee, the commanding general of the Confederate forces during the Civil War. The county was formed in 1874, shortly after Lee's death. The first known white settler was James Gotier, who settled on Rabbs Creek, in southern Lee County, in 1835. Before being killed by Indians in 1837, he laid out a pioneer trail known as Gotier's Trace, which is believed to have led from his cabin on Rabbs Creek to San Felipe and Bastrop, thus linking lower and upper Austin colonies.

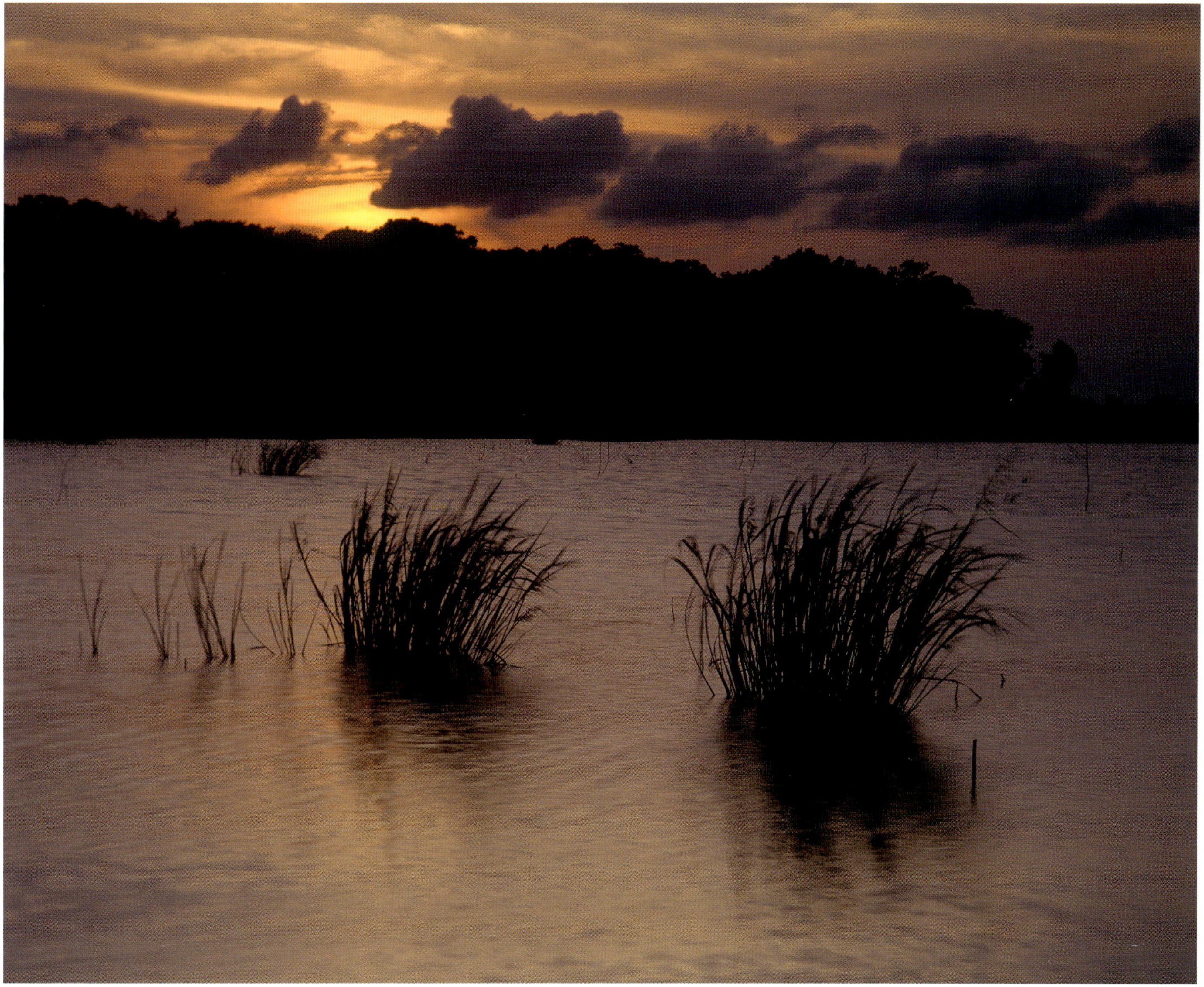

Leon County

Fort Boggy State Park

Leon County was formed in 1846. The name of the county is disputed. It is believed to be named either for Mexican impresario Martín de León, who founded Victoria, Texas, or the león, a local variety of yellow wolf. In 1837, settlers constructed a blockhouse on Boggy Creek and named it Fort Boggy. It offered protection to settlers who located nearby, and soon a small community developed adjacent to the fort.

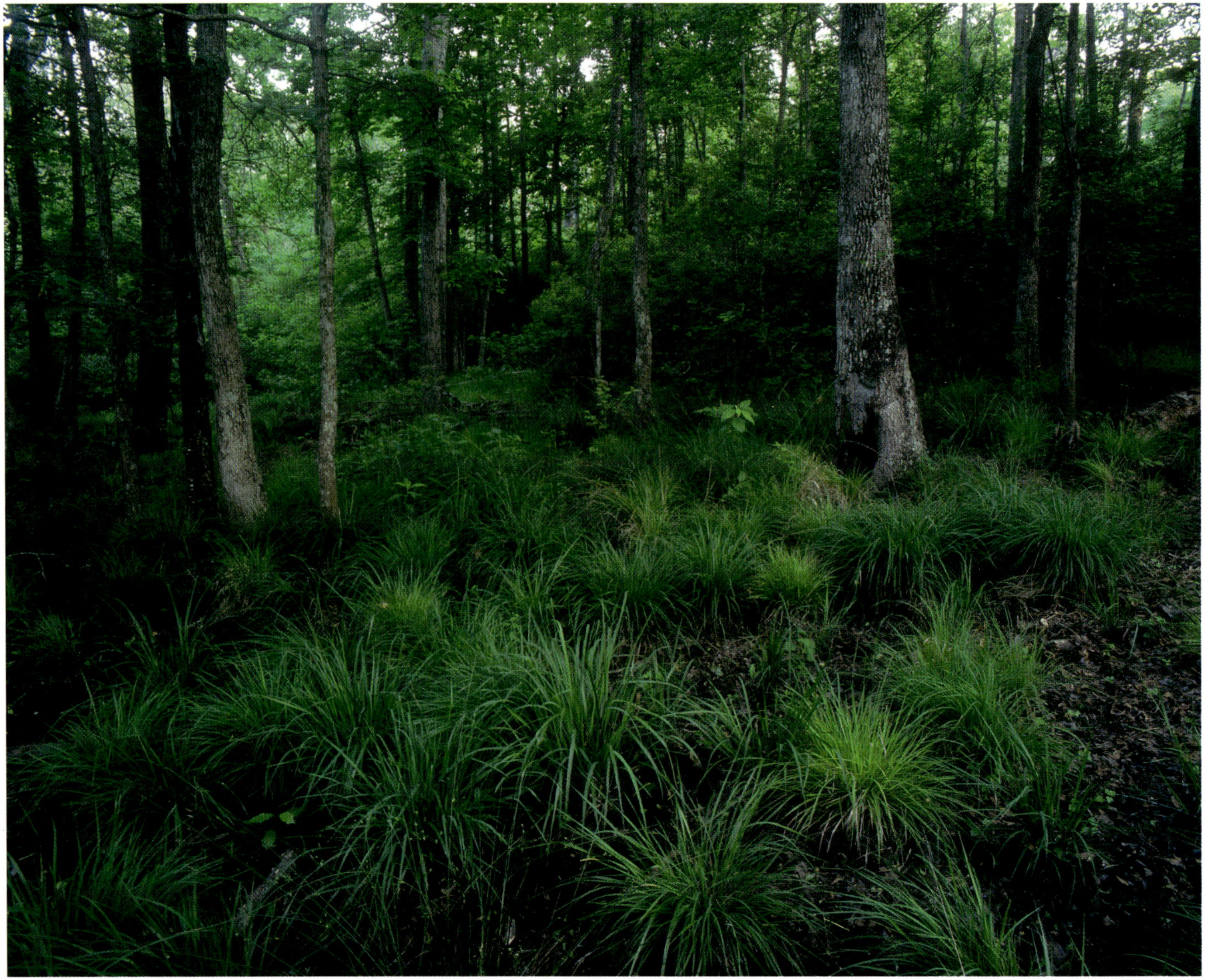

Liberty County

Trinity River Sunset

One of the original twenty-three Republic of Texas counties, Liberty County was established in 1836. The county is named for the success of the Mexican War of Independence or for Liberty, Mississippi. The northern portion of the county is part of the Big Thicket, a once-impenetrable wilderness wooded with pine, oak, ash, hickory, cypress, and walnut trees.

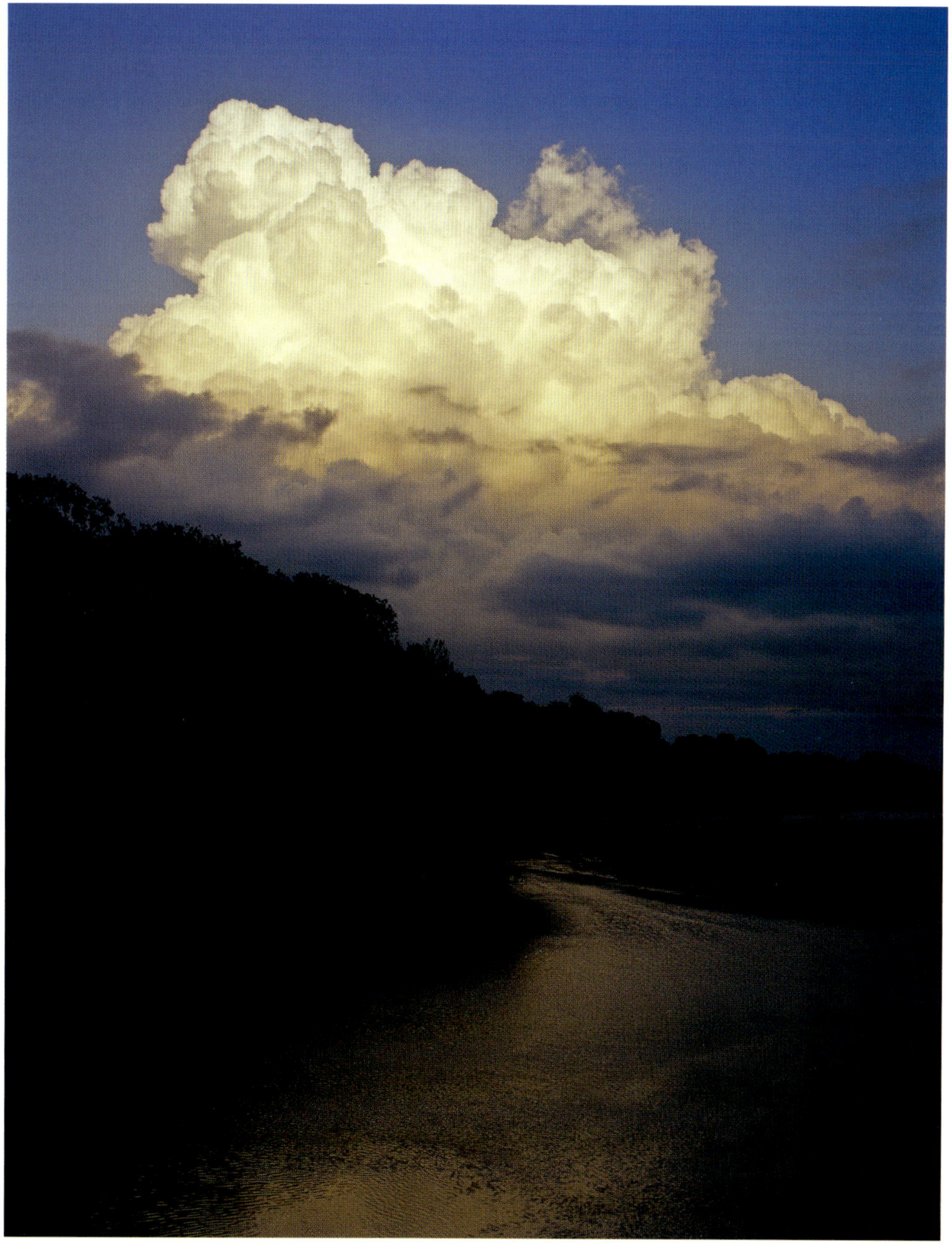

Limestone County

Fort Parker State Park

Limestone County is named for the limestone deposits in the area. The county was formed in 1846. Following the Civil War, Reconstruction in the county was so contentious, with racial violence and threats against the government, that on October 9,1871, Texas governor Edmund J. Davis declared the county to be under martial law.

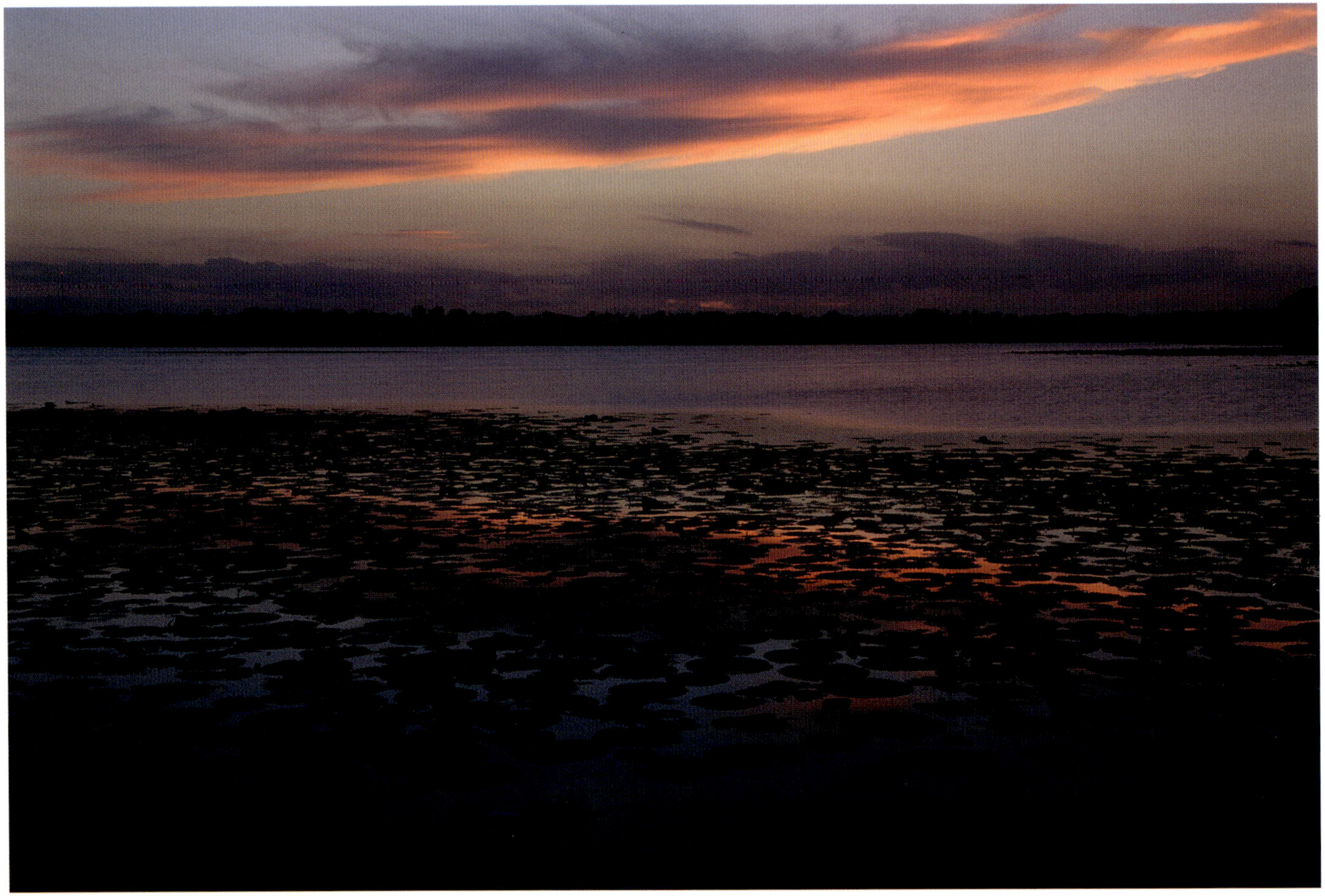

Lipscomb County

Sunrise on the High Plains

Formed in 1876, the county is named for Abner Smith Lipscomb, justice of the Texas Supreme Court (1846–1856) and secretary of state of the Republic of Texas (1840). Around 1919, many settlers of German origin from Kansas entered the northern part of the county, adding a distinctly ethnic atmosphere to any new towns formed.

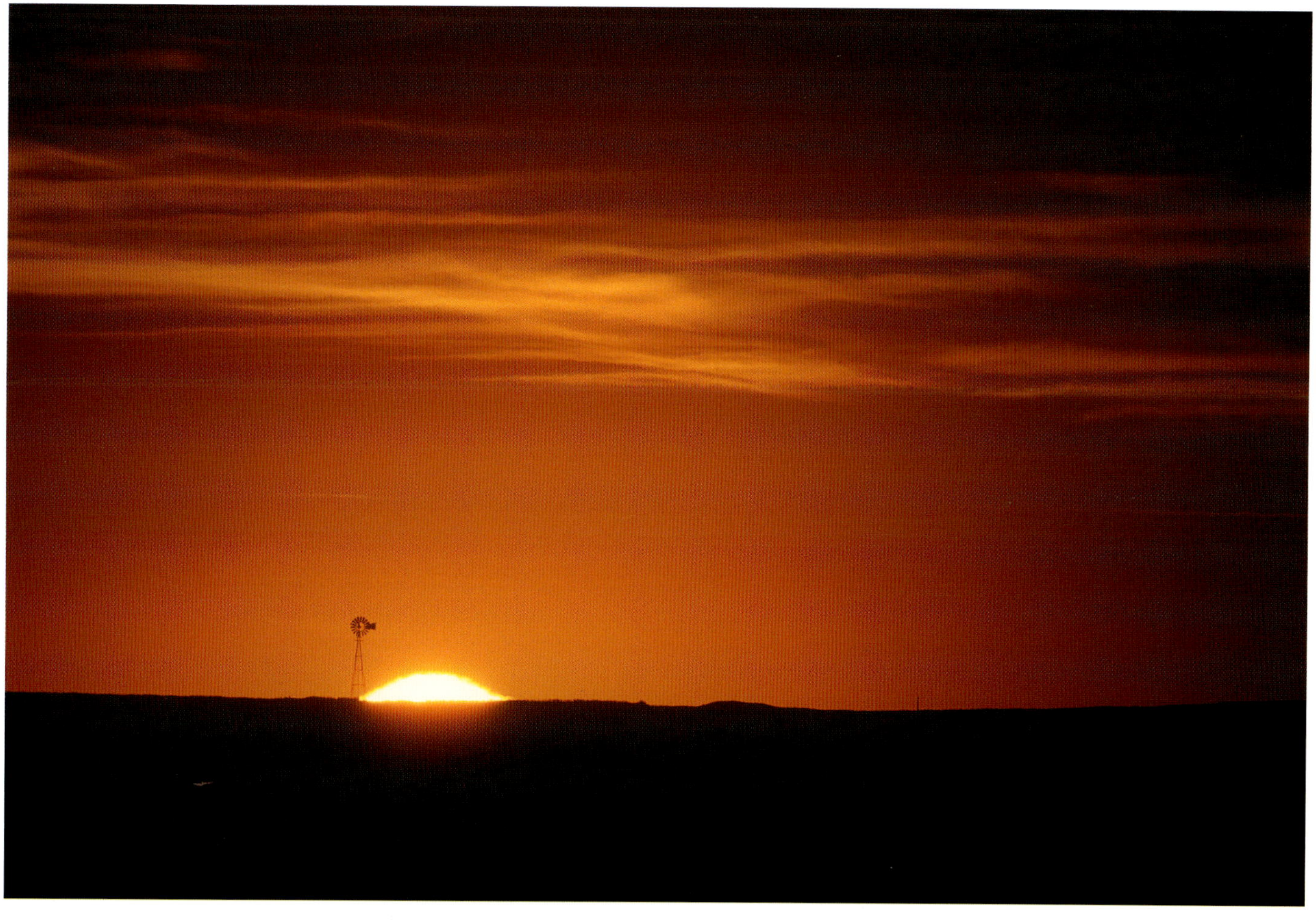

Live Oak County

Star Trails in Choke Canyon State Park

The county is named for the Texas live oak tree under which the petition for a new county was signed in 1856. At the time of the Texas Revolution and the end of the Mexican War in 1848, much of what is now Live Oak County lay in the disputed area between the Rio Grande and the Nueces. Neither the Republic of Texas nor the Mexican government could establish firm control over this strip of contested land, and it became a haven for fugitives and outlaws. When William Bollaert, an English land speculator, traveled through the area between the Nueces and Frio Rivers in 1844, the only people he encountered were convicts who had escaped from a prison in Laredo. The Republic of Texas finally asserted its claim to the disputed strip.

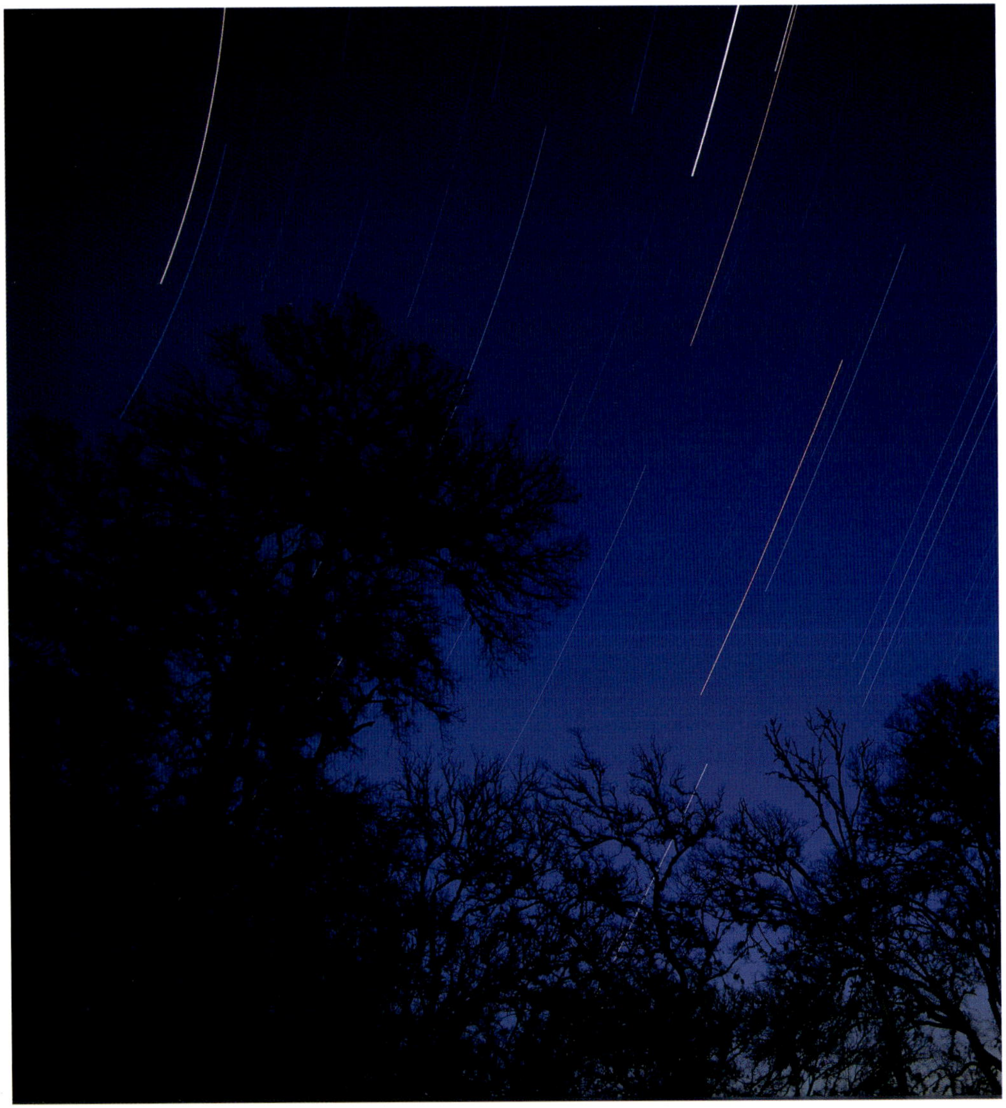

Llano County

Enchanted Rock State Natural Area

The county was founded in 1856, and it is named for the Llano River. *Llano* is Spanish for "plains." On August 4, 1873, Packsaddle Mountain became the site of the region's last battle with the Indians. The county's farming economy began to grow after threats of Indian attacks ceased.

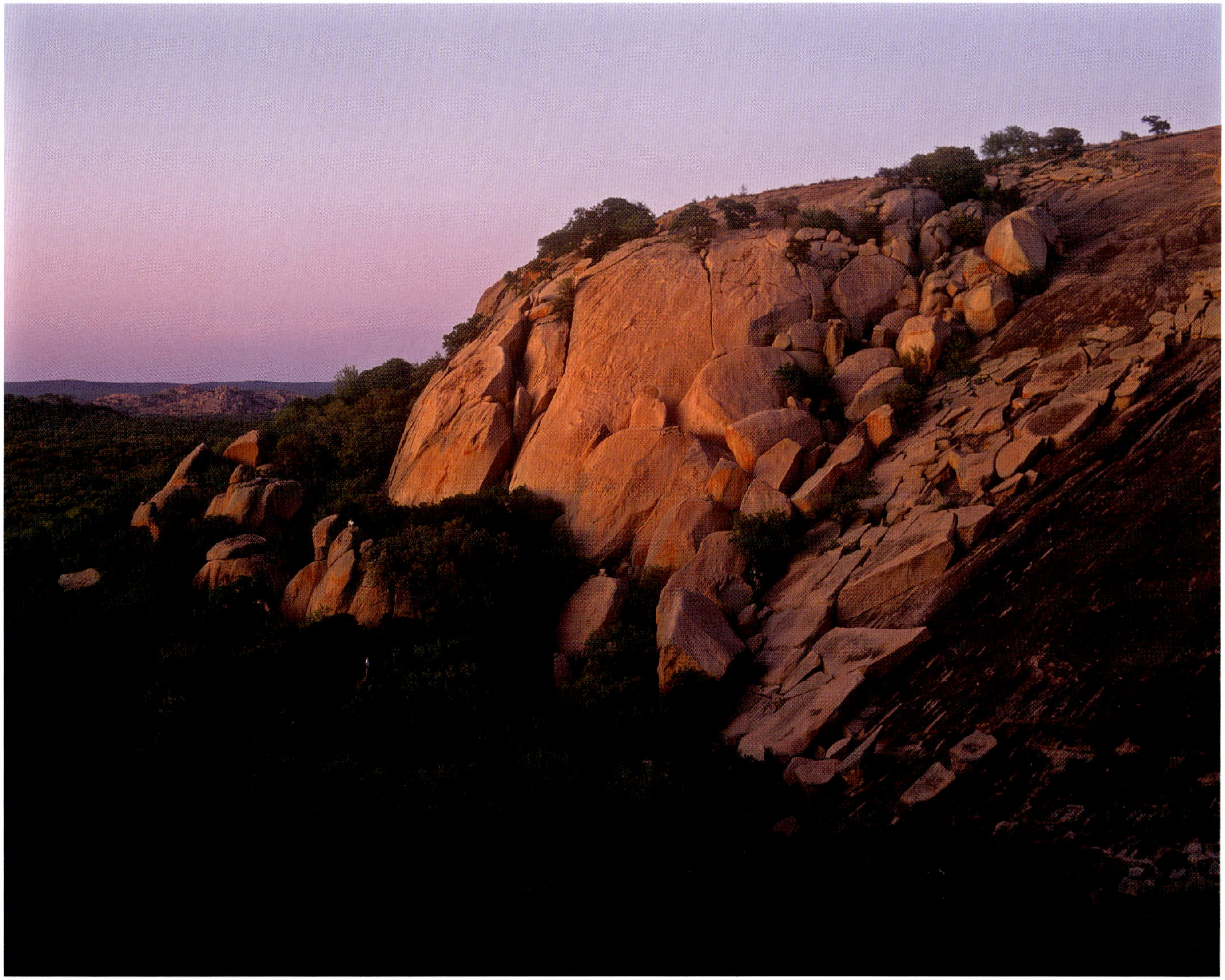

Loving County

Sunset over Red Bluff Lake

The county was established in 1931 and is named for Oliver Loving, a cattle rancher and pioneer of the cattle drive who, with Charles Goodnight, developed the Goodnight-Loving Trail. According to the 2010 US Census, Loving County had a population of eighty-two people, making Loving County the least populous county in the US.

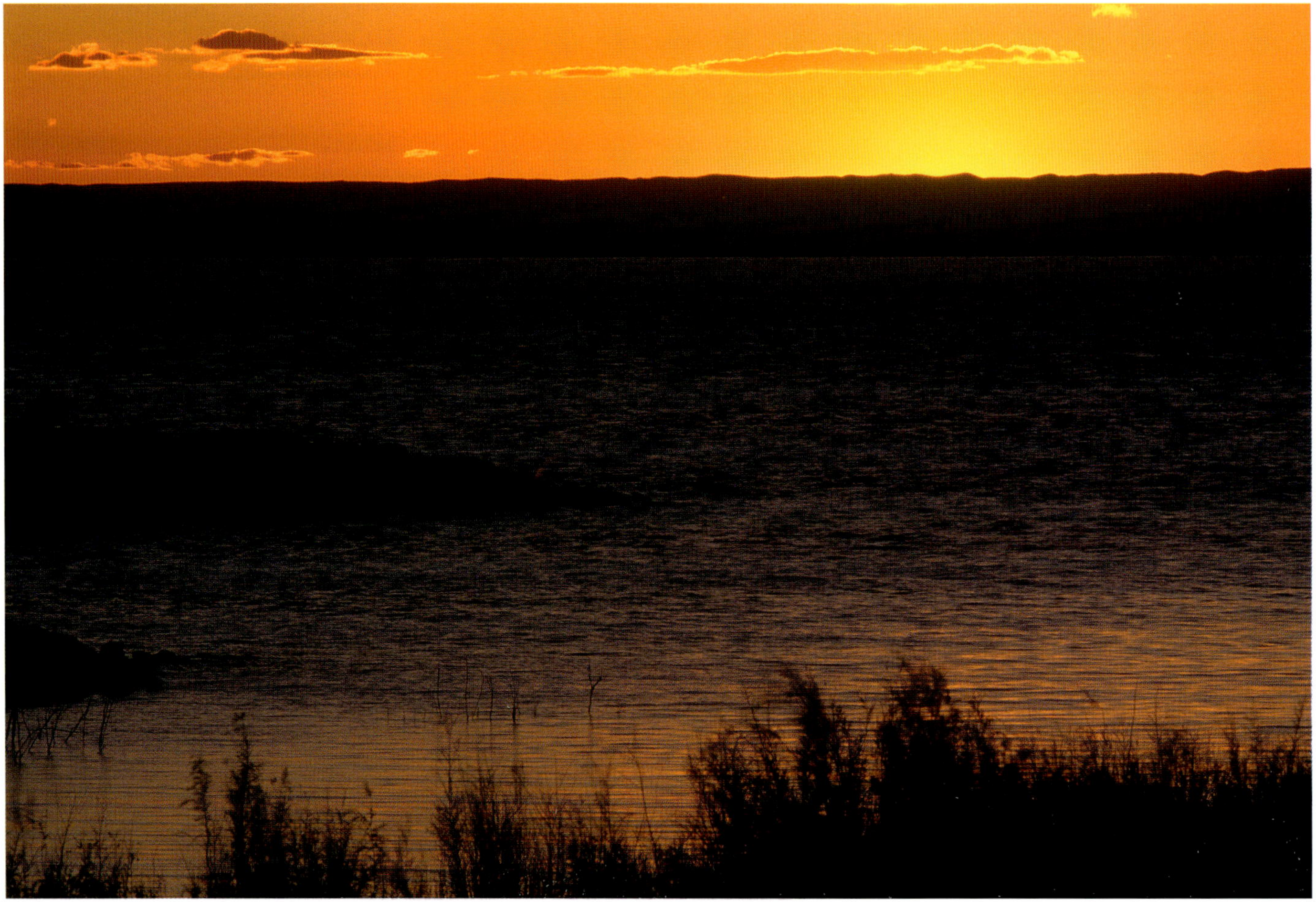

Lubbock County

Mackenzie Park inside the City of Lubbock

The county is named for Thomas Saltus Lubbock, a Texas Ranger and Confederate colonel during the Civil War. The county was formed in 1876. In the middle of the nineteenth century, West Texas was considered a part of the "Great American Desert." As Captain Randolph B. Marcy remarked after a reconnaissance trip through the area in 1849, "not a tree, shrub, or any other object, either animate or inanimate, relieved the dreary monotony of the prospects; it was a vast illimitable expanse of desert prairie . . . a land where no man, either savage or civilized, permanently abides; it spreads into a treeless, desolate waste of uninhabited solitude, which always has been, and must continue, uninhabited forever." Today, Lubbock County has a population of more than 290,000 residents.

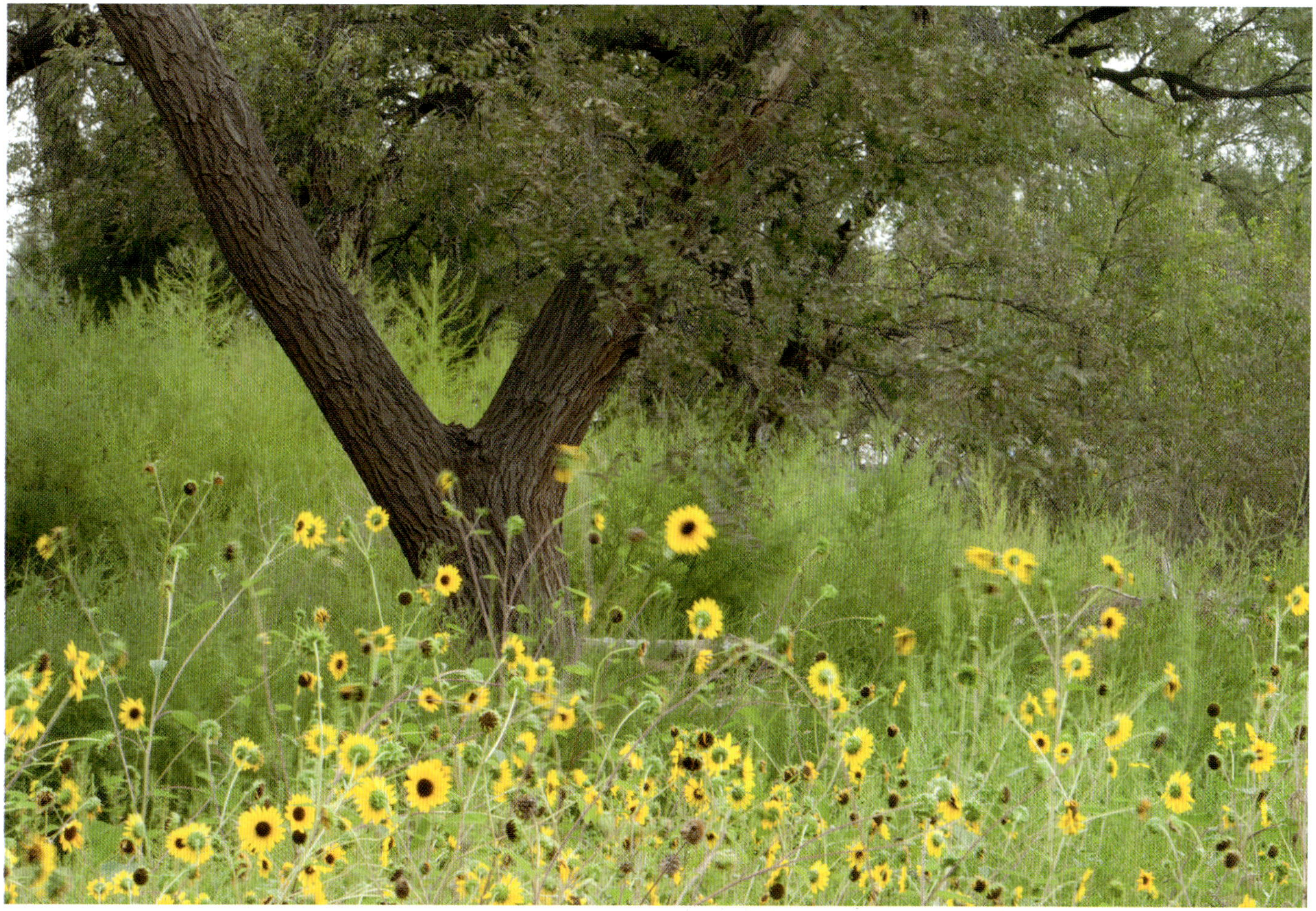

Lynn County

Sunrise over the Grasslands of the Panhandle

Lynn County was formed in 1876 and is named for William Lynn, a soldier in the Texas Revolution from Massachusetts who is believed to have died defending the Alamo. The county remained sparsely settled ranching territory for two decades after 1880. It had no towns; the population was nine in 1880, twenty-four in 1890, and seventeen in 1900. Later farmers began to move into the county and planted corn, grains, and cotton.

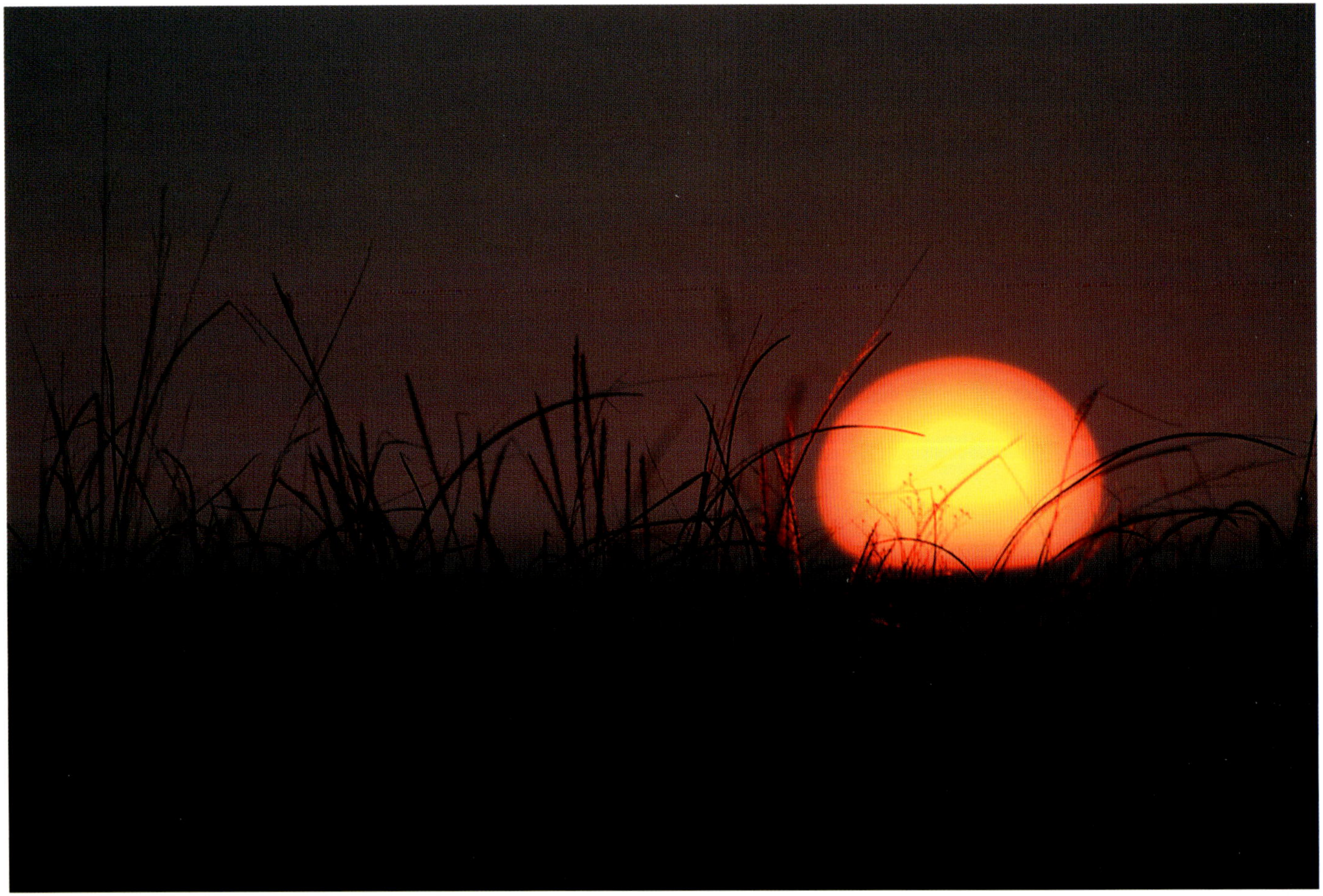

Madison County

Sunrise on a Ranchland Pasture

The county was created in 1853 and is named for James Madison, the fourth president of the United States. Settlers in the future Madison County witnessed the "Runaway Scrape" in 1836, as citizens of Texas rushed toward the Trinity River in an effort to escape the advance of Mexican general Santa Anna. News of the victory at San Jacinto caused them to turn back before many had crossed the river. Madison County reported having been "wild and woolly" before and after the Civil War and was referred to as the "Free State of Madison."

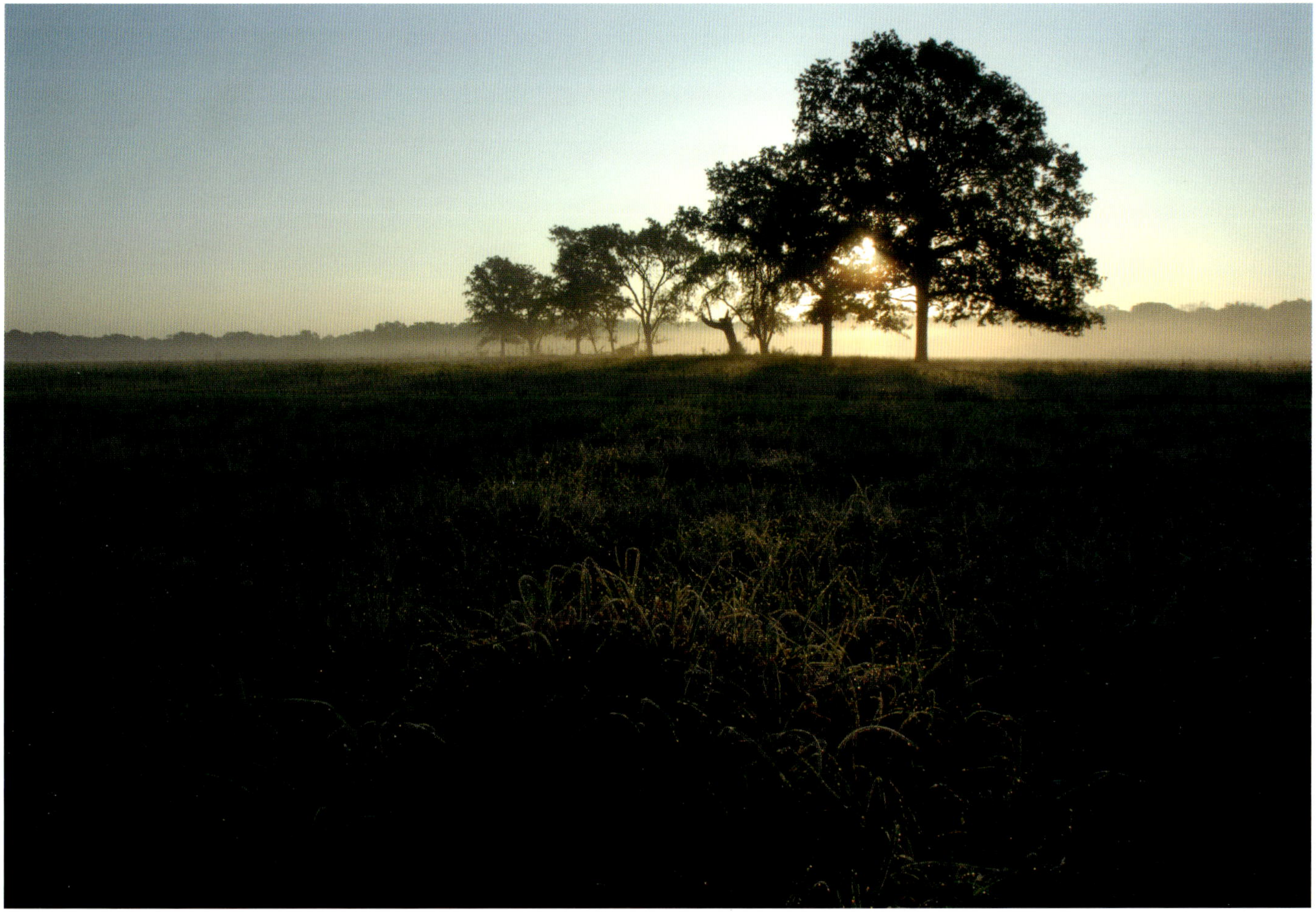

Marion County

Sunset over Lake O' the Pines

Marion County is named for Francis Marion, the Revolutionary War general from South Carolina who was nicknamed the "Swamp Fox." The county was established in 1860. One of the county's most famous disasters occurred in February 1869, when the steamboat *Mittie Stephens* caught fire from a torch basket that ignited a haystack onboard. Sixty-one people died, either from the fire or from being caught in the boat's paddle wheel as they jumped overboard.

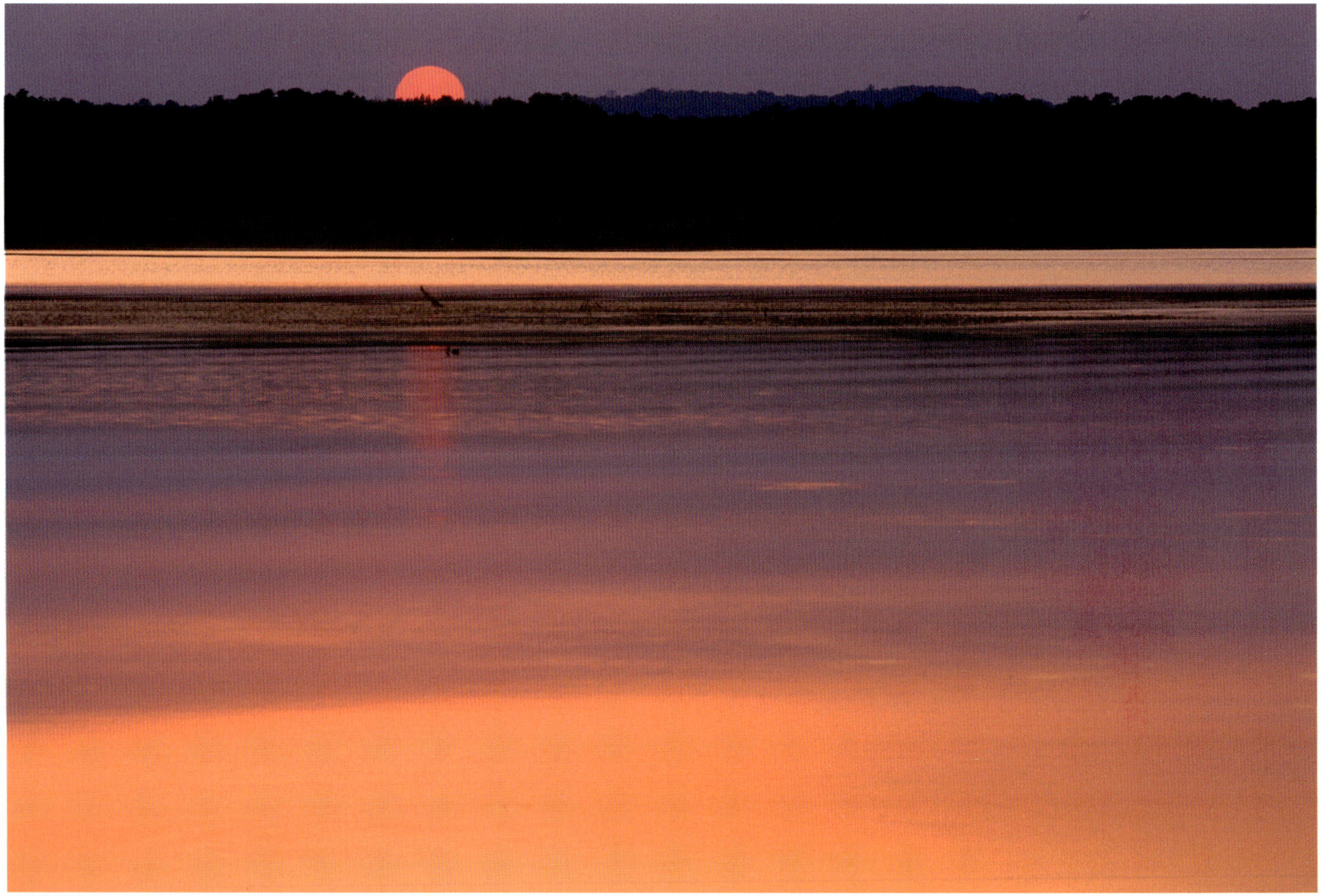

Martin County

Plowed Field and Yucca

The county was created in 1876 and is named for Wylie Martin, an early settler. By 1920, cotton had become the county's leading crop. Almost 7,000 acres were planted in cotton that year, while only 400 acres were devoted to corn production. Much of this expansion can be attributed to the high prices and demand stimulated by World War I.

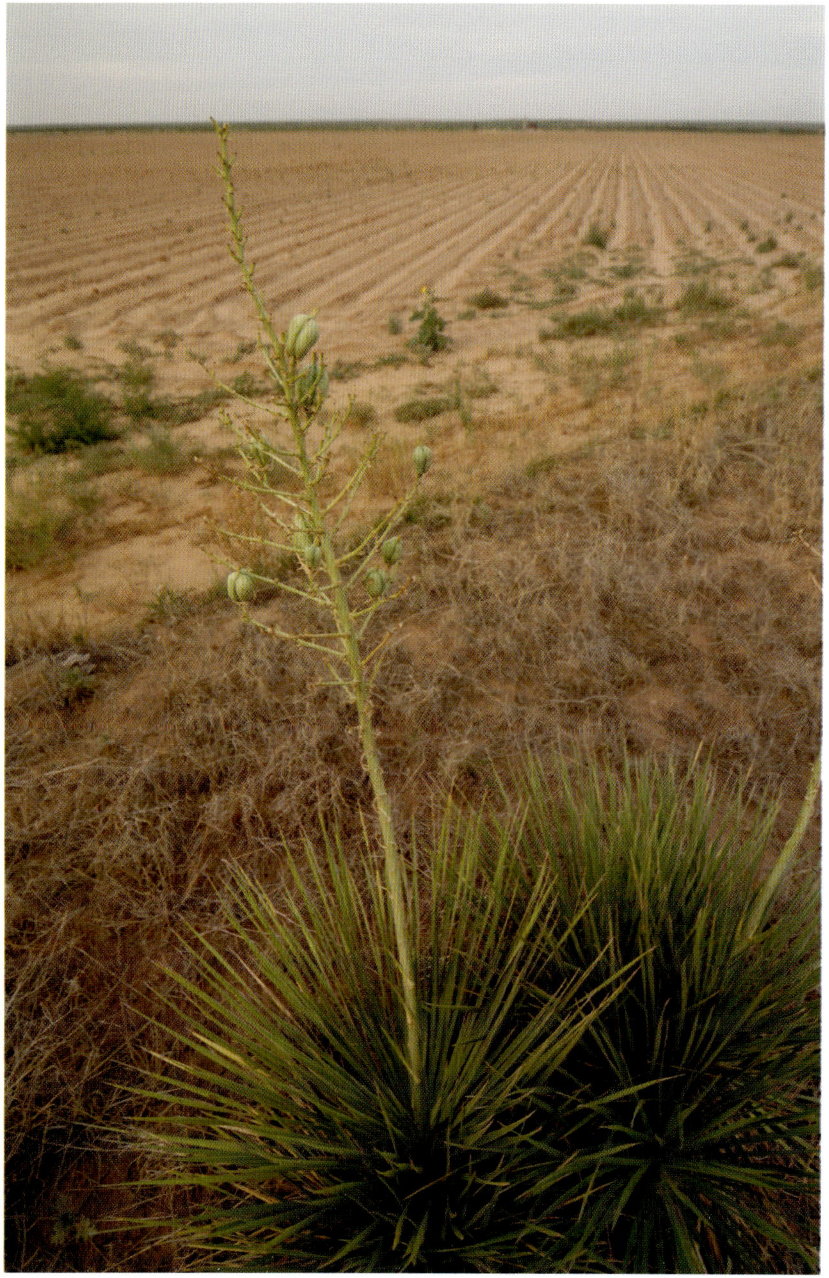

Mason County

Springtime Scene near the City of Mason

The county is named for Fort Mason, which was in the county. The county was created in 1858. In February 1861, the county, spurred in part by antislavery sentiments of German residents, overwhelmingly voted against secession from the Union. In March, following Texas secession, Fort Mason surrendered to the Confederacy, whose soldiers left it mostly vacant, causing an uptick in Indian attacks on the area.

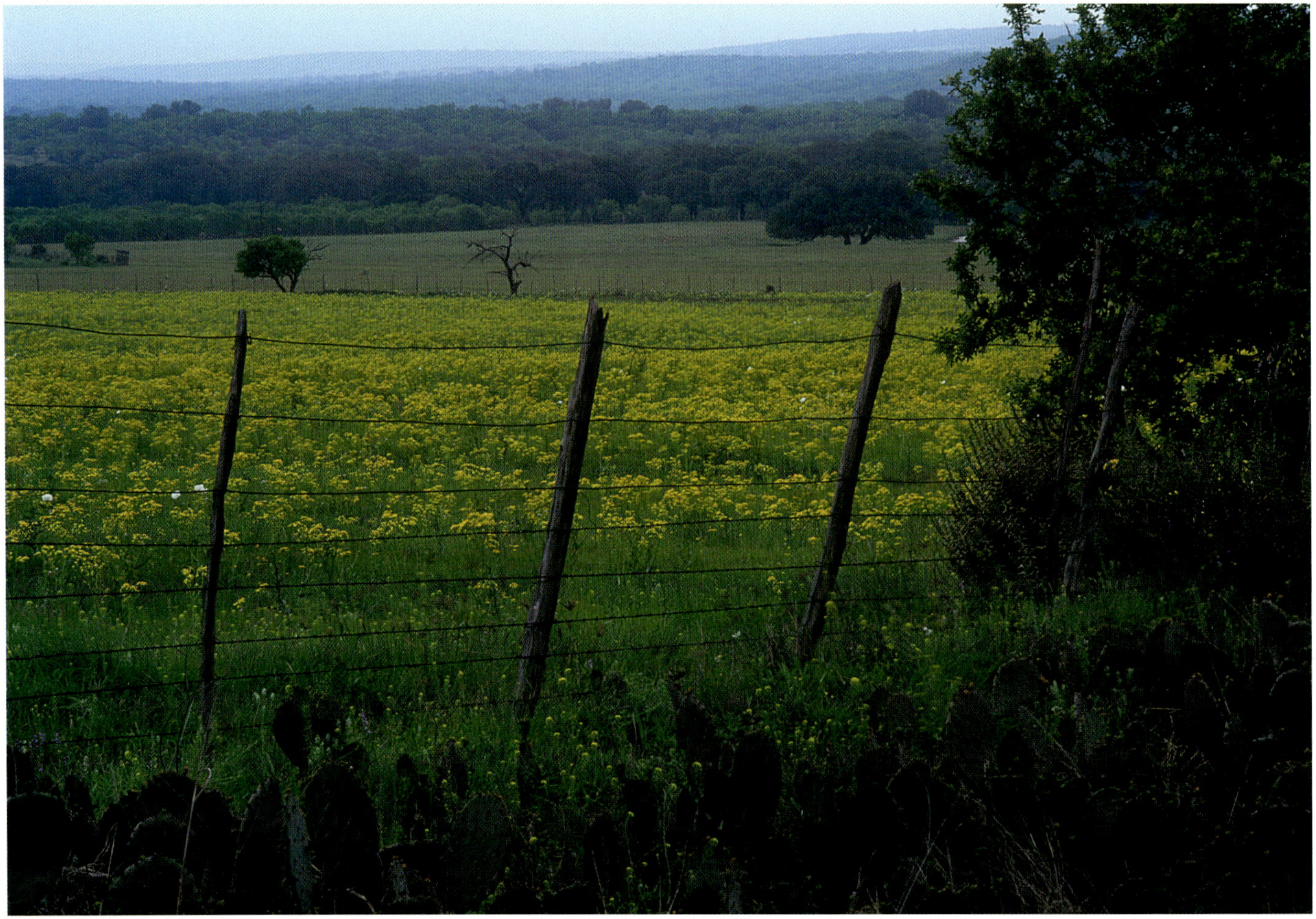

Matagorda County

Field of Indian Paintbrush

Matagorda County is named for the canebrakes that once grew along the coast. *Matagorda* is a Spanish word meaning "thick bush." The county was formed in 1836. The area harbors a variety of wildlife, including bobcats, coyotes, otters, white-tailed deer, and numerous smaller mammals, as well as oysters, shrimp, fish, snakes, and waterfowl. A number of protected wildlife habitats, including Big Boggy National Wildlife Refuge, the Mad Island Wildlife Management Area, the Runnels Family Mad Island Marsh, and the Nature Conservancy, are in the county.

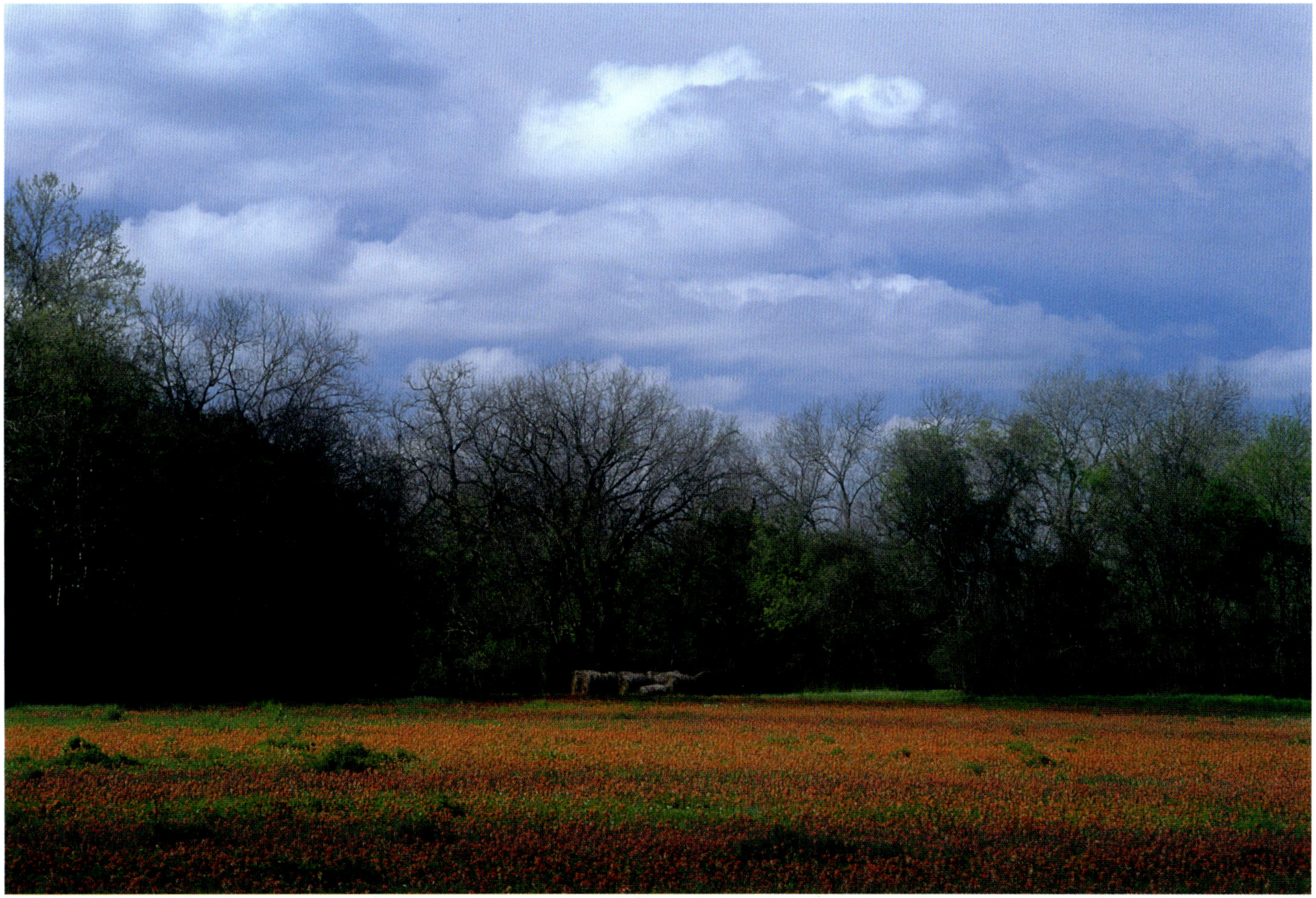

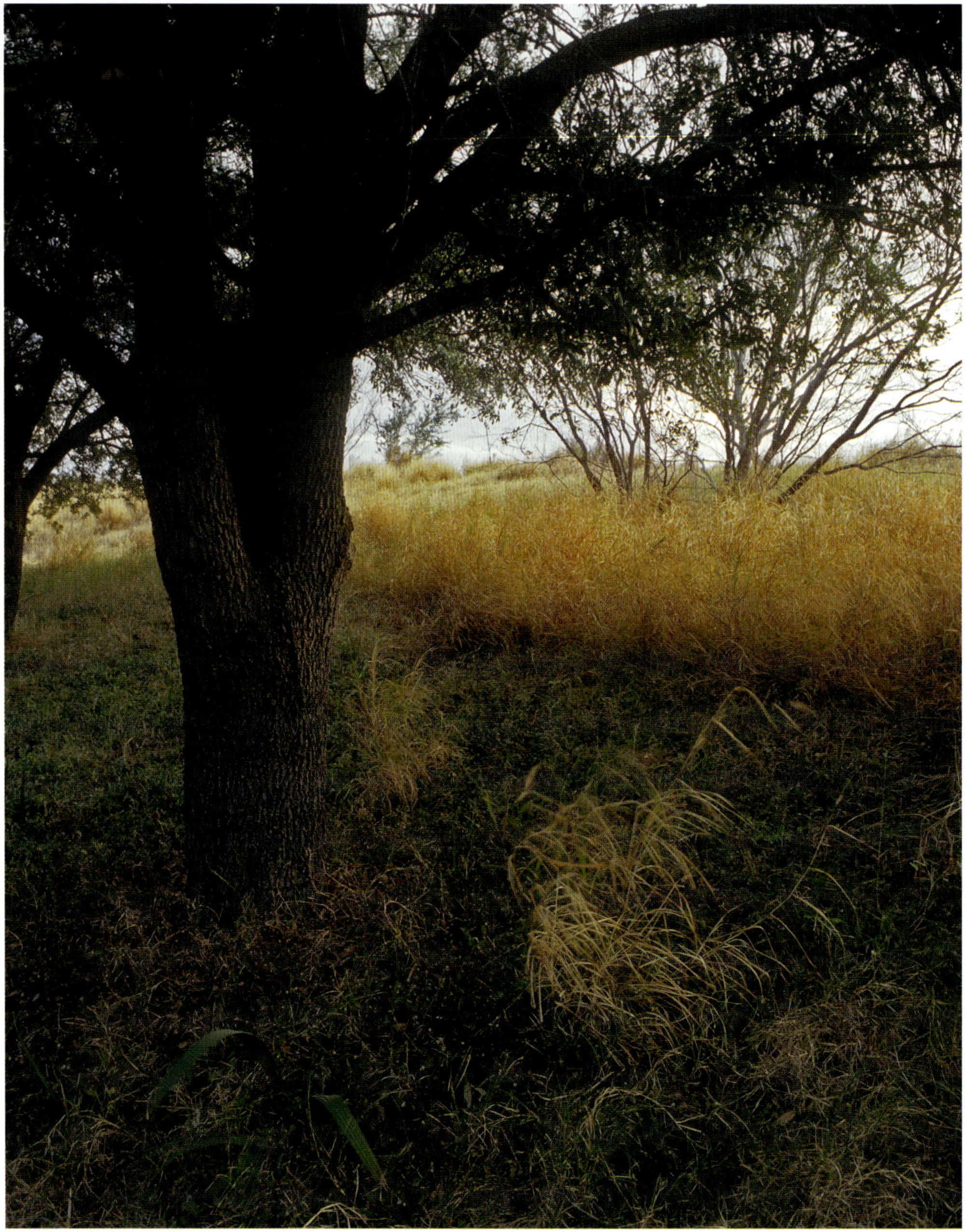

Maverick County

Scene near the Mexican Border

The county was created in 1856 and organized in 1871. It is named for Samuel Maverick, cattleman and state legislator. The coal industry of Maverick County is along a section of the Olmos Coal Formation immediately north of Eagle Pass. Mining operations developed by the Olmos Coal, Coke, and Oil Company at Olmos were the largest coal producers in Texas around the turn of the twentieth century.

McCulloch County

San Saba River

The county was created in 1856 and organized in 1876. It is named for Benjamin McCulloch, a famous Texas Ranger and Confederate general. In 1943, a county prisoner-of-war camp was set up and included prisoners from Rommel's Afrikakorps, as well as members of the SS and the Gestapo.

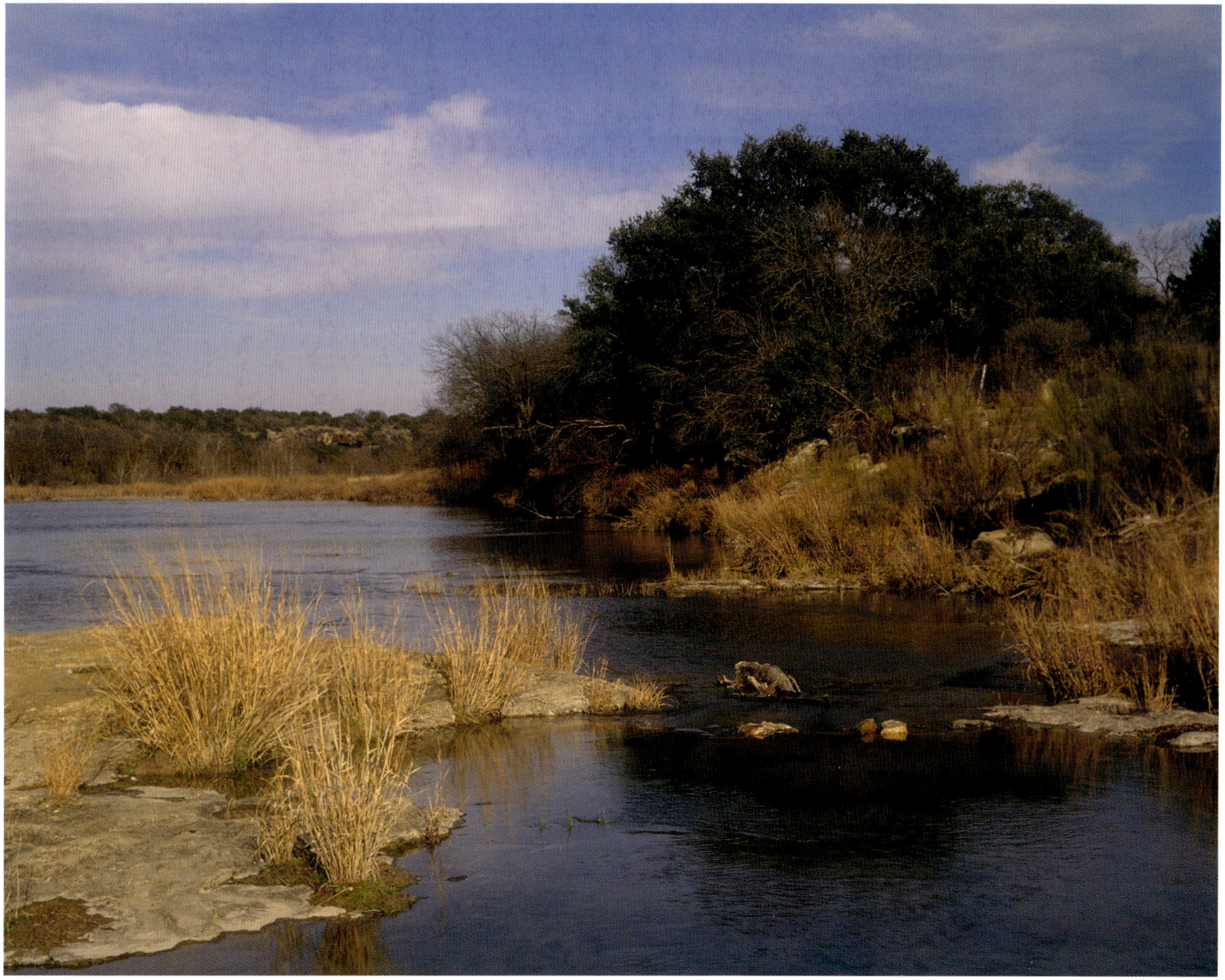

McLennan County

Lone Tree on a Rainy Winter Day

The county is named for Neil McLennan, an early settler. It was founded in 1880. Crush, Texas, was a short-lived town in McLennan County, about 15 miles north of Waco. It was established to stage a publicity stunt concocted by William George Crush and the Missouri-Kansas-Texas Railroad. The stunt involved the collision of two 35-ton steam locomotives in front of spectators whom the railway transported to the event for $2 each. After heavy promotion, on September 15, 1896, the event was delayed by several hours as the police maneuvered the crowd back to what was thought to be a safe distance. The crews of the two engines tied the throttles open and jumped off. The two engines, pulling wagons filled with railroad ties, traveled a 4-mile track and thunderously crashed into each other at a combined speed of up to 120 mph. The boilers exploded and sent steam and flying debris into the crowd. Three people were killed and about six were injured.

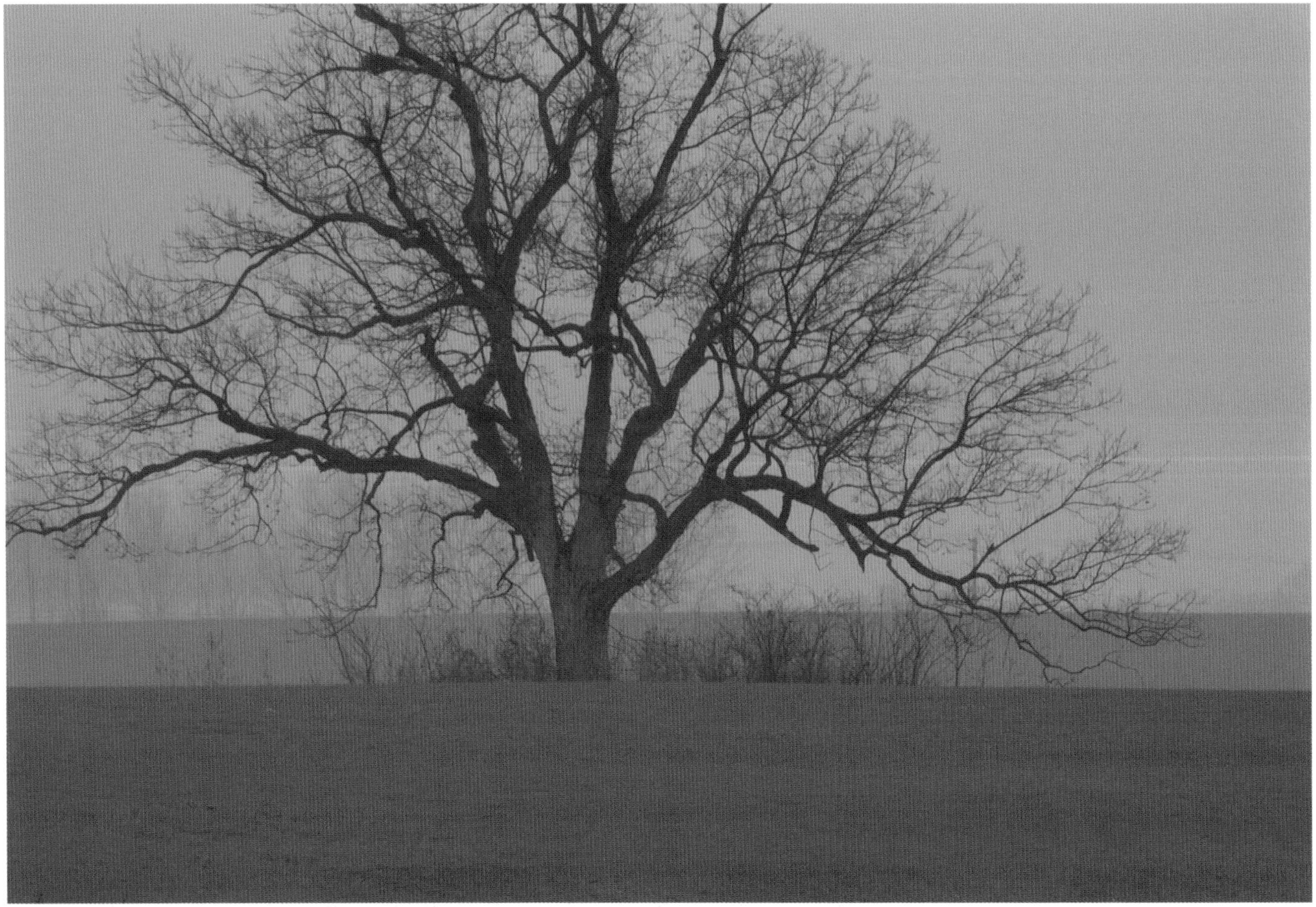

McMullen County

Choke Canyon State Park

The county was established in 1858 and organized in 1877. It is named for John McMullen, founder of a colony in Texas. In the years just prior to the Civil War, settlers began to move into northern McMullen County, particularly along the Frio River. The area's grasslands and many wild cattle and mustangs offered an economic opportunity for those willing to risk Indian attack.

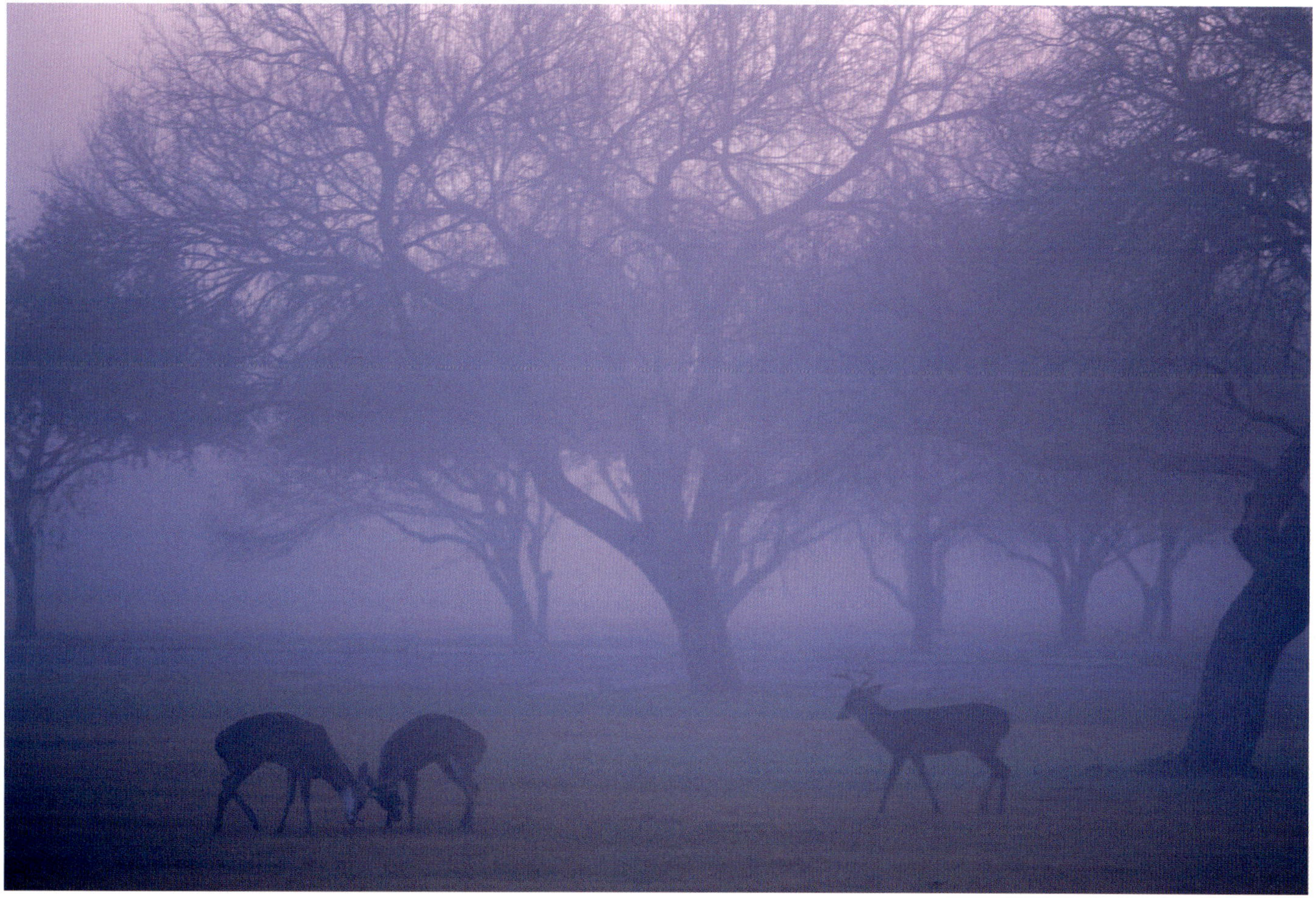

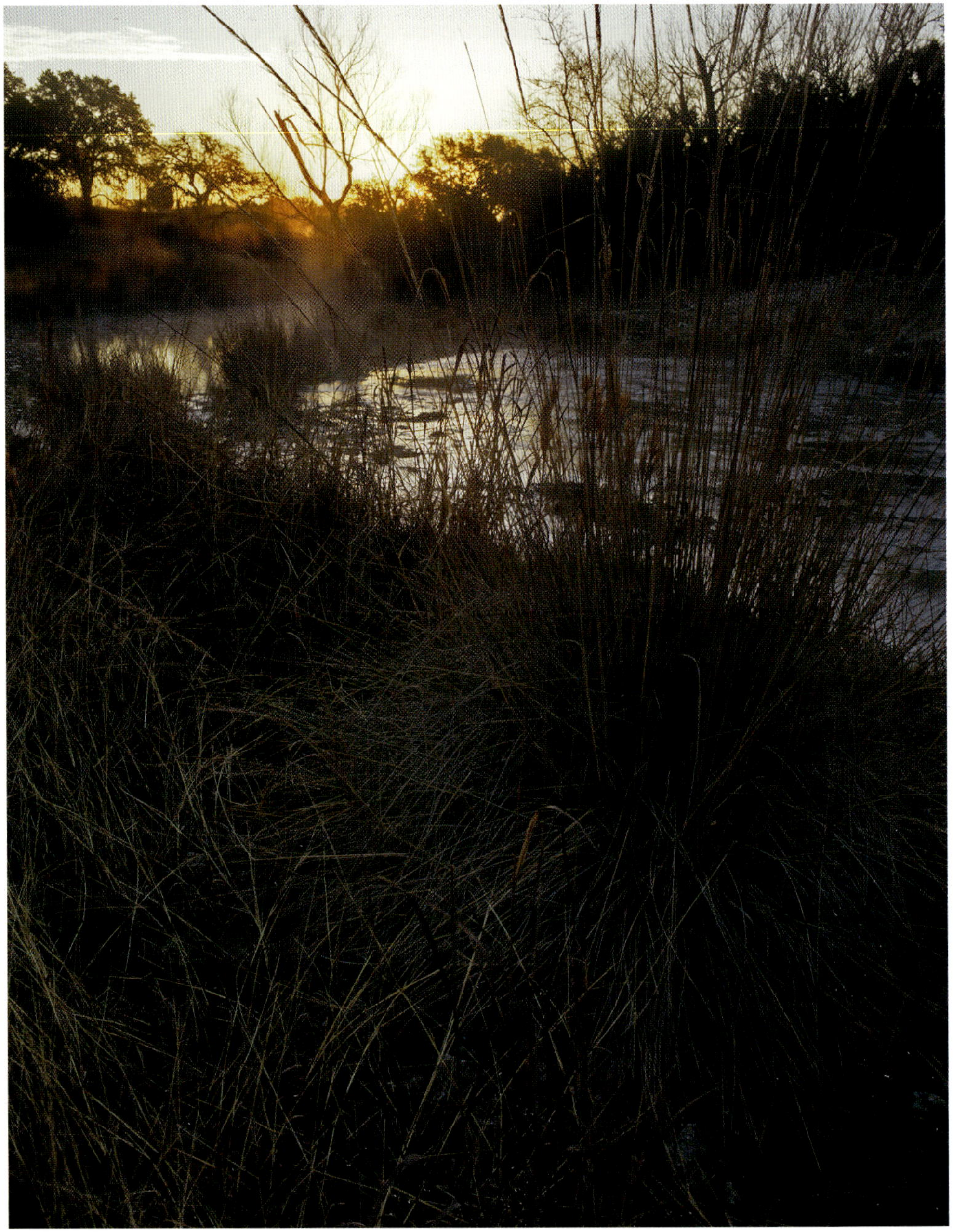

Medina County

West Verde Creek in Hill Country State Natural Area

The county is named for the Medina River and was founded in 1848. The Medina Dam, the fourth largest in the nation when completed in 1913, is listed on the National Register of Historic Places. The irrigation project, which created Medina Lake, was built by 1,500 skilled workers who worked in shifts, operating around the clock to complete the dam in two years.

Menard County

Late-Afternoon Light on the San Saba River

The county was created in 1858 and organized in 1871. It is named for Michel Branamour Menard, the founder of Galveston, Texas. The San Saba River was named by the governor of Spanish Texas, Juan Antonio Bustillo y Ceballos, in 1732. He called it Río de San Sabá de las Nueces because he and his troops had arrived on the feast day of St. Sabbas.

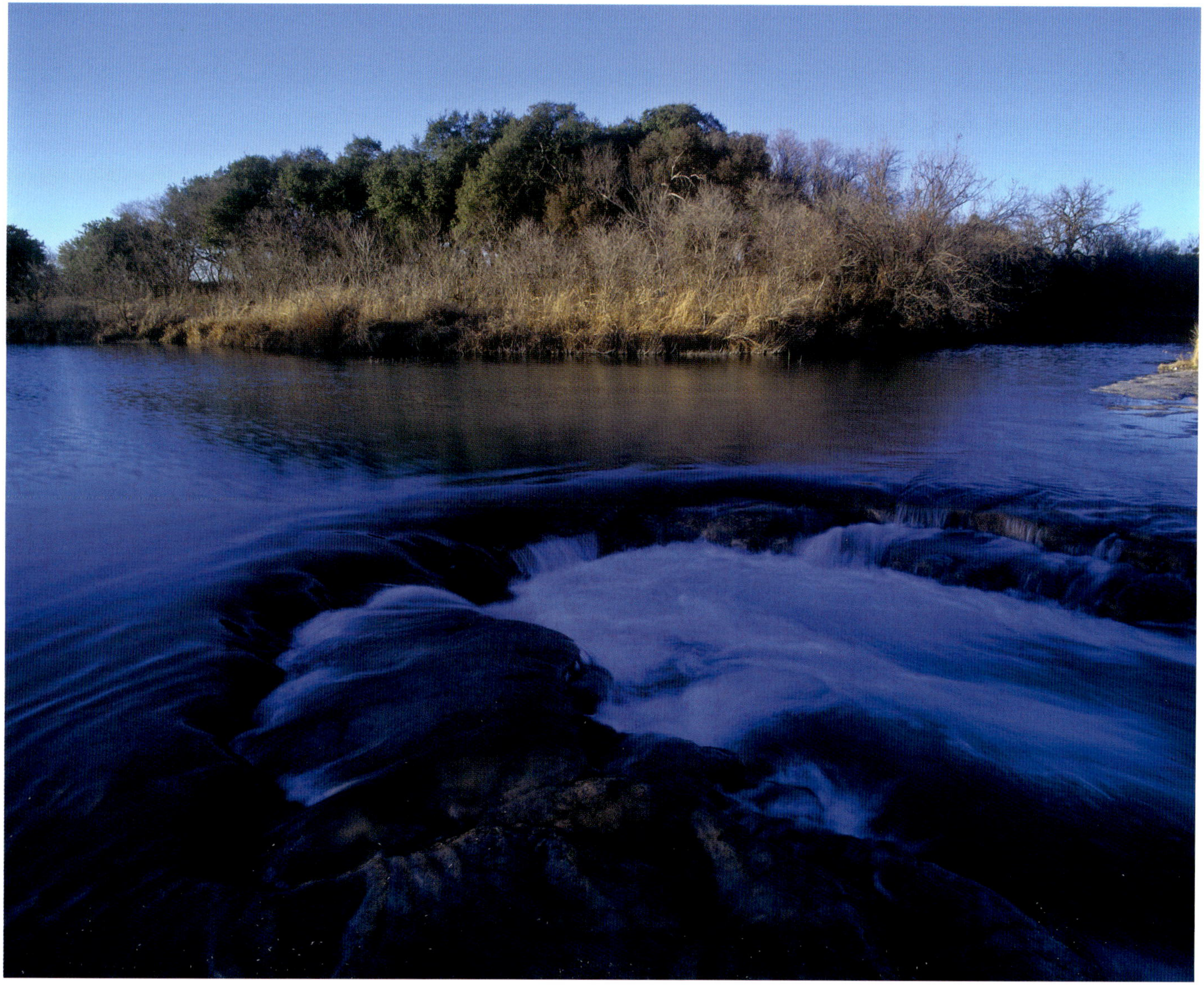

Midland County

Windlands Park inside the City of Midland

Formed in 1885, the county is named Midland because it is midway between Fort Worth and El Paso on the Texas and Pacific Railway. In 1968, the county lost its case before the Supreme Court in *Avery v. Midland County*, which required local districts to be nearly equal. The city of Midland had most of the county's population but elected only one of the five county commissioners, which was found to violate the Fourteenth Amendment.

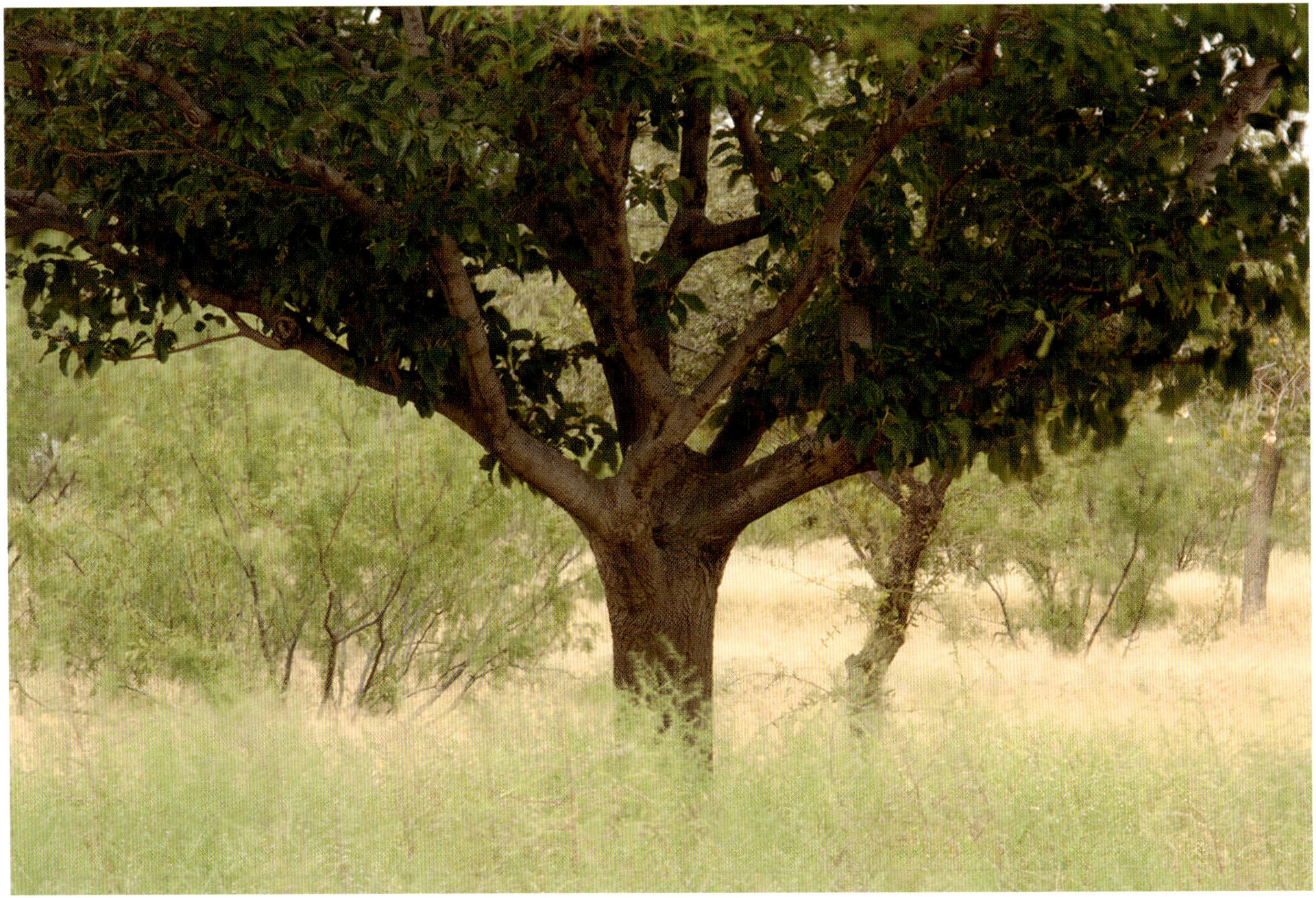

Milam County

Tussocks of Grass in a Ranch Pasture

The county, which was formed in 1837, is named for Benjamin Rush Milam (pronounced "MY-lum"), an early settler and a soldier in the Texas Revolution. During the Civil War, the Milam County Grays became Company G, Fifth Texas Regiment, Hood's Texas Brigade, and saw action in Tennessee and Virginia. Two other Milam County companies fought in the New Mexico campaign.

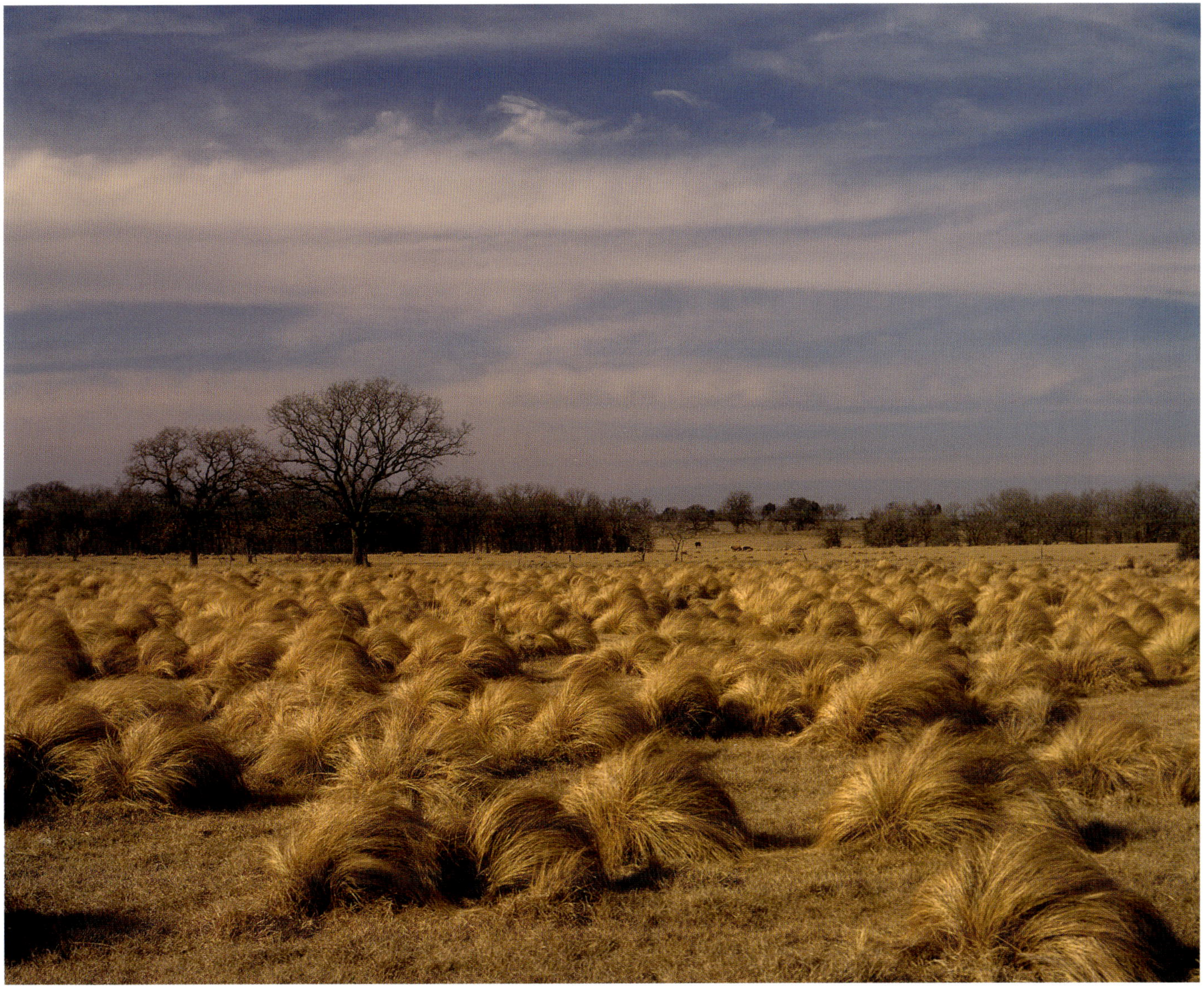

Mills County

Colorado River

The county was named for John T. Mills—a Texas Supreme Court judge—and was formed in 1887. From 1869 through 1897, lawlessness was rampant in the post–Civil War county. Vigilante committees created a reign of terror. Lynching and assassinations became commonplace. Ultimately the Texas Rangers were brought in to restore law and order.

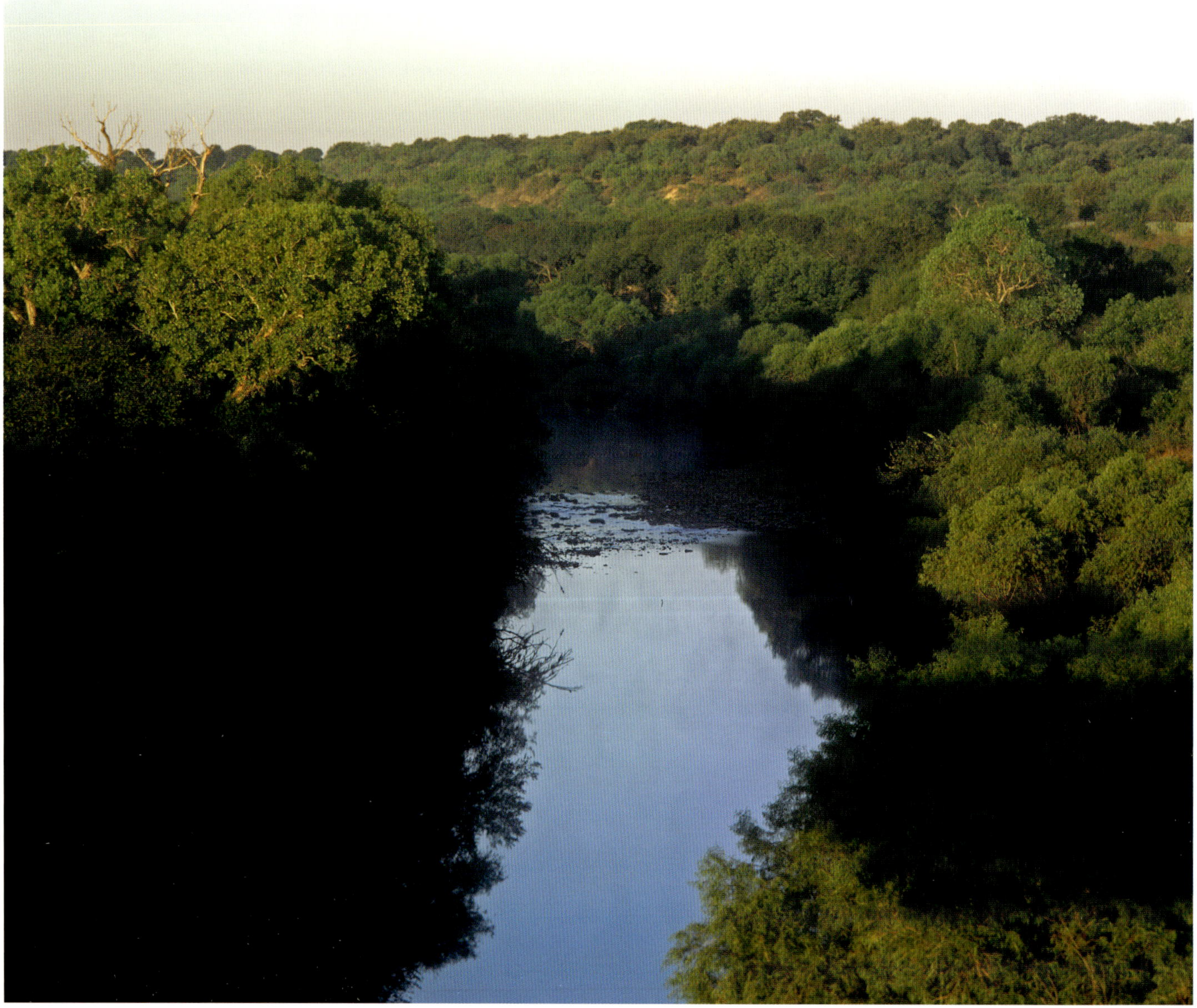

Mitchell County

Lake Colorado City State Park

The county was created in 1876 and organized in 1881. It is named for Asa Mitchell and Eli Mitchell, two early settlers and soldiers in the Texas Revolution. Cattlemen first moved into the county with their herds in the late 1870s. Until the early twentieth century the economy of Mitchell County was dominated by cattle ranching.

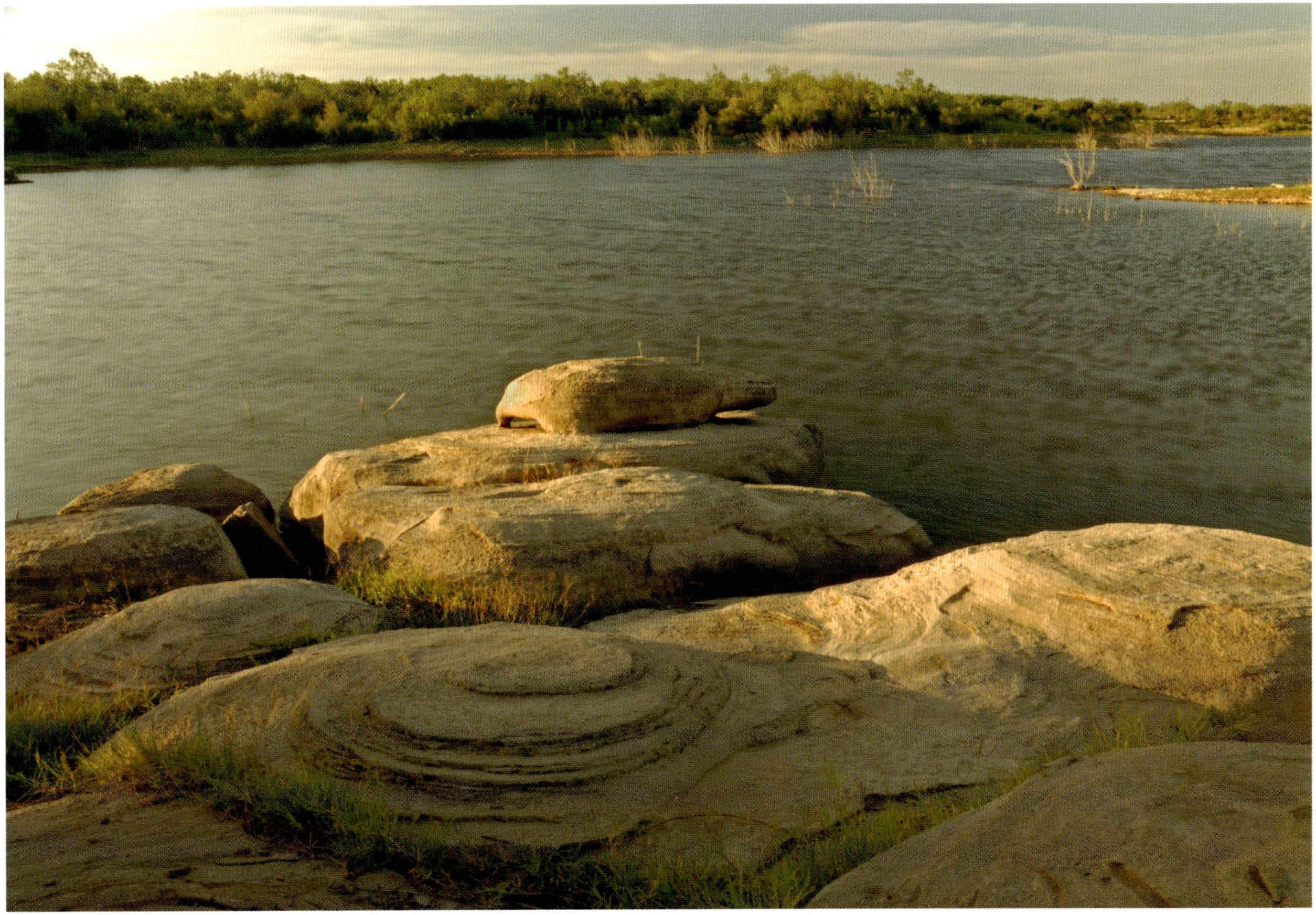

Montague County

Rocky Outcrop on Cougar Mound

The county was created in 1857 and organized the next year. It is named for Daniel Montague, a surveyor and soldier in the Mexican-American War. In fall 1867, Montague County was the last Texas county crossed by the Chisholm Trail before it entered Indian Territory.

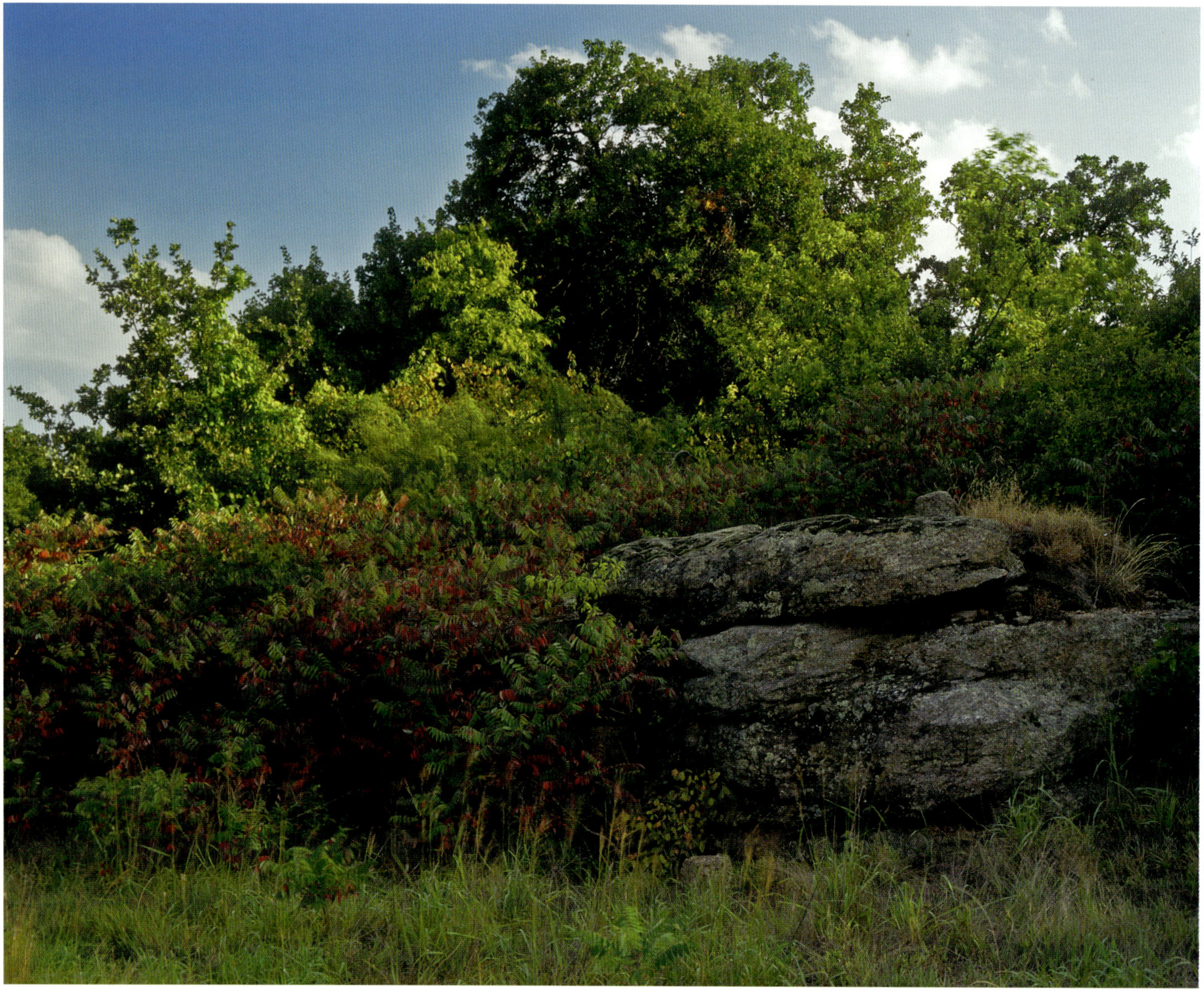

Montgomery County

Starry Night in the Piney Woods

The county was created by an act of the Congress of the Republic of Texas on December 14, 1837, and is named for the town of Montgomery. Natural resources of Montgomery include timber, lakes, gravel, and oil; the Conroe oil field was once the third largest in the United States. Lake Conroe is in the county.

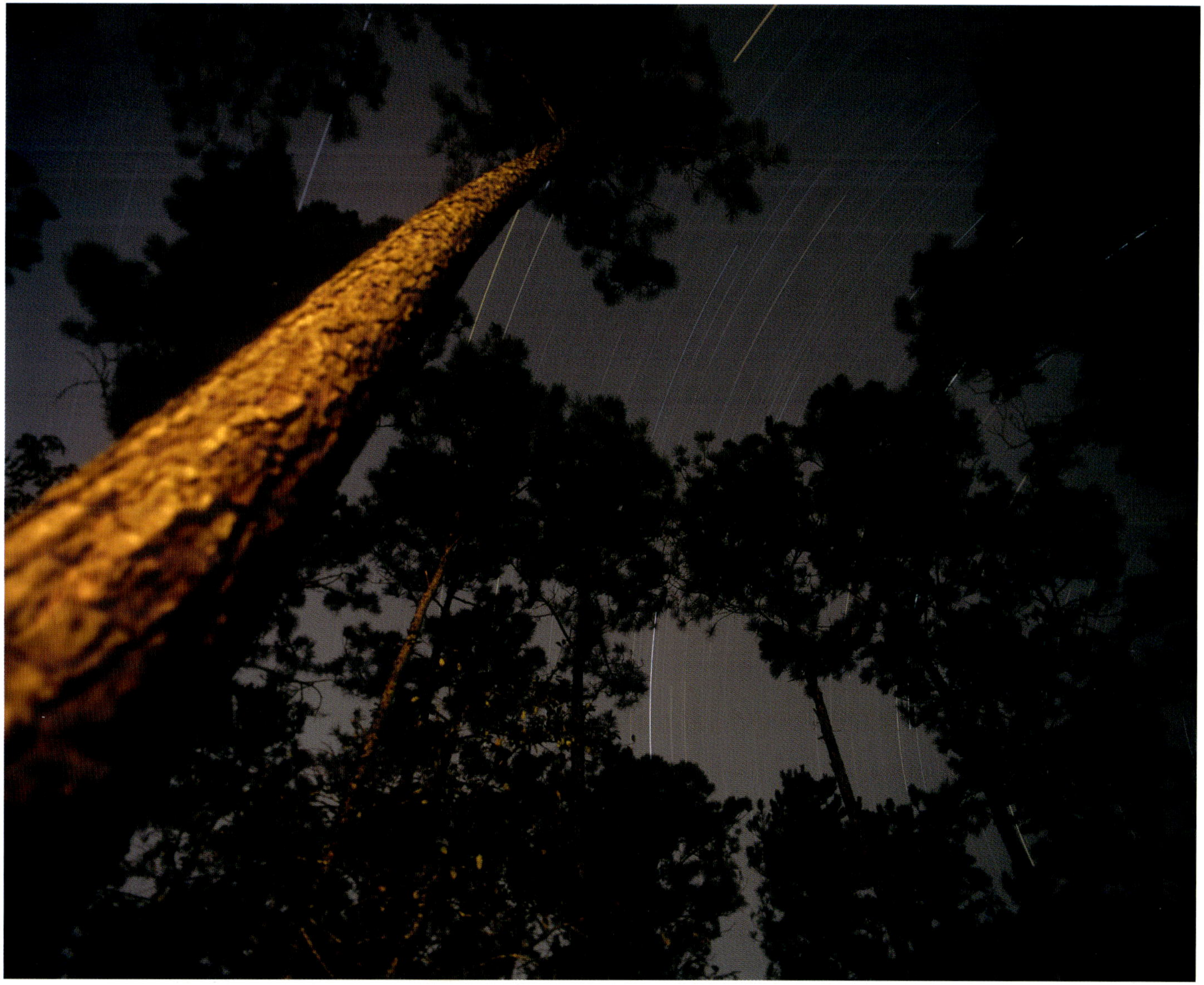

Moore County

Sunrise over Big Blue Creek Lake, Meredith National Recreation Area

The county was created in 1876 and organized in 1892. It is named for Edwin Ward Moore, the commander of the Texas navy. As early as the 1890s, local stock raisers and a few farmers began to plant small amounts of corn, wheat, and grain sorghums. Farming continued on a limited scale until the years during and just after World War I, when worldwide demand led to a boom in agriculture.

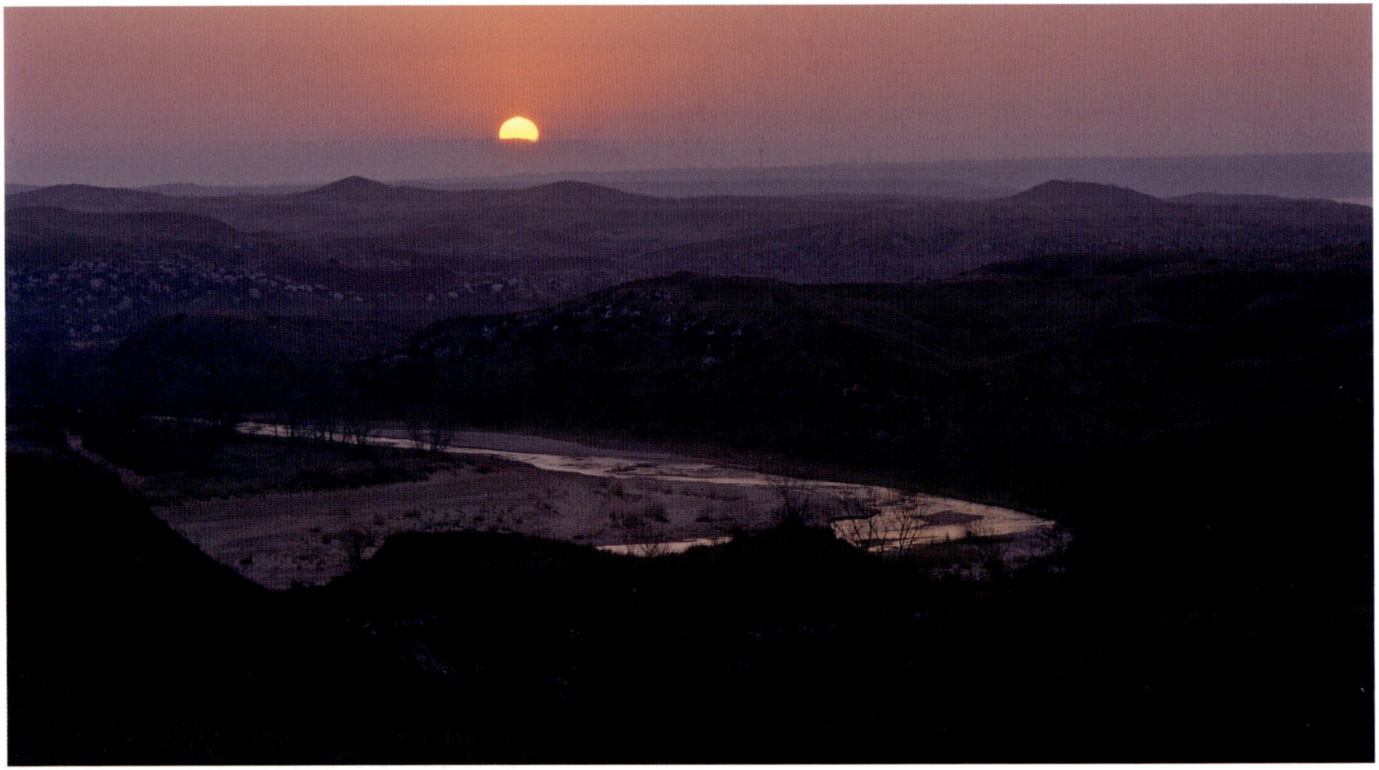

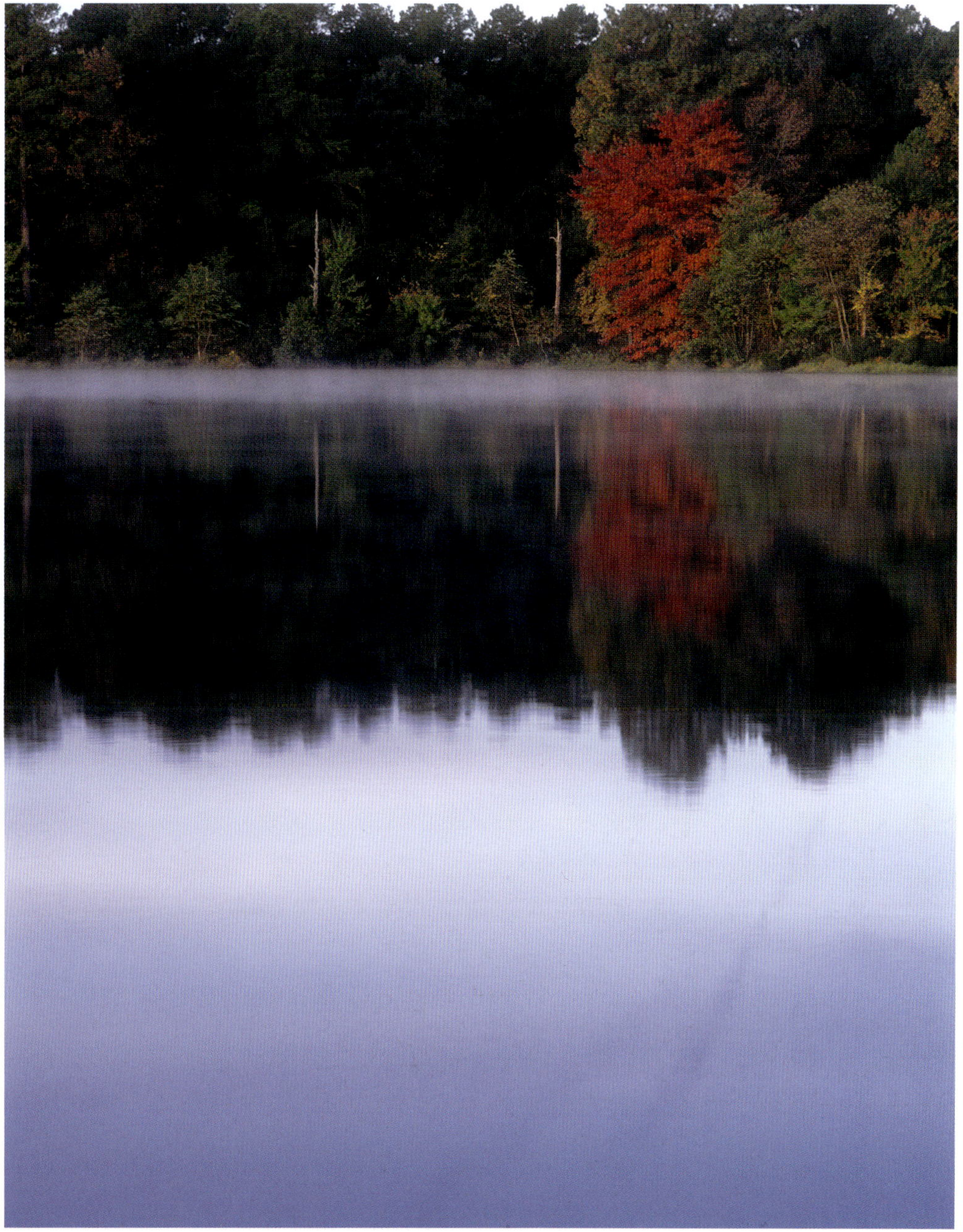

Morris County

Daingerfield State Park

Morris County is probably named for William Wright Morris, an early judge and planter from Henderson, also in Northeast Texas. The area had been noted as early as 1819, and crude mining operations were carried out in the area before the Civil War. The war effort in the 1940s demanded massive amounts of iron, and the federal government moved to tap these deposits through the United States Defense Plant Corporation with the construction of a blast furnace in 1943. The plant had a tremendous impact on the county's economy.

Motley County

Canyonlands in the Panhandle

The county was created in 1876 and organized in 1891. It is named for Junius William Mottley, a signer of the Texas Declaration of Independence. Mottley's name was misspelled in the bill establishing the county. The first white child in Motley County, Nora Cooper, was born in 1882, near what is now the ghost town of Tee Pee City. A camp operated by buffalo hunters and later the headquarters of the Texas Rangers under Captain G. W. Arrington existed from 1879 to 1881.

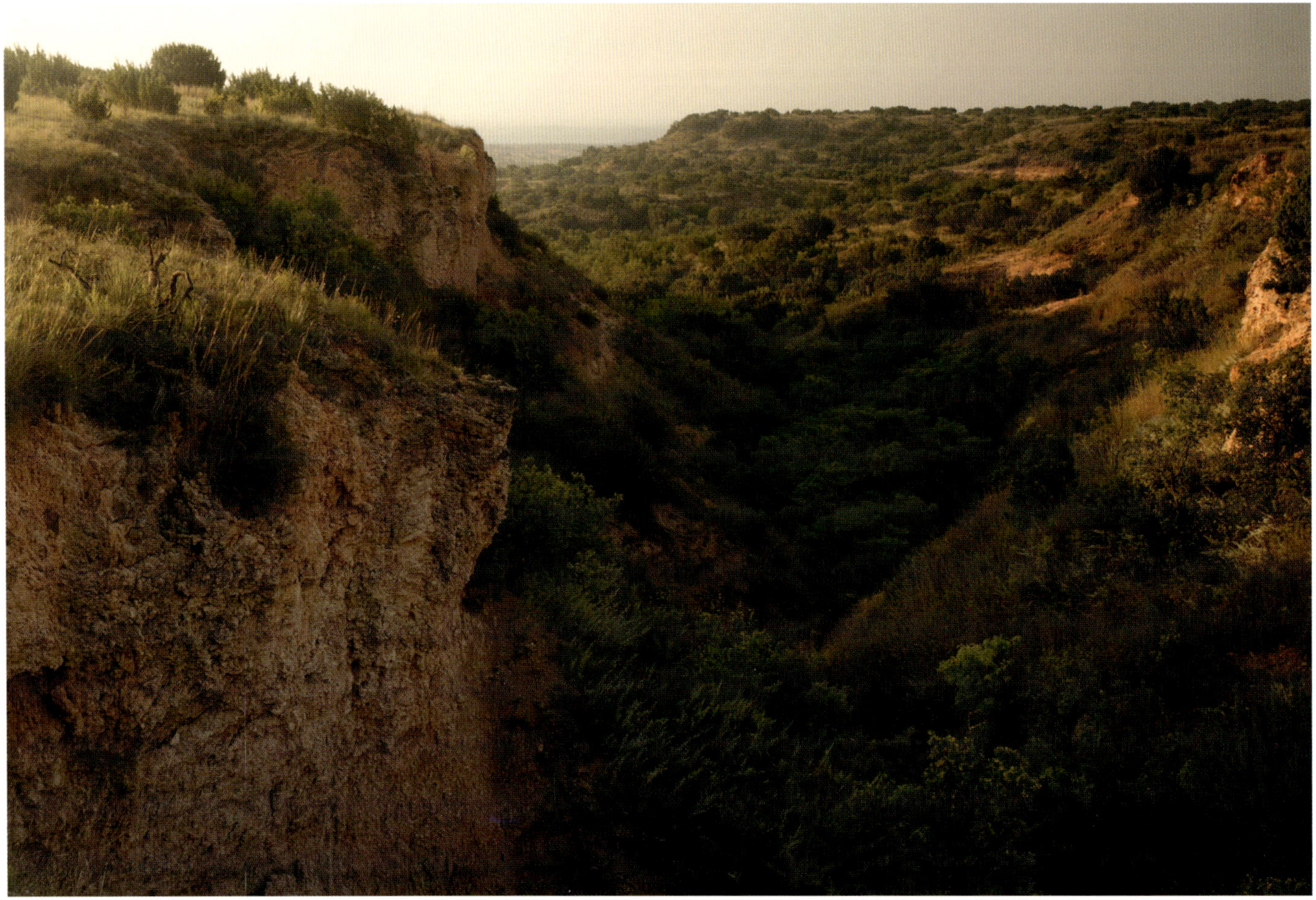

Nacogdoches County

Alazan Bayou Wildlife Management Area

The county was created in 1826 as a municipality of Mexico and was organized as a county in 1837. It is named for the Nacogdoches Native American tribe. In 1826, in an effort to assert their claims, Benjamin W. Edwards, his brother Harden, and some thirty followers rode into Nacogdoches, seized the Old Stone Fort, and declared the independence of Texas. The revolt, which became known as the Fredonian Rebellion, was quickly suppressed by Mexican militia, and the Edwards brothers and the others were forced to flee.

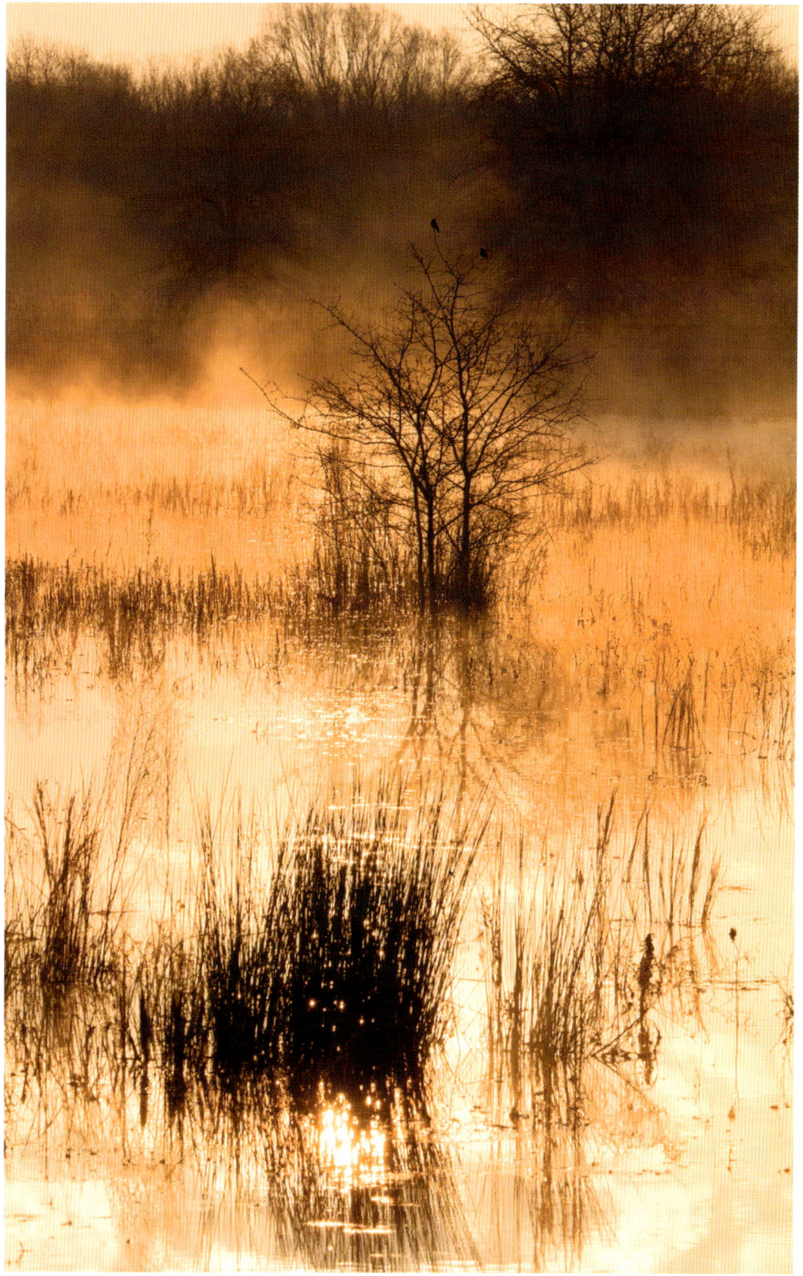

Navarro County

Mesquite Tree and a Ranchland Pathway

José Antonio Navarro (1795–1871)—a leading Tejano participant in the Texas Revolution and signer of the Texas Declaration of Independence—is the county's namesake. The county was formed in 1846. In 1860, after the election of Abraham Lincoln to the American presidency, Navarro County lowered the American flag at the courthouse in protest and instead hoisted the Texas flag. Thereafter, early in 1861, some 450 Navarro County men enlisted in the Confederate States Army.

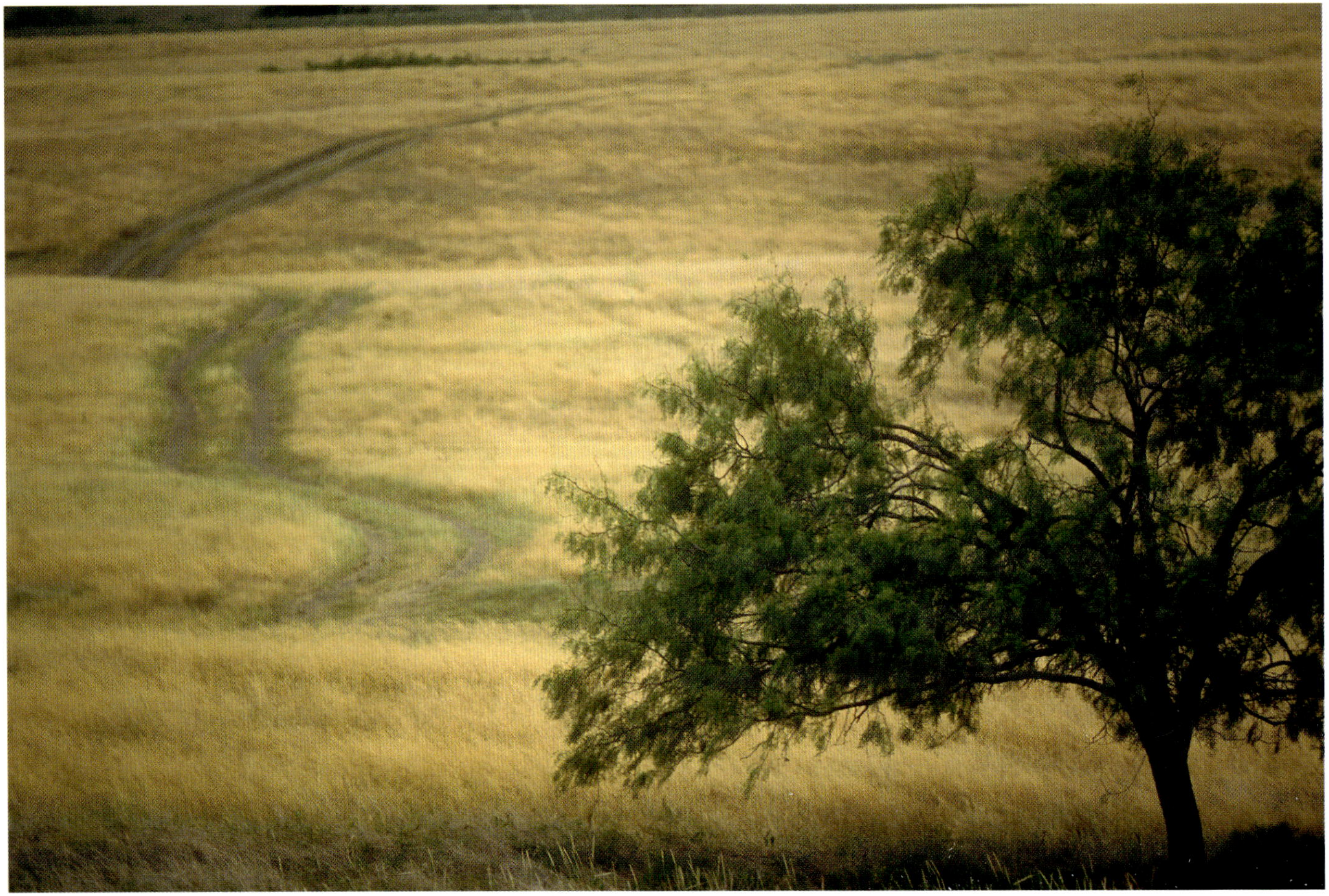

Newton County

Dogwood Tree in Bloom in Wild Azalea Canyon

The county is named for John Newton, a veteran of the American Revolutionary War. The county was formed in 1846. The lands that eventually composed Newton County were included in Lorenzo de Zavala's 1829 grant from the Mexican government. At least twenty-one settlers received title to land in the county in 1834 and 1835.

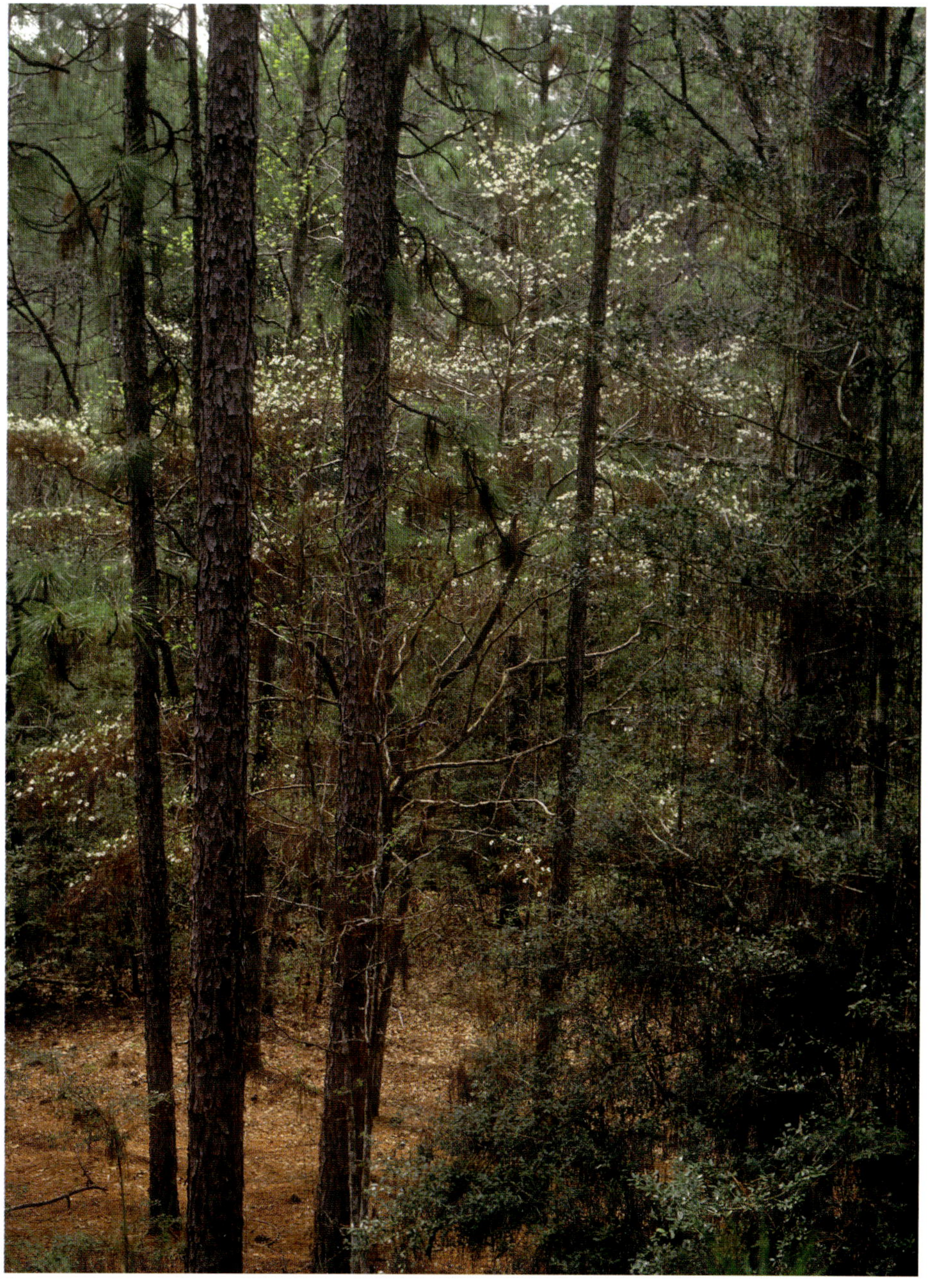

Nolan County

Lake Sweetwater

The county was created in 1876 and organized in 1881. It is named for Philip Nolan, one of the first American traders to visit Texas. Knight's store on Sweetwater Creek was started in a dugout in 1877 to serve buffalo hunters operating in the area. The county's first post office was opened in 1879 in the village of Sweetwater, which was two words until the spelling was officially changed in 1918.

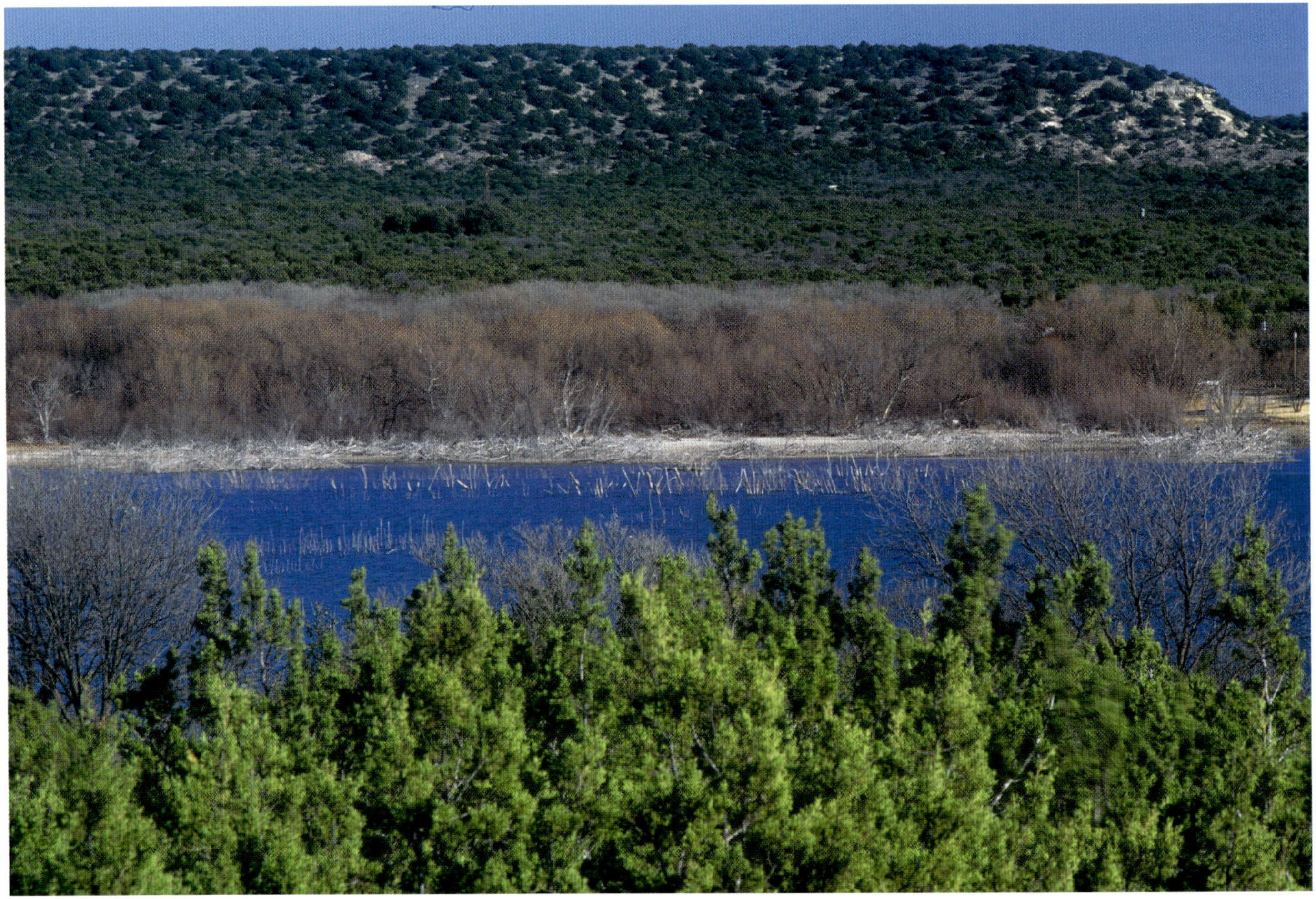

Nueces County

Sunset over Marsh near Fish Pass in Mustang Island State Park

The county was formed in 1846 from portions of San Patricio County and was organized the following year. It is named for the Nueces River, which flows through the county. During the early years of the Civil War, the Nueces community of Corpus Christi was an essential center for Confederate commerce. In 1859, no fewer than forty-five small vessels carried trade between Corpus Christi and Indianola. Small boats sailing inside the barrier islands transported goods from the Brazos River to the Rio Grande, while inland cotton was moved along the Cotton Road through Banquet to Matamoros, and on to the mills of England.

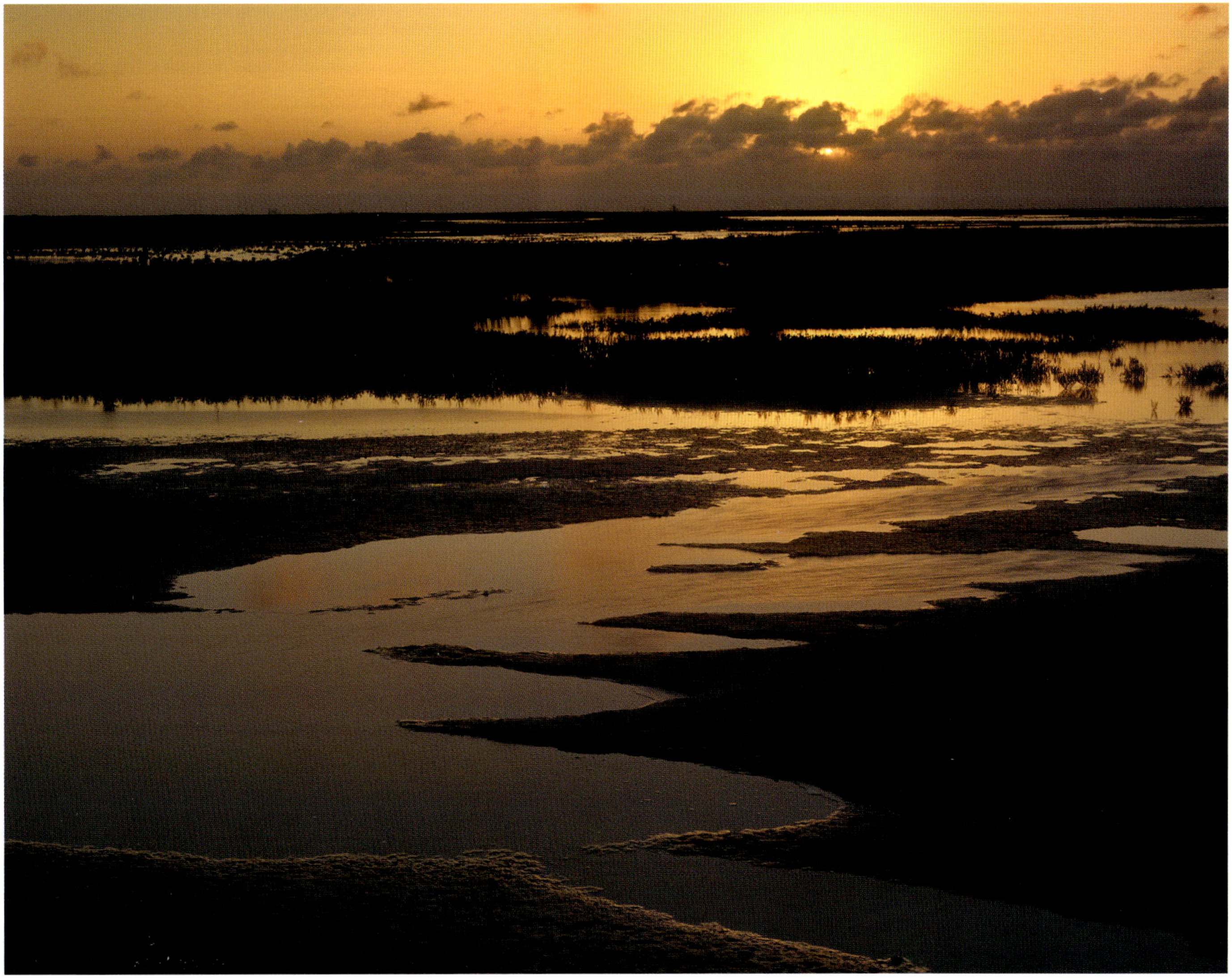

Ochiltree County

Lake Fryer in Wolf Creek Park

The county was created in 1876, was organized in 1889, and is named for William Beck Ochiltree, who was an attorney general for the Republic of Texas. Ochiltree County suffered from the effects of the Great Depression and the Dust Bowl of the 1930s. By 1940, there were just over five hundred farms in the county, and the number of acres devoted to wheat had declined substantially. Only 67,000 acres were planted in wheat that year. The population dropped from a little more than 5,000 in 1930 to 4,200 in 1940. The economy recovered during the 1940s, and the discovery of oil and gas in the southern part of the county in 1951 led to increased growth.

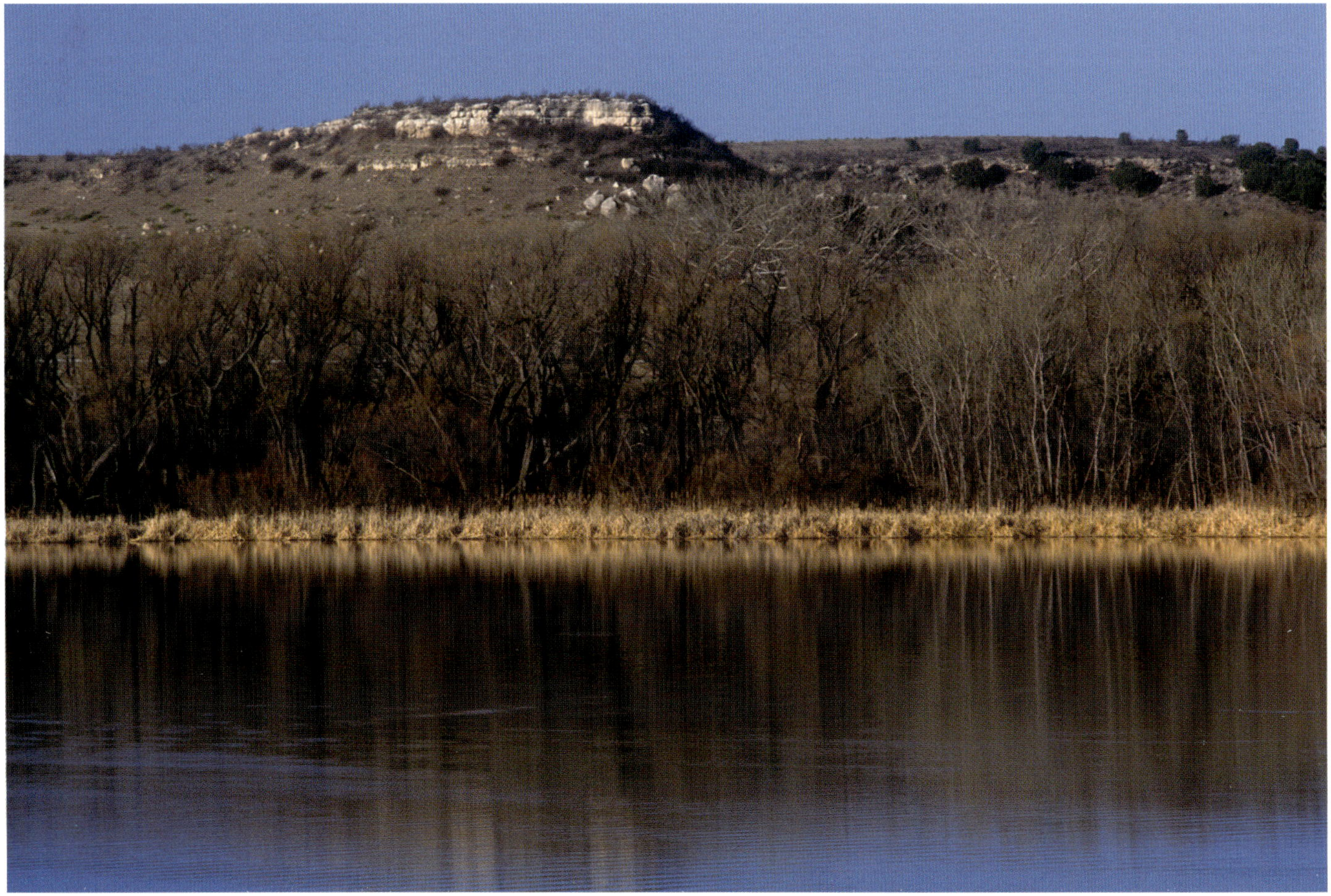

Oldham County

Rugged Country near the New Mexico Border

The county was created in 1876 and organized in 1881. The county is named for Williamson Simpson Oldham, a Confederate Texas senator. Oldham County is primarily ranch and farmland, with many thousands of acres planted in wheat, the primary crop. The county also has some petroleum production and large wind farms.

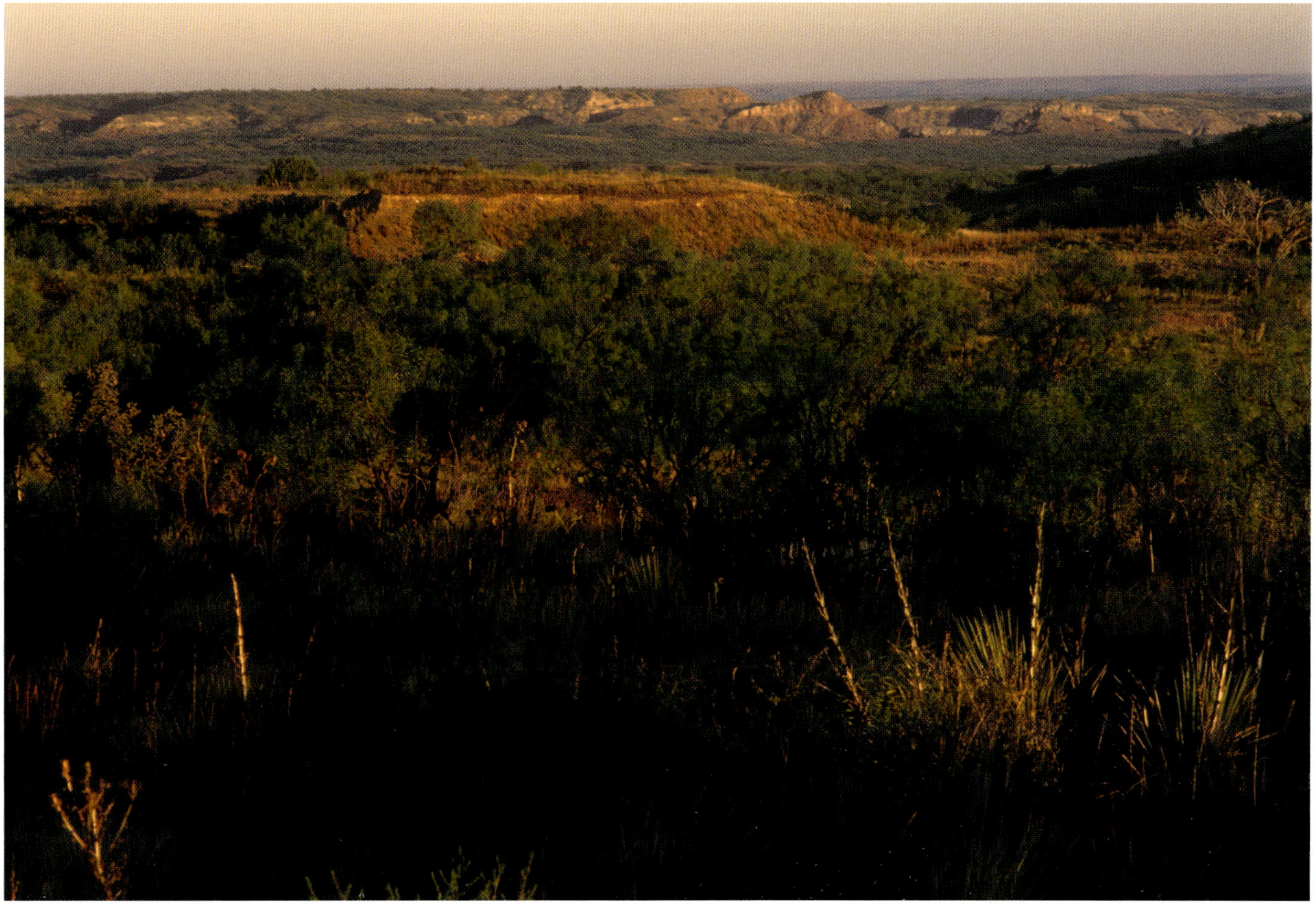

Orange County

Cypress Swamp

Orange County was founded in 1852 and is named for an orange grove planted by early settlers at the mouth of the Sabine River. During World War II, Orange County was the home of a large amount of shipbuilding for the navies of the United States and Allied countries. The major shipbuilder—the Consolidated Steel Corporation—was in the town of Orange and employed as many as 20,000 people during the war.

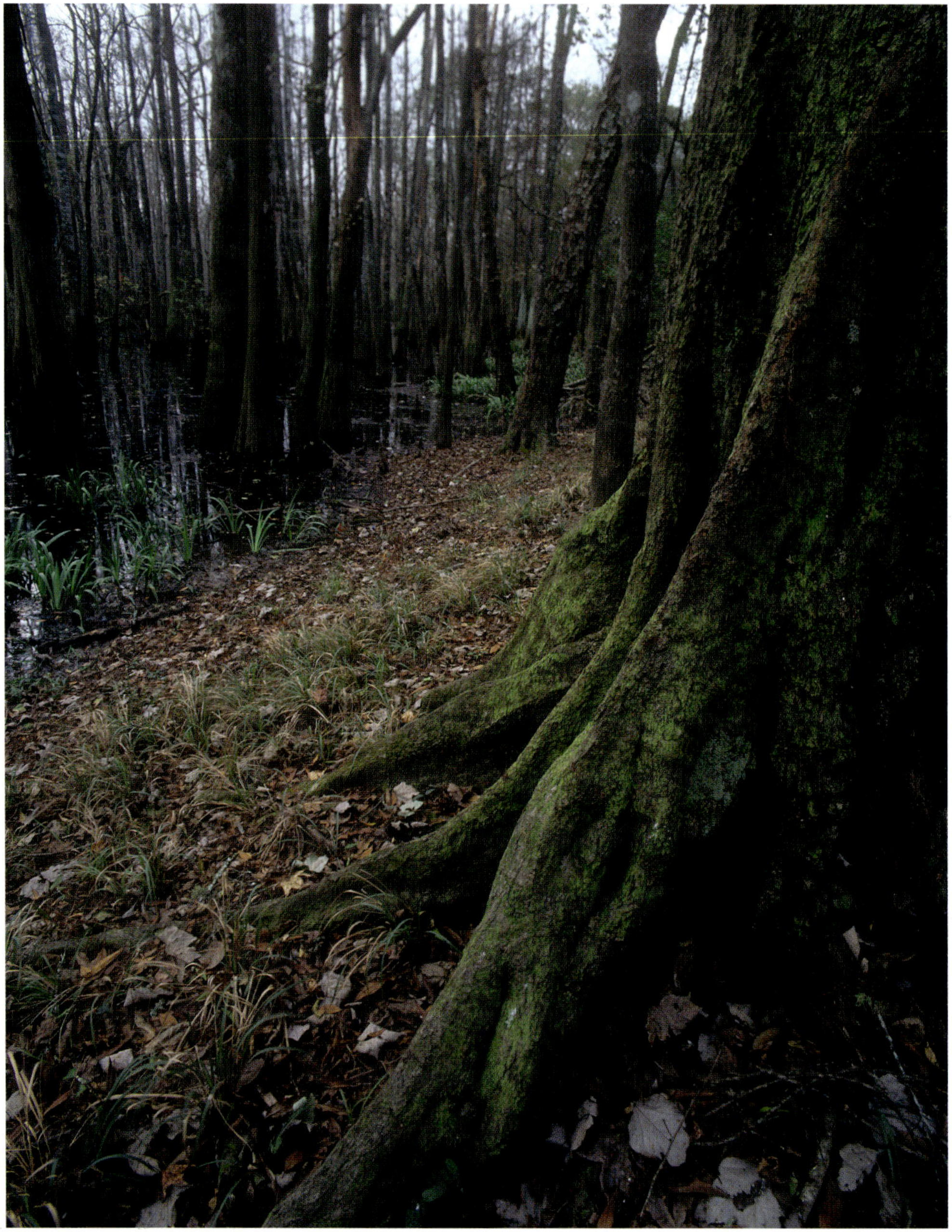

Palo Pinto County

Possum Kingdom State Park

The county is named for Palo Pinto Creek; *palo pinto* is Spanish for "painted stick." The county was formed in 1856. James and Amanda Lynch moved to the area in 1877, and in digging a well on their property, they discovered that the water seemed to benefit their well-being. Word spread about the water's healing powers, and people from all over came to experience the benefits. Eventually the town of Mineral Wells was platted.

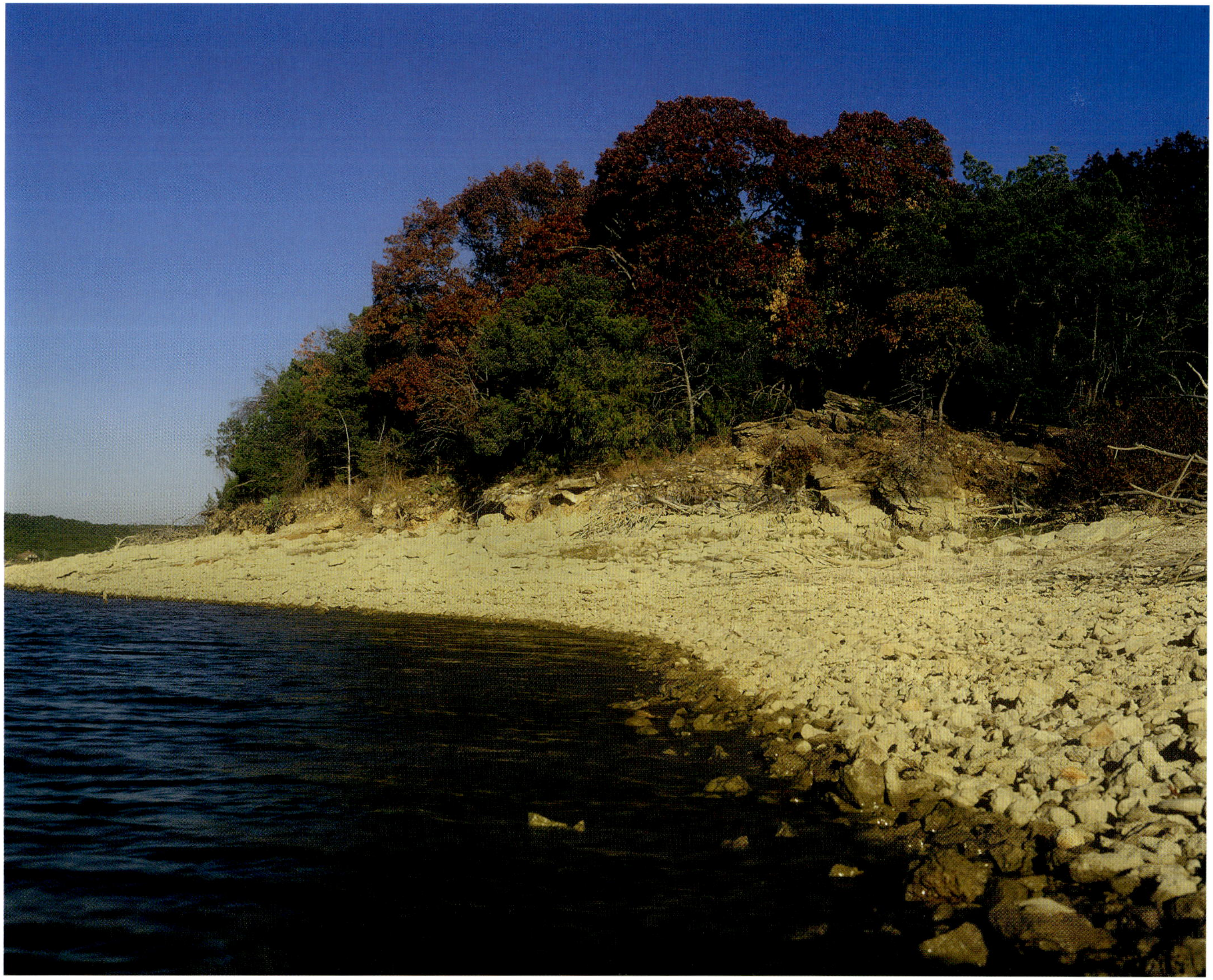

Panola County

Late-Afternoon Light on Pecan Trees

The county was formed in 1846, and the name of the county is derived from a Native American word for cotton. In the early 1840s, a feud erupted between two factions who called themselves Regulators and Moderators. For almost four years, skirmishes extended from Harrison County and the Caddo Lake area through Shelby and San Augustine Counties and into Sabine County. The so-called Regulator-Moderator War grew out of the unsettled border conditions. The Neutral Ground furnished a secure residence for lawless men, and their activities caused the growth of vigilante groups. The warfare ended in 1844, when President Sam Houston ordered the militia to stop it.

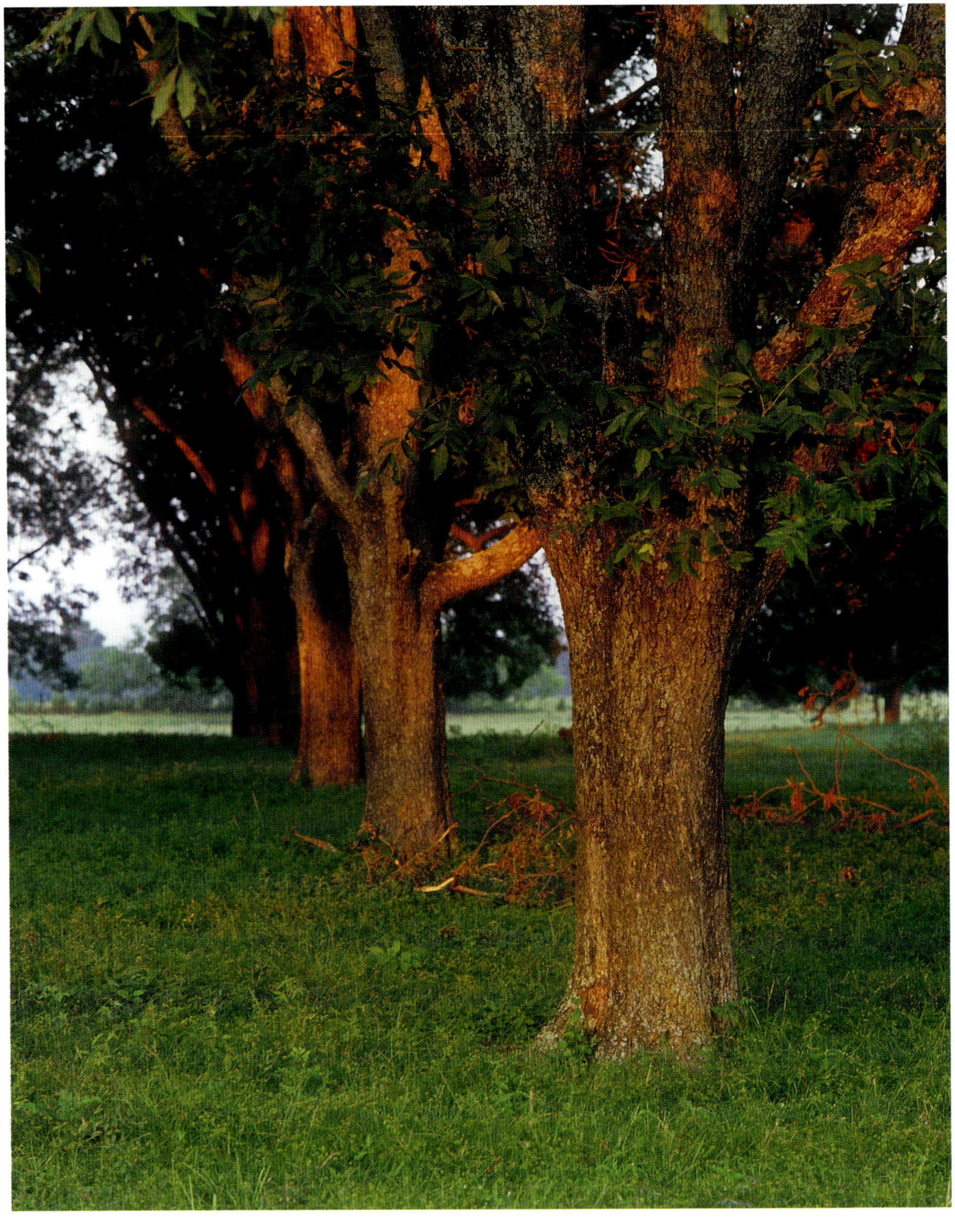

Parker County

Lake Mineral Wells State Park

The county was created in 1855 and organized the following year. It is named for Isaac Parker, a state legislator who introduced the bill that established the county in 1855. The economy grew rapidly in the first years of the twentieth century, partly because cotton cultivation continued to expand rapidly. By 1910 almost 90,000 acres in the county were planted in cotton.

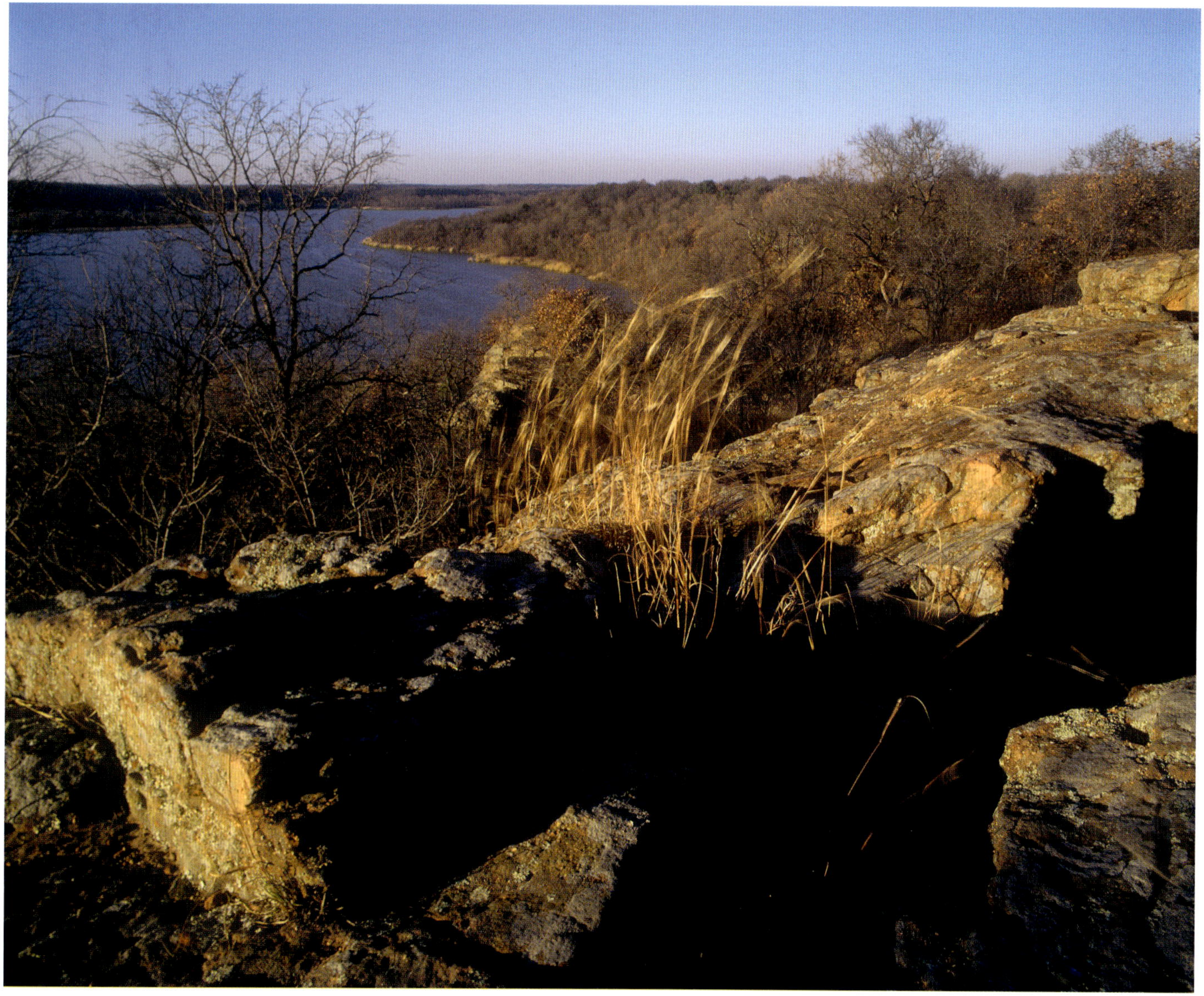

Parmer County

An October Sunrise

The county was created in 1876 and organized in 1907. It is named in honor of Martin Parmer, a signer of the Texas Declaration of Independence and an early judge. Kiowas and Comanches ruled the Texas High Plains between 1700 and the end of the Red River War in 1874. After their defeat and removal to the Indian Territory, the Parmer County region was opened for white settlement.

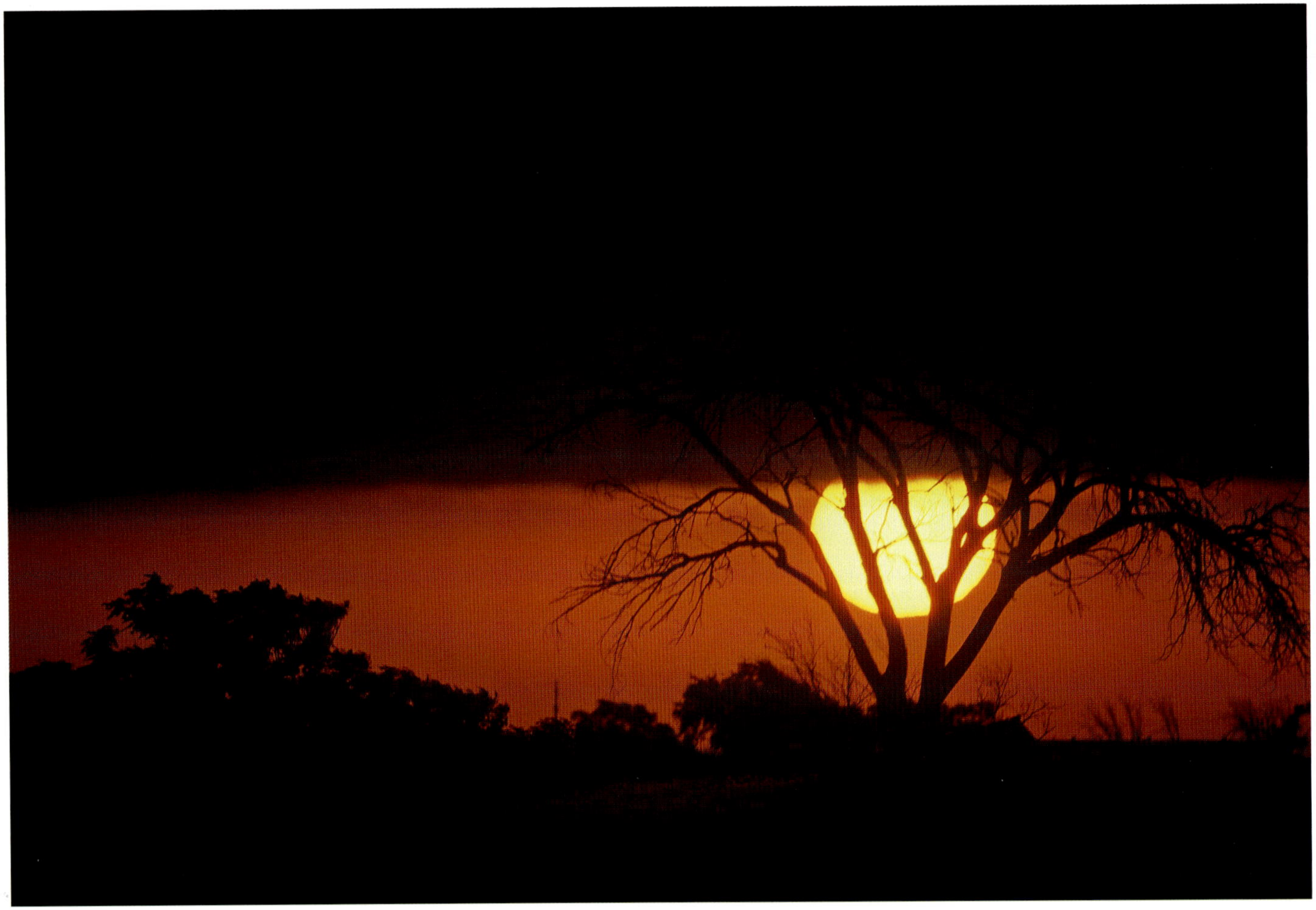

Pecos County

Pecos River

The county was created in 1871 and organized in 1875. It is named for the Pecos River. The town of Iraan, in Pecos County, prides itself on being the birthplace of cartoon caveman Alley Oop when creator V. T. Hamlin worked there in the oil fields. Although the cartoon strip was first published in the *Des Moines Register* in 1932, Hamlin claimed to have originated the idea while he watched dinosaur bones being dug up by oil equipment. Visitors to Iraan can visit the Alley Oop Museum, found on Alley Oop Lane.

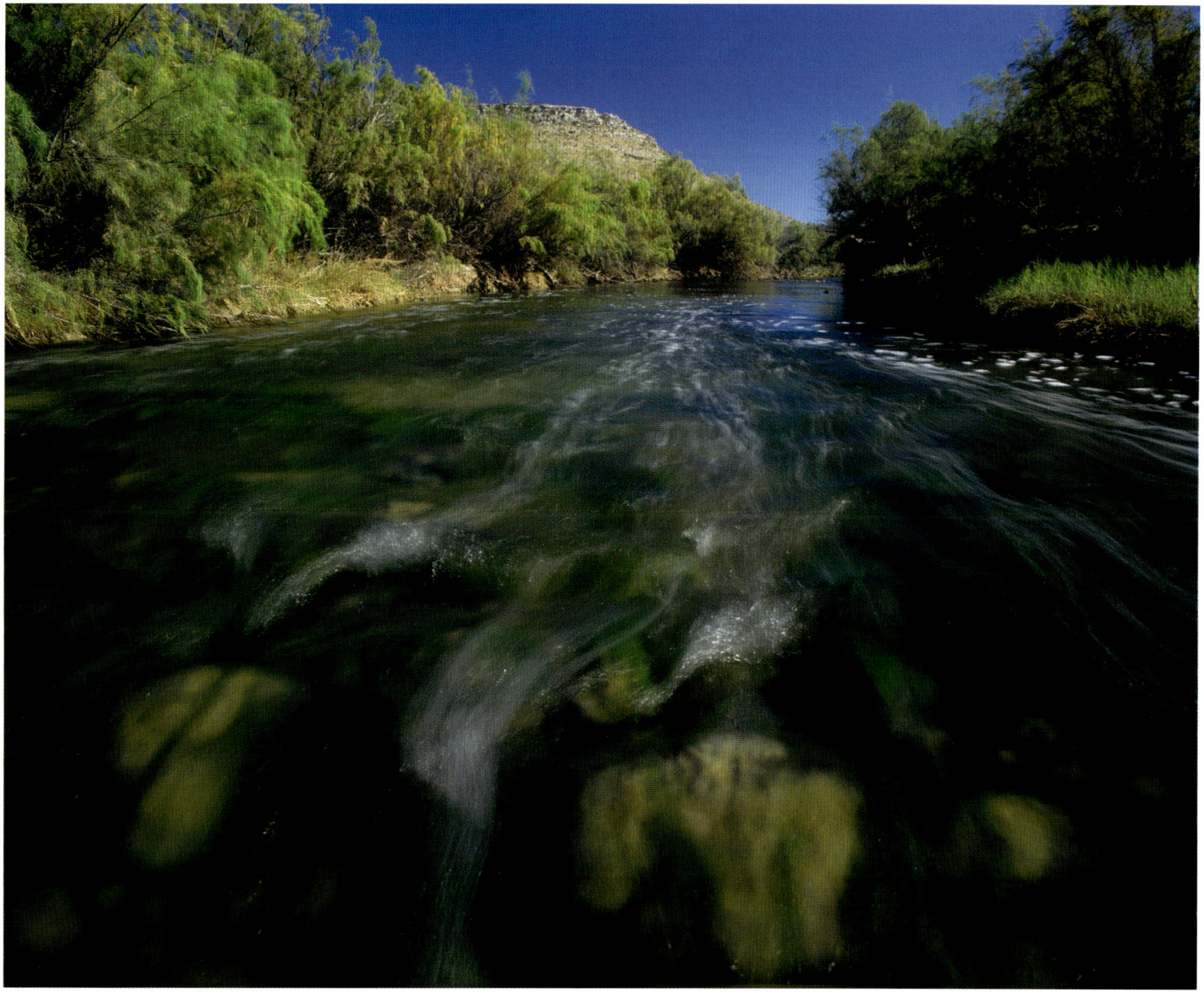

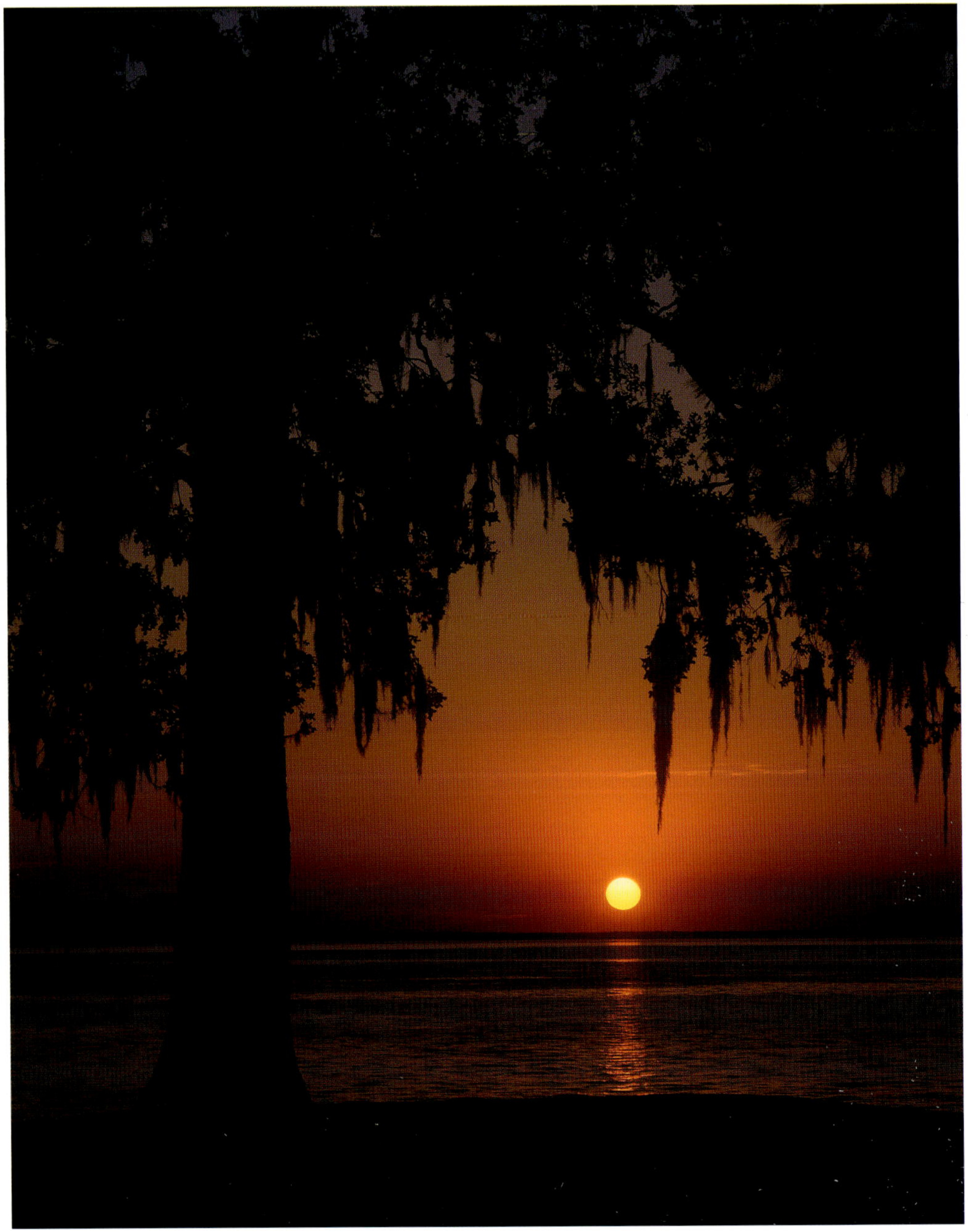

Polk County

Lake Livingston State Park

The county was founded in 1846 and is named for James Knox Polk, the eleventh president of the United States. The Alabama-Coushatta Indian Reservation of the federally recognized tribe is in eastern Polk County, where the people have been since the early nineteenth century after migrating from the Southeast.

Potter County

Lake Meredith National Recreation Area

The county was created in 1876 and organized in 1887. It is named for Robert Potter, a politician, signer of the Texas Declaration of Independence, and secretary of the Texas navy. The county area slopes to the Canadian River, which flows easterly across the northern part of Potter County. Lake Meredith, formed when the Canadian River was dammed in 1965, extends about 8 miles into the northwestern section of the county.

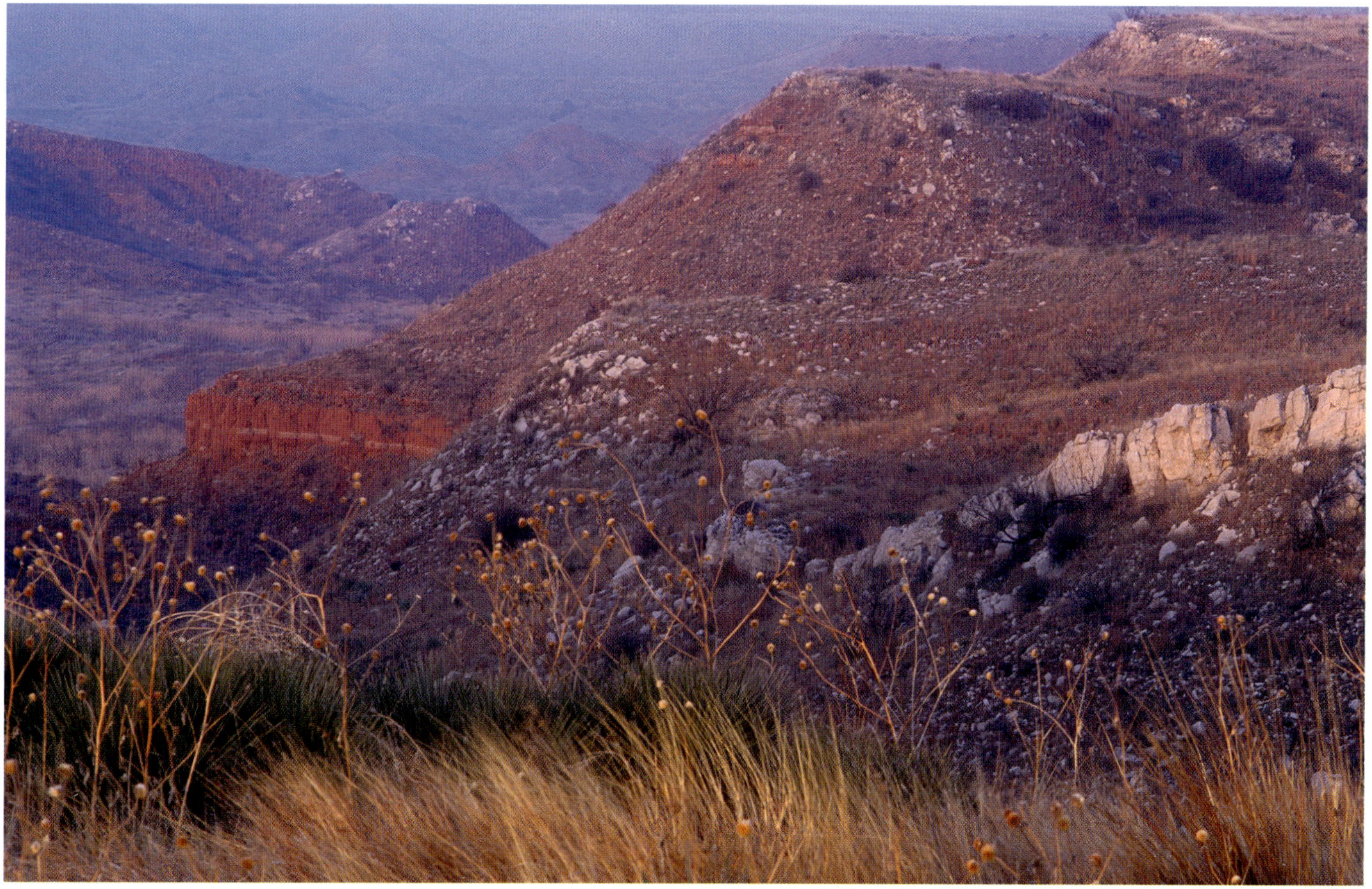

Presidio County

Rio Grande in Big Bend Ranch State Park

The county is named for Presidio del Norte, an eighteenth-century fort and settlement on the south side of the Rio Grande. The county was founded in 1850 and is home to Big Bend Ranch State Park, the largest state park in Texas. It is also home to the famous Marfa Lights. Wagon trains on the Chihuahua Trail reported seeing unexplained lights as early as the mid-nineteenth century. Since that time, the lights have continued to appear between Marfa and Paisano Pass. Speculation and fascination have sparked imaginations about the source. Some say they are caused by car headlights; some say extraterrestrial visitors. One theory is that the lights are similar to a mirage caused by atmospheric conditions. No one really knows for sure.

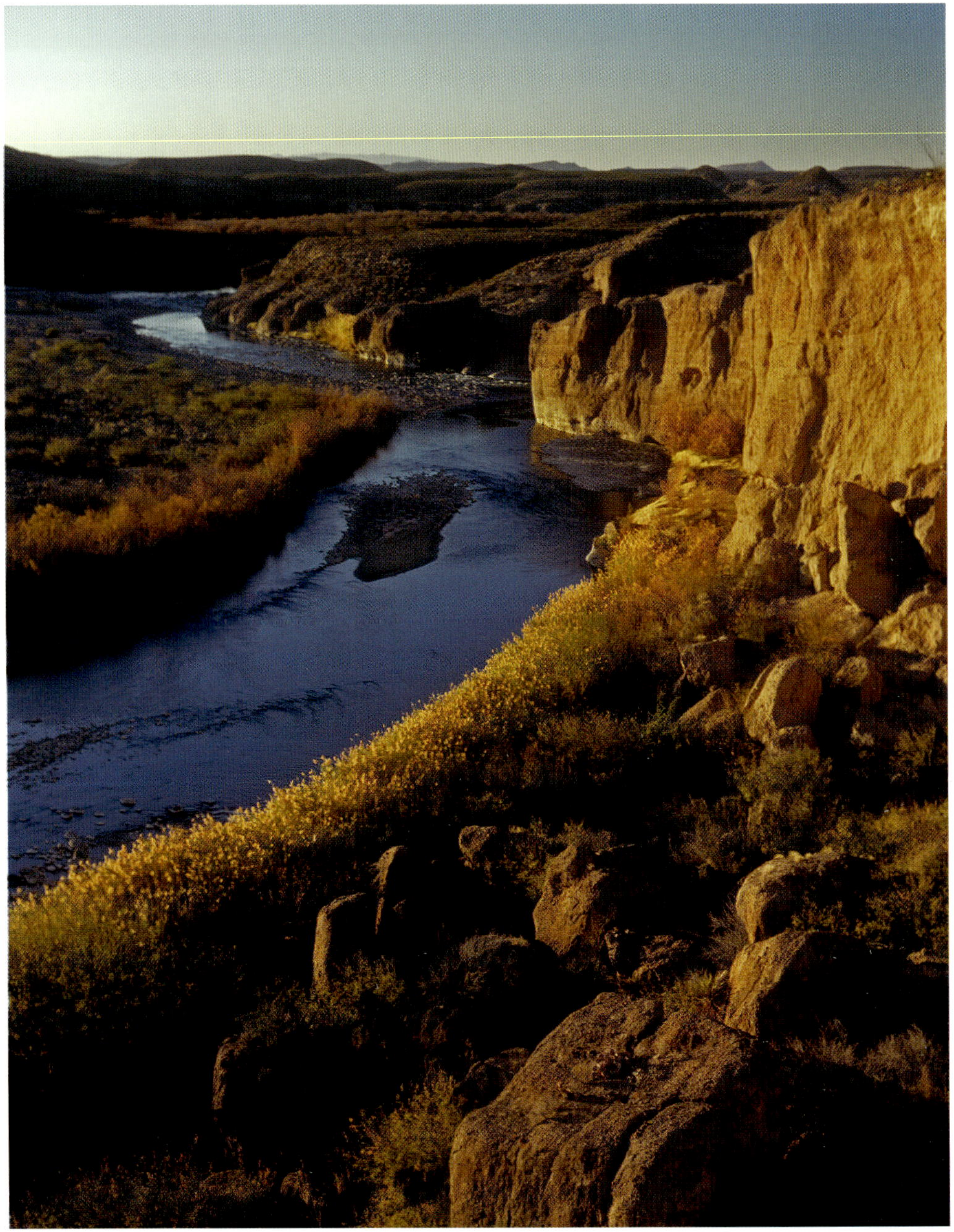

Rains County

Sunset over Lake Tawakoni

The county was founded in 1870 and is named for Emory Rains, a Texas state legislator. The late nineteenth century was a time of unrest in many rural areas, as farm owners and tenants rebelled against what they believed were unfair practices of banks and railroads. The agrarian populist movement was especially strong in Rains County. In the 1870s, many farmers organized granges—cooperative ventures aimed at bypassing the big-city middlemen.

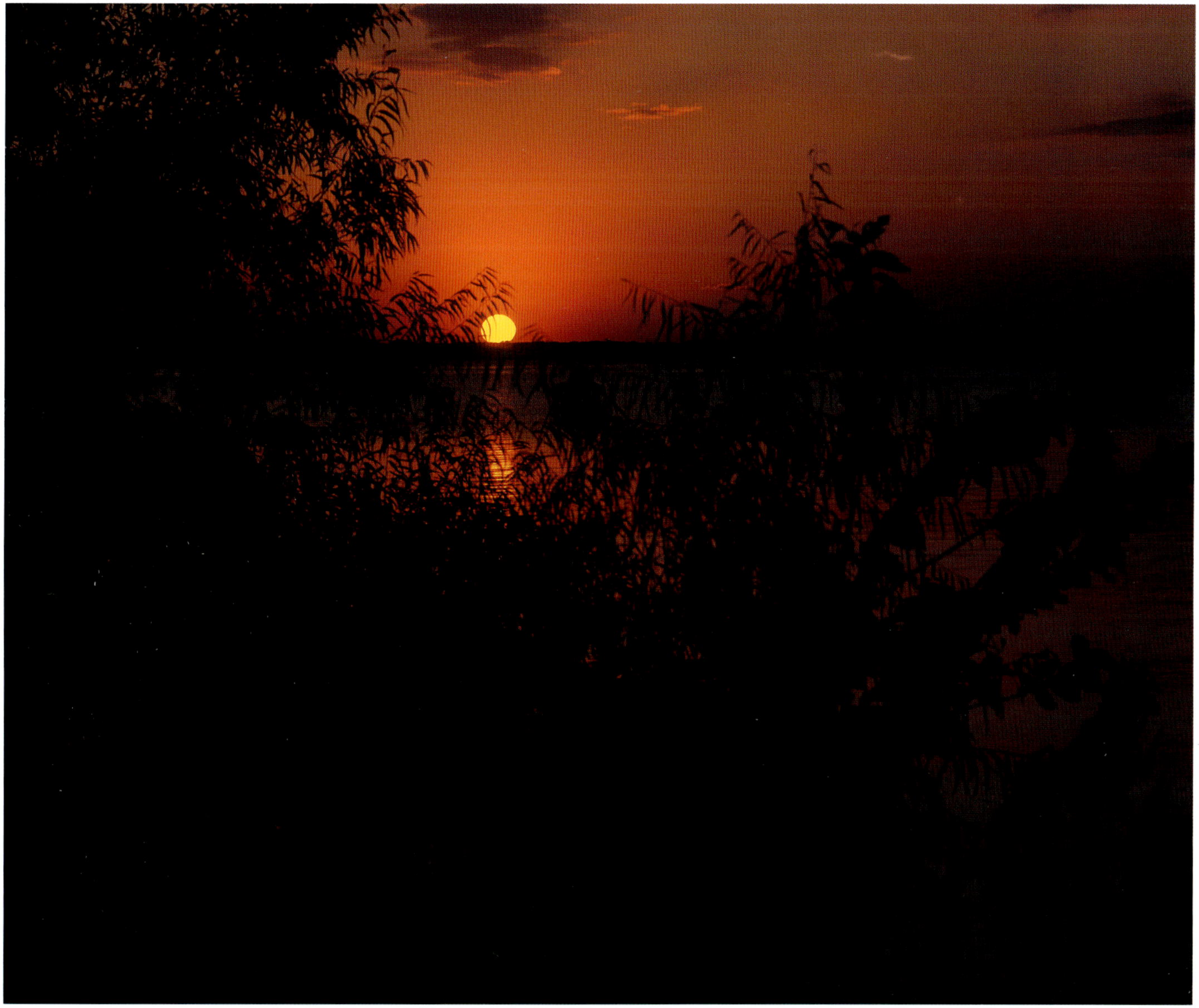

Randall County

Palo Duro Canyon State Park

The county was created in 1876 and organized in 1889. It is named for Horace Randal, a Confederate brigadier general killed at the Battle of Jenkins Ferry. The reason the county name differs from his is that the bill creating the county misspelled Randal's name. Settlement began in 1876, when Charles Goodnight drove 1,600 head of cattle into Palo Duro Canyon and established his Old Home Ranch. Goodnight's wife, Molly, became enshrined in the minds and hearts of countless cowboys as the "Mother of the Panhandle." Molly became doctor, nurse, homemaker, spiritual comforter, sister, and mother to the hands who worked for her husband. Rescuing and raising orphaned buffaloes, Mrs. Goodnight helped establish the Goodnight buffalo herd, which became well known throughout the world.

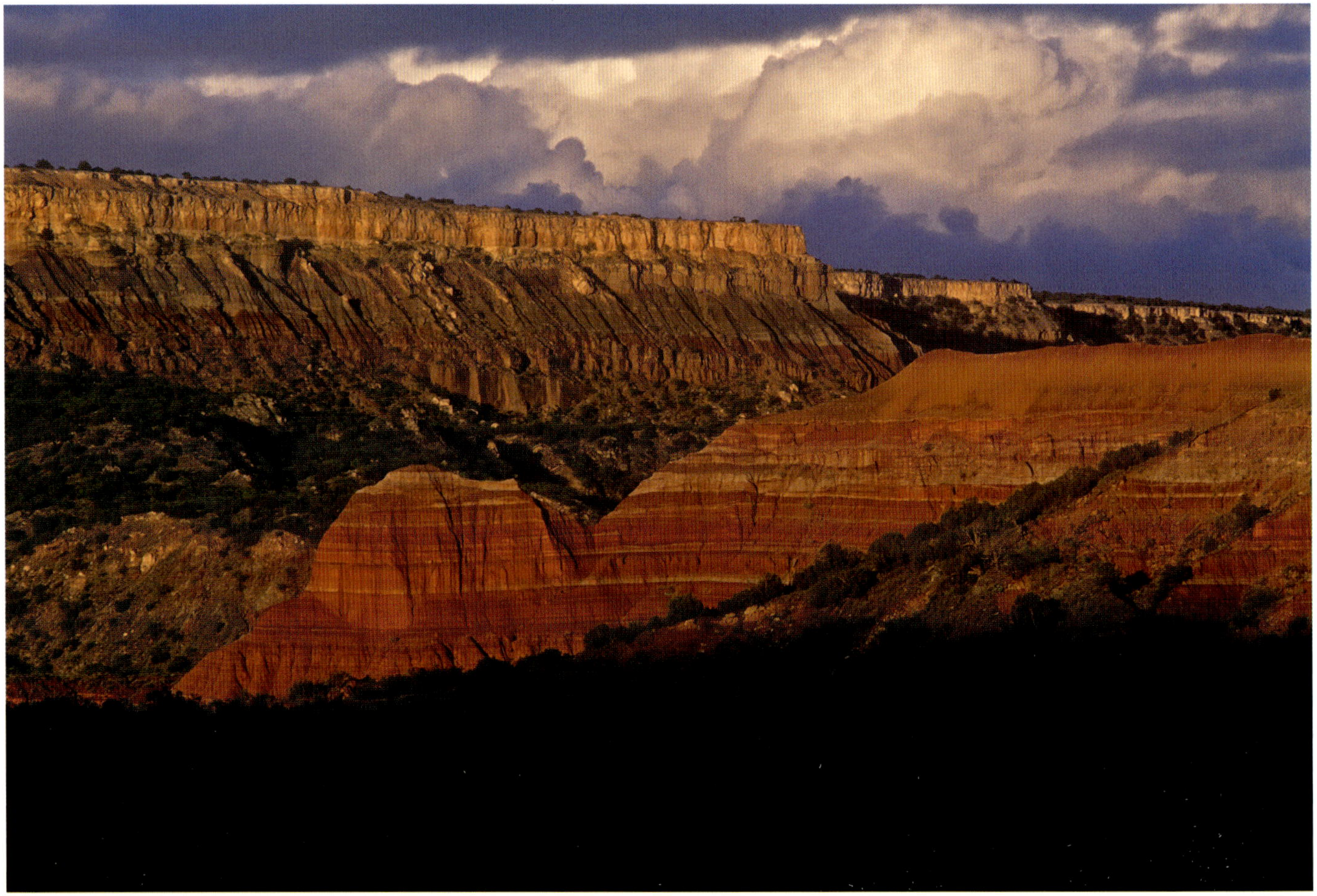

Reagan County

Windblown Mesquite Tree

The county, which was founded in 1903, is named in honor of John Henninger Reagan (1818–1905), who served as postmaster general of the Confederate States of America and also as a US senator, US representative, and first chairman of the Railroad Commission of Texas. In 1923, oil was discovered at the Big Lake Oil field in the Permian Basin; the discovery opened the Permian Basin to oil production. The original rig is named Santa Rita #1 for the Patron Saint of the Impossible.

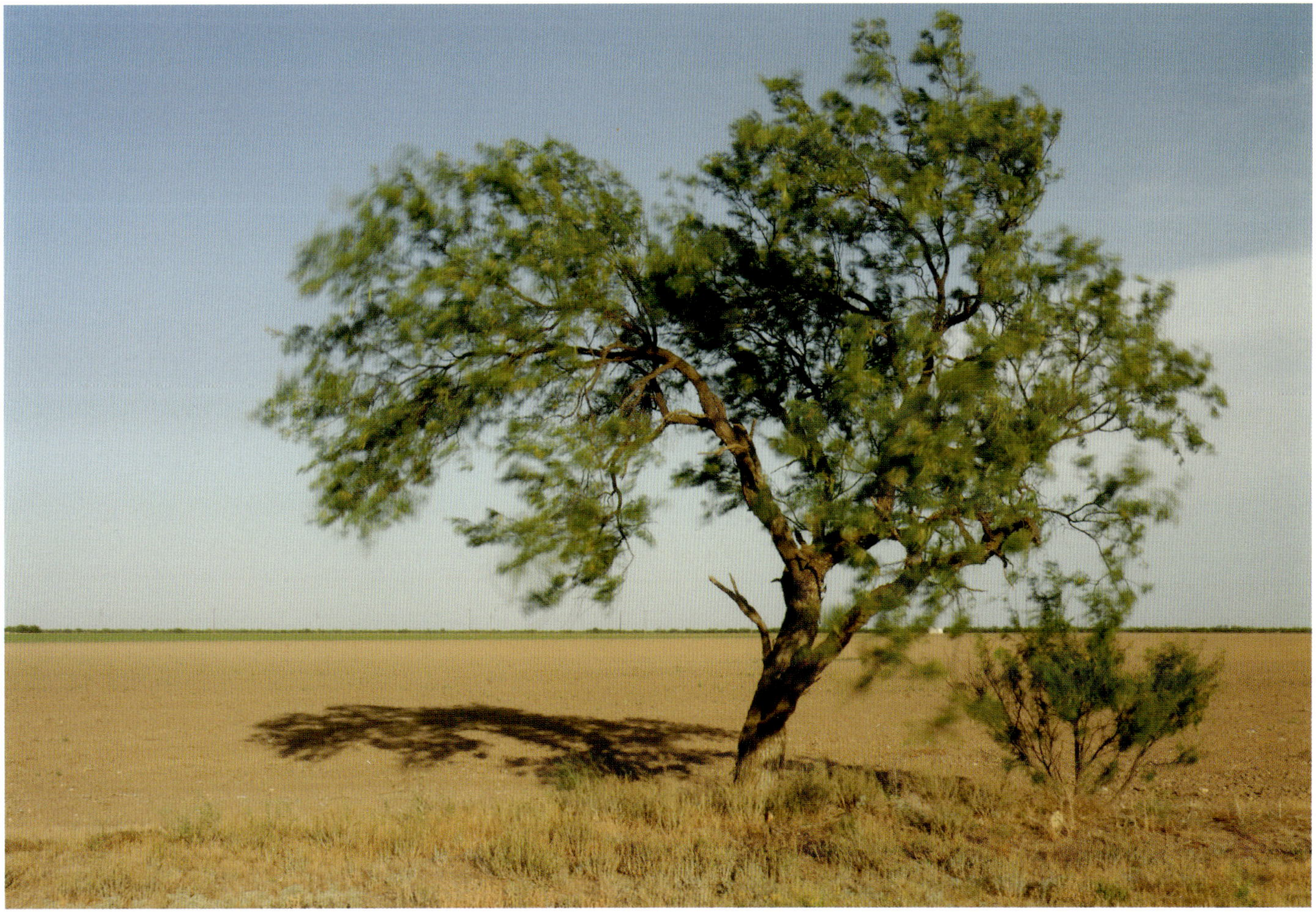

Real County

A Scene in the Heart of the Hill Country along RM 336

The county is named for Julius Real (1860–1944), a former member of the Texas state senate. The county was established in 1913. Angora was an essential part of the local economy. In the 1950s, there were more registered angora goats in Real County than any other county in the United States.

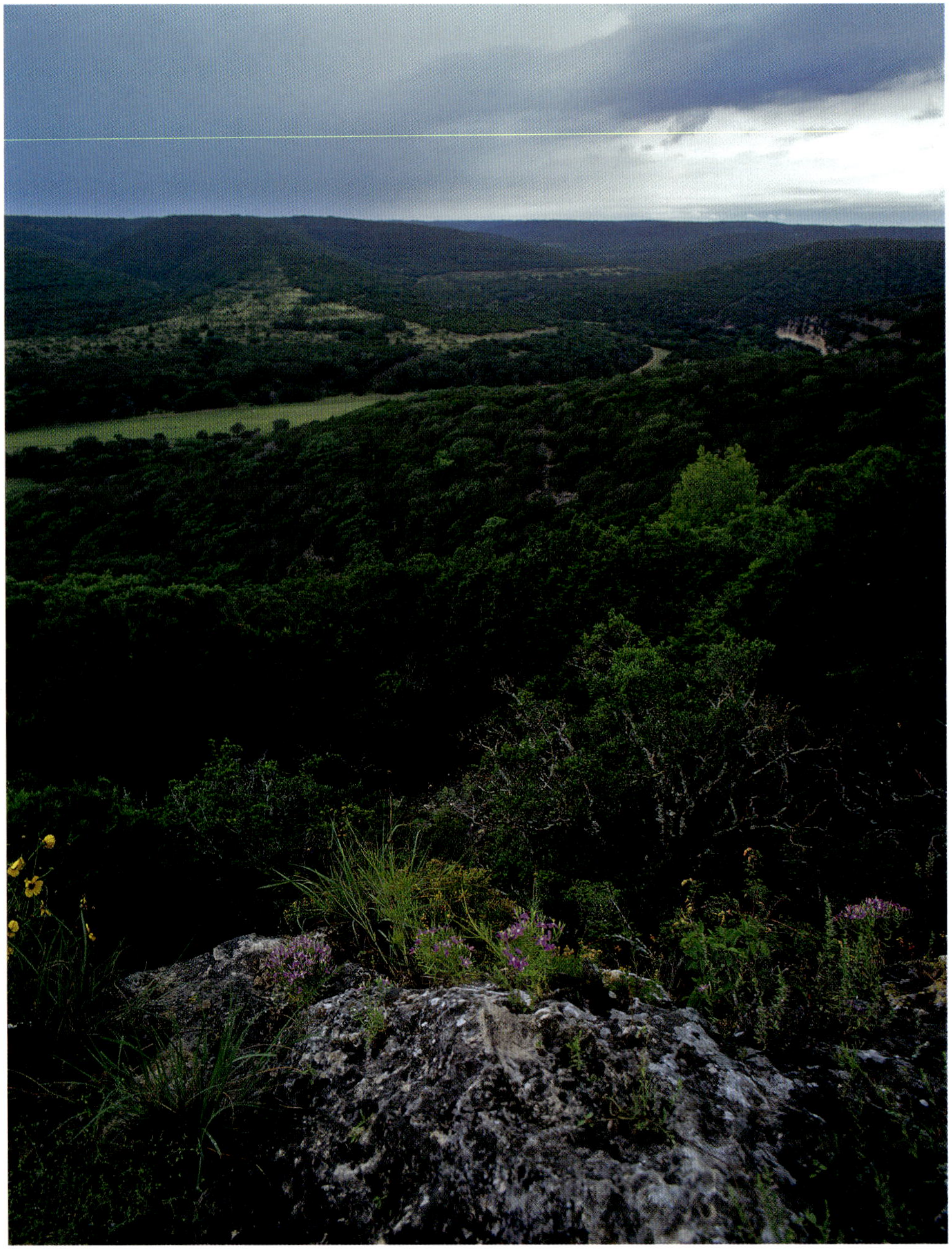

Red River County

Fall Color along a Fence Line

The county was created in 1835 and organized in 1837. It is named for the Red River, which forms its northern boundary. John "Cactus Jack" Garner—a vice president of the United States who served for eight years under President Franklin D. Roosevelt—was born in Red River County in 1868. He once described the vice presidency as "not worth a bucket of warm spit."

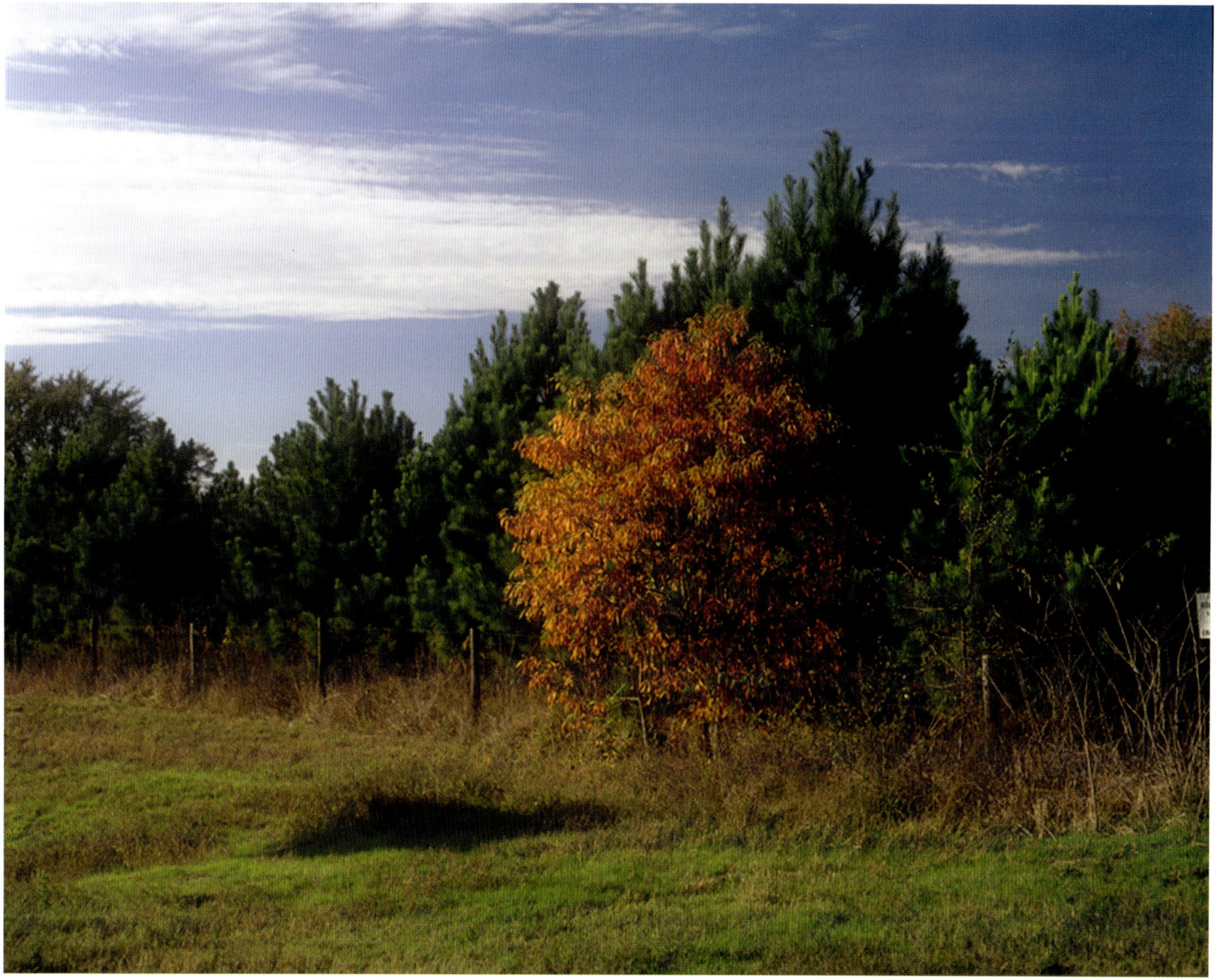

Reeves County

Springtime in the Desert with the Barilla Mountains in the Background

The county was created in 1883 and organized the following year. It is named for George R. Reeves, a Texas state legislator and colonel in the Confederate army. During WWII, Pecos Army Air Field was one of the 120 air bases that trained the pioneer Women Airforce Service Pilots (WASPs) to fly military aircraft for testing and transportation.

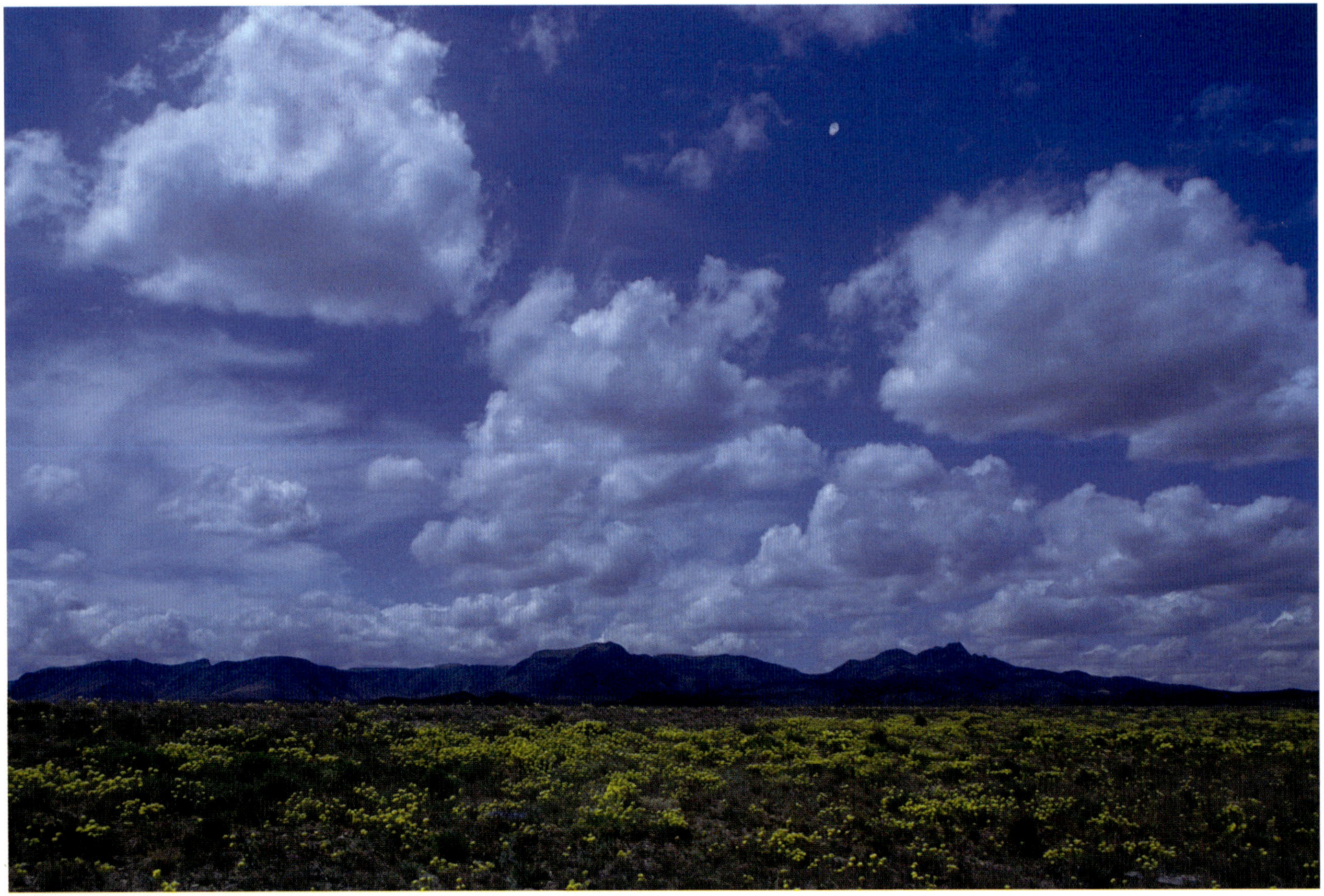

Refugio County

Sunrise over Capano Bay

The county was organized in 1837. It is named for the Spanish mission Nuestra Señora del Refugio, "Our Lady of Refuge." Observer James Murray Doughty captured the prevailing spirit of Refugio County progress as he described the county in the 1850s: "Refugio has three dry-goods stores, two public hotels, one private boarding house, three churches, two schools, two physicians, one dentist, and one lawyer, and no drinking shops and no paupers."

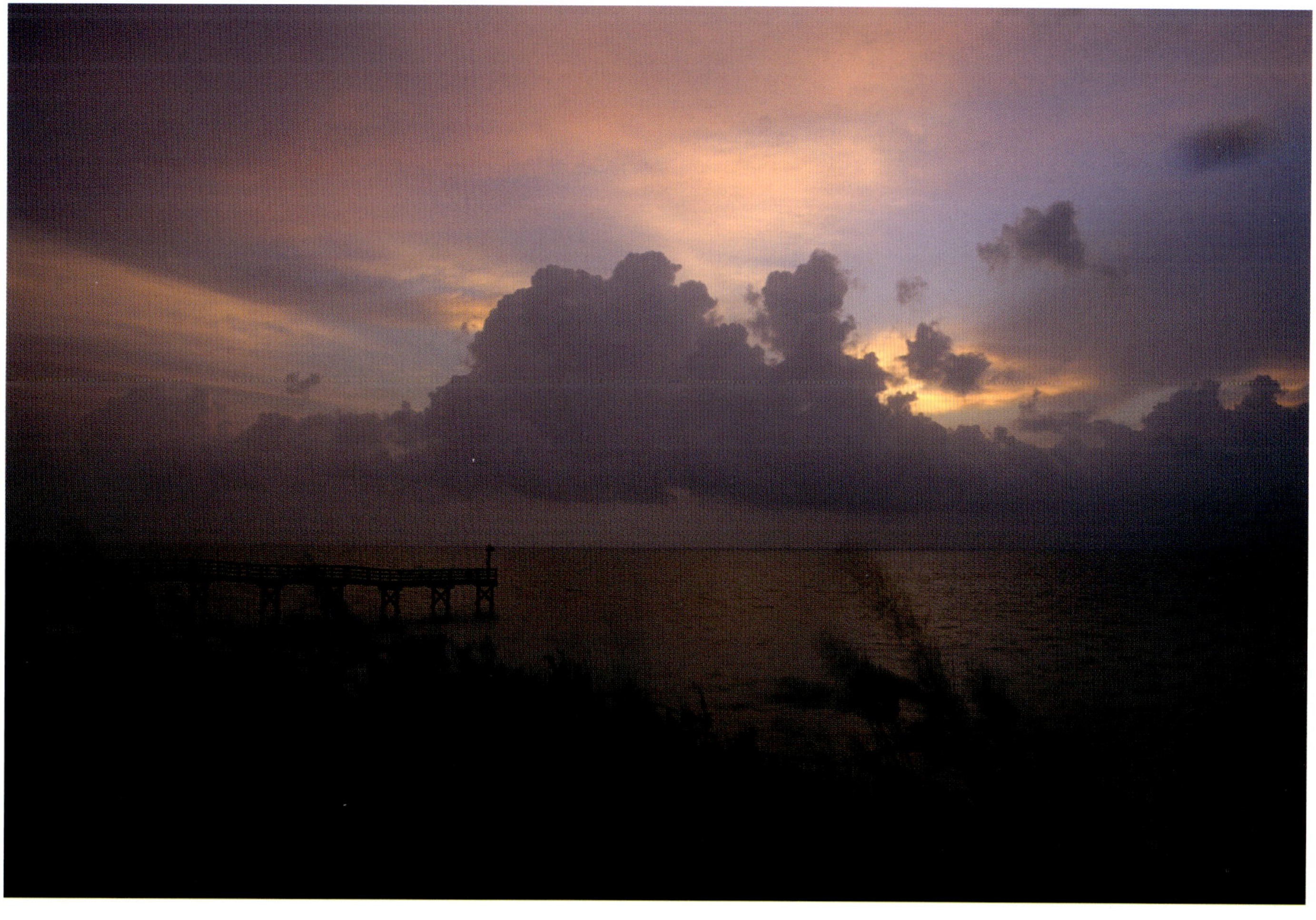

Roberts County

Late-Afternoon Light over Rugged Canyon Country

The county was created in 1876 and organized in 1889. It is named for Oran Milo Roberts, a governor of Texas. Roberts County was the scene of a battle for water rights, where the city of Amarillo, Texas; the Canadian River Municipal Water Authority; and T. Boone Pickens sought to purchase the water rights within the county. Between the three they own 80 percent of the county water rights.

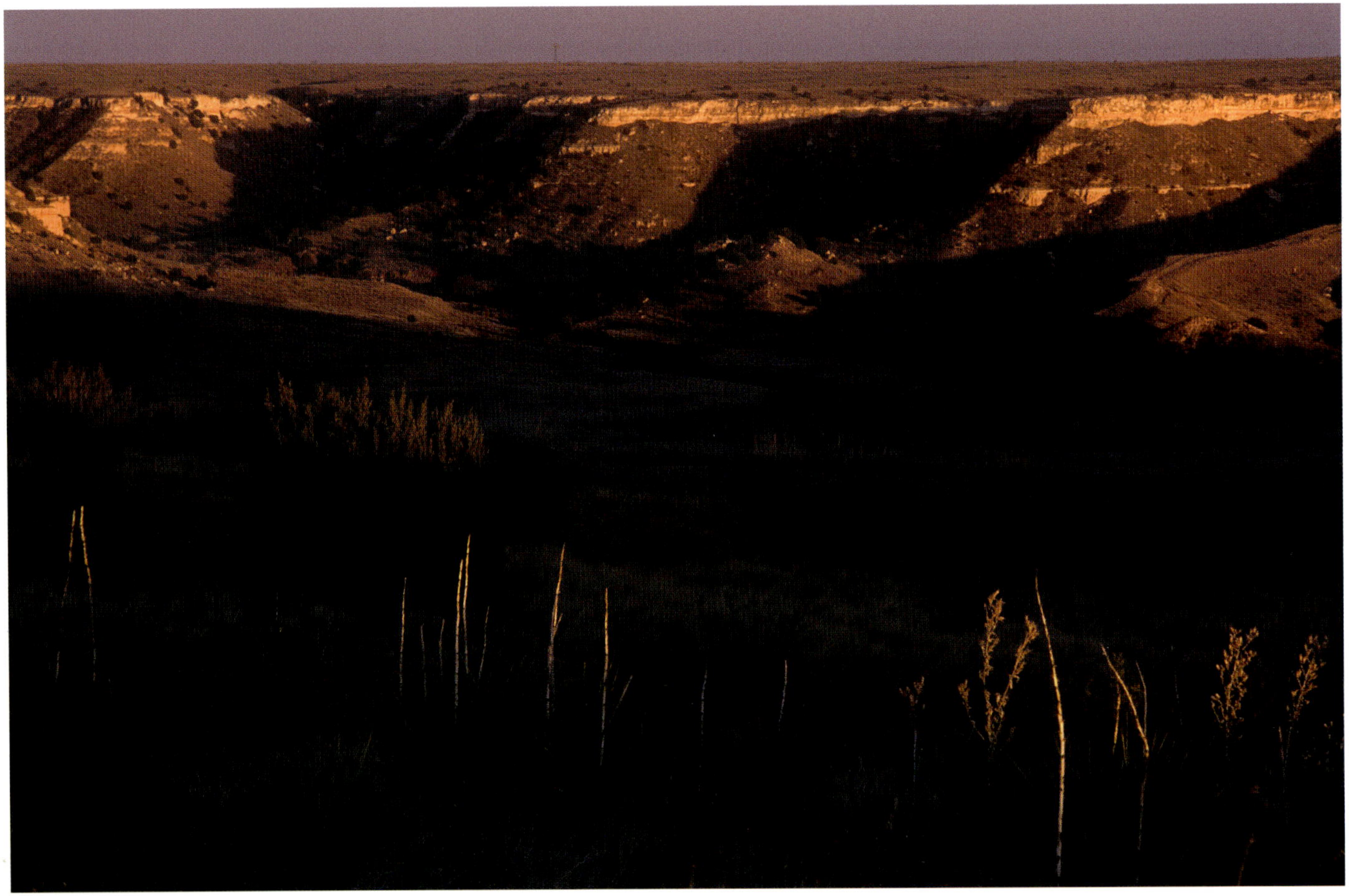

Robertson County

A Springtime Scene with Cedar Trees

The county was created in 1837 and organized the following year. It is named for Sterling C. Robertson, an early settler who signed the Texas Declaration of Independence. Because of a shortage of labor that followed the Civil War, Brazos valley farmers traveled to parts of the Old South to recruit black farmhands, who arrived in large numbers over the next decade and a half. As a result, by the 1880s blacks accounted for the majority of the population (53 percent), a position they would continue to occupy until the turn of the century.

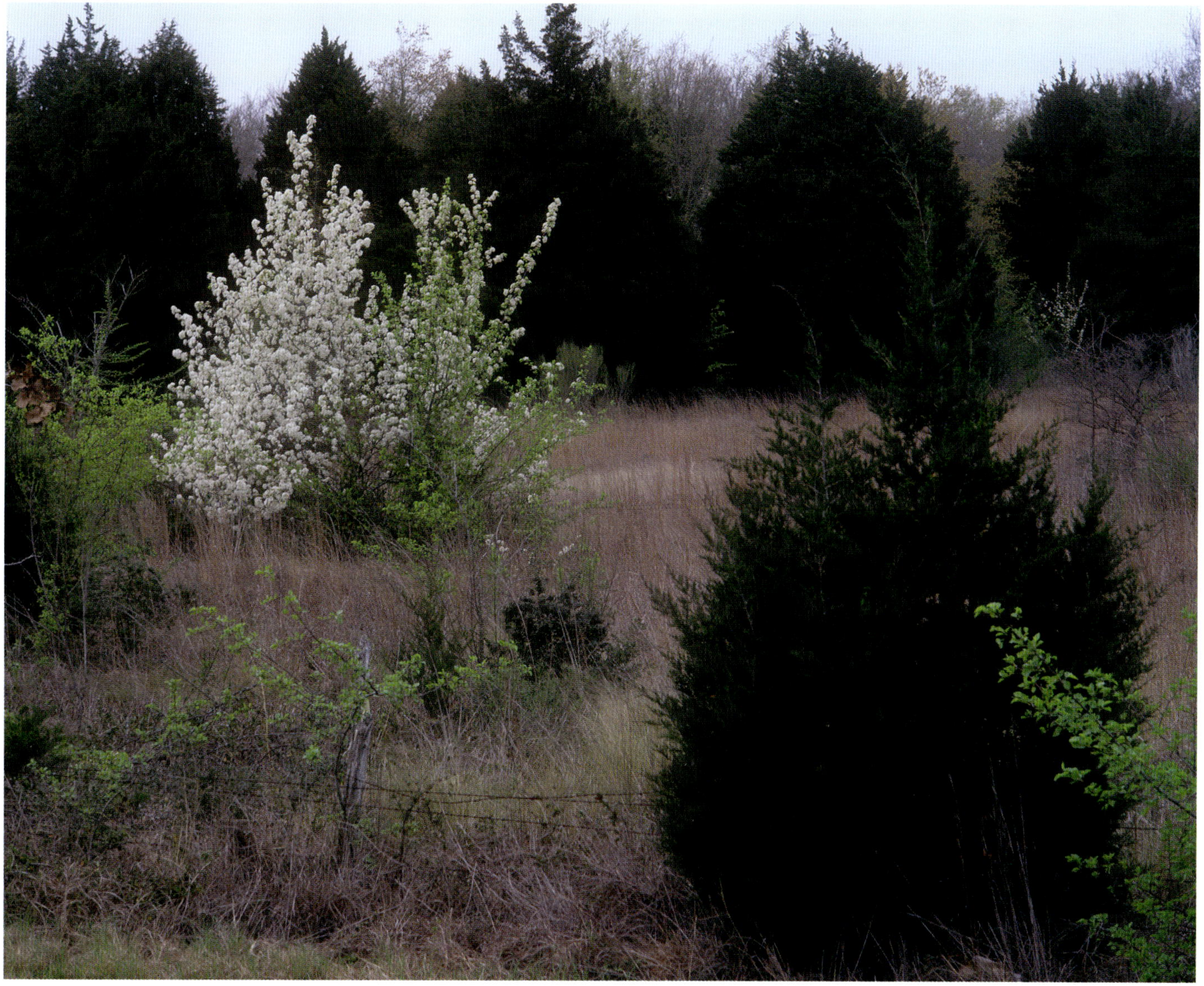

Rockwall County

Rolling Country East of Dallas

The county was founded in 1873 and is named for a wall-like subterranean rock formation that runs throughout the county. The economic structure of the area was altered in 1940 because of the high number of workers commuting to industrial jobs in Dallas. It was estimated that in 1948, one-third of the labor force living in Rockwall County was employed in Dallas.

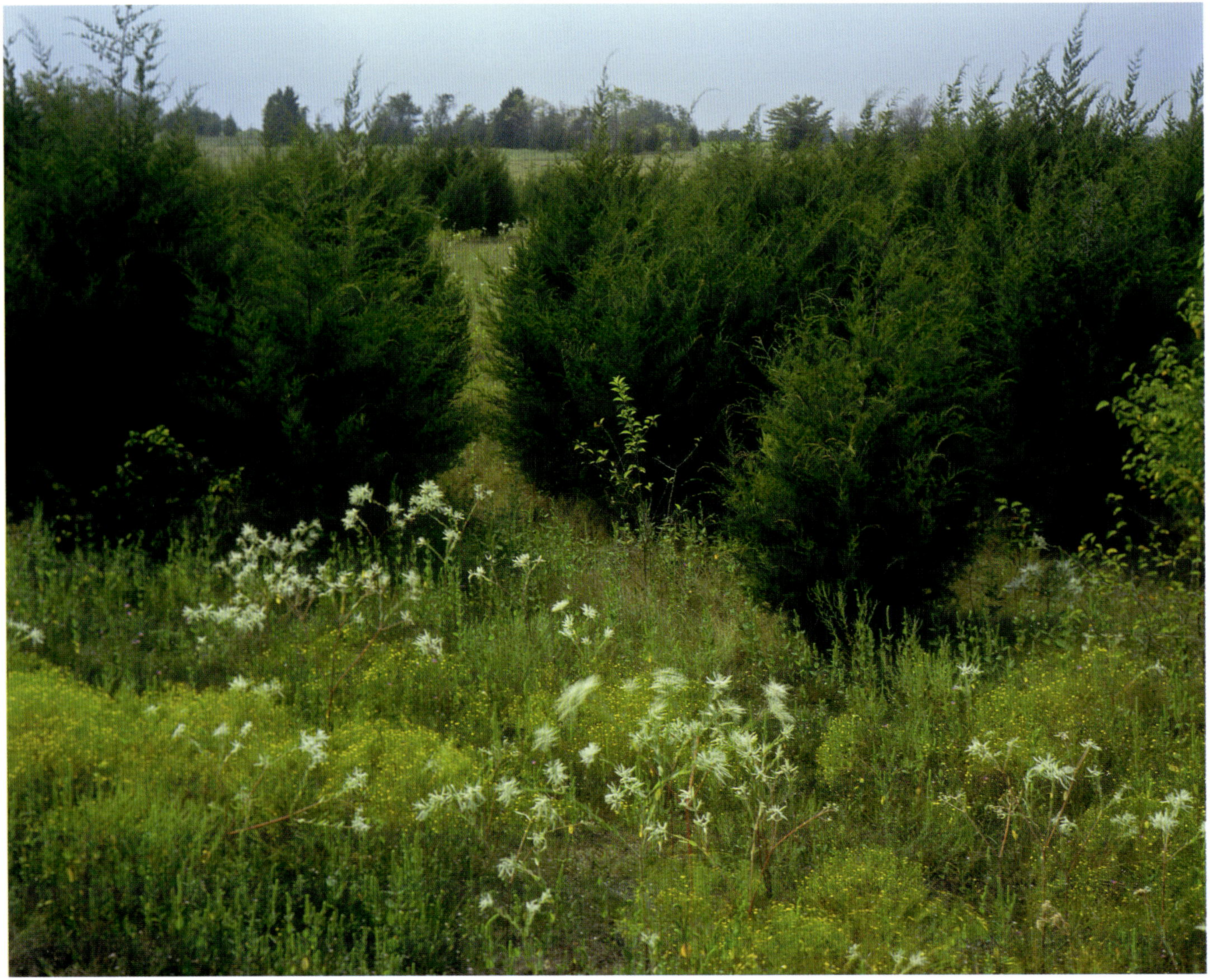

Runnels County

Quarry Creek

The county was created in 1858 and organized in 1880. It is named for Hiram G. Runnels, a Texas state legislator. One of the hardest-fought election issues in county history was over Prohibition. Time after time the county split. The southern third of the county was populated mainly by German Czech immigrants, and they voted against the northern two-thirds, largely native-born Anglos who voted for Prohibition. The election battle raged over the wet-dry controversy until the passage of the Volstead Act in 1919, which forbade the sale of alcohol on a nationwide basis, bringing the county debate to an end. Runnels County remained dry until September 1959.

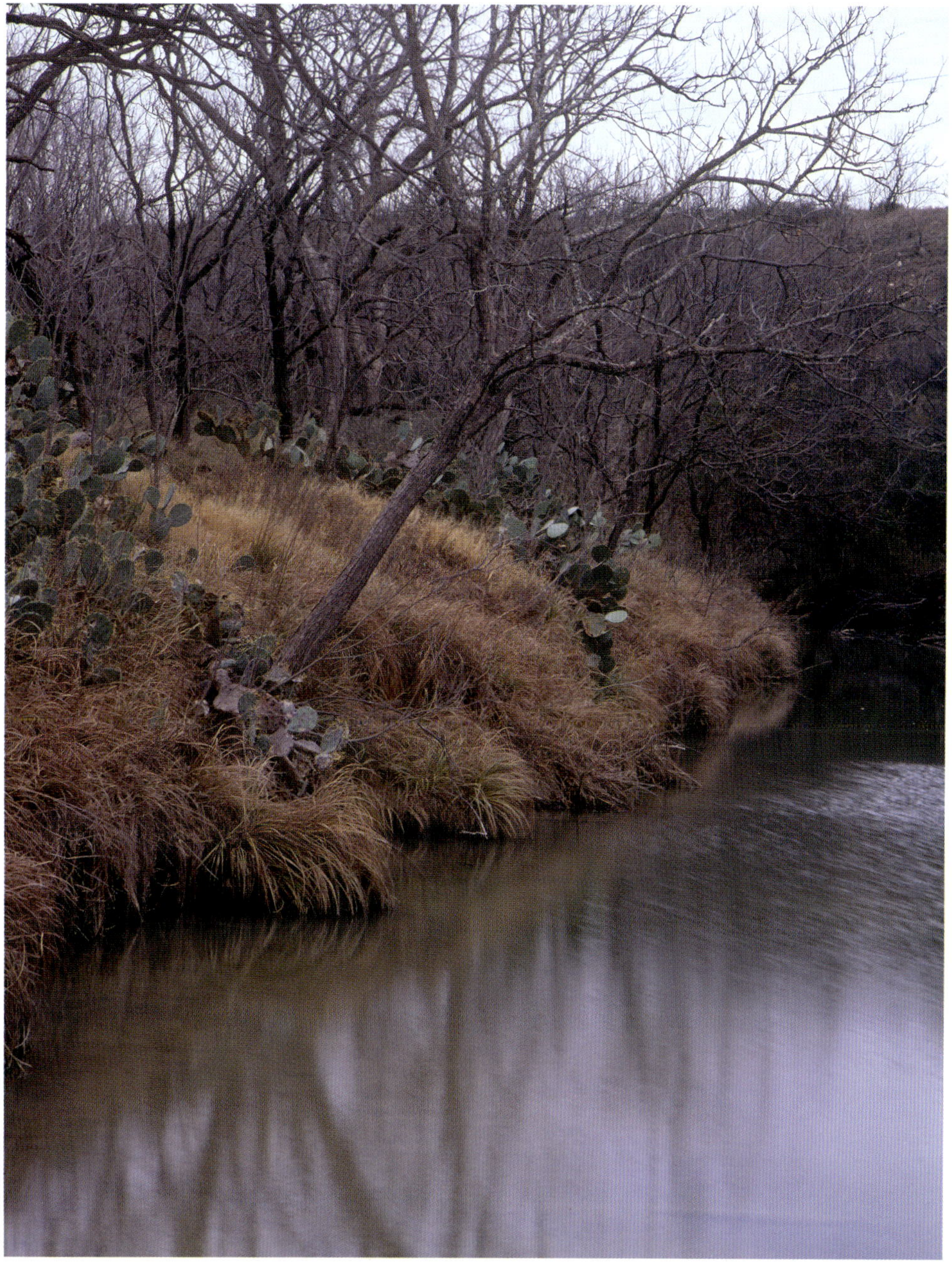

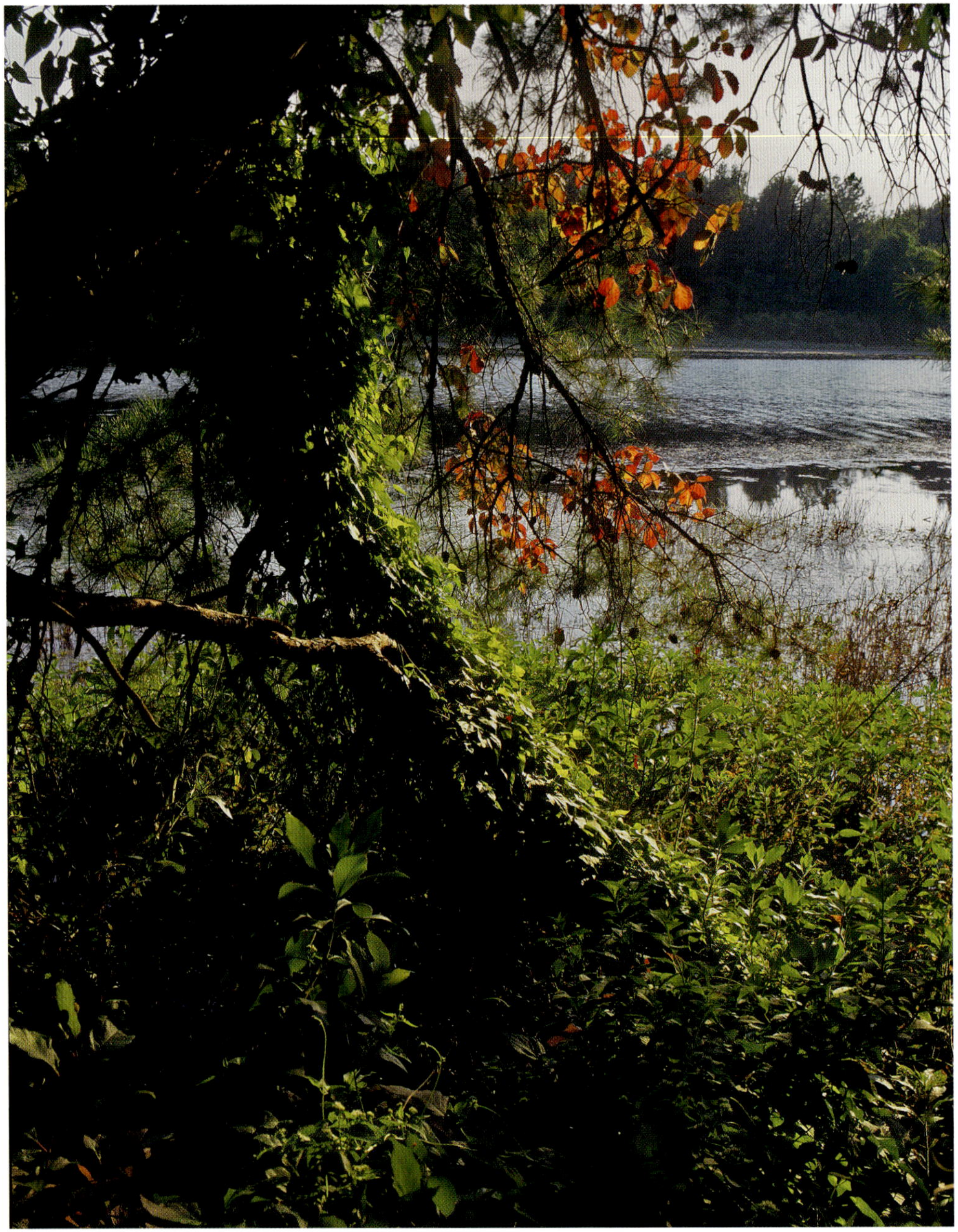

Rusk County

Martin Creek Lake State Park

The county is named for Thomas Jefferson Rusk, a secretary of war of the Republic of Texas. It was founded in 1843. With the discovery of oil in October 1930, an oil boom began that caused the county population to nearly double during the next decade. Rusk is one of the five counties that is part of the East Texas Oil Field, and oil production has been a significant part of the economy since that time.

Sabine County

Windblown Leaves in the Sabine National Forest

The county was organized on December 14, 1837, and is named for the Sabine River, which forms its eastern border. During the 1930s, two Civilian Conservation Corps camps—one near Pineland and one near Milam—helped the Texas Forest Service build fire watchtowers and roads and assisted in the planting of pine seedlings in the Sabine National Forest, which was established in 1933.

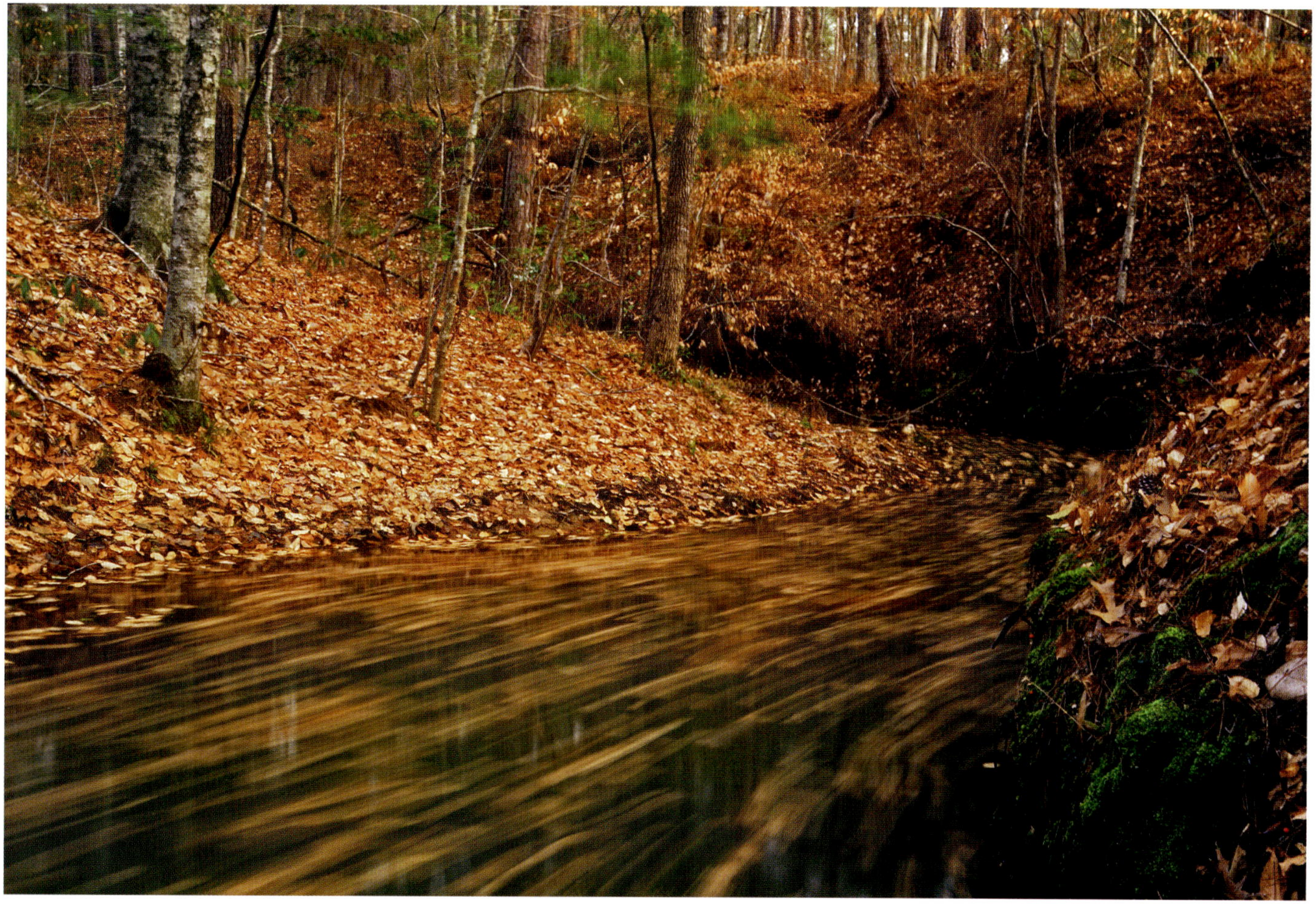

San Augustine County

Sunset over Sam Rayburn Reservoir

San Augustine County was formed in 1837. It was supposedly named after Saint Augustine of Hippo. However, it seems plausible that the county was named for the town of San Augustine, which was established five years earlier and whose name was based on an eighteenth-century Spanish presidio (fortress). The Sam Rayburn Reservoir is in the county. The reservoir is designed for flood control and power generation, is owned by the United States government, and is operated by the United States Army Corps of Engineers. It has become a top spot for bass fishermen.

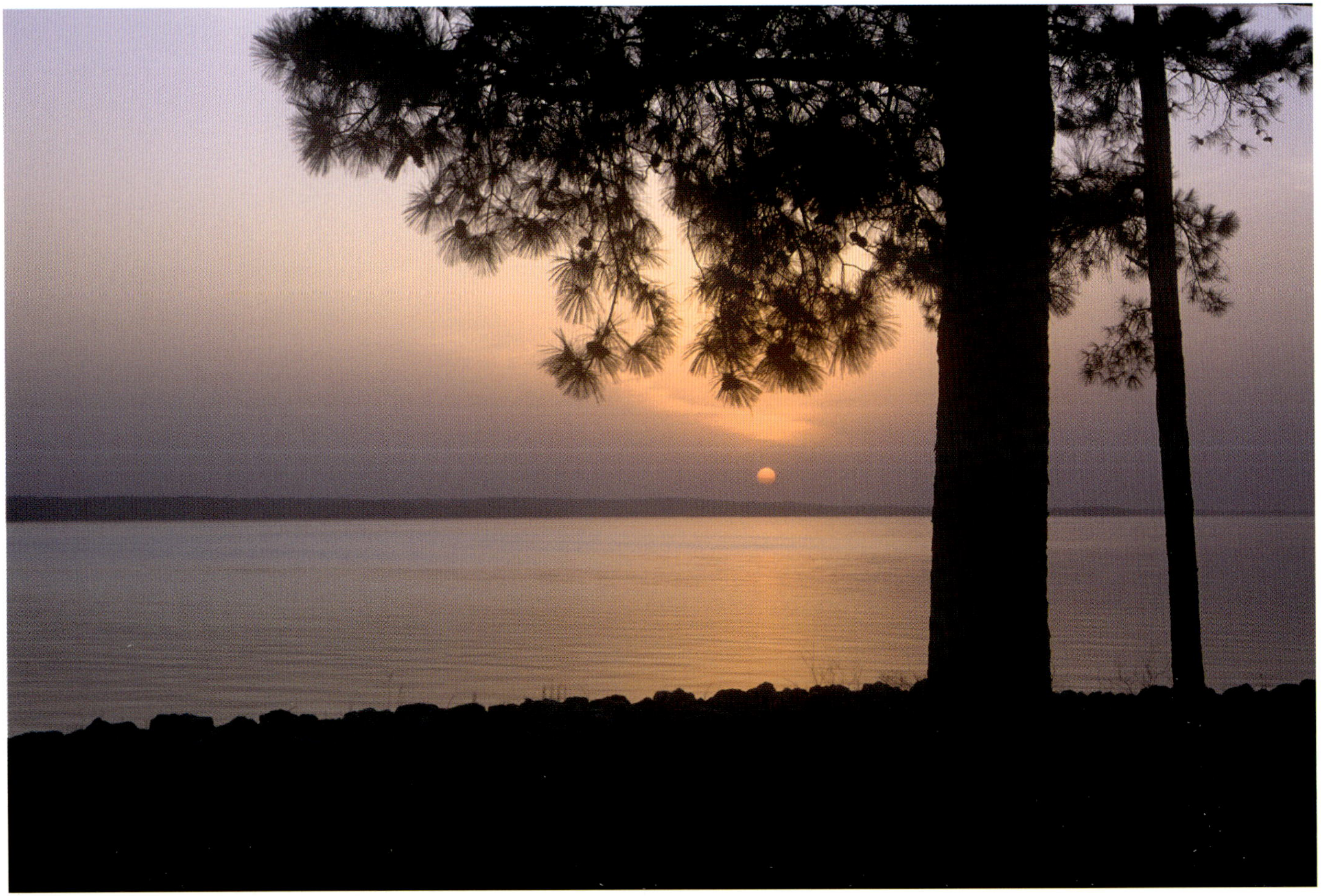

San Jacinto County

Magnolia Roots along the Four Notch Loop Trail in Sam Houston National Forest

The county was founded in 1870. The county's name comes from the Battle of San Jacinto, which, in 1836, secured Texas's independence from Mexico and established the Republic of Texas. At the Battle of San Jacinto, Sam Houston's men attacked General Santa Ana's Mexican army with shouts of "Remember the Alamo!" and "Remember Goliad!" The battle lasted but eighteen minutes. According to Houston's official report, the casualties were 630 Mexicans killed and 730 taken prisoner. Against this, only nine of the 910 Texans were killed and thirty were wounded less seriously.

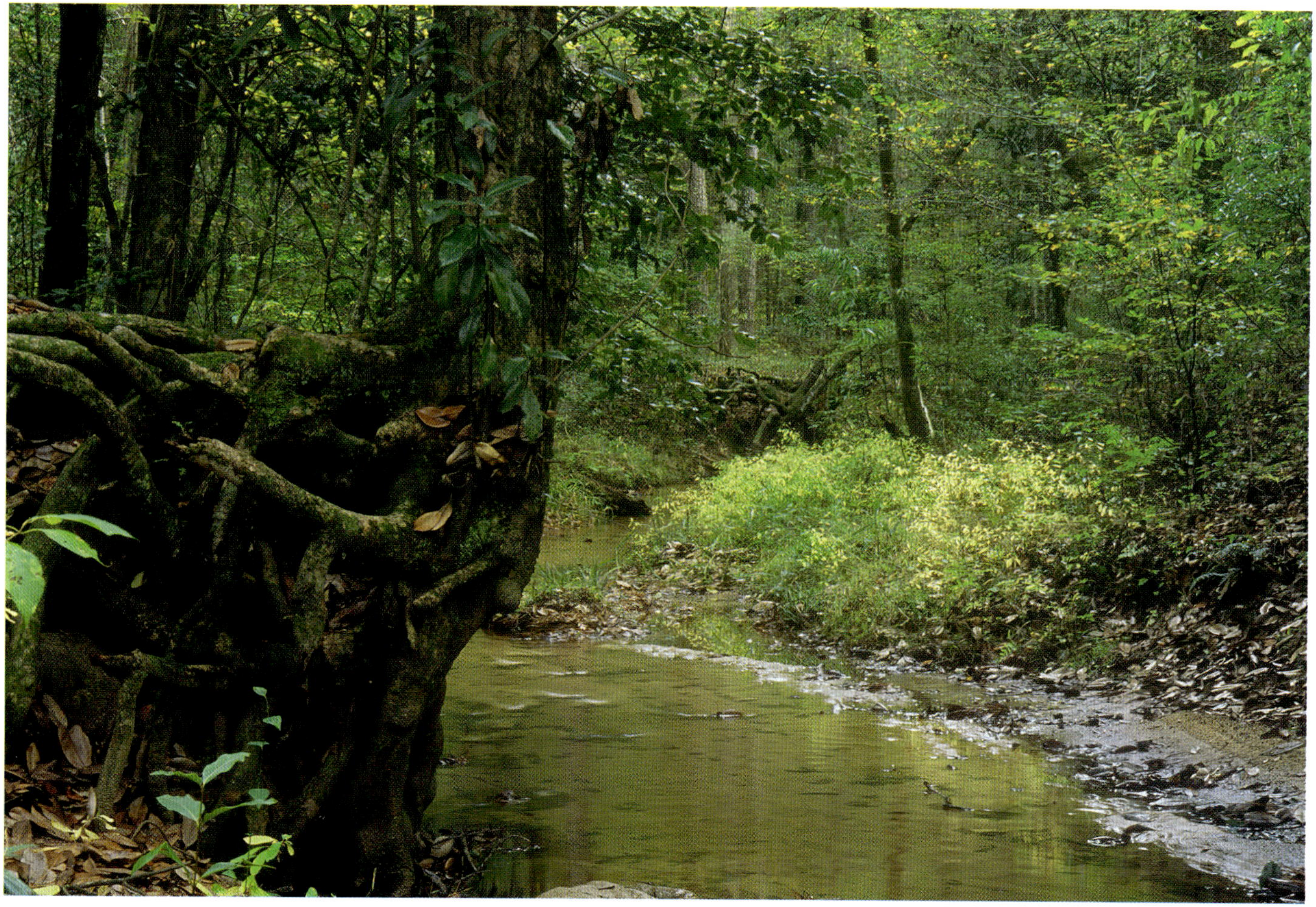

San Patricio County

Lake Corpus Christi State Park

Founded in 1836, the county is named San Patricio de Hibernia for an Irish colony named for Saint Patrick. In 1871, Thomas M. Coleman and George W. Fulton joined with J. M. and Thomas H. Mathis in a partnership that formed the largest cattle firm in Texas. The Coleman, Mathis, and Fulton partnership, which held acreage in San Patricio, Goliad, and Aransas Counties, flourished until an eighteen-month drought in 1878–79 wiped out much of its stock.

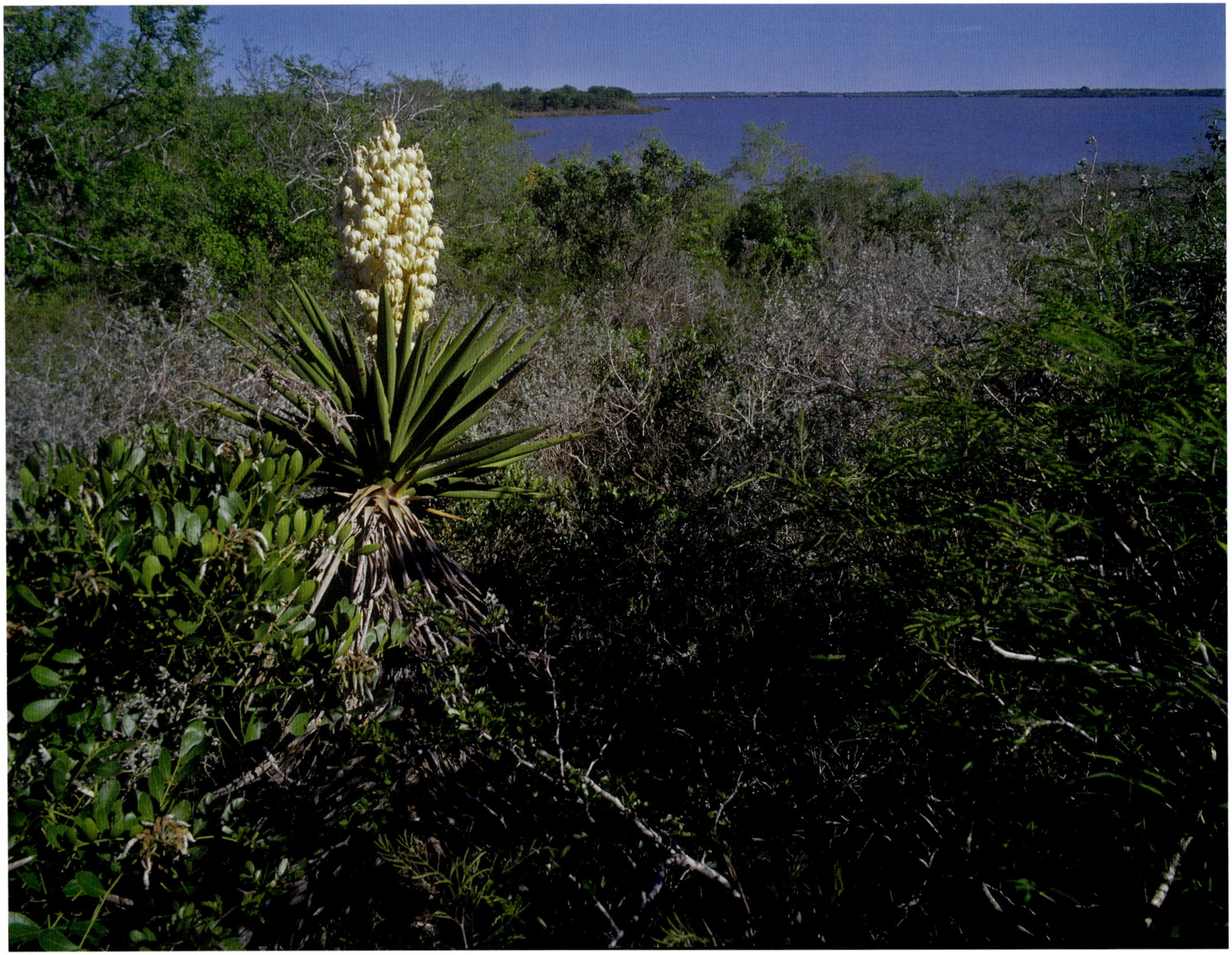

San Saba County

Colorado Bend State Park

The county is named for the San Saba River, which flows through the county. The county was formed in 1856. During the 1880s, a vigilante mob organized like a fraternal lodge killed a number of San Saba County settlers. In 1896, the Texas Rangers began an investigation. Uluth M. Sanderson, the editor of the *San Saba County News*, ran editorials against the mob. Ultimately the mob was broken by Ranger captain Bill McDonald and District Attorney W. C. Linder.

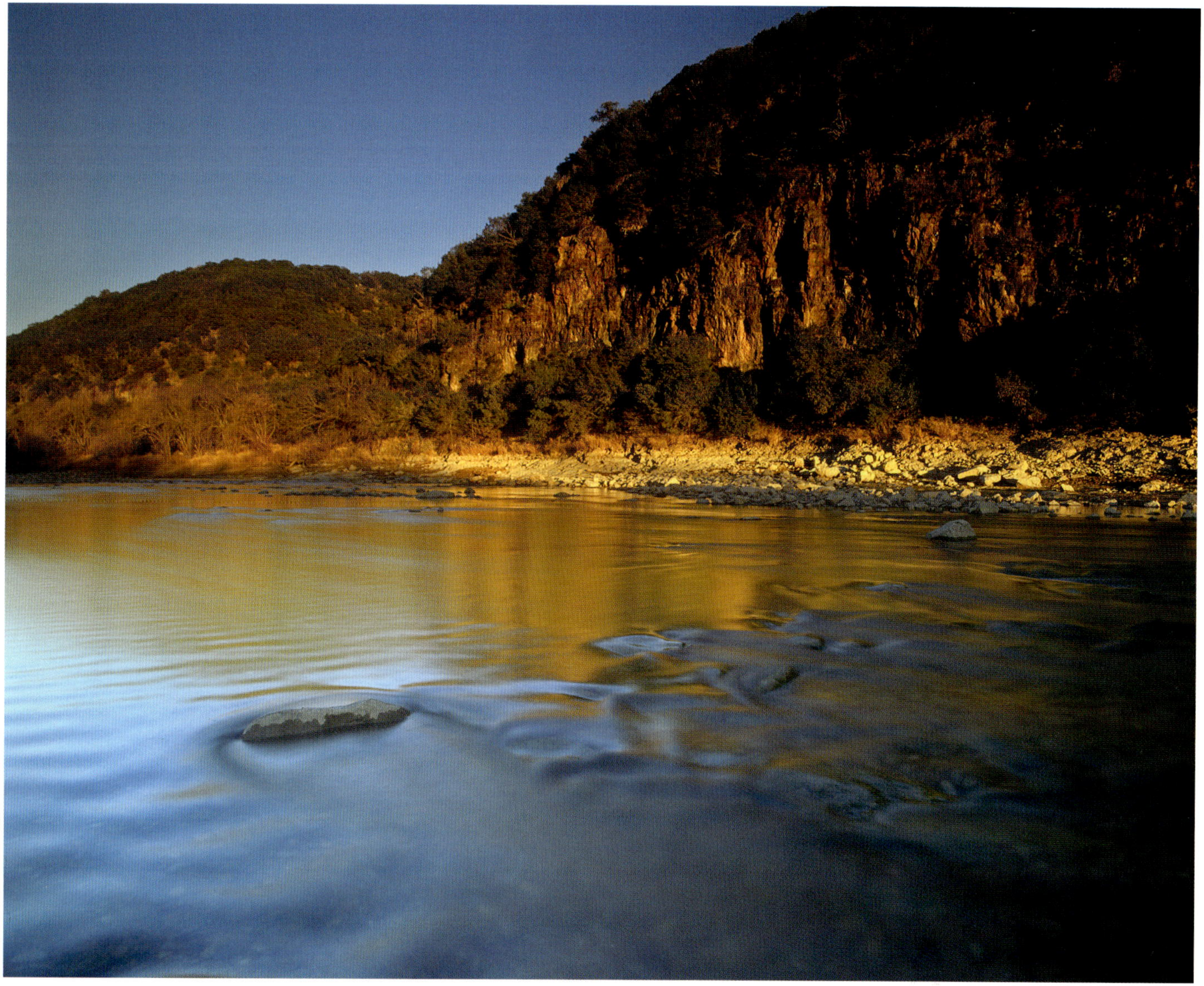

Schleicher County

Sunflowers along a Ranch Fence Line

The county was created in 1887 and organized in 1901. It is named for Gustav Schleicher, a German immigrant who became a surveyor and politician. In 1895, W. B. Silliman founded the Eldorado community and named it after the mythical city. To populate it he offered free town lots to residents of nearby Verand.

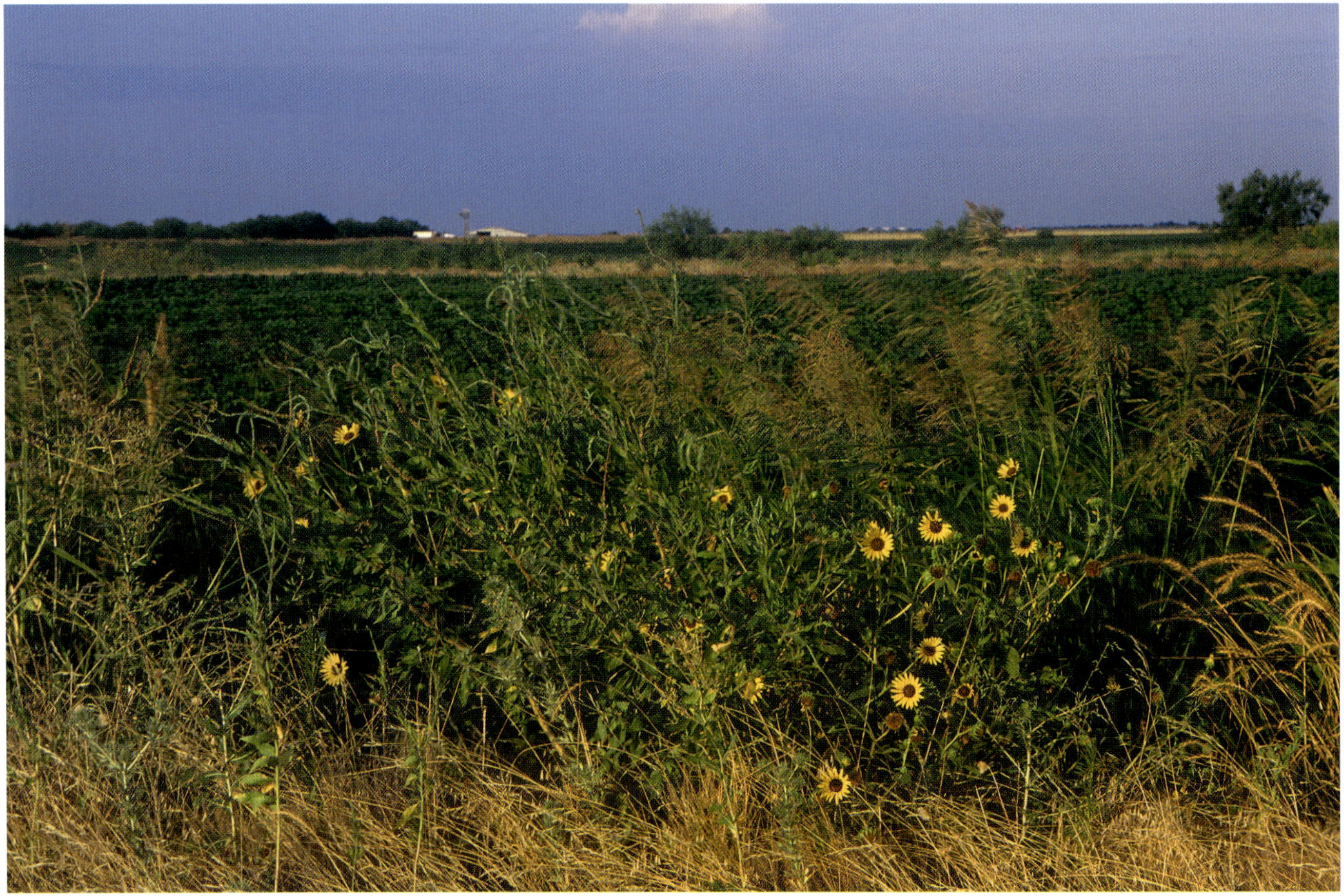

Scurry County

Pastel Dawn over Pasture

The county was created in 1876 and was organized on June 28, 1884. It is named for William Read Scurry, a lawyer and Confederate army general. The county is one of the leading oil-producing regions in Texas due to its location in the Permian Basin, one of the state's largest petroleum deposits. In 1982, more than 31 million barrels of crude oil and more than 53 million cubic feet of casing-head gas were produced in the county.

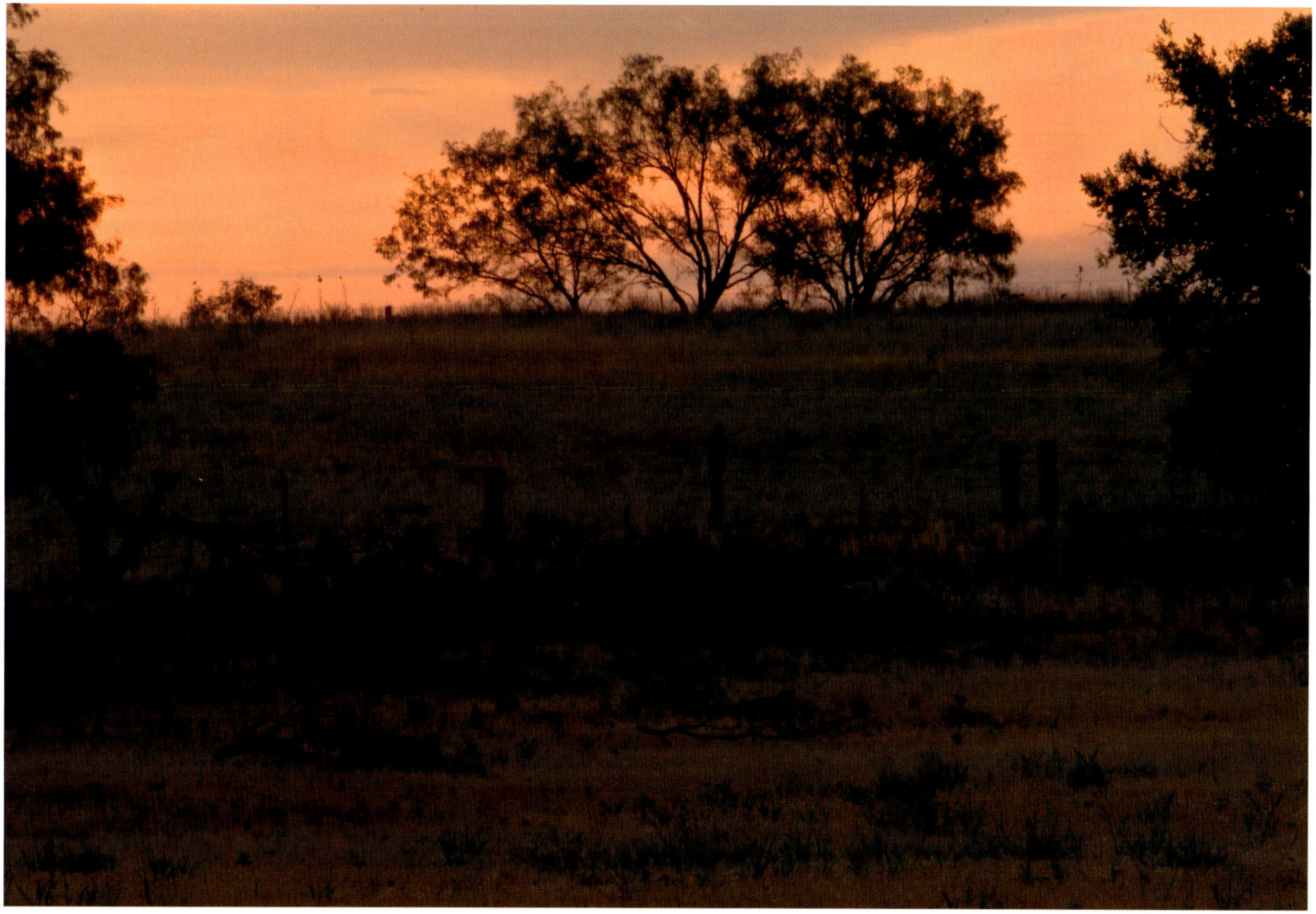

Shackelford County

A Sunny Afternoon on Ranchland near the Dallas-Ft. Worth Metroplex

The county was created in 1858 and organized in 1874. Shackelford County is named for Dr. Jack Shackelford, a Virginia physician who equipped soldiers at his own expense to fight in the Texas Revolution. In 1874, the civilian community of Fort Griffin—commonly called the Flat or Hidetown—served as a marketplace and supply point for buffalo hunters and as a watering place for soldiers, hunters, and trail hands driving cattle over the Western Trail, which crossed the Clear Fork nearby.

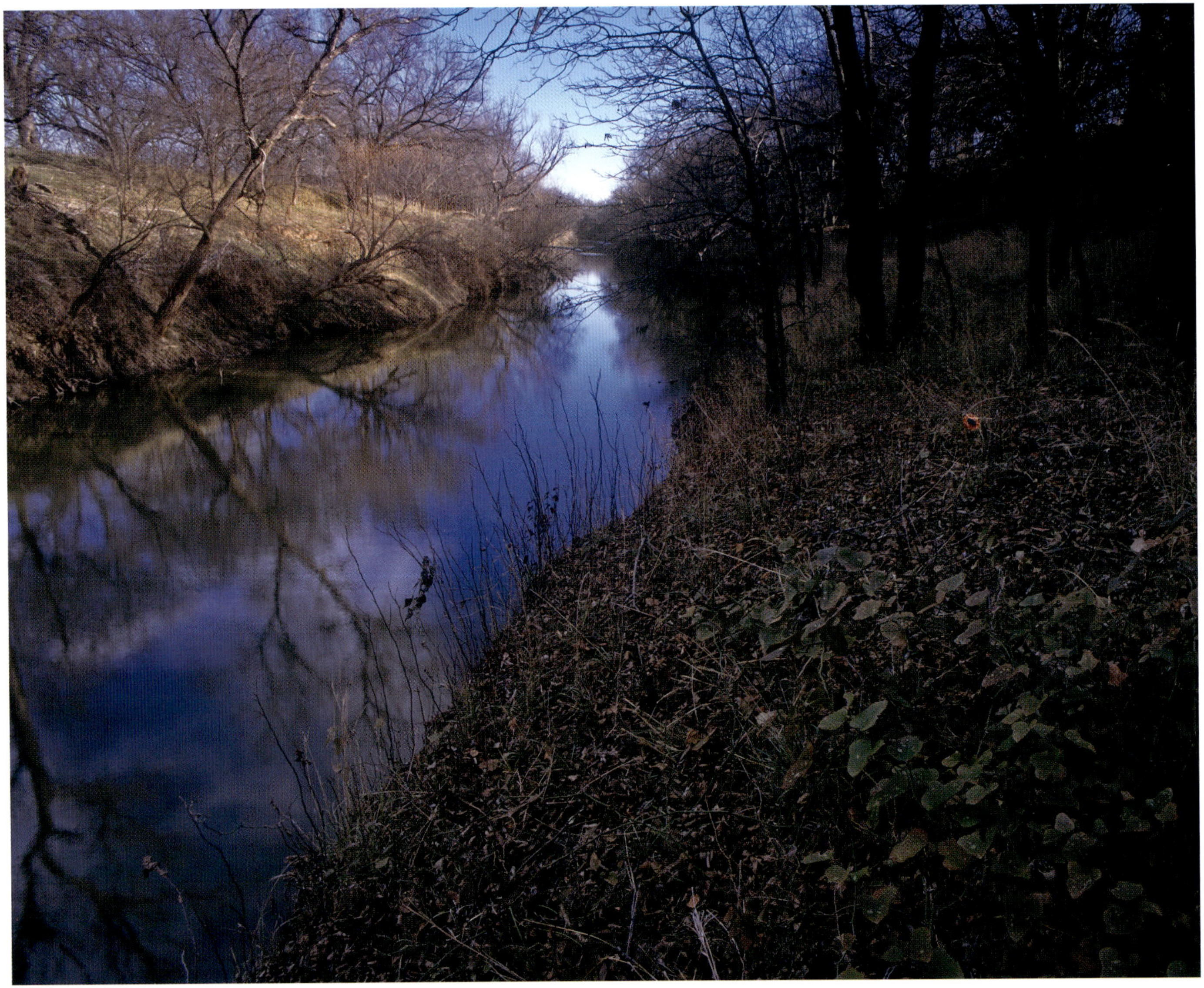

Shelby County

Toledo Bend Reservoir in the Sabine National Forest

The county was created in 1835 as a municipality of Mexico and was organized as a county in 1837. It is named for Isaac Shelby, a soldier in the American Revolution who became the first governor of Kentucky. Toledo Bend Reservoir—partially in Shelby County—is a reservoir on the Sabine River between Texas and Louisiana. The lake has an area of 185,000 acres. It is the largest man-made body of water in (or partially in) Texas. It is also the largest lake in the South, and the fifth largest by surface area in the United States. The dam is capable of generating 92 megawatts of electrical power. The lake is known for its excellent freshwater fishing.

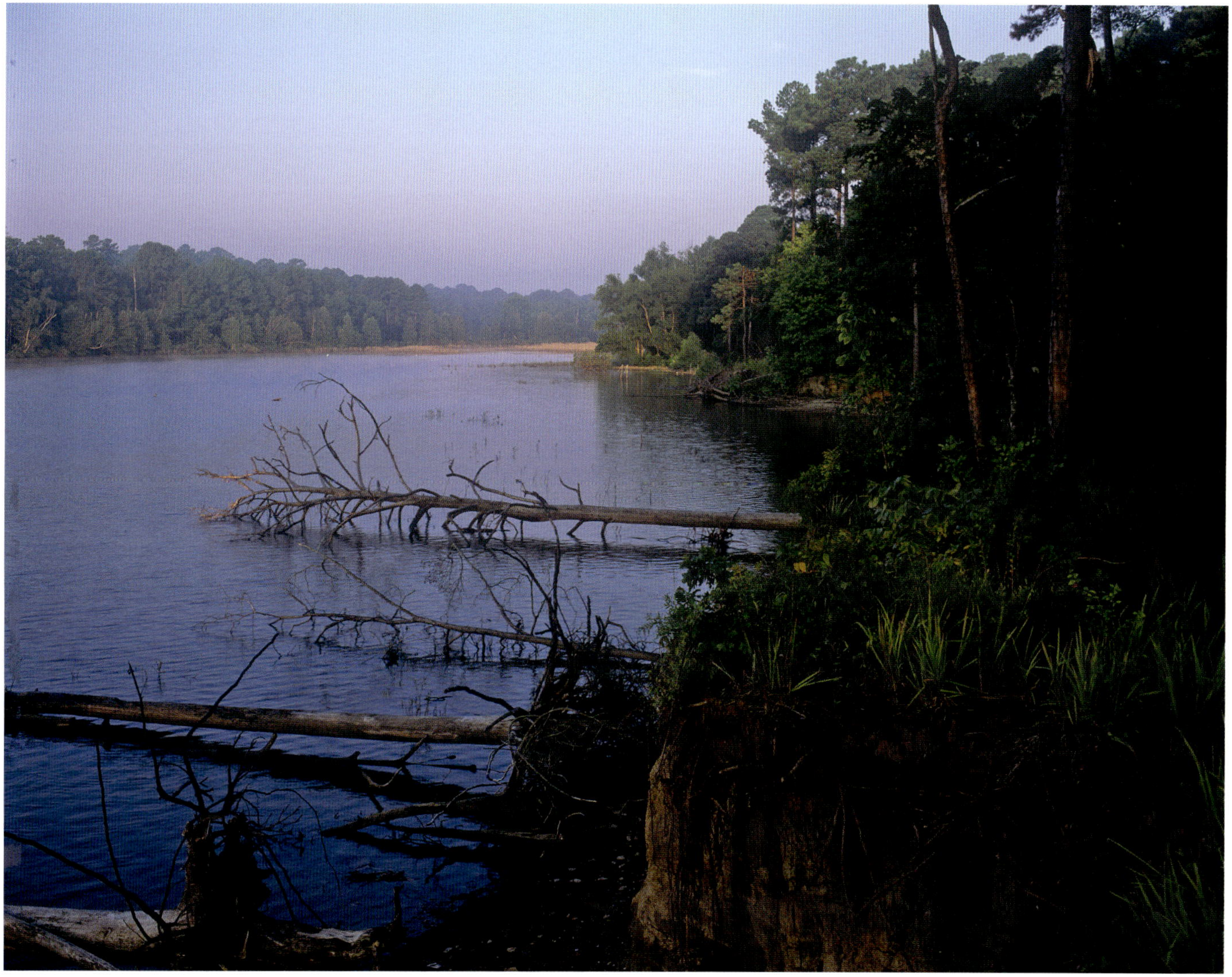

Sherman County

February Sunrise

The county was created in 1876 and organized in 1889. It is named for Sidney Sherman, who fought in the Texas Revolution. In 1933 the area received only 10 inches of rain, and during the mid-1930s its residents were caught in the Dust Bowl. Wheat production had fully recovered by 1940, however, when 130,000 acres were planted in wheat.

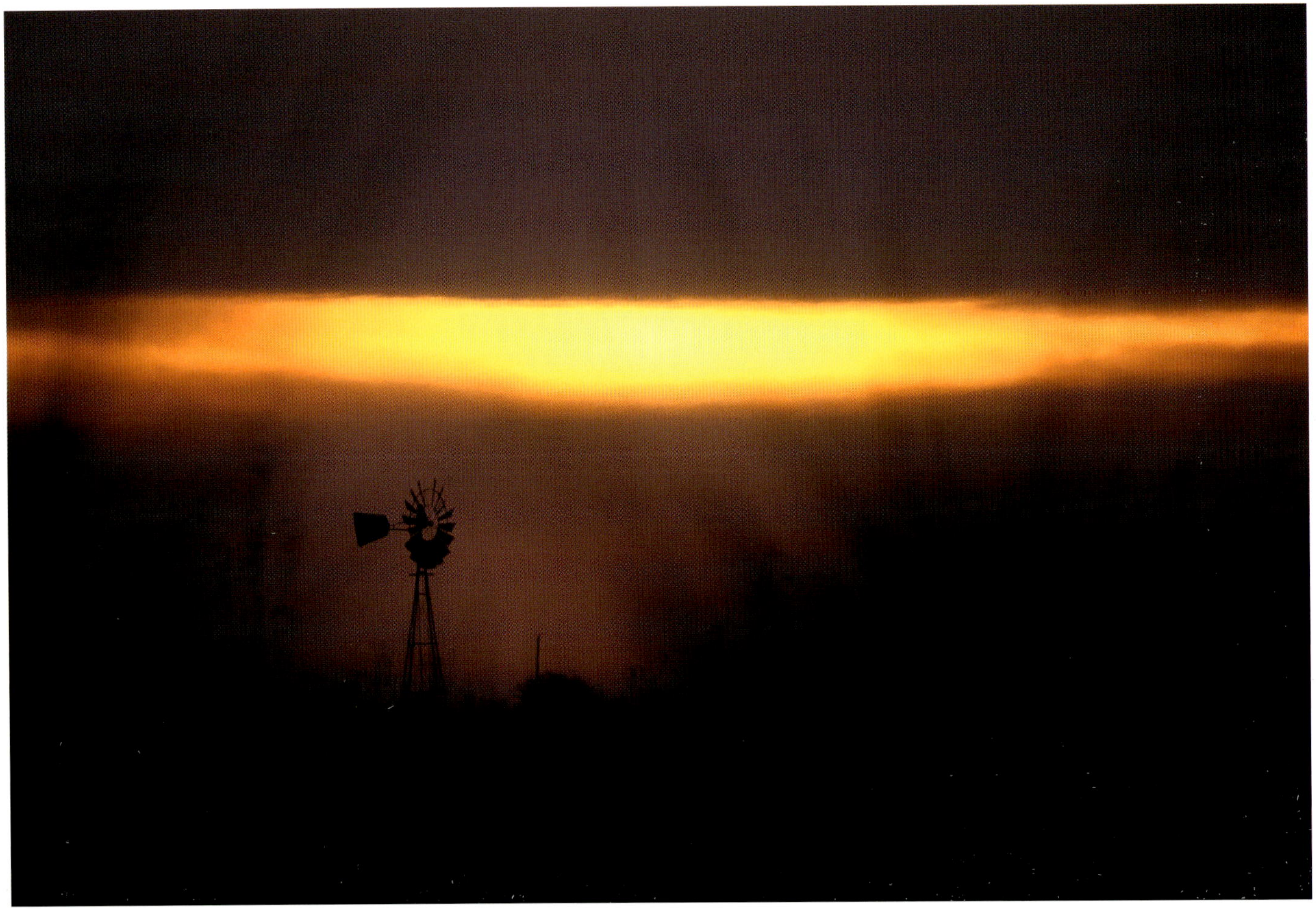

Smith County

Tyler State Park

Smith County is named for James Smith, a general during the Texas Revolution. The county was formed in 1846. Camp Ford, which is in the county, was the largest Confederate prisoner-of-war camp west of the Mississippi River during the American Civil War and was where Sheriff Jim Reed of Collin County and Judge McReynolds, former chief justice of the district, were seized and lynched by "Regulators."

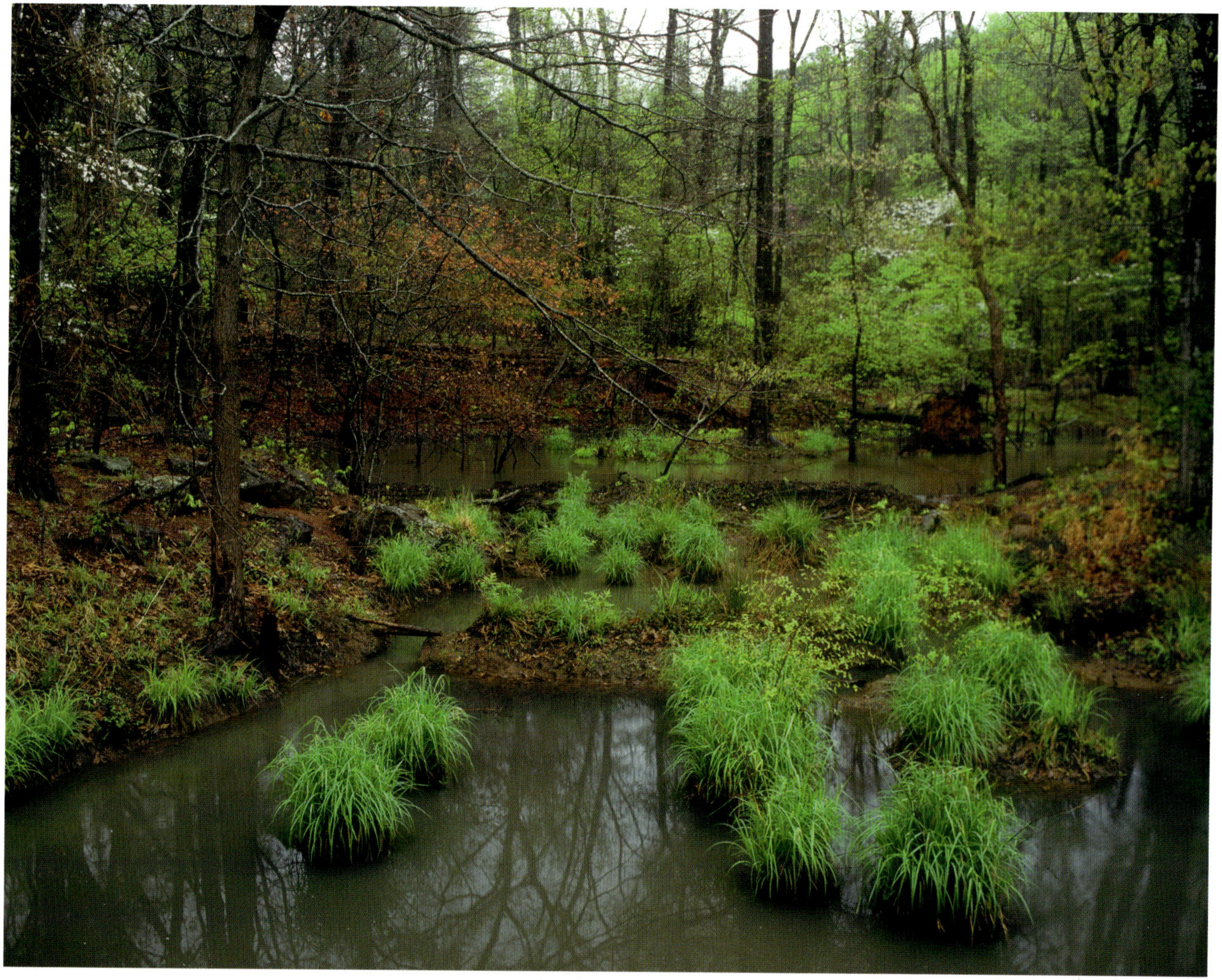

Somervell County

The Paluxy River in Dinosaur Valley State Park

The county was formed in 1875 and was named for Alexander Somervell, a secretary of war for the Republic of Texas. The tragic Paluxy River flood of 1908 uncovered three-toed prints from the Cretaceous period—possibly a dinosaur named *Acrocanthosaurus*—and was discovered by high school student George Adams in the limestone riverbed. The teenager related the discovery to his principal, Robert McDonald. Adams later ended up selling self-manufactured fake "giant-man tracks" to tourists sometime during the 1930s, sparking a debate about whether or not humans existed alongside dinosaurs.

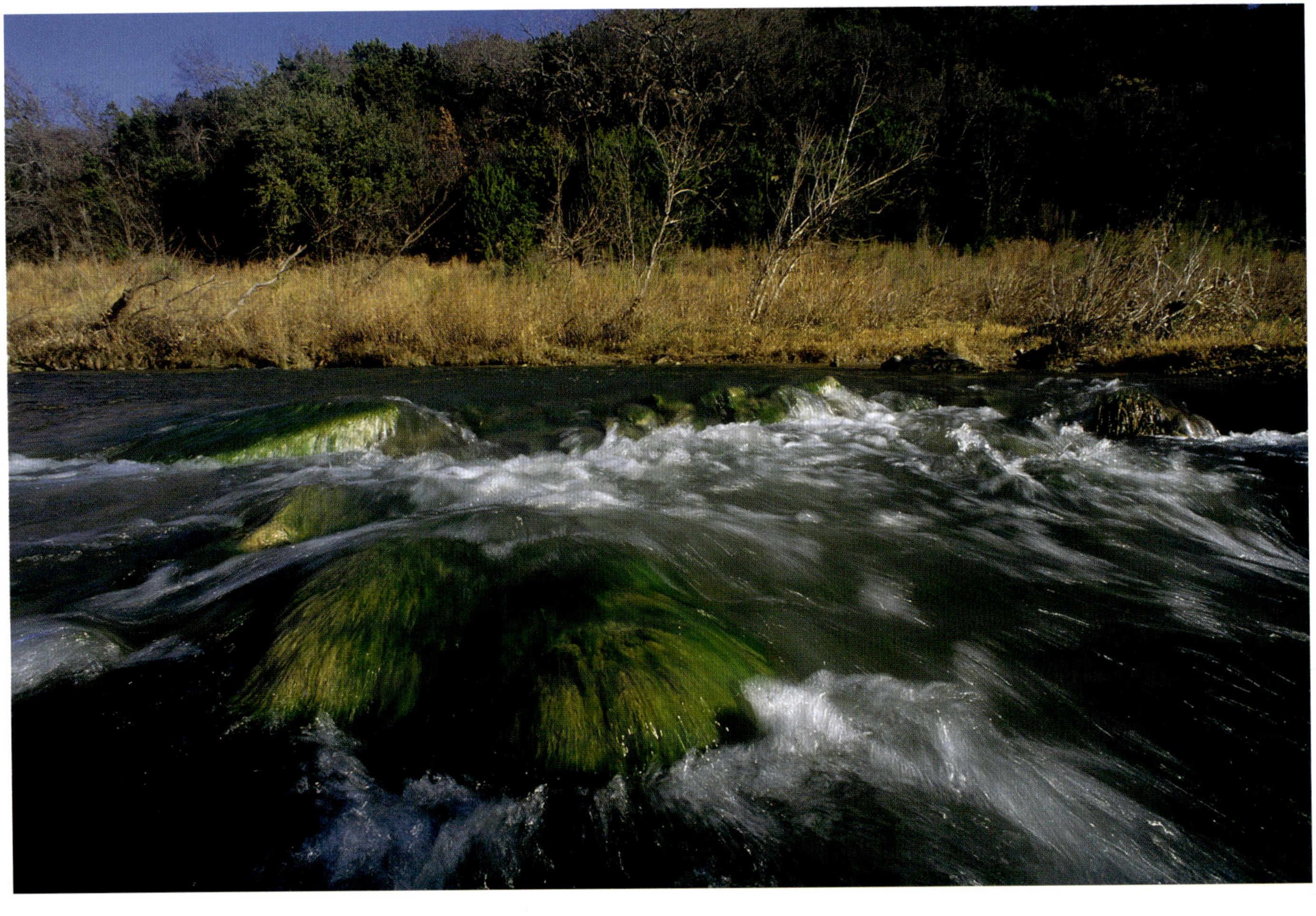

Starr County

Falcon State Park

The county was created in 1848. It is named for James Harper Starr, who served as secretary of the treasury of the Republic of Texas. The Rio Grande City Riot of September 1888 was set off by the arrest in May of Abraham Recéndez, a Mexican American resident of Rio Grande City. He was arrested for robbery by Starr County sheriff W. W. Sheley and after the arrest was killed by Victor Sebree, United States inspector of customs and Sheley's companion, while allegedly attempting to escape. The incident led to public anger, particularly against Sheley, who was previously implicated in the lynching of several Mexicans.

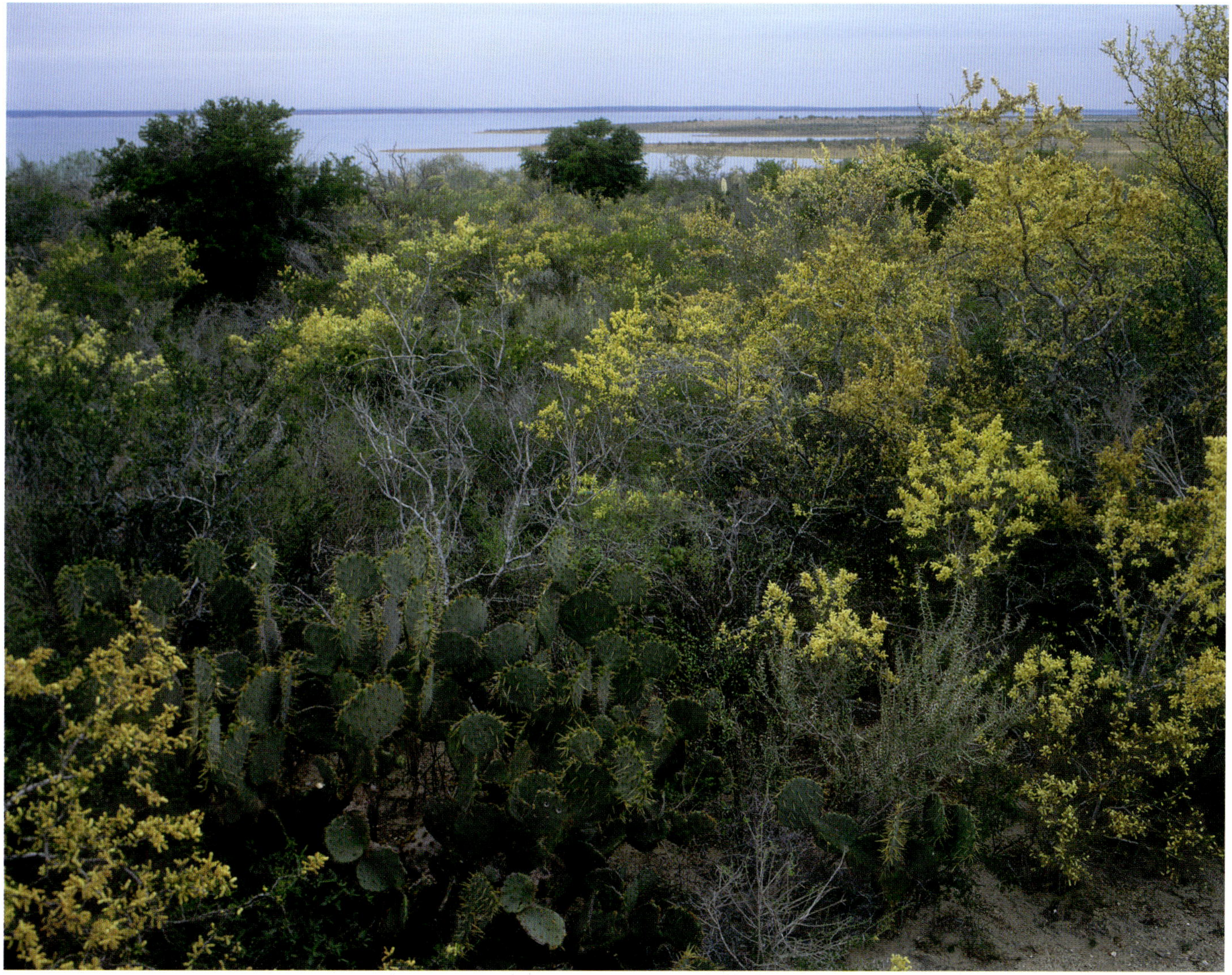

Stephens County

Early-Morning Light on Large Oak Tree

The county was created in 1858 and was organized in 1876. It is named for Alexander H. Stephens, the vice president of the Confederate States of America. A terrific boom centering on the Stephens County community of Breckenridge took off in 1921, when oil drillers brought in Stoker No. 1 just outside town. Breckenridge became a forest of wooden derricks; more than two hundred wells were drilled within the city limits. On September 1, 1921, Keithly No. 1 blew in at more than 3,000 feet with a huge flow that drenched the countryside until it was harnessed by the Humble Oil Company (later Exxon) after two weeks' work.

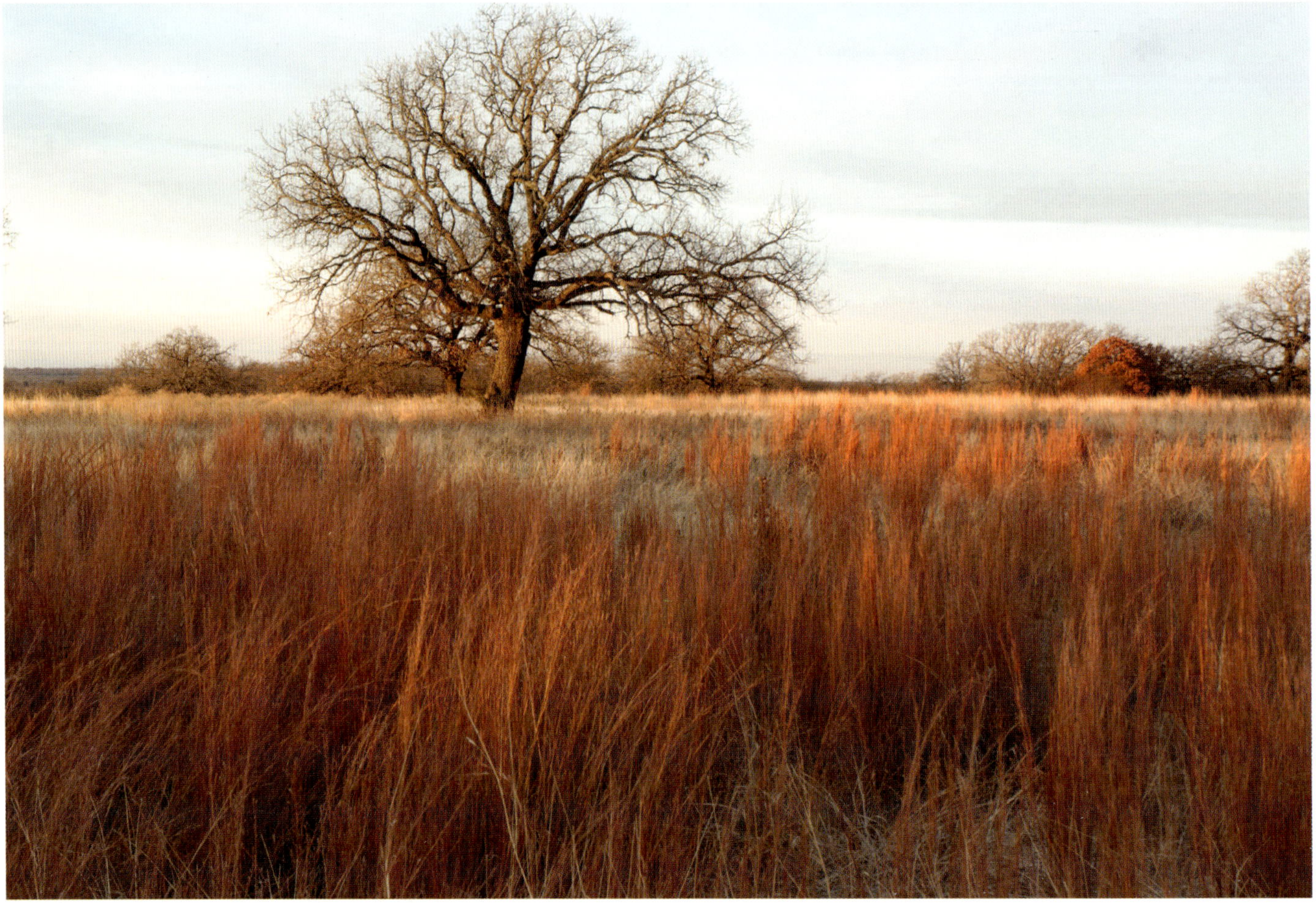

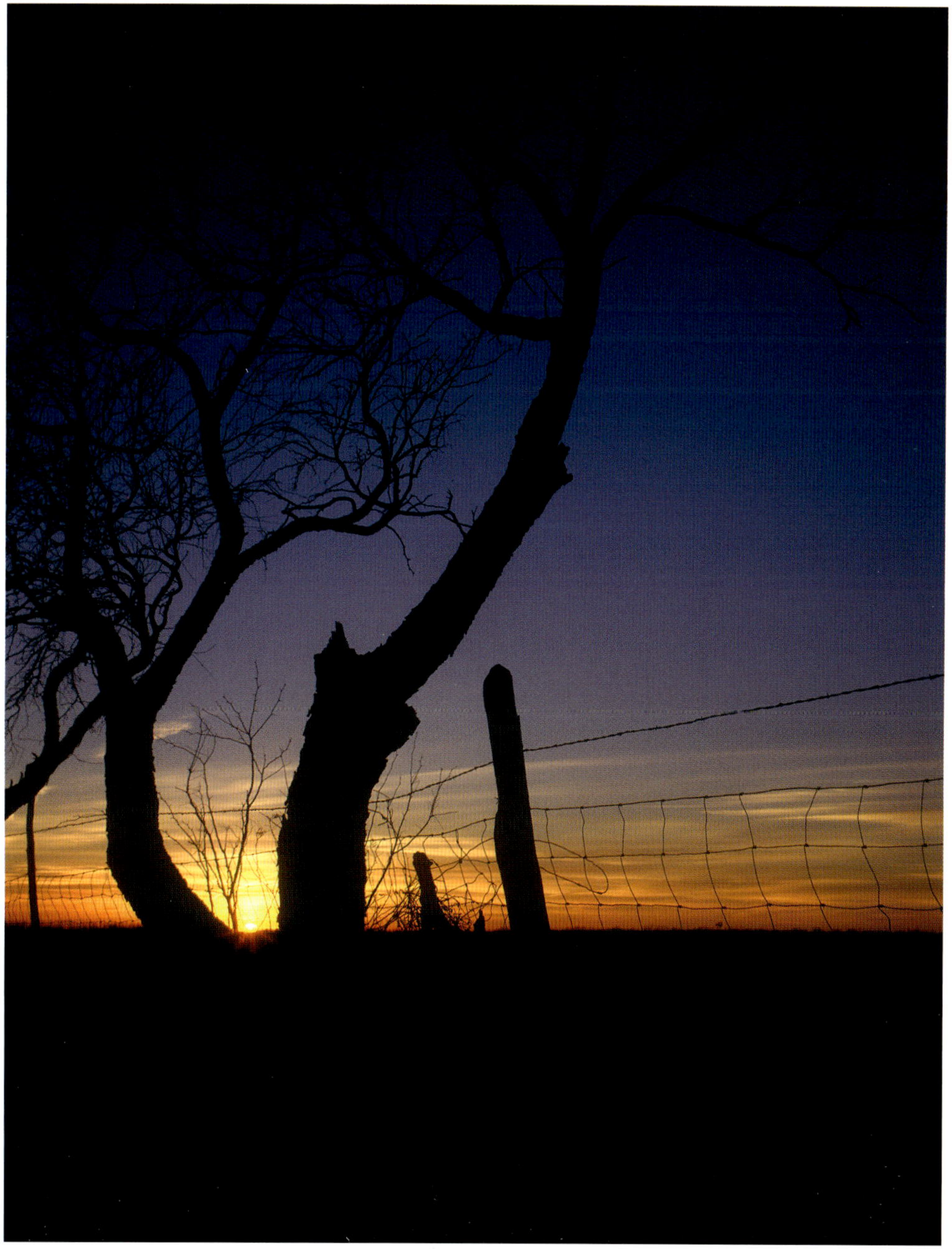

Sterling County

Mesquite Trunk along a Fence Line at Sunrise

The county is named for W. S. Sterling, an early settler in the area. The county was formed in 1891. The county suffered droughts in 1883, 1886, and 1887. The former ignited fence-cutting wars in the county, and the latter bankrupted the Half Circle S Ranch. Fence-cutting wars in Texas lasted for close to five years (1883–1888). As open range areas gave way to farming homesteaders who fenced their land, cattlemen found it more difficult to feed their herds. In some cases, large landowners also fenced public land as their property. As water and grass became increasingly scarce during droughts, homesteaders and ranch hands began cutting through fences.

Stonewall County

Double Mountain Fork of the Brazos River following a Thunderstorm

The county was created in 1876 and organized in 1888. It is named for Stonewall Jackson, a general of the Confederate States Army. Legends of buried treasure, Spanish missions, and gold and silver mines led to many explorations for ore along the Salt Fork of the Brazos. In the late 1890s a tent town, later known as Orient, was started by workers at the Orient copper mines. The town grew quickly after false claims of a silver strike, but both the copper and gold mines were closed after a very short period of operation, having yielded no riches.

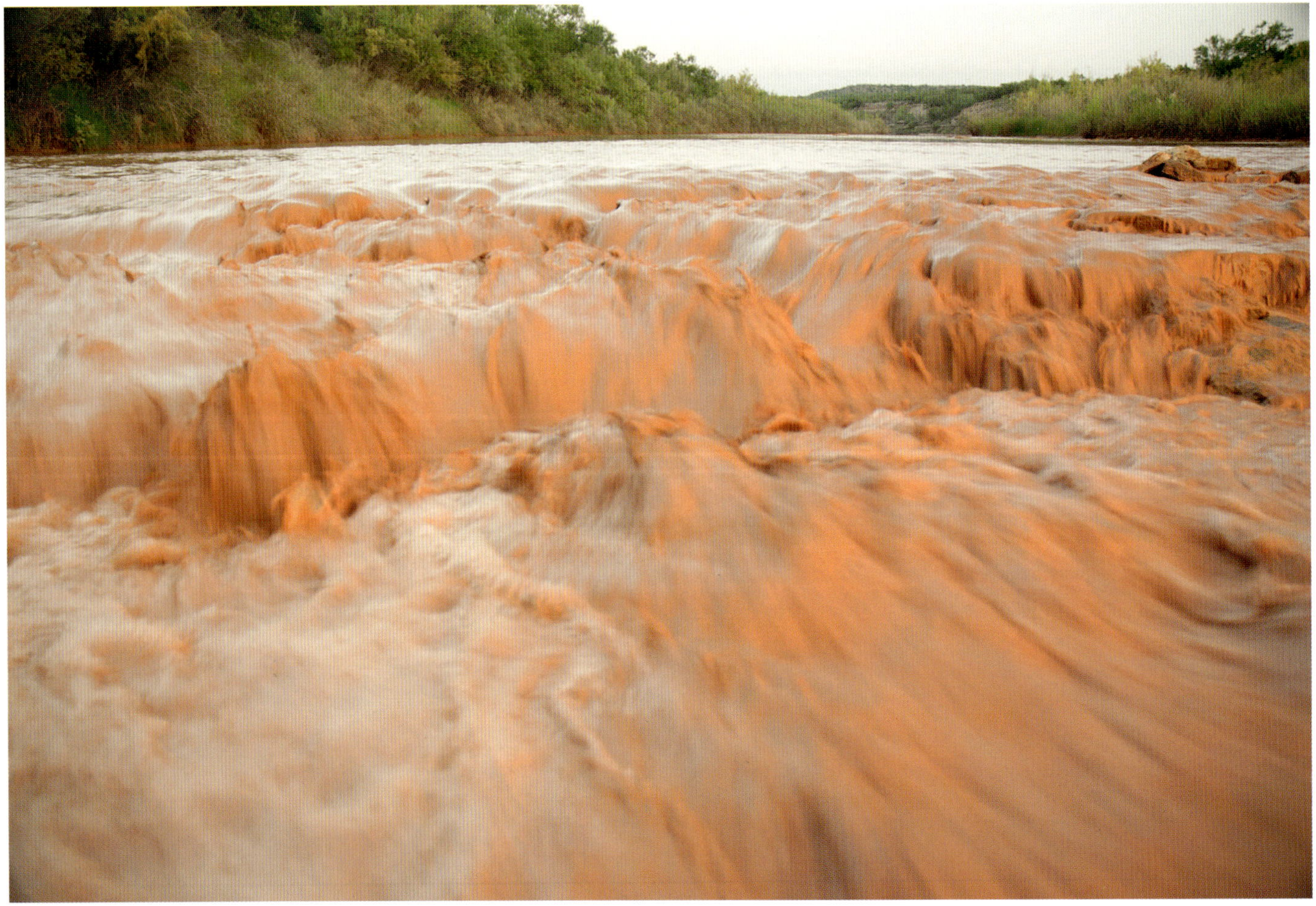

Sutton County

Gathering Storm and Windmill

The county was created in 1887 and organized in 1890. Sutton County is named for John S. Sutton, an officer in the Confederate army. In 1928, the Atchison, Topeka, and Santa Fe Railway acquired Kansas City, Mexico, and Orient Railway to connect Sonora with San Angelo, Del Rio, and the outside world by rail.

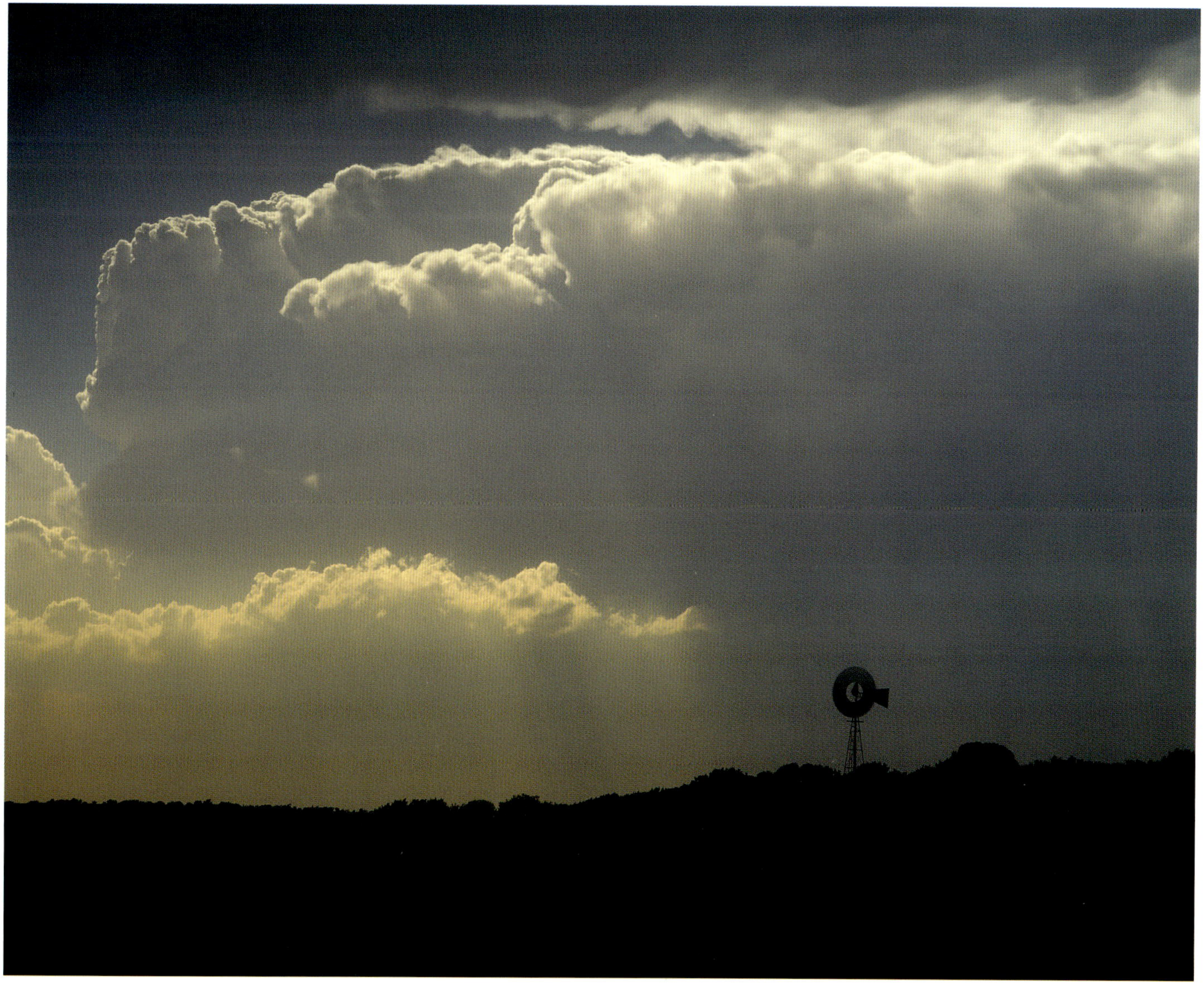

Swisher County

A Scene along Tule Creek

The county was created in 1876 and organized in 1890. It is named for James G. Swisher, a soldier of the Texas Revolution and a signer of the Texas Declaration of Independence. As the economy and population grew, so did the need for a useful road system. This was especially true after the automobile proved itself in the years before World War I. Until nearly 1920, roads in Swisher County consisted of crude paths scraped in the earth. In 1920, the Ozark Trail—a highway network from Arkansas and Missouri through Kansas, Oklahoma, Louisiana, and Texas, then to New Mexico—came to the plains of Texas. Collingsworth, Childress, Hall, Briscoe, Swisher, Castro, and Parmer Counties, along with Curry and Roosevelt Counties in New Mexico, cooperated in raising $10,000 in 1920 to erect markers along already existing roads to mark the Ozark Trail from Oklahoma across Texas to New Mexico.

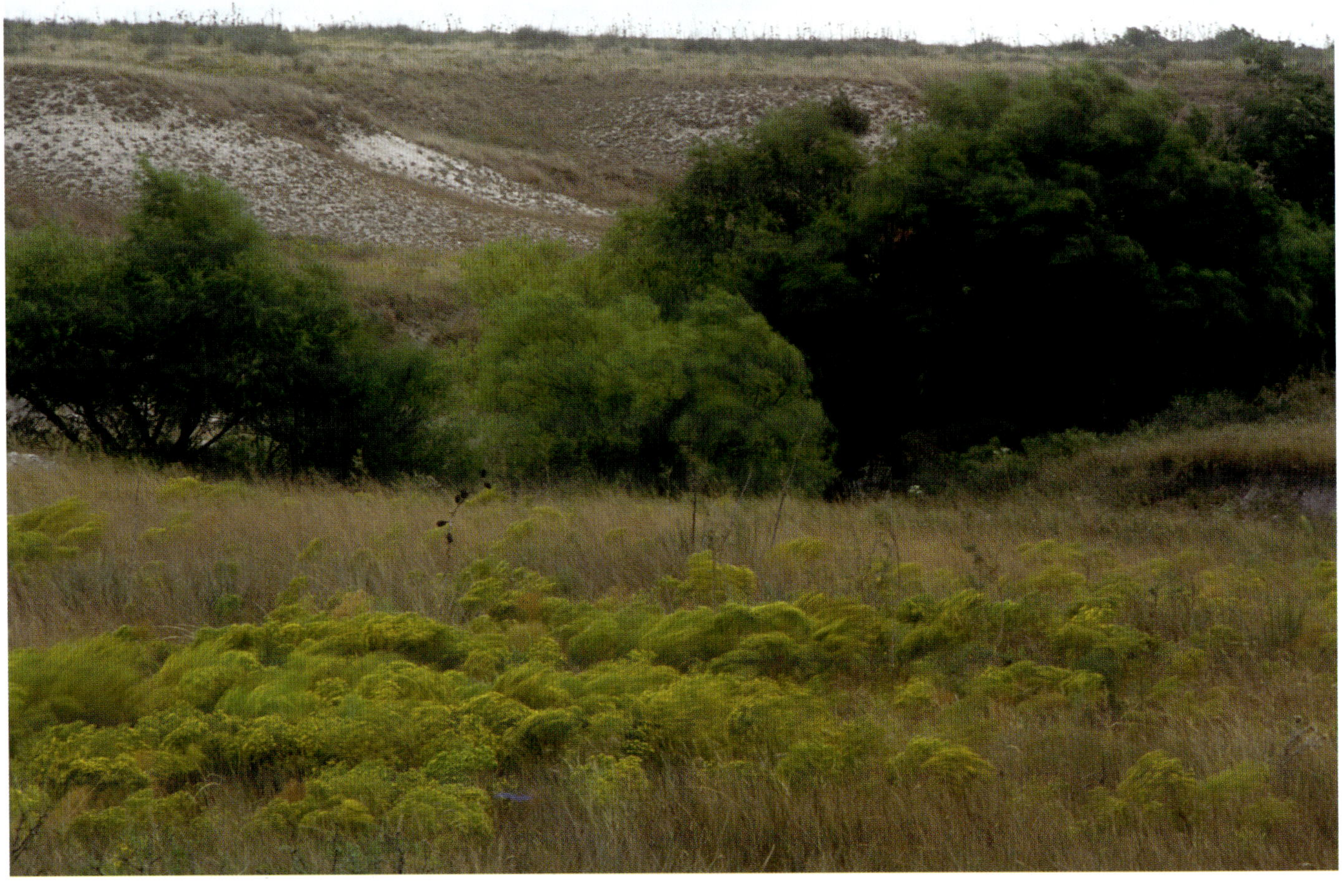

Tarrant County

Mixed Wildflowers in the Southern Portion of the County

Tarrant County was established in 1849 and organized the next year. The county was named in honor of General Edward H. Tarrant of the Republic of Texas militia. Settlement began in the vicinity of present-day Azle in 1846. In the late 1840s, Middleton Tate Johnson founded Johnson's Station 13 miles southeast of the site of the current Tarrant County Courthouse. These settlements pushed the frontier westward, and the need for a military post was recognized. In 1849, Maj. Ripley Arnold chose a site at the confluence of the Clear Fork and West Fork of the Trinity River. He named the post Camp Worth in honor of General William Jenkins Worth, who had won fame in the Mexican War, and the camp was officially named Fort Worth.

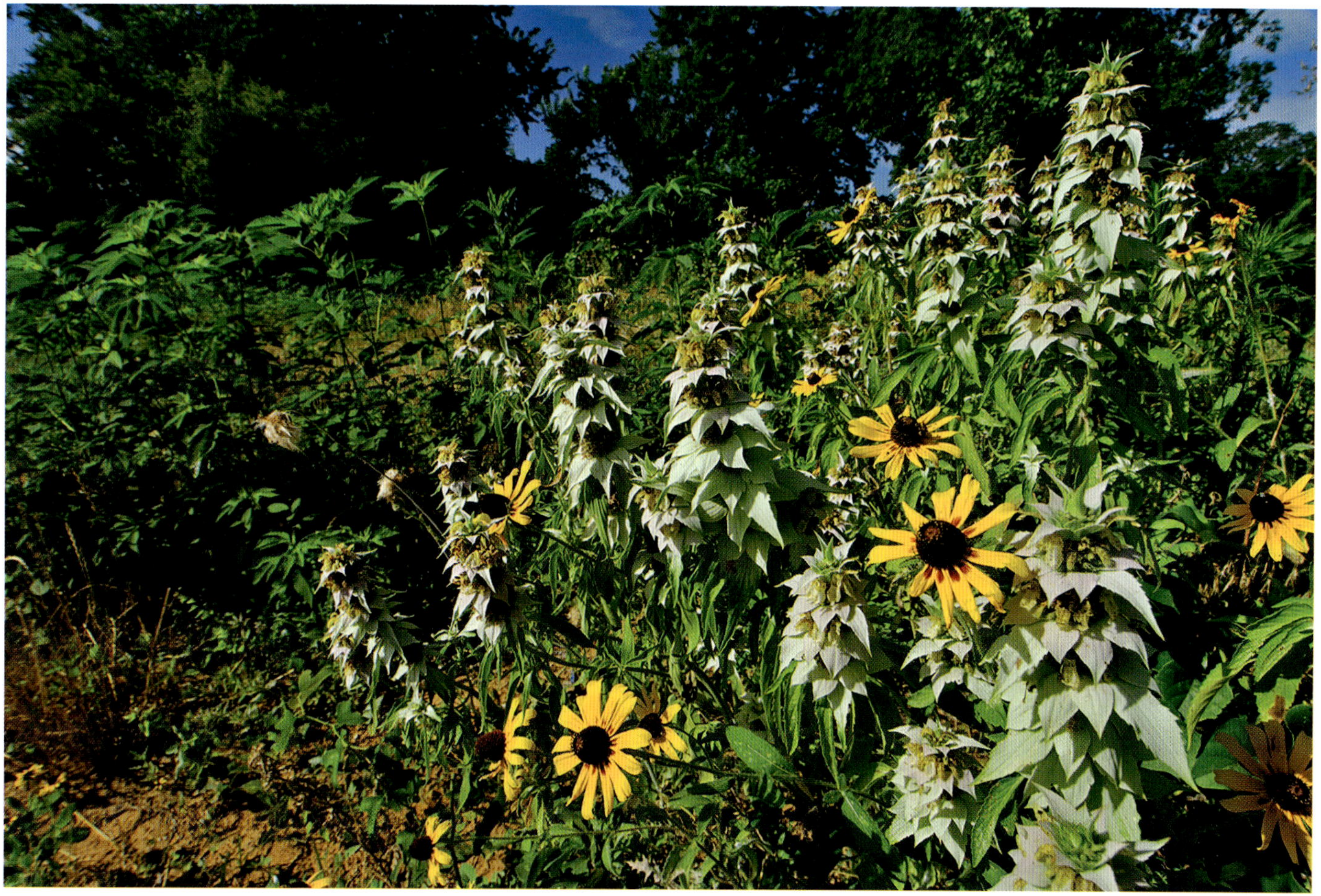

Taylor County

Abilene State Park

The county was created in 1858 and organized in 1878. It is named for Edward Taylor, George Taylor, and James Taylor, three brothers who died at the Battle of the Alamo. In 1942, Dyess Air Force Base was established as Abilene AFB. It is named in honor of Texas native and Bataan Death March survivor Lieutenant Colonel William Dyess.

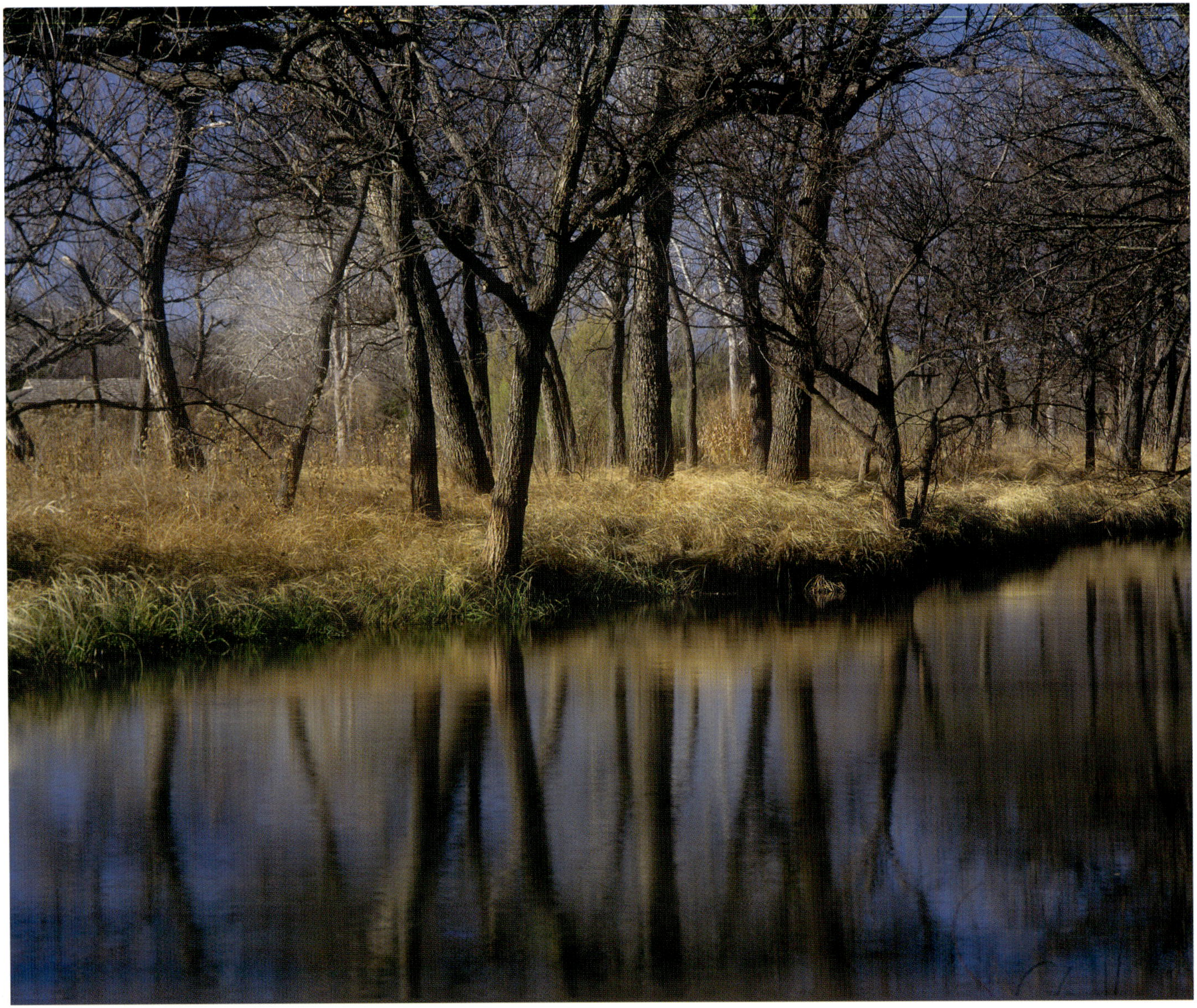

Terrell County

Independence Creek Preserve

The county, founded in 1905, was named for Alexander W. Terrell, a Texas state senator. In 1999, the Texas State Senate declared Sanderson and Terrell County the "Cactus Capital of Texas."

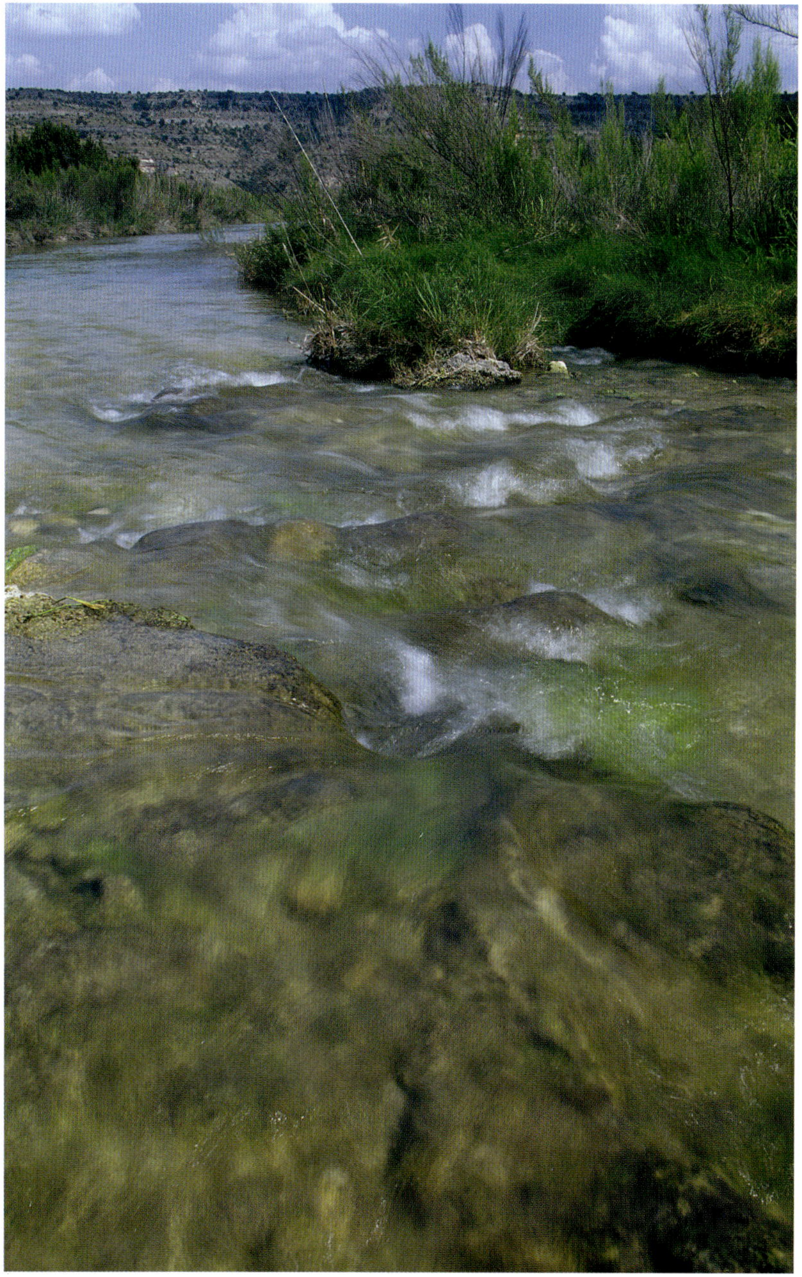

Terry County

Sunflowers along the Edge of a Plowed Field

The county was created in 1876 and organized in 1904. It is named for Benjamin Franklin Terry, a colonel in the Confederate army. Oil was discovered in the county in 1940. Terry County lies in the oil-rich northern Permian Basin, and the discovery of oil quickly led to production. By 1991, more than 363 million barrels of crude had been extracted from Terry County lands.

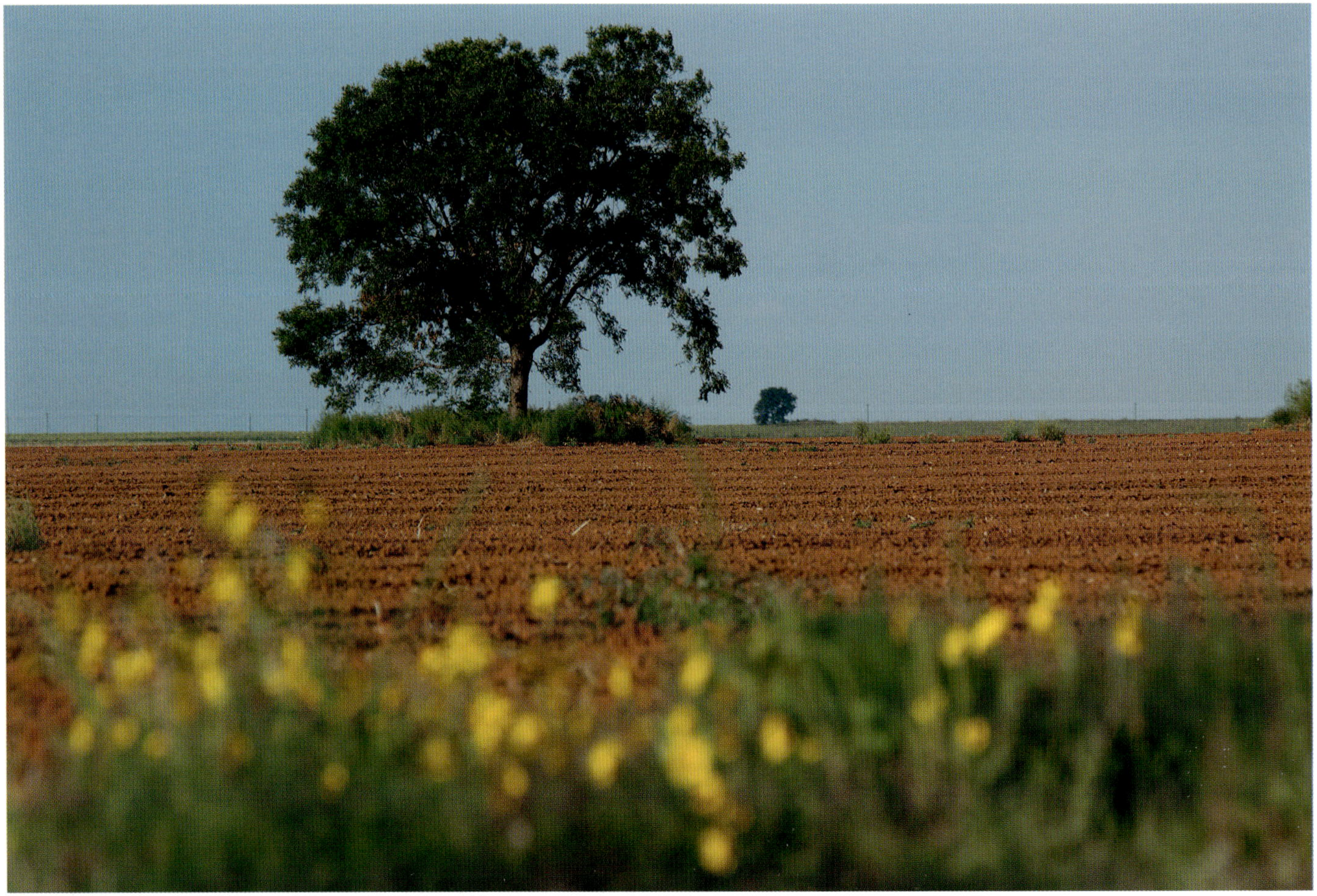

Throckmorton County

Deer Grazing at Sunrise

The county was created in 1858 and organized in 1879. The county is named for William Throckmorton, an early Collin County settler. Spanish explorer Pedro Vial is the earliest European to travel through what is known as Throckmorton County. Vial passed between the Clear Ford and the Main Fork of the Brazos River in 1786 while searching for a direct route between San Antonio and Santa Fe.

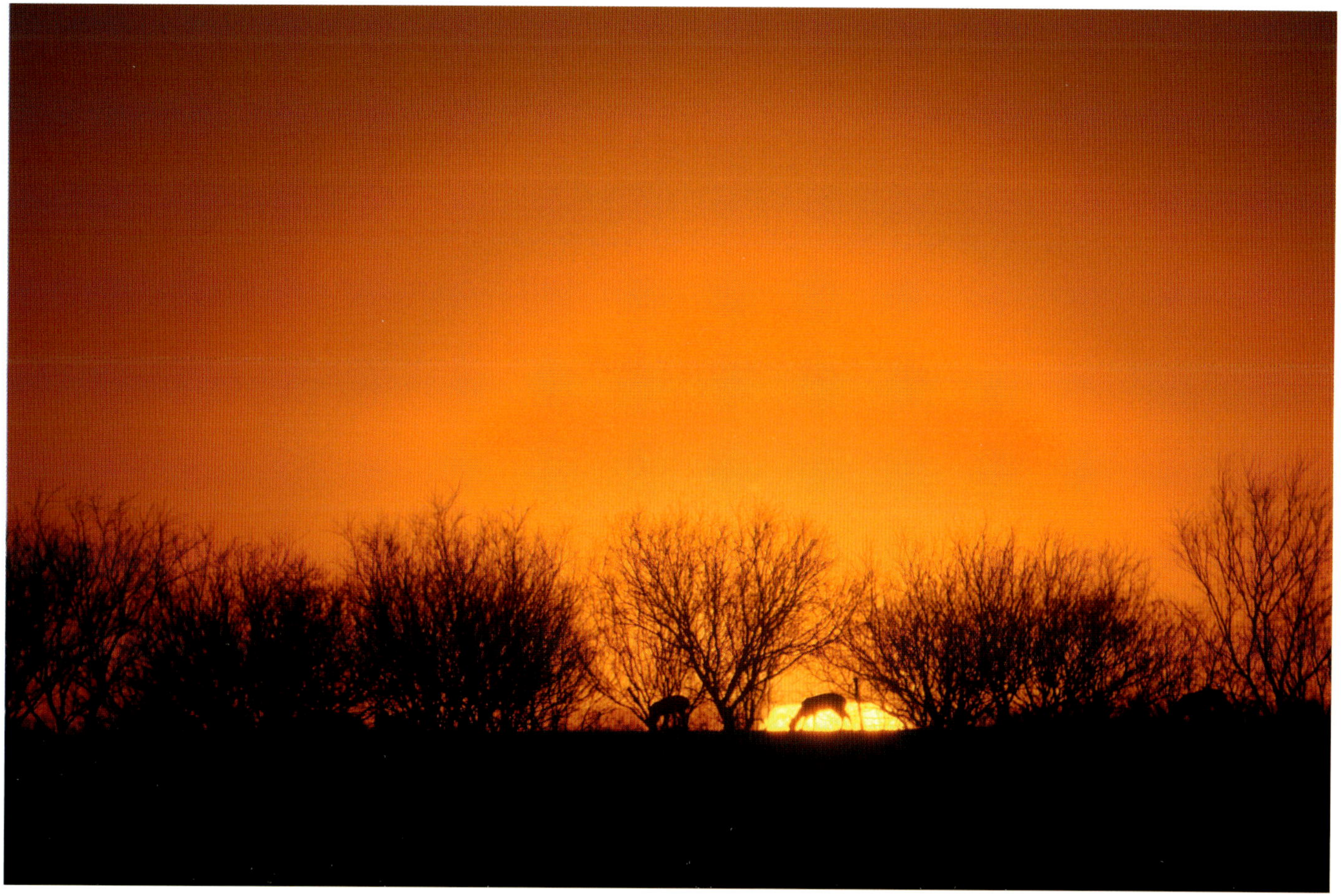

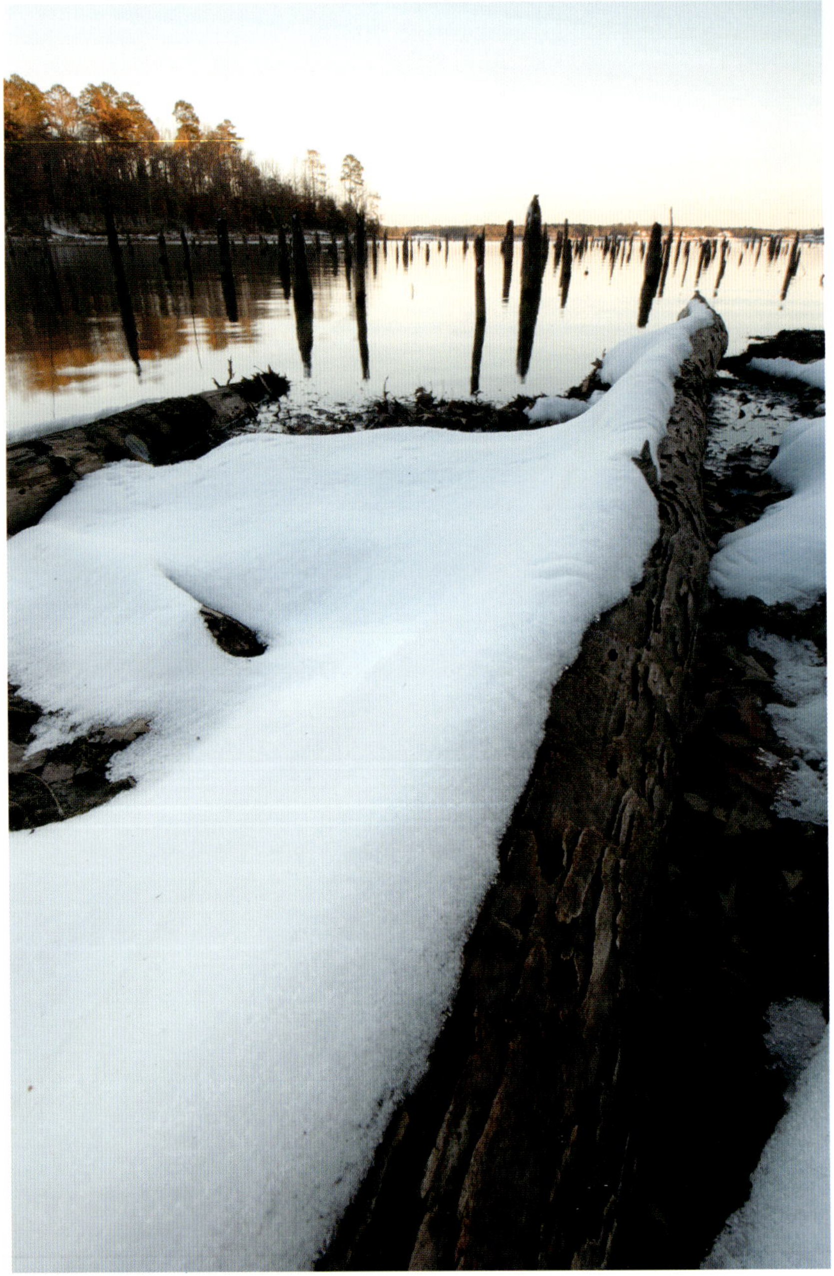

Titus County

Lake Bob Sandlin State Park

The county is named for Andrew Jackson Titus, an early settler. The county was founded in 1846. In the election of 1860, an overwhelming majority of Titus County voters supported the states'-rights candidate, John C. Breckinridge of Kentucky. When the election was held for delegates to the Secession Convention, however, one of the men elected from Titus County was Joshua F. Johnson—one of only eight delegates who opposed secession. Vigorous in his opposition, Johnson signed the "Address to the People of Texas," which urged Texans to reject the secession amendment, and he may have campaigned against the ordinance in the Titus County area. Despite the efforts of Johnson and a few other unionists, Titus County voters approved secession by a vote of 411 to 385.

Tom Green County

Rugged Scenery on a Sunny February Day

The county was created in 1874 and organized the following year. The county is named for Thomas Green (1814–1864), a Confederate brigadier general. The original county seat was the town of Bn Ficklin. In 1882, floodwaters of the Concho River destroyed the town and drowned sixty-five people. The county seat was then moved to San(ta) Angela. In 1883, the town's name was officially changed to San Angelo by the United States Post Office.

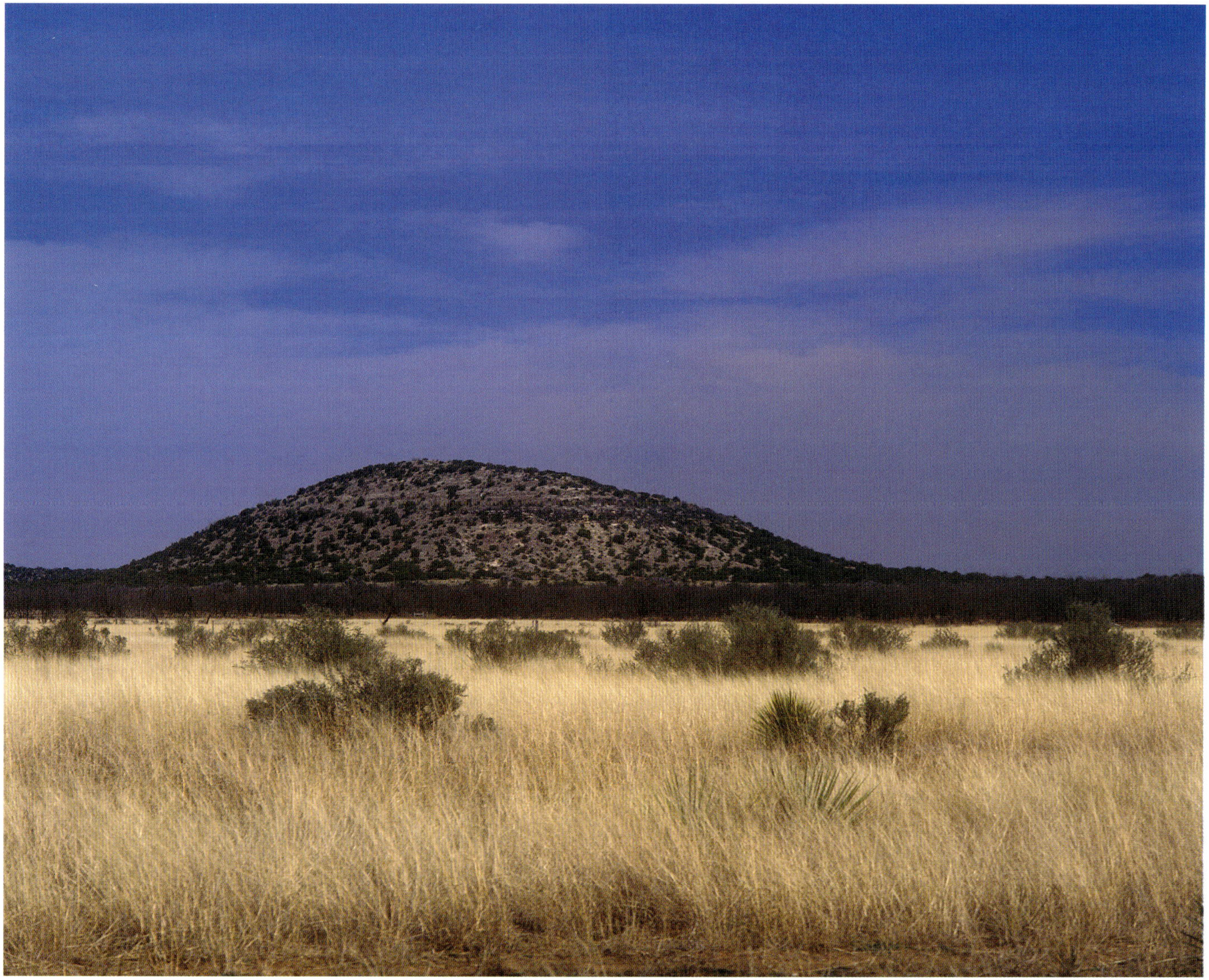

Travis County

Lower Falls at Dusk in McKinney Falls State Park

The county was established in 1840 and is named in honor of William Barret Travis, the commander of the Republic of Texas forces at the Battle of the Alamo. The state capital of Texas is in Travis County, in the city of Austin.

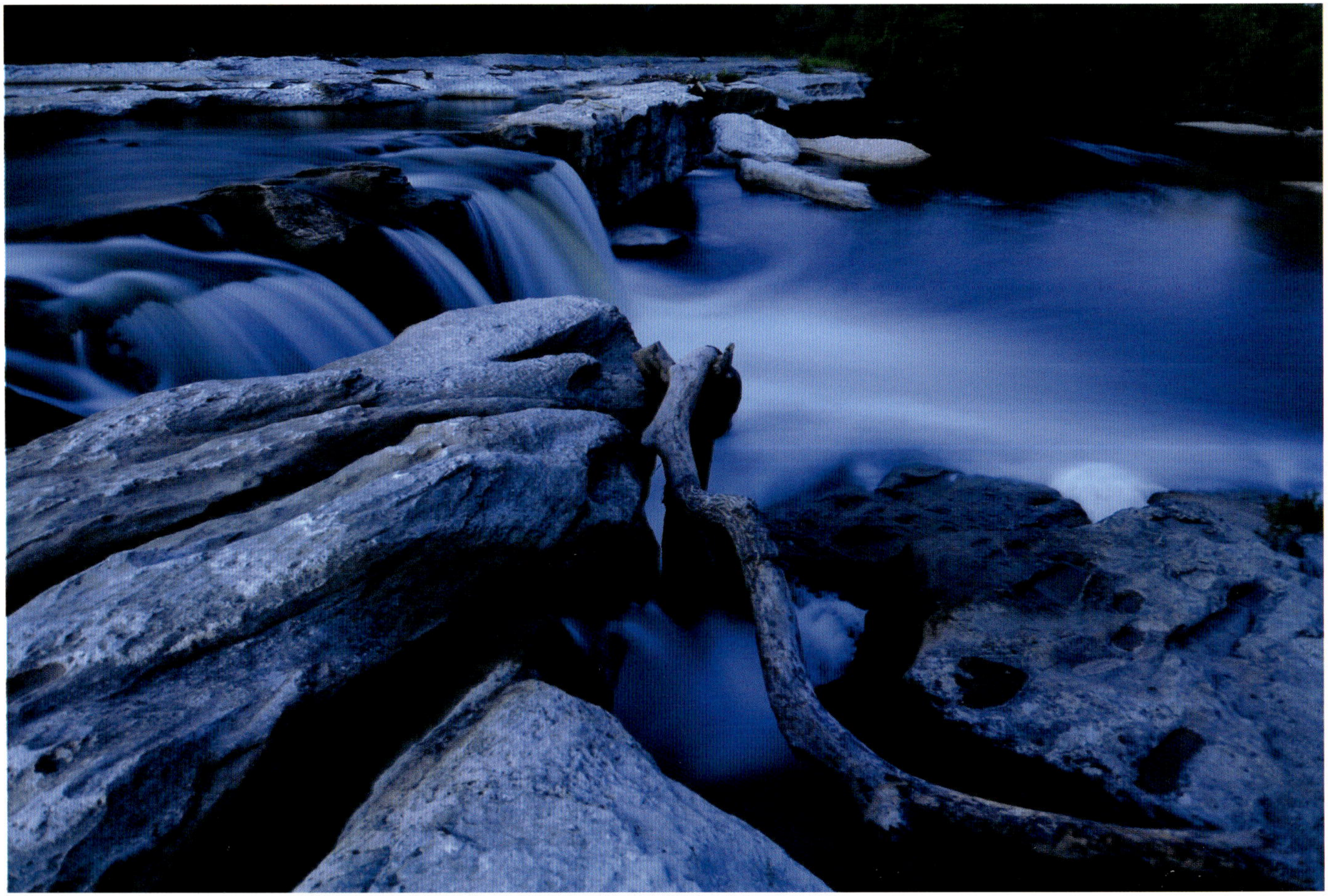

Trinity County

Sunset in the Alabama Creek Wildlife Management Area

The county is named for the Trinity River and was founded in 1850. Before the advent of the lumber industry in the 1880s, the area was covered by forests of immense trees as large as 50 inches in diameter, with first limbs 60 to 80 feet above the ground. Though these forests were destroyed, many areas are now reforested.

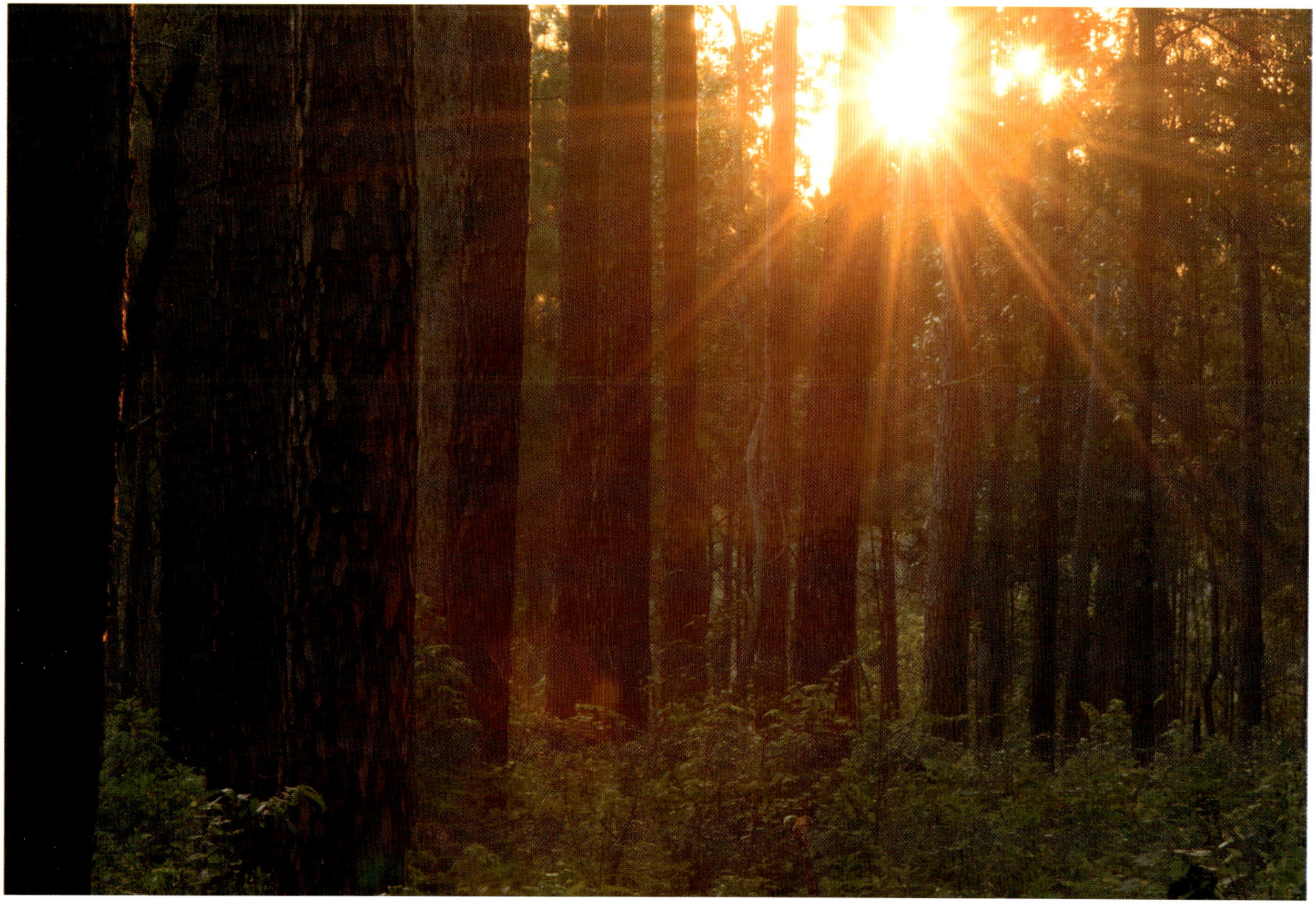

Tyler County

Carnivorous Pitcher Plants in the Big Thicket National Preserve

The county was founded in 1846 and is named for John Tyler, the tenth president of the United States. The county comprises 908 square miles of the East Texas Timberlands, an area densely forested with pine and a great variety of hardwoods. It contains two units and parts of two more of the twelve units of the Big Thicket National Preserve, established by Congress in 1974. The Big Thicket is known as the "biological crossroads of America" due to its diverse ecology.

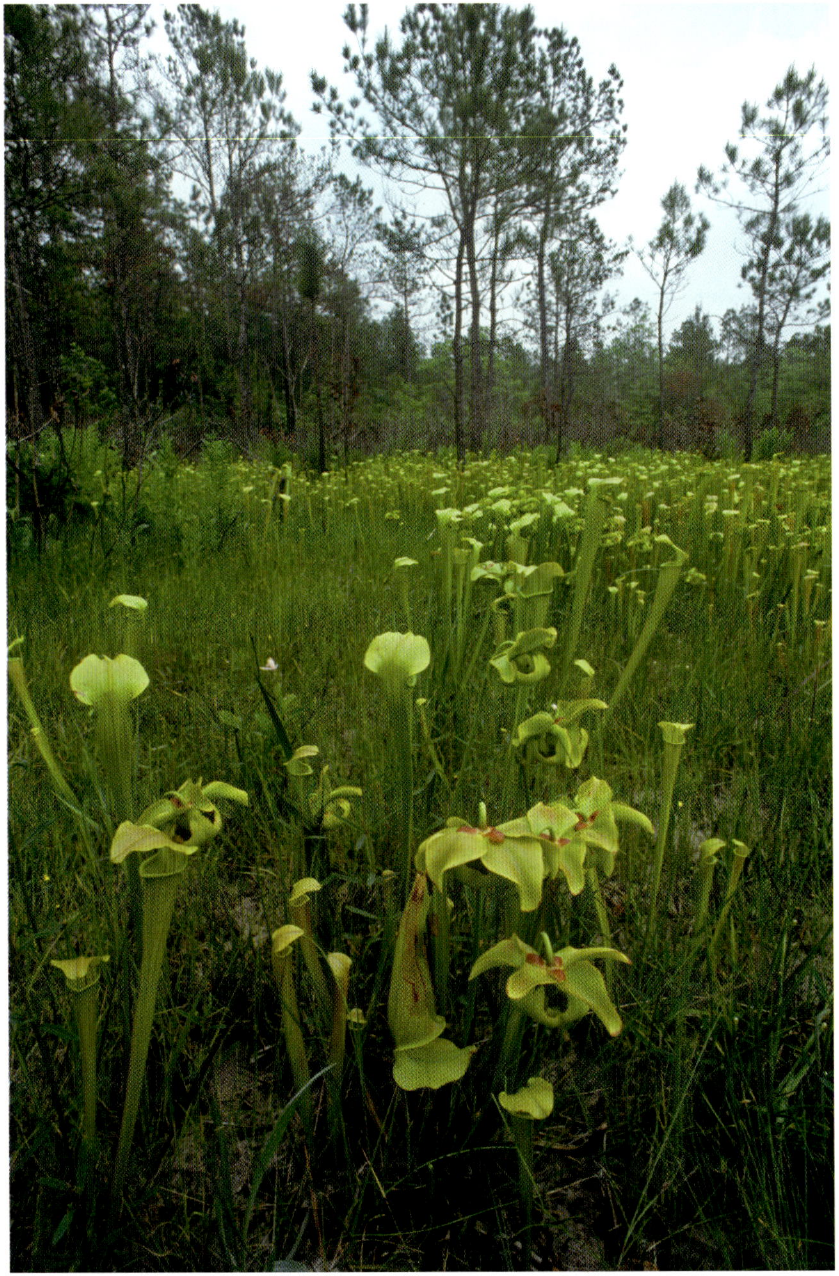

Upshur County

Wildflowers in a Forest Clearing

The county was named for Abel P. Upshur, who was US secretary of state during President John Tyler's administration. The county was founded in 1846. Upshur County has the distinction of being the Texas county that has the largest settlement organized by the Church of Jesus Christ of Latter-day Saints. In 1904, the Latter-day Saint South-western States Mission organized a colony at Kelsey, Texas.

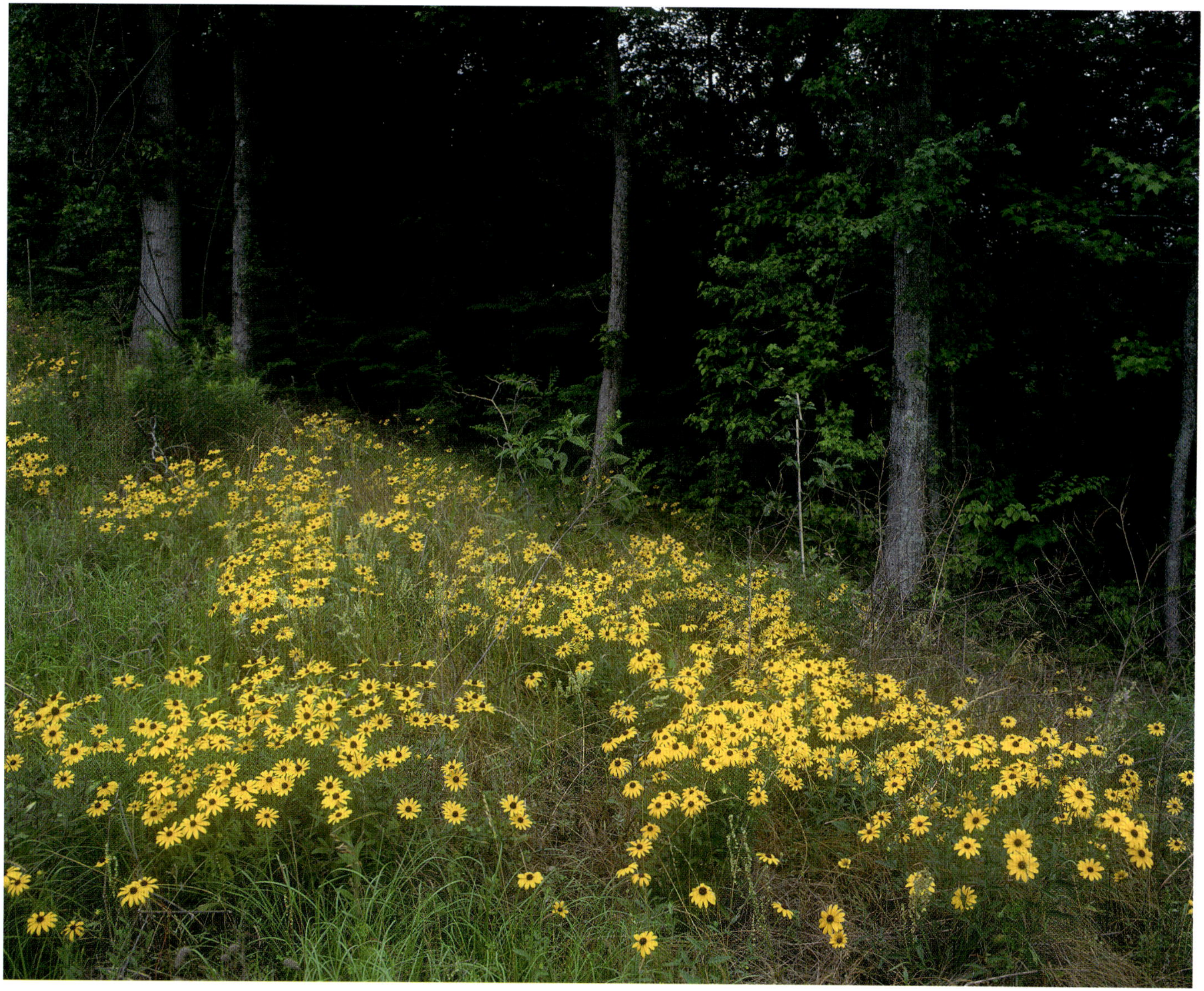

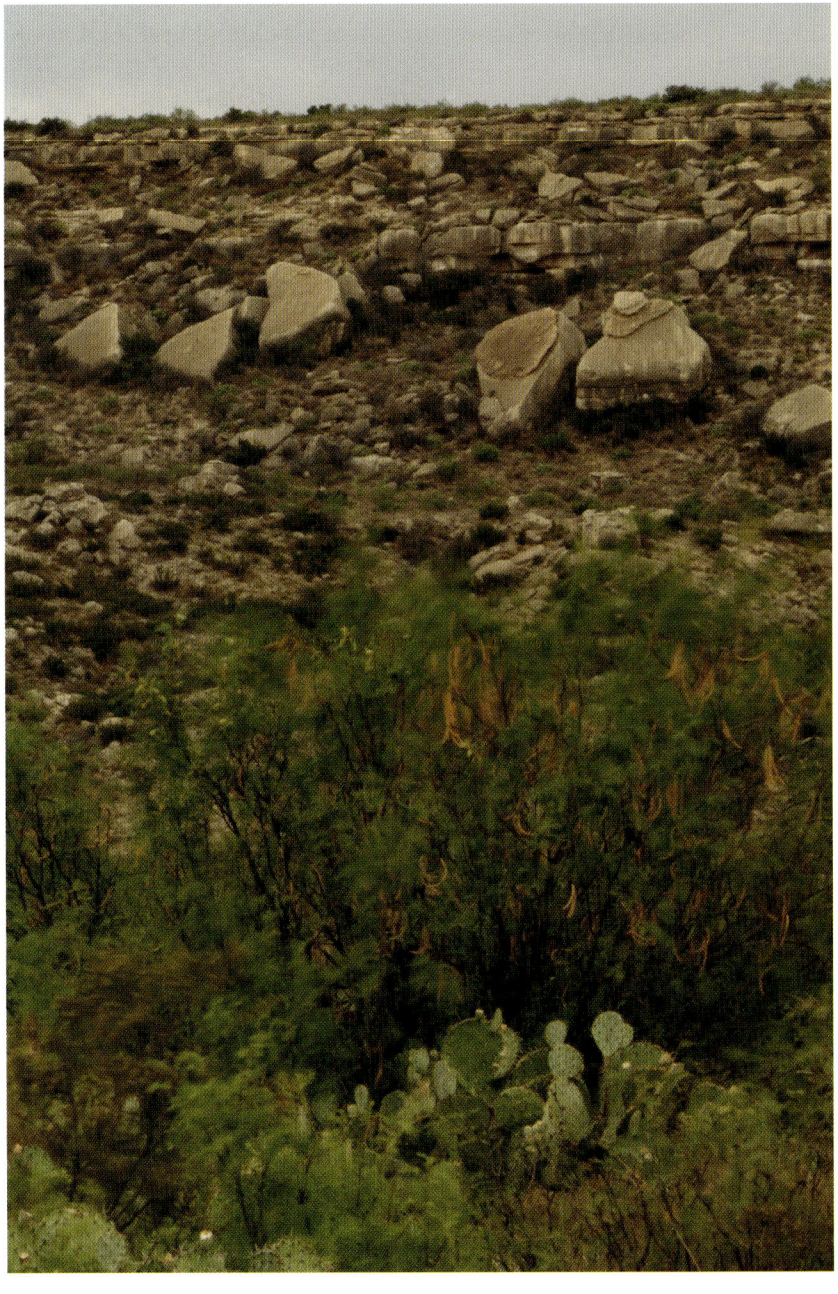

Upton County

Boulder-Strewn Hillside

The county was created in 1887 and organized in 1910. It is named for two brothers, John C. and William F. Upton, both colonels in the Confederate army. In the 1860s, the Chihuahua Trail from Mexico to Indianola, Texas—a significant trading route—crossed the region, as did the path of the Butterfield Overland Mail and the Goodnight-Loving Trail.

Uvalde County

Frio River in Garner State Park

The county was created in 1850 and organized in 1856. It is named for Juan de Ugalde, the Spanish governor of Coahuila. The conflict between Mexicans and Anglos during and after the Mexican War continued in Uvalde County with the reported lynching of eleven Mexicans near the Nueces River in 1855. Laws passed in 1857 prohibited Mexicans from traveling through the county.

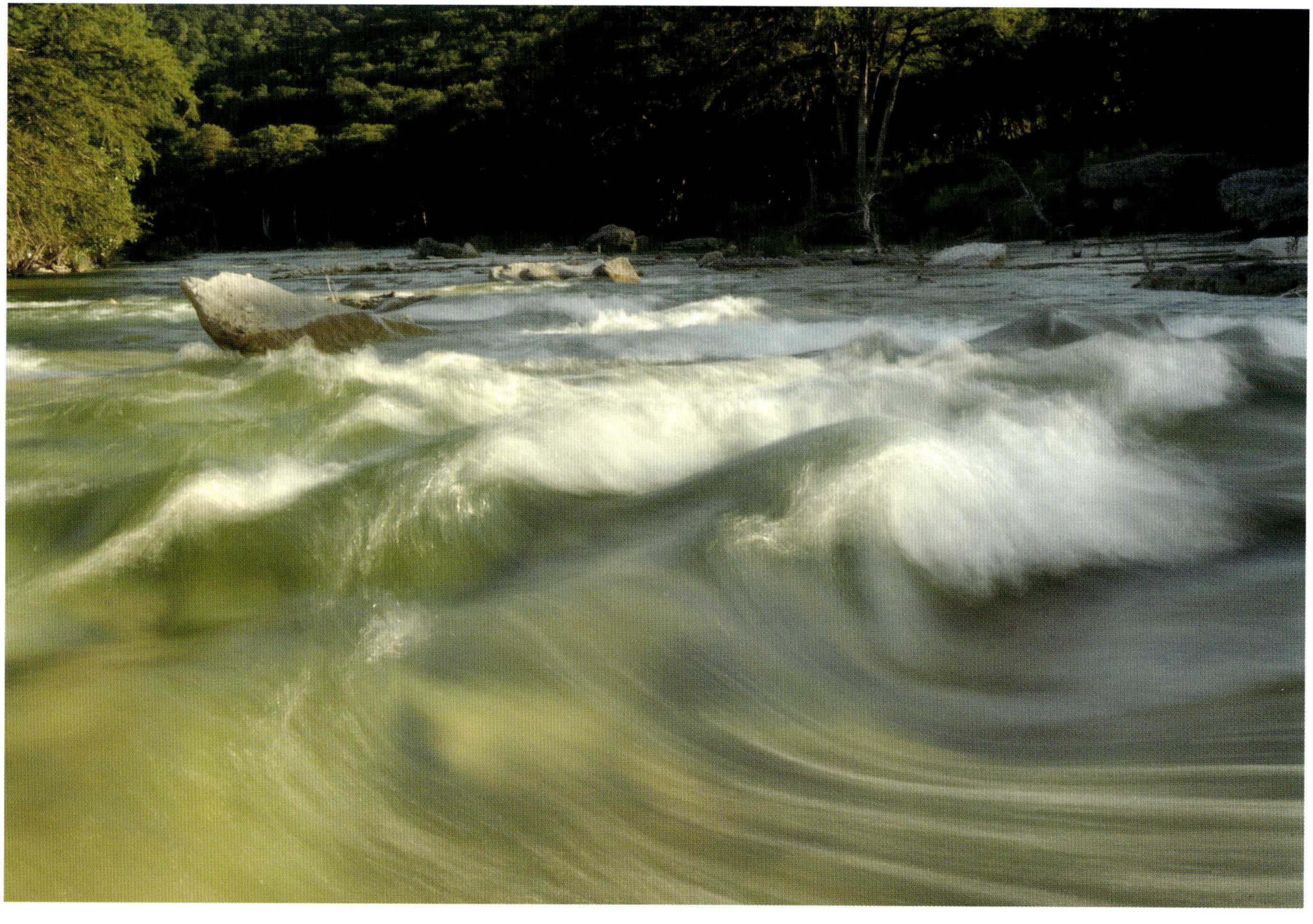

Val Verde County

Dolan Falls Preserve on the Devils River

The county was founded in 1885 and is named for the Civil War battle of Val Verde. In 1862, soldiers of Sibley's Brigade took part in the Texas invasion of New Mexico Territory, during which they captured several artillery pieces at the Battle of Val Verde.

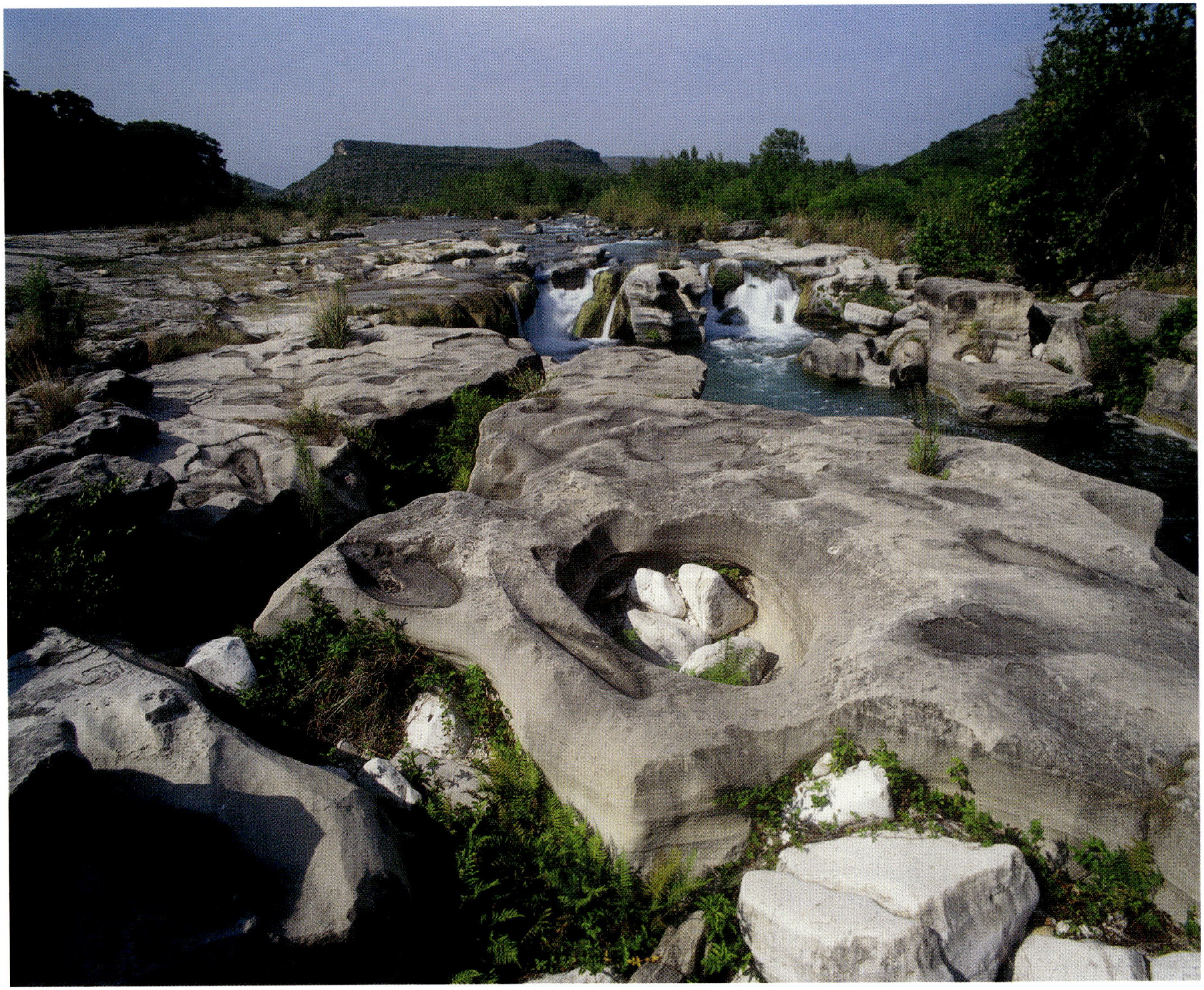

Van Zandt County

Beaver Lodge in Purtis Creek State Park

The county is named for Isaac Van Zandt, a member of the Congress of the Republic of Texas. The county was formed in 1848. Van Zandt County is commonly known as the "Free State of Van Zandt." The title was particularly prevalent through the Reconstruction Era but is still in use today. Many versions of the county's history may account for this name, and historians—even within the county and throughout its existence—do not agree on exactly how it became known as the "Free State."

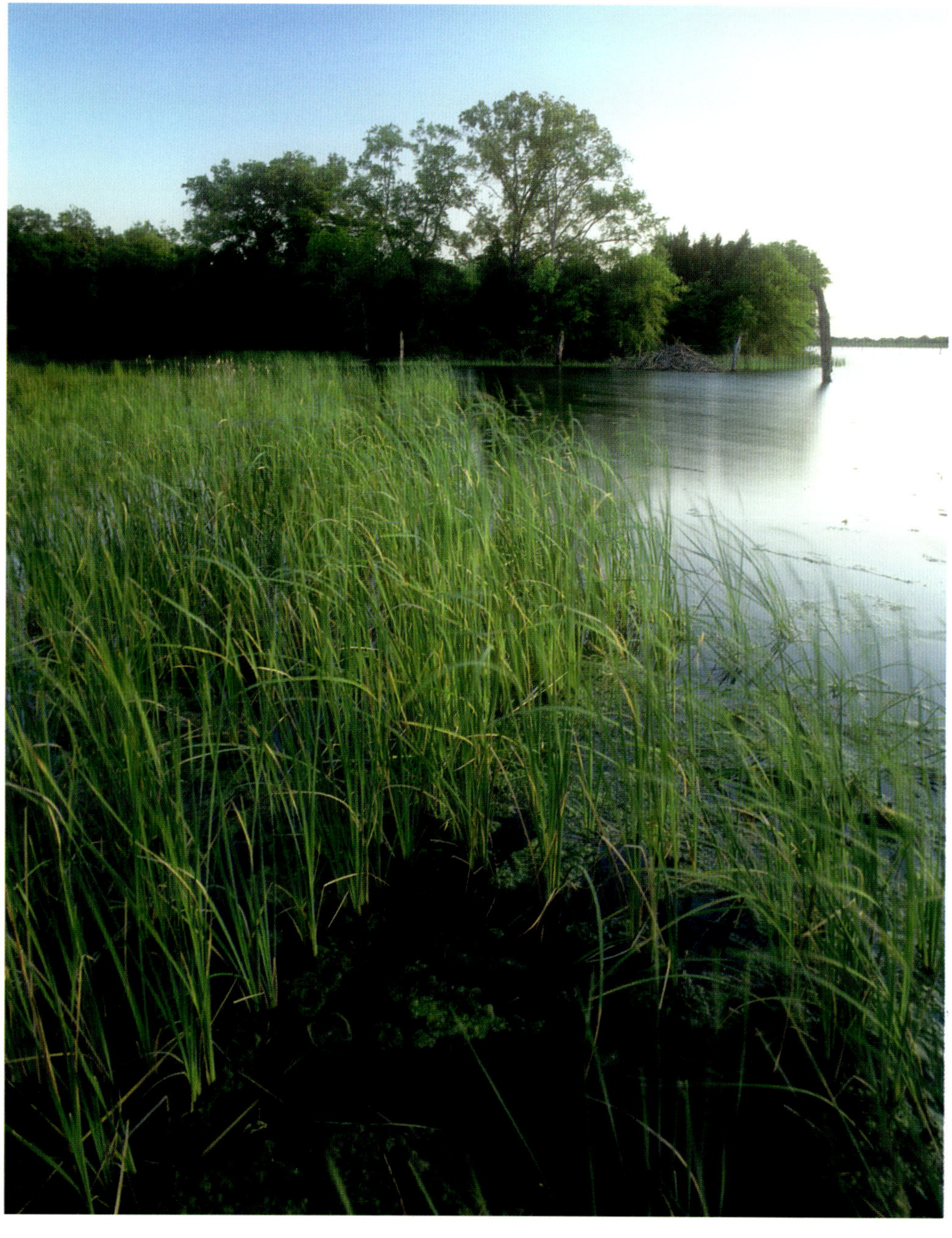

Victoria County

Oak Forest

Victoria—one of the original thirty-six counties—was organized in 1848. It is named for Isaac Van Zandt (1813–1847): attorney, Texas state representative, and diplomat. In 1835, Victoria's settlers supported the revolution against Antonio López de Santa Anna but were shunned by new incoming Americans, many of whom were adventurous soldiers or fortune hunters who wrongly profiled them as Mexican sympathizers and forced them to flee after the revolution in 1836. Anglo-Americans eventually resettled the area.

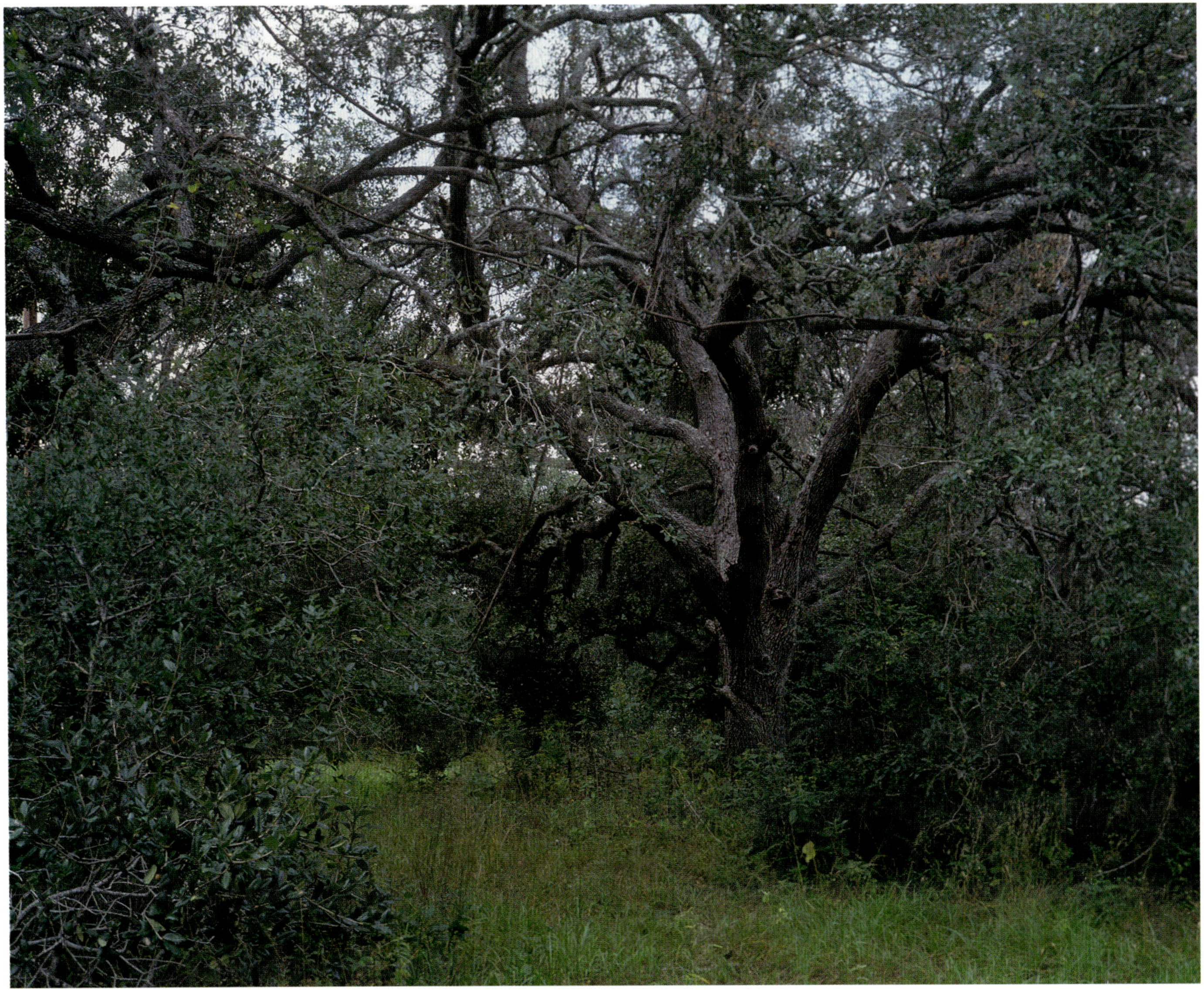

Walker County

Late-Afternoon Light on Lake Raven in Huntsville State Park

Formed in 1846, the county is named for Samuel Hamilton Walker (1815–1847), a Texas Ranger and soldier in the Mexican-American War. By 1847, there were 2,695 people living in the area. In 1848, the county became the designated site for what became the Texas State Penitentiary at Huntsville, which began operating in 1849 and is still in operation today.

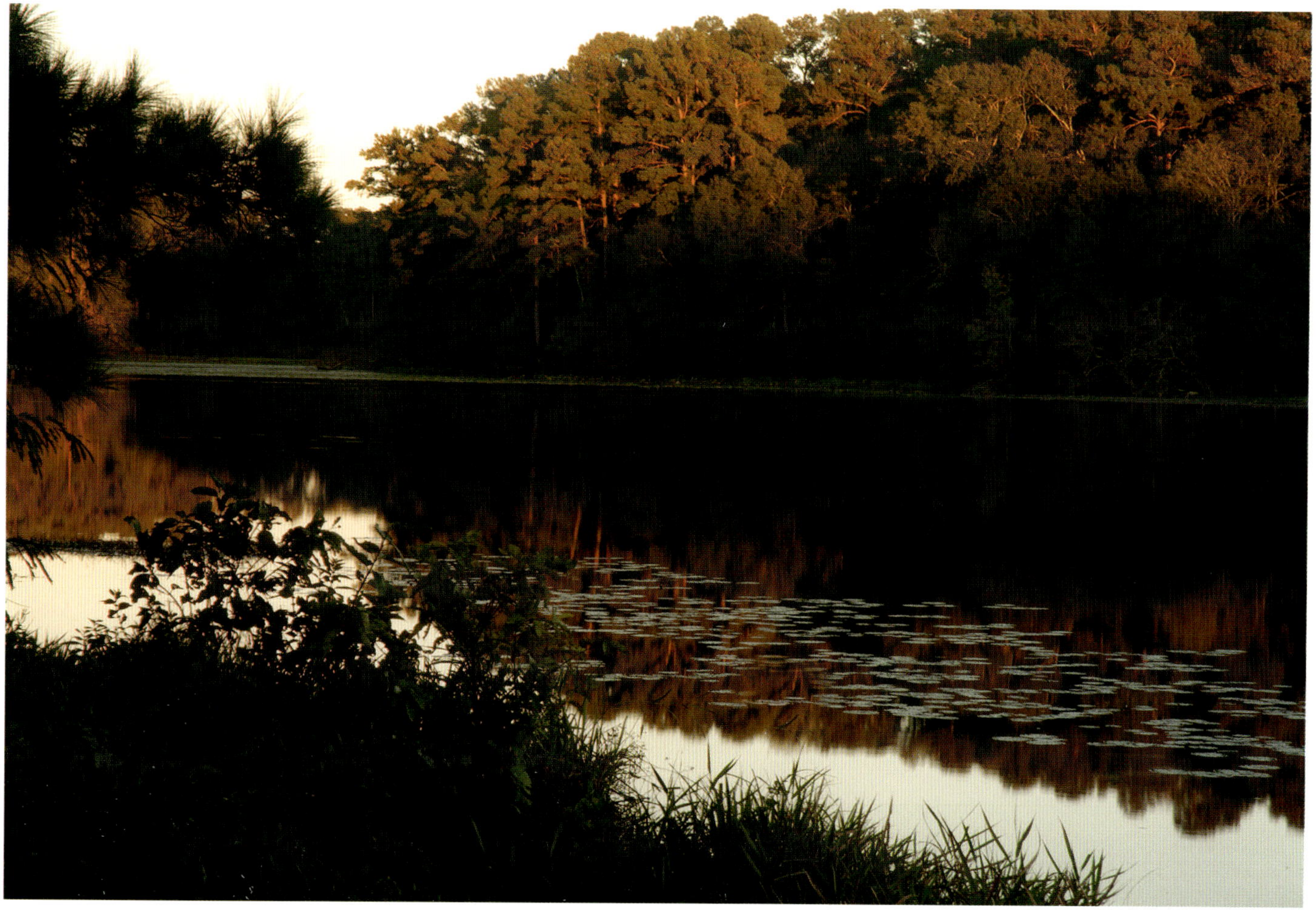

Waller County

Wildflowers in a Passing Storm

The county was named for Edwin Waller, a signer of the Texas Declaration of Independence and first mayor of Austin. The county was founded in 1873. During the Civil War, Confederate camps Carter, Groce, and Hebert were established near Hempstead; the town became a Confederate supply and manufacturing center, and a Confederate military hospital was established there. Camp Groce was one of two locations holding Union prisoners of war. Support was keen for the Confederacy in the area. Dr. Richard R. Peebles, a prominent local citizen who helped to found Hempstead, was imprisoned and exiled by Confederate authorities for speaking and writing against the war.

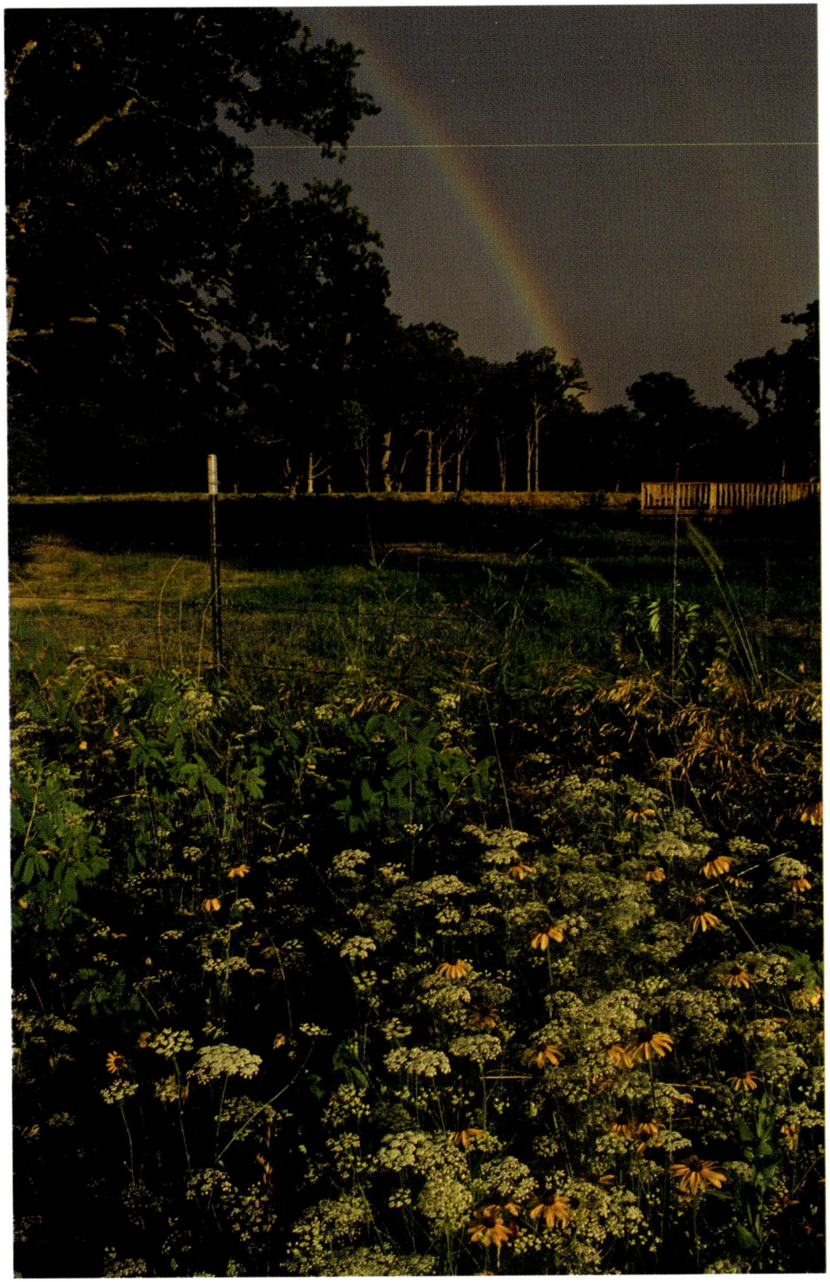

Ward County

Monahans Sandhills State Park

The county was created in 1887 and organized in 1892. It is named for Thomas W. Ward, a soldier in the Texas Revolution. Pyote Air Force Station opened in 1942, becoming the largest bomber installation in the United States. The plane Enola Gay, which dropped the atomic bomb on Hiroshima, was later stored here.

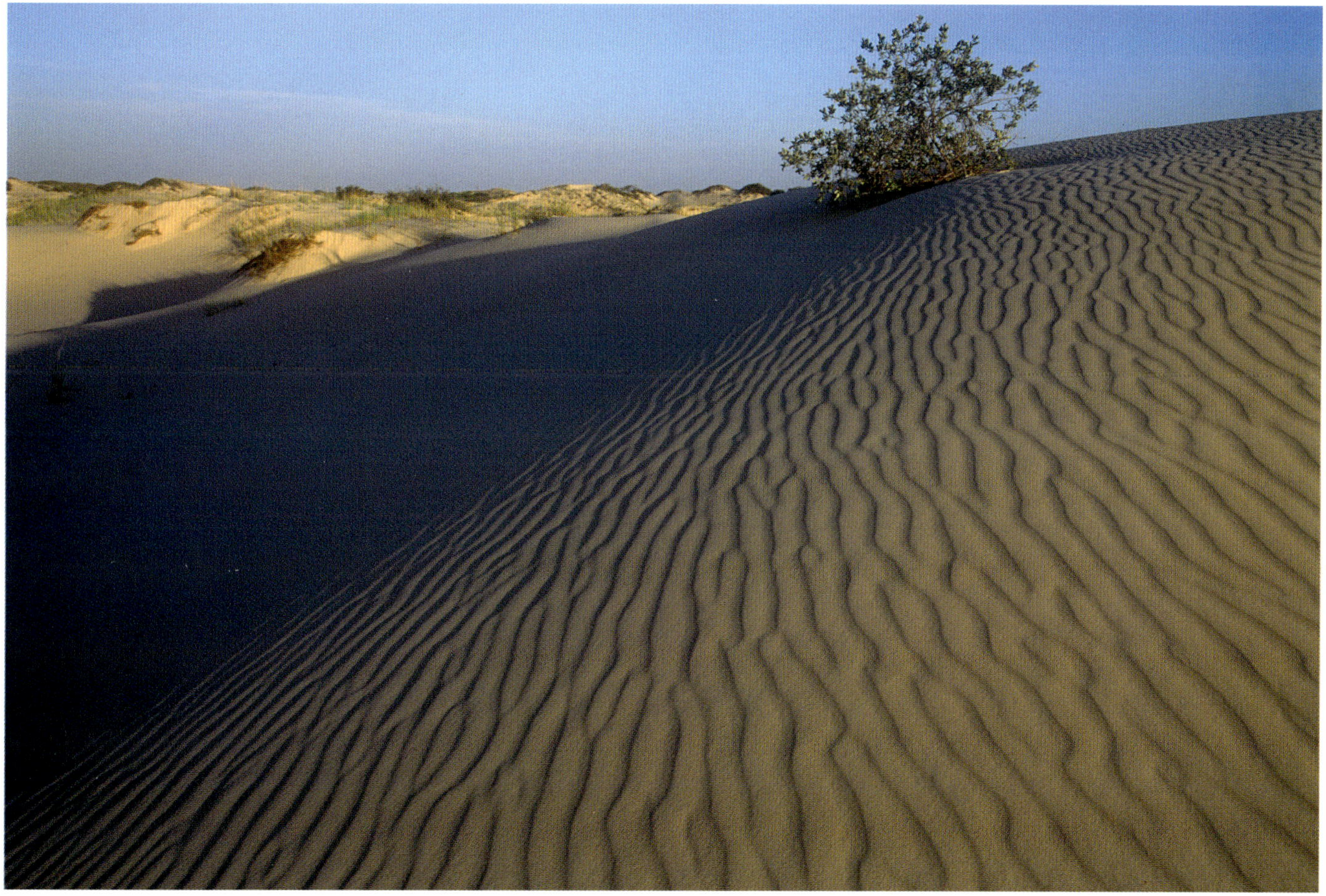

Washington County

Mixed Wildflowers near Independence

The county was created in 1835 as a municipality of Mexico and was organized as a Texas county in 1837. It is named for George Washington, the first president of the United States. Washington-on-the-Brazos is notable as the site of the signing of the Texas Declaration of Independence during the convention of 1836. The county is known as the "Birthplace of Texas." Each spring the county is blanketed in wildflowers, drawing large crowds of admirers.

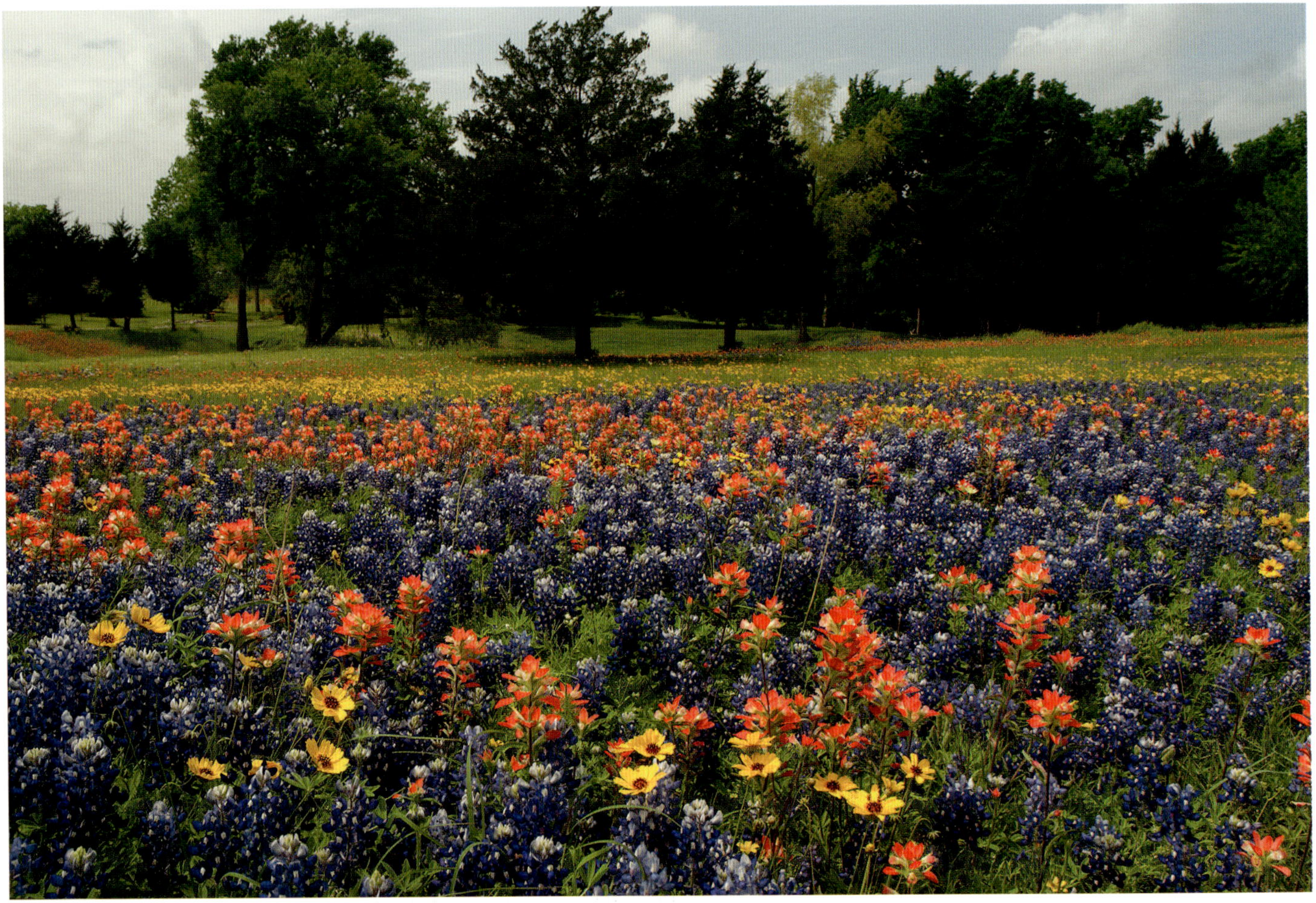

Webb County

Lake Casablanca State Park

Webb County was established in 1848. The county was named for James Webb, who served as secretary of the treasury, secretary of state, and attorney general of the Republic of Texas, and later as judge of the United States District Court following the admission of Texas to statehood. Indian attacks became a particular problem during and after the Mexican War of Independence. Writing for help in 1837, a Laredo official estimated that since 1813 the area had known "only three years of peace."

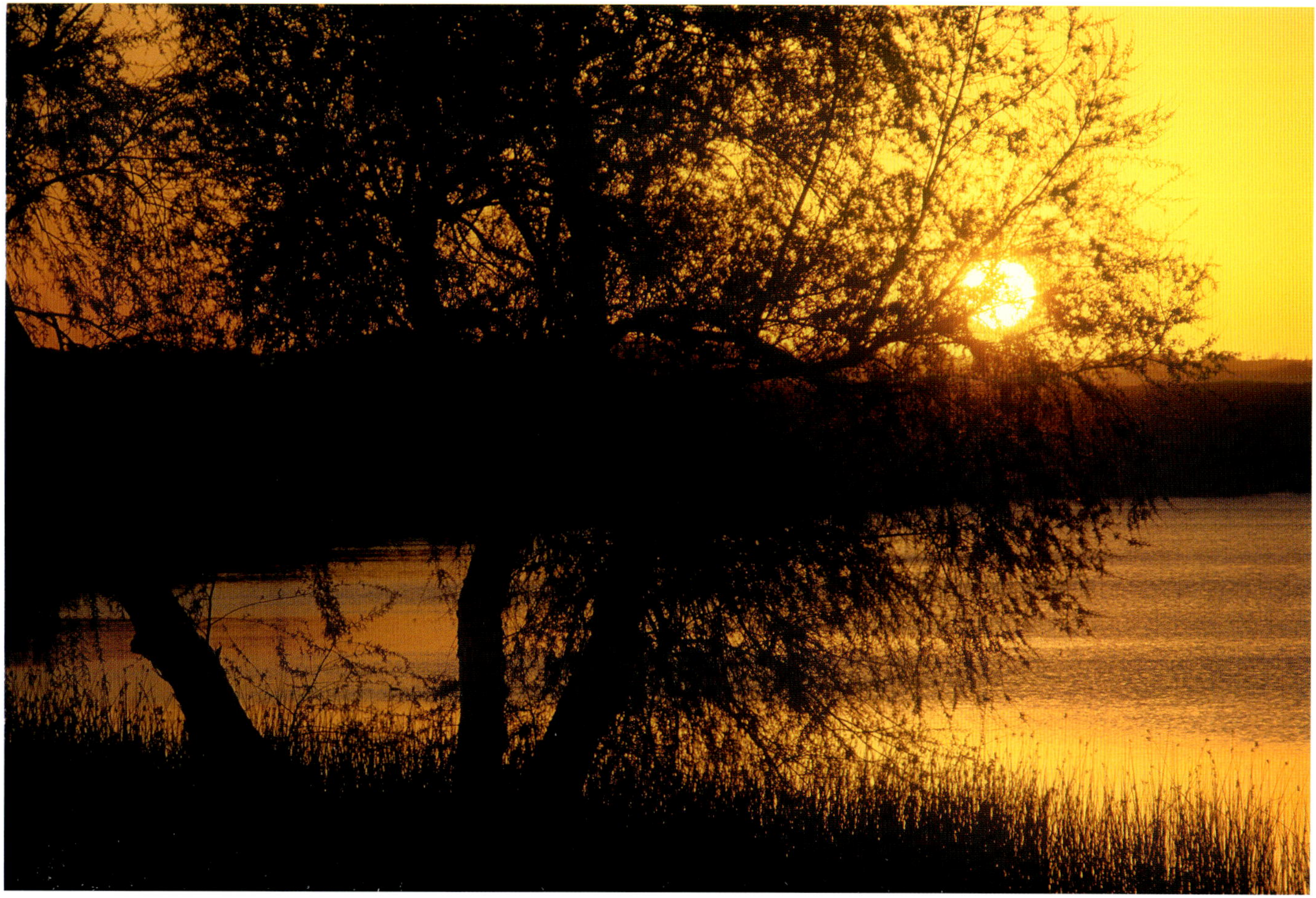

Wharton County

Late-Afternoon Light along the Colorado River

The county was named for brothers William Harris Wharton and John Austin Wharton and was formed in 1846. Cattle raising replaced the plantation system as Wharton County's primary industry after the Civil War and drew significant numbers of Mexicans into the area to serve as herdsmen. Herds were formed as residents bought cattle and rounded up strays that had multiplied on the prairies when access to markets was limited. Abel Head (Shanghai) Pierce took advantage of the times and acquired vast acreage on the west side of the Colorado, with a cattle empire that stretched over three counties, encompassing half a million acres, of which 30,000 were in Wharton County.

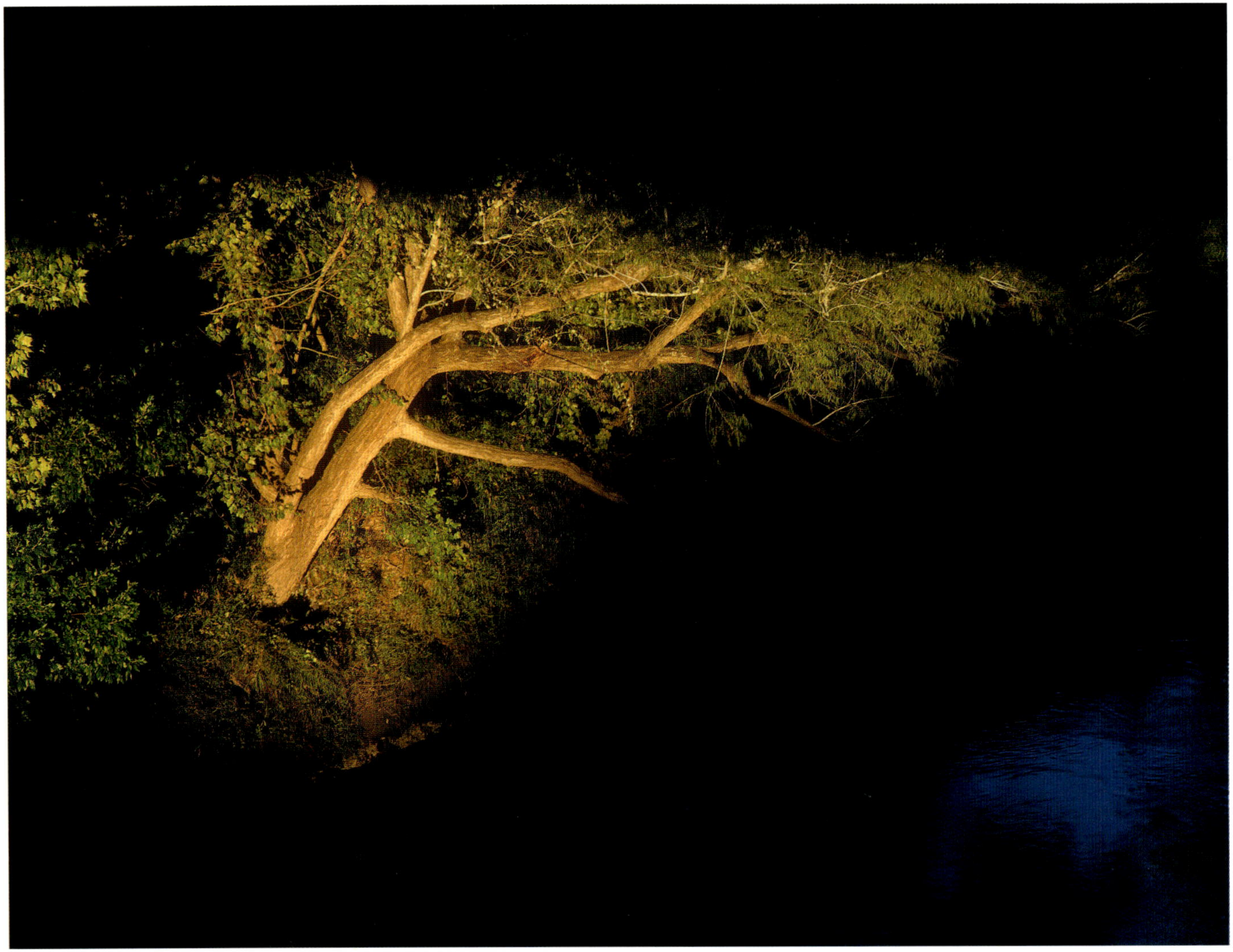

Wheeler County

Grove of Trees on a Sunny October Day

The county was formed in 1876 and organized in 1879. It is named for Royall Tyler Wheeler, a chief justice of the Texas Supreme Court. In the 1880s, Temple Lea Houston, the youngest son of Sam Houston, was the district attorney of the 35th Judicial District of Texas, which then encompassed twenty-six counties in the Texas Panhandle. The district was based at the time in the courthouse at Mobeetie, in Wheeler County.

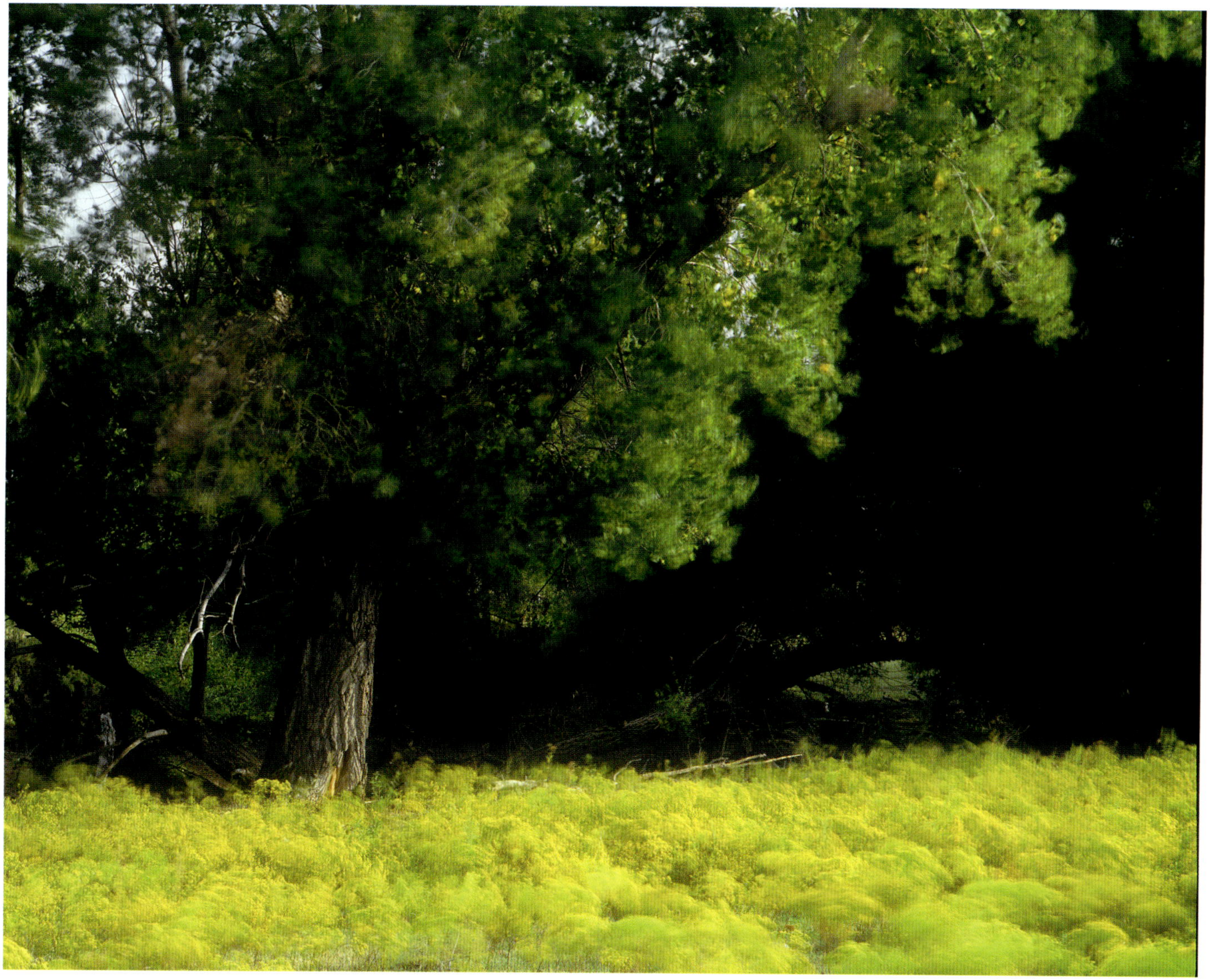

Wichita County

Approaching Storm near Iowa Park

The county was created in 1858 and is named for the Wichita Native American tribe. A benefit of the World War II years lay in the decision of the federal government to locate an Army Air Corps training facility just north of the county seat. Sheppard Field began operations in June 1941 and at its peak housed 46,000 men. It was used as a pilot-training, aircraft-maintenance-training, and basic-training facility. The facility added hundreds of jobs and millions of dollars to the local economy. Although it was deactivated in 1946, it reopened in 1950 as Sheppard Air Force Base and during the Korean War served as a training center for pilots and aircraft mechanics.

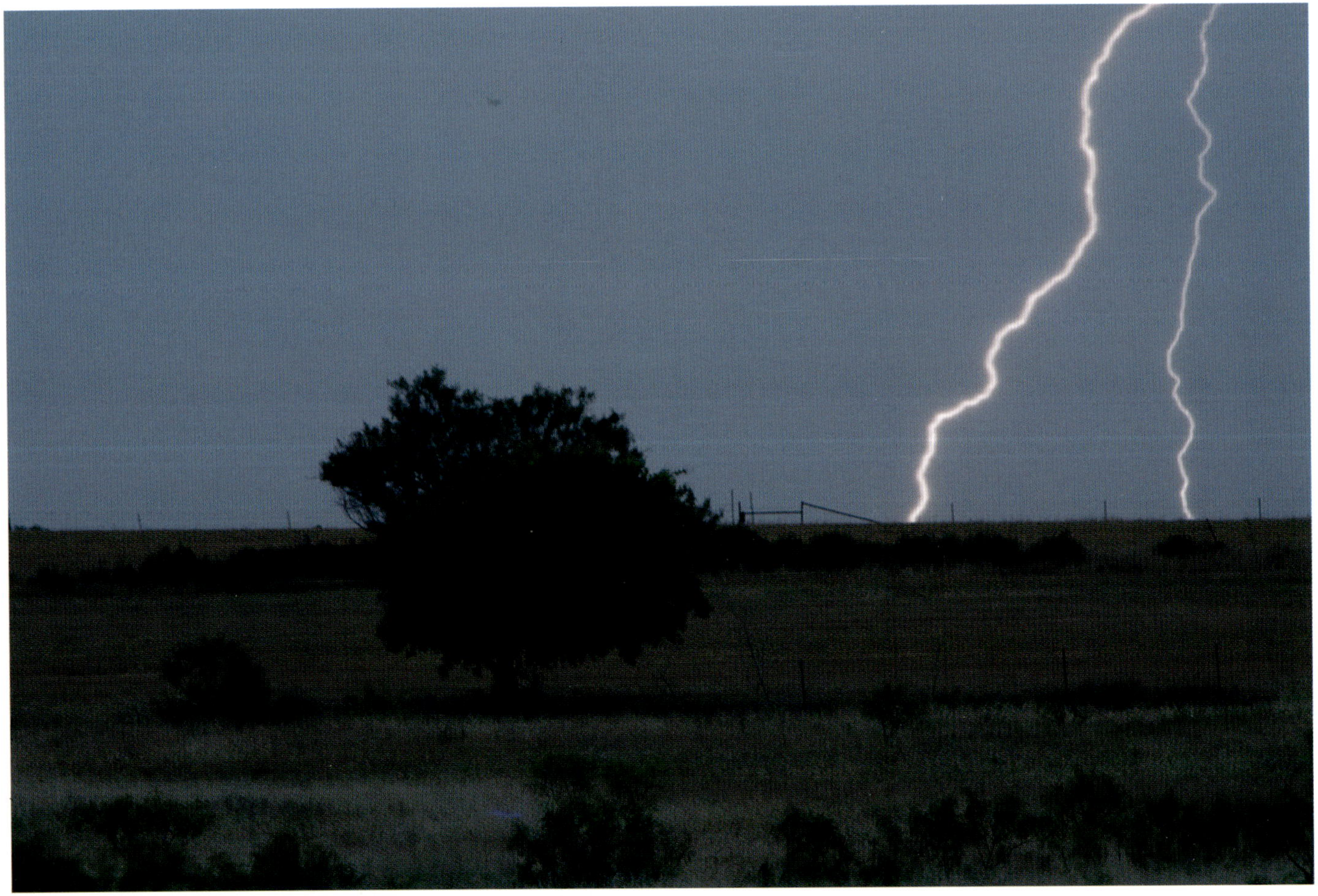

Wilbarger County

Wildflowers near the Oklahoma Border

The county was created in 1858 and organized in 1881. Wilbarger County was named for Josiah Pugh Wilbarger and Mathias Wilbarger, two early settlers. Notable people from the county include Roy Orbison, singer/songwriter, and Jack Teagarden, band leader and trombonist.

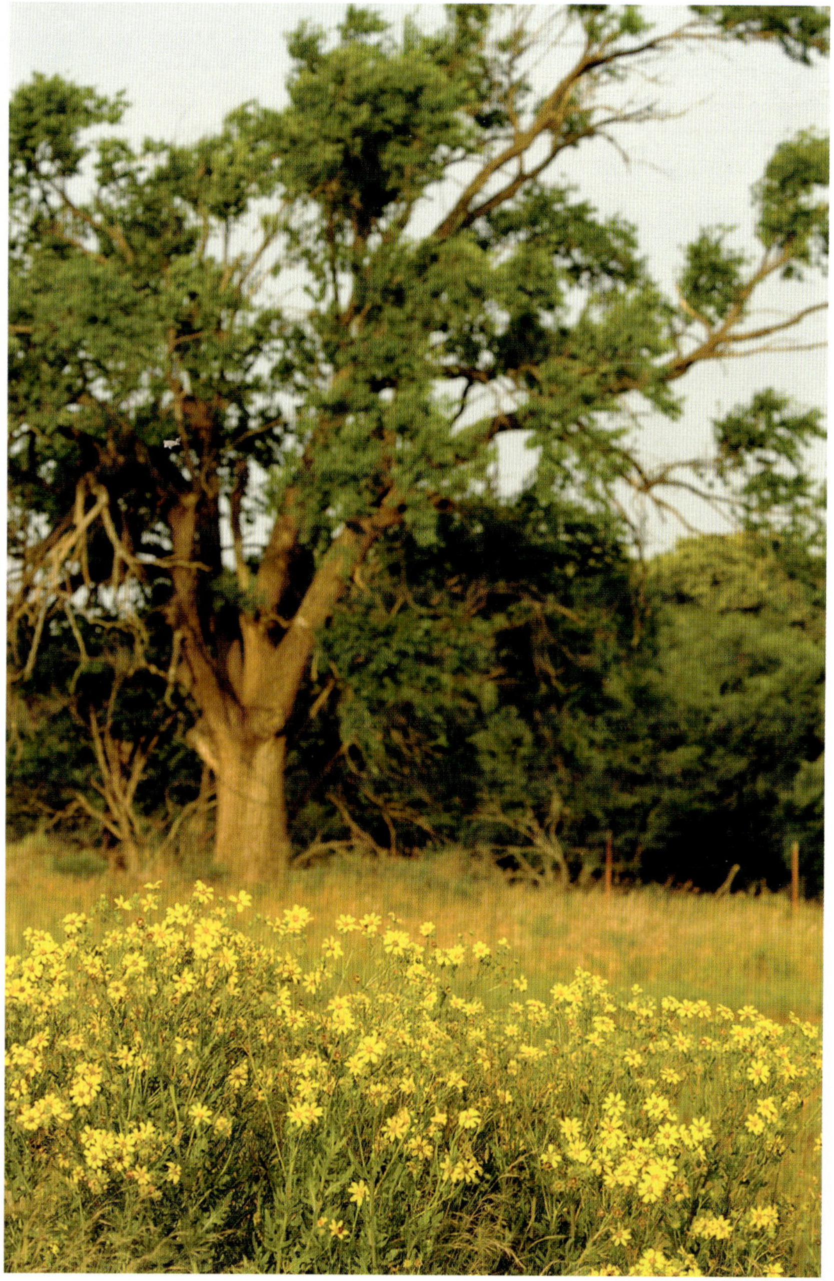

Willacy County

Placid Scene along the Gulf of Mexico near Port Mansfield

The county was created in 1911 and is named for John G. Willacy, Texas state senator, who was the author of the bill that established the county. The bays and coast are renowned for fishing. Port Mansfield, in Willacy County, is a coastal fisherman's mecca and hosts the Port Mansfield Fishing Tournament and the Port Mansfield Lady Anglers Tournament.

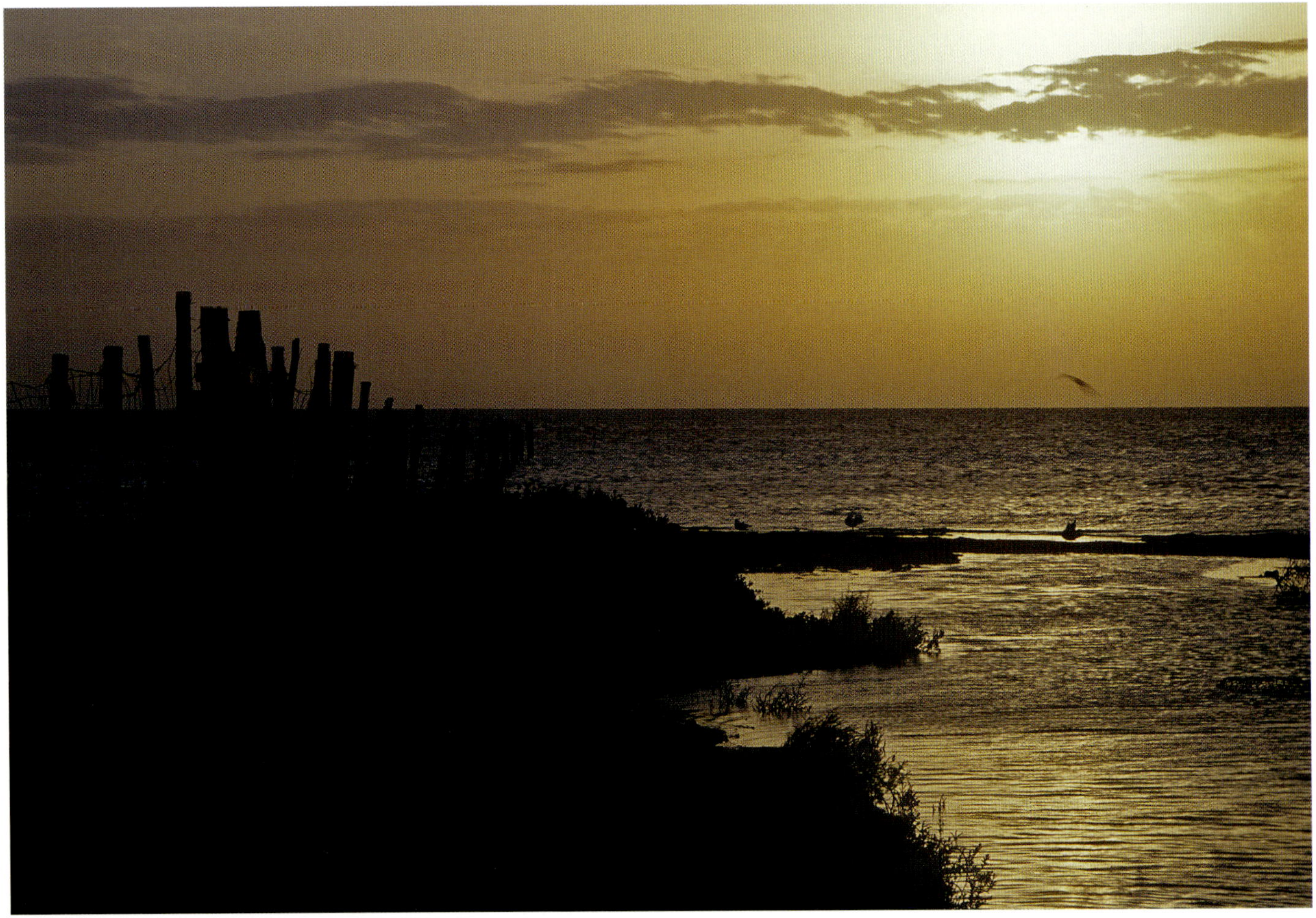

Williamson County

Late-Afternoon Scene along the North Fork of the San Gabriel River

The county was organized in 1848 and named for Robert McAlpin Williamson (1804?–1859), a community leader and veteran of the Battle of San Jacinto. On September 9 and 10, 1921, the remnants of a hurricane moved across Williamson County. The center of the storm became stationary over Thrall, a small farming town in eastern Williamson County, dropping a storm total of almost 40 inches of rain in thirty-six hours. The twenty-four-hour rainfall total remains the national official twenty-four-hour rainfall record.

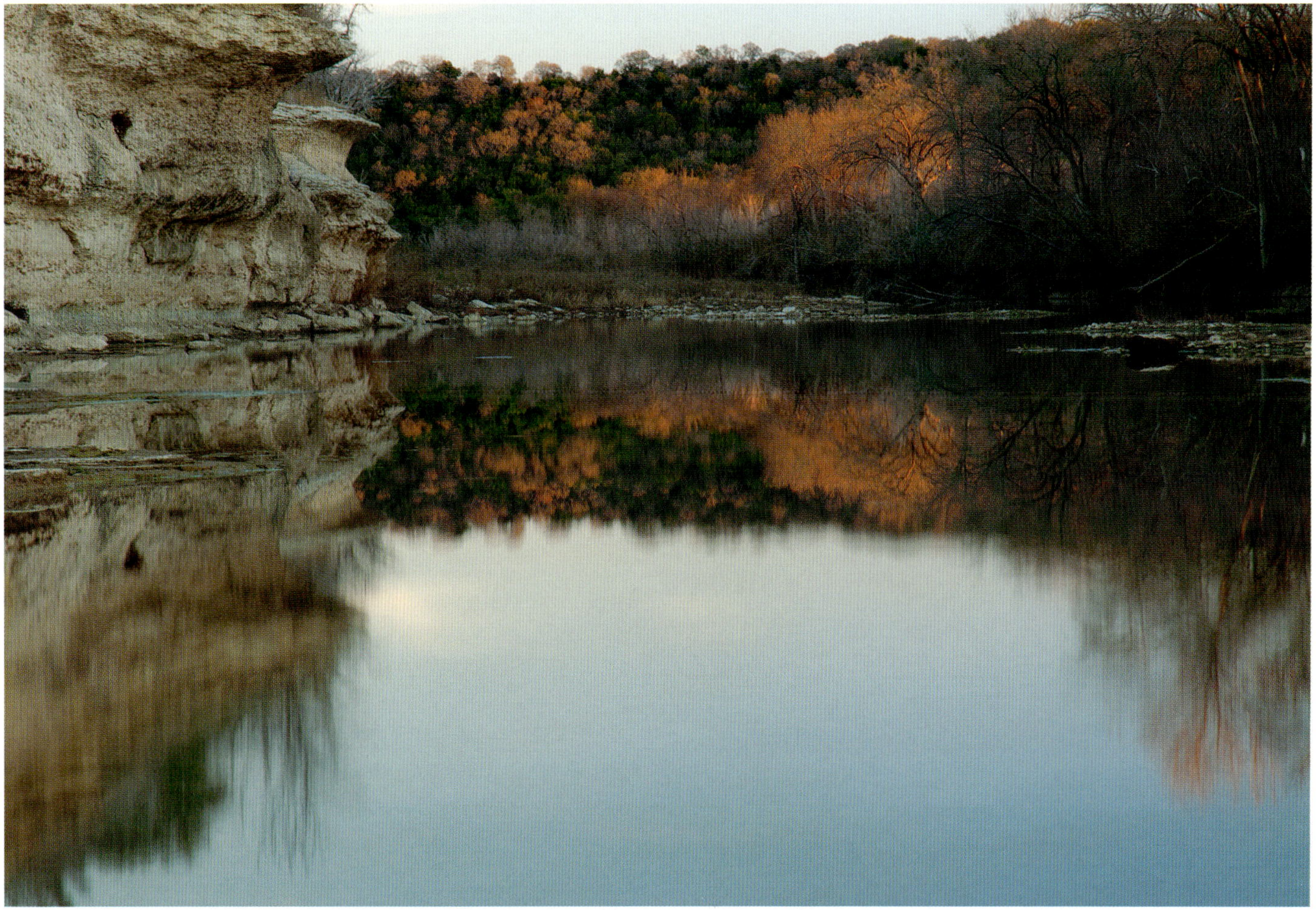

Wilson County

Sunflowers and Live Oak

The county is named for James Charles Wilson and was formed in 1860. John W. Longsworth, appointed judge and county clerk by the military government during congressional reconstruction, moved the county records to Lodi in 1867, beginning a controversy about the location of the county seat that lasted for more than a decade. The county seat was returned to Sutherland Springs in March 1871 but was moved back to Lodi in July 1871. An election was finally held in November 1873 to determine the location of county government, and the new town of Floresville, near the geographic center of the county, was selected as the county seat.

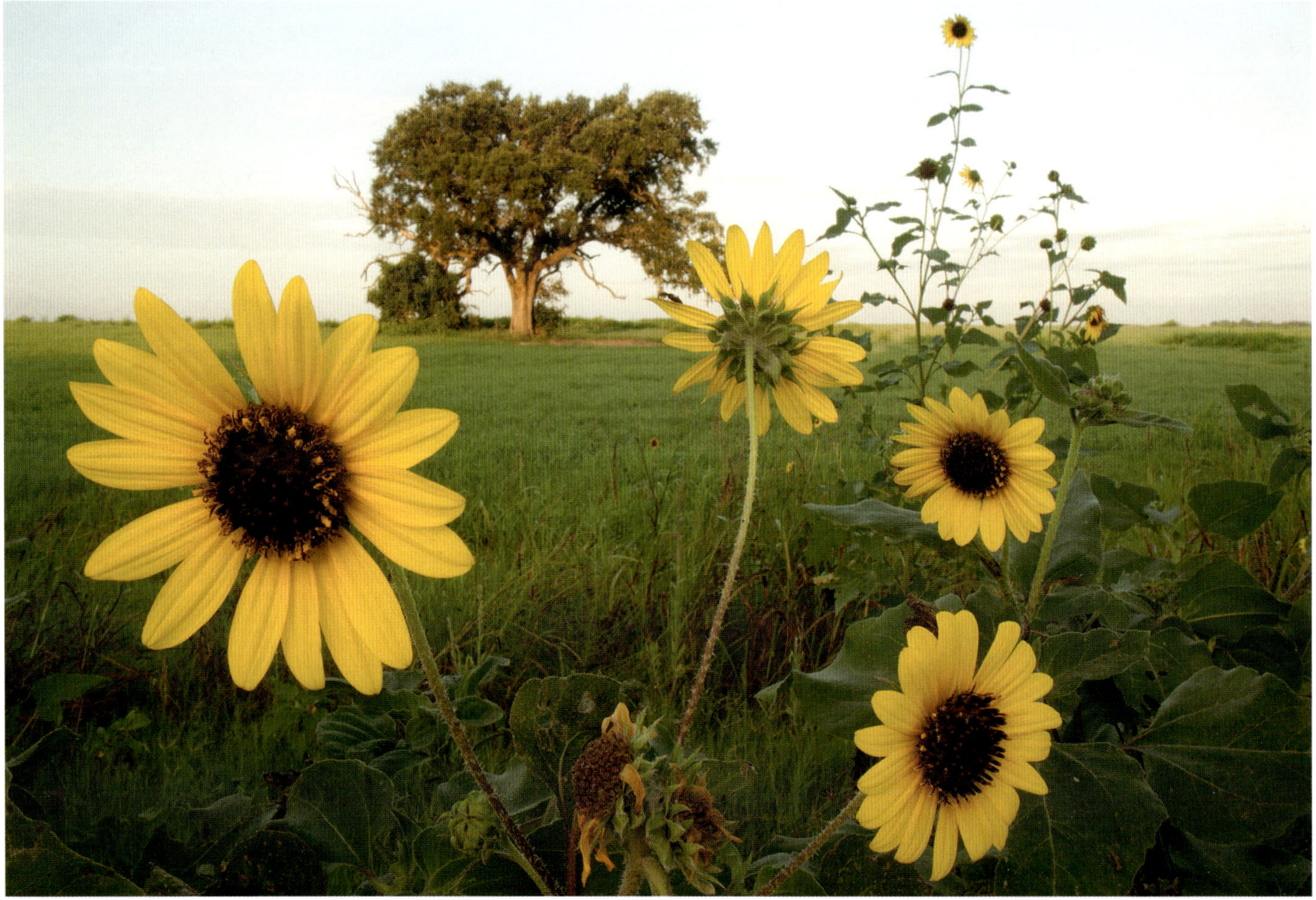

Winkler County

Monahans Sandhills State Park

The county was created in 1887 and organized in 1910. It is named for Clinton M. Winkler, a colonel in the Confederate army. In 2009, at Winkler County Memorial Hospital, two nurses—Anne Mitchell and Vicki Galle—were retaliated against for reporting physician Rolando Arafiles's inappropriate medical treatments to the Texas Medical Board. The story received national attention. The retaliation against the two nurses involved an investigation by county sheriff Robert Roberts, a friend and former business partner of Arafiles. The charges against Galle were ultimately dismissed at the last hour before trial. On February 11, 2010, Mitchell was acquitted by a jury that deliberated for less than an hour.

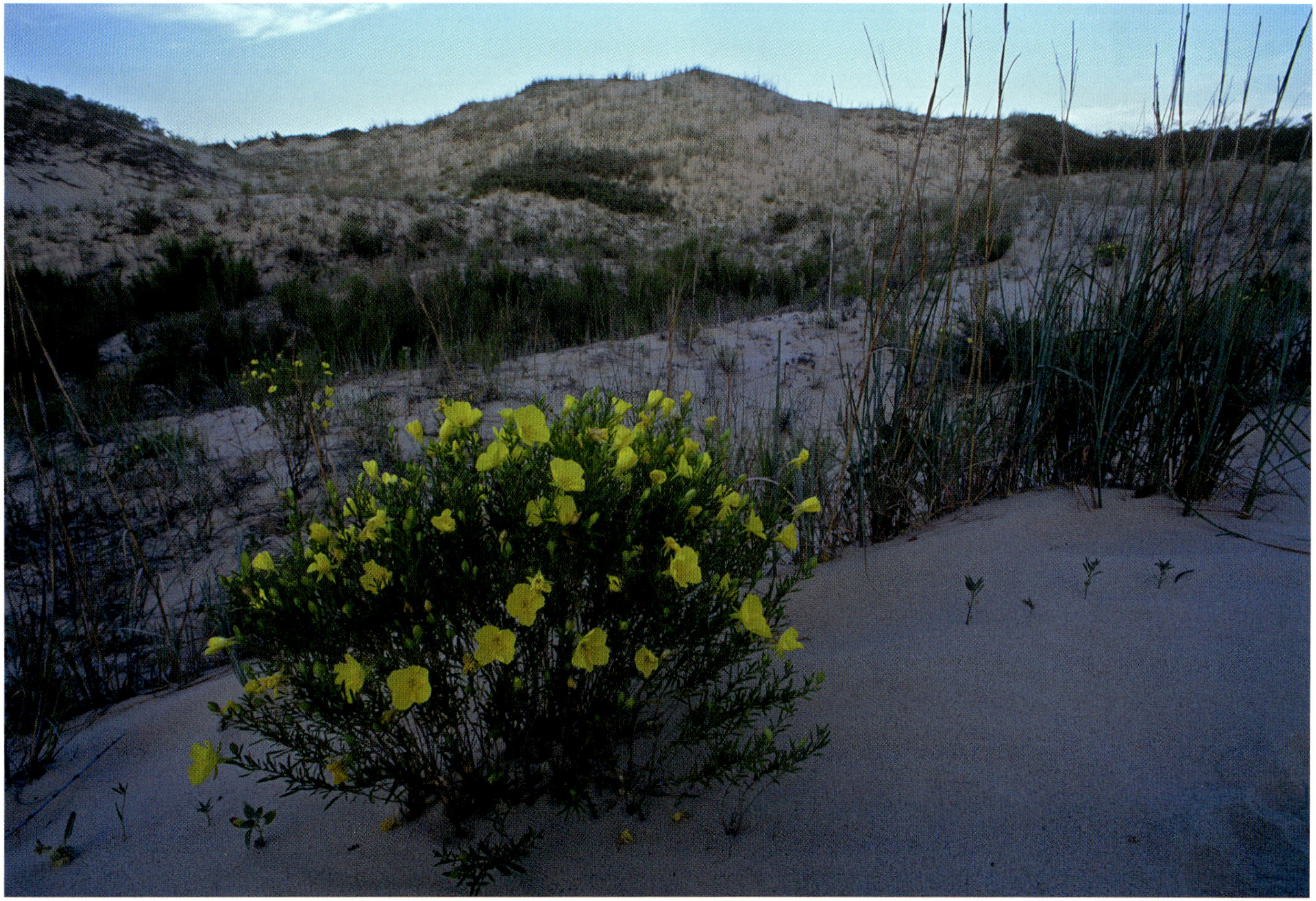

Wise County

Black Creek Lake in the Lyndon B. Johnson National Grassland

Wise County is named for Henry Alexander Wise, US congressman and future thirty-eighth governor of Virginia (1856–1860), who supported the annexation of Texas. The county was formed in 1856. On November 10, 1837, the Battle of the Knobs was fought in what is now Wise County between about 150 Indian warriors and just eighteen Republic of Texas soldiers under Lieutenant A. B. Benthuysen. Despite being heavily outnumbered, the Texas soldiers held their ground, and an estimated fifty Indians were killed or wounded and ten of the Texans were killed.

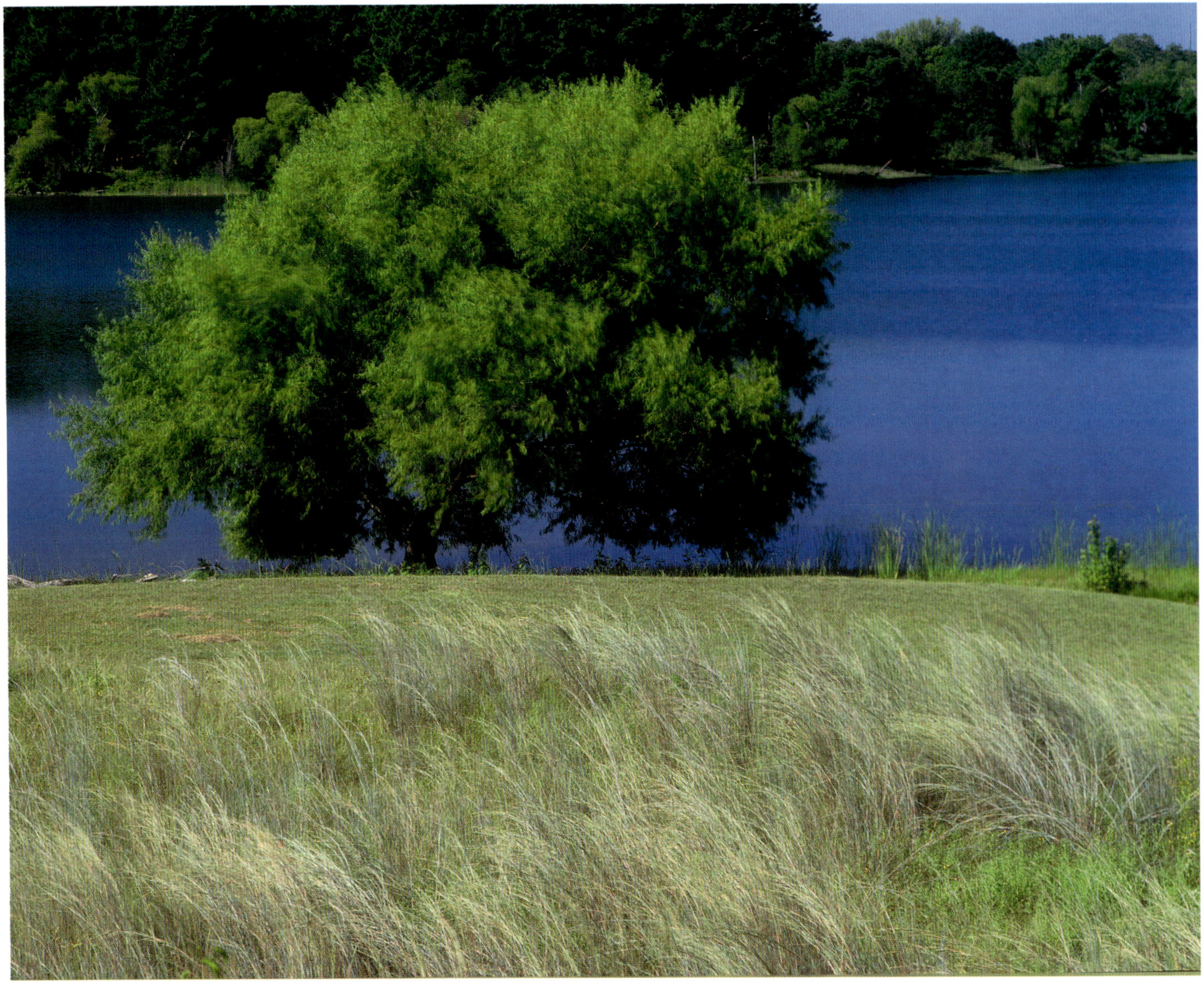

Wood County

Sunrise over Lake Fork

The county was named for George T. Wood, governor of Texas from 1847 to 1849. The county was founded in 1850. Lake Fork is in Wood County; it is known as one of the best bass-fishing lakes in the United States.

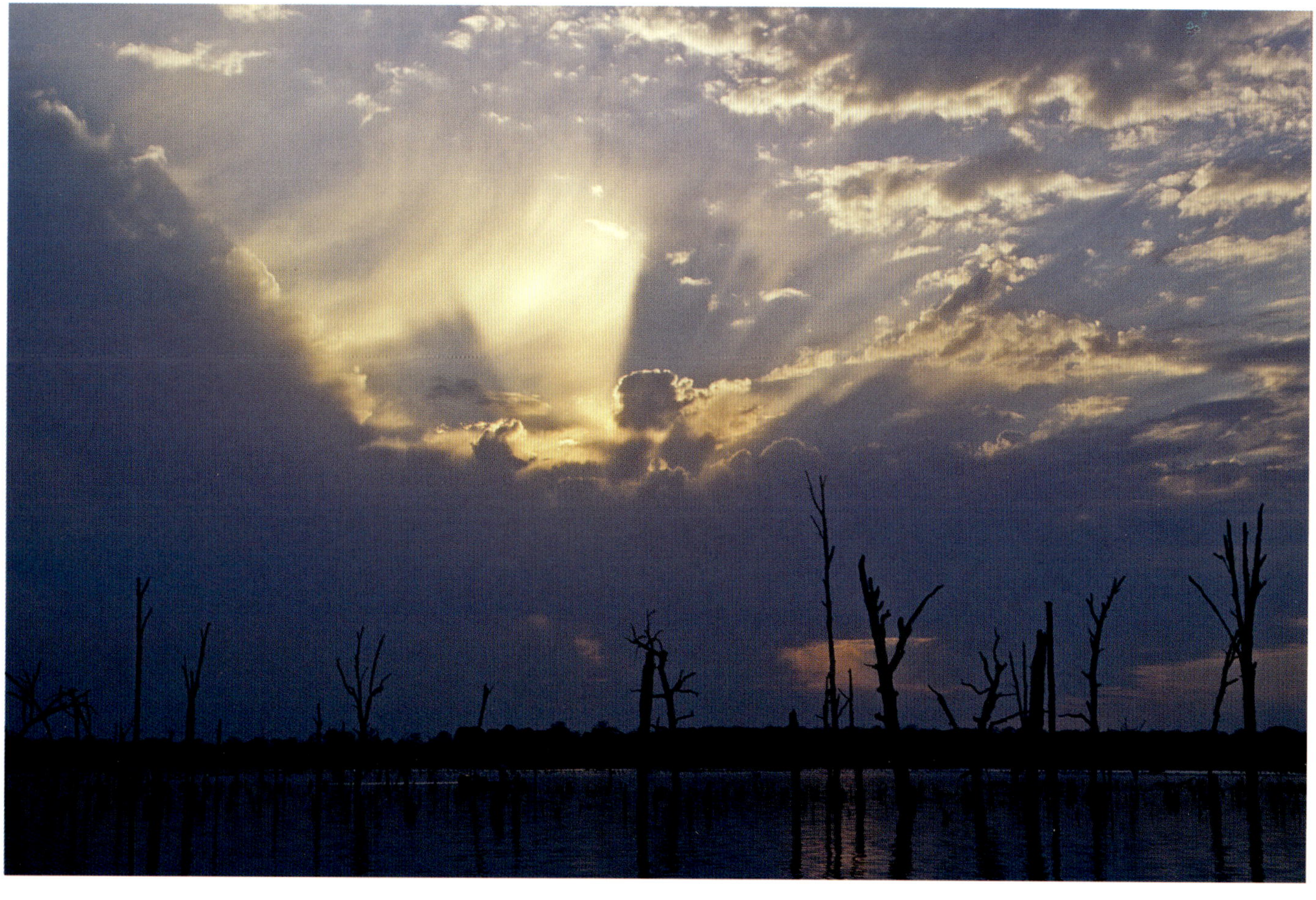

Yoakum County

Sunrise over an Agricultural Area

The county was created in 1876, was organized in 1907, and is named for Henderson King Yoakum, a Texas historian. Oil production began to intensify during the 1940s as Yoakum County became one of the leading oil-producing counties in the state. More than eighteen million barrels were produced in 1944, and almost twenty-five million barrels in 1948.

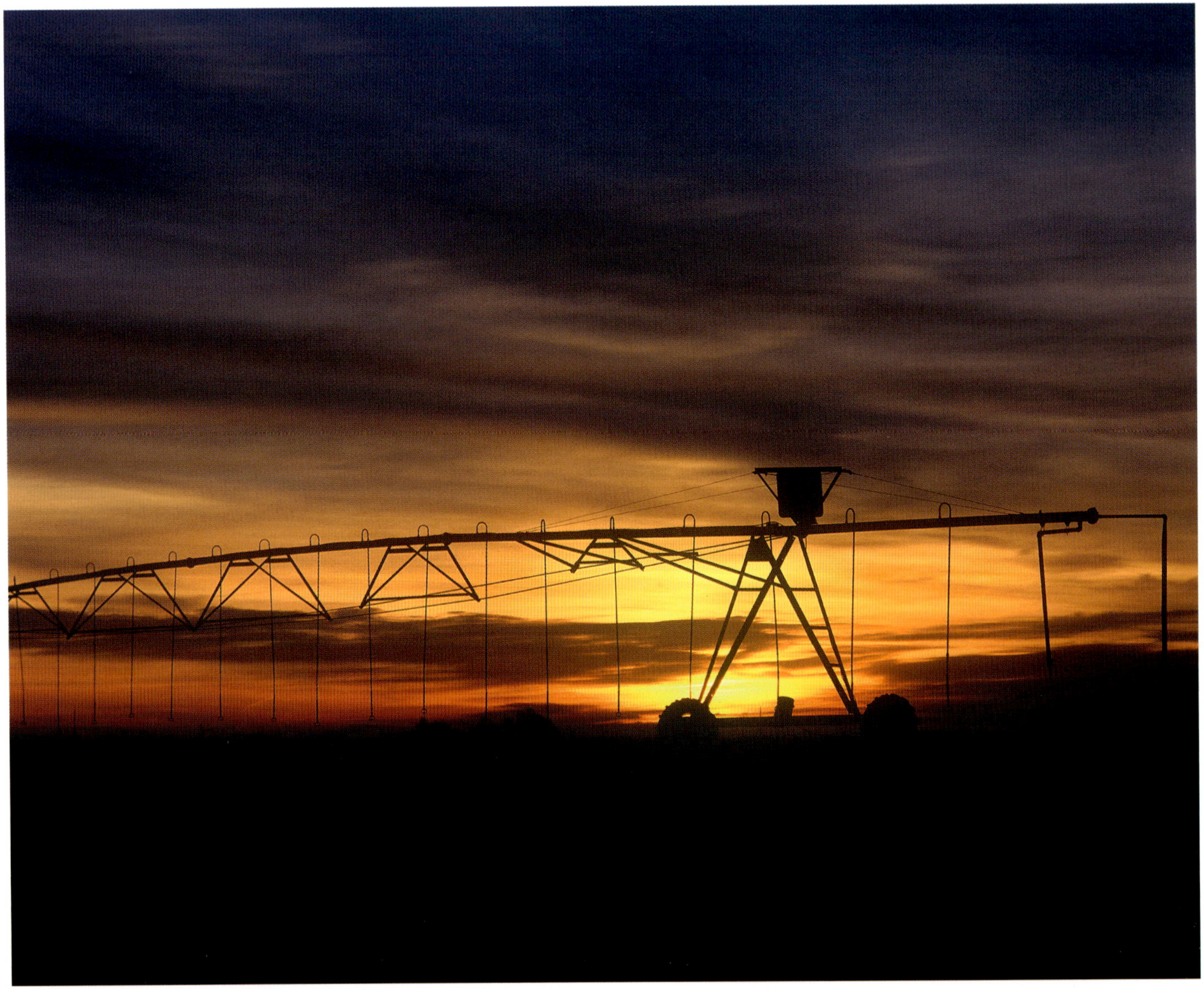

Young County

Mixed Wildflowers among Gently Rolling Country

The county was created in 1856 and organized in 1874. It is named for William Young, an early Texas settler and soldier. Federal programs came to the assistance of farmers and ranchers during the Great Depression. The Work Projects Administration (WPA) restored old Fort Belknap in 1936. In the 1930s, Young County also joined sixty-five other counties to form the Brazos River Conservation and Reclamation District.

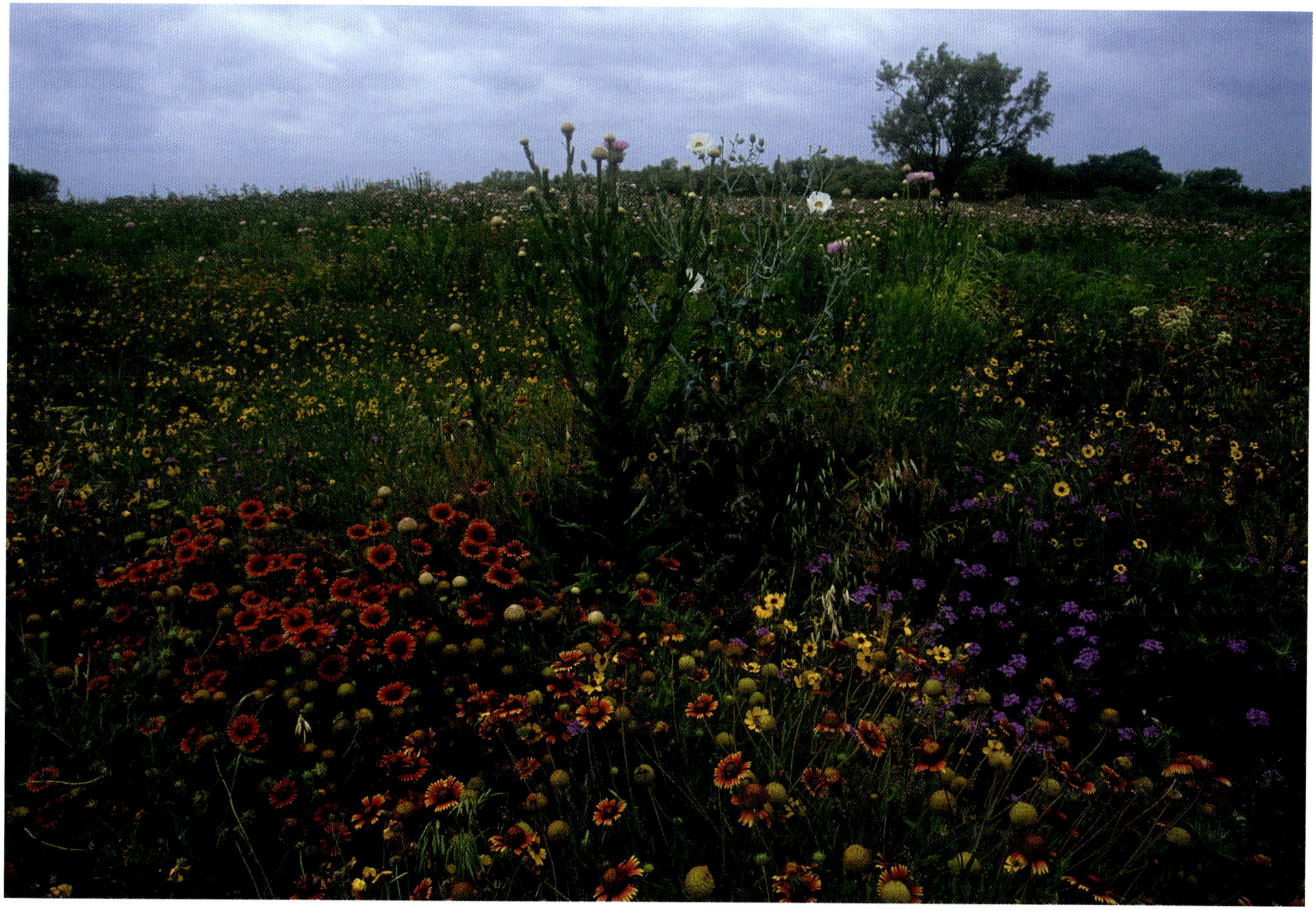

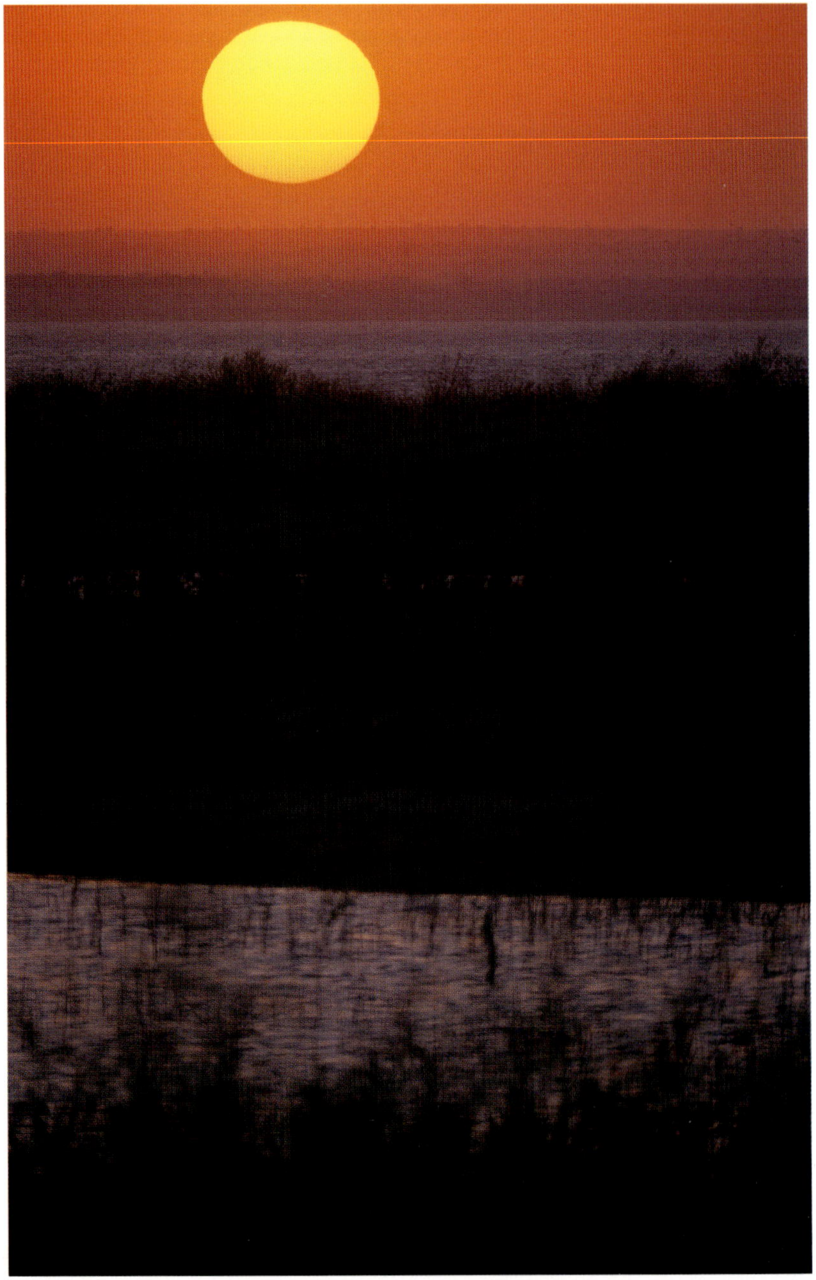

Zapata County

Falcon State Park

The county, formed in 1858, is named for Colonel José Antonio de Zapata, a rancher in the area who rebelled against Mexico. Among the earliest Anglo-Americans in the region was Henry Redmond, who in 1839 filed a claim for a headright (a legal grant to land) that became known as Habitación de Redmond. A small settlement eventually grew up at the site, which was called Habitación until 1858, when it was renamed Bellville.

Zavala County

Nueces River Cascade

The county is named for Lorenzo de Zavala (1788–1836), signer of the Texas Declaration of Independence and the first vice president of the Republic of Texas. The county was formed in 1846. The area between the Rio Grande and the Nueces River, including Zavala County, became a disputed territory known as the Wild Horse Desert, where neither the Republic of Texas nor the Mexican government had explicit control. Ownership was in dispute until the Mexican-American War. The area became filled with lawless characters who deterred settlers in the area. An agreement signed between Mexico and the United States in the 1930s put the liability of payments to the descendants of the original land grants on Mexico.

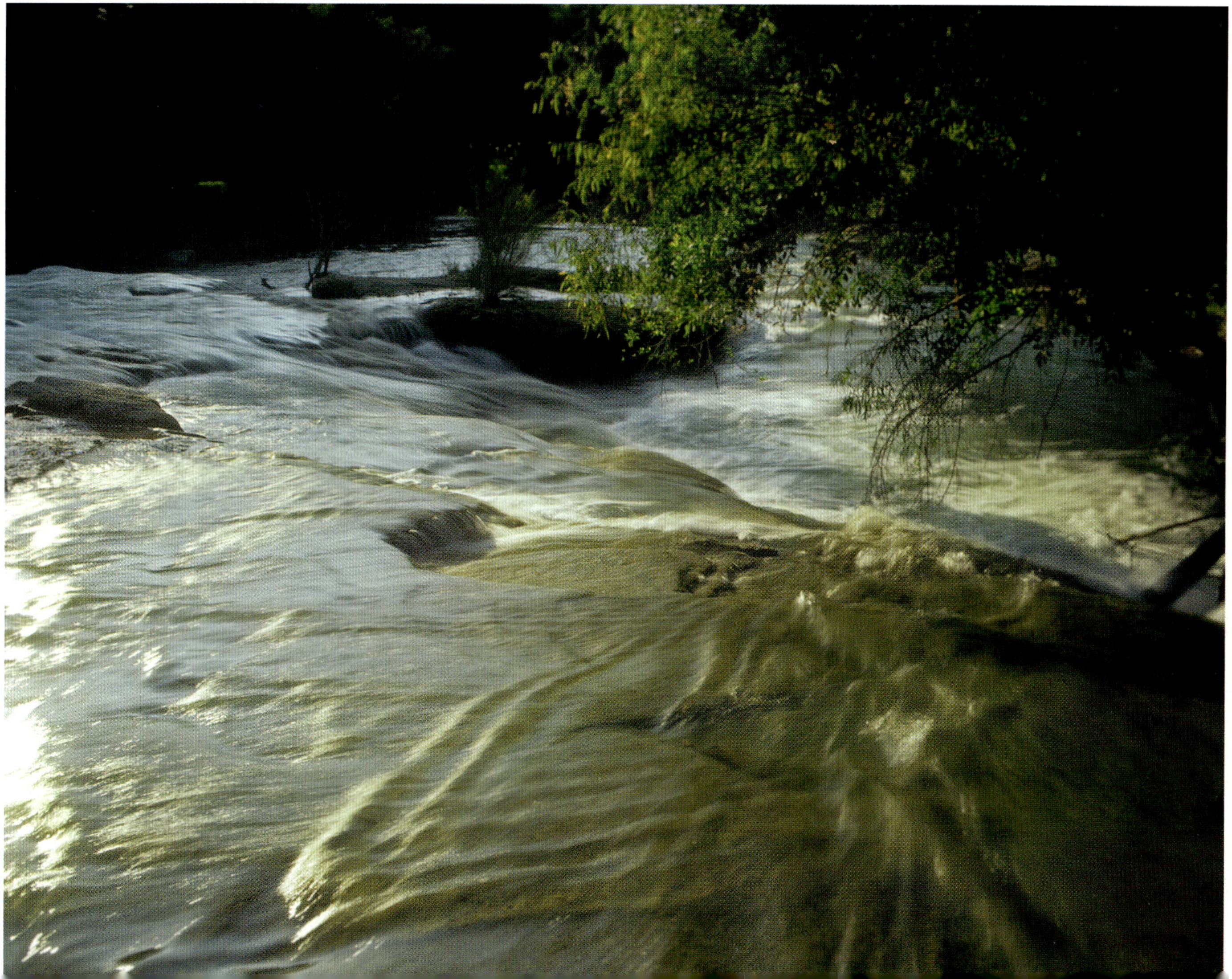

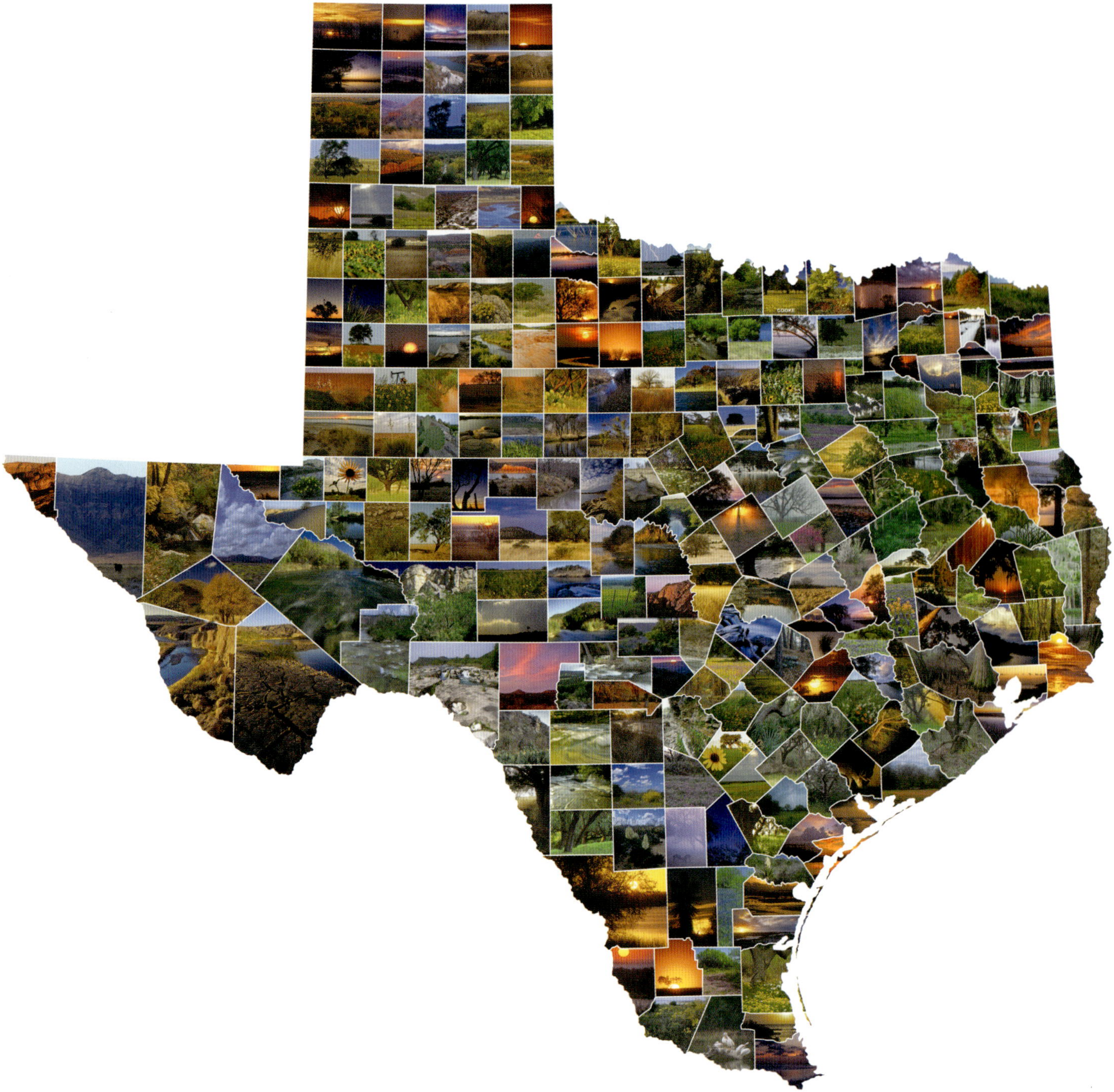
COOKE

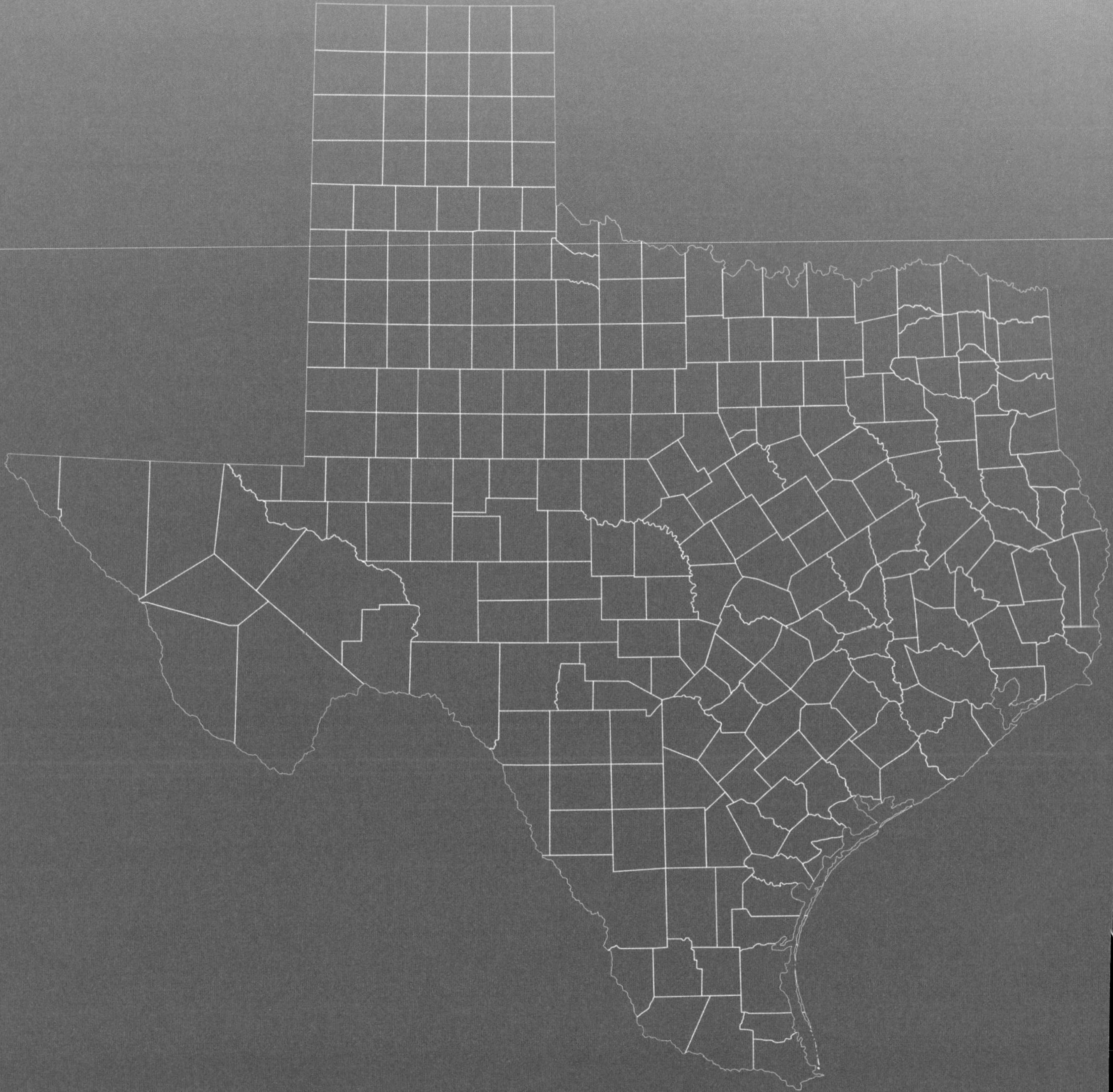